Skills for Living a Rich Life

Taken from:
Cornerstones for Professionalism, Second Edition
by Robert M. Sherfield and Patricia G. Moody

Personal Finance, Fourth Edition
by Jeff Madura

Professionalism: Skills for Workplace Success, Third Edition
by Lydia E. Anderson and Sandra B. Bolt

IDentity Series: Financial Responsibility
by ClearPoint Credit Counseling Solutions, Inc.

IDentity Series: Financial Literacy
by Farnoosh Torabi

Cover photograph: Copyright © Grischa Georgiew by Fotolia.

Taken from:

Cornerstones for Professionalism, Second Edition
by Robert M. Sherfield and Patricia G. Moody
Copyright © 2013, 2009 by Pearson Education, Inc.
Published by Pearson Education, Inc.

Personal Finance, Fourth Edition
by Jeff Madura
Copyright © 2011, 2007, 2004, 2002 by Pearson Education, Inc.
Published by Prentice Hall
Upper Saddle River, New Jersey 07458

Professionalism: Skills for Workplace Success, Third Edition
by Lydia E. Anderson and Sandra B. Bolt
Copyright © 2013, 2011, 2008 by Pearson Education, Inc.
Published by Prentice Hall

IDentity Series: Financial Responsibility
by ClearPoint Credit Counseling Solutions, Inc.
Copyright © 2012 by Pearson Education, Inc.
Published by Pearson Education, Inc.

IDentity Series: Financial Literacy
by Farnoosh Torabi
Copyright © 2012 by Pearson Education, Inc.
Published by Pearson Education, Inc.

This special edition is published in cooperation with Pearson Learning Solutions.

All trademarks, service marks, registered trademarks, and registered service marks are the property of their respective owners and are used herein for identification purposes only.

Pearson Learning Solutions, 501 Boylston Street, Suite 900, Boston, MA 02116
A Pearson Education Company
www.pearsoned.com

Printed in the United States of America

1 2 3 4 5 6 7 8 9 10 V011 18 17 16 15 14 13

000200010271770038

JL/JG

ISBN 10: 1-269-33132-9
ISBN 13: 978-1-269-33132-6

BRIEF CONTENTS

Part I: Character

Chapters taken from:
Cornerstones for Professionalism, Second Edition
by Robert M. Sherfield and Patricia G. Moody

chapter one

BUILD

BUILDING A STRONG CHARACTER WITH IMPECCABLE ETHICS

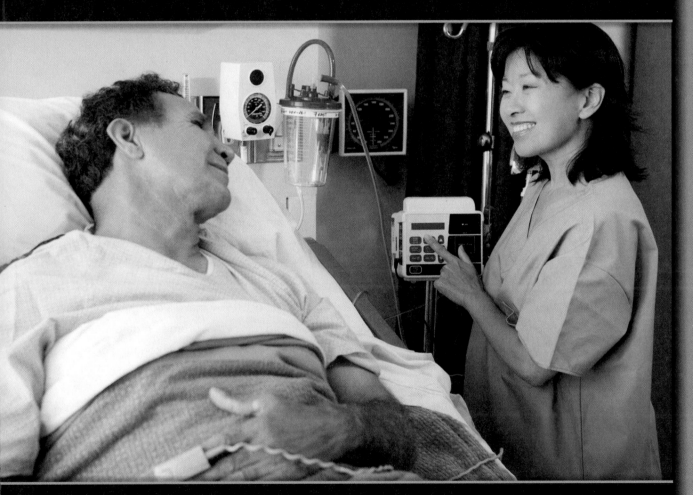

Ethics is knowing the difference between what you have a right to do and what is right to do.
—Potter Stewart

Why read this chapter?

Because you'll learn...

- How to develop your personal character and ethics
- The value of trustworthiness
- The importance of honoring commitments

Because you'll be able to...

- Discuss the six levels of ethical decision making
- Build a good name and reputation

PROFESSIONALS from the Field

Name: Sonya Lane

Business: Physical Therapist, In Shape Physical Therapy

You only have one reputation, and it's therefore very important to build one that you are proud of, one that will earn respect from your peers and coworkers, and one that is built on solid, ethical principles. Regardless of your position, you need to have a good ethical and moral character in order to earn people's trust in who you are and what you do. If you make a commitment to someone, you should honor that promise regardless of the circumstances, because someone is counting on you to keep your word. You need to respect and believe in yourself in order to develop a strong moral character and reputation. Build your personal character in such a way that you can look in the mirror every day, knowing that you are a good, decent person who has treated everyone fairly and in the way that you would want to be treated.

CULTIVATING YOUR CHARACTER AND ETHICS

How Do I Know How to Do the Right Thing?

Exactly what does *ethics* mean? Ethics is a set of moral principles that guide our decisions and behavior and help us make the appropriate decisions when faced with choices. Quite simply, ethics is how we choose to live our lives and how we treat other people. These decisions build our character. In the workplace, as in your social environment, you will be known by your character and ethics—or your lack of both. You only have one reputation, so it is very important to build a quality one, to be respected for the way you conduct your life day in and day out and for the way you treat others.

At a very early age, we begin to learn right from wrong, and we begin shaping our basic character and ethics. We learn not to hit our playmates, to share our possessions, to clean up after ourselves, and to not take things that don't belong to us; these are kindergarten mantras. Translated into workplace ethics, they might be stated this way: Treat your coworkers with respect, assist them when they need help with a project, keep your work area clean and organized, and don't take credit for someone else's work. While these statements are only a small part of the ethics puzzle, they are important to the process of getting along with others at work and making the right decisions.

Who Are You When No One Else Is Looking?

What if there were no rules or laws to govern your behavior? What if there were no consequences or ramifications for any of your actions? Let's pretend for a moment that you could never go to jail or face fines or be shunned for your actions or behaviors. If these statements came to pass, what would your life—or the lives of those you love—look like? This is one of the best ways to offer a practical definition of ethics. Basically, ethics is the accepted moral code or standard within a society by which we all live. Codes of ethics vary from culture to culture, country to country, and group to group, but each carries with it certain rules that members of that culture, country, or group are expected to follow.

Ethics, however, is about much, much more than following the law, adhering to your society's accepted code, or following your religion's teachings. Each will usually contain ethical standards, but as argued in the article "What Is Ethics?" (Velasquez, Andre, Shanks, & Meyer, 1987), following a corrupt society's "moral" standard can have dire consequences. Nazi Germany is a perfect example of this situation. Consider also slavery laws in the United States prior to the Civil War. Few people would now suggest those laws were "ethical." And think about the Crusades, in which hundreds of thousands of people were murdered in the name of religion. Was that ethical?

Think back in history for a moment (and you won't have to think back too far) and consider some national and international leaders, entertainers, sports figures, or even local professionals in your community who made monumental ethical mistakes that cost them dearly. Richard Nixon. Michael Vick. Barry Bonds. Bill Clinton. Martha Stewart. Prince Harry. Jerry Sandusky. O. J. Simpson. Each of these people, to varying degrees, failed to maintain the accepted moral code of his or her community and the consequences were grave. From jail sentences to public shame, each suffered a demoralizing defeat and a tarnished public image due

The word *ethics* is derived from the ancient Greek *ethos* (which loosely translates to "habit," "custom," or "character"). The study of ethics has also been called "moral philosophy." There are many factors that influence our ethics, from our family and friends to our teachers and relatives. TV, music, media, religion, and politics also play a tremendous role in how our ethical footprint is developed. We are constantly bombarded with conflicting messages about what is right and wrong or good and bad. Thus, more and more people slip into the gray twilight where it is hard to determine what the "right" thing to do really is. To prove this point, consider the following facts:

- 25 San Diego State University students failed a business ethics class because they were caught cheating.
- 75 percent of college students admit cheating at some point.
- According to a poll of Who's Who among American High School Students, 80 percent admitted to cheating to get to the top of his or her class.
- 61 percent of surveyed adults have gone against personal ethics for money.

As you enter the professional world, your moral conduct will become increasingly important to you, your managers, and your colleagues. The following are included to help you learn more about ethics, morality, and character to better enable you to make informed, logical, and smart decisions.

UNDERSTAND THE DYNAMICS OF ETHICS, INTEGRITY, AND CHARACTER

Do You Conduct Yourself in an Honorable Manner?

Ethics, integrity, and character can be hard to pin down because in today's discussions, they are all mixed up together. Basically, they all have to do with how you behave. Your actions are usually guided by a combination of your own personal ethical code, integrity, and character. As discussed earlier, ethics is a habit or a custom for behavior. Integrity, from the Latin *integri* (which means wholeness—as in wholeness of action and wholeness of thoughts), deals with fairness, courage, respect, temperance, and sound judgment. It is about choosing *right* over *easy* and *fairness* over *personal gain*.

Character, from the Greek *charakter* (which means "to stamp," "to scratch or mark," or "to engrave"), refers to the attributes that make up or distinguish you as an individual. In essence, your character is how your soul is "marked" or "engraved," and this is directly related to your ethical and moral behavior.

Making ethical choices usually involves three factors or levels: the law, fairness, and your conscience (Anderson & Bolt, 2008). You might also consider adding three other levels: time, pride, and publicity. When you are faced with

If given the opportunity to cheat in order to make a good grade, what would you do?

Shutterstock

a challenging professional or personal decision, ask yourself these vitally important questions: "Is it legal, is it fair, can I live with my decision, is this decision in my long-term best interest, could I tell my mama about it, and how would I feel if this showed up on the front page of the newspaper?" These questions will keep you on the right path if you just listen to your inner voice.

If you can answer yes to all six questions, this decision would most likely be in your best interest and the best interest of those around you. Ethics always includes the best interest of other people—not just yourself!

BE PROUD OF YOUR NAME AND REPUTATION

How Do You Build a Fine Reputation?

What's in a name? Smith. Johnson. Alexander. Ortiz. Aharonian. Brannon. "Nothing, really," you might say. "It's just a name. It was given to me when I was born." Few statements could be further from the truth. The pride that you have in your name and how protective you are of your name (your reputation) will drive many of your decisions. If you don't care what others think about your name or if your name has no value to you, then your decisions and actions will reflect this. If you are fiercely protective of your name's standing and meaning, your decisions and actions will reflect this. Having pride in your name and your reputation is paramount in considering ethics, integrity, and character.

Consider the play *The Crucible,* by Arthur Miller. It was written in 1953 and set in Salem, Massachusetts, during the 1692 witch trials. However, the play is really Miller's statement on McCarthyism in the United States (Congressman Joseph McCarthy's Committee on Un-American Activities intended to sniff out any Communists in the United States, and, in the process, ruined the lives and livelihoods of many innocent people.)

John Proctor, a main character in the play, is a husband, father, and farmer and one of the people accused of being a witch. Later in the play, he is convicted of witchcraft and sentenced to hang. During the last act of the play, another character from the play, Reverend Hale, begs those accused to confess to witchcraft so that they can be cleansed and not put to death. Hale sends John's wife, Elizabeth to try to convince him to confess so that he can save his life for the sake of his family. Reluctantly, he agrees to confess to the false charge and admits to witchcraft. Later, when he learns that the judges in the matter confession to the church door for all of Salem to see, he recants and refuses to confess.

> *Your character is determined by how you treat people who can do you no good and how you treat people who can't fight back.*
> —Abigail Van Buren

When the judges hear of this, they are angry and frustrated. They cannot understand why he won't simply sign the paper and choose life. They confront him again. Again, he refuses. In an angry confrontation, one judge, trying again to make him sign the paper, says, "I must have good and legal proof . . . explain to me, Mr. Proctor, why you will not let . . ."

To this, Proctor interrupts in a passionate, soul-wrenching scream, "Because it is my name! Because I cannot have another in my life . . . How am I to live without my name? I have given you my soul; leave me my name."

When you care this passionately about your reputation and character, your life is governed by protecting your name. Your actions, beliefs, and decisions are all tied to the belief, "My name and my reputation matter and I will do nothing to bring shame or embarrassment to them."

To protect your name and reputation, when in doubt about what to do, reflect on the Six Levels of Ethical Decision Making (Figure 1.1). You might also consider the following tips:

- Define what is right *before* you are faced with an ethical decision.
- Have faith in what you know to be right and just.
- Trust your heart and your conscience and that nagging little feeling in the pit of your stomach.

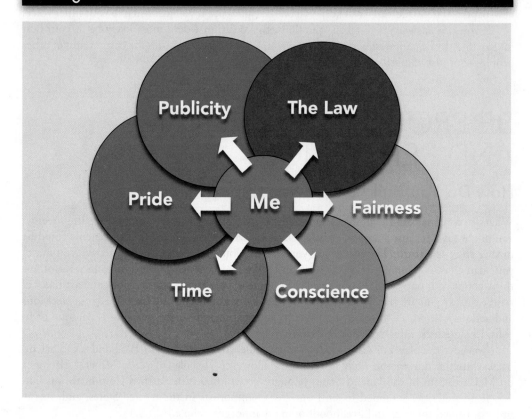

Figure 1.1 Six Levels of Ethical Decision Making

- Don't let your desires for bigger, better, faster, prettier, and greener cloud your judgment.
- Never let competition or the "need to win" overtake your knowledge of what you know is right.

DEVELOPING A STRONG MORAL CHARACTER

Why Is Character Important in the Workplace?

The word *morality* is associated with many terms such as ethics, principles, decency, honesty, integrity, honor, virtue, and goodness. So, what does it mean to have a strong moral character? As mentioned earlier, the word *character* comes from the Greek *charakter*, which means "to stamp or engrave." Therefore, in today's terms, your character is defined by the "markings or stamping" of honesty, virtue, decency, and goodness.

You might be asking yourself, "Why does character matter in the workplace?" Character matters because it is important that your employer be able to trust you, to know that you will keep your word and that you will honor the company's confidentiality policy. Character also matters because many professions require that records and information be kept private. If your character is suspect and you can't be trusted, most likely you will not remain employed very long.

> *Every time you make a choice, you choose your character.*
>
> *—Unknown*

Figure 1.2 Six Pillars of Character

Trustworthiness

Be honest • Don't deceive, cheat, or steal • Be reliable—do what you say you'll do • Have the courage to do the right thing • Build a good reputation • Be loyal—stand by your family, friends, and country

Respect

Treat others with respect • Be tolerant of differences • Use good manners, not bad language • Be considerate of the feelings of others • Don't threaten, hit, or hurt anyone • Deal peacefully with anger, insults, and disagreements

Responsibility

Do what you are supposed to do • Persevere: keep on trying! • Always do your best • Use self-control • Be self-disciplined • Think before you act—consider the consequences • Be accountable for your choices

Fairness

Play by the rules • Take turns and share • Be open-minded; listen to others • Don't take advantage of others • Don't blame others carelessly

Caring

Be kind • Be compassionate and show you care • Express gratitude • Forgive others • Help people in need

Citizenship

Do your share to make your school and community better • Cooperate • Get involved in community affairs • Stay informed; vote • Be a good neighbor • Obey laws and rules • Respect authority • Protect the environment

> *Always do right—this will gratify some people and astonish the rest.*
>
> —Mark Twain

Source: © 2011 CHARACTER COUNTS! The definitions of the Six Pillars of Character are reprinted with permission. Los Angeles: Josephson Institute of Ethics. www.charactercounts.org.

The CHARACTER COUNTS! Coalition, a project of the Josephson Institute of Ethics, suggests that there are Six Pillars of Character, as shown in Figure 1.2. By employing these Six Pillars of Character, you can begin to develop a strong moral character that will carry you far in the world of work and in your personal life as well.

Develop an Excellent Work Ethic

If you are in the right job, you will love your work and look forward to going to your workplace, and you will most likely demonstrate an excellent work ethic. Your work ethic is how you perform at work without a job description and without being told to do so. Your work ethic is not tied to what you do for a raise, what you do to impress others, or what you do to be promoted. Your work ethic is what you do at work because you know it is the right and just thing to do. Pride, ownership, and honor all play a role in one's work ethic.

Your work ethic can also be defined by how you approach the day. Do you only do what is required of you and the things that are laid out in your formal job description, or are you willing

GRADUATE *Quote*

Catherine Schleigh
Graduate!
The Katherine Gibbs School, Norristown, PA
Career: Customer Service Coordinator,
FedEx/Kinkos, Inc.

The most important thing I learned when interviewing was to truly assess my capabilities, my talents, and my skills. I learned that a resumé was not about big fancy words, but rather about being truthful and making your skills, training, and education stand out. I learned that you have to sell yourself as a product in this world.

to go "beyond" based on your own initiative and values? Do you bring a sense of energy and optimism to the workplace on a daily basis? Do you enjoy your colleagues and do all that you can to assist them without thinking of the rewards? Do you feel like what you do for a vocation is contributing to the good and whole of humanity? All of these questions get at the heart of the matter with regards to work ethic.

A work ethic is a set of values based on the ideals of hard work and discipline. Building a reliable work ethic means training yourself to follow these values. Training yourself so that work becomes automatic instead of a struggle. According to Lifehack (2007), work ethic is based on four habits:

- Persistence
- Focus
- Do it now
- Do it right

What strategies do you need to use to build positive relationships at work?

Stockbyte/Jupiter Images

With **persistence**, you are building a habit of working until the job is completed. Some days you may have to work 12 hours, whereas other days you may only have to work for seven hours. Persistence involves doing whatever it takes to get the job done.

Focus involves having clarity (and persistence) while working on a task. Focusing for one hour is better than working in a cloud for eight hours. Focus means that you have taken every precaution to eliminate distractions, interruptions, and needless wandering. An important part of focus is being sure you have chosen the right task to focus on.

The habit of **do it now** involves eliminating procrastination in your work and personal life. Yes, we advocate taking time for relaxation and joy, but those two things should come only when your work is done. If you procrastinate without completing a task *and* try to have time for joy, your spare time will be filled with stress and worry over not getting the work done.

Finally, **do it right** means that you are going to bring your very best to the table every time you do a task. It means that you have considered that your name is going to be attached to this project and it has to be the very best that it can be. Consider this: If your supervisor told you that your work would be posted or displayed for everyone to see and that your name would be displayed with your work, "do it right" takes on an entirely new meaning. There is only one way to perform a task: the right way!

Dale Dauten (2007) suggests that what is needed now is a "contribution ethic." By this, he suggests that those who make a valued contribution to their place of work are the "rare people who drive the economy and the world conversation." His contribution ethic includes the following:

- Just help. Make yourself useful. You aren't just there, waiting. There's no waiting. Just help.
- Your half is 60 percent.
- Innovation is a subversive activity. You can't expect management and/or coworkers to drool with excitement over your "I have an idea!" After all, most ideas and most suggestions are complaints. On the other hand, if an idea is truly original, then expect resistance; indeed, welcome it as a measure of originality.
- Giving time without attention is a gift-wrapped empty box.
- Being right is overrated. If your goal is usefulness, then what matters is progress.
- Being wrong is underrated. Admitting you were wrong is wisdom gained.
- Always bring something to read that is related to improving your job performance and yourself as a person.
- Think like a hero; work like an artist. When kindly attention meets curiosity, you move gracefully through the world. (Copyright © Dale Dauten, dauten.com)

> ## POSITIVE HABITS *at Work*
>
> Work hard to be a person who always gives more than is expected, works harder than is required, contributes more than you are obliged to do, and complains less than everyone else. Be the person who does the right thing just because it's right. "Just do it" is a very good motto.

THE IMPORTANCE OF RESPECT

How Do I Earn Respect?

The world is full of powerful people who have no respect. Conversely, the world is filled with people who have an abundance of respect, but no power and little money. Why? Because most people confuse the two or have no idea what either means. Few people understand that true respect can only be earned. Yes, there are people who think they are respected, but unless it was earned, they are only fooling themselves if they believe their respect is real or meaningful.

Respect can be earned many ways, including the following:

- Giving respect to others
- Being fair
- Being honest, even in difficult times
- Doing the right thing
- Listening
- Asking for opinions and suggestions and creating ownership
- Empowering others
- Standing up for those you see mistreated
- Helping others reach their dreams and goals
- Practicing open communication
- Being knowledgeable and constantly learning more
- Owning your mistakes and admitting when you are wrong
- Maintaining your principles, even when things are turbulent
- Treating people who are in positions lower than yours respectfully and honorably

Each of these acts shows that you care about not only other people, but that you care about yourself as well. If you think about your actions and what they mean to another person and your place of employment, you

> *Change occurs, progress is made, and difficulties resolved if people merely do the right thing. And rarely do people not know what is the right thing to do.*
> — *Father Hessburg, Notre Dame University*

How do you think this young woman will feel when others find out that she has been in jail?

Rhoda Sidney/PH College

will begin earning the respect of those around you. Respect is not an immediate gift to you from others. Respect comes with time, proven trust, open communication, and living a life above reproach. Respect is always earned.

AVOIDING MORAL BANKRUPTCY

Is The Price Worth the Prize?

You know who they are—the people you've met in your personal and professional life who will do anything, say anything, avoid anything, betray anyone, and change like a chameleon to get what they want. Seldom do we have positive or endearing things to say about these people because we see them as morally bankrupt. They have no scruples, no values, no guiding belief system, and no loyalty.

But worst of all, they have no continuity. You can't depend on them for anything because while you may have witnessed them being loyal or displaying values one day, you also saw them toss their loyalty and values aside for the sake of personal gain. They change from day to day, trying to carve out a power base, a leadership position, a promotion, or even to maintain their own status quo. Morally bankrupt people are impossible to befriend, depend on, or trust because you never know who they are from day to day.

Seldom do morally bankrupt people see themselves as "broken." They say to themselves, "I have done nothing to break the law or disobey the rules of our company." This may be completely true, but morality and integrity involve much more than following the written law or adhering to company policy. While those two factors are important, you need to understand that they are not the only two factors that make you moral and give you integrity.

There are many indicators to identify behaviors and traits of a morally bankrupt person, but the following are the most prominent:

- **They have unhealthy self-esteem.** Morally bankrupt people care little about themselves because they do not respect themselves; therefore, they cannot care about you or respect you. They value themselves so little that they can't even see how their actions damage their credibility and reputation.

- **They lack courage.** Morally bankrupt people only have the courage to stand up for what is right for them. They do not stand up for what is simply right. Courage is a quality of strong people, and morally bankrupt people are weak.

- **They use poor judgment.** Just as is the case with courage, morally bankrupt people make judgments and decisions that only affect them in a positive way. They base their judgments more on personal gain and loss than on right and wrong.

- **They are always looking for more (especially money).** Morally bankrupt people never have enough. They cannot be satisfied with abundance; they have to have super-abundance. They are driven by the pursuit of money or power and they will stop at nothing to have more of both.

- **They are untruthful.** "Truth is an expendable commodity to the morally bankrupt person" (Sherfield, 2004). Winning, money, power, and status always trump truth.

- **They are jealous and arrogant.** If morally bankrupt people see that you have more than them—more respect, more power, more money, a nicer car, a bigger home, more friends—they will work with diligence to take this from you, or at best, outdo you. They use what little status or power they have to make you look small so that

The hottest places in hell are reserved for those who, in times of great moral crisis, maintained their neutrality.

—Dante

your accomplishments pale in comparison to what they have. They mistakenly believe that by diminishing you, they improve their own stature.

- **They practice deception and betrayal.** Deception and betrayal are not necessarily loud and obvious. Morally bankrupt people know how to practice quiet deception and hushed betrayal. They will stab anyone in the back to get what they want and to advance as far as they can. They use blame, shame, and lies to quietly turn the tides in their favor. Often these people get other people to do their dirty work so they can keep up their outward appearances.

- **They are unfair.** *Fairness* is an unknown word to morally bankrupt people—unless, of course, the unfair act is directed toward them. They have learned how to convince themselves that any means justify a positive end for themselves—and fairness simply does not fit into the equation.

- **They put self-interest ahead of everything.** Self-interest is not a bad or morally wrong trait. In fact, it can be good and healthy to look out for yourself. However, when your every thought, action, and decision is based on what is good and right for you, this can be dangerous and immoral. When you look out for others and help them along, they will help you along.

We do not mean to suggest that every person with whom you come into contact will be morally bankrupt. In fact, the opposite is probably true. There are countless wonderful, remarkable, talented, truthful, honest people in the world of work and you will meet many of them. It is important, however, that you know the signs of moral bankruptcy so that you can avoid the personal and professional pitfalls of this deadly characteristic.

> *'tain't no law on earth dat can make a man be decent if it ain't in 'em.*
>
> —Zora Neale Hurston, "Sweat"

THE IMPORTANCE OF TRUSTWORTHINESS

How Do I Earn Trust?

Whether choosing a mate or someone to work closely with, trust really matters. University of Florida research finds that of all major character traits, people value trustworthiness the most in others (http://news.ufl.edu/2007/10/03/trustworthiness).

There are two types of people in the world: those who distrust everyone until it is proven they **can be trusted,** and those who trust everyone until it is proven that they **cannot be trusted.** Neither is right nor wrong, but rather a fact of life. Gaining trust and giving trust are both about time. It either happens immediately or is built over time.

Trustworthiness is a quality that most people admire and want in friends, employees, and coworkers. People want to know that you can be trusted to keep your word, that you adhere to moral standards, do what is right, remain ethical under dire pressure, and tell the truth even in times of struggle. If you are perceived as trustworthy, you will most likely be treated with respect and admiration. Trustworthiness earns respect and can be earned by acts as simple as delivering packages when you said you would or as complex as being loyal to your coworkers even when they are in trouble. Consider the following factors that promote trustworthiness.

> *Watch your thoughts; they become words. Watch your words; they become actions. Watch your actions; they become habits. Watch your habits; they become character. Watch your character; it becomes your destiny.*
>
> —Frank Outlaw

A Trustworthy Person:

1. Is truthful even in times of personal turmoil
2. Does the right thing even if it's not popular
3. Is courageous and does what they say they will do
4. Listens to his or her conscience

5. Supports and protects family, friends, and community
6. Works hard to build and maintain his or her reputation
7. Seeks advice from others when in doubt about the right thing
8. Is honorable in all actions
9. Does not go against his or her personal beliefs or ethics for gain
10. Constantly tries to improve

HONORING YOUR COMMITMENTS

Why Is It Important to Do What You Say You Will Do?

Commitments are a vital and real part of trust and character. Learning to honor your commitments is perhaps one of the most mature, rational, and loving things that you can do in this world. You should always think deeply and consider all angles before you make a commitment to another person—whether that commitment is picking up your friend from work or marrying a loved one. There are no degrees of commitment. It is black and white. Either you keep your word or you do not. You can't be a little pregnant, you can't be a little dead, and you can't be somewhat committed.

Making a commitment, whether in writing or verbal, means that you pledge to do something mutually agreed on. You can (and should) also have commitments with yourself. A commitment is an obligation. Some people consider the word *obligation* to be negative and restrictive. Yes, it can be, but you should view both commitment and obligation as an anchor. They are the characteristics that ground us—the qualities that make life worth living. When we are committed to others and ourselves, our lives begin to have purpose and meaning. Without commitment, we are kites in the wind with no strings attached. We are not connected to anyone or anything.

Strangely, however, being "anchored down" through a commitment or obligation is one of the most liberating feelings on earth. With commitment, we are still kites, free to fly and float and wander, but we are tethered to the earth and the people we love.

People who honor their commitments enjoy a variety of benefits that both enrich and improve the quality of life. For example, people who make a full and lasting commitment to their personal goals are among some of the most successful and notable in history (Arkoff, 1995).

Lee Foster/Alamy

Vincent Van Gogh, considered one of the world's greatest painters, only sold one of his works during his lifetime. He did not let this deter him from painting. Recently, a Van Gogh painting sold for over 75 million dollars. He was committed to his profession and his talents.

Zuma Press/Newscom

Lucille Ball was dismissed from drama school because her teacher thought she was too shy to ever do any effective stage work. She went on to earn 13 Emmys, was a Kennedy Center Honoree, and was awarded the Presidential Medal of Freedom. She was committed to her profession and her talents.

Photos 12/Alamy

The Beatles were turned down by Decca Recording Studio because the company's executives did not like their sound and felt that the guitar was a thing of the past. The Beatles went on to have over 40 number-one hits, sold over one billion songs worldwide, and are listed as the most successful recording act of all time. They were committed to their profession and their talents.

Michael Jordan was cut from his high school varsity basketball team and went home in tears. He later went on to join the Chicago Bulls, was named as the NBA's Most Valuable Player, holds

Greg Forwreck/Ai Wire Photo/Newscom

the NBA record for highest career regular season scoring average, and is considered by most basketball aficionados as the greatest basketball player of all time. He was committed to his profession and his talents.

Commitment, then, is a powerful and dynamic quality that can sustain you in times of doubt, lift you in times of defeat, inspire you in times of creative stillness, and guide you in times of turbulence. If you work to honor your commitments, the rewards will be powerful.

YOUR PERSONAL GUIDING STATEMENT AND INTEGRITY PLAN

What Philosophy Guides Your Actions?

You're wearing a t-shirt to class. It is not your normal, run-of-the-mill t-shirt, however. You designed this t-shirt for everyone to see and read. It is white with bright red letters. On the front of the t-shirt is written your personal guiding statement—the words by which you live. The words that govern your life. What will your t-shirt read? Perhaps you will use the golden rule, "Do unto others . . ." It might be an adaptation of the Nike slogan, "Just do it," or it might be something more profound such as, "I live my life to serve others and to try to make others' lives better."

Whatever your guiding statement, it must be yours. It can't be your parents', your professor's, or your best friend's statement. It must be based on something you value and it must be strong enough to motivate and carry you in tough times. Your guiding statement must be so powerful that it will literally *guide you* when you are ethically challenged, broke, alone, angry, hurt, sad, or feeling vindictive. It is a statement that will guide you in relationships with family, friends, spouses, partners, or would-be love interests. It is a statement that will earn you respect and rewards in the world of work.

As you've been reading, have you thought of your statement? If you already have a statement, great! However, if you do not, you are not alone. This is a very difficult question and most likely, you've never been asked to develop a guiding statement before. It may take you some time to write your statement, and this section is included to help you. Focus on keywords that are part of your personal makeup and character as you write your guiding statement.

For example, you may have chosen the words *respect, giving,* and *optimistic* as keywords that you value. These words become a basis for your guiding statement and might read something like this:

> "I will live my life as a positive, upbeat, motivated person who respects others and enjoys giving to others on a daily basis."

If you chose the words *integrity, truth,* and *fairness,* your statement may read something like:

> "My integrity is the most important value in my life and I will never act in any way that compromises it. I will be truthful, fair, and honest in all my endeavors."

As you can see, if one of these statements was your guiding statement, and you truly lived your life by that statement, your actions would be in alignment with your values. This is the purpose of a guiding statement—to give you direction and support in difficult, troubling times.

In the space on the next page, write the most important words you can think of that describe your values and strengths. You may want to review the list on page 27.

BIGGEST INTERVIEW Blunders

Michael was asked by the interview committee, "Suppose we offered you a position here at Ace Medical Supplies tomorrow with a 12-month contract. Then, in three months, another company offered you more money to move to their company. What would you do?" Michael responded, "Well, I hope you would understand that I have my family to consider and I'd have to seriously consider taking the other position. I know I'm under contract and all, but seriously, my future is important, too." The committee appreciated his honesty, but not his level of commitment.

LESSON: Once you have accepted a position and gone through training, you have an obligation to spend a reasonable amount of time working for that company.

I am my choices.
—Jean-Paul Sartre

My **dominant strengths include:**

_____

_____

_____

_____

The most important values are:

_____

_____

_____

_____

Draft of my guiding statement (Take your time and be sincere. You will need this statement to complete the following section.)

_____

_____

_____

_____

_____

_____

How Will Your Guiding Statement Help:

With your overall job search plan?

_____

_____

_____

If you have a disagreement with your supervisor at work?

_____

_____

_____

If you are asked to do something at work with which you fundamentally disagree?

_____

_____

_____

If you are having a disagreement with someone for whom you care deeply (friend, spouse, partner, parent, work associate, etc.)?

_____

_____

_____

Reflections: PUTTING IT ALL TOGETHER

Reflect on the words of John Proctor: "Because it is my name! Because I cannot have another in my life." If you allow these words to be your guiding mantra, you will begin to see a vast difference in how you approach work, relationships, commitment, fairness, and ethics. Being proud of yourself and your work is a powerfully important aspect of being fulfilled and happy. When you know that your moral compass is pointing in the direction of your dreams, you will have no trouble sleeping at night—or getting up in the morning.

DIGITAL BRIEFCASE

USING SOCIAL MEDIA TO COMBAT ELECTRONIC BULLYING

Some people have a good job, a nice circle of friends, and an interesting lifestyle, but they feel morally bankrupt and empty inside. In other words, they don't have a good inner feeling that makes them believe their life is counting for something other than just taking care of their own personal needs. We hope this chapter will instill in you the importance of giving back to others. As part of your ethics and character development, we want you to experience the wonderful feeling of knowing you have done something good for someone other than yourself. This exercise is designed to have you focus on helping people who may not be able to help themselves.

Assume that you write a personal blog devoted to combating electronic bullying. You want to find a way of creating interactivity among the people who read your blog, and you want to engage them in actively standing up against bullying via Facebook, Twitter, and other electronic media. One way to do this is to tell a compelling story. Using the Internet, identify a story in which someone has been bullied, one in which the bullying has led to a tragic ending. Develop your own blog if you do not have one and retell this story in your blog. Then list steps that you would like to have people take to counteract electronic bullying.

A good source to help you in developing your blog is this website www.dragonflyeffect.com/blog/model/focus-your-goal/. Another good source is the book *The Dragonfly Effect* by Jennifer Aaker and Andy Smith.

REFERENCES

Aaker, J., & Smith, A. (2010). *The dragonfly effect.* San Francisco: Jossey-Bass.

Anderson, L., & Bolt, S. (2008). *Professionalism: Real skills for workplace success.* Upper Saddle River, NJ: Pearson Prentice Hall.

Arkoff, A. (1995). *The illuminated life.* Boston: Allyn and Bacon.

Character Counts! Coalition (2011). *The six pillars of character.* Los Angeles: The Josephson Institute of Ethics. Retrieved from www.charactercounts.org.

Dauten, D. (March 25, 2007). Today's Work Ethic Just No Longer Works. *The Boston Globe.*

Hill, R. (1996). *Historical context of the work ethic.* Retrieved from www.coe.uga.edu/~rhill/workethic/hist.htm.

Lifehack.org. (2007). *How to build a reliable work habit*. Retrieved from www.lifehack.org/articles/management/how-to-build-a-reliable-work-ethic.html.

Miller, A. (1953/2003). *The crucible*. New York: Penguin Press.

Sherfield, R. (2004). *The everything self esteem book*. Avon, MA: Adams Media.

University of Florida. "Trustworthiness." Retrieved October 21, 2011, from http://news.ufl.edu/2007/10/03/trustworthiness.

chapter two

DISCOVER

DISCOVERING WHO YOU ARE

Believe you can and you are halfway there.
—Theodore Roosevelt

Why read this chapter?

Because you'll learn...

- The traits and characteristics that make you special
- The importance of establishing an excellent value system
- The power of optimism and positive self-esteem

Because you'll be able to...

- Complete a Personality Assessment Profile and identify your personality type
- Develop your own brand and know what qualities you need to market yourself to future employers

PROFESSIONALS from the Field

Name: Dawn Daniel Thompson

Business: Executive Assistant to the President, CEO, and Chairman of the Board, Haverty's

When you go to work in a new job, you are still trying to find out who you really are as a person, who you want to become, and what is expected of you. My advice to a person entering the workforce today is to learn everything you can about the company as quickly as you can. Learn all the technology you can; learn to read and interpret financial statements and balance sheets; pay attention to company reports. Work hard to become a good communicator and a team player. Work smart and use time-saving devices and strategies to produce more effectively. One of the most important things I can share with you is to be available and willing to work after hours if necessary to get the job done.

PROFESSIONALISM DEFINED

How Do I Become a Professional?

Professionalism is defined by a number of characteristics and traits: your character, which is who you are; your knowledge which is what you know and what experiences you can draw on; and your image which is how you project yourself and how others perceive you. A true professional cares deeply about what the job is and how well it is done, and, at the same time, cares about the company for which he or she works and the colleagues with whom they work. Professionals are willing to go above and beyond to be sure that customers and colleagues are taken care of in an exemplary manner.

SETTING YOURSELF APART AND FINDING YOUR DIRECTION

How Do You Separate Yourself from the Pack?

How do you distinguish yourself from the countless job seekers out there? What are you going to do that sets you apart from your competition? What do you have to offer that no one else can possibly offer to an employer? What unique skills do you have to help you thrive and survive in a rapidly changing world where outsourcing is commonplace and technology is constantly evolving? Answering these questions is the primary focus of this chapter, and indeed, this book and the course in which you are presently enrolled.

> You laugh at me because I am different. I laugh at you because you are all the same.
>
> —Unknown

In his book *The 2010 Meltdown,* Edward Gordon (2008) writes, "Simply stated, today in America, there are just too many people trained for the wrong jobs. Many jobs have become unnecessary, technically obsolete . . . or worse yet, the job/career aspirations of too many current and future workers are at serious odds with the changing needs of the U.S. labor market." An example of this disconnect between the workforce and the market place can be found in this fact: **Eight million U.S. workers speak English so poorly that they cannot hold high-paying jobs** (Center for Law and Social Policy). Conversely, people who are highly skilled, possess superb oral and written communication skills, know how to solve problems, have excellent technology skills, and can work well with others should be in great demand for many years to come.

Careers in the following areas are projected for high growth in the coming decade: **health sciences** (dental assistants, home health aids, physician assistants, medical assistants, occupational therapy, physical therapist, cardiovascular technologists, etc.), **aviation** (airplane mechanics and air traffic controllers), **skilled trades** (plumbers, electricians, mechanics, etc.); **teaching** (K–12 and college); **technology** (aerospace and GPS engineers, water and sanitation engineers, transportation services, systems analyst, programmers, interactive media designers, software engineers, desktop publishing, database administrators, etc.), and **management, marketing, and public relations** (business managers, human resource directors, advertising and public relations, accounting, etc.).

This chapter will help you discover your unique qualities and characteristics that can give you the competitive edge in today's workplace. Several solutions to help you kick-start your career and your personal development will be introduced here.

KNOW WHO YOU ARE AND WHERE YOU ARE GOING

Who Are You and What Do You Want to Do with Your One Lifetime?

When asked, "Who are you?" so many people answer with "I'm a student" or "I'm a mom" or "I'm a teacher." Often, we answer this question with *what* we are and not *who* we are. There is a huge difference between the two. What you are is your work, your position, and your family standing. Who you are is much deeper. Who you are involves your work and relationships, but it is also the basis for your core—your foundation. Who you are involves much more than your title as a brother, a mother, a nurse, a mechanic, or a friend. Who you are involves your morality, your intellect, your spirituality, your emotions, your beliefs, your values, your culture, your choices, and your dreams.

By understanding the difference between *what* you are and *who* you are, you can truly begin to understand yourself on a higher level. Few people are willing to take this journey. Fear, time pressures, or lack of motivation may cause people to avoid finding the answer, but finding out who you are can be one of the most rewarding opportunities in your life—and it can give you the competitive edge that you need to survive and thrive in today's world of work.

> *The Constitution only gives people the right to pursue happiness. You have to catch it yourself.*
> —Benjamin Franklin

In their book *The Dragonfly Effect*, Aaker and Smith (2010) state that "human beings have three basic needs in terms of their self-worth: competence (feeling that we are effective and able), autonomy (feeling that we are able to dictate our own behavior), and relatedness (feeling that we are connected to others)." As you go through this journey of discovering who you are and what you want to become, remember those thoughts.

Consider the "me puzzle" in Figure 2.1 As you can see, it involves nine different pieces. Understanding how each piece affects your actions, goals, relationships, work ethic, and motivation can mean the difference between success and failure in work . . . and in life. As you study the puzzle, consider your strengths and challenges in each area. How does each piece drive your choices and how does each piece help you understand more about who you are? Are there pieces of the puzzle that you have never considered? If so, how has this affected your life in the past? Has something been missing in your life because you did not address a certain piece of the overall puzzle? At this time and place in your life, which piece is the most or least important? Which pieces can you use to gain a competitive edge and which parts of your life need improvement?

As you look at each piece of the "me puzzle," think about **one strength** for each puzzle piece that you have to offer in the workplace and how it will help you in the future. Then, think about **one challenge** you will have to overcome for each piece of the "me puzzle" and how you plan to do so.

Example:

Moral Me

Strength: I am very grounded in my work ethic. I consider myself to be a loyal and dedicated employee and will do my best every day.

The Future: This strength will help me gain the trust of my superiors and peers. They will know that I am a person to whom they can turn in times of stress. They will know that I can make ethical and honest decisions.

Figure 2.1 Solving the "Me Puzzle"

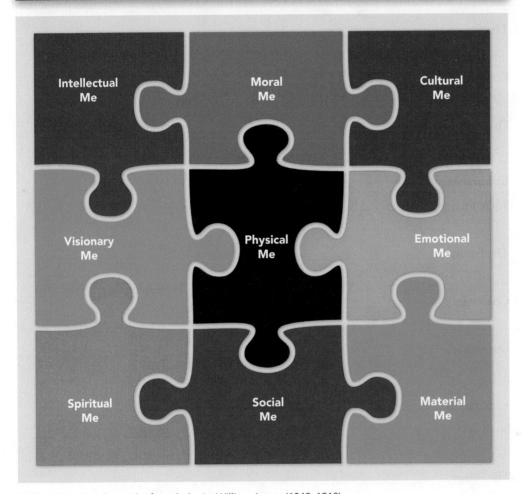

Source: Based on the work of psychologist William James (1842–1910).

Challenge: I sometimes judge others too harshly when they do not have the same work ethic that I possess. This can become a problem when I move up the ladder and begin supervising people.

Overcome: I plan to begin listening more and to try to understand others' backgrounds and problems before making judgments.

Intellectual Me

Strength: _____

_____

The Future: _____

_____

Challenge: _____

_____

Overcome: _____

_____

Moral Me

Strength: _____

_____

The Future: _____

_____

Challenge: _____

_____

Overcome: _____

_____

Cultural Me

Strength: _____

_____

The Future: _____

_____

Challenge: _____

_____

Overcome: _____

_____

Visionary Me

Strength: _____

_____

The Future: _____

_____

Challenge: _____

_____

Overcome: _____

_____

Physical Me

Strength: _____

_____

The Future: _____

_____

Challenge: _____

_____

Overcome: _____

_____

Emotional Me

Strength: _____

_____

The Future: _____

_____

Challenge: _____

_____

Overcome: _____

_____

Spiritual Me

Strength: _____

_____

The Future: _____

_____

Challenge: _____

_____

Overcome: _____

_____

Social Me

Strength: _____

_____

The Future: _____

_____

Challenge: _____

_____

Overcome: _____

_____

Material Me

Strength: _____

_____

The Future: _____

_____

Challenge: _____

_____

Overcome: _____

_____

Spiritual Me	**Social Me**	**Material Me**
What I believe	My relationships	What I have
My religion	My activities	What I want
Wisdom gained	My associations	What I need to survive
Meditation	My social involvement	Economic background
Altruistic notions		
My "grounding"		
Intellectual Me	**Moral Me**	**Cultural Me**
What I know	Character	How I interact with others
Common sense	Ethics/Values	Knowledge of my own culture, norms, heritage, environment, race, etc.
Skills I possess	Choices and decisions	
Critical thinking	Reactions	
Reasoning	Principles	
Problem solving		
Visionary Me	**Physical Me**	**Emotional Me**
Where I am going	My health	What I feel
My goals and dreams for the future	My appearance and grooming	How am I guided by emotions
What skills I need to be successful	My body	My heart vs. my head
	My habits	How I manage conflicts and challenges

CAPITALIZING ON YOUR STRENGTHS

What Do You Have Going for You?

Study the following statements carefully:

"I am super organized."　　　　　　"I can't find a thing on this desk."

"I am extremely good at my profession."　　"I feel so stupid at work."

"I know I can solve that problem."　　　"I don't even know where to begin."

Do you capitalize on all your strengths at work?

Shutterstock

Notice the difference between these perspectives? One person seems optimistic and appears to know his or her abilities and strengths, and the other is unsure, timid, and pessimistic. Who would you hire? Who would you like working on your team? Knowing what you're good at and owning those strengths can be an enormously positive attribute and can give you another competitive asset to highlight on your resumé. Basically, the question that must be answered is, "What do I have going for me?" If you don't know your strengths, it will be impossible to convey them to an employer. It is also impossible to use the strengths that you don't even know you have.

Perhaps you've never thought of yourself as a problem solver, but think again. Don't you do this on a daily basis with your personal budget? Your children? Your studies? Juggling schedules with work and classes? Making your iPad or smartphone work properly? You solve problems every day, and acknowledging these skills can only make it stronger.

You probably have strengths that you have never thoroughly identified. Take your time and consider the following list of traits and abilities. Circle your strengths and add any that are not listed. Be honest with yourself because you will return to this list later.

Accountable	Budget-minded	Organized
Positive attitude	Intuitive	Stable
Punctual	Inquisitive	Rational
Ethical	Reliable	Tolerant
Resourceful	Humorous	Compassionate
Hopeful	Self-reliant	Decisive
Courageous	Competent	Grateful
Loyal	Sincere	Open-minded
Stylish	Helpful	Friendly
Optimistic	Respectful	Trusting
Well-groomed	Neat	Prepared
Supportive	Honest	Strong
Reserved	Logical	Spiritual
Warm	Versatile	Motivated
Grounded	Trustworthy	Creative
Modest	Imaginative	Fair
Flexible	Persuasive	Analytical
Loving	Yielding	Fun-loving
Forgiving	Articulate	Giving

_____   _____   _____

_____   _____   _____

_____   _____   _____

IDENTIFY YOUR PERSONALITY TYPE AND USE IT TO BEST ADVANTAGE

Understanding your personality type enables you to use your best assets to your advantage. Having the knowledge of different personality types also helps you better understand others. In Figure 2.2 you will be able to take the PAP, a personality profile assessment that is designed to help you understand your personality type.

Figure 2.2 Take the PAP

The Personality Assessment Profile

Directions: Read each statement carefully and thoroughly. After reading the statement, rate your response using the scale below. There are no right or wrong answers. This is not a timed survey. The PAP is based, in part, on the Myers-Briggs Type Indicator (MBTI) by Katharine Briggs and Isabel Briggs-Myers.

3 = Often Applies   2 = Sometimes Applies   1 = Never or Almost Never Applies

_____ 1a. I am a very talkative person.

_____ 1b. I am a more reflective person than a verbal person.

_____ 2a. I am a very factual and literal person.

_____ 2b. I look to the future and I can see possibilities.

_____ 3a. I value truth and justice over tact and emotion.

_____ 3b. I find it easy to empathize with other people.

_____ 4a. I am very ordered and efficient.

_____ 4b. I enjoy having freedom from control.

_____ 5a. I am a very friendly and social person.

_____ 5b. I enjoy listening to others more than talking.

_____ 6a. I enjoy being around and working with people who have a great deal of common sense.

_____ 6b. I enjoy being around and working with people who are dreamers and have a great deal of imagination.

_____ 7a. One of my motivating forces is to do a job very well.

_____ 7b. I like to be recognized for, and I am motivated by, my accomplishments and awards.

_____ 8a. I like to plan out my day before I go to bed.

_____ 8b. When I get up on a non-school or non-work day, I just like to let the day "plan itself."

_____ 9a. I like to express my feelings and thoughts.

_____ 9b. I enjoy a great deal of tranquility and quiet time to myself.

_____ 10a. I am a very pragmatic and realistic person.

_____ 10b. I like to create new ideas, methods, or ways of doing things.

_____ 11a. I make decisions with my brain.

_____ 11b. I make decisions with my heart.

_____ 12a. I am a very disciplined and orderly person.

_____ 12b. I don't make a lot of plans.

_____ 13a. I like to work with a group of people.

_____ 13b. I would rather work independently.

_____ 14a. I learn best if I can see it, touch it, smell it, taste it, or hear it.

_____ 14b. I learn best by relying on my gut feelings or intuition.

_____ 15a. I am quick to criticize others.

_____ 15b. I compliment others very easily and quickly.

_____ 16a. My life is systematic and organized.

_____ 16b. I don't really pay attention to deadlines.

_____ 17a. I can be myself when I am around others.

_____ 17b. I can be myself when I am alone.

_____ 18a. I live in the here and now, in the present.

_____ 18b. I live in the future, planning and dreaming.

_____ 19a. I think that if someone breaks the rules, the person should be punished.

_____ 19b. I think that if someone breaks the rules, we should look at the person who broke the rules, examine the rules, and look at the situation at hand before a decision is made.

_____ 20a. I do my work, then I play.

_____ 20b. I play, then do my work.

Refer to your score on each individual question. Place that score beside the appropriate question number below. Then, tally each line at the side.

Score					Total Across	Code
1a _____	5a _____	9a _____	13a _____	17a _____	_____	E Extrovert
1b _____	5b _____	9b _____	13b _____	17b _____	_____	I Introvert
2a _____	6a _____	10a _____	14a _____	18a _____	_____	S Sensing
2b _____	6b _____	10b _____	14b _____	18b _____	_____	N Intuition
3a _____	7a _____	11a _____	15a _____	19a _____	_____	T Thinking
3b _____	7b _____	11b _____	15b _____	19b _____	_____	F Feeling
4a _____	8a _____	12a _____	16a _____	20a _____	_____	J Judging
4b _____	8b _____	12b _____	16b _____	20b _____	_____	P Perceiving

PAP Scores
Personality Indicator

Look at the scores on your PAP. Is your score higher in the E or I line? Is your score higher in the S or N line? Is your score higher in the T or F line? Is your score higher in the J or P line? Write the code to the side of each section below.

Is your higher score	E or I	Code _____
Is your higher score	S or N	Code _____
Is your higher score	T or F	Code _____
Is your higher score	J or P	Code _____

Source: © Robert M. Sherfield, Ph.D.

UNDERSTANDING PERSONALITY TYPING (TYPOLOGY)

What Do These Letters Mean to Me?

The questions on the PAP helped you discover whether you are extroverted or introverted (E or I), sensing or intuitive (S or N), thinking or feeling (T or F), and judging or perceiving (J or P). These questions were based, in part, on work done by Carl Jung, Katharine Briggs, and Isabel Briggs-Myers.

In 1921, Swiss psychologist Carl Jung (1875–1961) published his work *Psychological Types.* In this book, Jung suggested that human behavior is not random. He felt that behavior follows patterns, and these patterns are caused by differences in the way people use their minds. In 1942, Isabel Briggs-Myers and her mother, Katharine Briggs, began to put Jung's theory into practice. They developed the Myers-Briggs Type Indicator, which after more than 50 years of research and refinement has become the most widely used instrument for identifying and studying personality.

Please keep in mind that no part of this assessment measures your worth, your success factors, how smart you are, or your value as a human being. The questions on the PAP assisted you in identifying your type, but we do not want you to assume that one personality type is better or worse, more or less valuable, or more or less likely to be successful. What personality typing can do is to "help us discover what best motivates and energizes each of us as individuals" (Tieger & Barron-Tieger, 2001).

WHY PERSONALITY MATTERS

What Does My Personality Type Say about Me?

When all of the combinations of E/I, S/N, T/F, and J/P are combined, there are 16 personality types. Everyone will fit into one of the following categories:

ISTJ	ISFJ	INFJ	INTJ
ISTP	ISFP	INFP	INTP
ESTP	ESFP	ENFP	ENTP
ESTJ	ESFJ	ENFJ	ENTJ

Let's take a look at the four major categories of typing. Notice that the higher your score in one area, the stronger your personality type is for that area. For instance, if you scored 15 on the E (extroversion) questions, this means that you are a strong extrovert. If you scored 15 on the I (introversion) questions, this means that you are a strong introvert. However, if you scored 7 on the E questions and 8 on the I questions, your score indicates that you possess almost the same amount of extroverted and introverted qualities. The same is true for every category on the PAP.

E Versus I (Extroversion/Introversion)

This category deals with the way we interact with others and the world around us.

Extroverts prefer to live in the outside world, drawing their strength from other people. They are outgoing and love interaction. They usually make decisions with others in mind. They enjoy being the center of attention. There are usually few secrets about extroverts.

Introverts draw their strength from the inner world. They need to spend time alone to think and ponder. They are usually quiet and reflective. They usually make decisions by themselves. They do not like being the center of attention. They are private.

S Versus N (Sensing/Intuition)

This category deals with the way we learn and deal with information.

Sensing types gather information through their five senses. They have a hard time believing something if it cannot be seen, touched, smelled, tasted, or heard. They like concrete facts and details. They do not rely on intuition or gut feelings. They usually have a great deal of common sense.

Intuitive types are not very detail-oriented. They can see possibilities, and they rely on their gut feelings. Usually, they are very innovative people. They tend to live in the future and often get bored once they have mastered a task.

T Versus F (Thinking/Feeling)

This category deals with the way we make decisions.

Thinkers are very logical people. They do not make decisions based on feelings or emotion. They are analytical and sometimes do not take others' values into consideration when making decisions. They can easily identify the flaws of others. They can be seen as insensitive and lacking compassion.

Feelers make decisions based on what they feel is right and just. They like to have harmony, and they value others' opinions and feelings. They are usually very tactful people who like to please others. They are very warm people.

J Versus P (Judging/Perceiving)

This category deals with the way we live.

Judgers are very orderly people. They must have a great deal of structure in their lives. They are good at setting goals and sticking to their goals. They are the type of people who would seldom, if ever, play before their work was completed.

Perceivers are just the opposite. They are less structured and more spontaneous. They do not like timelines. Unlike the judger, they will play before their work is done. They will take every chance to delay a decision or judgment. Sometimes, they can become involved in too many things at one time.

HOW PERSONALITY AFFECTS CAREER CHOICE

What Do I Want to Be When I Grow Up?

Taking personality and career tests and using them to help you decide which career you want to pursue is somewhat like playing the childhood game of "What Do I Want to Be When I Grow Up?" When taking career and personality tests, you need to remember that the results are indicators that will help you narrow the choices related to your personality, skills, and abilities; tests won't provide you with a specific career choice. Tests cannot pinpoint exactly what career you should pursue, but they can provide additional information to help you find your way. There are many free personality/career tests online and others you can access for a fee. To locate sites that will provide additional information related to personality types and career choices, use your Internet browser and type in keywords such as "careers for different personality types." Figure 2.3 provides suggestions of the types of careers that are best for specific personality types.

Figure 2.3 **A Closer Look at Your Personality Type**

Type	Attributes	Possible Careers
ISTJ—The Dutiful (7–10% of Americans)	Have great power of concentration; very serious; dependable; logical and realistic; take responsibility for their own actions; not easily distracted.	Accountant, purchasing agent, real estate, IRS agent, corrections officer, investment counselor, law researcher, technical writer, judge, mechanic
ISTP—The Mechanic (4–7% of Americans)	Very reserved; good at making things clear to others; interested in how and why things work; like to work with their hands; can sometimes be misunderstood as idle.	Police officer, intelligence officer, firefighter, athletic coach, engineer, technical trainer, logistic manager, EMT, surgical technician, banker, office manager, carpenter, landscape architect
ISFJ —The Nurturer (7–10% of Americans)	Hard workers; detail-oriented; considerate of others' feelings; friendly and warm to others; very conscientious; down-to-earth and like to be around the same.	Dentist, physician, biologist, surgical technician, teacher, speech pathologist, historian, clerical, bookkeeper, electrician, retail owner, counselor
ISFP—The Artist (5–7% of Americans)	Very sensitive and modest; adapt easily to change; they are respectful of others' feelings and values; take criticism personally; don't enjoy leadership roles.	Artist, chef, musician, nurse, medical assistant, surgeon, botanist, zoologist, science teacher, travel agent, game warden, coach, bookkeeper, clerical, insurance examiner
INFJ—The Protector (2–3% of Americans)	Enjoy an atmosphere where all get along; do what is needed of them; have strong beliefs and principles; enjoy helping others achieve their goals.	Career counselor, psychologist, teacher, social worker, clergy, artist, novelist, filmmaker, health care provider, human resource manager, agent, coach, crisis manager, mediator

(continued)

Figure 2.3 A Closer Look at Your Personality Type (*continued*)

Type	Attributes	Possible Careers
INFP—The Idealist (3–4% of Americans)	Work well alone; must know others well to interact; faithful to others and their jobs; excellent at communication; open-minded; dreamers; tend to do too much.	Entertainer, artist, editor, musician, professor, researcher, counselor, consultant, clergy, dietitian, massage therapist, human resources manager, events manager, corporate leader
INTJ—The Scientist (2–3% of Americans)	Very independent; enjoy challenges; inventors; can be skeptical; perfectionists; believe in their own work, sometimes to a fault.	Economist, financial planner, banker, budget analyst, scientist, astronomer, network specialist, computer programmer, engineer, curriculum designer, coroner, pathologist, attorney, manager
INTP—The Thinker (3–4% of Americans)	Extremely logical; very analytical; good at planning; love to learn; excellent problem solvers; don't enjoy needless conversation; hard to understand at times.	Software designer, programmer, systems analyst, network administrator, surgeon, veterinarian, lawyer, economist, architect, physicist, mathematician, college professor, writer, agent, producer
ESTP—The Doer (6–8% of Americans)	Usually very happy; don't let trivial things upset them; have very good memories; very good at working with things and taking them apart.	Police officer, firefighter, detective, military, investigator, paramedic, banker, investor, promoter, carpenter, chef, real estate broker, retail sales, insurance claims
ESTJ—The Guardian (12–15% of Americans)	"Take charge" people; like to get things done; focus on results; very good at organizing; good at seeing what will not work; responsible; realists.	Insurance agent, military, security, coach, credit analyst, project manager, auditor, general contractor, paralegal, stockbroker, executive, information officer, lawyer, controller, accounts manager
ESFP—The Performer (8–10% of Americans)	Very good at sports and active exercises; good common sense; easygoing; good at communication; can be impulsive; do not enjoy working alone; have fun and enjoy living and life.	Nurse, social worker, physician assistant, nutritionist, therapist, photographer, musician, film producer, social events coordinator, news anchor, fund raiser, host, retail sales
ESFJ—The Caregiver (11–14% of Americans)	Enjoy many friendly relationships; popular; love to help others; do not take criticism very well; need praise; need to work with people; organized; talkative; active.	Medical assistant, physician, nurse, teacher, coach, principal, social worker, counselor, clergy, court reporter, office manager, loan officer, public relations, customer service, caterer, office manager
ENFP—The Inspirer (6–7% of Americans)	Creative and industrious; can easily find success in activities and projects that interest them; good at motivating others; organized; do not like routine.	Journalist, writer, actor, newscaster, artist, director, public relations, teacher, clergy, psychologist, guidance counselor, trainer, project manager, human resources manager
ENFJ—The Giver (3–5% of Americans)	Very concerned about others' feelings; respect others; good leaders; usually popular; good at public speaking; can make decisions too quickly; trust easily.	Journalist, entertainer, TV producer, politician, counselor, clergy, psychologist, teacher, social worker, health care provider, customer service manager
ENTP—The Visionary (4–6% of Americans)	Great problem solvers; love to argue either side; can do almost anything; good at speaking/motivating; love challenges; very creative; do not like routine; overconfident.	Entrepreneur, manager, agent, journalist, attorney, urban planner, analyst, creative director, public relations, marketing, broadcaster, network solutions, politician, detective
ENTJ—The Executive (3–5% of Americans)	Excellent leaders; speak very well; hardworking; may be workaholics; may not give enough praise; like to learn; great planners; enjoy helping others reach their goals.	Executive, senior manager, administrator, consultant, editor, producer, financial planner, stockbroker, program designer, attorney, psychologist, engineer, network administrator

GRADUATE *Quote*

Nancy Kirkess
Graduate!
Empire College, Santa Rosa, CA
**Career: Concierge, River Rock Casino Visitors
and Convention Center**

As I was investigating and applying for employment during this stage in my life, I found that my criteria for the perfect job had changed from when I was younger.

I realized that an environment of mutual respect, where value and a sense of dignity were given to coworkers as well as clients, had risen to the top of my list.

KNOW WHAT YOU WANT FROM LIFE AND WORK

Are You Prepared to Go Get What You Want?

Some of the strongest, most dedicated people in the world struggle in their work and personal lives. Why? Because they have never really thought about what they want out of life or from their careers. They have never done the work required to answer this question—and it is work. What is it that you really want and need to be happy, fulfilled, and successful? What is the main thing that you really need to focus on? You may have never thought about the questions below, but consider them as you try to formulate an answer to the question, "What do I want from my life and my work?"

- Is my success tied to the amount of money I make?
- Are my friends and family more important than my career?
- What would I be willing to do to get ahead?
- What can I contribute to the world through my career?
- What really makes me happy? Will my career choice give this to me?
- Does my career choice suit my genuine interests?
- Does my current career choice really motivate me?
- Am I working toward this career for convenience or passion?
- Would I rather work inside or outside?
- Am I more of a leader or a follower?
- Do I want to travel with my work?
- Am I truly grounded in my ethics?
- Am I focused on the things that are life changing?

There is an old quote that says, "If you don't know where you're going, it doesn't matter which path you take." Many people have found this to be true in their personal and professional lives. Knowing what you want and need from your career and your life will be ultimately important to your happiness and success.

In the space below, jot down a few things that you think you want and need from your career. Remember, the two categories are different.

I need . . .	I want . . .
_____	_____
_____	_____
_____	_____
_____	_____

IDENTIFY AND EMULATE YOUR ROLE MODELS

Whom Do You Admire Most?

Whom do you admire most in your life right now? Is it a parent or grandparent who struggled to raise you and offer you things he or she never had? Is it your current supervisor who treats people well and with respect? Is it a famous person, such as Oprah Winfrey, who overcame adversity to help make life better for others?

We all have role models in our lives for a reason. They help us see what is possible. They help us see a better future. Think about a person that you greatly admire. Who is that person?

_____

What personal and professional qualities do they possess that you would like to someday have?

Personal Qualities	Professional Qualities
_____	_____
_____	_____
_____	_____
_____	_____
_____	_____

Choose one of the qualities from the list you created above. How will this quality help you become successful and advance in your chosen career? Be specific in your answer.

_____

_____

_____

_____

_____

Who is your best role model?

IndexOpen

DETERMINE WHAT YOU VALUE

What Really Matters to You?

Values are unique to each individual. What you value and consider important to your life and success may be at the bottom of the list for someone else. A value is simply a principle or quality that you think is worthwhile and regard highly. You may value honesty or love or friendship in your life. Others may put primary importance on money or possessions. Others' values might include family, children, or career.

So, why are values important to us? They usually drive our decisions, determine how we treat others, guide us in reacting to certain situations, and help direct our moral behavior. When we act in a way that goes against what we value, our conscience begins to gnaw at us. That little voice inside our head begins to let us know that what we have done, or what we are about to do goes against our moral code—our values. When we make decisions or act in a way that goes against the values established by society or our workplace, we begin to suffer in different ways, such as being terminated or reprimanded. Therefore, knowing what you value *and* what society and your workplace value will be exceedingly important to your success and mobility.

Our personal value system also serves as a motivational force in our lives. What we value, we work to keep, protect, enrich, and get more of. We are motivated by what brings us joy and peace, and unless we hold a firm picture of our value system in our hearts and minds, we may be working for the wrong things.

Take a moment and circle the words in the following list that best indicate what you value. If one or more of your personal values is not on the list, add them to the bottom.

Service to others	Privacy	Interaction
A healthy love relationship	Money	Honesty
Fairness	Challenges	Respect
The environment	Family	Friends
Justice	Success	Education
Leisure time	Faith	Money
Leadership abilities	Fun activities	Beauty
A nice home	Fine car	Stylish clothes
Safety	Health	Comfort
Fame/popularity	Independence	Control
Reputation	Physical activity	Pets
Decision making	Speaking	Writing

_____   _____   _____

_____   _____   _____

Now for the hard part—if you could only have one thing in your life that you valued and this value had to sustain you in your personal and professional life, which value above would you choose? _____

Why? _____

_____

How will this one value help you be successful in your career? _____

_____

_____

_____

THE POWER OF YOUR VALUES AND BELIEFS

What Do You Believe In and Hold in High Esteem?

It has been said, "If you think you can't, you can't. If you think you can, you can." Countless studies have been conducted on the power of personal beliefs and positive thinking. A belief is what we consider to be true or false. A belief is a conviction that we hold so dearly that it literally causes us to act in one way or another. If you believe that you are going to fail your math test, you probably will. If you believe that you have nothing to offer to the world, you probably do not. Our beliefs are powerful and central to our self-esteem and personal motivation. Consider the following examples:

Abraham Lincoln lost eight elections, went bankrupt twice, lost two children, and had a complete nervous and mental breakdown all before he became president of the United States. He believed that he could govern this country . . . and he did. He helped change the world.

Walt Disney was fired from his first job because his boss thought he did not have any creativity or good ideas and considered him to be a poor sketch artist. Disney believed that he was much more talented than his boss gave him credit for.

Tina Turner, raped and beaten by her own husband, Ike, had to sue in a court of law to keep her identity—her name. Ike believed that she would never be successful without him. She believed otherwise. After their divorce and business partnership ended, she recorded many songs, won several Grammys, and has sold over 300 million albums. Her beliefs paid off.

Ray Romano was fired from the TV show *NewsRadio* while it was still in rehearsal. He believed that he had talent as a comedian and went on to develop, produce, and write the Emmy-winning series *Everybody Loves Raymond*.

Maya Angelou has won three Grammys for the spoken word and has been nominated twice for Broadway's prestigious Tony Award. However, as a young girl, she was raped by her mother's boyfriend and did not speak again for four years. By the time she was in her twenties, she had been a cook, streetcar conductor, cocktail waitress, dancer, madam, high school dropout, and unwed mother. However, she believed that she had talent as a writer and poet. Her beliefs paid off, too. She became only the second poet in U.S. history to write and deliver an original poem at a presidential inauguration (for Bill Clinton).

Some examples of beliefs are:

- I believe that honesty is always the best policy.
- I believe that it is important to save 10 percent of my paycheck each month.
- I believe that hard work will always pay off in the end.
- I believe that people are basically good, not evil.
- I believe in God.

I am somebody. I am me. I like being me. And I need nobody to make me somebody.
—Louis L'Amour

Our beliefs can guide us through many troubled times. They can help us when everything seems to be going against our hopes and dreams. They influence our attitudes and behaviors. However, even though they are very powerful, beliefs alone will not get you an Emmy or the presidency of the United States. Beliefs must be followed by hard work, active goals, and many sacrifices.

Think about a belief that you hold dear. What is that belief? _____

_____

_____

_____

_____

How can this belief help guide you in your career or job-making decisions? _____

_____

_____

_____

CREATING YOUR OWN PERSONAL BRAND—ME, INC.

Who Do You Want to Become?

Brands are everywhere. The Nike swoosh, the Starbucks cup, Levi rivets, the AT&T globe—the list goes on and on. Big companies understand the importance of establishing a distinctive brand. You need to take a lesson from big companies and establish a brand for yourself. You are literally the CEO of your own company: Me, Inc. As you prepare to interview for a job, you need to be preparing to market yourself. You should be striving to "develop the micro equivalent of the Nike Swoosh" (Peters, 1997). You need to develop your brand!

You have an opportunity to stand out and to develop your own brand, to become exactly what you want to be. You have to figure out how to create a distinctive role for yourself, a message that conveys who you are. As you work through this book, you may want to change parts of your brand, but the main thing for you to focus on right now is getting started.

> The remarkable thing we have is a choice every day regarding the attitude we will embrace for that day. We cannot change our past . . . We cannot change the fact that people will act in a certain way. We cannot change the inevitable. The only thing we can do is play on the one string we have, and that is our attitude.
>
> —Charles R. Swindoll

THE POWER OF OPTIMISM AND THE RIGHT ATTITUDE

What Do You Need to Improve?

You've heard it all your life: "You have a great attitude." Or maybe "You have a bad attitude." Or "You need to improve your attitude." Perhaps you have heard it said this way: "Attitude is not important—attitude is everything." Parents, teachers, coaches, and bosses all talk constantly about attitude. Why are attitude and optimism so important? Perhaps it is because what you think and how you feel about yourself has so much to do with how your perform at school and later at work. Attitude is important in all aspects of your life: school, work, relationships. A recent national survey asked the question, "What counts more: Employee aptitude; hard skills and technical competencies; employee attitude; or relational skills, motivation and positive outlook? Nearly 60% of corporations said attitude was the no. 1 concern" (Teamwork Newsletter, 2008).

Exactly what is attitude? Attitude is the manner in which you act or your views toward whatever is happening. For example, you may care about your schoolwork, or you may not be interested. You might treat people with respect, or you may be disrespectful toward some people. You either come to school on time and listen, or you get there late and slouch in your desk and look disgusted. You have a willing attitude at work or you have a "let somebody else do it" disposition. All of this has to do with your personal attitude.

Your attitude affects your performance at school and at work; it also affects others' performance because one person with a bad attitude can have a negative effect on everyone around him

Figure 2.4 Working on Yourself

■ **Smile** even when you really just want to sit down and cry or when being grouchy and hurtful is easier than being nice. Greet everyone with a smile and good thoughts and feelings.

■ **Push yourself** to be outgoing and friendly even when you feel shy and want to withdraw. Remember that most people feel shy and insecure at times. By being friendly, you will be helping others who are struggling.

■ **Try to avoid worrying** about things that *might* happen. Deal with the here and now—that will usually be more than enough to keep you busy. It has been said that only 8 percent of our worries actually come true and they are usually small worries when they happen. Instead of worrying, focus your energy on doing great work at school or on your job.

■ **Give people sincere compliments.** Tell them how nice they look or specifically what a great job they did. Look right at the person and brag on him or her. Being nice to someone else takes nothing away from you, and it wins friends and influences people if you are sincere.

■ **Avoid getting caught up in the gossip mill.** Volunteer nice remarks about people when they are not present, especially if someone else is running them down. Stand up for people who are being mistreated when you can.

■ **Try to be helpful to others**, especially someone who is having a really bad day or a difficult time in their

Only 8 percent of our worries are actually over legitimate troubles. 40 percent of our worries never happen. 30 percent of our worries concern the past. 12 percent are needless worries about health. 10 percent are insignificant.
—Dr. Walter Cavert

lives. Offer to pick up something for them or buy them lunch or just listen. Kindness is never forgotten, and everyone needs it.

■ **Get up early and exercise for a few minutes** to get your adrenaline working. Meditate and concentrate on all the good things in your life. Count your blessings instead of your problems.

■ **Rid yourself of negative baggage** that you have been carrying around with you—bad things that happened, and you keep bringing them up in your mind. Forgive yourself and others for things that happened in the past that hurt you. It is very important for you to forgive yourself! In your mind, put all the negative things you are still holding onto in a big suitcase. Take this suitcase into the forest and leave it there with all the negativity that you have been carrying around way too long. Now, pretend that you are walking out of the forest into the sunshine.

■ **Be aware that everyone you meet is carrying some kind of burden or dealing with a problem.** A negative reaction from someone may be a reflection of a difficult problem they are struggling with rather than the fact they are simply not nice people. Try to listen to people's words but also their body language. Look at people around you. What can you do to help them? You will find that if you help others, you will feel better about yourself, and they will help you when you need it.

or her. Not only must you work on your personal attitude, you also have to learn not to let others make you feel bad about yourself or to put a damper on your day. So how do you get this magical attitude that makes things so much better for you and everyone with whom you come in contact? Consider the tips in Figure 2.4.

GETTING RID OF NEGATIVISM AND AVOIDING NEGATIVE PEOPLE

Who Drags You Down and Makes You Feel Small?

One thing you need to know is that you can't change anyone unless he or she wants to change—that includes people with negative attitudes. You can only change yourself and how you allow other people's negative attitudes to affect you. As you deal with certain people who make you feel small or put you down, consider your feelings after you have interacted with them. What was the result of your being in contact with that person? Did you feel worse or distressed or depressed? Did talking to a certain person make you begin to doubt your ability to do something that you really wanted to do? This is what attitude is all about—you simply can't let those people control you and your emotions. So what do you do to rid yourself of this negativism and negative people's attitudes? Study the tips in Figure 2.5.

Shutterstock

Do you allow people with negative attitudes to rub off on you?

Figure 2.5   Working on Relationships

- Make up your mind that you are in control of yourself and that you will not let anyone else steal your joy and optimism. This may take time. The person who makes you feel bad could be your mother or your significant other or a good friend. Is there a person or people who make you feel bad almost every time you interact with them? Sometimes you simply have to distance yourself from these people so you can get healthy yourself—even if it is someone whom you love very much.

- Try to be helpful to negative people. Point out the positive. Try to offer them constructive solutions, but don't let them become destructive to you.

- Be aware of how you feel after you have been in contact with certain people. Who lifts you up? Makes you laugh? Encourages you? Increase your time with these people, and decrease your time with those who bring you down.

- When faced with challenges that are very difficult, think about all the good things and the good people you have in your life. Spend time with a person who really cares about you. Remember to listen to them as well as talk about your own problems.

- Remember that you have to get along with negative people, especially at work. You might put this advice under the category "social diplomacy." "Employees who have good professional skills but do not relationally get along with co-workers, clients or management are now considered incompetent" (Teamworks Fall Newsletter, 2008). More people are terminated because of attitude-related problems than lack of job skills. Social diplomacy can take you a long way at work and in life.

> *The optimist sees opportunity in every danger; the pessimist sees danger in every opportunity.*
> *—Winston Churchill*

Do you use the power of positive people to improve your own attitude?

Shutterstock

CHOOSE OPTIMISM AND SURROUND YOURSELF WITH OPTIMISTIC PEOPLE

What Can I Gain by Surrounding Myself with Positive People?

Your attitude is yours. It belongs to you. You own it. Good or bad, happy or sad, optimistic or pessimistic, it is yours and you are responsible for it. However, your attitude is greatly influenced by situations in your life and by the people with whom you associate. Developing a winning, optimistic attitude can be hard, yet extremely rewarding work. Motivated and successful people have learned that one's attitude is the mirror to one's soul.

Optimism has many benefits beyond helping you develop a winning attitude. Researchers have found that people who are optimistic live longer, are more motivated, survive cancer treatment at a greater rate, have longer and more satisfying relationships, and are mentally healthier than pessimists. This would suggest that developing and maintaining a winning, optimistic attitude can help you have a longer and more satisfying quality of life.

Listen to yourself for a few days. Are you more of an optimist or a pessimist? Do you hear yourself whining, complaining, griping, and finding fault with everything and everybody around you? Do you blame others for things that are wrong in your life? Do you blame your bad grades on your professors? Is someone else responsible for your unhappiness? If these thoughts or comments are in your head, you are suffering from *"I CAN'T" Syndrome* (**I**rritated, **C**ontaminated, **A**ngry, **N**egative **T**houghts). This pessimistic condition can negatively influence every aspect of your life, from your self-esteem and your motivation level to your academic performance, your relationships, and your career success.

If you want to eliminate *"I CAN'T"* from your life, consider the following tips:

- Work every day to find the good in people, places, and things.
- Discover what is holding you back and what you need to push you forward.
- Visualize your success—visualize yourself actually being who and what you want to be.
- Locate and observe positive, optimistic people and things in your life.
- Make a list of who helps you, supports you, and helps you feel positive; then make a point to be around them more.
- Take responsibility for your own actions and their consequences.
- Force yourself to find five positive things a day for which to be thankful.

You've seen the difference between an optimist and a pessimist. Both are everywhere—at work, at school, and probably in your own family. Positive, upbeat, and motivated people are easy to spot. You can basically see their attitude in the way they walk, the way they carry themselves, the way they approach people, and the way they treat others. Negative people are also easy to spot—they are grouchy, late, and depressing.

Learn from both as you move through the days and months ahead. Choose your friends carefully. Seek out people who have ambition, good work habits, positive attitudes, and high ethical standards. Look for those who study hard, enjoy learning, are goal oriented, and don't mind taking a stand when they believe strongly about something. Befriend people who have interests and hobbies that are new to you. Step outside your comfort zone and add people to your circle of friends who are from a different

POSITIVE HABITS *at Work*

When you hear someone gossiping and spreading rumors, do not participate in the conversation. It can only lead to resentment and trouble. If you feel it is appropriate, say something positive about the person who is being maligned.

culture, are of a different religion, or who have lived in a different geographic region. You'll be happily surprised at how much enrichment they can bring to your life and how much you grow personally and professionally in the process.

Be wary, however, of *the others*. Whiners. Degraders. Attackers. Manipulators. Pessimists. Back-stabbers. Abusers. Cowards. Two-faced racists, sexists, ageists, homophobes, ethnocentrists. These people carry around an aura so negative that it can almost be seen as a dark cloud above them. They degrade others because they do not like themselves. They find fault with everything because their own lives are unrewarding. Many of these people will do nothing to use their potential but will attack you for being motivated and trying to improve your life. We call them contaminated people.

Examine the two lists that follow. As you read through the lists, consider the people with whom you associate. Are the majority of your friends, family, peers, and work associates positive or contaminated?

Positive People:	Contaminated People:
■ Bring out the best in you	■ Bring out the worst in you
■ Find the good in bad situations	■ Find the bad in every situation
■ Are gracious and understanding	■ Are rude and uncaring
■ Build people up	■ Sabotage people, even loved ones
■ Support your dreams	■ Criticize your hopes and plans
■ Make you feel comfortable and happy	■ Make you feel uneasy, nervous, and irritable
■ Tell you the truth and offer constructive criticism	■ Are two-faced and use harsh language to "put you in your place"
■ Are open-minded and fair	■ Are narrow and ethnocentric
■ Are patient	■ Are quick to anger
■ Are giving	■ Are jealous and smothering
■ Love to learn from others	■ Think they know everything

As you think about the list above and the people in your life, ask yourself, "Do I surround myself with more positive or contaminated people?" As you consider your friends, family, class-mates, and work associates, use the space below to compare and contrast one *positive person* with one *contaminated person* in your life.

Positive Person _____

His/Her Attributes _____

_____

_____

Contaminated Person _____

His/Her Attributes _____

_____

_____

Compare and Contrast _____

_____

_____

UNDERSTAND YOUR EMOTIONAL RESPONSES

Who Pushes Your Buttons?

Should evolution be taught in the public school system? Should the drinking age be lowered to 18? Should 16-year-olds be allowed to drive? Should hate crime laws be abolished? Should same-sex couples be allowed to marry and adopt children? What emotions are you feeling right now? Did you immediately formulate answers to these questions in your mind? Do your emotions drive the way you think or act?

Your mentality shapes your reality.
—Bert Goldman

Emotions play a vital role in our lives. They help us feel compassion, offer assistance to others, reach out in times of need, and relate with compassion and empathy. On the other hand, our emotions can cause problems in our thinking process. They can cloud issues and distort facts. They can make us act in inappropriate ways when normally, we would not—and this can affect our performance and attitude in the workplace. Emotions are not bad—as a matter of fact, they are good and help us be human. However, it is of paramount importance that you know how to identify when your emotions are calling the shots and how to control them. You do not have to eliminate emotions from your thoughts or actions, but it is crucial that you know when your emotions are clouding an issue.

ARTICULATE YOUR HOPES AND GOALS

BIGGEST INTERVIEW *Blunders*

Rosalynn had done a very good job with her resumé and cover letter and had secured an interview with her dream company. Things got off to a good start at the interview, but Rosalynn knew she had blown it when the interviewer asked her to tell her what she knew about the company. Rosalynn realized too late that she should have made the effort to learn a great deal about the company before going to an interview!

LESSON: Always research the company and be prepared to talk about the positive things you know about it and to ask thoughtful questions. If the interviewer doesn't ask you about the company, try to find ways to weave some of your knowledge related to the company's policies into the conversation.

Where Are You Going with Your One Lifetime?

"Go tell it on the mountain, over the hills and everywhere . . . " "Why would I want to do that?" you might ask. "If I tell everyone my hopes and dreams and goals, they'll know if I don't make it." Yes, but they will also know when you do—and they can help you make it.

If others know what you want from your life or your career, they can help you bring it to fruition. When you share what type of position you want or where you would like to work, others can be on the lookout for you, and you can do the same for your peers.

Consider this: You have a secret desire to become an animation artist for Pixar Animation Studios. Yes, it is a major film company producing such hits as *Finding Nemo, Cars,* and *Toy Story.* "How stupid to think that someone from Newell, Iowa (population 887) could ever go to work for one of Disney's major studios," you might think. Wrong. Wrong. Wrong. Everyday people get fabulous dream jobs. Someone became the veterinarian for Lady Gaga's pets, someone became Oprah's personal trainer, and someone became an animator for an upcoming Disney/Pixar film. Others became the head mechanic for Delta Airlines and a chef at MGM Grand in Las Vegas, a nurse at Mercy Hospital, a firefighter for New York City, and a fashion design intern for Versace. Why? Because they had talent, they worked hard, they had a belief that they could do it, and they let others know of their hopes and dreams.

Consider this. You told your classmate that you really want to become a physical therapist. Your peer takes his mother to physical therapy one day and overhears a conversation between two staff members about an opening. She mentions this to you. You stop by the therapy center to inquire, and they are very impressed that you knew about the position and took the initiative to stop by. You fill out an application, leave your resumé, and two days later, you're called in for an interview to become an intern.

> *You are fast becoming what you are going to be.*
> —Patricia G. Moody

Reflections: PUTTING IT ALL TOGETHER

A great deal of your success in the workplace depends on the characteristics and qualities you bring with you. Your attitude, optimism, and personality type will all affect your performance at work. It is important that you find good role models to emulate, that you build a strong set of values and beliefs, and that you rid yourself of negativity about yourself and others. Knowing what you want, staying focused on your goals, and working hard will be valuable assets in the workplace.

DIGITAL BRIEFCASE

PERSONAL BRANDING

Review the information on personal branding on page 37. Answer the following questions as you think about creating your own brand: Me, Inc.

- ■ What is unique about you? (Do you have special talents? Are you loyal and dedicated to your company and coworkers? Do you have unique technology talents?)
- ■ What is a feature benefit about you? (Are you always on time? Do you deliver high-quality work? Do you get along well with team members? Are you great at problem solving?)
- ■ What have you done that you are most proud of? (Were you on the debate team? Did you lead a team? Did you succeed at a part-time job? Did you volunteer for a charitable activity?)
- ■ How do you sell the "sizzle" about yourself? (What can you do to be noticed and appreciated? Can you take on a project for an organization? Can you volunteer for tasks at work? Are you careful what you send out via technology that can easily be passed on to anybody else? (How about your personal advertisements when you text, e-mail, or post something to your Facebook wall? Do you stop and think before engaging in popular pastimes like "sexting?" Are you thinking when you post pictures on Facebook that might come back to haunt you later?)
- ■ Do you volunteer or participate in things that give you power? If your meetings are disorganized, can you volunteer to write an agenda that keeps your group on track? Can you put together an informal user's group that can give you honest feedback on how your brand is doing? Ask them to give you an honest assessment of how you are perceived and what they think you need to do differently.)
- ■ How do you measure up against four important benchmarks?
    - ■ Are you a great team member and supportive colleague?
    - ■ What are you a real expert at that adds value to your personal brand?

- What are you doing that adds to your ability to apply vision to everything you do?
- Are the things you are trying to accomplish practical and doable?

If you are smart, you will figure out the answer to all these questions and create a brand for which you are known, a brand that sells the best features of who you are and what you have to offer. It takes time, and it's not easy, but it is absolutely essential to your success. Know who you are! Know what you want! Build the brand that takes you there!

By thinking about who you really are, what you want, what you need, and what you have to offer an employer, you can better determine the type of position you will need in order to be happy, successful, and continue growing. If you focus on matching your vocation together with your passion, you will never face a day of "work" in your life. Work hard on developing your personal brand (Peters, 1997).

So, let's get to work on creating your personal brand.

Complete the following questions about yourself as you begin to work on developing your special brand—Me, Inc.

1. Write at least three things that you think are unique about you.

   _____

   _____

2. Name at least one major benefit about you.

   _____

3. What special talent can you add to a company's everyday function that will make you stand out? When answering this question, consider the list you developed on page 27.

   _____

   _____

4. Name something you have done that you are very proud of.

   _____

   _____

5. What can you do to get noticed in a subtle, positive way without appearing that you are bragging?

   _____

   _____

6. Do the personal messages you send reflect positively on you? Which things do you need to start doing or stop doing?

   _____

   _____

7. What can you volunteer to do at work or school that will give you positive visibility?

   _____

   _____

8. Name at least three people who can serve as your "user's group" and who will tell you honestly what you need to know and what you need to do differently.

   _____

   _____

9. Measure yourself against the four benchmarks mentioned on pages 43–44. How are you doing? For each one, give yourself a grade from A to F.

1. _____   3. _____

2. _____   4. _____

You should now be ready to focus on developing your brand, an important step in discovering who you are and what you have to offer.

REFERENCES

Aaker, J., & Smith, A. (2010). *The dragonfly effect.* San Francisco: Jossey-Bass.

Center for Law and Social Policy. (2003). *The language of opportunity: Expanding employment for adults with limited English skills.* Washington, DC: Author

Gordon, E. (2008). *The 2010 meltdown: Solving the impending job crisis.* Lanham, MD: Rowman & Littlefield Education.

Peters, T. (August 31, 1997). "The Brand Called You." *Fast Company.*

Teamworks Newsletter. (2008). Retrieved on March 3, 2011, from www.iwolff.com/files/teamworks/Newsletter-attitudeIsEverythingInTheWorkplace.pdf.

Tieger, P., & Barron-Tieger, B. (2001). *Do what you are: Discover the perfect career for you through the secrets of personality type* (3rd ed.). Boston: Little, Brown.

Part II:
Communication

Chapters taken from:
Cornerstones for Professionalism, Second Edition
by Robert M. Sherfield and Patricia G. Moody

Professionalism: Skills for Workplace Success, Third Edition
by Lydia E. Anderson and Sandra B. Bolt

chapter three

COMMUNICATE

EFFECTIVE COMMUNICATION FOR THE SOCIAL MEDIA GENERATION

The way we communicate with others and with ourselves ultimately determines the quality of our lives.
—Anthony Robbins

Why read this chapter?

Because you'll learn...

- The key elements of the communication process
- How to make a positive first impression
- The difference between formal and informal communications

Because you'll be able to...

- Engage in appropriate verbal and nonverbal communication
- Compose a variety of written communication documents

PROFESSIONALS from the Field

Name: Leo G. Borges

Business: CEO/Founder Borges and Mahoney, Inc.

Successful businesses are built on communication. There is no substitute for it. There is no way around it. And there is no excuse for not doing it well. One of the most important things you will encounter in any business, small or large, is how strong communication plays a vital role not only in the big strategic plans of a company but also in the day-to-day workings between people. Lack of clear and strong communication skills can cost you dearly in the workplace and I would encourage you to learn everything you can about communicating well in writing, orally, nonverbally, and online. Then, practice it!

THE IMPORTANCE OF COMMUNICATING WELL

How Does It Affect Your Life?

Effective communication skills are constantly rated among the top five attributes that employers seek in today's workforce. According to the National Association of Colleges and Employers (2011), verbal communication skills topped the list of soft skills companies seek in college graduates. Good communication skills set you apart from others.

Communication is not something we do **to people**; rather, it is something that is done **between people.** Communication encompasses every aspect of your personal life, your work life, and your social life and takes up most of your time—in fact, the typical person spends up to 75 percent of every day communicating. Even though this process is so important, most of us were never taught to communicate properly; therefore, many go through life feeling frustrated, misunderstood, involved in conflicts, and not measuring up to their potential simply because they didn't learn to communicate well.

Communication involves what you are thinking and saying, but just as important, it involves what the other person is thinking and saying. To become a good communicator, you have to put yourself in the other person's position. This chapter will discuss the communications process and will show you how to co-create better outcomes with people in all aspects of communications. To co-create good communication outcomes, you have to take responsibility not just for what you are saying or writing, but also for how the other person interprets your messages. Quite often we think we have communicated something to another person, and they interpreted the message in an entirely different way from what we intended. It is a mistake to assume that the other person understood your message exactly as you meant it.

When you go to work, you will be communicating all day—talking on the phone; responding and generating e-mails; meeting face-to-face; using social media; attending meetings; interfacing with customers; working with colleagues; writing memos, letters, and reports; and interacting with your supervisors. In other words, everything you do will be affected by how well you speak, write, listen, interpret nonverbal communications, and make good decisions about what is communicated to you by others.

> *The single biggest problem in communication is the illusion that it has taken place.*
> —George Bernard Shaw

> *You can have brilliant ideas, but if you can't get them across, your ideas won't get you anywhere.*
> —Lee Iacocca, former CEO of Chrysler Corporation

THE COMMUNICATION PROCESS

How Does Communication Work?

Basically, the communications process involves **six elements:** the source, the message, the channel, the receiver, barriers, and feedback. Consider Figure 3.1.

Barriers (represented by the lines in Figure 3.1) are factors that can interfere with the source, the message, the channel, or the receiver. Barriers can occur anywhere within the communication

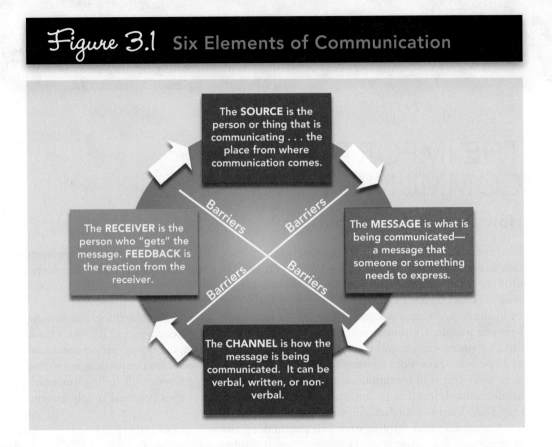

Figure 3.1 Six Elements of Communication

The **SOURCE** is the person or thing that is communicating . . . the place from where communication comes.

The **RECEIVER** is the person who "gets" the message. **FEEDBACK** is the reaction from the receiver.

The **MESSAGE** is what is being communicated— a message that someone or something needs to express.

Barriers

Barriers

Barriers

Barriers

The **CHANNEL** is how the message is being communicated. It can be verbal, written, or non-verbal.

process and can include external noise (others talking, cell phones, and traffic) and internal noise (self-talk, doubt, and questioning). Your emotions, past experiences, social norms, communication expectations, and prejudices can also be barriers to effective communications. **Feedback** is the verbal and nonverbal responses the receiver gives you.

MAKING AN IMPRESSIVE FIRST IMPRESSION

How Do People Judge You Face-to-Face?

You never get a second chance to make a good first impression. So what do you need to do to impress people? First, remember that the impression starts the moment someone sees you, hears you on the telephone, or receives your written communication. You may not like it, but first impressions stick, and they are very hard to change and virtually impossible to erase. So you need to get it right the first time!

According to Susan Bixler and Nancy Nix-Rice (2005), "Books are judged by their covers, houses are appraised by their curb appeal, and people are initially evaluated on how they choose to dress and behave. In a perfect world, this is not fair, moral or just. What's inside should count a great deal more. And eventually, it does, but not right away. In the meantime, a lot of opportunities can be lost." If you don't make a good first impression, you may not get a chance to make another one.

It doesn't take long to make an impression. "You have about 30 seconds, at the most. When someone first sees you, they will be deciding about your education level, competence and success, personality, level of sophistication, confidence, trustworthiness, sense of humor and social heritage" (Bixler & Nix-Rice, 2005). People may not even realize they are judging you, but it is a natural human reaction to do just that.

So exactly what do people notice when they meet you? From several feet away, they first see you. They notice if you are standing tall or slouching, neatly groomed or sloppy, smiling or frowning, walking briskly or dragging along, acting confident or shy. The person meeting you sees all these things at once. Their eyes are like little cameras, snapping picture after picture and saving them. They are deciding if you are likeable, assertive, and friendly. They are drawing conclusions about your ability, communication style, manners, etiquette, and attitude—and they haven't even met you yet!

Then the person hears your voice and makes another judgment. Is your voice well modulated? Is it pleasant? Is it too loud or too soft? Do you use good grammar? Do you have an accent? Is there a smile in your voice? Do you appear to be educated? All of this is taken in by the other person in an instant.

And finally, you shake hands with the other person and he or she notices immediately if you have a firm handshake or a "cold fish" grip. So, in less than 30 seconds, you have made a first impression that will be very difficult to change. Not only are overall impressions, dress, and grooming significant factors when getting a job and working with clients and colleagues, they are also very important when it comes to being considered for a promotion. That's why all of this is important!

Do yourself a big favor. Take a few minutes, look in the mirror, and judge yourself as though you are looking at someone else. Use the questions in Figure 3.2 to assess your first impression profile.

In the space below, identify the one thing you need to work on most to improve your first impression profile.

_____

_____

_____

_____

Employers expect you to have an excellent professional appearance and behavior because you are representing their company. When you interview looking your best and presenting yourself as a professional, it's like "money in the bank." Employers pay more for people who look and act professional. When you greet clients with a smile, a firm handshake, and appropriate dress, you are representing yourself and your company well and making a lasting positive impression. Because of technology, we have fewer face-to-face meetings, making the ones that we do have all the more important.

Figure 3.2 First Impression Profile

- If you are honest, what do you really see when you look in the mirror? What can you improve?

- Is something about your appearance holding you back? How are your grooming and hygiene? Do you need to change anything?

- What do your posture and facial expressions say about you? Do you smile or frown often?

- Do you dress appropriately for a person about to enter the business world, or do you need to spruce up your wardrobe?

- Are you friendly and engaging? Are you nice to everyone you meet?

- Do you shake hands firmly and confidently?

Making a Good Impression on the Telephone

Later, you will learn about nonverbal communication and the importance of body language. When talking on the phone, you lose the power of body language, including facial expressions. All you have to represent yourself is your voice. How you sound is more important than what you say. When you answer, put a smile in your voice and make the other person feel that you are glad he or she called. Identify yourself properly, speak clearly with a well-modulated tone of voice, and provide accurate and timely information. If you say you will get back to someone by a certain time, do it! If you don't know the answer to his or her questions, say, "I don't know, but I will find out and get back to you right away." If the person calling is irate, do not return anger. Perhaps he or she is just having a bad day. If you stay calm and polite, the other person will often apologize for being rude.

Making a Good Impression in Written Documents

If you have never met someone or talked to them on the telephone, all they have to judge you on when they receive a document from you is the document itself. This is what he or she will automatically notice: Is the document professional? Is it formatted correctly? Is the paper of good quality? Are the spelling and grammar correct? Were you polite, clear, and concise?

It is very important to remember that you are always making impressions on people, and they are saving them like pictures in an album. Most people really don't know you, but they have an opinion of you because of what you choose to let them see. The good news? You can shape those opinions and impressions.

Is the woman likely to make a good first impression? Why or why not?

Shutterstock

FORMAL AND INFORMAL COMMUNICATION

Why Is It Important to Understand the Difference?

At work we communicate to share information for several different purposes: persuading, influencing, motivating, or informing. Information is delivered in two basic ways—**formal** and **informal.** Formal communications flow through an organization's lines of authority. You receive information based on your role in the company and where you are located on the organizational chart. This information is distributed through formal networks in order to get action from everyone who needs to be involved.

Formal information may come through your direct supervisor, a division supervisor, or a company officer. This type of important information can be delivered either vertically or horizontally and is important for keeping employees informed. Formal messages flowing through the organization need to be carefully planned, because such information may have a dramatic impact on employees. **Formal vertical information** often flows from the top down—from executives and directors to managers and then to staff—and may be delivered in oral messages, company newsletters, procedures manuals, policy directives, or management decisions. Formal vertical information can also flow up the organizational chart in the form of reports, budgets, and suggestions from staff to managers to directors to executives. It is important for you to follow the chain of command when communicating formal information. **Formal horizontal information** usually occurs between people or departments who work closely together and are located near each other on the organizational chart.

The second major type of communication is **informal.** This type of communication is not planned or managed in an organized manner but is nevertheless very important. Informal communication follows no lines of authority and tends to be spread by word of mouth. This information can spread quickly throughout a department and even a company because no one is restricted from hearing it and no formal lines of communication are used.

Frequently, you will hear informal communication referred to as *the grapevine.* This type of information may be considered as gossip or rumors. Grapevine messages usually escalate when employees feel threatened or vulnerable about their jobs or a policy that they think is coming down from the top. If situations are ambiguous or uncertain or if big changes are being planned without employees having enough knowledge, the grapevine will kick into high gear. Rumors can spread information very quickly, and the danger is that exaggerations and deletions happen as the story is passed from one person to another.

Regardless of whether the grapevine is accurate or not, it cannot be eliminated. People simply cannot be stopped from talking, but wise managers can learn to understand and influence it. After conducting a survey about informal communications, Carol Gorman (2005) concluded: "Formal communication focuses on messages the company wants to deliver, with a scope management feels is appropriate, and at a time management feels is right. The reason the grapevine plays such an important role is that it delivers the information employees care about, provides the details employees think they should know, and is delivered at the time employees are interested." According to Gorman (2005), "80 percent of information coming down the grapevine is true."

Answer the questions in Figure 3.3 to determine how well you are helping to co-create effective formal and informal communication.

Shutterstock

How does informal communication such as the "grapevine" affect the work environment?

Figure 3.3 Taking Responsibility for Co-Creating Effective Communication

- Am I sure I understood how the other person interpreted my message?

- Did I make the other person feel acknowledged and important?

- Did I really hear the other person, or did I show some reaction that caused me not to get the right message?

- Did I speak in the other person's language/communication style to make him or her feel comfortable?

- Was I open, honest, and sincere in my message?

- Did I prejudge the other person for any reason that may have caused me not to understand his or her message?

- If I asked someone to do something, was I clear in my expectations and deadlines?

- Did I make the other person feel that his or her viewpoints were appreciated and respected?

- Did I listen well enough to get a better understanding of the other person's feelings and positions?

- If the conversation did not go as I wished, did I gain anything from the conversation that will help me improve my relationship with the person?

VERBAL COMMUNICATION

Are You Sending the Right Message?

Verbal communication includes any type of interaction that uses the spoken word. Knowing a great deal of information is important, but the ability to use words and enthusiasm to bring those ideas to life is highly valued in the business world. You will need to be able to use effective verbal communication in business meetings, staff meetings, interactions with customers, telephone discussions, and informal conversations with colleagues.

Learning to deliver powerful and considerate oral communication messages can be very important to your career, as well as in your personal life. Communicating verbally can be a little tricky. If you use basic words or slang, you may not appear to be well-educated; on the other hand, if you use big words that most people don't understand, you may be considered arrogant, and you probably won't be understood.

The goal of verbal communication is to be heard and understood, so you have to think about your listener. How old is the receiver of your message? How well educated is the person? What is the person's mood at the time? Listen to what is not being said, as well as what is. Look at the person and be sure you are establishing eye contact. Do you sense anger? Is it better to leave things unsaid for now?

> *It is better to remain silent and be thought a fool than to open one's mouth and remove all doubt.*
> —Abraham Lincoln

Speak with Authority and Clarity

While nonverbal communication is extremely important, you cannot ignore that what you say and how you say it matters, too. The "power of words" is staggering. They can make a person's day or break a person's spirit. They change nations, free masses, and even start wars. The most interesting thing about words is that they must have a medium—they must be written or spoken—and here is where you come into the picture. In truth, the phrase "the power of words" is a misnomer. Words have little power until they are used by humans. *You* determine how words and phrases are to be used, and in turn, you determine their power.

If you have to deliver bad news, remember the lesson you probably experienced when you were a child: When you had to take bad medicine, it went down easier when it was in orange juice. Wrap up bad messages in "orange juice" by sharing a compliment first, which should make your words more palatable for the receiver.

Your ability to speak with confidence, clarity, and sincerity will be paramount to your success. To improve the *quality* of your oral communication skills when interacting with others or interviewing, use these simple strategies:

- Be sincere and honest
- Be clear, accurate, and detailed
- Mean what you say and work hard to say what you mean
- Choose your words carefully
- Use examples to clarify your point
- Ask for feedback during the discussion
- Get to the point as quickly as possible
- Make sure you emphasize your main points
- Pay attention to others' feelings and emotions
- Respect others' opinions
- Don't use language that is threatening or demeaning to you or others
- Try to put other people at ease
- Remember the power of silence; force yourself to listen

Think about your own communication efforts at this point in your life. Below, make a list of three positive communication strategies you now use. An example might be, "I am very good at making my point clear."

1. _____

2. _____

3. _____

Now consider the areas where you may need improvement. List three areas and at least one strategy for improvement in each area. Example: "I am not a very good listener." Strategy for improvement: "I plan to make it a point to stop talking when others are talking."

1. _____

Strategy for Improvement: _____

_____

2. _____

Strategy for Improvement: _____

_____

3. _____

Strategy for Improvement: _____

> *The real art of conversation is not only to say the right thing at the right place but to leave unsaid the wrong thing at the tempting moment.*
>
> —Dorothy Nevill

Dealing with Language Diversity in the Workplace

"When the 2000 census results were publicized, many customer service companies received a jolt: Hispanics now made up nearly 13 percent of the U.S. population and had surpassed African Americans as the largest minority group in the country" (Holmes, 2003). In 2011 over 16 percent of the population, the Hispanic population has continued to thrive in this country and is expected to increase to 30 percent of the U.S. population by 2050. Because of the rapid growth of the Hispanic population and other nationalities, the language of business has changed.

Astute companies are bringing the Spanish language to their English-speaking employees through in-house classes while simultaneously teaching English as a second language to their Spanish-speaking employees. In response to increased diversity in the workplace, companies are making Spanish ATMs available, providing call centers with Spanish-speaking employees, and introducing Spanish-language credit cards. Several other minority cultures have grown significantly in recent years and are making their mark on the U.S. workplace as well.

Communication among employees and between employees and customers and clients is critical in any well-run business, but it is complicated when you are dealing with a culturally diverse workforce. Language diversity can be a serious problem in the workplace. On the other hand, used properly, language diversity can be a great asset because a business can relate more directly to large populations. Communicating well with all employees affects employee morale, improves understanding of safety regulations, helps build good relationships with a diverse customer base, and exposes all employees to a rich internal corporate culture.

If you are a native-born U.S. citizen, you have the advantage of understanding the language and the culture, and you can be very helpful and accommodating to non-English-speaking employees in helping them understand the culture. If you are viewed as a friendly, helpful team player, this will bode well for you in terms of getting promoted.

Some people say the United States has no real culture, that we are merely a conglomeration of cultures from other worlds. "There are many reasons why it is important to remember that America does have a culture. The first reason, quite simply, is a question of pride. Having cultural self-awareness gives us all, regardless of our culture, a sense of identity and core values that allows us to function more successfully in both our personal and professional lives. Equally important, however, is that knowing our own culture makes it possible to more accurately interpret the needs and behaviors of colleagues, patients, and families who might be new arrivals to this country" (Thiederman, 2011). Our pride, culture, and language are all important to us. We need to remember that the same can be said of people who come to this country from other countries.

NONVERBAL COMMUNICATION

Does Your Body Language Match Your Words?

The typical working adult spends about 75 percent of waking hours communicating knowledge, thoughts, and ideas to others and making an effort to transfer information to another person. Most of us, however, do not realize that a large part of what we communicate to each other comes through nonverbal communications or body language.

The most important thing in communication is to hear what isn't being said.
—Peter Drucker

What you're doing speaks so loudly I can't hear what you're saying.
—Anonymous

Nonverbal communication includes facial expressions, tone of voice, body posture and motions, eye contact, and positioning within groups. It may also include the way we wear our clothes or the fact that we remain silent or how we use space. It could be a look, a glare, a wince, a pulling back, or a crossing of arms. You need to be very aware of this fact: As much as 90 percent of what you are saying is not coming from your mouth.

Because we function in a global society today, it is important to remember that nonverbal communication is powerful in any language or culture. Some researchers believe that facial expressions convey 55 percent of a message. Facial expressions are similar in many different cultures. A smile, for example, is universally understood.

Study Figure 3.4 carefully for information about different aspects of nonverbal communication.

Understanding all kinds of communication is very important to your career and personal success, but perhaps none is more important than nonverbal communication.

WRITTEN COMMUNICATION

Did I Get My Message Across?

Although written communication is not used as much as verbal communication or nonverbal communication, it is very important to your career success. The forms of written communication used in business include letters, reports, e-mails, memos, and notes. These documents can be printed, handwritten, or sent electronically. All business documents should be typed, unless you are writing a personal note such as a thank you or a congratulatory note.

One of the major differences in written and verbal communication is that the document alone conveys the message—you are not there in person to smile, be friendly, or listen and answer questions. When the recipient gets your written document, he or she will automatically judge you on the appearance and the content. If you wrote a letter, what kind of stationery did you use? Was it heavy bond paper or did you scrawl it on notebook paper? Did you use correct grammar and spelling? Is the document formatted well? Is the content clear and complete? Were you respectful of the other person? All these points matter when you are communicating in writing.

Study the tips for written communication in Figure 3.5.

Figure 3.4 The Important Messages of Nonverbal Communications

Eye Contact	Eye contact is one of the most powerful communication tools. Eyes convey emotion; they may signal when to start or finish and may show anger, disgust, friendliness, happiness, or sadness.
Facial Expressions	Facial expressions often convey the attitude of the person. This could be a smile, a frown, a sneer, a yawn, a raising or lowering of the eyebrows, a doubtful look, squinting the eyes, or a blank stare.
Voice	The quality and tone of your voice and how fast or slow you speak conveys a message. Your voice should be pitched deep; you should speak with a strong voice; and you should speak fluently and knowledgeably to be believable.
Gestures	Gestures are often a reflection of the individual and may be somewhat difficult to understand. Some gestures, such as a raised, clenched fist, are universally understood and some, such as pointing, are considered rude and unmannerly. Gestures include waving the arms, crossed arms, tapping the fingers, and cracking knuckles.
Space	Respect the other person's space. The distance you stand away from someone may indicate attraction, the intensity of the conversation, or status of the person. Pulling back from someone might mean that something has been said or done that the other person finds offensive.
Kinesics	People's movements while they are talking sometimes convey hidden messages.
Forward, Backward, and Vertical Movements	It is considered good practice to lean slightly forward in an interview, as it conveys interest. Similarly, it is considered positive to stand up straight and tall when you are meeting someone or greeting someone at an interview. Slumping conveys a message of laziness or a lack of self-confidence.
Handshake	A firm, full handshake is considered extremely important as you interview, meet people, or greet clients.
Tactile	Touch can convey much more than mere words if used correctly. A gentle touch on the arm, an arm around the shoulder, or a firm handshake can be positive nonverbal communications. On the other hand, improper touching and invading someone's personal space can be harmful.
Personal Space	Personal space varies according to each person's needs. Some people are not offended if you stand close, while others are. You have to judge how the person responds and guards his or her personal space. Because of their status, executives are afforded more space than others. The president can put his or her arm around an employee, if done properly, but the employee most likely should not invade the president's personal space.
Environment	The way you arrange your office conveys a message. Is your desk neat or messy? Do you have pictures of your family on your desk? The size of one's office or desk, the number of windows, or a corner office may convey one's status in the organization. Some people recommend putting your professional items on your desk and personal items such as children's pictures behind the desk on a credenza or bookcase.
Silence	You do not have to be talking to convey a message. The fact that you remain silent may indicate that you disagree or that you are thinking. It is better to remain silent if you are not sure of your opinions at the moment. You may need to say, "I need to think about this more" to indicate that you have heard the other person.
Appearance of Documents	The appearance of your written documents sends a nonverbal message. Are your documents well-written? Are they reader-friendly and courteous? Do you have spelling and grammatical errors? Are your documents too brief or too wordy?

Figure 3.5 Important Tips for Writing Business Documents

1. Be very careful what you put in writing and what you promise in writing because it might become a legal document.

2. Write a draft first, especially if it is a very important document. Read and edit the draft carefully.

3. Be very specific about the goal of your written document.

4. Select the best and most appropriate communication form, and include all necessary details—dates, times, and places.

5. Tell the person who is receiving your communication exactly what you want him or her to do. Include contact information and give the reader a deadline so he or she knows how to help you.

6. Be clear about any benefits to the reader if he or she does what you ask.

7. Be succinct and respectful of the reader and of his or her time.

8. If appropriate, establish your credibility in a modest way. Avoid overusing "I," "my," and "our."

9. Send the document to everyone who needs the information, but avoid sending out blanket messages to busy people who are not involved. Be sure to keep your supervisor informed and do not leave out anyone who might be offended if he or she did not receive a copy.

10. If you are angry or upset, do not send the document until you have calmed down and had time to rewrite your message. A good rule to remember is to send good news in a written document and deliver bad news in person. If possible, avoid putting bad news in written form, especially if you are angry.

How to Write a Business Letter

A business letter is a formal document that is written to someone outside your company, such as a person in another organization, a customer, a vendor, a member of the local community, or a company with which you conduct business. Business letters are written for a variety of purposes, including to extend an offer, accept an offer, provide information to a customer, and extend or cancel a contract.

Since business letters represent your company, as well as yourself, you want to be sure that they are well written, error free, and grammatically correct. Your formal business letters should be typed on the company letterhead using a quality paper and professional font (such as Times New Roman), formatted correctly, and signed by you. Check to be sure you have made it clear what follow-up response by the recipient is needed. Always proofread letters before you mail them; if the letter is very important and contains binding information such as prices or quotes, you might want to get someone else to proofread it as well.

Figure 3.6 shows the correct format for writing a business letter.

BIGGEST INTERVIEW *Blunders*

Jocelyn was in a rush and did not proofread her cover letter very carefully. To her horror, she discovered later that the letter had several typos and grammatical errors and that the interviewer's name was spelled incorrectly. Needless to say, she didn't get an interview. Interviewers believe you put your best foot forward before an interview; if you have errors in your resume and cover letter, they tend to think you will be careless at work.

LESSON: Never mail any written document without carefully proofreading and correcting errors.

The Business Envelope

The envelope for your letter makes the very first impression so it, too, needs to be done correctly. Number 10 envelopes (9.5" x 4" in size) are used by most businesses. The recipient's name, title, and address are typed in the middle of the envelope and the writer's name, title, and address are typed in the upper left-hand corner. Be sure names and addresses are typed correctly and that your envelope is formatted properly.

Figures 3.7 and 3.8 show examples of a correctly written and formatted business letter and envelope.

Figure 3.6 Format for Business Letters

The information at the top is the company letterhead

Type the date about two inches from the top of the page

The inside address should include the recipient's name, title, company, and address

The salutation should include the person's title and last name. Use a colon after the name.

Begin all lines of the document at the left margin.

"Sincerely" is the best way to end a business letter. It is followed by a comma.

The writer's full name and title should be typed four spaces below the closing.

If someone other than the writer types the letter, his or her initials should be here. "Enclosure" or "Attachment" is used only if something else is included with the letter.

VISION COMPUTER COMPANY
4568 Main Street
Columbia, SC 29087

April 15, 2012

Mr. Jack Rogers
President
Skyler Electronics
58 Main Street
Columbus, OH 38765

Dear Mr. Rogers:

The first paragraph of your letter should tell the reader why you are writing. If you do not know the person, you may want to introduce yourself or tell where you met the recipient.

The second paragraph (and sometimes a third, if necessary) should provide the details of why you are writing. The main reason you are writing should be detailed here.

Use the last paragraph to end your letter in a respectful manner. If you need to include a deadline or contact information, it should be done in this paragraph.

Sincerely,

Mary S. Thompson

Mary S. Thompson
General Manager

jku
Attachment

Figure 3.7 Sample Business Letter

SKYLER ELECTRONICS
58 Main Street
Columbus, OH 38765

April 20, 2012

Ms. Mary S. Thompson
General Manager
Vision Computer Company
4568 Main Street
Columbia, SC 29087

Dear Ms. Thompson:

Thank you for your recent letter inviting me to meet with you and your sales representative for a demonstration of your new XJZ printers. I was very impressed with your products when I saw them at the trade show in Myrtle Beach. Your salesman, Jamaal Greenwood, did a very good job convincing me that I should take a look at them.

My staff and I will be able to meet with you on the date you requested, May 16, at 10:30. I will invite all six of our department managers to be present for your demonstration. We will allow one hour for your demonstration and questions followed by lunch in the conference room for further discussion.

I look forward to your and Jamaal's visit and hope that our managers will be as impressed with your printers as I was. I am enclosing directions to our facility. If you need additional information, please call me at 404-555-5555. Please give my regards to Jamaal.

Sincerely,

Jack Rogers

Jack Rogers
President

mjk
Enclosure

Figure 3.8 Sample Business Envelope

President
Skyler Electronics
58 Main Street
Columbus, OH 38765

Ms. Mary Thompson
General Manager
Vision Computer Equipment
4568 Main Street
Columbia, SC 29087

How to Write a Business Memo

Business memoranda (or memos) are used for interoffice correspondence between employees in one location or between employees who work in different branches of a company. They are used to share ideas, inform people of decisions, or make announcements or requests. Memos are considered less formal than a business letter but are usually more private and important than an e-mail. As with all business documents, memos communicate a nonverbal message about you; therefore, the content should be given the same attention as a business letter although the format is less formal. You should be sure to include all the necessary details for your recipients while being as brief as possible. Refrain from writing volatile information in a memo or anything that might be misconstrued by those receiving it. As with any written document, some things are better said face-to-face rather than putting them in writing.

Figure 3.9 shows an example of how to format and write a business memorandum. Figure 3.10 shows an example of a business memo that is correctly written.

How to Write a Business E-Mail

E-mails have become a mainstay of business communication and are by far the most frequently used form of internal and external communication. Writing an e-mail is quicker, easier, and more efficient than writing a formal document, making this type of communication very acceptable in the business community.

E-mails are usually brief and informal, but this doesn't mean you can relax your standards of good grammar, composition, and spelling. You are judged by the quality of your e-mails just as you are by your formal letters. E-mails may be written in a more relaxed, informal manner, but you should still be careful to demonstrate professionalism. Write the purpose of the e-mail

---

Figure 3.9 Format for Business Memoranda

Some people like to type "MEMORAN-DUM" at the top, but that is a matter of preference. If it is confidential, type "CONFIDENTIAL MEMORANDUM."

Begin the actual memo about one to one and a half inches from the top of the page. Bold the headings but not the information that follows. Write your initials above your typed name to indicate that you have read the memo and approve. Capitalize all words in the subject line.

Add an extra line space between headings and paragraphs. Single space the body of the memo.

Add initials of the typist if someone else typed it, and add "Attachment" or "Enclosure" if you attach or enclose anything.

THE SILVER EMPORIUM
MEMORANDUM

TO: Kenneth Rosemond, Vice President
FROM: Carmella Esperanza, Sales Manager
DATE: July 14, 2012
SUBJECT: Format for Memorandum

Memoranda (memos) are documents that are sent within the company or to employees in other branches of the company. They provide a record of a variety of company actions, policies and procedures, meetings, and other items.

Many companies used printed forms that are saved and retrieved when needed to ensure a uniform look and to save time for employees. Your word-processing software has a memo template that can be used, if you prefer. Some companies prefer that the company name be typed or printed at the top of the memo.

jkl
Enclosure

Figure 3.10 Sample Business Memo

THE SILVER EMPORIUM
MEMORANDUM

TO: Kenneth Rosemond, Vice President
FROM: Carmella Esperanza, Sales Manager
DATE: July 14, 2012
SUBJECT: Sales Report for June, 2012

The sales figures for June 2012 were up 18 percent over June 2011. Our internal and external sales forces did an outstanding job. The American Silver Eagle coins have been an amazing product for us during this past few months, and demand continues to increase steadily.

The entire sales force is looking forward to having you attend our next meeting on July 21 at 10:00 in the main third-floor conference room. Thank you for your support and leadership. We are all proud of our division and glad to be working for you.

---

in the subject line. If you know the person well, you can write as though you are speaking to him or her. Avoid the temptation to use emoticons, smiley faces, or other unprofessional inserts that may take away from your document's message and your professionalism.

While it is very tempting to share stories, jokes, and cartoons with your colleagues, you should refrain from doing so. First, you are on company time, and managers frown on having people waste time. Second, if you are constantly forwarding this type of information, you will not be taken seriously by anyone. You also need to be aware of the fact that your work computer belongs to the company, and anything on that computer can be accessed by high-level corporate officers if they feel the need to do so. Further, a court of law can subpoena your documents if the need arises, so you should never put anything on a work computer that you would mind being made public.

Finally, you need to remember that anything you write in an e-mail can be forwarded to anyone else. Be especially careful not to put anything in an e-mail that you would mind seeing passed along to others. By all means, do not forward anything that might be offensive to a colleague or customer, and do not forward anyone else's e-mail without asking their permission. Figure 3.11 shows an example of a proper business e-mail.

Professionalism in Social Media

Social media such as Facebook, Twitter, LinkedIn, Jing, Bing, Hulu, YouTube, Google+, and blogs have taken the younger generation—and many of the older—by storm! Many people use social media only for personal communications and entertainment, but the business world has caught on to the benefits of using social media to promote their products and services. Your ticket to a good job might very well be your ability to use social media for professional reasons.

Most big companies and many smaller ones now have a social media strategy. Social media in business is used primarily for marketing and promotions. One of the major differences in traditional marketing and social media marketing is that social media belong to the consumers. People don't just receive messages from social media; they create them and respond to them and interact with them. This form of communication is not a one-way street. "Social media is multiple online mediums all controlled by the people participating within them, people who are

Figure 3.11 Example of a Business E-Mail

From: Xia Guang
To: Marketing Department
cc: Jill Henderson, President
Subject: Marketing XJS5 Mainframe

Please plan to meet with me on July 14 from 10:00 until noon in my conference room to discuss promotion options for our new XJS5 mainframe computer, which will be released in November. I realize that this meeting is longer than our typical meetings, but I want us to get a head start on the promotion package because the XJS5 is going to be marketed heavily in international markets as well as domestic. Baahir Boparai will address the group at 10:30. Baahir is an expert on the Indian domestic and corporate computer markets and will share his expertise with us as we prepare to move into that arena.

Lunch will be served following the meeting.

busy having conversations, sharing resources, and forming their own communities" (Kabani, 2010).

There are many social media platforms, but here we will focus on four of the major platforms: Facebook, Twitter, LinkedIn, and blogs. Since social media have become important in so many arenas, both social and professional, it is important for you to demonstrate professionalism and etiquette when communicating via media such as Facebook, Twitter, and LinkedIn. Many of the rules of netiquette apply to social media.

Facebook is one of the most popular social media sites and now boasts over 600 million users. Marketers use Facebook to attract customers to their websites. "Facebook is like a coffee shop. Everyone is there for his or her own reasons, but it is a great place to strike up a conversation" (Kabani, 2010). Facebook allows you to create a profile and promote it online. This is an opportunity for you to create your own identity, so develop it carefully.

A Facebook profile is a good way to make yourself known, but you want to be sure that you are known for the right reasons. Pictures you think are amusing today may not be so funny five years from now when they show up on YouTube or some other medium. Employers searching your Facebook profile will not be impressed with pictures of you and your friends partying—and many do check your profile. Be selective in posting photos for the world to peruse. You don't want to look like "Good Time Susie" who appears to do nothing but party.

You should avoid putting anything in writing that you would not want to see in the headlines of the newspaper. Don't use language on Facebook or any other social medium that you would not want your grandmother to read. If your boss is one of your friends on Facebook, he or she can read what you post about him or her, so you have to use good judgment. Many people have been fired for posting inappropriate remarks on social media. Many interviewers check Facebook pages today, so you want to have a professional image in case your profile is checked. Likewise, you should refrain from sending any sexually explicit messages or pictures via any form of social media—you have no control over where the receiver might forward your message or pictures. The boyfriend or girlfriend of today may not even be a friend next year, and who knows what may happen with your personal messages and photos at that point!

We suggest that you invest in a professional photo to use on your Facebook profile along with pertinent information that you want to share. You may want to protect your personal information from everyone except those you choose to accept as friends. Be very careful what you put on Facebook that might attract the wrong kind of people.

> *What happens in Vegas stays on Facebook, Twitter, and other Social Media.*
> —*Social Media Revolution 2*

Twitter is another rapidly growing and popular social medium. "Twitter is like a giant, colorful bazaar" (Kabani, 2010). Marketers use Twitter to attract customers directly, and it is also a very popular social interaction platform. You can send direct "tweets" (messages limited to 140 characters each) to friends as well as reply to other people's tweets. Begin by selecting a short Twitter name and posting an attractive headshot. Capture attention with your profile, for which you are allowed 160 characters. You might say something like this: "Soon-to-be college graduate with excellent social media marketing experience. Seek full-time position with progressive company in Atlanta region."

Perhaps the most helpful social medium for career purposes is **LinkedIn,** a network for professionals. The main purpose of LinkedIn is to give businesspeople a platform for connecting. While it is important to be professional on all social media sites, it is crucial that you put your best foot forward on LinkedIn. This might be the source of your first big job if you can connect with the right person.

LinkedIn is much more formal than Facebook or Twitter. You might consider LinkedIn as an interactive online resume. As with other social media, use a good headshot. Ask your references to post recommendations that might attract an employer who is searching for someone with your skills. Your summary is very important and should be written to impress and attract professionals who might read it. It should be professional and truthful. Use keywords that make it easy for other professionals to locate you, such as *social media expert.*

Text language (LOL, OMG, BFF, :-(BTW, FYI) is fine when texting or IMing with your friends, but not for e-mails (or class/work projects). Use them sparingly. Proofread your summary carefully to be sure your grammar and spelling are perfect.

As part of your LinkedIn network, you might want to connect with previous colleagues and bosses, former customers, vendors, and bloggers who may be related to your field. You will be surprised how quickly your network of professionals grows.

Finally, you need to understand blogs. A blog is a personal website that can be updated anytime you want. You might want to experiment with developing your own blog, using directions from many sources on the Internet. If you have a blog, you need to refresh it with new content fairly often if you want people to keep coming back. Blogs are used for many purposes and can be recognized by the following characteristics:

- They resemble websites, but not all websites are blogs.
- A blog can be accessed using a web address.
- Blogs usually consist of posts, which are like miniature articles.
- Readers can read blogs and post their comments and reactions.

As with all social media, you should be sure your blog represents you well as a professional and that you post nothing that others may find offensive.

POSITIVE HABITS *at Work*

Go to work every day with the attitude that you are going to be nice to everyone you meet, that you are going to look your best, that you are going to smile and be friendly to colleagues and customers, and that you will make a good first impression on new coworkers and customers. Resolve to do all these things even when you don't feel well or are in a bad mood. Resolve to use positive communication in your personal relationships as well as your verbal and nonverbal communication.

How to Write Thank You Notes and Congratulatory Notes

One of the most important of all written communications is the handwritten note. Nothing grabs an employee's attention more than a sincere, handwritten thank you note from the boss. People who get notes from their bosses usually save them and read them several times. On the other hand, bosses are people, too, and they also like to get an occasional thank you note. For example, if your boss recommended you for a nice raise, you should take time to write a sincere thank you note. If someone does something thoughtful or nice for you, take a few minutes and write the person a note. If a colleague achieves an unusual accomplishment or gets a promotion, write a sincere note congratulating him or her. Thank you notes and other similar notes should be brief and handwritten on note paper. Figure 3.12 demonstrates the correct format and main parts of a thank you note.

Figure 3.12   Sample Thank You Note

Write the date at the top of the paper.

Use an appropriate salutation, along with the person's name.

Tell the person how his or her actions made you feel, and extend your thanks specifically for what he or she did.

Use an appropriate closing and remember to sign the note.

> August 18, 2012
>
> Dear Jacquelyn,
>
> Thank you so much for the lovely flowers you sent me while I was in the hospital! What a thoughtful surprise! When I awoke on Wednesday afternoon, I was so pleased to see the beautiful arrangement of my favorite flowers. They lasted several days, and I enjoyed them immensely.
>
> You are a wonderful colleague, and I am fortunate to call you friend.
>
> Sincerely,
> Jamie

THE IMPORTANCE OF INTERPERSONAL COMMUNICATION

Do You Have Good People Skills?

Interpersonal communication is your personal interaction with other people. This form of communication is very complicated because it comes with so many variables. "Theorists note that whenever we communicate there are really at least six 'people' involved: 1) who you think you are; 2) who you think the other person is; 3) who you think the other person thinks you are; 4) who the other person thinks s/he is; 5) who the other person thinks you are; and 6) who the other person thinks you think s/he is" (King, 2000).

As you have already learned, communication can take on a variety of forms, such as oral speech, the written word, body movements, and even yawns. All of these actions communicate something to another person. When thinking about your interpersonal communication encounters, remember this—communication is continuous and irreversible. Communication happens all the time; you can't take back words you have said because they have already made an impact. People judge us on our actions, not our good intentions. Consider the tips about interpersonal communications in Figure 3.13.

How to Make a Powerful Business Presentation—Prepare, Prepare, Prepare

The secret to a good presentation is to begin with a specific goal that you want to accomplish and then prepare to the point that you are comfortable with your remarks. While you may not have to speak to hundreds of

> *The #1 Rule for Effective Interpersonal Communication: Be nice. Be nice. Be nice.*
>
> *—Patricia G. Moody*

Figure 3.13 General Tips for Interpersonal Communication

- You never know what type of day, month, year, or life a person has had—act accordingly. Everyone you meet is carrying a burden of some type. Be kind.

- Ask people about themselves. This puts them at ease.

- Interpersonal communication involves a great deal of trust on your part.

- Never try to diminish another's self-worth, because you diminish yourself when you do.

- Try to greet and treat everyone as if he or she was your personal friend.

- Show empathy for others and, most of the time, you will be treated the same.

- Always choose your words carefully. They are immensely powerful tools.

- Pay very close attention to your nonverbal communication, including gestures, facial expressions, clothing, proximity, posture, touch, and eye contact.

- Understand that first impressions are not always correct. Get to know the person and the situation.

- Remember to listen very carefully and read between the lines. Listen to what is not being said.

- Eliminate distractions such as cell phones, other conversations, and outside noise.

- Never use your power or position to control a person just because you can.

people, you will most likely have to present information to your colleagues, your managers, or your customers. Regardless of how relaxed a speaker might appear to be, almost no one is born with the innate ability to speak in front of a group without being nervous. The more you speak, the better you will get and the more confident you will become. A list of important points about making a business presentation follows:

- Prepare, prepare, prepare. Get ready to do a good job.
- Prepare three major parts to your presentation: the opening, the body, and the ending. Plan for a powerful opening, such as a story, a question, or an example. Deliver the main message in the body of your presentation. End powerfully, again with a story, a question, or a quote. You want to touch your participants' emotions so they will remember your remarks.
- Do your homework. Find just the right illustrations to make your presentation interesting.
- If humor is appropriate (and don't overdo it), find the perfect story to complement your presentation. Never use off-color, ethnic, or religious jokes; they are sure to offend someone.
- Make an outline but speak from the heart. Never read your presentation!
- Speak clearly and distinctly and use professional language.
- State the purpose of your presentation and use major points to support the purpose.
- Avoid uncomfortable sounds like "Uh," "umm," or "you know." You do not have to fill up every second with words.
- Be aware of your nonverbal communication. Establish eye contact with your audience. Look up—not down at your notes. Get an "eyeful" and look up.

In my field of information technology, there is something new that comes along every day. Every day! Without my training and education, I would not be able to process all of the changes that are required to be successful. I would not be able to keep up. My education taught me how to expect the unexpected and know the unknown. Use every tool in your box to be able to meet the demands of your position. Never stop learning. Never stop growing.

- Do not lean on the podium, if you are using one.
- Wear an outfit that makes you feel confident. Avoid loud colors and/or patterns that may be distracting.
- Choose supporting visual content carefully. If you are using presentation software, do not overdo it with too many graphics, tables, cartoons, pictures, or page after page of small print. Limit the number of words you put on one slide. Never read word for word from your screen! Visual content should support your presentation, not dominate it.
- Test all equipment before you begin. If it malfunctions, it may not be your fault, but it's your problem.
- If you have activities designed to engage your audience, think them through carefully to be sure they will work as you want them to. Provide simple, complete directions.
- If you use a handout, include activities that involve the audience as you proceed through your remarks. If not, distribute the handout at the end so as not to distract the participants during your presentation.
- Be brief, be good, and be gone. Never drag out a presentation until everyone has glazed over with boredom.

Reflections: PUTTING IT ALL TOGETHER

As you prepare to go to work, nothing will be more important to your success than improving all aspects of your communication profile. Begin now by learning to make a good first impression—this will serve you well when interviewing and later when you are in the workplace. Hone your speaking and writing skills by focusing more attention on all your writing and speaking and intentionally thinking about improving.

DIGITAL BRIEFCASE

OPENING A FACEBOOK ACCOUNT

This exercise is designed to walk you through the steps in registering for a Facebook account and learning to use some of the simpler options available. Even if you already have an account, you should be able to learn some new things by completing this exercise. Follow the steps below:

1. **First, register your account.** Go to www.facebook.com. In the top right of the screen, on the blue taskbar, click on "Register." This will take you to the registration screen. Type in your name, identify what you do for a living if you are working, and enter a valid e-mail address. Facebook needs your e-mail address to contact you and occasionally send updates on new things. Then, follow instructions to choose a secure password, agree to the terms and conditions, and click "Register now."

2. **Confirm your e-mail.** Open the e-mail sent to you by Facebook and click on the link that will take you to your new Facebook profile.

3. **Next, personalize your Facebook profile and find friends.** All you have to do is enter your e-mail address, and Facebook will search for your friends for you. You have the option of selecting the people you want from the "friends" Facebook locates for you. Click on the box to the left of each person you want to add as a friend. This means they will have access to you and your postings. Then you'll be given the option of befriending others who are not in your e-mail address book. You can send e-mails inviting them to join and be your friend.

4. **You can search for coworkers by clicking on "Search for coworkers."** Write the person's company and the name of the person for whom you are searching. Then click on "Search for coworkers," and Facebook will search for you.

5. **Next, click on your name in the upper right corner to access your profile.** Here you will find empty sections waiting for you to complete. You can enter your sex, if you are interested in men or women, your relationship status, and why you are accessing Facebook (for dating, friendship, etc.). Then enter your birthday, hometown, state, and religious views, if you so desire. When you like what you have done, click "Save changes."

6. **The next step is to click on "Contact Information" under "Info" on your profile.** You can now enter a screen name and a telephone number, if you want to. You can click on "Personal" and enter activities, interests, music, sports, TV shows, books, and the like. You can tell things about yourself if you choose to. You might want to keep this short, because people tend not to read long items. You can also enter your educational background and your work information.

7. **You do not have to complete every field unless you want to.**

8. **You can upload a picture from your hard drive for your profile picture. Click on the "Photo" tab to upload a picture.** Now that you have registered and completed your profile, your assignment is to create a group. On the left side of the screen, under "Groups," is a tab called "Create a Group." Click on this tab and create a group of 10 people. This group can be a study group, a group of colleagues at work, or a group of friends. Once you have created the group, ask each member to send in one tip for using Facebook safely and professionally. Then share the list with the group.

REFERENCES

Bixler, S., & Nix-Rice, N. (2005). *The new professional image: From corporate casual to the ultimate power look.* Avon, MA: Adams Media Corporation.

Gorman, C. K. (2005). I heard it through the grapevine. Retrieved April 3, 2011, from www.communitelligence.com/clps/clprint.cfm?adsid=329.

Holmes, T. (2003). Diversity in the workplace: The changing language of business. Retrieved April 18, 2011, from www.boston.com/jobs/diversity/062003.

Kabani, S. H. (2010). *The zen of social media marketing.* Dallas: BenBella Books, Inc.

King, D. (2000). Four principles of interpersonal communication. Retrieved April 7, 2011, from www.pstcc.edu/facstaff/dking/interpr.htm.

National Association of Colleges and Employers. (2011). Job outlook report for 2011. Retrieved July 25, 2011, from http://www.naceweb.org/s04142011/job_outlook_ spring_update/

Thiederman, S. (2011). American culture: Knowing yourself in order to understand others. Retrieved February 18, 2011, from www.diversityworking.com/diversityManagement /americanc-ulture.php.

chapter four

RELATE

RELATIONSHIPS, DIVERSITY, AND MULTIGENERATIONAL DISTINCTIONS

*We must learn to live together as brothers
or perish together as fools.
—Martin Luther King, Jr.*

Why
read this chapter?

Because you'll learn...

- Why it is important to respect people from diverse backgrounds
- To respect opinions that are different from yours
- The concept of globalization and the impact on personal and work relationships

Because you'll be able to...

- Work more effectively in a company that has a diverse, multigenerational workforce
- Determine the type of workplace culture in which you feel most comfortable

PROFESSIONALS
from the
Field

Name: Bert Pooser

Business: CEO, IMIC Hotels

I have been in the hotel business for many years and have learned that the ability to build good relationships with all kinds of people is one of the most important skills you can have. When we are hiring new employees, we look for personalities whom we think will be engaging and friendly with our customers. We can teach someone to use a computer and work at the front desk, but we can't teach them how to be personable, friendly, helpful, and willing to serve our customers so these are the qualities we seek when interviewing. We also look for people who can interact with a very diverse customer base. We have people of all ages, from all parts of the world, from many different religious backgrounds, and who represent a great variety of ethnicities. Our employees have to be able to relate to all of them and to treat them as our respected guests.

DEVELOPING STRONG WORKPLACE RELATIONSHIPS

How Do You Build Relationships at Work?

Building solid relationships is one of the most important jobs you have in the workplace. If you cannot get along with other people, you will not be promoted and you certainly will not be placed in a management position. There are so many ways to work and play well with others, and many are detailed here. There is one rule you can apply consistently—you need to be nice, be nice, be nice to everyone with whom you come in contact. Civility will go a long way toward building positive relationships. Do the little things—send a sympathy or get well card, write a congratulatory note, do something for someone's children, buy donuts for the department occasionally, smile often, and learn to give sincere compliments and accept them in return.

Working and playing well with others can be spelled out in hundreds of simple ways that make a difference in people's lives. Simple actions done over and over again build good relationships. Some of these actions are listed below:

- Catch people doing good things and tell them about it—in front of others if you can.
- Compliment someone on making a difficult decision and having the character to do the right thing.
- Be a good listener and a good confidante. If someone shares their personal feelings with you, they trust you and have paid you a high compliment.
- Accept feedback even when it is painful, and try to learn from it.
- If you must criticize, wrap the criticism up in praise. Deliver the criticism quickly and let it drop.
- Take time for yourself, but also take time for others. Do the little things that make a big difference in others' lives.
- If you harm someone, apologize quickly and sincerely. Admit when you are wrong.
- Always treat others fairly, even when it is not the best thing for you.
- Be generous with your praise for others and be sincerely happy for them when good things happen.
- Tell the truth, even when it is painful and not to your advantage.

Think about this discussion and add a few simple, powerful actions to the list that you can do for your colleagues in your workplace:

> The closer you get to the top, the nicer people are.
> —J. W. Marriott

_____

_____

_____

_____

GRADUATE *Quote*

Sakeenah Pendergrass
Graduate!
The Art Institute of Philadephia, Philadelphia, PA
Career: Culinary Arts, Saucier and Pastry Development

My advice to anyone in college and in the workforce is to learn how to take criticism. When you get a piece of criticism, ask "Why?" Learn to use the advice and criticism to get better. Also, learn to listen. Listen to what they are telling you so that you can grow and improve. Take the criticism as a piece of advice from someone who cares and wants you to grow. Usually, constructive criticism is not given to stifle you, but to make you stronger and better at what you do.

Why Is It Important to Understand People Who Are Different from You?

A truly educated person knows how to listen to others, learn from many different people, and grow from others' experiences and cultures. This chapter will provide a chance for you to rethink and evaluate some of your long-held beliefs and offer a challenge to open yourself and your thinking to new possibilities regarding diversity, different generations of coworkers, and relationships with a variety of people—indeed, to learn to celebrate differences and to relate to and enjoy all kinds of people.

Today's workplace requires interactions with people from all walks of life. You may have a boss who is different from you in many ways, and you will certainly have colleagues who think differently from you. You will probably serve on committees and teams with people who have diverse backgrounds. Although you don't have to love everybody at work, you have to be able to work with all of them—even the difficult ones. The sooner you begin learning how to build strong workplace relationships with all kinds of people, the more successful you will become.

Few things will do more to make you an educated, sophisticated, and competitive person than to expand your thinking about diversity and to be able to build lasting and rewarding relationships with people from many walks of life. Many people think diversity is only about culture and race, but diversity encompasses so many more differences than just those two areas. You will be working with people who are different from you in many respects: They may be older; they may be from a different country; their religion may be very different from your personal beliefs; they may come from a different part of the country; their sexual orientation may be different from yours; their social status may differ. The list of differences is very long, and your job is to learn to relate to all types of people who embrace different backgrounds, philosophies, and beliefs than yours and to learn to work with them.

UNDERSTANDING YOUR COMPANY'S WORKPLACE CULTURE

What Kind of Personality Does Your Company Have?

Workplace culture means the same thing as *corporate* or *organizational culture*—you will see all of these terms used. *Corporate culture* seems to infer big, multinational companies, so we prefer *workplace culture.* "Corporate culture, sometimes also called organizational culture, refers to the shared values, attitudes, standards, codes, and behaviors of a company's management and employees. Some would argue that the corporate culture extends to the broader circle of relationships a business maintains, such as with customers, vendors, strategic partners, and so forth. Corporate culture is rooted in an organization's goals, strategies, structure, and approaches to business activities" (Encyclopedia for Business, 2011).

Workplace Cultures—How We Do Things Around Here

Workplace cultures can be very diverse. Some would describe it simply "as the way we do things around here." You might say that workplace culture is what life is really like at work; it is the glue that holds the company together. Workplace culture can be very difficult to define, but everyone who works at the same place soon understands exactly what it is. The culture is usually established by upper management but can be heavily affected by employees. The values and expectations of the management group tend to trickle down to the employees until everyone "gets it" and operates using unwritten rules.

Workplace cultures can be casual, friendly, and fun-loving; they can be stiff, closed, and formal; or anything in between. Employees may feel free to take a break and discuss a project in a room with comfortable furniture and a pool table, or they may be restricted to cubicles with little or no communication. In some organizations, lower-level employees have a great deal of interaction with higher-level executives, whereas in others, there is very little contact between ranks. Employees may come to work in jeans and tennis shoes or they may be required to have on dress clothes. In hospitals and in some small businesses, employees may be required to wear uniforms, either for a consistent look or because of the nature of the work. In some companies, employees may be asked to share their opinions and ideas, or they may simply be expected to follow orders from their boss. The company may value innovation and togetherness or they may have high regard for structure and working alone. No two companies have exactly the same workplace culture. A large corporation's culture will be very different from a small business environment where everyone knows each other and works closely on a daily basis.

> *Every company has two organizational structures; the formal one is written on the charts; the other one is the everyday relationship of the men and women in the organization.*
> —Harold S. Geneen, former CEO of ITT Corporation

Part of your job when interviewing is to check out the workplace culture and see if you are a good fit for a particular environment. Observe carefully as you walk around, and ask questions that give you information but are not offensive. Every business has a personality, and it is important for you to find the one that matches your goals, skills, and temperament.

Remember, you are there to interview the company while they are interviewing you. Study the checklist in Figure 4.1 and use it to evaluate a company's workplace culture as it relates to you and your needs and goals.

After studying Figure 4.1, write a brief statement about your personal needs in a corporate culture. Not every company will be a good match for you.

_____

_____

_____

_____

_____

Figure 4.1 Is This Workplace Culture a Match for You?

Workplace Observation	YES	NO	COMMENTS
Do you like the size of the company?			
Would you be able to get to know everyone?			
Is the company so small that everyone would know your business?			
Do people seem friendly and engaged with each other?			
Is it a cold, formal environment?			
Are the company's values readily visible in the way employees act and perform?			
Is the basic dress formal?			
Do the people wear uniforms?			
Is the workforce diverse in terms of generations, ethnicity, and other important categories?			
Does the company have many layers of managers in its organizational structure?			
Do you see opportunities for advancement?			
Are the working hours fairly routine?			
Is the heaviest part of the work seasonal, requiring you to work longer hours?			
Does the company appear to embrace work/life balance?			
Do the company and employees appear to value customers, both internal and external?			
Do you feel tension between individuals and/or groups?			
Does the company appear to value independent thinking?			
Does the work you would be doing require field work and travel?			

Workplace Observation	YES	NO	COMMENTS
Do you think power is invested in only a few people?			
Do you think this is an adaptive company that can change quickly if necessary?			
Does the benefits package reflect the fact that owners/managers value employees?			
Is there a 401(k) or other retirement package?			
Does the company provide child care, break room, exercise facility, or play rooms?			
Is the atmosphere quiet and sterile as is necessary in some medical settings?			
Is the atmosphere lively and informal as in some technology companies?			
Does management interact with employees?			
Do supervisors travel with and train new employees if the company is a small business, such as an air-conditioning company?			
Does the company provide a comprehensive educational program?			
If the company is a small business, such as electrical installation, does it provide an apprentice program?			
Do people seem to enjoy coming to work?			
If the company is a relatively small business, such as an automobile dealership, do the mechanics have enough time to do a good job?			
Do you know what a typical day at work would be like for you?			
Do employees seem to have a can-do spirit?			
Can you tell if the company appears to be based on long-term goals that include caring for employees, as opposed to short-term, profit-based goals?			
Do you think this company can provide the kind of opportunity you are seeking?			

CELEBRATING AMERICA'S DIVERSE HERITAGE

How Can You Strengthen Relationships with a Diverse Workforce?

The U.S. culture is the most diverse of any on earth! We are a nation of immigrants that still welcomes people from all over the world to our shores. This fact is one of our greatest strengths—ideas from all over the world can come together in an environment that allows anyone to pursue his or her dreams and ambitions. On the other hand, all this diversity is accompanied by the problems of throwing so many people from diverse cultures together and expecting them to function together as one society.

Although U.S. society is called the "melting pot," it is not so simple to mix all these people together and not have problems. Perhaps the best way to think of U.S. society is not as a melting pot but as a mixed salad, with each item remaining intact but still complementing each other. Regardless of what we symbolically call ourselves, this country offers the greatest opportunities of any on earth. As we grow as a nation and as individuals, we must all seek to become so good at dealing with differences that it really doesn't matter that we are not alike. In fact, we should learn to celebrate differences as strengths and as unique opportunities to expand our thinking.

How comfortable would you be working with a diverse group?

iStockPhoto

LEARNING TO THINK GLOBALLY WHILE MAKING LOCAL APPLICATIONS

Is It Really a Small World after All?

iStockPhoto

"Think globally, act locally" was a phrase that emerged from an international conference on environmental issues in the early 1970s. In today's world, that phrase encompasses so much more than just the environment. Today we are connected by technology and economics, as well as social networks. Because we are so mobile and interconnected, what happens in another part of the world can have immediate implications for our part of the world. For example, war in a Middle Eastern country can interrupt oil supplies and thus affect our economy. As we have seen, a meltdown in U.S. financial markets can severely affect the world markets because other countries' citizens own a significant portion of U.S. stocks and bonds.

Figure 4.2 Global Connectivity over the Years

RADIO:
It took 38 years for radio to reach 50 million users

TELEVISION:
It took 13 years for television to reach 50 million users

INTERNET:
It took 5 years for the Internet to reach 50 million users

Because of technology, primarily the Internet, we are now connected with people all over the world. "Internet users are roughly 35 percent English and 65 percent Non-English with Chinese at 14 percent. Google's Index now stands at over 8 billion pages. Today we have over a billion internet users, and that number is growing rapidly" (Internet in Numbers, 2011). Consider the statistics in Figure 4.2.

Technology has opened the doors to the world and brought with it amazing opportunities and difficulties. But it has also brought a new set of problems and concerns as it exposes our differences to a greater degree than in the past and pits us against each other as competitors for jobs, business ventures, and tourists. So we all have work to do to become good global citizens in this brave new world. As a citizen and an employee, you will need new skills and knowledge to function at your best capacity. Some ideas to consider as you begin to *think globally and act locally* are:

> *I am not a citizen of Athens or Greece but of the world.*
>
> —Socrates

- To act with compassion and understanding for people who are different from you
- To develop a good understanding of the different cultures, beliefs, and issues embraced by people from locations all over the world
- To travel internationally and experience first-hand people from other parts of the world
- To examine multiple viewpoints and philosophies and make decisions that are respectful of many types of differences
- To listen carefully, think differently, and solve problems that emerge in the workplace and in communities because of cultural differences
- To study historical perspectives to grasp reasons for tensions between different cultures

> *We don't see things as they are; we see things as we are.*
>
> —Anaïs Nin

RELATING TO YOUR SUPERVISOR

How Can I Best Support My Supervisor?

Supervisors come in all sizes and shapes and bring with them a great diversity of personalities, likes and dislikes, and expectations. Some are warm and friendly; others are distant and cool. Some are hard-driving and goal-oriented; others are laid back and nonchalant. Some are supportive; some are tyrants. Some supervisors want people to love each other and work together as a team in an open and relaxed environment; others don't care if you like each other or not as long as you get the job done. So the first thing you have to do is to learn who your supervisor is as a person, and then you have to adjust to his or her likes and dislikes. The main things most supervisors want is for you to do your job and to do it well—the first time. Below is a list of ways to support your supervisor and win his or her approval:

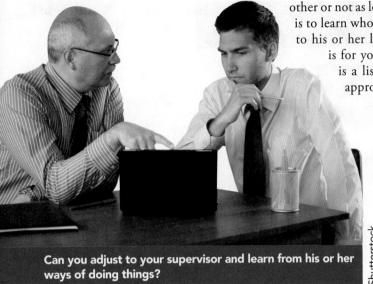

Can you adjust to your supervisor and learn from his or her ways of doing things?

Shutterstock

- Know exactly what your job duties are and what is expected of you. Find out if there is anyone to whom you can delegate or if you should do everything yourself.
- Always be sure to get your job done before you volunteer to help someone else. You will be judged on your personal assignments, so they have to come first. Once your supervisor learns that you are dependable, you will most likely be given bigger and more important tasks. Let the boss know that you are willing to learn more and that you don't mind taking on more responsibilities. Supervisors love people who are willing to do whatever it takes to get the job done.

- Keep your supervisor informed of what is going on around the office. Bosses don't like surprises, and they certainly don't want to be surprised by hearing negative information from their bosses. You don't have to be a sneak or a tattletale, but supervisors need to know certain things before they get out of hand. Some people may have hidden agendas and will actually work against the boss. This is the kind of thing the boss needs to know. You need to be absolutely sure you are right and have concrete evidence before you share such information with your boss.

- If you can't meet a deadline although you have worked overtime, tell your supervisor before he or she comes to you. Ask for more time, and then focus on getting that task completed quickly and well.

- If you have questions, make a list of things you want to discuss with your supervisor and get an appointment. Get answers to all your questions so you don't have to keep going back again and again.

- If you uncover a problem, let the boss know, but also give him or her a potential solution to the problem. Supervisors have a lot on their plates, so they value people who can solve problems.

- Above all, be loyal to your supervisor. Do everything you can do to make your boss look good. Supervisors know who is really on their team, and they will reward loyal, hard-working employees.

RELATING TO YOUR COLLEAGUES

How Can I Please All These People?

The first thing to understand is that you simply can't please everyone all the time, but you can always treat everyone professionally and respectfully. You will really like and relate to some colleagues; others will seem complicated and unlike you. Nevertheless, you still have to find a way to work with them. Since you will spend so much time at work, you are likely to be more productive if you are happy with your relationships. Some helpful hints follow that will guide you in "playing well" with others.

- **Use good manners with everyone.** Be as nice and friendly to the janitor as you are the CEO. Use e-mail properly and refrain from using your cell phone during work hours. Avoid all personal business at work unless you have to take care of something; then do it quickly and efficiently.

- **Be friendly and engaging.** Take time to inquire about how your colleagues are doing. Don't be nosy about their personal business. If someone shares something personal with you, treat it as confidential information. If someone asks you how you are doing, the only answer is "I feel great!"

- **Avoid engaging in gossip.** Don't be snared by the head gossip who talks about everyone and is loyal to no one. Stay away from the areas and offices where malicious gossip often takes place. Be seen as someone who is there to work, not gossip.

- **Manage your time and priorities well.** Meet your deadlines, and be sure you don't inconvenience someone else by not doing what you are supposed to do.

- **Deal well with the unexpected.** Sometimes things happen suddenly and everyone needs to stop what they are doing and pitch in to handle a crisis. Be one of the first to go to work to solve the problem.

- **Stay away from certain topics.** There are so many different viewpoints about religion and politics that you should refrain from discussing them at work. You are sure to offend someone even if you are careful. Don't ever tell off-color or race-based jokes, and don't forward offensive e-mails.

- **Do not forward anyone's e-mail message unless you ask permission.** If someone sends you an e-mail message, assume it is meant only for you unless you ask.

- **Do not discuss your personal business or problems at work.** Everyone has problems and issues, but they do not belong at work. When you have problems, discuss them with friends with whom you do not work. Never put your personal business "on the streets." Some people will be glad you have a problem and others will use it against you. Only your close personal friends should know your business.

- **If you make a mistake, admit it and don't pass the blame to someone else.** Everyone makes mistakes sooner or later. Admit the mistake and fix it as quickly as you can. Apologize to everyone concerned and don't do it again.

- **If you are really sick, stay at home; if you just feel bad, go to work.** No one wants to be around people who have the flu or a virus, so stay at home. If your head hurts or you feel groggy, take some medicine and go to work. Go to bed early that night so you can recover for the next day.

- **Dress appropriately and in a manner that reflects well on you and the company.** You should always dress neatly and appropriately at work. Some jobs may have specific requirements about what you should wear, while others will allow you to use your judgment. Regardless of what you choose or need to wear to work, look your best. Your clothes should be clean and pressed, and you should be well-groomed. People judge us on what they see, so it is up to you to shape your business image.

- **Limit the amount of time you spend socializing with work colleagues.** You can't avoid spending some social time with colleagues, but your best friends should be outside of work. If you get promoted over a friend, he or she may be jealous or expect certain favors. If you have a disagreement, it will be magnified at work.

- **Make a good impression at business meetings.** Be prepared by studying the agenda. Make at least one constructive suggestion or ask one thought-provoking question. If you are very new to the company, listen more than you talk. Never text while in a business meeting or allow your cell phone to ring.

- **Make a good impression on customers by going out of your way to serve them.** Customers pay your salary, so try to always provide good service. If you don't know the answer, get up and find it. Return calls in a timely manner. Always deliver more than you promise.

LIVING AND WORKING IN THE BRAVE NEW WORLD

What Are the Dimensions of Diversity?

Both managers and employees must learn to work and manage in an environment that includes great diversity in terms of ethnicity, age, and gender. Older workers are staying longer because they are living longer, and many cannot afford to retire. "The U.S. workforce is in the midst of a transformation. From 1980 to 2020, Caucasian workers in the United States will decline from 82 percent to 62 percent . . . the non-Caucasian portion of the workforce is projected to double from 18 percent to 37 percent, with the Latino portion almost tripling from 6 percent to 17 percent" (Meister & Willyerd, 2010). In the future, as many as five generations will be working side by side in the workplace. This means that everyone—managers and employees alike—will have to learn to work together productively.

The kinds of diversity you might encounter include race, religion, gender, age, ethnicity, nationality, culture, sexual orientation, social class, geographic region, and physical ability (see Figure 4.3). It is important for you to become open and accepting of individuals in all categories of diversity. The most significant thing you can do is to think of people who are different from you as individuals, not as groups. Some of you will need to make bigger changes in your overall belief system than others; it all depends on what kind of background you come from and what experiences you have had. An explanation of some major types of diversity follows.

Figure 4.3 Dimensions of Diversity Wheel

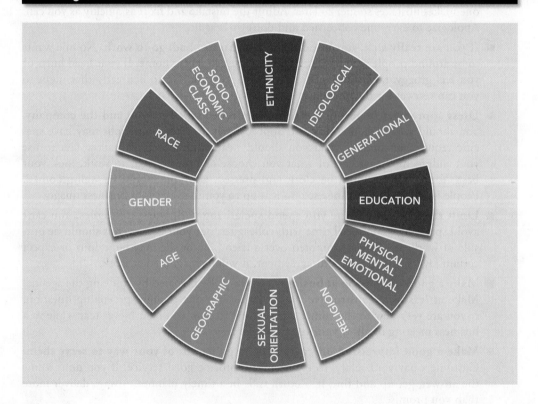

Racial Diversity

Racism is a prejudice that exists when an individual has a negative attitude about any race or ethnic group. Racism can be institutionalized in actions such as racial profiling or refusal to hire certain races except for menial manual labor. It can also mean that certain races are charged higher interest rates when borrowing money or have to pay more for an automobile than another race. Racist language usually implies that an individual or group is inferior in some way. In many cases, races that are discriminated against have been relegated to inferior positions in society due to economic and political oppression.

iStockPhoto

What have you learned about a culture other than your own since beginning your studies?

Religious Diversity

Many religions are practiced in this country and around the world. Ranging from orthodox practices that have been in place for hundreds of years to newly formed religions, people who practice each of these forms of worship are sensitive to unkind remarks about their beliefs. There are actually three major beliefs about other religions: *exclusivism, inclusivism*, and *pluralism.* Those who believe in exclusivism think that other faiths are in grave error and often view them as opponents. Those who practice inclusivism believe other faiths have some truth in them, but are only partly developed. Finally, those who believe in pluralism think that all faiths are legitimate and valid—when viewed from within their particular culture.

The biggest problem, quite simply, is that people tend to believe their religion is the only right one and is superior to all others. Such a position can also be dangerous, as wars frequently break out over religious differences. The terrible events that took place on September 11, 2001, were perpetrated by individuals who no doubt believed they were martyring themselves in the name of their religion. You live in a free country where you are free to worship as you choose. We must all grow to the point that we can allow others the same choice without judgment or hate. Regardless of what your religion is, you should not discuss it at work, nor should you try to recruit colleagues to your religion.

Gender Diversity

Since the 1960s and the women's rights movement, women in the United States have made steady gains toward being treated equally to men. However, there are still biases to be found among some institutions and certainly with some individuals. The fact that Hillary Clinton was a strong contender for the 2008 Democratic Party presidential nomination and that Sarah Palin was named as the Republican vice presidential candidate marks the fact that women have made significant gains. There are still a large number of both men and women, however, who will make the statement, "I just can't vote for a woman for president."

Just a few years ago, boys were expected to grow up to be masculine and to pursue certain types of careers, whereas girls were expected to be

Zuma Press/Newscom

What are your personal feelings about diverse groups of people succeeding in areas where there were previous limitations?

What do you think a person older than you could teach you about the world and about work?

iStockPhoto

feminine and perhaps pursue a role as a homemaker, nurse, or teacher. Many of the women who ventured out and did become involved in the business or academic world ran up against the "glass ceiling." Today men and women are attending college in record numbers, with more women actually in attendance than men. Although dramatic progress has been made to improve gender bias, there is still some confusion regarding "women's roles," as well as stigma attached to certain careers for men, such as nursing.

Age Diversity

In your coursework, you have probably had classmates of all ages, so you have had some experience dealing with age diversity. In today's workforce, you will experience a community with people of all ages, and you need to learn to relate to and work with all of them. Older people are very much like other employees of all ages. They want to be treated with respect; most want to laugh and have fun; some want to see the latest movies; many are likely to enjoy sporting events; some will enjoy travel; and they want to be included in discussions. Study Figure 4.4 to determine how to work with diverse age groups.

List two other ways to work with a diverse age group of colleagues:

_____

_____

Figure 4.4 Working with Diverse Age Groups

- Learn to mix well with all age groups.

- Treat people of all ages and backgrounds with respect.

- Do not restrict your group of closest company colleagues only to people of your age.

- Seek the advice of older colleagues and those who have been with the company longer.

- Be sure to watch your language carefully at work. You might easily offend people of older generations as well as younger workers.

- Invite colleagues of varying ages and backgrounds to lunch. It is an asset for you to be seen as one who brings diverse groups together.

- If a group is going to lunch or for drinks after work, you might extend an invitation to your immediate supervisor.

- Take time to listen to people of all ages and backgrounds. This is the nicest compliment you can give anyone, and it will help you form positive relationships at work.

Ethnic Diversity

The word *ethnic* is derived from the Greek work *ethnos,* meaning "nation"; some people refer to ethnic groups simply by the country from which they originated. Scholars don't always agree on exactly what constitutes an ethnic group. An ethnic group is considered by some to be a social group that is typically distinguished by race, religion, or national origin. These groups may be marked or identified by distinguishing features and physical characteristics. But in some cases, they can be identified by their religion or language even when physical differences do not exist. Ethnicity might mean to others simply national origin. According to Feagin and Feagin (2008), an ethnic group is "a group socially distinguished or set apart, by others or by itself, primarily on the basis of cultural or national-origin characteristics."

Sexual Orientation Diversity

In your workplace, you will most likely encounter people of a variety of sexual orientations. Actually, work is not the place for this topic to be openly discussed. A person's sexual orientation is really no one else's business. Regardless of your personal sexual orientation, this should be a private matter. If other people choose to discuss their personal business with you, you should not share this with others, and you are not required to discuss your own personal business because they did. Ideally, all sexual orientations are respected in the workplace and people are treated as individuals rather than a member of a group. Actually, there are intelligent, engaging, attractive people of all sexual orientations—people who can become good friends and colleagues if you are open to accepting them and open to being accepted.

Social Class Diversity

Socioeconomic status or social class can be defined using the parameters of a person's income, education level, type of work, and family heritage. Someone may have social status because his or her grandfather was a senator, yet still not have large wealth. In the United States, the following terminology is generally used: upper class (wealthy), middle class (people who have jobs requiring considerable education or who own businesses that afford them a certain level of income), and lower class (people who are unemployed or hold low-level jobs that do not provide them with a good standard of living).

 If you follow our advice and consider people as individuals rather than part of a class, you will meet great people from all classes. Wealth and status certainly provide opportunities and advantages not enjoyed by everyone, but you can find outstanding people in all classes to add to your personal community.

Generational Diversity

While you may have heard of many different types of diversity, you are less likely to have been informed about generational diversity. Different generations have been labeled with names such as the "Traditionals," "Boomers," "Generation X," and the current generation, "Generation Y" or "Millennials." You do need to remember that just because a person fits a particular age group, it does not mean that he or she will automatically embrace all the characteristics of that generation. A good rule to remember when considering all types of diversities is to treat people as individuals. Figure 4.5 explains the categories for age groups of different generations.

 For the first time, four distinctly different generations, each with their own loyalties, priorities, and expectations, are working side by side in the workplace (Glenn, 2007). Naturally, with such a wide range of ages and different viewpoints, there are conflicts over how work should be processed, what constitutes company loyalty, how many hours one should work after closing time, and how best to communicate.

Figure 4.5 The Multigenerational Workforce

TRADITIONALS OR VETERANS

They believe in following the chain of command and are typically very loyal to their company and bosses. They may not function as well in collaborative efforts as some of your younger colleagues. They are not very tech savvy, as a rule, and usually prefer formal memos or phone calls rather than text messages or e-mail. They don't believe in accumulating large debts.

- Born between 1927–1945
- Most have retired, but some are still in the workforce
- Strong work ethic
- May not have strong technology skills

- Respect experience
- Believe in following the chain of command
- Very respectful of their bosses

BOOMERS

Boomers are often thought of as "climbers," and they tend to be ambitious. They are usually more tech-literate than people older than they are and handle voicemail and e-mail well. They know about social media and texting but are not likely to use them very often. They tend to believe in "face time" at work and don't put much faith in people working from home.

- Born between 1946–1964
- Very hard working
- Motivated by prestige and position
- Tend to handle their business in meetings

- Like to feel valued by their supervisors and colleagues
- Tend to be optimistic about their future

GENERATION X

This generation is fairly savvy when it comes to using technology. They are not overly fond of face-to-face meetings. You might hear them grumble after a meeting, "This could have been handled in an e-mail." They tend to be independent and don't necessarily enjoy working in groups. Many of them were reared as "latchkey" children, so they value family time. Because they grew up in times of recession, they tend to be savers.

- Born between 1965–1980
- Smaller in numbers than other generations
- Independent thinkers

- Many suffered through the recession and limited job market
- Value informality and fun at work
- Enjoy freedom to work in their own way

GENERATION Y/MILLENNIALS

Having been in school more recently, they are usually tech-savvy and especially enjoy social media. Their favorite way of communicating is texting, and they are very attached to their smartphones. They do not care for e-mail or phone calls, but are very adept at using the Internet. They usually exhibit a strong degree of confidence and tend to be social. They went to school at a time when tuition was on the rise, and many have big student loans.

- Born in mid-1980s
- Fastest-growing group in workforce
- Technology savvy
- Work to make money so they can spend freely
- Like to work with creative people

- Tend to be good at multitasking
- May be more tolerant of people who are different from them
- 96 percent of them have joined a social network
- Spend 16 hours a week online

You may very well go to work with an older person from the "traditional" generation who is very focused on a chain-of-command approach. In the same group, you might have a "boomer" who believes strongly in visibility or face time at the office and equates that as time spent working. Your team might include a member of Generation X who believes that his or her time is as important as money and that it doesn't matter if you don't work overtime as long as you do the job and do it well. If you work with Generation Y employees, you may find them to be focused on technology and finding a job that makes them happy.

Geographic Region Diversity

As strange as it seems, there are some who are prejudiced against people from certain geographic regions in this country. It is true that there are people in all parts of our country who have very different ideas from the masses; however, we should not label an entire section of the country based on the actions of a few. In the case of geographic regions, as in all cases, you should determine the characteristics of an individual rather than judge him or her as a member of a group. You might find that a friend from California could open up all kinds of new ideas and thinking for you, a friend from the South could show you beautiful beaches and golf courses, or a friend from New York could introduce you to Broadway or Central Park. As you expand your personal community of friends, make a special effort to get to know people from other regions of the country and learn to consider their character rather than where they came from.

Physical, Mental, and Emotional Diversity

You will encounter a number of colleagues who suffer from physical, mental, and emotional challenges. They could be visually impaired, deaf, or confined to a wheelchair. Quite a few people have depression, and others deal with bipolar disorders. Research shows that around 15 to 20 percent of all people experience some kind of learning disability such as dyslexia (National Institutes of Health, 2010). We assume that people who are labeled legally blind cannot see, when in fact, 80 percent can read large or regular print books. They may have a problem in only one eye. Truthfully, these colleagues are just like everyone else, except they have a physical problem that makes life a little more difficult. They have feelings just like the rest of us; they want to be included in social life and activities, and they don't want to be treated as disabled, different, and unable to participate. Consider getting to know a physically, mentally, or emotionally challenged person and bringing this person into your social network.

Ideological Diversity

The fact that we all have different opinions and ideas that are rooted in our family backgrounds, socioeconomic status, religious beliefs, cultural experiences, political beliefs, educational levels, and travel experiences creates great diversity and can cause difficulties between individuals and groups of people. "Individuals tend to come to more extreme views if they deliberate a given issue with like-minded people" (Kallock, 2009). In other words, internal diversity tends to be squelched by the forces of group polarization. People tend to remain moderate in expressing their beliefs until they are confident that others agree with them, and then they tend to become more extreme in their beliefs. These personal beliefs

BIGGEST INTERVIEW *Blunders*

When Jack Richardson interviewed with a large international company, he was interested in a position in logistics. During the interview he was asked this question: "Our logistics division employee base is made up of people from many different nationalities, many of whom have excellent computer skills. How do you think you will function working in an environment with Asians, Hispanics, Indians, and others?" Jack made a crucial mistake when he answered: "I'm from a small Midwest town where most people were Caucasian, so I think I might fit in another department better." The interviewer then told him that all their departments were highly diverse, and that they were proud of this fact and how well their employees worked together. Jack learned that day that he had a great deal of growing to do and that he needed to open up his mind to being able to work with people from a wide variety of backgrounds if he was going to be successful.

LESSON: When you go to work, you are unlikely to work in a company where everyone has the same background, race, and religion that you do. Learn to be open to relating and accepting all kinds of people. Judge them on their character and work ethic.

How could your ideological differences cause you a problem at work?

iStockPhoto

create diversity in thoughts, reasoning, ideas, and creativity. Political beliefs, for example, can be quite polarizing between individuals and groups. As an educated, enlightened individual, you will need to practice patience and understanding of other people's viewpoints and why they believe them even when you are diametrically opposed to their beliefs.

THE LAW PROTECTS PEOPLE FROM DISCRIMINATION AT WORK

What Is EEOC and What Does It Have to Do with You?

The Equal Employment Opportunity Commission (EEOC) is a part of the sweeping civil rights legislation passed after President Kennedy was assassinated. This legislation was actually being debated when he was assassinated, and President Johnson picked up the torch and managed its passage in 1964. The EEOC is charged with the responsibility of protecting people from being discriminated against in many different areas of employment, including recruiting, hiring, unlawful terminations, wages and salaries, and promotions. "The Equal Employment Opportunity Commission (EEOC) is an independent federal law enforcement agency that enforces laws against workplace discrimination. The EEOC investigates discrimination complaints based on an individual's race, color, national origin, religion, sex, age, perceived intelligence, disability and retaliation for reporting and/or opposing a discriminatory practice. It is empowered to file discrimination suits against employers on behalf of alleged victims and to adjudicate claims of discrimination brought against federal agencies" (Wikipedia, 2011).

If you experience discrimination, your first step is to read the legislation and be sure that you have a legitimate case. Then contact your human resources division and seek their help in resolving the problem.

Everything we shut our eyes to, everything we run away from, everything we deny, denigrate or despise, serves to defeat us in the end. What seems nasty, painful, and evil, can become a source of beauty, joy, and strength, if faced with an open mind.

—Henry Miller

If that fails, go to the EEOC in your state and ask for assistance in resolving the problem and in determining if your situation is a legitimate claim.

UNDERSTANDING STEREOTYPES AND PREJUDICE

Why Is Having an Open Mind So Powerful?

As you seek to develop an open mind and become an educated citizen, you need to be aware of the terms *discrimination* and *prejudice*. If you discriminate against someone, you make a distinction in favor of or against a person on the basis of the group or class to which the person belongs, rather than according to an individual's merit. For example, you might discriminate against a person who is highly qualified for a job because he or she is of a certain race or religion, rather than consider his or her qualifications. Prejudice, on the other hand, is an unreasonable opinion or feeling formed beforehand or without knowledge, thought, or reason; it is a preconceived opinion of a hostile nature regarding a racial, religious or national group (*Webster's College Dictionary*, 1995).

If you discriminate against someone, it is because you are prejudiced against him or her for preconceived ideas that are based on insufficient knowledge, irrational feelings, or inaccurate stereotypes. As you can see, prejudice is usually not based on reason or knowledge, but on opinions most likely shaped by someone who influenced you or a region of the country where you grew up. Finally, prejudice is not an illegal act, whereas discrimination is illegal in employment, housing, loans, and many other areas outlined in the Civil Rights Act of 1964.

To receive the benefits of knowing someone, you need to enter all relationships with an open mind. If you have a derogatory mindset toward a race, an ethnic group, a sexual orientation, or a religion, for example, you have internal barriers that can keep you from getting to know who a person really is.

POSITIVE HABITS *at Work*

You will be expected to interact and work well with people from many different backgrounds. From the beginning, take time to get to know people who are different from you. Accept them as individuals, rather than judging them as members of a larger group. Ask people who have different viewpoints from you to go to lunch, and make an effort to understand their perspectives. Go out of your way to be known as a person who is not prejudiced or biased toward anyone. The more engaging and open you are to other people, the more open they will be to you.

Reflections: PUTTING IT ALL TOGETHER

Remember, we are motivated by what we value. As you establish your career and work toward personal and professional growth and change, consider the following ideas:

- Examine your personal values and beliefs to determine if cultural adjustments are needed.
- Listen to people and try to understand them before you form opinions.
- Stand up against intolerance and bigotry of any kind.

- Help others understand the importance of organizing against hate crimes.
- Develop relationships with people from a variety of backgrounds.
- Learn to appreciate and celebrate differences.
- Maintain close friendships with people who share your values and beliefs, as well as others who bring new and different ideas to the mix.

DIGITAL BRIEFCASE

ADJUSTING TO A GLOBAL ECONOMY

One of the many ways you can grow at work is to educate yourself on issues resulting from a global economy. Regardless of what position or workplace you are in, you will be affected by what is happening in other parts of the world. A good place to begin is to learn as much as you can about what is happening in China and India, two of our fastest-growing international competitors—and sometimes partners.

Access YouTube and identify several videos that show how employees in China work. As you view these videos, try to determine how their workplace differs from yours. Do you see any advantages Chinese businesses have over U.S. businesses because of a difference in regulations and laws? What reasons can you find that would cause U.S. businesses to ship certain jobs overseas to China rather than keeping the jobs here at home?

REFERENCES

Encyclopedia for Business. (2011). Corporate culture. Retrieved May 17, 2011, from www .referenceforbusiness.com/encyclopedia/Con-Cos/Corporate-Culture.html.

Feagin, J. R., & Feagin, C. B. (2008). *Racial and ethnic relations.* Upper Saddle River, NJ: Pearson/Prentice Hall.

Glenn, J. M. L. (2007). Generations at work: The new diversity. *Business Education Forum* (62)1.

Kallock, A. (April 16, 2009). Sunstein: Lack of ideological diversity leads to extremism. *The Harvard Law Review.*

Meister, J. C., & Willyerd, K. (2010). *The 2020 workplace.* New York: HarperCollins.

National Institutes of Health. (2010). Learning disabilities. Retrieved October 27, 2011, from http://www.nichd.nih.gov/health/topics/learning_disabilities.cfm.

Royal Pingdom. 2010. "Internet 2010 in numbers." Retrieved July 28, 2011, from http://royal.pingdom.com/2011/01/12/internet-2010-in-numbers.

Webster's College Dictionary. (1995). New York: Random House.

Wikipedia. (2011). Equal employment opportunity commission. Retrieved May 16, 2011, from http://en.wikipedia.org/wiki/Equal_Employment_Opportunity_Commission.

Electronic Communications

Be a yardstick of quality. Some people aren't used to an environment where excellence is expected.

Steve Jobs (1955–2011)

Objectives

- Explain the basics of utilizing modern workplace telecommunication tools
- Demonstrate proper business e-mail etiquette
- Display professionalism when utilizing both the telephone and mobile communication devices (including texting and call behaviors)
- Demonstrate professionalism when utilizing social media tools
- Demonstrate proper behaviors when participating in *video- and teleconferences*

How-Do-You-Rate

	Are you addicted to your smart phone?	Yes	No
1.	Within five minutes of waking, do you check your device for messages?	❏	❏
2.	Do you have to view/check your device at least once every hour?	❏	❏
3.	Do you use/view your device in locations/situations where you know it is not appropriate to use/view your device?	❏	❏
4.	Do you always have your device visible or easily accessible?	❏	❏
5.	Are you unable to go an entire day without access to your smart phone?	❏	❏

If you answered "yes" to two or more of these questions, you may be addicted to your smart phone.

Electronic Communications at Work

We live in a multitasking, fast-paced world that has resulted in technology addiction. The traditional workplace of the past has evolved into a virtual workplace where most people are connected electronically. Today's workplace communicates through venues including e-mail, mobile devices, texting, instant messaging, blogs, wikis, and audio and video conferencing. The more we are connected technologically, the greater the opportunity for disconnected messages. This chapter focuses on electronic communications in the workplace. Due to the frequency and speed of message transmission, those who communicate through today's virtual workplace need to take great care to ensure all electronic communications are sent in a clear and professional manner.

Telecommunication Basics

With the increase of technology in the workplace, the proper use of electronic communication tools, devices, and equipment becomes increasingly important. Common communication tools include various forms of computers, software, e-mail, Internet, and mobile (smart) devices. Employers may provide these tools to employees free of charge. If you utilize company-provided tools (including a computer, company server, or e-mail address), the tools, equipment, and messages are company property. Use these items only for company business. This includes the use of the Internet and electronic messaging. Many organizations have technology-use policies that outline expectations including privacy, liability, and potential misconduct issues. Ensure the messages you send and receive do not violate confidentiality and that they represent the company in a favorable light.

With a wide variety of electronic device options, keep in mind that there are proper times and places for their use. In some work situations, it is perfectly appropriate to utilize a laptop, tablet, or mobile device. In other situations, it is highly inappropriate. Only utilize the communication tool when it is relevant to the discussion or issue you are addressing. The communication tool should not distract from the conversation at hand. When in doubt, ask permission to use the device and explain why you want to use it to assist in the discussion.

Cory was in a company meeting. During the meeting, there was disagreement on whether the company's competitor had specific information on its website. Cory quickly pulled out a smart phone and began pulling up the competitor's website. One of the company executives glared at Cory, assuming Cory was being rude by texting or tending to personal business. Catching the executive's glare, Cory immediately held up the device and said, "I don't want to appear rude. I am quickly checking our competitor's site." Cory quickly retrieved and reported on the site and was able to contribute valuable information to the discussion.

Practice good computer hygiene. If possible, routinely scan your equipment for viruses, cookies, and other malicious coding that can be potentially harmful. Just as you would not show up to work when you are sick, you do not want to be responsible for contaminating others' communication tools when sharing information electronically. Regularly back up documents for preservation should a storage device fail.

Talk It Out

How might Cory have better handled the situation of using a smart phone during a meeting?

The Business E-mail

Electronic mail (e-mail) is the most common form of internal and external electronic communications in the workplace. With e-mail messages, you can directly type a message or attach a business document to your e-mail. E-mail creates more efficient communication within an organization and with individuals outside of the organization.

When sending an e-mail, ensure the subject line clearly describes the purpose of the e-mail message to let the reader know your message is not spam or a virus. Include a descriptive subject in the subject line that makes the receiver want to read the message. Do not leave the subject line blank nor use the words "Hi" or "Hello." It is also inappropriate to use the words "Urgent," "Important," or "Test" in a subject line. Most e-mail software contains a command that tags a message as important or urgent. The common tag is an exclamation point (!). Tag only important messages. A proper business e-mail subject line is formatted the same as a hard-copy memo subject line, which uses initial capitalization of words and no abbreviations.

As with all workplace equipment, business e-mail should be used only for business purposes. When composing or responding to e-mails, emoticons (faces made and embedded in e-mail messages) are inappropriate in business messages. Including emoticons in business messages reduces your professional image. Refrain from forwarding messages that are not work-related. These non-business-related messages clutter up company servers and may contain viruses and cookies. Maintain an organized and updated electronic address book and make every attempt to preserve the confidentiality of your address book.

When you receive a work-related message that requires a reply, respond to the message. Ignoring a message is rude and communicates to the sender that you do not care. You also run the risk of being excluded from future messages.

Writing E-mail Messages

E-mail is a necessary technology in nearly every workplace and can be easily misused. As with formal correspondence written on company letterhead, an e-mail should utilize proper layout, spelling, and grammar. Just like writing a business letter, composing a successful e-mail message involves planning and identifying the purpose of your message. Include what specifically needs to be communicated and what action you want the receiver(s) to take. Your message may be informational, or it may be a topic for discussion, or the message may require a decision.

Identify who should receive your e-mail message and include only individuals who need to know the information you are sharing. When sending an e-mail message, you have the option of sending the message directly to individuals on the "To:" line to the main recipient. You can also copy (cc:) the message to individuals by listing them in the "cc:" line. Any individual to whom the message is directed should be listed in the "To" line. Individuals who are named in the message and are not included in the "To:" line should be listed in the "cc:" line, as well as individuals who may be affected by the message. It is not necessary to include your boss in every e-mail. E-mail software has the option of blind copying (bcc:) your message to others through the use of "bcc:"; when an individual is blind copied on an e-mail, the bcc: recipient can see the main and cc: recipients, but the main and cc: recipients do not see the bcc: recipient. Not all recipients are aware of who is included in the message, and this creates a sense of mistrust. The use of blind copying (bcc:) is discouraged, except in the case of sending an e-mail to a mailing list where you do not want the recipients to see the other names due to privacy issues.

Exercise 5-1   Create an E-mail

Your boss (Austin@workspace.star) asks you to send a copy of a meeting memo to your coworkers: Charlie@workspace.star, Ben@workspace.star, and Audrey@workspace.star. Fill in the proper entries.

To:

Cc:

Bcc:

Subject:

After you have planned your message, begin writing a draft message. As you write your draft, clearly communicate your primary message early in the e-mail so as to capture and keep the reader's attention. Include the key points you want to communicate and the specific action you are requesting from the reader(s). Consider the reader's perspective and communicate the message in a positive manner. If your message contains several points, bullet or number each item and/or use subheadings to make it easier for the reader to follow and properly respond to your message. After you have finished composing your message, edit the message. Delete unnecessary words, and review the message for clarity and conciseness. People often judge others' professionalism based upon their writing skills. When you are satisfied, proofread the entire message. Most business e-mail software contains both spelling and grammar check—use them. If your message refers to an attachment, do not forget to include the attachment. Before sending your e-mail, give your message one final review, ensure the proper file is attached (if relevant), and check that you are sending the message to the appropriate parties. Also, review that the subject line concisely summarizes your message. After you have taken these steps, send your e-mail.

When sending e-mail messages practice positive e-mail habits:

- Mark only important time-sensitive messages "Urgent" (!). Marking all outgoing messages as urgent weakens your credibility, as it becomes hard for individuals to identify which of your messages truly are urgent. People may stop reading your messages immediately or altogether.
- Check all outgoing messages for proper spelling and grammar. Nothing lessens credibility faster than receiving a message filled with spelling and grammatical errors, especially since the majority of e-mail software comes with tools to correct them.
- E-mail messages written in all capital letters or with large and colorful letters are interpreted as yelling and are considered rude.
- Business e-mail should not have decorative backgrounds or use emoticons.
- If your e-mail software has the ability to embed a permanent signature, use it. Include your first and last name, title, company, business address, contact phone, and e-mail address.
- Some software has the capability of requesting a "return receipt" whenever a message is read and received. Some individuals consider this an invasion of privacy. Use this function only when necessary.
- If you will be out of the office and unable to access and/or respond to your e-mail message within a reasonable time, utilize an automated response to all e-mail messages informing the senders that you are unavailable. Remember to retract the automated response when you return.

Talk It Out

When is an appropriate time to use the return receipt feature in an e-mail message?

A common practice when utilizing workplace e-mail is that of forwarding business messages. If misused, this practice can cause conflict and/or embarrassment. Forwarding messages saves time and brings parties into the loop on a subject they may have not originally been involved with. When forwarding messages, include only individuals for whom the information is relevant. Prior to forwarding a message, ensure that none of the earlier information in the string of e-mails could embarrass anyone and does not contain information that should not be shared with others. If you are unsure the information has the potential to embarrass someone, do not forward the message. Simply summarize the situation in a new e-mail with (potentially) new recipients and copy (cc:) the original parties if appropriate.

Using business e-mail was a common activity for Cory. Cory was careful to always include an appropriate subject line, ensured that the content was professionally and concisely written, requested an action or follow-up activity, and sent it to the appropriate people. Cory was taken aback one day when a coworker sent Cory a negative e-mail for including inappropriate recipients in an e-mail message. The individual scolding Cory had sent his negative e-mail to everyone in the department, which embarrassed Cory. Cory reviewed the e-mail in question and did not see anything wrong with the message or the recipient list. As Cory reflected on how best to respond, Cory decided that the individual

Talk It Out

Did Cory appropriately handle the negative e-mail sent by the coworker? Why or why not?

who sent the negative message acted on emotion and embarrassed himself to all of his coworkers in the process of trying to embarrass Cory. Therefore, Cory felt it best to not respond.

Mobile (Portable) Communication Devices

Today's business environment relies on current technologies to improve communication. This is achieved through the use of mobile (portable) communication devices. Common devices include cell phones, smart phones, personal digital assistants (PDAs), portable music/entertainment devices, and wireless computers. While the use of these tools is acceptable in most business situations, employees need to be aware of the proper etiquette regarding the use of these devices. Just as it is impolite to verbally interrupt someone who is talking, it is also impolite to interrupt a conversation or meeting with incoming or outgoing electronic communications. There are two basic guidelines for using electronic communication devices. First, you may use your communication device if you are alone, in a private area, and its use is permitted at your workplace. Second, you may use your device when attending a meeting or business activity and it is necessary for communication. If the use of the device is not relevant to the activity, silence your device and place it screen down on the table, or turn it off and put it away. Do not answer calls. If you are expecting and receive an important call, politely excuse yourself from the room and take the call in private. If you forget to turn off the sound and it rings, apologize and immediately silence the device or turn it off. Although these guidelines are for business purposes, they should pertain to personal use, as well. Please review the information regarding telecommunication etiquette detailed in chapter 4.

In some situations, texting is a valuable communication tool. When you are in the presence of others, a general rule of thumb is to text only if the texting is related to the business at hand. For example, if you are negotiating a deal, you may text your boss to identify terms to present. Prior to texting, inform those present of your activity. Just as with all written communication, when texting for business purposes, the use of proper spelling and grammar is essential. Constant texting and utilizing a mobile device has become a habit for many. If you give in to the temptation to utilize your device as a distraction, you will display unprofessional behavior. Therefore, when in meetings, turn off or silence and put your communication device away unless it is explicitly necessary for the meeting. If not, the mere presence of the device may be tempting and will divert your attention from the business at hand. If you are anticipating an important message, if possible, inform the leader of the meeting and explain the situation and apologize ahead of time for the potential interruption. When the message is received, quietly step out of the meeting to respond to the message. It is rude to use your communication device while dining or attending meetings or performances. It is also not polite to take calls in front of others. Doing so implies that the individuals you are with are not important. When taking a call, apologize for the interruption, excuse yourself, and step away for privacy. Many people utilize text slang, text shorthand, acronyms, and codes in personal e-mails and texts. The use of these styles is not appropriate for business communications. In the workplace, texting should be used only for brief, informal communications, always utilizing proper spelling. Just as with other portable communication devices, it is not appropriate and is considered rude behavior to view and send text messages while with others (including discreetly during meetings).

It is inappropriate to use or display portable music/entertainment devices in the workplace unless the device provides quiet background music appropriate for a professional workplace and it does not disturb others.

Phone Etiquette

The phone is one of the most common workplace communication tools. Phone etiquette, whether land-line or wireless, is something every individual must practice to create and maintain a professional image for his or her company. Because the individual(s) on the other end of the phone cannot see you, it is important to communicate properly through the words you choose, your tone of voice, the pitch of your voice, and your rate of speech.

When answering a call, try to answer on the first or second ring. Start with a salutation such as "Good morning," and identify yourself and the company. Convey a positive, professional attitude when speaking on the phone. Smile when you speak, to create a friendly tone. Speak clearly and slowly, and do not speak too softly or too loudly. If you take a call and need to place the first caller on hold, politely tell the individual on the phone that you are placing him or her on hold. If an individual is placed on hold for more than one minute, get back on the line and ask if you can return the call at a later time.

Taking a call without explanation in the presence of others implies that the individual in your presence is not important. When with others, let the call go into voice mail. If you are expecting an important call and are in the presence of others, inform those you are with that you are expecting an important call and will need to take it when it arrives. When the call is received, politely excuse yourself. If you are in your office, politely ask your office guest to excuse you for one moment while you quickly take the call.

When making a phone call, identify yourself to the receiver. The call should be for a brief interaction unless you make sure the receiver has time to talk. If you expect the discussion to be lengthy, ask the individual on the other end of the line if he or she has time to talk or if there is a more convenient time. When you are having a phone conversation, do not eat or tend to personal matters.

Speaker phones are useful communication tools for specific situations and also require proper etiquette. A speaker phone should be used only when you are on a conference call with other participants in the same room or when you require a hands-free device. Use a speaker phone only when you are in a private room where your call will not be distracting to others in your work area. When you use a speaker phone, ask individuals included in the call for permission to use the speaker phone. Alert those included in the call that others are in the room with you and make introductions. This ensures confidentiality and open communication between all parties. Those using a speaker phone should be aware that any small noise they make may be heard and distracting to those on the other end of the line.

Voice mail messages are a part of business communication. A voice mail impression is equally as important as communicating in person. When leaving a voice mail message, keep the message brief and professional. State your name and the purpose of the call, and leave a return number at the beginning of the message. Speak slowly and clearly and leave a short but concise message. After you have left your message, repeat your name and return number a second time before ending the call. When you receive voice mail messages, it is proper and important to promptly return messages left for you. Routinely check and empty your voice mail box.

On both portable and land-line phones, keep your voice mail greeting professional. Include your name and the company name in the message. Clever voice mail greetings are not professional. Musical introductions or bad jokes do not form favorable impressions when employers or customers are attempting to contact you.

Exercise 5-2 Create a Professional Voice Mail Greeting

You are the account clerk at Garret and Danielle Accounting Firm. Create a professional voice mail greeting for your work phone.

_____

_____

Web Quiz

Are you addicted to social media? Use the following quiz to identify if you are addicted to social media, or find another online quiz related to social media addiction.

http://www.blueglass.com/widgets/social-media-expert.php

Social Media Tools

Companies commonly use social media tools such as Facebook, video/photo file sharing, blogs, and micro-blogs for marketing purposes. Some companies hire professionals to maintain and manage their image through social media outlets. While it may be tempting to post a video or vent about an irate customer, coworker, or administrator online, such behavior is not only unprofessional, but could be a violation of the company's technology-use policy. The behavior could also pose potential legal issues for both you and your employer. An increasing number of employers consider any employee use of social media that reflects poorly on the employer as a violation of its technology-use policy. Individuals using social media for personal reasons need to separate personal sharing from professional sharing. Many organizations regard the posting of company-related information by employees as divulging confidential or competitive information. Regardless of your company's policy, it is best to refrain from identifying and/or speaking poorly of the company, employees, vendors, and customers in all social media communications.

A growing number of companies are moving away from e-mail as a primary means of communicating brief electronic business messages and are utilizing wikis, blogs, and instant messaging for both internal and external communications. A wiki is a collaborative website where users have the ability to edit and contribute to the site. Blogs, also called web logs, are online journals where readers are often allowed to comment. Instant messaging (IM) is a form of online communication that occurs between two or more parties in real time. Business etiquette regarding the use of these communication methods is similar to that of e-mail. When at work, use these venues only for business purposes. Proper spelling and grammar and clear and concise communications are necessary. As with all forms of written communication, professionalism and tone matter. View your participation in a wiki as a form of teamwork. When making edits to the wiki, be sensitive to how others are receiving your comments and, in turn, accept the suggestions of others. Your goal is to provide an accurate web page that properly communicates your message. Business blogs are used as both marketing and education tools. The purpose of a blog is to create and enhance relationships, so keep blog posts and comments positive and meaningful. The difference between IM and e-mail is that you are able to identify who is online at the same time you are. Utilize IM only for brief business interactions. While it is tempting to IM individuals when you see they are online at their workstations, remember that

IM at work is not intended as a workplace social tool. You do not want to become disruptive or annoying when utilizing IM. Whatever electronic communication venue you utilize, remember that you are representing your company.

While it is perfectly common and acceptable to utilize social media tools for personal reasons, remember to maintain a positive and professional online image. We refer to this as an electronic image. An **electronic image** is the image formed when someone is communicating and/or researching you through electronic means. It is becoming common to refer to your electronic image as an **e-dentity.** Routinely conduct an Internet search of yourself to ensure you have a clean online image. If there are negative photos, videos, blogs, or other information that reflect poorly on you, have them removed. Maintain a professional electronic personality by utilizing a professional voice mail message and e-mail address.

Cory's friend Gigi recently got a new job in sales that required her to train and job-shadow her manager for the first few weeks. Cory knew Gigi was addicted to both texting and her social media site, so Cory was glad that she now had something to keep her mind focused. During a sales call, Gigi was not focused and was using a company laptop to play on her social media site instead of reviewing sales figures. Gigi and her client stepped away from the conference table for a minute, and Gigi's boss tried to quickly retrieve a figure from the computer. Unfortunately, all the boss saw was Gigi's social media site. To make matters worse, the site contained a photo of Gigi in a crazy pose outside of her new company headquarters, which included the company's name in the picture.

Talk It Out

If you were Gigi and you knew your new boss saw the social media site open on your computer, how would you respond?

Exercise 5-3 Identify a Professional Personal E-mail Address for Yourself

Create a professional personal e-mail address

Video and Teleconferencing

It is common for meetings to take place through video or teleconference venues such as Skype, WebEx, and Google Talk. A **video conference** is an interactive communication using two-way video and audio technology. It allows individuals in another location to see and hear all meeting participants. A **teleconference** is also an interactive communication; however, it connects participants through the telephone without the opportunity of visually seeing all participants. When participating in a video conference, a computer, a web cam, and a reliable Internet connection are needed. An individual participating in a teleconference requires a reliable phone line and a quiet location. When taking part in a video or teleconference, the participant will receive a designated time and specific instructions on how to establish connection. In addition to following the phone interview tips that the meeting participant needs to prepare for and treat the telecommunication meeting as if it were a face-to-face meeting. Follow these basic tips for a successful electronic meeting:

- Plan ahead. Research the venue you will be using to address any unforeseen issue. If possible, arrange a pre-meeting trial to ensure all equipment works properly (including your volume and microphone).
- Dress professionally (if you are visible to other participants). As with face-to-face meetings, visual impressions matter.

- Maintain a professional environment. Conduct your meeting in a quiet and appropriate location. When you are visible to other participants, a bedroom, public place, or outside location is not appropriate.
- Speak to the camera (if you are participating in a video conference). Focus on the web cam as if you were speaking directly to the other participants. Without interrupting or distracting others, feel free to ask questions, take notes, and use hand gestures.
- Avoid distracting noises. Turn off music or any other items that create distracting noises. Do not eat or drink during the meeting.

When teleconferencing, state your name each time you speak. For example, prior to contributing, say, "Hi, this is Ted. I would like to provide a status report on the Phoenix project." Because virtual meetings require a special emphasis on listening, be quiet when others are speaking and do not do anything distracting. Take your turn speaking and do not interrupt. As with face-to-face meetings, be prepared and actively contribute.

The number of technology-related workplace tools continues to grow, as do their applications. While our means of communicating at work may change, the need for professional communication remains the same. Be respectful and concise in your communication and represent your organization in a professional manner.

Workplace Dos and Don'ts

Do utilize company technology tools only for company business	*Don't* violate your company's technology-use policy
Do practice good computer hygiene by routinely backing up documents	*Don't* forget to routinely scan your computer for viruses and other malicious software
Do recognize the appropriate time and place for workplace technologies	*Don't* allow technology to distract from business matters
Do demonstrate professionalism in business e-mail and texts	*Don't* become addicted to workplace technologies by sharing inappropriate messages
Do practice good meeting habits in video conferencing and teleconferencing	*Don't* let the fact of not being face-to-face in a video or teleconference interfere with practicing professionalism

Concept Review and Application

Summary of Key Concepts

- Send electronic communications in a clear and professional manner.
- Many organizations have technology-use policies that address privacy, liability, and potential misconduct issues.
- Do not forward messages at work that do not involve work-related issues.
- Just as with written communication, when texting for business purposes, the use of proper spelling and grammar is essential.
- When utilizing social media for personal use, refrain from identifying your company and/or speaking poorly of the company and/or its customers.
- Maintain a clean e-dentity.
- Practice good meeting habits in technology-based meetings.

Key Terms

e-dentity   electronic image
teleconference   video conference

If You Were the Boss

1. One of your employees has been sending personal texts during meetings. How should you handle this issue?
2. Many employees are taking photos and/or videos at department meetings and company events. Should you be concerned? Why? As the boss, what should you do?

Web Links

http://www.forbes.com/2010/07/27/internet-email-workplace-technology-privacy.html
http://www.helium.com/items/436615-what-is-the-impact-of-new-technology-in-the-workplace
http://www.businessweek.com/technology/ceo_guide/

Activities

Activity 5-1

Name two specific technology devices that are used in your job (current or future). How are they used to improve communication?

Device	What Use?

Activity 5-2

Check your e-dentity. Conduct an Internet search on yourself. Is there anything you need to change?

_____

_____

Activity 5-3

What should you say to someone who is inappropriately using his or her mobile device (e.g., during a meeting)?

_____

_____

Activity 5-4

Research at least two different smart phones and explain which is best for a job that requires smart-phone technology for traveling (calls, e-mails, texting, viewing documents).

_____

_____

1. The more the workplace is connected technologically, the greater opportunities for

   _____.

2. Many organizations have _____ that outline expectations including privacy, liability, and potential misconduct issues.

3. Practice _____ to ensure you do not contaminate others' communication tools.

4. When in doubt about the proper use of a technology device, _____.

5. The use of _____ is inappropriate for business messages.

6. Blind copying someone in a business e-mail creates a sense of _____.

7. It is impolite to interrupt a conversation or meeting with _____ electronic communications.

Part III: Leadership

Chapter 6: *LEAD*: Teamwork-How to Lead and How to Follow
Chapter 7: *RELATE*: Managing Conflict and Dealing with Difficult People

Chapters taken from:
Cornerstones for Professionalism, Second Edition
by Robert M. Sherfield and Patricia G. Moody

chapter six

LEAD

TEAMWORK—HOW TO LEAD AND HOW TO FOLLOW

Leadership is a potent combination of strategy and character. If you must be without one, be without the strategy.
—Gen. H. Norman Schwarzkopf

Why read **this chapter?**

Because you'll learn...

- The characteristics of a good leader
- The types of power
- The steps in becoming a good follower

Because you'll be able to...

- Discuss how to work in a virtual team
- List steps in effective delegation

PROFESSIONALS from the *Field*

Name: *Mike Collins*

Business: *CEO and founder, IMI Living*

Learning to lead and to follow are equally important. There are times when I need to step up as the CEO of my company and lead my colleagues with a clear vision and motivational strategy. There are other times when I need to sit back and let someone else who may be more of an expert in a particular area take the lead. I advise you to learn to lead a good meeting—one that has a clear agenda, that is focused, moves quickly and decisively, has good complementary visuals and graphs, and ends with a clear action plan. You also need to be a good meeting participant—do your homework and come prepared to make valuable comments or ask questions that focus the group on the right targets. I also encourage you to learn about the different kinds of power—some of which you have as a new employee—and to use power wisely and effectively. You should never abuse power just because you have it.

LEADING WITH PASSION, POWER, AND PROMISE

How Do I Find the "Right Stuff" to Lead?

Everyone recognizes good leadership and strong leaders. Sometimes we refer to leaders as having "the right stuff." We observe outstanding leadership in dynamic corporate presidents, in good teachers, in football stars, and in effective politicians. Leadership qualities can be found in class presidents, military platoon leaders, or organizations' officers. At times we can almost see leadership as it is happening. Certainly, we feel the presence of a great leader, but leadership remains somewhat intangible.

Before we go further, we need to define *leadership*. There are many definitions, but the one we like best is this one: Leadership is the ability to establish a culture where people can make contributions, use their unique talents, and feel that they have been part of something bigger than they are. The influence potential of leaders is determined largely by how well they get other people to willingly and enthusiastically do what they want them to do.

Leadership is not playing a role, acting a part, wearing a uniform, or holding an office. Leadership is caring about people and an organization, putting others' needs ahead of your own, giving more of yourself than just enough to get by, and working as hard on "dirty work" as on "glory work." Leadership is knowing when to follow, sharing successes, understanding people's innate needs to achieve and to feel good about themselves, and helping others develop their potential. Finally, leadership is having the ability to craft a vision that is bigger than any one person's goals, and that, when accomplished, is worthy of having done the work to get there. We will discuss leading and following here to help prepare you for your future leadership roles, as well as for your role as a member of a team—both very important to your career.

You may be thinking, "I'm not interested in being a leader, and my degree won't lead me to a leadership role." However, you will be working in teams and with others in every position, and there will be times when you may have to lead in order to complete a task, help others, or just keep your job.

> If your actions inspire others to dream more, learn more, and become more, you are a leader.
> —John Quincy Adams, sixth President of the United States

Embrace Outstanding Leadership Qualities

The leader's job is to secure the cooperation of a group of followers, stimulate them to work together for common goals, guide them using previous experience, encourage them to become a dedicated member of the team, and set such a positive example that people willingly do what the leader wishes. You can only teach what you model yourself; if you don't do what you are telling everyone else to do, they won't do it. Leadership should never be confused with power, adoration, and seizing recognition for oneself. Although good leaders come in many shapes and sizes and rise from a multitude of backgrounds, they share common characteristics.

Major points for becoming an outstanding leader are listed in Figure 6.1.

> Remarkable leaders never build pyramids in their own backyards.
> —Wes Roberts

Figure 6.1 **Qualities of Outstanding Leaders**

Outstanding Leaders:

- Have the ability to shape a vision that is compelling enough to make other people believe in it and see themselves participating in making it happen.

- Are goal oriented and demonstrate direction in their own lives. Leaders must never allow their personal goals to supersede the goals of the organization, nor should an organization be used as a vehicle to serve the leader's personal ambitions. Goals must be jointly shared by the leader and the people.

- Can establish a climate of success, where people feel they can achieve and find fulfillment. This climate is inviting, encouraging, and rewarding to individuals. Leaders are able to involve all people and make them feel a part of an organization.

- Have a strong system of values and morals. As a leader, one must be an example for others to follow, meaning that one must be a decent, ethical, honest, and trustworthy person and must treat people consistently and fairly.

- Are great communicators. They are outstanding listeners as well as talkers. They know how to communicate up and down the chain of command, and can deliver a compelling inspirational message.

- Help others feel good about themselves, assist others in sharing in successes, and help others be a part of something bigger than themselves. A good leader is a diplomat who can navigate through the difficult situations confronted by decision makers.

- Know the basic underlying truth of leadership: leaders serve others. They meet the needs of others ahead of their own. Albert Schweitzer, Mother Teresa, and Martin Luther King, Jr., are all recognized as great leaders because they were servant leaders.

- Understand that leadership is caring about people and an organization, putting others' needs ahead of your own, and giving more of yourself than just enough to get by.

- Know that they must step aside and let others lead sometimes. They realize that they may be leaders today and followers another day. They know that they must first be good followers and good teammates in order to become a leader.

- Must be courageous, decisive, bold, imaginative, creative, and strong. They must be able to develop plans that are daring and different, and then they must have the strength and staying power to make them happen. Good leaders are "can do" people.

- Are able to display confidence in themselves and others. They must look, act, and speak like leaders. The ability to speak well is a great asset to anyone trying to lead. Leaders must look and act the part if people

are going to follow them. They must stand tall, walk briskly, and speak decisively.

- Must be courageous and able to stand adversity. They must be able to look at a bad situation and find a way to capitalize on it and overcome it.

- Do what they say they will do. Good leaders "keep their promises and follow up on their commitments" (Berko, Welvin, & Ray, 1997). They honor their word.

- Are able to compromise on some issues. One cannot always get everything he or she wants. People who are unyielding, unbending, and uncompromising will accomplish very little. The leader's job is to get the group to reach a consensus and then implement the plan.

- Must be open-minded and able to hear competing viewpoints and separate the good ideas from the bad. Leaders must be able to keep arguments from getting personal. No members should be allowed to attack other individuals. The leader's job is to give everyone a forum in which to express ideas and opinions, bring the group to a satisfactory conclusion, get disagreeing members to accept the compromise, and not take criticisms of an idea too personally.

- Are willing to share the victory! This can be accomplished by celebrations that involve everyone and by making statements such as, "This was a great team effort. We all made sacrifices and worked very hard. This is a victory for all of us, and I am proud to be a part of this team."

- Praise people and present awards publicly. Make people feel good and recognize them when they have worked hard and made outstanding contributions. Leaders know how to "make a difference in the lives of others—and liberate the leader in everyone" (Berko, Welvin, & Ray, 1997).

- Know that winning nobly and with class is a must. Leaders don't gloat or take the credit when they win. They are humble and always share the credit. The more you give credit away, the more it comes back to you.

- Are cheerleaders for their team members. Leaders write notes of personal congratulations; they thank people sincerely in front of groups; they tell people, "I appreciate you." Leaders spend a great deal of their time cheering others' accomplishments and no time cheering their own. If you are good, you don't have to tell people; they will know.

- Have the ability to get along well with all kinds of people and see the best in all people. They don't judge people by their race, religion, color, ethnic background, sexual orientation, or level of education. They cherish diversity! Leaders must be passionate about their vision, their followers, and their goals.

112

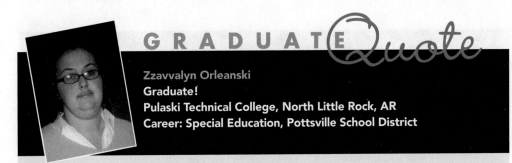

A positive attitude will help you so much more than a negative attitude when it comes to reaching your goals and working at your best. When you face challenging times, dig in and hold on. If you let negative thoughts and self-talk derail you, you won't survive in this world. Approach every day in your position as a chance to learn something new and help someone along the way.

GOOD LEADERS USE POWER CAREFULLY

How Can I Use Power Without Being Heavy Handed?

Many people confuse management with leadership, just as many confuse power with force. Real leadership power and respect must be earned. They cannot be bought, inherited, or bestowed on someone. The strangest thing about power is that the less you use it, the more you seem to have. Power is a precious commodity that few people know how to use. Conversely, if you have power, you must use it at times when a hard decision has to be made, or people will lose their respect for you and you will lose your power. The worst leaders are those who use their power for trivial reasons, personal gain, or vindictiveness. Weak leaders use force rather than leadership. Remember, leadership is the ability to get people to follow you voluntarily. Good leaders use their power to develop other leaders and take pride in seeing people they have led become successful.

Nearly all people can stand adversity, but if you want to test their true character, give them power.

— Abraham Lincoln

Categories of Leadership Power

Power comes to us through a variety of means. Specifically, we can view the acquisition of leadership power in six categories, illustrated in Figure 6.2. Each category is numbered in increasing order of significance in acquiring power for a leadership role. Category 1 is the weakest and most short-lived, whereas Category 6 is the strongest and most long-lasting. However, Categories 1 through 5 are actually part of Category 6. Each one builds on the other and strengthens Category 6. Viewed separately, we can describe each category as such.

CATEGORY 1: WHAT YOU HAVE. Category 1 is the weakest category for acquiring power. Many people are drawn to materialistic goods and place people who have a variety of these goods on a pedestal. Some people who are wealthy and have valuable property, spacious homes, or other commodities viewed as "important" use these objects to attract and gain temporary power. Unfortunately, some people are swayed by "things" and will step back and let wealthier people

Figure 6.2   Professional Development Puzzle

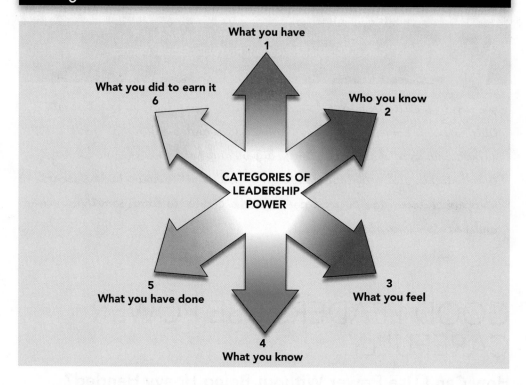

make all the decisions. If a person's power base is built only on material objects, his or her power base will soon crumble.

CATEGORY 2: WHO YOU KNOW.   Who you know is Category 2. You probably have heard the expression, "It's not **what** you know, but **who** you know." In today's workplace, this is often true. Networking and making contacts are of ultimate importance to most employees today. Nevertheless, a power base built only on "who you know" is weak. Managers, supervisors, and leaders who acquired their positions because they "knew the boss" are familiar to us. Many people who acquire power this way quickly learn that the boss or the owner can make you a supervisor or assign you a title, but they cannot give you real power. True power is earned through the respect of the people you lead.

CATEGORY 3: WHAT YOU FEEL.   What you feel, Category 3, is much more abstract than what you have or who you know. Acquiring power by what you feel can be summed up as "leading with a soul." People respect leaders who are reflective and thoughtful. When leaders make decisions with their souls, those who are being led know the difference. This is the beginning of earned power. People begin to respect and appreciate that the leader has taken the time to look at every option, explored many solutions—and taken the human side of matters into consideration. Earning true power begins with soul leadership. This category includes leaders who care about the people they are leading; they feel their pain and frustrations and try to help them overcome their problems. Leaders who care also try to help people get promoted and find their strengths so they, too, can become leaders. Leaders with soul build other people.

Surround yourself with the most brilliant, talented, and optimistic people possible.

—Steve Brannon

CATEGORY 4: WHAT YOU KNOW.   What you know, Category 4, goes a long way with people who are being led. Sometimes older people have difficulty being led by younger people. The younger person feels threatened and sometimes uses too much force, and the older person sees the younger leader as a "hotshot" fresh out of college with no real life experience, just "book knowledge." To a large extent, leadership power is gained through competence, experience, and expertise. When people know that the leader is intelligent, bright, studious, resourceful, clever, and concerned about them, respect and earned power follow. It is important to understand that good leaders with real power are knowledgeable students, too. They continue to learn from their surroundings, and they learn from the people they lead. If you are a young leader, it is wise to ask older people for their advice and suggestions. If you are an older leader, it is wise to learn the new ideas that young people bring to the table. In all cases, good leaders must keep people informed of what they know that needs to be shared. What people are not up on, they are down on.

CATEGORY 5: WHAT YOU HAVE DONE. What you have done, Category 5, might be referred to as life experience. Used properly, life experience is one of the most powerful tools in leadership and can earn you great respect and power. Leaders should be careful, however, not to rely too heavily on the past and, in doing so, overlook current trends and new options. Using what you know is one of the strongest tools for gaining respect and acquiring power. People like working for leaders who have experience, knowledge, background, and training. They also like working with leaders who know how to use past situations to develop solutions to current problems. People also admire and respect leaders who stay up to date and are always looking forward and learning emerging trends and tools that will help them compete.

CATEGORY 6: WHAT YOU DID TO EARN IT. What you did to earn power, Category 6, is the most important category. Coming full circle, true power is always earned. Power may come from what you have, who you know, what you feel, what you know, and what you have done, but, ultimately, true power is earned. Power can be earned by:

- Respecting other people
- Appreciating the work that people do and what they know
- Making good, solid, fair decisions that people respect
- Demonstrating a genuine interest in colleagues and their families
- Appreciating and calling on others' life experiences
- Being courageous and willing to take calculated risks
- Giving others the power to help themselves (empowering and enlarging)
- Remaining calm and getting the facts in the face of crisis
- Being a positive, optimistic, and engaging force
- Using creativity and asking for help
- Providing employees with the tools, support, and training to help them do the best job possible
- Living the motto, "I am a part of a bigger picture."

Powerful leaders enable others to be the very best they can be. They enlarge other people and their abilities. They encourage others to explore options and to create new paths. Last, powerful leaders are not challenged or threatened by people who excel, but they learn from them and celebrate their successes.

The Use of Power from Leaders' and Followers' Perspectives

Power is the ability to make things happen or to prevent things from happening. Power is also the ability to cause people to act in certain ways. People sometimes label power as being a bad thing, but power, in and of itself, is not bad. The issue is how someone gets power and how he or she uses it. Actually, everyone has some form of power, although some people don't understand how to use the power they have. Study the types of power illustrated in Figure 6.3.

> *Power is like being a lady. If you have to tell people you are, you aren't.*
>
> —Margaret Thatcher, former Prime Minister of England

Figure 6.3 Power from Leaders' and Followers' Perspectives

Types of Power	From Leader's Perspective	From Follower's Perspective
Reward	Has power because he or she has control of the finances and resources—can reward through money, promotion, increased visibility	Complies in order to get the resources that he or she believes a person has
Coercive	Has power because he or she can deliver punishment	Complies to avoid punishment by the person he or she thinks can wield it; fears the consequences of not following this person's orders
Legitimate	Has power based on one's position or title; given by the company and carries authority to make decisions	Believes power is granted by the company and he or she must carry out the directives given by this person
Expert	Has power because this person is an expert at something that is valued in the company (for example, technology knowledge)	Admires this person's knowledge and thus assigns him or her power
Referent/ Charisma	Has power that is gained from charm, humor, and engaging personality that causes people to want to emulate him or her	Complies because he or she wants to be liked by this person and accepted in his or her circle of friends
Information/ Knowledge	Has power that is gained from special knowledge that others need; related to skills, practice, experience, expertise	Believes that this person has information he or she needs and therefore, must stay on his or her good side
Connection	Gains power through the legitimate power of others (for example, an executive assistant to the president has the power to allow people in to see the boss); has the ear of powerful people	Believes this person has access to someone who is powerful and therefore, he or she must be obeyed
Support	Has ability to gain support from peers, subordinates, superiors, and customers outside the formal organization	Complies because he or she perceives this person to have internal and external power
Ethical/Character	Has respect and thus power because his or her word can always be trusted; treats everyone with respect and dignity; when this person speaks, he or she usually has something worthwhile to say	Complies from respect of who this person is and how well he or she is respected in the company

OUTSTANDING FOLLOWERS AND TEAM PLAYERS

How Do You Become a Great Team Member?

It has been said that "power corrupts and absolute power corrupts absolutely." In so many cases, this statement proves to be true. In the space below, explain that statement:

_____

_____

_____

_____

If you become a leader/manager of people, what can you learn from this statement and how can you avoid becoming corrupt simply because you have power over people?

Certainly, you must have a great leader to accomplish major goals, but great leaders cannot lead without great team members. According to Maxwell (2002), "Team players are enlargers, meaning they have the ability to see their teammates in the best light and make those around them better." If you are an enlarger, you believe in your teammates and want the best for them. You delight in seeing them grow. If you are a good, solid team player, others will work better because of you and your contributions to the team. Good team members who are also good followers care about their colleagues, and they have a burning desire to succeed together. A good team member is committed to giving his or her all to making the team succeed. The characteristics listed in Figure 6.4 are always found in good team members.

> *A team is many voices with a single heart.*
> —John C. Maxwell

Figure 6.4 Characteristics of Great Team Members

- Great team members love to win, to do a job better than any other team, and to win with their teammates. It's not so much that they love to beat someone else; the fact is that they simply love to strive together, to learn and improve together, and to reach goals together. Winning is simply the visible fact that they have worked hard and accomplished something great together. Winning together is bigger than any one of them winning separately.

- Great team members are excellent communicators. They are friendly, engaging, and able to express themselves and their ideas well. They are adept at listening and reading body language. They speak up when they have a point to make; they disagree with their teammates if they feel they should, but they do it in a respectful and careful manner. Great team members speak up candidly and openly, being careful not to offend intentionally. They own what they say and take responsibility for it.

- Great team members are intentional. *Intentional* is a word one hears a lot in business settings today. It simply means that people are acting deliberately, purposefully, and in a calculated manner with intentional goals and motives, rather than wandering around with no direction. They know where they are headed. Team members who act with intention take responsibility for keeping themselves mentally, physically, and emotionally in top condition.

- Great team members are adaptable and flexible. They are able to change directions if they need to, stop what they are doing and pick up something else if they are needed urgently in another place, and keep a lid on their emotions when things get stressful.

- Great team members are able to collaborate and cooperate. They learn to love being together as a team and to value what they can achieve together. Together they create a synergy that none of them has alone, and this is the glue that holds them together and makes them care about each other. They are able to work in a group and give and take on ideas.

- Great team members have a sense of humor. If you really love your work and your colleagues and you are in the right place, work becomes fun. Work is challenging, fulfilling, educational, and rewarding. Everyone loves people who can laugh and have fun, especially at their own expense. Laughter can diffuse tension and anger and cause people to release stress that is building up in their bodies; laughter is healing. A leader or follower who can evoke laughter into the mix has power.

- Great team members are committed to the vision and the goals. They place the team's goals ahead of their own. They know where they are headed and they will not take "no" for an answer. Failure is not an option!

- Great team members are disciplined. They stay and do the job no matter how tired they are. They are determined and tenacious and go above and beyond to be sure they don't let their team down. In a championship playoff game between the Dallas Mavericks and the Miami Heat, Dirk Nowitzski played with a temperature of 102 degrees—he was that committed to his team and to winning with them. Not only did he play, he led a comeback that enabled his team to win the game.

- Great team members are enthusiastic and excited about the team and what they are accomplishing together. They come to work fired up and ready to go to work. They don't drag others down with negativism, whining, and complaining. They bring an "I feel great" attitude to everything they do, and they are a joy to be around.

- Great team members are supportive of their colleagues. No matter how strong or private a person is, everyone needs help at one time or another. Good team members understand this fact, and they take care of each other during good times and bad. If one team member is having a bad day or a particularly difficult time in life, the others step up and take up the slack. It is said about geese that if one is shot or has to fall out of formation, another goose will follow and stay with him until he is OK or until he is dead. Good team members look after each other this way.

LEAD WITH VISION

How Can I Sell the Big Picture?

A vision portrays how the future is supposed to look. It provides people with a framework to help them understand. A leader's vision gives direction and asks: *What* should we be? *Where* should we be? *When* should we be there? *Why* should we be there? *Where* will we concentrate our resources? *How* will our lives be changed?

"Vision, quite simply, is a way of spelling out for your listeners the big picture, to help them understand the effort in which they are engaged, and to win their buy-in" (Barnes, 2005). A good leader must be able to paint a picture that is compelling for the people who are following. The vision must be something that is worth working for together and something that will challenge people to work for a common goal.

> *Leadership is the capacity to translate vision into reality.*
> —Warren Bennis

Good leaders understand that there can be no leadership without followers. Leaders and followers ideally bring out the best in each other. A visionary leader must capture the imagination of followers by painting a picture of some worthy achievement. Leaders are the kind of people who draw others to them, often because of the visions they lay out.

Followers are not likely to get excited about a plan that accomplishes very little or that is not much different from what they have always done. In other words, they don't want a leader who "majors in the minors." Big plans and big changes may frighten people, but they also grab them. Being able to comprehend, design, and sell a challenging vision that is built in conjunction with team members is one of the hallmarks of a great leader.

LEADING AND FOLLOWING IN A GLOBAL WORKPLACE

How Do You Work with a Virtual Team?

The use of virtual teams is becoming increasingly popular in today's modern workplace. Team members may work very effectively together while living in different time zones or even different countries. Virtual work teams can be part of an ideal job for people with certain requirements

Shutterstock

How do you think you would function as a member of a virtual team?

Figure 6.5 Guidelines for Virtual Team Members

- Establish a clear system for communicating, taking notes and sharing them in an accessible medium, and a sequence of participating so that everyone has an opportunity and an expectation to participate.

- Take time to get to know each other on personal and professional levels. Have "water cooler conversations" using Skype, WebEx, GoToMeeting, or some other system and pretend you are all together sharing likes and dislikes, hobbies and interests, and special skills and knowledge.

- Use a shared calendar system that allows people to schedule meetings and to have discussions with each other across multiple time zones. Designate core or mutual time slots when everyone must be available to confer. Use systems such as Google Apps and Google Calendar to assist in the scheduling process.

- Use instant messaging instead of e-mail—it is more effective. Some virtual teams always have Skype or some other system running to use for quick conversations.

- Share documents through tools such as Dropbox.

- Plan a "workplace happy hour" where you share new ideas and create together. You might consider using Second Life as a channel for having these meetings. Explore the use of new technologies, ideas that other companies are using, and how you can better work together as a virtual team.

and needs. The major key in making virtual teams work is that everyone is comfortable and productive working in this situation. Certainly, it is not for everyone. Figure 6.5 provides several important guidelines for making this happen.

THINK BEFORE YOU ACT

How Do I Make Good Decisions as a Leader?

Good leaders have to be decisive! Most of the time they don't have to make snap judgments, but at times a leader must make a quick decision. In 1955, Ruth and Eliot Handler, the cofounders of Mattel Toys, bet their company on television advertising when they signed on with ABC's *Mickey Mouse Club* for the sum of $500,000—the net worth of the company at that time. They had only a few hours to make this monumental decision. The payoff was immediate and significant. Orders came in by the sackful, all because of leaders who were willing to take a chance and make a decision at just the right time.

Most decisions won't be this urgent or important. However, sometimes a decision could mean life and death, or it could involve a piece of equipment that is needed right now, or it might be necessary to stop something being done by an employee. Most decisions, however, can wait until you have had time to think about the end results and the process needed to accomplish an objective. Being decisive and able to make a rational decision under pressure is very important, but being smart enough to take your time and weigh all possibilities is smarter if you have the luxury of time.

Here are some points to consider before you act:

- Can it wait so you can have a little more time to think about your decision? (But don't let decisions sit on your desk forever.)

- Do you have all the facts? Or at least most of them?

- Have you asked other leaders how they would handle this situation?

- Have you thought through how your decision will affect everyone concerned?

- Have you heard from everyone the decision might affect?
- Have you talked to members of your team and listened to their opinions? Do you have "buy-in" from them?

The best advice to be offered here is simply, "Stop and think!" Don't make rash decisions that can come back to haunt you. Sometimes you may not have much time to make a decision before you act. You can't hear opposing viewpoints; you can't take a vote; you can't read a good book—you simply have to act. Stay calm, think, and make the best decision you can make. **Remember, however, that not making a decision *is* a decision.**

CREATIVE PROBLEM SOLVING

How Can You Learn to Make Good Decisions Using Creativity and Logic?

> *Nothing is more difficult, and therefore more precious, than to be able to decide.*
>
> *—Napoleon*

The word *decision* comes from the Latin word *decidere,* meaning to "cut off." In other words, you have decided on something, and all other options have been canceled. Life is a series of choices, and the ones we make affect our lives in many different ways. Therefore, we need to learn to make good, logical, and creative choices.

Decisions mean letting uncertainty enter your life because the results usually happen somewhere in the future. For example, you could decide suddenly, without thinking the decision through, to drop out of school. The result might be that you can't get a good job or that you aren't earning the salary you had hoped for. If you had taken time to think about this decision and weigh all the possible results, you might have decided not to leave school. We all make poor decisions at one time or another, but we can learn to make good decisions most of the time by using the right strategies. The leader's job is to make the hard decisions, the decisions that can't be delegated, and the right decisions. Some decisions are amazingly smart; others are painfully embarrassing, and in hindsight, you wonder how you could have made such a bad decision. The scary part of leadership is that we don't have a crystal ball to see how our decisions are going to turn out.

As you lead and make decisions, approach difficult problems as though you are trying on a new pair of glasses. Try to see things you have never seen before; look beneath people's hidden agendas—secret motives different from the group's agenda—and fears and try to find their strengths; and be sensitive to others' feelings. Consciously try to see things in a new light, and you might be able to devise a new solution.

Here are some things to consider when making decisions:

- Set high standards and have big expectations of everyone. Expect people to perform at their highest level of ability.
- Surmount your anxieties (Useem, 2005).
- Create an atmosphere where information flows freely and decisions are transparent, unless it must be kept confidential to protect employees' rights.
- Use logic to solve problems. Think through your decisions step by step. Analyze the potential outcome and effect on other people. Weigh all the information. Look before you leap, if you have time to study the situation.
- Use creativity to solve problems. Just because it has never been done before doesn't mean it isn't a good idea. Remember that people resist change, even good change.
- "Don't put paint on a rotten board." This means that glossing over a difficult problem or trying to "fix" an incompetent employee is only going to cover up the problem temporarily; it won't solve the problem. Address the problem—not the symptoms!
- Get other people's ideas and tap into their creativity—but you make the decision. You don't have to take a vote or get a consensus if you are the decision maker. The leader makes the call and bears the responsibility, so take charge.

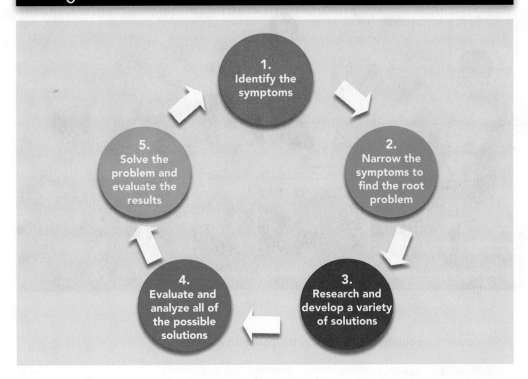

Figure 6.6 Steps in the Problem-Solving Process

- Quit being a perfectionist. Understand that you cannot please everyone. Do what you know in your heart is right.
- Don't become paralyzed with indecision until the decision is made by lack of a decision.
- The decision you make should match with the overall goals of the organization, or with your personal goals if the decision is personal.
- Remember that decisions are very much about "who" rather than "what" (Collins, 2005).
- Once a decision has been made, execution becomes crucially important. Ideas without action don't get the job done. Just do it!
- Forgive yourself when you make a bad decision and move on.

To assist you in solving problems and making difficult decisions, you might want to examine the chart in Figure 6.6

PARTICIPATING IN AND LEADING EFFECTIVE MEETINGS

How Can I Be Sure I Won't Lead a Worthless Meeting?

People tend to hate meetings because so many are poorly planned, accomplish nothing, and waste people's time. If you haven't already done so, sooner or later, you will find yourself at the head of the table discussing an agenda. There is a true "art" to leading (and participating in) an effective meeting. Productive meetings do not "just happen." Good meetings take planning, research, and careful preparation. If you can lead a good meeting in which people can honestly say, "I really got something out of that meeting," you will shine.

Do you know how to lead and participate in an effective meeting?

Here are some tips for leading and participating in a meeting.

Before the Meeting

- Prepare to do well by developing a folder with an agenda, supporting documents, minutes, and handouts for each committee or group with whom you have meetings. Before the first meeting, read previous minutes so you will be prepared. Do your homework!
- Bring all necessary supplies to the meeting (pen, paper, personal calendar, highlighter, and supporting folder).

During the Meeting

- Take good notes, highlighting any items that require your personal action.
- Participate in the meeting if you have relevant information.
- Ask a thought-provoking question to enable your committee to think through critical decisions.
- Listen twice as much as you talk.
- Don't make commitments for something over which you have no authority.

After the Meeting

- Read your notes to ensure that you understand them. Transfer highlighted items that are your assignments to your personal planner so that they become a part of your to do list. Develop an action plan that enables you to complete your tasks prior to the next meeting.
- Provide an overview of the meeting for your superior in writing, through e-mail, or through a meeting.

Following Good Meeting Manners and Established Protocol

- Arrive at least five minutes early. Late arrivals irritate some bosses greatly. In any case, it makes you look slack.

- Never smoke or eat in a meeting unless everyone is eating.

- If refreshments are served, choose only items you can eat inconspicuously, and don't talk with your mouth full.

- Choose your seating carefully. The seat to the right of the leader is usually reserved for the next-in-command. Sit close so you can hear. Avoid sitting by people who talk to each other during the meeting. This behavior is rude, and the boss—and everyone else—will notice.

- Never use inappropriate language in a meeting.

- If you have to leave early for any reason, inform the chair prior to the meeting. Leave as quietly and as inconspicuously as you can. Call the committee chair during the day to determine what you missed.

- Leave your seat and work area free of debris. The committee chair is not your mother and will be irritated if he or she has to clean up after you.

> *A stream of decisions over time, brilliantly executed, accounts for great outcomes.*
> —Jim Collins, *Fortune* author

Leading an Effective Meeting

The first thing you must always consider is this: Do we really need a meeting? If you are leading or chairing a meeting, there are several questions you should ask yourself:

1. Do I need the group to accomplish the task, or is this something I could handle by phone or e-mail with a few key people? If you can handle the situation in a satisfactory manner electronically, do it and don't have a meeting.

2. Will a meeting save time by allowing us to accomplish more faster?

3. Do I need the group to meet to allow me to gain their commitment and to be transparent in an important decision?

4. Do I have everything I need to conduct this meeting properly (time, answers to questions, supplies, handouts)?

5. Do my committee members have the time to meet? Will they have enough time to prepare adequately for the meeting?

Before the Meeting

- Set goals and objectives.

- Plan and disseminate an agenda to your committee members in time for them to study and prepare details carefully. People are watching your leadership skills in action.

- Secure meeting space and supplies. Notify members of the meeting and inform them of when, where, what, how, and why.

During the Meeting

- Arrive early for the meeting to be sure everything is ready.

- Conduct the meeting in an organized way. Own the meeting! Take charge!

- Tell the group how long this meeting will last, and end it on time. This helps keep the agenda on track.

- Review decisions and assign tasks to members with deadlines.

- Determine the committee's next meeting time.

BIGGEST INTERVIEW *Blunders*

Wanda wrote on her resumé that she spoke Spanish fluently. When Wanda arrived the interviewer talked for a few minutes and then began conducting the interview in Spanish. Wanda's Spanish was mediocre at best, so naturally she did not perform well on the interview. She did not get the job, and she made a bad impression because she had stretched the truth.

LESSON: You should always tell the truth on your resumé and when you are interviewing. The people in HR departments and others have a great deal of experience in interviewing, and they can usually tell if someone is lying.

After the Meeting

- Have someone transcribe the minutes of the meeting and disseminate them as soon as possible.
- Minutes should include a comprehensive action plan that describes an overview of important discussion items, action items, responsible parties, and due dates.

Participating in and leading impressive meetings gain positive recognition with your bosses and colleagues.

LEARN TO DELEGATE EFFECTIVELY

How Can I Get All This Work Done?

If you cannot delegate, you cannot lead! Many leaders have a very difficult time giving up control. You cannot hold everything close to yourself; you must trust others to help get the work done. When you delegate, you simply hand work over to someone else, usually someone who reports to you and whom you trust. This person needs to be someone on whom you can depend, someone who has proved himself or herself to you by past actions. The opposite of delegation is "dumping," the process of giving bad jobs to someone who has no choice in the matter. Delegation, done properly, should be considered an opportunity to assume more responsibility and to develop leadership skills that will prepare one for promotion. If you view delegation as job enrichment, the chances are good that the person to whom you are delegating will be motivated to do a good job because people like responsible jobs over which they have control.

Many people use this excuse not to delegate: "By the time I could teach someone else to do this, I could have done it twice." That may be true, but the next time you need it done, you already have someone trained to do the task, and a simple review of the steps is all that is required.

People need clear goals. They need their managers to sit down with them periodically and help them understand exactly what is expected of them. Many employees don't have a clue. They may be doing what they think the boss wants, and it may not even be close. If your employees don't know where you want them to go, any road will be fine. You have to lay out the path, especially when you delegate.

Conversely, if you have responsibilities delegated to you, appreciate the opportunity and learn from it. Someone had to have confidence in you in order to decide to delegate to you.

Here are steps in delegating work to someone else:

1. First, remember that you are still responsible for getting the work done. If it doesn't happen, the responsibility is still yours. Likewise, if it is done poorly, you will be held accountable by your boss.

2. When you delegate a task, delegate authority to get it done along with the responsibility. For example, if you ask someone to collect data from all your colleagues, you have to make it known that you, as the boss, have asked this person to collect data.

3. When you delegate a task to someone, begin by telling the person that you have a job that you need help with and that you need him or her to help get this done. Make the person feel that you value what you are asking him or her to do, not dumping a bad task. Tell the person you trust him or her and believe he or she has the skills to do the job well. Be positive.

POSITIVE HABITS *at Work*

If your boss delegates a job to you, consider it an opportunity to showcase your abilities. Meet and exceed all deadlines and do more than expected. Check with your boss intermittently, even if he or she does not contact you to be sure you are on track. Sometimes your boss doesn't know exactly what you are doing—in this case, the boss will know exactly how well you are doing.

It is better to lead from behind and put others in front, especially when you celebrate victory when nice things occur. You take the front line when there is danger.

—Nelson Mandela

4. Let the person know that you look on this as an opportunity for him or her to grow and that these are the kinds of tasks that he or she will need to be able to do in order to move up the ladder. In other words, you are grooming this employee to be promoted. Be careful, however, not to go overboard, since promotion may not be imminent and may not be your decision.

5. Once you have described the task, you then need to work with the employee to set realistic goals and deadlines. Set intermediate steps to achieve, deadlines, and checkpoints.

6. It may be necessary to provide training to the person to whom you are delegating to ensure that he or she is able to do the job according to your expectations. Discuss the quality that is expected.

7. If the employee is not meeting deadlines and not doing quality work, constructive criticism and more direction needs to come as soon as you are aware of the problem.

8. Establish a timeline. Set an ending date that allows you time to recover if the assignment is not completed or done to your expectations. Remember, your name is on the line!

9. Establish intermediate checkpoints to be sure the person is on target, especially if this is a big, time-consuming task.

10. Encourage the delegatee to ask questions if concerns arise.

11. Evaluate the project and provide feedback to the person who did the job.

12. When the job is completed, give the person the credit for doing the job. Praise him or her openly in front of other colleagues.

> *Everybody wants to be somebody.*
> —Patricia G. Moody

Reflections: PUTTING IT ALL TOGETHER

You may be thinking, "Leadership? I'm just trying to find a job and survive." That may be true, but never doubt that you, your talents, your communication skills, and your overall decorum are constantly being evaluated by your superiors.

There will always be a need for effective, fair, honest, and hard-working leaders and followers in the workplace. You may be the next leader of a team, a department, a division, an entire shift, or even a company. It is never too early to begin thinking about your leadership abilities. Being a good follower will always be important throughout your career.

DIGITAL BRIEFCASE

WORKING COLLABORATIVELY IN A VIRTUAL TEAM

Select two people to work on a virtual, collaborative team that you will lead. They can be members of your class or two friends. Using Google Docs, Dropbox, or another collaborative program, work together to write a brief, two-page, double-spaced paper on teamwork. As the leader, you should furnish the outline and begin the draft. Assign one part of the outline to each participant. Give your teammates a deadline for making any adjustments to the draft before you finalize it as the team's leader.

REFERENCES

Barnes, J. (2005). *John F. Kennedy on leadership: The lessons and legacy of a president.* New York: AMACON/American Management Association.

Berko, R., Welvin, A., & Ray, R. (1997). *Business communication in a changing world.* New York: St. Martin's Press.

Collins, J. (2005, June 27). Jim Collins on tough calls. *Fortune.*

Maxwell, J. (2002). *The 17 essential qualities of a team player.* Nashville, TN: Thomas Nelson Publishers.

Useem, J. (2005, June 27). Decisions, decisions. *Fortune.*

RELATE

MANAGING CONFLICT AND DEALING WITH DIFFICULT PEOPLE

Good leaders first get the right people on the bus, the wrong people off the bus, and the right people in the right seats.

—Jim Collins, Good to Great

Why read this chapter?

Because you'll learn...

- To identify sources of conflict in the workplace
- To understand how the amygdala functions
- To assess how well you manage conflict

Because you'll be able to...

- Resolve certain types of conflict
- Deal with different types of difficult people

PROFESSIONALS from the Field

Name: Dr. Patricia G. Moody

Business: Dean Emerita
University of South Carolina

No matter what profession or job you are in, you will experience conflict, and you will encounter some very difficult people. On the other hand, you will have relationships with many wonderful employees and customers, and fortunately, there are many more nice people than rude ones. As a dean leading a large college at a major university, I have had to deal with rather difficult situations. My advice is to always try to keep your cool; try to make fair and consistent decisions when arguments arise; and try to treat everyone as you want to be treated. Our college prides itself on excellent internal relationships with our faculty and staff and outstanding external customer service and relationships with our students and parents. My goal was to try to take care of internal and external customers, even the difficult ones, in such a way that our employees love working in our college and that our students leave us with a feeling that they were well cared for and respected. It's a tough job at times—but our college does it well!

CONFLICT—THE MOST AVOIDED AREA IN THE WORKPLACE

Exactly What Is Conflict and What Do You Do about It?

As much as we all hate conflict, it is a natural part of life, and sooner or later, you will experience it in the workplace. Conflict is never pleasant, but the sooner you face this demon, the quicker and more effectively you can resolve it. *Conflict* is from a Latin word, *conflictus*, meaning "to strike together with force." This is basically what happens when two people—or sometimes more—have conflict. Their opinions and ideas and ways of doing things are at direct odds with each other, and conflict arises as a result. Conflict causes some people to be intimidated and withdrawn, brings out the worse in some of us, but actually is not a bad thing if handled properly. When conflict arises at work, someone has to deal with it, and the sooner, the better.

THE AMYGDALA AND ITS ROLE IN CONFLICT

What in the World Is an Amygdala?

The amygdala plays a major role in how each of us responds to conflict. A part of the brain's emotional system, the amygdala, shown in Figure 7.1, can cause us to go into default behavior based on past experiences.

So one of the first steps in understanding conflict is to know that sometimes people are reacting to something in which you had no role—they are just fighting for their emotional survival. They are reacting to a past trauma that has been brought to the forefront by this new experience. In recognizing how the amygdala functions, you will be able to understand the causes of some conflict.

DR. PHIL'S ANALOGY OF WRITING ON A SLATE

What's That Got to Do with Me and Resolving Conflict?

In a television interview, Dr. Phil McGraw, noted television personality, discussed the former Duchess of York's childhood and her difficulty in loving herself and believing she was OK. In the course of this conversation, he described to Sarah Ferguson his belief that we all have a "slate" that we and other people write on all the time. After a while, it begins to be the picture

Figure **7.1** The Amygdala

Don't let this word or concept frighten you. If you have never heard the word **amygdala** (pronounced ah-MIG-da-la), you're not alone. Most people have not. But this term and concept are important for you to be able to understand the overall aspects of your emotions. The amygdala, simply a part of the brain's emotional system, can cause us to go into default behavior based on what we remember from a similar experience. Do I use **fight** or **flight**? Basically, the amygdala is there to protect us when we become afraid or emotionally upset. When influenced by the amygdala, everything becomes **about us**. We become more judgmental. We don't stop to think about differences or the other person's feelings or the relationship. The amygdala can trigger an emotional response **before** the rest of the brain has had time to understand what is happening, and this situation causes us to have problems with others.

The amygdala remembers frustrations, fears, hurt feelings, and anger from our past. The tension from these past experiences causes the amygdala to go into default behavior—we **feel** before we **think**—and this can create a potentially explosive situation. If you had a bad experience several years ago and are placed in a similar situation today, the amygdala will remember and trigger emotions that cause the body to respond. These feelings often cause people to bypass critical thinking (the logical brain) and to respond with angry words or actions (the emotional brain). For example:

- They get angry—you get angry.
- They curse you—you curse them.
- They use physical violence—you use physical violence.

However, if you remain calm and level-headed, you will begin to see that the other person usually begins to calm down, too. He or she will follow your emotional lead, positive or negative, and if you're calm and rational, anger and violence become out of place for most people.

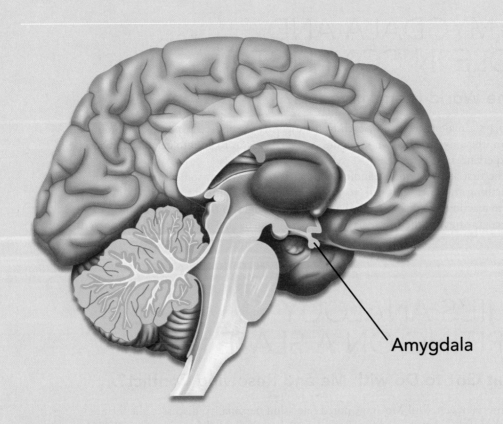

Amygdala

of the person we believe we are. According to reports, Sarah's mother looked nothing like her daughter and would make disparaging remarks such as "Sarah comes from the postman" because of her red hair and blue eyes. When Sarah was 12, her mother left her family and ran away to Argentina with a polo player, and Sarah rarely ever saw her. Sarah Ferguson had it all and lost it because of poor decisions and, according to herself, her "low self-worth." Perhaps if Sarah had had positive things written on her slate, she might have been a much happier person. Certainly, she would not have had as much conflict in her life or caused as much conflict in the lives of her loved ones.

We share this story with you as we discuss conflict and difficult people as a reminder that people are rarely who they appear to be. Many difficult, contrary people are not mean; they are just hurt. Bill Cosby said, "Hurt people, hurt people." In other words, they fight back even when there is no real reason to fight. We have no idea what was "written on someone's slate" that causes him or her to behave in a bad manner. So we begin by encouraging you to listen to people before you make judgments and try to understand why they do the crazy things they do—because there is always a reason.

CAUSES OF PERSONAL CONFLICT

Why Can't People Just Get Along?

What causes conflict between people? "The short answer to the question of what causes conflict is quite simply, life. Bringing people together in social interaction necessarily involves a set of interpersonal dynamics which sooner or later will lead to conflict" (Thompson, 2011). When one considers what a diverse population mix we have in this country, it is easy to see why many conflicts arise. First, we are free to express ourselves, and most of us do. We come from a melting pot of races, ethnic backgrounds, religious beliefs, customs, values, and backgrounds, so sometimes we simply don't see eye to eye. Because we are so different, we are unlikely to co-exist without conflicts, so we have to learn to manage our disagreements in a civil manner and as acceptably to both parties as possible. Conflict is simply a fundamental part of human relationships—often a very misunderstood part.

Conflict is inevitable. But conflict itself is not the problem; the breakdown in organizations' productivity and the inability of people to work together is the dangerous part of conflict. Conflict is difficult, uncomfortable, and stressful, but used properly, as a learning tool, conflict can actually help you learn and grow. Believe it or not—conflict can even be essential to an organization's improvement. An organization that encourages transparency, honesty, openness, and expression of ideas and feelings can expect conflict. On the other hand, an organization that tries to restrict honesty and openness and centralizes all the power within a few people can also expect conflict. Conflict may arise simply from having people view problems or actions from different perspectives. Chances are they may both be partially right, and by combining both opinions, you might arrive at a potentially great idea—but first the people have to calm down and communicate. Communications is key to solving conflict.

Please hear what I am not saying.
—Old Indian Proverb

So conflict is going to happen. How do you deal with it? The first step in dealing with conflict is to determine the root causes—not the symptoms of the problem, but what is at the bottom of the problem. There are many causes of conflict. Sometimes conflict is caused by difficult people (which we will discuss later) and sometimes it can be caused by people who are

If you were able to have an internship during your college studies, use this experience to best advantage. Always list your internship experience on your resumé and talk about your experiences during the interview. Having real-life, on-the-job experience goes a long way in an interview. If an internship is not required for your degree, try to do one anyway. It will benefit you greatly.

typically calm. There is no "one size fits all" solution to handling conflict. It all depends on the people who are involved, where they are coming from, what past experiences they have had, and numerous other factors.

> *If you are patient in one moment of anger, you will save yourself a hundred days of sorrow.*
> —Chinese Proverb

We all have our "hot buttons"—those touchy topics that make our blood boil and cause us to say things we wish we hadn't. And let's face it—some people just rub us the wrong way. We simply find some people's habits, actions, and demeanor annoying. Maybe they don't carry their load; maybe they act like know-it-alls; maybe they flaunt their possessions and brag too much to suit us. What causes one person to go off the deep end may only slightly irritate another person. We've all experienced the unpleasant feelings that conflict stirs in each of us. It creeps up on us like the flu. We never expected it to happen, but before we know it, in a moment of anger, during a misunderstanding, dealing with a difficult colleague, or in a jealous rage, we lose control, and the door to conflict has been opened. Conflict can happen between any people, even the best of friends.

SYSTEMIC SOURCES OF CONFLICT

Does Anyone Around Here Know What Is Going On?

> *Stepping on someone's feelings and ideas hurts just as bad as stepping on their toes, and it lasts a lot longer.*
> —Unknown

Not all conflict is the result of people not getting along or not liking each other. "Conflict in the workplace is often blamed on personalities and misbehavior, but in reality, much workplace conflict is systemic and endemic to the workplace environment. **Systemic conflict** is conflict that is caused by the system's policies and procedures. **Endemic conflict** is conflict that is common in a particular kind of business or setting. Ineffective organizational systems, unpredictable policies, incompatible goals, scarce resources, and poor communication can all contribute to conflict in the workplace. Workplace conflict causes loss of productivity, distractions, and employee dissatisfaction. However, management can produce positive results by paying attention to and addressing the true causes of conflict in their organizations" (Cardenas, 2011). Management is the key to systemic conflict. Workplaces need highly organized systems and controls and clearly communicated policies that are consistently applied to all people.

Let's give you a chance to try your hand at solving systemic conflict. Assume you are a manager and have been put in charge of solving systemic conflicts. If you were in charge, how would you solve the systemic sources of conflict listed in Figure 7.2? Write your answers in the right-hand column. You may need to do some research to solve some of these problems. The Internet has excellent resources on conflict management.

Now that you have been introduced to systemic causes of conflict, you need to understand some basic causes of personal conflict, as shown in Figure 7.3.

Sometimes it helps to resolve conflict by just being calm and deliberate and thinking things through. Approach conflict with an open mind. This is not about trying to prove one person wrong and another right. The goal is to have a win–win solution. You won't always have that option, but if you do, some good questions to ask yourself are outlined in Figure 7.4.

iStockPhoto

How does conflict hurt your chances of promotion?

Figure 7.2 What Would You Do to Solve Systemic Sources of Conflict?

Systemic Source of Conflict	How Would You Solve the Problem If You Were in Charge?
Competition for scarce resources (people, time, money, space, travel)	
Interdependence conflicts (when one person depends on another who is not producing)	
People who have overlapping responsibilities with no clear delineation	
Two bosses giving conflicting directions and simultaneous deadlines to the same person	
Unequal application of policies with favoritism shown to some	
Unnecessary change that keeps people off balance, irritated, and confused	
Poor communication by management that has the grapevine running wild with rumors	
Skill deficits by some employees	
Conflict among teams because of incompatible goals with no clear vision or leadership from management	

Figure 7.3 Causes of Personal Conflict

- Failure to understand and respect an individual's needs, background, culture, sex, age, or values.

- Competing interests and perspectives.

- Hidden agendas—perhaps someone is fighting against an idea because it introduces a major paradigm change and makes him or her feel threatened and insecure.

- Passive-aggressive communication style and use of sarcasm to make an underhanded "dig" at someone.

- Killing people's ideas without giving them an opportunity to "sell" their thoughts.

- Interpersonal conflicts—sometimes people simply don't get along. Interpersonal communication is complicated; often this type conflict has to be mediated.

- Harsh criticism and lack of appropriate feedback.

- Gender differences that create different ways of looking at things.

- Bullying and intimidation, which are forms of harassment. These sources of conflict are an abuse of power that always cause conflict and unhappiness among employees.

Figure 7.4 Ask the Right Questions When Resolving Conflict

- Does the cause appear to be systemic or personal?

- Is it because you or someone needs a scarce resource?

- Is there a conflict in work and personality styles?

- Is there a communications breakdown?

- Is there a clear picture of what management expects of these people who are involved in conflict?

- Are there conflicting pressures because of two managers' expectations?

- Is the policy clear, and is it being applied consistently to everyone?

Cultivate the Mavericks

Conflict, handled properly, can actually be a good thing for a person or a company. If everyone at your workplace had total agreement, the ideas would become stagnant. There are always "mavericks" at work who frequently take an opposing view to a decision or direction. Although they may be annoying, mavericks are often the people who move the organization faster than it might have moved and in new and rewarding directions. On the other hand, if there is too much conflict, work is disrupted, and people focus on the conflict rather than their work. If you are a maverick, be careful of how you say things; be aware of stepping on other people's ideas; present your ideas in a rational, well-thought-out manner; and don't surprise your boss with something that he or she might not like discussed openly at a meeting before you talk to him or her.

As a result of being forced to work through a situation, good things can actually occur:

- The relationship may become more viable, and both parties' work might actually improve.
- A discussion might clear the air.
- People might examine the issues and develop new strategies and solutions that lead to growth and progression.
- Perhaps both parties can compromise and get most of what they want.
- Talking together and listening to each other can provide a better understanding of each other.
- Communications in the future might be improved.
- Policies might be revamped and made more fair and consistent.
- Stress can be reduced if the conflict is resolved.

> *Cultivate the mavericks in your organization. This doesn't mean to turn them loose and let them run wild. It means to pay attention to their ideas even when they may seem a little bizarre. They may have come up with the next "star" to replace the idea that is fading.*
>
> —Pat Moody

CONFLICT RESOLUTION

How Can I Settle Disputes and Keep the Peace?

Conflict resolution is a way of settling disputes and disagreements in a peaceful manner through discussions that lead to an understanding of the cause of problems. Ideally, conflict resolution resolves the problem without name-calling, violence, fights, or long-term hostilities. While some conflicts are easy to resolve, others may take months. As a leader, you can be assured that you will be called on to resolve conflicts and disputes.

There is no common denominator for solving conflict issues. Some are very complex, deep-seated, and difficult to eradicate; they may not be resolved quickly or easily. Some may require professional counseling, and in some cases, people have to be terminated because they are such a disruption in the workplace. An extreme example of deep-seated conflict is the conflicts between Catholics and Protestants in Northern Ireland that can be traced back to 1690. While this is an extreme example, it illustrates how conflict can be passed along from one generation to another. Different types of racial conflict in this country, for example, are deep-seated and not easily solved overnight. There are ways, however, to deal with more common conflict situations that arise in the workplace. Figure 7.5 details some of them.

Shutterstock

Can you think of situations where you can create a "win–win" solution?

Dealing with Conflict as a Manager

When resolving interpersonal conflict and incompatibility in a leadership role, you will need to discover ways that all parties can win at least some measure of satisfaction. This is not an easy task! If you have to resolve a conflict, these suggestions should be helpful, whether the dispute is between two other people or between you and someone else:

- Conflict just won't go away. Putting your head in the sand and ignoring it is the worst thing to do. The quicker you face it, the better.
- As the mediator, you need to be objective and show no favoritism. Don't attack either person or let one attack the other.

> *A leader is needed who can listen to both sides and propose a model for a problem solving session in which both sides come together and mediate a solution.*
>
> —Warren Bennis and Joan Goldsmith

Figure 7.5 Ways to Resolve Conflict

- Accept the fact that conflict is a natural occurrence, one that will happen in all areas of your life. Work hard to learn to deal with it and not let it control your life. Remember, no one can control you unless you let them—and you should never allow this to happen!

- Don't be afraid of conflict—if you do, you will always be a victim.

- Provide a forum where people can be heard when conflict arises.

- Allow the other person to vent fully before you begin any negotiation or resolution. Breathe deeply.

- Don't meet anger with anger. Sometimes firmness is required, but be firm, not volatile.

- Try to see the world through the other person's eyes. You have no idea who wrote what on his or her "slate" or who has imprinted negative thoughts on his or her amygdala.

- Try to create win–win situations where everyone can walk away having gained something. It is always best not to have a loser.

- Try to reach an agreement that uses part of both people's ideas, if possible.

- Determine if the conflict is a "person conflict" or a "situation conflict."

- Ask the other person what he or she needs. Try to understand the situation.

- Realize that you (or your company or office) may very well be in the wrong.

- Try to face the conflict head-on and quickly. To avoid conflict only makes it worse. Most conflict will not go away quietly, so deal with it before it escalates.

- Don't become the same type of difficult person as the ones with whom you are dealing. Fighting fire with fire will only make the flame hotter. In most situations, you will need to be the "cool" one.

- Don't take the other person's attitude or words personally. Most of the time, the person doesn't know you or your life. You are his or her sounding board.

- Avoid physical contact with others at every expense.

- If you must give criticism, try to do so with a positive tone and attitude. If possible, provide some positive comments to the person before you offer your criticism.

- Don't save up a list of the person's faults and problems and "sandbag" him or her all at once.

- Never verbally attack the other person.

- Allow the other person to save face. Don't back the other person into a corner and give him or her no way out except to fight.

- If you have a problem with a person or his or her actions, be specific and state your concerns before things get out of hand. The person can't read your mind.

- Ask yourself, "If this were my last action on earth, would I be proud of how I acted?"

- If someone shows signs of becoming physically aggressive toward you, get help early, stay calm, talk slowly and calmly to the other person, and if necessary, walk away to safety.

- Own your words. If you're making a statement, let it come from you, not "them."

- Show your concern for the other person.

- Try with all your might to end on a positive note. It is far better to make a friend—or at least build a relationship with a colleague with whom you can work—than it is to make an enemy who will always be a problem for you.

- Define the conflict. Get to the root of the problems, not the symptoms. Is this a people argument or an issue conflict?

- Try to set up an ending scenario where an agreement can be reached.

- If you are the boss, let the conflicting parties know that you expect them to resolve their differences and be able to work together. The workplace cannot be disrupted by constant conflict.

- Ask them to state their opinions in respectful language. Don't let the parties get off track, accuse each other in threatening tones, or use improper language toward each other.

- Try to avoid having a winner and a loser. You should try for win–win if possible. Both parties will more than likely have to compromise.
- Diffuse anger with humor if possible, but don't make light of the situation.
- Never make a decision without hearing both sides. There are always two sides, at least.
- Provide constructive criticism and feedback to both parties. Avoid accusing and finger-pointing. State feedback in positive terms.
- Your goal is to reach a mutually desirable end. Suggest some possible solutions that do not favor one over the other.
- You cannot change either party; you can only try to get each to see the other person's side.
- Sometimes you have to get people to make trade-offs.
- Occasionally, you have to allow for a cooling-off period before people are able to settle down and perhaps reach an agreement.
- Don't expect someone else to read your mind. You have to state your opinions in a modulated, even voice. Avoid yelling or shrill-pitched words. Stay cool!
- Allow both parties to save face. Humiliation is never a good tactic in any circumstance!
- Try to end the meeting in a positive manner.

Is there ever a time when one should resort to physical violence to solve a conflict? How can such a situation be avoided?

iStock

Resolving conflicts is never easy. It takes a level-headed person who is able to see all sides of a situation and who can use strategies for diffusing the situation and reaching a mutually satisfying conclusion.

The assessment on conflict management in Figure 7.6 will help you determine how well you personally manage conflict.

HARASSMENT IN THE WORKPLACE

What Are These People Thinking?

The most important thing you need to know about harassment is that it is illegal. Exactly what constitutes workplace harassment? "Workplace harassment is any unwelcome or unwanted conduct that denigrates or shows hostility or an aversion toward another person on the basis of any characteristic protected by law, which includes an individual's race, color, gender, ethnic or national origin, age, religion, disability, marital status, sexual orientation, gender identity, or other personal characteristic protected by law. A conduct is unwelcome if the employee did not solicit, instigate or provoke it, and the employee regarded the conduct as undesirable or offensive" (Strategic HR Services, 2010). Any kind of behavior toward another employee that creates a hostile workplace is in violation of the law. Some of the major points you need to know about harassment as an employee and as a potential manager are outlined in Figure 7.7.

BIGGEST INTERVIEW *Blunders*

James was asked a question that he considered inappropriate; in fact, he thought the question was illegal. Instead of approaching the question calmly or the interviewer respectfully, James barked, "What business is that of yours? I don't have to answer that question." He learned later that the question was legal. While the question may not have been in the best taste, the interviewer had the right to ask the question.

LESSON: Know what questions are illegal and determine in advance how you will respond if someone asks you such a question. Don't be caught off guard and don't be too quick to snap at an interviewer. You might say, "I prefer not to answer that question because I don't see how it is relevant to this job."

Figure 7.6   Conflict Management Assessment

Read the following questions carefully and respond according to the key below. Take your time and be honest with yourself.

1 = Never typical of the way I address conflict   3 = Often typical of the way I address conflict
2 = Sometimes typical of the way I address conflict   4 = Almost always typical of the way I address conflict

1. When someone verbally attacks me, I can let it go and move on.	1	2	3	4
2. I would rather resolve an issue than have to "be right" about it.	1	2	3	4
3. I try to defuse arguments and verbal confrontations at all costs.	1	2	3	4
4. Once I've had a conflict with someone, I can forget it and get along with that person just fine.	1	2	3	4
5. I look at conflicts in my relationships as positive growth opportunities.	1	2	3	4
6. When I'm in a conflict, I will try many ways to resolve it.	1	2	3	4
7. When I'm in a conflict, I try not to verbally attack or abuse the other person.	1	2	3	4
8. When I'm in a conflict, I try never to blame the other person; rather, I look at every side.	1	2	3	4
9. When I'm in a conflict, I try not to avoid the other person.	1	2	3	4
10. When I'm in a conflict, I try to talk through the issue with the other person.	1	2	3	4
11. When I'm in a conflict, I often feel empathy for the other person.	1	2	3	4
12. When I'm in a conflict, I do not try to manipulate the other person.	1	2	3	4
13. When I'm in a conflict, I try never to withhold my love or affection for that person.	1	2	3	4
14. When I'm in a conflict, I try never to attack the person; I concentrate on his or her actions.	1	2	3	4
15. When I'm in a conflict, I try to never insult the other person.	1	2	3	4
16. I believe in give and take when trying to resolve a conflict.	1	2	3	4
17. I understand and use the concept that kindness can solve more conflicts than cruelty.	1	2	3	4
18. I am able to control my defensive attitude when I'm in a conflict.	1	2	3	4
19. I keep my temper in check and do not yell and scream during conflicts.	1	2	3	4
20. I am able to accept "defeat" at the end of a conflict.	1	2	3	4

Total number of 1s _____   Total number of 3s _____

Total number of 2s _____   Total number of 4s _____

If you have more 1s, you do not handle conflict very well and have few tools for conflict management. You have a tendency to anger quickly and lose your temper during the conflict.

If you have more 2s, you have a tendency to want to work through conflict, but you lack the skills to carry this tendency through. You can hold your temper for a while, but eventually, it gets the best of you.

If you have more 3s, you have some helpful skills in handling conflict. You tend to work very hard for a peaceful and mutually beneficial outcome for all parties.

If you have more 4s, you are very adept at handling conflict and do well with mediation, negotiation, and anger management. You are very approachable; people turn to you for advice about conflicts and their resolution.

Figure 7.7 Frequently Asked Questions on Workplace Harassment

1. What law(s) does workplace harassment violate?

Workplace harassment is a violation of Title VII of the Civil Rights Act of 1964, the Age Discrimination in Employment Act, and the Americans with Disabilities Act.

2. What constitutes sexual harassment?

Sexual harassment is any advancement toward another person of a sexual nature that is unwanted and uninvited. "This applies to harassment by a person against another person of the opposite sex as well as harassment by a person against another person of the same sex" (Strategic HR Services, 2010). It includes gender harassment against employees because of pregnancy, childbirth, or any other violations of a related nature. The law also applies to what is known as "quid pro quo" sexual violations, in which a person is promoted, given a raise, or offered other special rewards in exchange for sexual favors.

Some examples of sexual harassment are verbal abuse or harassment (e.g., dirty jokes, unwanted letters, e-mails, sexually explicit pictures, telephone calls, or written materials); unwelcome sexual overtures or advances; pressure for dates or to engage in sexual activity; remarks about a person's body, clothing, or sexual activities; personal questions of a sexual nature; touching of any kind; or referring to people as *babes, hunks, dolls, honey, boy toy*, and so forth.

3. How does one know when a violation has occurred?

If an employee is required to work in a hostile environment where he or she is intimidated or treated in an offensive manner, a violation has most likely occurred. Employees cannot be discriminated against for any reason, nor can they be retaliated against if they file a complaint or ask for an investigation.

Is taking a chance on sexual harassment worth losing your job and embarrassing yourself and your family?

Shutterstock

4. To whom does one report a violation?

First, tell the offender directly to stop harassing you and that you will report it if it doesn't stop immediately. To whom you report the offense depends, of course, on who is making the violation. If it is your boss, you can go directly to his or her boss, or you can report it to human resources. You should have the offenses carefully documented and dated. If you can find another person who has experienced the same offense and will go with you, your case will be strengthened. If it is a colleague, go to your boss. The person to whom the offense is reported is required by law to address the violation immediately. Supervisors should report the claim of violation to management immediately. The law requires that all claims of sexual harassment be investigated. File a formal complaint with the HR department.

5. Can the employee who commits the offense be held accountable?

You most likely will not be successful in suing an individual unless you work in a state that has a statute that authorizes a suit against an individual.

6. What happens to the person who commits the harassment?

The chances are good that the person will be fired if the offense can be proved. Companies do not want the liability of a person who violates others' rights.

7. What happens if you report an offense and nothing happens?

If you believe you have a good case and you have tried to resolve this through proper channels, hire an attorney. Harassment is against the law, and you may have to bring legal charges if necessary.

DEALING WITH DIFFICULT PEOPLE

What Causes People to Be So Ornery?

According to Brinkman and Kirschner (2002), "we all have varying degrees of knowledge and ignorance in our repertoire of communications skills, with their consequent interpersonal strengths and weaknesses." You may get upset with a whiner, while your friend gets upset with a procrastinator. Overly aggressive people may set you off, while a "yes person" may drive someone else crazy. You may not be able to stand people who boast about their accomplishments and belongings. Chances are pretty good that each of us has characteristics that drive someone crazy. The truth is that most people are OK once you get beneath the surface and understand why they do what they do. Of course, that takes lots of time and lots of listening, and you won't ever be able to get to the bottom of every person's reasons for being ornery, so you have to deal with him or her and move on. Honest answers and responses, delivered in a kind, rational manner, often provide the best results. Figure 7.8 provides some insight into how to deal with certain types of difficult people.

Understand, Relate to, and Lead Difficult People

If you are a leader or an employee, you will deal with difficult people. We can all be difficult at times and under certain situations, but some people excel at being difficult. They resist everything; they think every rule is made to get them; they can't get along with their colleagues; they won't carry their loads; they don't get paid enough—on and on the list goes.

As you try to motivate people and give everyone a fair chance, one important principle to remember is this: Reinforce the behavior you want. When someone performs well—even if it's for a day—recognize and praise him or her. Many people have never had praise at work or at home. Having you notice them can be enough to get some people to change their behavior. Say things like: "I really appreciate your staying late to help Jack today. You were a real team player." "I'm very impressed with the way you handle irate customers on the phone. You are making a great difference in helping us resolve problems." Write a personal, handwritten note thanking the person for his or her achievement. Catch people doing something right and tell them about it!

If people don't do well, don't ignore the behavior. Bring the behavior to their attention as soon as you can. If a person is late, for example, let him or her know you know as soon as it happens. Certainly, everyone has a problem sooner or later, but if this becomes a habit, others notice that one person is getting away with it and that the policies are being applied inconsistently and with favoritism. If people need training in order to perform their duties, get it for them. If people are having personal problems and you can provide company counseling, recommend it. Do everything in your power to help the difficult person be successful. First, you try to salvage difficult people, but you need to know that you can't save everyone. Sometimes you have to perform surgery; in other words, you may have to follow company policy, document unacceptable behavior and work performance, and terminate the person.

Difficult people come in all shapes and sizes, all ages and backgrounds. They may have a Ph.D. or they may have a middle school education. They may be loud and obnoxious or sly and underhanded. Regardless of what their tactics and habits may be, they are a disrupting force in the workplace and cannot be ignored. Some tips for dealing with difficult people are detailed in Figure 7.9.

POSITIVE HABITS *at Work*

Build a reputation as a level-headed thinker who never loses your cool. Stay calm when others are getting out of control, and you will earn respect. Learn all you can about mediating disagreements and managing difficult people, even though it may not be the most pleasant thing to do. Gaining respect from your fellow workers is one way to gain power and be recognized as management potential.

Figure 7.8 Types of Difficult People

	Type of Difficult Person	Behavior of This Type	How to Deal with This Person
	Bulldozer	Loud, obnoxious, bully; delights in intimidating people and getting his or her way.	Stand your ground; show no signs of weakness; take deep breaths; look him or her right in the eye and calmly state your position. You might say, "I'll listen to you when you calm down and treat me with respect." If a superior is bullying you, you may need to take formal action.
	Saboteur	Undercuts colleagues to make him- or herself look good; stabs people in the back; goes behind your back instead of talking directly.	You want to bring this person out in the open. Ask him or her in front of other people, "Exactly what are you trying to say or do with that remark?" If you don't know who is sabotaging you, ask around. Go to the person's office and confront him or her. Tell the person, "I have a problem with what I hear you or saying or doing." This is another type of bully. Expose the person, and he or she will back off.
	Procrastinator	Can't make a decision; afraid of doing the wrong thing; poor time management skills; occasionally they will use procrastination as a way of getting attention.	Many procrastinators just need coaching on better work habits; some need help in overcoming fear of making a mistake. Negative remarks may have been written on their "slates" in the past. Give them false deadlines so they get their work done on time. Help them be successful and get positive attention. Teach them time management.
	Whiner	Everything is always wrong; bad things always happen to these people; they are overworked but spend most of their time complaining.	Nobody likes to be around whiners. You certainly don't want to listen to them, but try. When you hear anything that you might be able to be positive about, stop them and tell them that is a good idea. Try to find solutions without listening to too much whining. Seek ways for this person to get positive attention so he or she can feel a part of the team.

(continued)

Figure 7.8 Types of Difficult People (*Continued*)

	Type of Difficult Person	Behavior of This Type	How to Deal with This Person
	Exploder	Loses temper all the time over little things; uses explosions to get his or her way; has probably been doing this since he or she was a child.	You may have to raise your voice to be heard. Stand your ground. This person probably has a damaged amygdala and is reacting to something you know nothing about. You just happened to touch the nerve. Don't try to solve the problem today. Give it some time and tell the person you'll resume talking when he or she is under control.
	Pleaser	Agrees with everyone; will never have an opinion; may be passive-aggressive; the consummate "yes" person.	Force this person to make a decision. In a meeting, go around the room and call on everyone. Try to establish a "fail-safe" atmosphere where there are no wrong answers. These people have had others write on their "slates" with negativism so much that they are afraid to even have a decision. Build confidence by helping them have successes.
	Grandstander	Insecure; needs to feel good about himself or herself; knows a little about everything but has no in-depth knowledge on anything.	The know-it-all will try to block your ideas by always having a different idea or finding a reason why something won't work the way you think it will. Remember, this is usually an insecure person, so tread gently and choose your words carefully. You might say, "What if we used this part of your idea and add my idea to it?"
	Doomsayer	Expects the worst and usually gets it.	First, you need to know these people will always be complainers and you can't change that about them. Don't let them change you, because they are always looking for a teammate with whom to gripe and complain. Try saying, "Oh, surely things aren't that bad. Can you name one good thing that has happened to you today?" If you are the boss, you need to tell the person directly that his or her complaining is affecting everyone. Tell the person directly, "Stop complaining!"

© Robert Sherfield and Patricia Moody.

Figure 7.9 Tips for Dealing with Difficult People

- Create a climate where people feel they are heard.

- Assess the situation. Identify the difficult person or people, study their behavior, and see if you can determine why they are causing trouble.

- If someone tells you about the problem, get the other side before making a decision or an accusation. There are always two sides to every story. Remember, some people are very cunning and underhanded, and everyone does not tell the whole story. People usually omit their own wrong behaviors. Don't jump to conclusions. Nothing is ever exactly as it seems at first glance. Never react—act!

- Don't sit around and hope they will change. They won't! Chances are, difficult people have been acting this way for a long time and getting away with it. Wishing for a different behavior will get you nothing and provide no relief. You must confront the person and be very specific about the behavior and your expectations.

- If this is a difficult person for you to get along with personally, ask for a time to discuss the situation and try to resolve it by calling it to the person's attention, letting the person know you want to get along with him or her and to be a good colleague.

- If it is an employee under your supervision, develop a plan that includes exactly what the offensive behavior is, what needs to be done, and what you expect and by when.

- If a difficult person has been getting away with offensive behaviors for a long time, the other employees will appreciate having a boss who takes care of it, and they will respect you for doing so. Take a stand!

- Confront the employee in a private setting. Never embarrass or humiliate anyone in public. They will never forget or forgive you. These people are often fragile and easily hurt and offended—even the bullies. Talk to the offender in private, and you may see a different person. Tell him or her in a strong, assertive, forceful voice that this behavior has been documented, and it has to stop *now.* Remember to address the criticism to the behavior, not the person.

- Stick to the one behavior you are discussing. Don't load up the employee with all kinds of criticisms.

- Let the person explain his or her feelings and reasons. Tell the person how you feel: "I am disappointed that you would say that to your colleague" or "I was shocked that you would say that in an open meeting. What were you thinking?"

- Stay in control of the meeting. If the person gets loud and obnoxious, ask him or her to speak more quietly and to treat you with respect. If the person is not respectful, ask him or her to leave and come back after regaining self-control.

- If the person cries, offer him or her a tissue, and leave the room for awhile.

- Don't let the meeting deteriorate into a gripe session. Explain that the person needs to work more and complain less.

- Try to include the employee in designing a solution. Ask the person to stop the offensive behavior, and give him or her a deadline.

- If a formal disciplinary action is necessary, state the action in writing, following your company's policies. Tell the employee that you are summarizing this meeting and placing a copy in his or her file.

- Monitor the effectiveness of your meeting. Pay close attention to the employee's behavior.

- If you see positive results, praise the employee. Your goal is to salvage the employee, not isolate him or her.

Reflections: PUTTING IT ALL TOGETHER

Because we are all so different and come from such a variety of backgrounds, it stands to reason that there will be conflict. The major lesson to be learned is that most conflicts can be resolved either by listening and improving communications so you can understand other people, or by fixing something that is wrong with the system. If you are involved in a conflict, try not to let it consume you. Be reasonable and be sure you are not part of the problem. Remember the amygdala and the role it plays in how we act and react. As you work with people, think about what may have been written on their "slates" and how that may be affecting their actions. Sometimes it pays just to be quiet, ask the right questions, and listen.

DIGITAL BRIEFCASE

WHAT KINDS OF CONFLICT HAVE YOU EXPERIENCED?

Access Poll Everywhere at www.polleverywhere.com and click "Create your first poll." Follow the directions at this site and create a series of questions on conflict management that can be answered with "yes" or "no." Then send your poll to five people, record their answers, and share your poll with your friends.

REFERENCES

Brinkman, R., & Kirschner, R. (2002). *Dealing with people you can't stand: How to bring out the best in people when they are at their worst.* New York: McGraw-Hill.

Cardenas, H. (2011). What are the causes of conflict in the workplace? Retrieved June 14, 2011, from www.ehow.com/list5801672causes-conflict-workplace.html.

Stretegic HR Services. (2010). Workplace harassment. Retrieved June 21, 2011, from www.strategichr.com/shrsweb2/harassment01.shtml.

Thompson, N. (2011). How conflicts arise. Retrieved June 17, 2011, from www.humansolutions.org.uk/conflict-1.html.

Part IV:
Money

Chapters taken from:
Personal Finance, Fourth Edition
by Jeff Madura

IDentity Series: Financial Responsibility
by ClearPoint Credit Counseling Solutions, Inc.

IDentity Series: Financial Literacy
by Farnoosh Torabi

CHAPTER 8

Overview of a Financial Plan

Imagine that you are taking a vacation next year. You have many financial choices to make. How big is your vacation budget and how do you want to allocate it? The more money that you save now, the more you will have to spend on your vacation.

Now, imagine that you are planning your financial future. You have many choices to make. What type of house should you buy? How much of your budget should be allocated to food and utilities? How much can you afford to spend on clothes? Should you spend all of your money as you earn it, or should you use some money for investment opportunities? Should you buy a new car? Should you buy a house? When do you want to retire? Do you want to leave an estate for your heirs? All of these decisions require detailed planning.

In a world where there are few guarantees, thorough financial planning, prudent financial management, and careful spending can help you achieve your financial goals.

The personal financial planning process enables you to understand a financial plan and to develop a personal financial plan. The simple objective of financial planning is to make the best use of your resources to achieve your financial goals. The sooner you develop your goals and a financial plan to achieve those goals, the easier it will be to achieve your objectives.

The objectives of this chapter are to:

- Explain how you benefit from personal financial planning
- Identify the key components of a financial plan
- Outline the steps involved in developing your financial plan

HOW YOU BENEFIT FROM AN UNDERSTANDING OF PERSONAL FINANCE

personal finance
The process of planning your spending, financing, and investing to optimize your financial situation.

Personal finance (also referred to as **personal financial planning**) is the process of planning your spending, financing, and investing to optimize your financial situation. A **personal financial plan** specifies your financial goals and describes the spending, financing, and investing plans that are intended to achieve those goals. Although the U.S. is one of the wealthiest countries, many Americans do not manage their financial situations well. Consequently, they tend to rely too much on credit and have excessive debt. Consider these statistics:

personal financial plan
A plan that specifies your financial goals and describes the spending, financing, and investing plans that are intended to achieve those goals.

- More than 1.2 million people filed for personal bankruptcy in 2008.
- The level of savings in the U.S. is only about 1 percent of income earned. (Some investments, including retirement accounts, are not included as savings.)
- About half of all surveyed people in the U.S. who are working full-time state that they live from one paycheck to the next, without a plan for saving money.
- About 40 percent of people who work full time do not save for retirement. Those who do typically save a relatively small amount of money.

The lack of savings is especially problematic given the increasing cost of health care and other necessities. You will have numerous options regarding the choice of bank deposits, credit cards, loans, insurance policies, investments, and retirement plans. With an understanding of personal finance, you will be able to make decisions that can enhance your financial situation.

How much do you know about personal finance? Various government agencies of various countries have attempted to assess financial literacy in recent years. Surveys have documented that people tend to have very limited personal finance skills. In addition, surveys have found that many people who believe they have strong personal finance skills do not understand some basic personal finance concepts. Take the Financial Literacy Test, provided just before this chapter. Even if your knowledge of personal finance is limited, you can substantially increase your knowledge and improve your financial planning skills by reading this text. An understanding of personal finance is beneficial to you in many ways, including the following:

Make Your Own Financial Decisions

opportunity cost
What you give up as a result of a decision.

An understanding of personal finance enables you to make informed decisions about your financial situation. Each of your spending decisions has an **opportunity cost,** which represents what you give up as a result of that decision. By spending money for a specific purpose, you forgo alternative ways that you could have spent the money and also forgo saving the money for a future purpose. For example, if your decision to use your cell phone costs $100 per month, you have forgone the possibility of using that money to buy concert tickets or to save for a new car. Informed financial decisions increase the amount of money that you accumulate over time and give you more flexibility to purchase the products and services you want in the future.

Judge the Advice of Financial Advisers

The personal financial planning process will enable you to make informed decisions about your spending, saving, financing, and investing. Nevertheless, you may prefer to rely on advice from various types of financial advisers. An understanding of personal finance allows you to judge the guidance of financial advisers and to determine whether their advice is in your best interest (or in their best interest).

EXAMPLE	You want to invest $10,000 of your savings. A financial adviser guarantees that your investment will increase in value by 20 percent (or by $2,000) this year, but he will charge you 4 percent of the investment ($400) for his advice. If you have a background in personal finance, you would know that no investment can be guaranteed to increase in value by 20 percent in one year. Therefore, you would realize that you should not trust this financial adviser. You could either hire a more reputable financial adviser or review investment recommendations made by financial advisers on the Internet (often for free).

Become a Financial Adviser

An understanding of personal finance may interest you in pursuing a career as a financial adviser. Financial advisers are in demand because many people lack an understanding of personal finance or are not interested in making their own financial decisions. A single course in personal finance is insufficient to start a career as a financial adviser, but it may interest you in taking additional courses to obtain the necessary qualifications.

■ COMPONENTS OF A FINANCIAL PLAN

A complete financial plan contains your personal finance decisions related to six key components:

1. Budgeting and tax planning
2. Managing your liquidity
3. Financing your large purchases
4. Protecting your assets and income (insurance)
5. Investing your money
6. Planning your retirement and estate

These six components are very different; decisions concerning each are included in separate plans that, taken together, form your overall financial plan. To begin your introduction to the financial planning process, let's briefly explore each component.

A Plan for Your Budgeting and Tax Planning

budget planning (budgeting)
The process of forecasting future expenses and savings.

Budget planning (also referred to as **budgeting**) is the process of forecasting future expenses and savings. That is, it requires you to decide whether to spend or save money. If you receive $750 in income during one month, your amount saved is the amount of money (say, $100) that you do not spend. The relationship between income received, spending, and saving is illustrated in Exhibit 8.1. Some individuals are "big spenders": they focus their budget decisions on how to spend most or all of their income and therefore have little or no money left for saving. Others are "big savers": they set a savings goal and consider spending their income received only after allocating a portion of it toward saving. Budgeting can help you estimate how much of your income will be required to cover monthly expenses so that you can set a goal for saving each month.

assets
What you own.

liabilities
What you owe; your debt.

net worth
The value of what you own minus the value of what you owe.

The first step in budget planning is to evaluate your current financial position by assessing your income, your expenses, your **assets** (what you own), and your **liabilities** (debt, or what you owe). Your **net worth** is the value of what you own minus the value of what you owe. You can measure your wealth by your net worth. As you save money, you increase your assets and therefore increase your net worth. Budget planning enables you to build your net worth by setting aside part of your income to either invest in additional assets or reduce your liabilities.

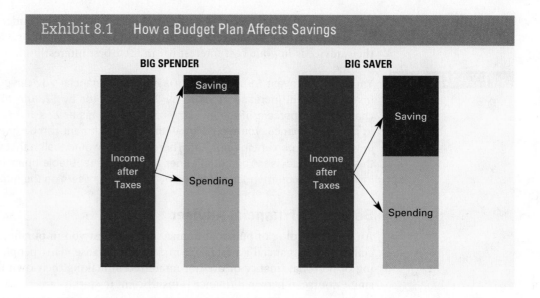

Exhibit 8.1   How a Budget Plan Affects Savings

Your budget is influenced by your income, which in turn is influenced by your education and career decisions. Individuals who pursue higher levels of education tend to have smaller budgets during the education years. After obtaining their degrees, however, they typically are able to obtain jobs that pay higher salaries and therefore have larger budgets.

A key part of budgeting is estimating the typical expenses that you will incur each month. If you underestimate expenses, you will not achieve your savings goals. Achieving a higher level of future wealth requires you to sacrifice by keeping spending at a lower level today.

Many financial decisions are affected by tax laws, as some forms of income are taxed at a higher rate than others. By understanding how your alternative financial choices would be affected by taxes, you can make financial decisions that have the most favorable effect on your cash flows. Budgeting and tax planning are discussed in Part 1 because they are the basis for decisions about all other parts of your financial plan.

A Plan to Manage Your Liquidity

liquidity
Access to funds to cover any short-term cash deficiencies.

You should have a plan for how you will cover your daily purchases. Your expenses can range from your morning cup of coffee to major car repairs. You need to have **liquidity**, or access to funds to cover any short-term cash needs. You can enhance your liquidity by utilizing money management and credit management.

money management
Decisions regarding how much money to retain in a liquid form and how to allocate the funds among short-term investment instruments.

Money management involves decisions regarding how much money to retain in a liquid form and how to allocate the funds among short-term investments. If you do not have access to money to cover your cash needs, you may have insufficient liquidity. That is, you have the assets to cover your expenses, but the money is not easily accessible. Finding an effective liquidity level involves deciding how to invest your money so that you can earn a return, but also have easy access to cash if needed. At times, you may be unable to avoid cash shortages because of unanticipated expenses.

credit management
Decisions regarding how much credit to obtain to support your spending and which sources of credit to use.

Credit management involves decisions about how much credit you need to support your spending and which sources of credit to use. Credit is commonly used to cover both large and small expenses when you are short on cash, so it enhances your liquidity. Credit should be used only when necessary, however, as you will need to pay back borrowed funds with interest (and the interest expenses may be very high). The use of money management and credit management to manage your liquidity is illustrated in Exhibit 8.2.

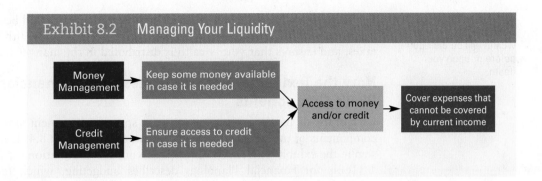

Exhibit 8.2   Managing Your Liquidity

A Plan for Your Financing

Loans are typically needed to finance large expenditures, such as the payment of college tuition or the purchase of a car or a home. The amount of financing needed is the difference between the amount of the purchase and the amount of money you have available, as illustrated in Exhibit 8.3. Managing loans includes determining how much you can afford to borrow, deciding on the maturity (length of time) of the loan, and selecting a loan that charges a competitive interest rate.

A Plan for Protecting Your Assets and Income

insurance planning
Determining the types and amount of insurance needed to protect your assets.

To protect your assets, you can conduct **insurance planning**, which determines the types and amount of insurance that you need. In particular, automobile insurance and homeowner's insurance protect your assets, while health insurance limits your potential medical expenses. Disability insurance and life insurance protect your income.

A Plan for Your Investing

risk
Uncertainty surrounding the potential return on an investment.

Any funds that you have beyond what you need to maintain liquidity should be invested. Because these funds normally are not used to satisfy your liquidity needs, they can be invested with the primary objective of earning a high return. Potential investments include stocks, bonds, mutual funds, and real estate. You must determine how much of your funds you wish to allocate toward investments and what types of investments you wish to consider. Most investments are subject to **risk** (uncertainty surrounding their potential return), however, so you need to manage them so that your risk is limited to a tolerable level.

A Plan for Your Retirement and Estate

retirement planning
Determining how much money you should set aside each year for retirement and how you should invest those funds.

Retirement planning involves determining how much money you should set aside each year for retirement and how you should invest those funds. Retirement planning must begin well before you retire so that you can accumulate sufficient money to invest and support yourself after you retire. Money contributed to various kinds of retirement plans is protected from taxes until it is withdrawn from the retirement account.

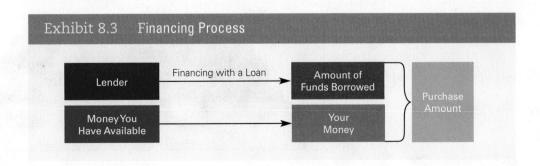

Exhibit 8.3   Financing Process

estate planning
Determining how your wealth will be distributed before or upon your death.

Estate planning is the act of planning how your wealth will be distributed before or upon your death. Effective estate planning protects your wealth against unnecessary taxes, and ensures that your wealth is distributed in the manner that you desire.

How the Text Organization Relates to the Financial Plan's Components

Each of the six parts of this text covers one specific component of the financial plan. The components of the financial plan are illustrated in Exhibit 8.4. Each part is shown as a step in the exhibit with the lower steps serving as a foundation for the higher steps. Part 1 (Tools for Financial Planning) describes budgeting, which focuses on how cash received (from income or other sources) is allocated to saving, spending, and taxes. Budget planning serves as the foundation of the financial plan, as it is your base for making personal financial decisions.

The next component is liquidity management (Part 2) because you must have adequate liquidity before financing or investing. Once your budget plan and your liquidity are in order, you are in a position to plan your financing (Part 3) for major purchases such as a new car or a home. Part 4 explains how to use insurance to protect your assets and your income. Next, you can consider investment alternatives such as stocks, bonds, and mutual funds (Part 5). Finally, planning for retirement (Part 6) focuses on the wealth that you will accumulate by the time you retire.

An effective financial plan enhances your net worth and therefore builds your wealth. In each part of the text, you will have the opportunity to develop a component of your financial plan. At the end of each chapter, the Building Your Own Financial Plan exercise offers you guidance on the key decisions that you can make after reading that chapter. Evaluate your options and make decisions using the Excel-based software on the CD-ROM available with your text. By completing the Building Your Own Financial Plan exercises, you will build a financial plan for yourself by the end of the school term. Exhibit 8.5 lists examples of the decisions you will make for each component.

How the Components Relate to Your Cash Flows. Exhibit 8.6 illustrates the typical types of cash inflows (cash that you receive) and cash outflows (cash that you spend). This exhibit also shows how each component of the financial plan reflects decisions on how to obtain or use cash. You receive cash inflows in the form of income from your employer and use some of that cash to spend on products and services. Income (Part 1) focuses on the relationship between your income and your spending. Your budgeting decisions determine how much of your income you spend on products and services. The residual funds can be allocated for your personal finance needs. Liquidity management (Part 2) focuses on depositing excess cash or obtaining credit if you are short on cash. Financing (Part 3) focuses on obtaining cash to support your large purchases. Protecting your assets and income (Part 4) focuses on determining your insurance needs and

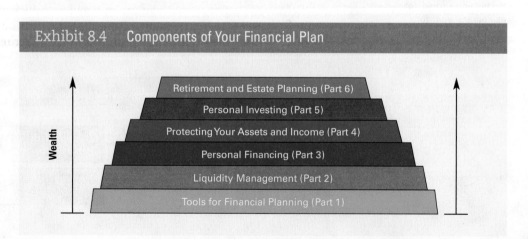

Exhibit 8.4   Components of Your Financial Plan

Retirement and Estate Planning (Part 6)

Personal Investing (Part 5)

Protecting Your Assets and Income (Part 4)

Personal Financing (Part 3)

Liquidity Management (Part 2)

Tools for Financial Planning (Part 1)

Wealth

Exhibit 8.5	Examples of Decisions Made in Each Component of a Financial Plan
A Plan for:	**Types of Decisions**
1. Managing your income	What expenses should you anticipate?
	How much money should you attempt to save each month?
	How much money must you save each month toward a specific purchase?
	What debt payments must you make each month?
2. Managing your liquidity	How much money should you maintain in your checking account?
	How much money should you maintain in your savings account?
	Should you use credit cards as a means of borrowing money?
3. Financing	How much money can you borrow to purchase a car?
	Should you borrow money to purchase a car or should you lease a car?
	How much money can you borrow to purchase a home?
	What type of mortgage loan should you obtain to finance the purchase of a house?
4. Protecting your assets and income	What type of insurance do you need?
	How much insurance do you need?
5. Investing	How much money should you allocate toward investments?
	What types of investments should you consider?
	How much risk can you tolerate when investing your money?
6. Your retirement and estate	How much money will you need for retirement?
	How much money must you save each year so that you can retire in a specific year?
	How will you allocate your estate among your heirs?

Exhibit 8.6	How Financial Planning Affects Your Cash Flows

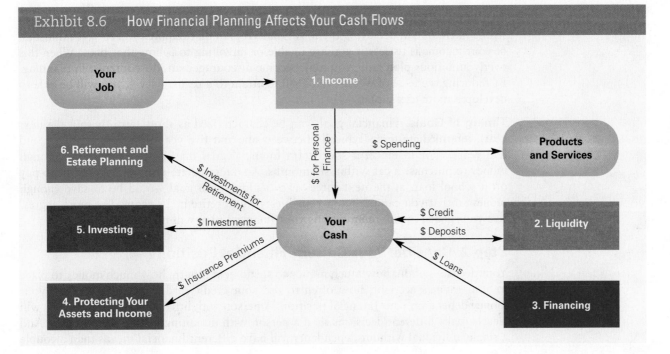

spending money on insurance premiums. Investing (Part 5) focuses on using some of your cash to build your wealth. Planning for your retirement (Part 6) focuses on periodically investing cash in your retirement account.

If you need more cash inflows beyond your income, you may decide to rely on savings that you have already accumulated or obtain loans from creditors. If your income exceeds the amount that you wish to spend, you can use the excess funds to make more investments or to repay some or all of the principal on existing loans. Thus, your investment decisions can serve as a source of funds (selling your investments) or a way of using additional funds (making additional investments). Your financing decisions can serve as a source of funds (obtaining additional loans) or a use of funds (repaying existing loans).

■ DEVELOPING THE FINANCIAL PLAN

Six steps are involved in developing each component of your financial plan.

Step 1. Establish Your Financial Goals

You must determine your financial goals.

First, determine your general goals in life. These goals do not have to be put in financial terms. For example, you may have goals such as a family, additional education, a vacation to a foreign country for one week every year. You may envision owning a five-bedroom house, or having a new car every four years, or retiring when you reach age 55.

Types of Financial Goals. Your general goals in life influence your financial goals. It takes money to support many of your goals. If you want to have a family, one of your financial goals may be that you and your spouse earn enough income and save enough money over time to financially support a family. If you want a vacation to a foreign country every year, one of your financial goals may be that you earn enough income and save enough money to financially support your travel. If you want a large home, one of your financial goals should be that you earn enough income and save enough money over time to make a substantial real estate purchase. If you want to retire by age 55, this will require you to save enough money by then so that you could afford to stop working. You may also establish financial goals such as helping a family member or donating to charities.

Set Realistic Goals. You need to be realistic about your goals so that you can have a strong likelihood of achieving them. A financial plan that requires you to save almost all of your income is useless if you are unable or unwilling to follow that plan. When this overly ambitious plan fails, you may become discouraged and lose interest in planning. By reducing the level of wealth you wish to attain to a realistic level, you will be able to develop a more useful plan.

Timing of Goals. Financial goals can be characterized as short term (within the next year), intermediate term (typically between one and five years), or long term (beyond five years). For instance, a short-term financial goal may be to accumulate enough money to purchase a car within six months. An intermediate-term goal would be to pay off a school loan in the next three years. A long-term goal would be to save enough money so that you can maintain your lifestyle and retire in 20 years. The more aggressive your goals, the more ambitious your financial plan will need to be.

Step 2. Consider Your Current Financial Position

Your decisions about how much money to spend next month, how much money to place in your savings account, how often to use your credit card, and how to invest your money depend on your financial position. A person with little debt and many assets will clearly make different decisions than a person with mounting debt and few assets. And a single individual without dependents will have different financial means than a couple with children, even if the individual and the couple have the same income. The appropriate plan also varies with your age and wealth. If you are 20 years old with zero funds in your bank account, your financial plan will be different than if you are 65 years old and have saved much of your income over the last 40 years.

Since your financial planning decisions are dependent on your financial position, they are dependent on your education and career choice, as explained next.

How Your Future Financial Position Is Tied to Your Education. Your financial position is highly influenced by the amount of education you pursue. The more education you have, the higher your earnings will likely be. As Exhibit 8.7 shows, the difference in annual income between a high school graduate and a bachelor's degree holder in 2007 was more than $18,000. Before you choose a major, consider your skills, interests, and how your choice can prepare you for different career paths. A major in biology or chemistry may allow you to pursue careers in the biotechnology industry, while a major in English may allow you to pursue a career in journalism.

How Your Future Financial Position Is Tied to Your Career Choice. Your career choices also affect your income and potential for spending and saving money. If you become a social worker, you will be in a different financial position than if you choose to work as an electrical engineer. As a social worker, you will need to save a much higher proportion of your income to achieve the same level of savings that you could amass as an electrical engineer. If you choose a career that pays a low income, you will need to set attainable financial goals. Or you may reconsider your choice of a career in pursuit of a higher level of income. However, be realistic. You should not decide to be a doctor just because doctors' salaries are high if you dislike health-related work. You should choose a career that will be enjoyable and will suit your skills. If you like your job, you are more likely to perform well. Since you may be working for 40 years or longer, you should seriously think about the career that will satisfy both your financial and personal needs.

The fastest-growing occupations are identified in the first column of Exhibit 8.8. The expected change in the employment level for each of these positions is shown in the second column, while the required degree is shown in the third column. Notice that an associate or bachelor's degree is needed for many of the occupations.

Many people change their career over time. As the demand for occupations changes, some jobs are eliminated and others are created. In addition, some people grow tired of their occupation and seek a new career. Thus, career choices are not restricted to students who are just completing their education. As with your initial career decision, a shift to a new career should be influenced by your views of what will satisfy you.

Various Web sites can help you estimate the income level for a specific career. Even if the income level in a particular career you desire is less than what you expected, you

Exhibit 8.7	Comparison of Income among Education Levels
Education	**Median Level of Annual Income**
Master's degree	$55,426
Bachelor's degree	45,773
Associate degree	36,333
Some college, no degree	33,837
High-school graduate	27,240
Some high school, no degree	20,398

Source: U.S. Census Bureau, 2007.

Exhibit 8.8   Fastest-Growing Occupations, 2000–2010

Occupation	Percentage Change in Employment	Degree Required
Network systems	53%	Bachelor's degree
Personal and home health aides	51	
Computer software engineers	45	Bachelor's degree
Veterinary technicians	41	
Personal financial advisors	41	Bachelor's degree
Makeup artists, theatrical, and performance	40	
Medical assistants	35	
Veterinarians	35	Associate degree
Substance abuse and behavioral disorder counselors	34	Bachelor's degree
Skin care specialists	34	
Financial Analysts	34	Bachelor's degree
Social and human service assistants	34	
Gaming surveillance officers and investigators	34	
Physical therapy assistants	32	Associate degree
Pharmacy technicians	31	
Forensic science technicians	31	Bachelor's degree
Dental hygienists	30	Associate degree
Mental health counselors	30	Master's degree
Mental health and substance abuse social workers	30	Master's degree
Marriage and family therapists	30	Master's degree
Dental assistants	29	
Computer systems analysts	29	Bachelor's degree
Database administrators	29	Bachelor's degree
Environmental science and protection technicians	28	Associate degree

Source: Bureau of Labor Statistics, U.S. Department of Labor, 2008–2009 Occupational Handbook.

may be able to maintain the same financial goals by extending the period in which you hope to achieve those goals.

FINANCIAL IMPACT

How Your Future Financial Position Is Tied to the Economy

Economic conditions affect the types of jobs that are available to you, and the salary offered by each type of job. They affect the price you pay for services such as rent. They affect the value of assets (such as a home) that you own. They also affect the return that you can earn on your investments.

The financial crisis of 2008–2009 affected the financial position of individuals in many ways. First, it resulted in lower housing prices. Second, it resulted in lower values of many types of investments, such as stocks. Third, it caused a reduction in new job opportunities. Fourth, it resulted in the elimination of some jobs. Fifth, it resulted in lower salaries for the existing job positions, as employers could not afford to give high raises to their employees.

Overall, the financial crisis reduced the asset values and wealth of individuals. At the beginning of 2008, the wealth of households in the U.S. was estimated by the federal government to be about $62 trillion. By 2009, the wealth of households in the U.S. was estimated to be about $51 trillion, reflecting a reduction of $11 trillion, or 18 percent of total wealth. The financial crisis also resulted in a higher level of debt for individuals. The total debt of households was about 23 percent larger than the annual income. In other words, if households used all of their annual income just to repay debt, they would not be able to pay off all of the debt. Overall, the financial crisis may force individuals to revise their financial goals in order to make them attainable. Alternatively, the crisis might require that individuals allow a longer period of time in order to reach their financial goals.

QUESTIONS

a. **Economic Impact on Net Worth**. Assume that you have established a plan to achieve a particular level of wealth in three years, but the economic conditions suddenly cause your existing income to decline and the value of your existing assets to decline. Should you leave your financial plan as it is, or adjust it?

b. **Economic Impact on Job Strategy**. During a weak economy, jobs are scarce, and some individuals may consider starting their own businesses. What is the disadvantage of this idea during a weak economy?

Step 3. Identify and Evaluate Alternative Plans That Could Achieve Your Goals

You must identify and evaluate the alternative financial plans that could achieve your financial goals (specified in Step 1), given your financial position (determined in Step 2). For example, to accumulate a substantial amount of money in 10 years, you could decide to save a large portion of your income over those years. This plan is likely to achieve your goal of accumulating a substantial amount of money in 10 years. However, this plan requires much discipline. Alternatively, you could plan to save only a small portion of your income, but to invest your savings in a manner that earns a very high return so that you can accumulate a substantial amount of money in 10 years. This alternative plan does not require you to save as much money. However, it places more pressure on you to earn a high return on your investments. To earn such a high return, you will likely have to make risky investments in order to achieve your goals. You might not achieve your goals with this alternative plan because your investments might not perform as well as you expected.

Step 4. Select and Implement the Best Plan for Achieving Your Goals

You need to analyze and select the plan that will be most effective in achieving your goals. For example, if you are disciplined and conservative, you will likely select the first of the two plans identified in the previous paragraph. The type of plan you select to achieve your financial goals will be influenced by your willingness to accept risk and your self-discipline.

Using the Internet. The Internet provides you with valuable information for making financial decisions. Your decision to spend money on a new stereo or to save the money may be dependent on how much you can earn from depositing the money. Your decision of whether to purchase a new car depends on the prices of new cars and financing rates on car loans. Your decision of whether to purchase a home depends on the prices of homes and financing rates on home loans. Your decision of whether to invest in stocks is influenced by the prices of stocks. Your decision of where to purchase insurance may be influenced by the insurance premiums quoted by different insurance agencies. All of these financial decisions require knowledge of prevailing prices or interest rates, which are literally at your fingertips on the Internet.

The Internet also provides updated information on all parts of the financial plan, such as:

- Current tax rates and rules that can be used for tax planning
- Recent performance of various types of investments
- New retirement plan rules that can be used for long-term planning

Many Web sites offer online calculators that you can use for a variety of financial planning decisions, such as:

- Estimating your taxes
- Determining how your savings will grow over time
- Determining whether buying or leasing a car is more appropriate

Special features in each chapter called Financial Planning Online illustrate how the Internet can facilitate the creation of the various parts of the financial plan. Financial Planning Online exercises are also provided at the end of each chapter so that you can practice using the Internet for financial planning purposes. URLs in this text are available and updated on the text's Web site for easy navigation.

When you use online information for personal finance decisions, keep in mind that some information may not be accurate. Use reliable sources, such as Web sites of government agencies or financial media companies that have a proven track record for reporting financial information. Also, recognize that free personal finance advice provided online does not necessarily apply to every person's situation. Get a second opinion before you follow online advice, especially when it recommends that you spend or invest money.

Financial Planning Online 8.1: **Financial Planning Tools for You**

Go to
finance.yahoo.com/

This Web site provides much information and many tools that can be used for all aspects of financial planning, including tax rates, bank deposit rates, loan rates, credit card information, mortgage rates, and quotations and analysis of stocks, bonds, mutual funds, and insurance policies. It also provides information for creating retirement plans and wills.

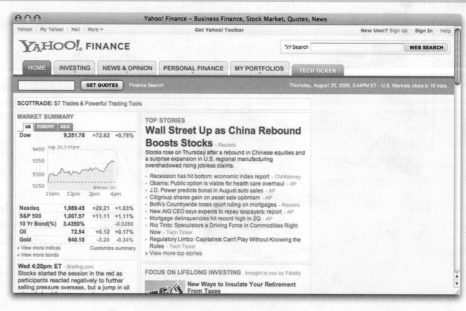

FOCUS ON ETHICS: Personal Financial Advice

Many individuals have a limited background in financial planning and rely on professionals in the financial services industry for advice when developing their financial plan. While most advisers take their responsibilities seriously and are very ethical, there are some unethical and incompetent advisers.

One of the aspects of financial services products that creates a potential conflict of interest for your adviser is the variety of fee and commission structures available on even a single product such as a life insurance policy. Your objective is to get the best advice appropriate for your needs. The adviser's objective should be the same, but the method (or product) selected could possibly be chosen because of the commission structure the product offers. There is a potential conflict of interest any time a salesperson charges a fee or commission.

Check the credentials of the adviser. Financial services professionals are licensed for the products they sell and they must meet continuing education requirements to maintain those licenses. There are special certifications such as the CFP®, the Certified Financial Planner designation, and the CLU, Chartered Life Underwriter, that indicate a level of competence in some aspects of financial planning.

While most financial services professionals are indeed professional and knowledgeable in their field, it is still your responsibility to ensure that their advice serves your needs. It should be your decision which product to buy, how much insurance coverage you should have, and when to change investments. Educating yourself on these financial products will help you make sound decisions.

Step 5. Evaluate Your Financial Plan

After you develop and implement each component of your financial plan, you must monitor your progress to ensure that the plan is working as you intended. Keep your financial plan easily accessible so that you can evaluate it over time.

Step 6. Revise Your Financial Plan

If you find that you are unable or unwilling to follow the financial plan that you developed, you need to revise the plan to make it more realistic. Of course, your financial goals may have to be reduced as well if you are unable to maintain the plan for achieving a particular level of wealth.

As time passes, your financial position will change, especially upon specific events such as graduating from college, marriage, a career change, or the birth of a child. As your financial position changes, your financial goals may change as well. You need to revise your financial plan to reflect such changes in your means and priorities.

The steps in developing a financial plan are summarized in Exhibit 8.9. To see how the steps can be applied, consider the following example.

EXAMPLE

Stephanie Spratt graduated from college last year with a degree in marketing. After job searching for several months, she was just hired by the sales department of an advertising firm at an annual salary of $38,000. She is eager to have money from her salary to spend and to give up her interim part-time job waiting tables.

Stephanie plans to save a portion of every paycheck so that she can invest money to build her wealth over time. She realizes that by establishing a financial plan to limit her spending today, she can increase her wealth and therefore her potential spending in the future. At this point, Stephanie decides to develop an overview of her current financial position, establish her goals, and map out a plan for how she might achieve those goals, as shown in Exhibit 8.10.

Exhibit 8.9   Summary of Steps Used to Develop a Financial Plan

1. Establish your financial goals.

   - What are your short-term financial goals?
   - What are your intermediate-term financial goals?
   - What are your long-term financial goals?

2. Consider your current financial position.

   - How much money do you have in savings?
   - What is the value of your investments?
   - What is your net worth?

3. Identify and evaluate alternative plans that could achieve your goals.

   - Given your goals and existing financial position described in the previous steps, how can you obtain the necessary funds to achieve your financial goals?
   - Will you need to reduce your spending to save more money each month?
   - Will you need to make investments that generate a higher rate of return?

4. Select and implement the best plan for achieving your goals.

   - What are the advantages and disadvantages of each alternative plan that could be used to achieve your goals?

5. Evaluate your financial plan.

   - Is your financial plan working properly? That is, will it enable you to achieve your financial goals?

6. Revise your financial plan.

   - Have your financial goals changed?
   - Should parts of the financial plan be revised in order to increase the chance of achieving your financial goals? (If so, identify the parts that should be changed, and determine how they should be revised.)

Key decisions that relate to Stephanie's financial plan will be summarized at the end of each chapter. Your financial planning decisions will differ from Stephanie's or anyone else's. Nevertheless, the process of building the financial plan is the same. You need to establish your goals, assess alternative methods for reaching your goals, and decide on a financial plan that can achieve your goals.

Exhibit 8.10   Overview of Stephanie Spratt's Financial Plan

Step 1. Current Financial Position:

I have very little savings at this time and own an old car. My income, which is about $30,000 a year after taxes, should increase over time.

Step 2. Financial Goals:

I would like to:

- *buy a new car within a year,*
- *buy a home within two years,*
- *make investments that will allow my wealth to grow over time, and*
- *build a large amount of savings for retirement in 20 to 40 years.*

Step 3. Plans to Achieve the Goals:

Since my current financial position does not provide me with sufficient funds to achieve these financial goals, I need to develop a financial plan for achieving these goals. One possible plan would be to save enough money until I could purchase the car and home with cash. With this plan, however, I would not have sufficient savings to purchase a home for many years. An alternative is to save enough money to make a down payment on the car and home and to obtain financing to cover the rest of the cost. This alternative plan allows me to allocate some of my income toward investments.

My financing decisions will determine the type of car and home that I will purchase and the amount of funds I will have left to make other investments so that I can build my wealth over time.

Step 4. Selecting and Implementing the Best Plan:

Financing the purchase of a car and a home is a more appropriate plan for me. I will prepare a budget so that over time I can accumulate savings that will be used to make a down payment on a new car. Then, I will attempt to accumulate savings to make a down payment on a new home. I need to make sure that I can afford financing payments on any money that I borrow.

Step 5. Evaluating the Plan:

Once I establish a budget, I will monitor it over time to determine whether I am achieving the desired amount of savings each month.

Step 6. Revising the Plan:

If I cannot save as much money as I desire, I may have to delay my plans for purchasing a car and a home until I can accumulate enough funds to make the down payments. If I am able to exceed my savings goal, I may be able to purchase the car and the home sooner than I had originally expected.

SUMMARY

- Personal financial planning is the process of planning your spending, financing, and investing to optimize your financial situation. Your financial planning decisions allow you to develop a financial plan, which involves a set of decisions about how to manage your spending, financing, and investments.

- A financial plan has six components: (1) budgeting, (2) managing your liquidity, (3) financing large purchases, (4) protecting your assets and income, (5) investing, and (6) planning beyond your career.

- The financial planning process involves six steps: (1) establishing your financial goals, (2) considering your current financial position, (3) identifying and evaluating alternative plans that could achieve your goals, (4) selecting and implementing the best plan for achieving your financial goals, (5) evaluating the financial plan over time to ensure that you are meeting your goals, and (6) revising the financial plan when necessary.

REVIEW QUESTIONS

1. **Personal Finance Decisions.** Define personal financial planning. What types of decisions are involved in a personal financial plan?

2. **Opportunity Cost.** What is an opportunity cost? What might be some of the opportunity costs of spending $10 per week on the lottery?

3. **Personal Finance Benefits.** How can an understanding of personal finance benefit you?

4. **Financial Plan Components.** What are the six key components of a financial plan?

5. **Budget Planning.** Define budget planning. What elements must be assessed in budget planning?

6. **Net Worth.** How is your net worth calculated? Why is it important?

7. **Tax Effects on Planning.** What factors influence income? Why is an accurate estimate of expenses important in budget planning? How do tax laws affect the budgeting process?

8. **Liquidity.** What is liquidity? What two factors are considered in managing liquidity? How are they used?

9. **Financing.** What factors are considered in managing financing?

10. **Investing.** What is the primary objective of investing? What else must be considered? What potential investment vehicles are available?

11. **Protecting Your Assets.** What are the three elements of planning to protect your assets? Define each element.

12. **Your Cash Flows.** How does each element of financial planning affect your cash flows?

13. **Steps in Financial Planning.** What are the six steps in developing a financial plan?

14. **Financial Goals.** How do your financial goals fit into your financial plan? Why should goals be realistic? What are three time frames for goals? Give an example of a goal for each time frame.

15. **Your Financial Position.** Name some factors that might affect your current financial position.

16. **Financial Goals and Planning.** How do your current financial position and goals relate to your creation of alternative financial plans?

17. **Implementing Your Plan.** Once your financial plan has been implemented, what is the next step? Why is it important?

18. **Revising Your Plan.** Why might you need to revise your financial plan?

19. **Online Information.** List some information available on the Internet that might be useful for financial planning. Describe one way you might use some of this information for financial planning purposes.

20. **Financial Advisers.** Offer an example of unethical behavior that financial advisers might engage in. How can an understanding of personal financial planning help you deal with this potential behavior?

FINANCIAL PLANNING PROBLEMS

1. **Estimating Savings.** Julia brings home $1,600 per month after taxes. Julia's rent is $350 per month, her utilities are $100 per month, and her car payment is $250 per month. Julia is currently paying $200 per month to her orthodontist for her braces. If Julia's groceries cost $50 per week and she estimates her other expenses to be $150 per month, how much will she have left each month to put toward savings to reach her financial goals?

2. **Estimating the Opportunity Cost.** Julia (from problem 1) is considering trading in her car for a new one. Her new car payment will be $325 per month, and her insurance cost will increase by $60 per month. Julia determines that her other car-related expenses (gas, oil) will stay about the same. What is the opportunity cost if Julia purchases the new car?

3. **Estimating Net Worth.** Mia has $3,000 in assets, a finance company loan for $500, and an outstanding credit card balance of $135. Mia's monthly cash inflows are $2,000, and she has monthly expenses of $1,650. What is Mia's net worth?

4. **Estimating Net Worth.** At the beginning of the year, Arianne had a net worth of $5,000. During the year she set aside $100 per month from her paycheck for savings and borrowed $500 from her cousin that she must pay back in January of next year. What was her net worth at the end of the year?

5. **Estimating Net Worth.** Anna has just received a gift of $500 for her graduation, which increased her net worth by $500. If she uses the money to purchase a stereo, how will her net worth be affected? If she invests the $500 at 10 percent interest per year, what will it be worth in one year?

6. **Estimating Cash Flows.** Jason's car was just stolen, and the police informed him that they will probably be unable to recover it. His insurance will not cover the theft. Jason has a net worth of $3,000, all of which is easily convertible to cash. Jason requires a car for his job and his daily life. Based on Jason's cash flow, he can't currently afford more than $200 in car payments. What options does he have? How will these options affect his net worth and cash flow?

7. **ETHICAL DILEMMA:** Sandy and Phil have recently married and are both in their early 20s. In establishing their financial goals, they determine that their three long-term goals are to purchase a home, to provide their children with

college education, and to plan for their retirement.

They decide to seek professional assistance in reaching their goals. After considering several financial advisers who charge an annual fee based on the size of their portfolio, they decide to go to Sandy's cousin Larry, who is a stockbroker. Larry tells them that he is happy to help them, and the only fee he will charge is for transactions. In their initial meeting, Larry recommends stocks of several well-known companies that pay high dividends, which they purchase. Three months later, Larry tells them that due to changing market conditions, they need to sell the stocks and buy several others. Three months later, the same thing happens. At the end of the year Phil and Sandy, who had sold each of the stocks for more than they had paid for them, were surprised to see that the total dollar value of their portfolio had declined. After careful analysis, they found the transaction fees exceeded their capital gains.

a. Do you think Larry behaved ethically? Explain.

b. Would Larry have a personal reason for handling Sandy and Phil's portfolio as he did? Explain.

FINANCIAL PLANNING ONLINE EXERCISE

1. The purpose of this exercise is to familiarize you with the wide variety of personal finance resources on Yahoo!. Go to finance.yahoo.com/ personal-finance.

   a. Determine how inflation and taxes will affect your investments. Click "Taxes" and using the calculator "How do taxes and inflation impact my return?" answer this question: Assuming a before-tax return on your savings of 8%, a state marginal tax rate of 5%, a federal marginal tax rate of 25%, no itemized deductions, and an annual inflation rate of 3%, what would a $10,000 investment be in 10 years?

   b. Return to finance.yahoo.com/ personal-finance. Click on "Banking and Budget" and using the calculator "Value of reducing or foregoing expenses" determine how much you could save in 10 years if you stopped buying soft drinks from a vending machine. Assume you currently spend $35 per month on soft drinks and you could invest this money at a rate of return of 8%.

   c. Now click "Loans" and using the calculator "What would my loan payments be?" determine what your loan payment would be if you borrowed $30,000 at 6% for 60 months and made monthly payments. For your 10th payment, how much of the loan payment would be interest? (*Hint*: Find the loan amortization table.)

   d. Click "Retirement" and using the calculator "How much will I need to save for retirement?" complete the following exercise: Assuming an inflation rate of 3%, a desired retirement age of 65, 30 years of retirement income, income replacement of 100%, and returns both pre- and post-retirement of 8%, use your current age and other current information to compute how much you will need to save for retirement. (*Hint*: If you are not currently working and have no income, use your estimated income upon graduation.) Make this calculation both including and excluding Social Security.

   e. Using the section entitled "Rates," click each of the tabs. Have interest rates on home mortgages increased or decreased over the last week? On home equity loans? On savings? On auto loans? On credit cards? How do national auto loan rates compare to auto loan rates in your local area? (*Hint*: Click "View rates in your area" to answer this question.)

VIDEO EXERCISE: Benefits of Financial Planning

Go to one of the Web sites that contain video clips (such as www.youtube.com) and view some video clips about financial planning. Conduct a search of the site using phrases such as "value of financial planning" or "benefits of financial planning." Select one video clip on this topic that you would recommend for the other students in your class.

1. Provide the Web link for the video clip.

2. What do you think is the main point of this video clip?

3. How might you change your financial planning as a result of watching this video clip?

BUILDING YOUR OWN FINANCIAL PLAN

These end-of-chapter exercises are designed to enable you to create a working lifelong financial plan. Like all plans, your personal plan will require periodic review and revision. In this first exercise, you should review your current financial situation. If you are a full-time student, base your review on what you anticipate your financial situation will be upon your graduation. After carefully reviewing your current or anticipated financial situation, create three short-term goals and three intermediate-term and long-term goals.

Your short-term goals should be goals that you can realistically accomplish in one year. They may include, but are not limited to, paying off credit card balances, beginning a 401(k) or other retirement-type savings program, or getting your cash inflows and outflows in balance.

Your intermediate-term goals are goals that you should realistically be able to accomplish in one to five years. They may include, but are not limited to, purchasing a new vehicle or paying off school loans.

Long-term goals will take longer than five years to accomplish realistically. They may include, but are not limited to, purchasing a home, taking a major trip (such as a summer in Europe), or saving sufficient funds to retire at a predetermined age.

The goals that you develop are a first draft and may be added to or modified as you proceed through this course. This course is designed to provide you with information and insight that will help you make informed decisions about your financial future. As you gain experience in financial planning, new goals may emerge, and existing goals may change. Once you have completed your financial plan, you should review your goals annually or whenever a significant change occurs in your life (e.g., marriage, divorce, birth of a child, or a significant change in employment circumstances).

Go to the worksheets at the end of this chapter and to the CD-ROM accompanying this text to begin building your financial plan.

THE SAMPSONS—A CONTINUING CASE

Dave and Sharon Sampson are 30 years old and have two children, who are five and six years old. Since marrying seven years ago, the Sampsons have relied on Dave's salary, which is currently $48,000 per year. They have not been able to save any money, as Dave's income is just enough to cover their mortgage loan payment and their other expenses.

Dave and Sharon feel they need to take control of their finances. Now that both children are in school, they have decided that Sharon will look into getting a part-time job. She was just hired for a part-time position at a local department store at a salary of $12,000 per year. Dave and Sharon are excited by the prospect of having additional cash inflows—they now feel they have the leeway to start working toward their financial goals.

The Sampsons own a home valued at about $100,000, and their mortgage is $90,000. They have a credit card balance of $2,000. Although they own two cars and do not have any car loans, Sharon's car is old and will need to be replaced soon. Sharon would really like to purchase a new car within the next year; she hopes to save $500 each month until she has accumulated savings of $5,000 to use for a down payment.

The Sampsons are also concerned about how they will pay for their children's college education. Sharon plans to save an additional $300 each month that will be set aside for this purpose.

The Sampsons also know they need to save for their retirement over time. Yet they do not have a plan right now to achieve that goal because they are focused on saving for a new car and their children's education. If the Sampsons were to start saving for retirement, they would probably consult a financial adviser.

The Sampsons have decided to develop a financial plan. They realize that by formally identifying their main goals, they will be able to implement and monitor their plan over time. At the end of every chapter, you will help the Sampsons develop their financial plan using the key concepts presented in the chapter.

Go to the worksheets at the end of this chapter, and to the CD-ROM accompanying this text to begin this case.

Chapter 8: Building Your Own Financial Plan

GOALS

1. Evaluate your current financial situation.
2. Set short-term, intermediate-term, and long-term goals.

ANALYSIS

1. Complete the Personal Financial Goals worksheet below.

Personal Financial Goals

Financial Goal	Dollar Amount to Accomplish	Priority (Low, Medium, High)
Short-Term Goals		
1.		
2.		
3.		
Intermediate-Term Goals		
1.		
2.		
3.		
Long-Term Goals		
1.		
2.		
3.		

2. A key part of the process of establishing your goals is evaluating your financial situation and career choices. Go to the "Occupational Outlook Handbook, 2004–05 Edition" (www.bls.gov/oco/home.htm) and research two careers that interest you. Complete the worksheet on the next page with the information you find on this Web site.

Personal Career Goals

	Career One	Career Two
Job Title		
Educational Requirements		
Advancement Potential		
Job Outlook		
Salary Range		
Continuing Education Requirements		
Related Occupations		
Brief Description of Working Conditions		
Brief Job Description		

DECISIONS

Describe your strategies for reaching your goals.

_____

_____

_____

_____

_____

_____

_____

_____

_____

_____

_____

_____

_____

_____

_____

_____

Chapter 8: The Sampsons—A Continuing Case

CASE QUESTION

Help the Sampsons summarize their current financial position, their goals, and their plans for achieving their goals by filling out the following worksheets.

Current Financial Position

Major Assets	Amount
Savings (High, Medium, or Low)	
Money Owed	
Salary	

Financial Goals

Goal 1. Purchase a new car for Sharon this year

How to Achieve the Goal	
How to Implement the Plan	
How to Evaluate the Plan	

Goal 2. Pay for the children's college education in 12–17 years from now

How to Achieve the Goal	
How to Implement the Plan	
How to Evaluate the Plan	

Goal 3. Set aside money for retirement

How to Achieve the Goal	
How to Implement the Plan	
How to Evaluate the Plan	

CHAPTER 9

Planning with Personal Financial Statements

Where does it all go? It seems like the last paycheck is gone before the next one comes in. Money seems to burn a hole in your pocket, yet you don't believe that you are living extravagantly. Last month you made a pledge to yourself to spend less than the month before. Somehow, though, you are in the same position as you were last month. Your money is gone. Is there any way to plug the hole in your pocket?

What are your expenses? For many people, the first obstacle is to correctly assess their true expenses. Each expense seems harmless and worthwhile. But combined they can be like a pack of piranhas that quickly gobble up your modest income. What can you do to gain control of your personal finances?

Just read on in this chapter and you will see how to take control of your finances. However, your task is not easy because it takes self-discipline and there may be no immediate reward. The result is often like a diet: easy to get started, but hard to carry through.

Your tools are the personal balance statement, the personal cash flow statement, and a budget. These three personal financial statements show you where you are, predict where you will be after three months or a year, and help you control expenses. The potential benefits are reduced spending, increased savings and investments, and peace of mind from knowing that you are in control.

The objectives of this chapter are to:

- Explain how to create your personal cash flow statement
- Identify the factors that affect your cash flows
- Show how to create a budget based on your forecasted cash flows
- Describe how to create your personal balance sheet
- Explain how your net cash flows are related to your personal balance sheet (and therefore affect your wealth)

■ PERSONAL CASH FLOW STATEMENT

You may commonly ask whether you can afford a new television, a new car, another year of education, or a vacation. You can answer these questions by determining your financial position. Specifically, you use what you know about your income and spending habits to estimate how much cash you will have at the end of this week, or quarter, or year. Once you obtain an estimate, you can decide if there are ways in which you can either increase your income or reduce your spending in order to achieve a higher level of cash.

As mentioned in Chapter 8, budgeting is the process of forecasting future expenses and savings. When budgeting, the first step is to create a **personal cash flow statement**, which measures your cash inflows and cash outflows. Comparing your cash inflows and outflows allows you to monitor your spending and determine the amount of cash that you can allocate toward savings or other purposes.

personal cash flow statement
A financial statement that measures a person's cash inflows and cash outflows.

Cash Inflows

The main source of cash inflows for working people is their salary, but there can be other important sources of income. Deposits in various types of savings accounts can generate cash inflows in the form of interest income. Some stocks also generate quarterly dividend income.

Cash Outflows

Cash outflows represent all of your expenses. Expenses are both large (for example, monthly rent) and small (for example, dry cleaning costs). It is not necessary to document every expenditure, but you should track how most of your money is spent. Recording transactions in your checkbook when you write checks helps you to identify how you spent your money. Using a credit card for your purchases also provides a written record of your transactions. Many people use software programs such as Quicken and Microsoft Money to record and monitor cash outflows.

Creating a Personal Cash Flow Statement

You can create a personal cash flow statement by recording how you received cash over a given period and how you used cash for expenses.

EXAMPLE

Stephanie Spratt tried to limit her spending in college but never created a personal cash flow statement. Now that she has begun her career and is earning a salary, she wants to monitor her spending on a monthly basis. She decides to create a personal cash flow statement for the last month.

Stephanie's Monthly Cash Inflows. Stephanie's present salary is about $3,170 per month ($38,000 annually) before taxes. For budgeting purposes, she is interested in the cash inflow she receives from her employer after taxes.

About $670 per month of her salary goes to taxes, so her disposable (after-tax) income is:

Monthly Salary	$3,170
– Monthly Taxes	– $670
Monthly Cash Inflow	$2,500

Then Stephanie considers other potential sources of cash inflows. She does not receive any dividend income from stocks and she does not have any money deposited in an account that pays interest. Thus, her entire monthly cash inflows come from her paycheck. She inserts the monthly cash inflow of $2,500 at the top of her personal cash flow statement.

Stephanie's Monthly Cash Outflows. Stephanie looks in her checkbook register to see how she spent her money last month. Her household payments for the month were as follows:

- $600 for rent
- $50 for cable TV
- $60 for electricity and water
- $60 for telephone expenses
- $300 for groceries
- $130 for a health care plan provided by her employer (this expense is deducted directly from her pay)

Next Stephanie reviews several credit card bills to estimate her other typical expenses on a monthly basis:

- About $100 for clothing
- About $200 for car expenses (insurance, maintenance, and gas)
- About $600 for recreation (including restaurants and a health club membership)

Stephanie uses this cash outflow information to complete her personal cash flow statement, as shown in Exhibit 9.1. Her total cash outflows were $2,100 last month.

Stephanie's Net Cash Flows. Monthly cash inflows and outflows can be compared by estimating **net cash flows**, which are equal to the cash inflows minus the cash outflows. Stephanie estimates her net cash flows to determine how easily she covers her expenses and how much excess cash she has to allocate to savings or other purposes. Her net cash flows during the last month were:

Net Cash Flows	= Cash Inflows	– Cash Outflows	
	= $2,500	– $2,100	
	= $400		

Stephanie enters this information at the bottom of her personal cash flow statement.

net cash flows
Cash inflows minus cash outflows.

■ FACTORS THAT AFFECT CASH FLOWS

To enhance your wealth, you want to maximize your (or your household's) cash inflows and minimize cash outflows. Your cash inflows and outflows depend on various factors, as will be described next.

Factors Affecting Cash Inflows

Cash inflows are highly influenced by factors that affect your income level. The key factors to consider are the stage in your career path and your job skills.

Stage in Your Career Path. The stage you have reached in your career path influences cash inflows because it affects your income level. Cash inflows are relatively low for

Exhibit 9.1	Personal Cash Flow Statement for Stephanie Spratt

Cash Inflows	Last Month
Disposable (after-tax) income	$2,500
Interest on deposits	0
Dividend payments	0
Total Cash Inflows	**$2,500**

Cash Outflows	Last Month
Rent	$600
Cable TV	50
Electricity and water	60
Telephone	60
Groceries	300
Health care insurance and expenses	130
Clothing	100
Car expenses (insurance, maintenance, and gas)	200
Recreation	600
Total Cash Outflows	**$2,100**
Net Cash Flows	**+$400**

people who are in college or just starting a career (like Stephanie Spratt). They tend to increase as you gain job experience and progress within your chosen career.

Your career stage is closely related to your place in the life cycle. Younger people tend to be at early stages in their respective careers, whereas older people tend to have more work experience and are thus further along the career path. It follows that cash inflows tend to be lower for younger individuals and much higher for individuals in their 50s.

There are many exceptions to this trend, however. Some older people switch careers and therefore may be set back on their career path. Other individuals who switch careers from a low-demand industry to a high-demand industry may actually earn higher incomes. Many women put their careers on hold for several years to raise children and then resume their professional lives.

The final stage in the life cycle that we will consider is retirement. The cash flows that come from a salary are discontinued at the time of retirement. After retirement, individuals rely on Social Security payments and interest or dividends earned on investments as sources of income. Consequently, retired individuals' cash inflows tend to be smaller than when they were working. Your retirement cash inflows will come from income from your investments and from your retirement plan. The manner in which age commonly affects cash inflows is summarized in Exhibit 9.2. Notice that there are three distinct phases.

Type of Job. Income also varies by job type. Jobs that require specialized skills tend to pay much higher salaries than those that require skills that can be obtained very quickly and easily. The income level associated with specific skills is also affected by the demand for those skills. The demand for people with a nursing license has been very high in recent years, so hospitals have been forced to pay high salaries to outbid other hospitals for nurses. Conversely, the demand for people with a history or an English literature degree is low because the number of students who major in these areas outnumber available jobs.

Exhibit 9.2   How Your Cash Inflows Are Related to Your Age

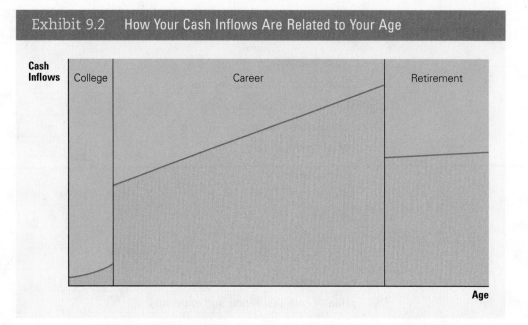

Number of Income Earners in Your Household. If you are the sole income earner, your household's cash inflows will typically be less than if there is a second income earner. Many households now have two income earners, a trend that has substantially increased the cash flows to these households.

Factors Affecting Cash Outflows

The key factors that affect cash outflows are a person's family status, age, and personal consumption behavior.

Size of Family. A person who is supporting a family will normally incur more expenses than a single person without dependents. The more family members, the greater the amount of spending, and the greater the cash outflows. Expenses for food, clothing, day care, and school tuition are higher for families with many dependents.

Age. As people get older, they tend to spend more money on expensive houses, cars, and vacations. This adjustment in spending may result from the increase in their income (cash inflows) over time as they progress along their career path.

Personal Consumption Behavior. People's consumption behavior varies substantially. At one extreme are people who spend their entire paycheck within a few days of receiving it, regardless of the size of the paycheck. Although this behavior is understandable for people who have low incomes, it is also a common practice for some people who have very large incomes, perhaps because they do not understand the importance of saving for the future. At the other extreme are "big savers" who minimize their spending and focus on saving for the future. Most people's consumption behavior is affected by their income. For example, a two-income household tends to spend more money when both income earners are working full-time.

■ CREATING A BUDGET

budget
A cash flow statement that is based on forecasted cash flows for a future time period.

The next step in the budgeting process is an extension of the personal cash flow statement. You can forecast net cash flows by forecasting the cash inflows and outflows for each item on the personal cash flow statement. We refer to a cash flow statement that is based on forecasted cash flows for a future time period as a **budget.** For example, you may develop a budget to determine whether your cash inflows will be sufficient to cover your cash outflows. If you expect your cash inflows to exceed your cash outflows, you can also use the budget to determine the amount of excess cash that you will have available to invest in additional assets or to make extra payments to reduce your personal debt.

EXAMPLE

Stephanie Spratt wants to determine whether she will have sufficient cash inflows this month. She uses the personal cash flow statement she developed last month to forecast this month's cash flows. However, she adjusts that statement for the following additional anticipated expenses:

1. Total health care expenses will be $430 this month, due to a minor health care procedure she had done recently that is not covered by her insurance.
2. Car maintenance expenses will be $500 this month, mainly due to the need to purchase new tires for her car.

Stephanie revises her personal cash flow statement from last month to reflect the expected changes this month, as shown in Exhibit 9.3. The numbers in boldface type show the revised cash flows as a result of the unusual circumstances for this month.

The main effects of the unusual circumstances on Stephanie's expected cash flows for this month are summarized in Exhibit 9.4. Notice that the expected cash outflows for this month are $2,700, or $600 higher than the cash outflows in a typical month. In this month, the expected net cash flows are:

Expected Net Cash Flows = Expected Cash Inflows – Expected Cash Outflows

= $2,500   – $2,700

= –$200

The budgeting process has alerted Stephanie to this $200 cash shortage.

Exhibit 9.3   Stephanie Spratt's Revised Personal Cash Flow Statement

Cash Inflows	Actual Amounts Last Month	Expected Amounts This Month
Disposable (after-tax) income	$2,500	$2,500
Interest on deposits	0	0
Dividend payments	0	0
Total Cash Inflows	**$2,500**	**$2,500**

Cash Outflows	Actual Amounts Last Month	Expected Amounts This Month
Rent	$600	$600
Cable TV	50	50
Electricity and water	60	60
Telephone	60	60
Groceries	300	300
Health care insurance and expenses	130	**430**
Clothing	100	100
Car expenses (insurance, maintenance, and gas)	200	**500**
Recreation	600	600
Total Cash Outflows	**$2,100**	**$2,700**
Net Cash Flows	**+$400**	**–$200**

Exhibit 9.4	Summary of Stephanie Spratt's Revised Cash Flows		
	Last Month's Cash Flow Situation	**Unusual Cash Flows Expected This Month**	**This Month's Cash Flow Situation**
Cash inflows	$2,500	$ 0	$2,500
Cash outflows	$2,100	$600	$2,700
Net cash flows	$ 400	–$600	–$200

Anticipating Cash Shortages

In a month with a large amount of unexpected expenses, you may not have sufficient cash inflows to cover your expected cash outflows. If the cash shortage is small, you would likely withdraw funds from your checking account to make up the difference. If you expect a major deficiency for a future month, however, you might not have sufficient funds available to cover it. The budget can warn you of such a problem well in advance so that you can determine how to cover the deficiency. You should set aside funds in a savings account that can serve as an emergency fund in the event that you experience a cash shortage.

Assessing the Accuracy of the Budget

Periodically compare your actual cash flows over a recent period (such as last month) to the forecasted cash flows in your budget to determine whether your forecasts are on target. Many individuals tend to be overly optimistic about their cash flow forecasts. They overestimate their cash inflows and underestimate their cash outflows; as a result, their net cash flows are lower than expected. By detecting such forecasting errors, you can take steps to improve your budgeting. You may decide to limit your spending to stay within your budgeted cash outflows. Or you may choose not to adjust your spending habits, but to increase your forecast of cash outflows to reflect reality. By budgeting accurately, you are more likely to detect any future cash flow shortages and therefore can prepare in advance for any deficiencies.

EXAMPLE

Recall that Stephanie Spratt forecasted cash flows to create a budget for this coming month. Now it is the end of the month, so she can assess whether her forecasts were accurate. Her forecasted cash flows are shown in the second column of Exhibit 9.5. She compares the actual cash flows (third column) to her forecast and calculates the difference between them (shown in the fourth column). This difference between columns two and three is referred to as the *forecasting error*. A positive difference means that the actual cash flow level was less than forecasted, while a negative difference means that the actual cash flow level exceeded the forecast.

Reviewing the fourth column of Exhibit 9.5, Stephanie notices that total cash outflows were $100 more than expected. Her net cash flows were –$300 (a deficiency of $300), which is worse than the expected level of –$200. Stephanie assesses the individual cash outflows to determine where she underestimated. Although grocery expenses were slightly lower than expected, her clothing and recreation expenses were higher than she anticipated. She decides that the expenses were abnormally high in this month only, so she believes that her budgeted cash flows should be reasonably accurate in most months.

Forecasting Net Cash Flows over Several Months

To forecast your cash flows for several months ahead, you can follow the same process as for forecasting one month ahead. Whenever particular types of cash flows are

Exhibit 9.5   Comparison of Stephanie Spratt's Budgeted and Actual Cash Flows for This Month

Cash Inflows	Expected Amounts (forecasted at the beginning of the month)	Actual Amounts (determined at the end of the month)	Forecasting Error
Disposable (after-tax) income	$2,500	$2,500	$0
Interest on deposits	0	0	0
Dividend payments	0	0	0
Total Cash Inflows	**$2,500**	**$2,500**	**$0**
Cash Outflows	**Expected Amounts**	**Actual Amounts**	**Forecasting Error**
Rent	$600	$600	$0
Cable TV	50	50	0
Electricity and water	60	60	0
Telephone	60	60	0
Groceries	300	280	+20
Health care insurance and expenses	430	430	0
Clothing	100	170	–70
Car expenses (insurance, maintenance, and gas)	500	500	0
Recreation	600	650	–50
Total Cash Outflows	**$2,700**	**$2,800**	**–$100**
Net Cash Flows	**–$200**	**–$300**	**–$100**

expected to be normal, they can be forecasted from previous months when the levels were normal. You can make adjustments to account for any cash flows that you expect to be unusual in a specific month in the future. (For example, around the winter holidays you can expect to spend more on gifts and recreation.)

Expenses such as health care, car repairs, and household repairs often occur unexpectedly. Although such expenses are not always predictable, you should budget for them periodically. You should assume that you will likely incur some unexpected expenses for health care as well as for repairs on a car or on household items over the course of several months. Thus, your budget may not be perfectly accurate in any specific month, but it will be reasonably accurate over time. If you do not account for such possible expenses over time, you will likely experience lower net cash flows than expected over time.

Creating an Annual Budget

If you are curious about how much money you may be able to save in the next year, you can extend your budget out for longer periods. You should first create an annual budget and then adjust it to reflect anticipated large changes in your cash flows.

EXAMPLE

Stephanie Spratt believes her budget for last month (except for the unusual health care and car expenses) is typical for her. She wants to extend it to forecast the amount of money that she might be able to save over the next year. Her cash inflows are predictable because she already knows her salary for the year. Some of the monthly cash outflows (such as rent and the cable bill) in her monthly budget are also constant from one month to another. To forecast these types of cash outflows, she simply multiplies the monthly amount by 12 (for each month of the year) to derive an estimate of the annual expenses, as shown in the third column of Exhibit 9.6.

Some other items vary from month to month, but last month's budgeted amount seems a reasonable estimate for the next 12 months. Over the next 12 months Stephanie expects net cash flows of $4,800. Therefore, she sets a goal of saving $4,800, which she can place in a bank account or invest in stocks.

Improving the Budget

As time passes, you should review your budget to determine whether you are progressing toward the financial goals that you established. To increase your savings or pay down more debt so that you can more easily achieve your financial goals, you should identify the components within the budget that you can change to improve your budget over time.

EXAMPLE

Recall that Stephanie Spratt expects to spend about $2,100 and invest the remaining $400 in assets (such as bank accounts or stocks) each month. She would like to save a substantial amount of money so that she can purchase a new car and a home someday, so she considers how she might increase her net cash flows.

Stephanie assesses her personal income statement to determine whether she can increase her cash inflows or reduce her cash outflows. She would like to generate more

Exhibit 9.6   Annual Budget for Stephanie Spratt

Cash Inflows	Typical Month	This Year's Cash Flows (equal to the typical monthly cash flows × 12)
Disposable (after-tax) income	$2,500	$30,000
Interest on deposits	0	0
Dividend payments	0	0
Total Cash Inflows	**$2,500**	**$30,000**

Cash Outflows	Typical Month	This Year's Cash Flows
Rent	$600	$7,200
Cable TV	50	600
Electricity and water	60	720
Telephone	60	720
Groceries	300	3,600
Health care insurance and expenses	130	1,560
Clothing	100	1,200
Car expenses (insurance, maintenance, and gas)	200	2,400
Recreation	600	7,200
Total Cash Outflows	**$2,100**	**$25,200**
Net Cash Flows	**+$400**	**$4,800 (difference between cash inflows and outflows)**

cash inflows than $2,500, but she is already paid well, given her skills and experience. She considers pursuing a part-time job on weekends, but does not want to use her limited free time to work. Therefore, she realizes that given her present situation and preferences, she will not be able to increase her monthly cash inflows. She decides to reduce her monthly cash outflows so that she can save more than $400 per month.

Stephanie reviews the summary of cash outflows on her budget to determine how she can reduce spending. Of the $2,100 that she spends per month, about $1,500 is spent on what she considers necessities (such as her rent and utilities). The remainder of the cash outflows (about $600) is spent on recreation; Stephanie realizes that any major reduction in spending will have to be in this category of cash outflows.

Most of her recreation spending is on her health club membership and eating at restaurants. She recognizes that she can scale back her spending while still enjoying these activities. Specifically, she observes that her health club is upscale and overpriced. She can save about $60 per month by going to a different health club that offers essentially the same services. She also decides to reduce her spending at restaurants by about $40 per month. By revising her spending behavior in these ways, she can reduce her cash outflows by $100 per month, as summarized here:

	Previous Cash Flow Situation	Planned Cash Flow Situation
Monthly cash inflows	$2,500	$2,500
Monthly cash outflows	$2,100	$2,000
Monthly net cash flows	$400	$500
Yearly net cash flows	$4,800	$6,000

This reduction in spending will increase net cash flows from the present level of about $400 per month to a new level of $500 per month. Over the course of a year, her net cash flows will now be $6,000. Although Stephanie had hoped to find a solution that would improve her personal cash flow statement more substantially, she believes this is a good start. Most importantly, her budget is realistic.

Financial Planning Online 9.1: **Budgeting Tips**

Go to
www.moneycrashers.com/
five-steps-to-effective
-budgeting/

Click
"Budget to Save"

This Web site provides
tips on effective budgeting
based on your goals.

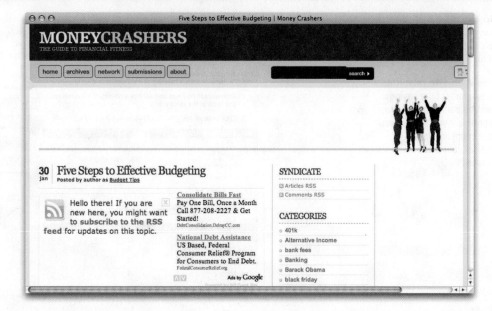

FOCUS ON ETHICS: **Excessive Financial Dependence**

Have you ever been faced with a large unexpected expense that forced you to ask for financial assistance from your family or your friends? Such a situation could result from a failure to maintain a budget or to even set a budget. Other causes are unexpected expenses. Perhaps your car breaks down and needs some expensive repairs. Or perhaps you see something that you would really like to buy, but you know you cannot afford it. If you have not planned for such a large expenditure, you may not have money to pay for it. Faced with a looming debt, it may seem easy to fall back on your family for support. Beware of relying too much on such support. When you fail to control your own budget, your reliance on others over long periods of time can create tension with your relatives and can ultimately destroy family relationships.

You must become self-reliant. While there are times when an emergency may force you to rely on family or friends for financial assistance, you should not take such help for granted on a regular and long-term basis. Create a budget and stay within it. Build and maintain an emergency fund so that you need not rely on others in times of financial crisis. Before you seek help from family members or friends, ask yourself if you have done all you can on your own. Is your financial crisis an unforeseen emergency or did you spend the money earlier instead of saving it for this expense? Careful budgeting and controlled spending lead to self-reliance and a feeling of financial freedom.

■ PERSONAL BALANCE SHEET

personal balance sheet
A summary of your assets (what you own), your liabilities (what you owe), and your net worth (assets minus liabilities).

The next step in the budgeting process is to create a personal balance sheet. A budget tracks your cash flows over a given period of time, whereas a personal balance sheet provides an overall snapshot of your wealth at a specific point in time. The **personal balance sheet** summarizes your **assets** (what you own), your **liabilities** (what you owe), and your net worth (assets minus liabilities).

Assets

The assets on a balance sheet can be classified as liquid assets, household assets, and investments.

Financial Planning Online 9.2: **The Impact of Reduced Spending**

Go to
www.calculatorweb.com/
calculators/savingscalc
.shtml

This Web site provides an estimate of the savings that you can accumulate over time if you can reduce your spending on one or more of your monthly expenses.

Savings Calculator – CalculatorWeb

SAVINGS CALCULATOR

INSTRUCTIONS

This calculator is designed to help you estimate your interest earned and final balance from a monthly savings investment.

1. Enter your investment and savings amounts, the interest rate and term of the investment.

2. Click once on the "Calculate" button to calculate your result.

ENTER DETAILS HERE

Initial Lump Sum Investment	$	
Monthly Savings	$	
Interest Rate		%
Term of Investment		years

Calculate   Reset

RESULT

Total Amount Invested	$	
Interest Earned	$	
Final Balance	$	

Free Tools Online
Book Club
Send A Postcard
Discussion Forums
Live Chat
News Headlines

From

CLICK DAY TRADING

MoneyWeb

liquid assets
Financial assets that can be easily sold without a loss in value.

Liquid Assets. **Liquid assets** are financial assets that can be easily sold without a loss in value. They are especially useful for covering upcoming expenses. Some of the more common liquid assets are cash, checking accounts, and savings accounts. Cash is handy to cover small purchases, while a checking account is convenient for larger purchases. Savings accounts are desirable because they pay interest on the money that is deposited. For example, if your savings account offers an interest rate of 4 percent, you earn annual interest of $4 for every $100 deposited in your account.

household assets
Items normally owned by a household, such as a home, car, and furniture.

Household Assets. **Household assets** include items normally owned by a household, such as a home, car, and furniture. These items tend to make up a larger proportion of your total assets than the liquid assets.

When creating a personal balance sheet, you need to assess the value of your household assets. The market value of an asset is the amount you would receive if you sold the asset today. For example, if you purchased a car last year for $20,000, the car may have a market value of $14,000 today, meaning that you could sell it to someone else for $14,000. The market values of cars can easily be obtained from various sources on the Internet, such as kbb.com. Although establishing the precise market value of some assets such as a house may be difficult, you can use recent selling prices of other similar houses nearby to obtain a reasonable estimate.

Investments. Some of the more common investments are in bonds, stocks, and rental property.

bonds
Certificates issued by borrowers to raise funds.

Bonds are certificates issued by borrowers (typically firms and government agencies) to raise funds. When you purchase a $1,000 bond that was just issued, you provide a $1,000 loan to the issuer of the bond. You earn interest while you hold the bond for a specified period. (Bonds are discussed further in Chapter 16.)

stocks
Certificates representing partial ownership of a firm.

Stocks are certificates representing partial ownership of a firm. Firms issue stock to obtain funding for various purposes, such as purchasing new machinery or building new facilities. Many firms have millions of shareholders who own shares of the firm's stock.

The investors who purchase stock are referred to as shareholders or stockholders. You may consider purchasing stocks if you have excess funds. You can sell some of your stock holdings when you need funds.

Financial Planning Online 9.3: **Financial Planning Online: Budgeting Advice**

Go to
www.calculatorweb.com/calculators/budgetcalc/

This Web site provides a means for comparing your actual budget versus your desired budget (based on your income and spending habits) and shows how you could improve your budget.

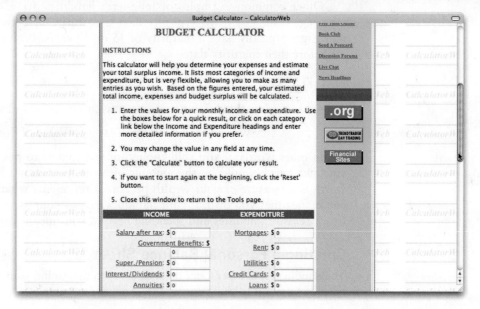

The market value of stocks changes daily. You can find the current market value of a stock at many Web sites, including finance.yahoo.com. Stock investors can earn a return on their investment if the stock's value increases over time. They can also earn a return if the firm pays dividends to its shareholders.

Investments such as stocks normally are not considered liquid assets because they can result in a loss in value if they have to be sold suddenly. Stocks are commonly viewed as a long-term investment and therefore are not used to cover day-to-day expenses. (Stocks will be discussed in detail in Chapter 16.)

Mutual funds sell shares to individuals and invest the proceeds in an overall portfolio of investment instruments such as bonds or stocks. They are managed by portfolio managers who decide what securities to purchase so that the individual investors do not have to make the investment decisions themselves. The minimum investment varies depending on the particular fund, but it is usually between $500 and $3,000. The value of the shares of any mutual fund can be found in periodicals such as *The Wall Street Journal* or on various Web sites. We'll examine mutual funds in detail in Chapter 16.

Real estate includes holdings in rental property and land. **Rental property** is housing or commercial property that is rented out to others. Some individuals purchase a second home and rent it out to generate additional income every year. Others purchase apartment complexes for the same reason. Some individuals purchase land as an investment.

mutual funds
Investment companies that sell shares to individuals and invest the proceeds in investment instruments such as bonds or stocks.

real estate
Rental property and land.

rental property
Housing or commercial property that is rented out to others.

Liabilities

Liabilities represent debt (what you owe) and can be segmented into current liabilities and long-term liabilities.

Current Liabilities. **Current liabilities** are debt that you will pay off in the near future (within a year). The most common example of a current liability is a credit card balance that will be paid off in the near future. Credit card companies send the cardholder a monthly bill that itemizes all the purchases made in the previous month. If you pay your balance in full upon receipt of the bill, no interest is charged on the balance. The liability is then eliminated until you receive the next monthly bill.

current liabilities
Debt that will be paid within a year.

Long-Term Liabilities. **Long-term liabilities** are debt that will be paid over a period beyond one year. A common long-term liability is a student loan, which reflects debt that a student must pay back to a lender over time after graduation. This liability requires you to pay an interest expense periodically. Once you pay off this loan, you eliminate this liability and do not have to pay any more interest expenses. In general, you should limit your liabilities so that you can limit the amount of interest owed.

Other common examples of long-term liabilities are a car loan and a mortgage (housing) loan. Car loans typically have a maturity of between 3 and 5 years, while mortgages typically have a maturity of 15 or 30 years. Both types of loans can be paid off before their maturity date.

long-term liabilities
Debt that will be paid over a period longer than one year.

Net Worth

Your net worth is the difference between what you own and what you owe.

Net Worth = Value of Total Assets − Value of Total Liabilities

In other words, if you sold enough of your assets to pay off all of your liabilities, your net worth would be the amount of assets you would have remaining. Your net worth is a measure of your wealth because it represents what you own after deducting any money that you owe. If your liabilities exceed your assets, your net worth is negative. Excessive liabilities and spending beyond your means can lead to bankruptcy.

Creating a Personal Balance Sheet

You should create a personal balance sheet to determine your net worth. Update it periodically to monitor how your wealth changes over time.

EXAMPLE

Stephanie Spratt wants to determine her net worth by creating a personal balance sheet that identifies her assets and her liabilities.

Stephanie's Assets. Stephanie owns:

- $500 in cash
- $3,500 in her checking account
- Furniture in her apartment that is worth about $1,000
- A car that is worth about $1,000
- 100 shares of stock that she just purchased for $3,000 ($30 per share), which does not pay dividends

Stephanie uses this information to complete the top of her personal balance sheet, shown in Exhibit 9.7. She classifies each item that she owns as a liquid asset, a household asset, or an investment asset.

Stephanie's Liabilities. Stephanie owes $2,000 on her credit card. She does not have any other liabilities at this time, so she lists the one liability on her personal balance sheet under "Current Liabilities" because she will pay off the debt soon. Since she has no long-term liabilities at this time, her total liabilities are $2,000.

Stephanie's Net Worth. Stephanie determines her net worth as the difference between her total assets and total liabilities. Notice from her personal balance sheet that her total assets are valued at $9,000, while her total liabilities are valued at $2,000. Thus, her net worth is:

$$
\begin{aligned}
\text{Net Worth} &= \text{Total Assets} - \text{Total Liabilities} \\
&= \$9,000 - \$2,000 \\
&= \$7,000
\end{aligned}
$$

Changes in the Personal Balance Sheet

If you earn new income this month but spend all of it on products or services such as rent, food, and concert tickets that are not personal assets, you will not increase your net worth. As you invest in assets, your personal balance sheet will change. In some cases, such as when you purchase a home, your assets increase while at the same time your liabilities may increase from taking on a mortgage. In any case, your net worth will not grow unless the increase in the value of your assets exceeds the increase in your liabilities.

EXAMPLE

Stephanie Spratt is considering purchasing a new car for $20,000. To make the purchase, Stephanie would do the following:

- She would trade in her existing car, which has a market value of about $1,000.
- She would write a check for $3,000 as a down payment on the car.
- She would obtain a five-year loan for $16,000 to cover the remaining amount owed to the car dealer.

Her personal balance sheet would be affected as shown in Exhibit 9.8 and explained next.

Change in Stephanie's Assets. Stephanie's assets would change as follows:

- Her car would now have a market value of $20,000 instead of $1,000.
- Her checking account balance would be reduced from $3,500 to $500.

Thus, her total assets would increase by $16,000 (her new car would be valued at $19,000 more than her old one, but her checking account would be reduced by $3,000).

Exhibit 9.7	Stephanie Spratt's Personal Balance Sheet	
Assets		
Liquid Assets		
Cash		$500
Checking account		3,500
Savings account		0
Total liquid assets		$4,000
Household Assets		
Home		$0
Car		1,000
Furniture		1,000
Total household assets		$2,000
Investment Assets		
Stocks		$3,000
Total investment assets		$3,000
Total Assets		**$9,000**
Liabilities and Net Worth		
Current Liabilities		
Credit card balance		$2,000
Total current liabilities		$2,000
Long-Term Liabilities		
Mortgage		$0
Car loan		0
Total long-term liabilities		$0
Total Liabilities		**$2,000**
Net Worth		**$7,000**

Change in Stephanie's Liabilities. Stephanie's liabilities would also change:

- She would now have a long-term liability of $16,000 as a result of the car loan.

Therefore, her total liabilities would increase by $16,000 if she purchases the car.

Change in Stephanie's Net Worth. If Stephanie purchases the car, her net worth would be:

Net Worth	=	Total Assets	–	Total liabilities
	=	$25,000	–	$18,000
	=	$7,000		

Stephanie's net worth would remain unchanged as a result of buying the car because her total assets and total liabilities would increase by the same amount.

Stephanie's Decision. Because the purchase of a new car will not increase her net worth, she decides not to purchase the car at this time. Still, she is concerned that her old car will require expensive maintenance in the future, so she will likely buy a car in a few months once she improves her financial position.

Exhibit 9.8	Stephanie's Personal Balance Sheet if She Purchases a New Car

Assets

Liquid Assets	Present Situation	If She Purchases a New Car
Cash	$500	$500
Checking account	3,500	500
Savings account	0	0
Total liquid assets	$4,000	$1,000
Household Assets		
Home	$0	$0
Car	1,000	20,000
Furniture	1,000	1,000
Total household assets	$2,000	$21,000
Investment Assets		
Stocks	$3,000	$3,000
Total investment assets	$3,000	$3,000
Total Assets	**$9,000**	**$25,000**
Liabilities and Net Worth		
Current Liabilities		
Credit card balance	$2,000	$2,000
Total current liabilities	$2,000	$2,000
Long-Term Liabilities		
Mortgage	$0	$0
Car loan	0	16,000
Total long-term liabilities	$0	$16,000
Total Liabilities	**$2,000**	**$18,000**
Net Worth	**$7,000**	**$7,000**

How Cash Flows Affect the Personal Balance Sheet

The relationship between the personal cash flow statement and the personal balance sheet is shown in Exhibit 9.9. This relationship explains how you build wealth (net worth) over time. If you use net cash flows to invest in more assets, you increase the value of your assets without increasing your liabilities. Therefore, you increase your net worth. You can also increase your net worth by using net cash flows to reduce your liabilities. So, the more of your income that you allocate to investing in assets or to reducing your debt, the more wealth you will build.

Your net worth can change even if your net cash flows are zero. For example, if the market value of your car declines over time, the value of this asset is reduced and your net worth will decline. Conversely, if the value of a stock that you own increases, the value of your assets will rise, and your net worth will increase.

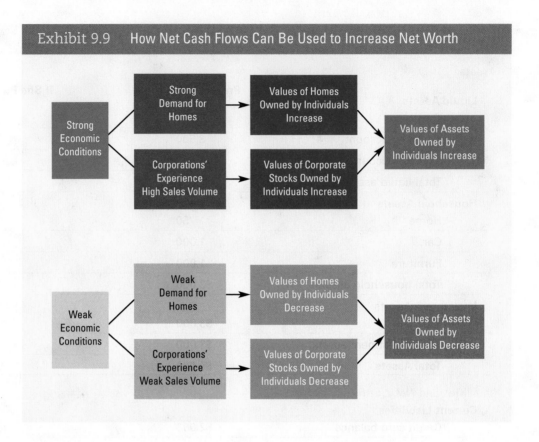

Exhibit 9.9   How Net Cash Flows Can Be Used to Increase Net Worth

ECONOMIC IMPACT

Impact of the Economy on the Personal Balance Sheet

Economic conditions can affect your cash flows, and therefore affect your personal balance sheet, as illustrated in Exhibit 9.10. Favorable economic conditions can increase job opportunities and therefore your income. Conversely, unfavorable economic conditions such as the financial crisis of 2008–2009 can result in the elimination of jobs and reduced income for some individuals.

Economic conditions also affect the value of your assets. Favorable economic conditions result in a high demand to purchase homes, which increases the values of homes. In addition, the values of stocks rise when economic conditions are favorable, because corporations experience higher sales of the products or services they produce. Conversely, weak economic conditions such as the financial crisis result in lower values of assets. Home prices declined substantially during the financial crisis, as demand for homes declined. Stock prices declined because the corporations experienced a reduction in sales. Many individuals experienced such a large decline in their asset value during the crisis that their assets were worth less than their liabilities. That is, their net worth became negative.

QUESTIONS

a. **Economic Impact on Asset Values.** Explain in logical terms why values of assets such as homes and stocks may decline during a weak economy.

b. **Economic Impact on Net Worth.** Explain in logical terms why a weak economy can cause the net worth of individuals to decline.

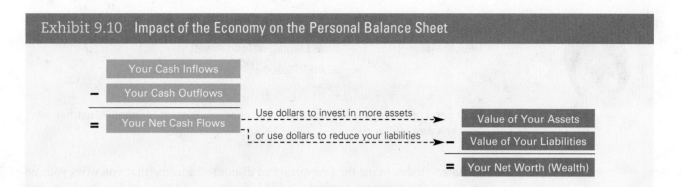

Exhibit 9.10 Impact of the Economy on the Personal Balance Sheet

Analysis of the Personal Balance Sheet

The budgeting process helps you monitor your cash flows and evaluate your net worth. In addition, by analyzing some financial characteristics within your personal balance sheet or cash flow statement, you can monitor your level of liquidity, your amount of debt, and your ability to save.

Liquidity. Recall that liquidity represents your access to funds to cover any short-term cash deficiencies. You need to monitor your liquidity over time to ensure that you have sufficient funds when they are needed. Your liquidity can be measured by the liquidity ratio, which is calculated as:

$$Liquidity\ Ratio = Liquid\ Assets/Current\ Liabilities$$

A high liquidity ratio indicates a higher degree of liquidity. For example, a liquidity ratio of 3.0 implies that for every dollar of liabilities that you will need to pay off in the near future, you have $3 in liquid assets. Thus, you could easily cover your short-term liabilities.

A liquidity ratio of less than 1.0 means that you do not have sufficient liquid assets to cover your upcoming payments. In this case, you might need to borrow funds.

EXAMPLE

Based on the information in her personal balance sheet shown in Exhibit 9.7, Stephanie measures her liquidity:

Liquidity Ratio	=	Liquid Assets/Current Liabilities
	=	$4,000/$2,000
	=	2.0

Stephanie's liquidity ratio of 2.0 means that for every dollar of current liabilities, she has $2 of liquid assets. This means that she has more than enough funds available to cover her current liabilities, so she is maintaining sufficient liquidity to cover her current liabilities.

Debt Level. You also need to monitor your debt level to ensure that it does not become so high that you are unable to cover your debt payments. A debt level of $20,000 would not be a serious problem for a person with assets of $100,000, but it could be quite serious for someone with hardly any assets. Thus, your debt level should be measured relative to your assets, as shown here:

$$Debt\text{-}to\text{-}Asset\ Ratio = Total\ Liabilities/Total\ Assets$$

A high debt ratio indicates an excessive amount of debt and should be reduced over time to avoid any debt repayment problems. Individuals in this position should review their cash flows to maximize inflows and minimize outflows.

EXAMPLE

Based on her personal balance sheet, Stephanie calculates her debt-to-asset ratio as:

Debt-to-Asset Ratio	=	Total Liabilities/Total Assets
	=	$2,000/$9,000
	=	22.22%

This 22.22 percent debt level is not a cause for concern. Even if Stephanie lost her job, she could still pay off her debt.

Savings Rate. To determine the proportion of disposable income that you save, you can measure your savings over a particular period in comparison to your disposable income (income after taxes are taken out) using the following formula:

Savings Rate = Savings during the Period/Disposable Income during the Period

EXAMPLE

Based on her cash flow statement, Stephanie earns $2,500 in a particular month and expects to have net cash flows of $400 for savings or investments. She calculates her typical savings rate per month as:

Savings Rate	=	Savings during the Period/Disposable Income during the Period
	=	$400/$2,500
	=	16%

Thus, Stephanie saves 16 percent of her disposable income.

■ HOW BUDGETING FITS WITHIN YOUR FINANCIAL PLAN

The key budgeting decisions for building your financial plan are:

- How can I improve my net cash flows in the near future?
- How can I improve my net cash flows in the distant future?

These decisions require initial estimates of your cash inflows and outflows and an assessment of how you might change your spending behavior to improve your budget over time. By limiting your spending, you may be able to increase your net cash flows and your net worth. Exhibit 9.11 provides an example of how the budgeting decisions apply to Stephanie Spratt's financial plan.

Exhibit 9.11   Application of Budgeting Concepts to Stephanie Spratt's Financial Plan

GOALS FOR A BUDGETING PLAN

1. Determine how I can increase my net cash flows in the near future.
2. Determine how I can increase my net cash flows in the distant future.

ANALYSIS

Present Situation:

Cash Inflows = $2,500 per month

Cash Outflows = $2,100 per month

Net Cash Flows = $400 per month

Estimated Savings per Year = $4,800 ($400 per month × 12 months)

Increase Net Cash Flows by:

Increasing my salary? (New job?)	*No. I like my job and have no plans to search for another job right now, even if it would pay a higher salary.*
Increasing my income provided by my investments?	*No. My investments are small at this point. I cannot rely on them to provide much income.*
Other? (If yes, explain.)	*No.*

Reduce Cash Outflows by:

Reducing my household expenses?	*No.*
Reducing my recreation expenses?	*Yes (by $100 per month).*
Reducing my other expenses?	*No.*

Overall, I identified only one adjustment to my budget, which will increase monthly net cash flows by $100.

DECISIONS

Decision to Increase Net Cash Flows in the Near Future:

I initially established a budget to save $4,800 per year. During the next year, I can attempt to save an additional $100 per month by reducing the amount I spend on recreation. I can increase my savings if I reduce cash outflows. By reducing cash outflows by $100 per month, my savings will increase from $400 to $500 per month. The only way that I can reduce cash outflows at this point is to reduce the amount I spend for recreation purposes.

Decision to Increase Net Cash Flows in the Distant Future:

My cash inflows will rise over time if my salary increases. If I can keep my cash outflows stable, my net cash flows (and therefore my savings) will increase. When I buy a new car or a home, my monthly cash outflows will increase as a result of the monthly loan payments. If I buy a new car or a home, I need to make sure that I limit my spending (and therefore limit the loan amount) so that I have sufficient cash inflows to cover the monthly loan payments along with my other typical monthly expenses.

If I get married someday, my husband would contribute to the cash inflows, which would increase net cash flows. We would be able to save more money and may consider buying a home. If I marry, my goal will be to save even more money per month than I save now, to prepare for the possibility of raising a family in the future.

DISCUSSION QUESTIONS

1. How would Stephanie's budgeting decisions be different if she were a single mother of two children?

2. How would Stephanie's budgeting decisions be affected if she were 35 years old? If she were 50 years old?

SUMMARY

- The personal cash flow statement measures your cash inflows, your cash outflows, and their difference (net cash flows) over a specific period. Cash inflows result from your salary or from income generated by your investments. Cash outflows result from your spending.

- Your cash inflows are primarily affected by your stage in your career path and your type of job.

Your cash outflows are influenced by your family status, age, and personal consumption behavior. If you develop specialized skills, you may be able to obtain a job position that increases your cash inflows. If you limit your consumption, you can limit your spending and therefore reduce your cash outflows. Either of these actions will increase net cash flows and thus allow you to increase your wealth.

- You can forecast net cash flows (and therefore anticipate cash deficiencies) by creating a budget, which is based on forecasted cash inflows and outflows for an upcoming period.

- The budgeting process allows you to control spending. Comparing your forecasted and actual income and expenses will show whether or not you were able to stay within the budget. By examining the difference between your forecast and the actual cash flow, you can determine areas of your budget that may need further control or areas of your budget that required less in expenditures than you predicted. This analysis will help you modify your spending in the future or perhaps adjust your future budgets.

- The personal balance sheet measures the value of your assets, your liabilities, and your net worth. The assets can be categorized into liquid assets, household assets, and investments. Liabilities can be categorized as current or long-term liabilities. The difference between total assets and total liabilities is net worth, which is a measure of your wealth.

- The net cash flows on the personal cash flow statement are related to the net worth on the personal balance sheet. When you have positive net cash flows over a period, you can invest that amount in additional assets, which results in an increase in your net worth (or your wealth). Alternatively, you may use the net cash flows to pay off liabilities, which also increases your wealth.

REVIEW QUESTIONS

1. **Personal Financial Statements.** What two personal financial statements are most important to personal financial planning?

2. **Cash Flows.** Define cash inflows and cash outflows and identify some sources of each. How are net cash flows determined?

3. **Changing Your Cash Flows.** In general, how can you modify your cash flows to enhance your wealth?

4. **Factors Affecting Cash Inflows.** Identify some factors that affect cash inflows.

5. **Factors Affecting Cash Outflows.** Identify some factors that affect cash outflows.

6. **Purpose of a Budget.** What is a budget? What is the purpose of a budget? How can a budget help when you are anticipating cash shortages or a cash surplus?

7. **Budget Accuracy.** How do you assess the accuracy of your budget? How can finding forecasting errors improve your budget?

8. **Unexpected Expenses.** How should unexpected expenses be handled in your budget? How might these expenses affect your budget for a specific month? Over time?

9. **Creating an Annual Budget.** Describe the process of creating an annual budget.

10. **Changing Your Budget.** Suppose you want to change your budget to increase your savings. What could you do?

11. **Cash Deficiencies.** How do you think people who do not create a budget may deal with cash deficiencies? How can this affect their personal relationships?

12. **Personal Balance Sheet.** What is a personal balance sheet?

13. **Asset Classifications.** Name three classifications of assets. Briefly define and give examples of each.

14. **Types of Investments.** What are bonds? What are stocks? What are mutual funds? Describe how each of these provides a return on your investment.

15. **Real Estate Investment.** Describe two ways real estate might provide a return on an investment.

16. **Types of Liabilities.** What are liabilities? Define current liabilities and long-term liabilities.

17. **Measuring Net Worth.** How is net worth a measure of wealth?

18. **Change in Net Worth.** When does your net worth increase? Will the purchase of additional assets always increase your net worth? Why or why not?

19. **Financial Characteristics.** What three financial characteristics can be monitored by analyzing your personal balance sheet?

20. **Liquidity Ratio.** What is the liquidity ratio? What does it indicate? How is the debt-to-asset ratio calculated? What does a high debt ratio indicate? How is your savings rate determined? What does it indicate?

21. **Personal Financial Statements.** Describe how wealth is built over time. How do your personal cash flow statement and your personal balance sheet assist in this process?

FINANCIAL PLANNING PROBLEMS

1. **Estimating Disposable Income.** Angela earns $2,170 per month before taxes in her full-time job and $900 before taxes in her part-time job. About $650 per month is needed to pay taxes. What is Angela's disposable income?

2. **Estimating Net Cash Flow.** Angela (from problem 1) inspects her checkbook and her credit card bills and determines that she has the following monthly expenses:

Rent	$500
Cable TV	30
Electricity	100
Water	25
Telephone	40
Groceries	400
Car expenses	350
Health insurance	200
Clothing and personal items	175
Recreation	300

What is Angela's net cash flow?

3. **Impact on Net Cash Flow.** Angela makes a budget based on her personal cash flow statement. In two months, she must pay $375 for tags and taxes on her car. How will this payment affect her net cash flow for that month? Suggest ways that Angela might handle this situation.

4. **Estimating Savings.** From the information in problems 1 through 3, how much can Angela expect to save in the next 12 months?

5. **Change in Savings.** Angela analyzes her personal budget and decides that she can reduce her recreational spending by $50 per month. How much will that increase her annual savings? What will her annual savings be now?

6. **Savings Rate.** If Angela is saving $350 per month, what is her savings rate (i.e., savings as a percentage of disposable income)?

7. **Estimating Liquidity.** Jarrod is a college student. All of Jarrod's disposable income is used to pay his college-related expenses. While he has no liabilities (Jarrod is on a scholarship), he does have a credit card that he typically uses for emergencies. He and his friend went on a shopping spree in New York City costing $2,000, which Jarrod charged to his credit card. Jarrod has $20 in his wallet, but his bank accounts are empty. What is Jarrod's liquidity ratio? What does this ratio indicate about Jarrod's financial position?

8. **Estimating Debt.** Jarrod (from problem 7) has an old TV worth about $100. Jarrod's other assets total about $150. What is Jarrod's debt-to-asset ratio? What does this indicate about Jarrod's financial position?

9. **Asset Levels.** Ryan and Nicole have the following assets:

	Fair Market Value
Home	$85,000
Cars	22,000
Furniture	14,000
Stocks	10,000
Savings account	5,000
Checking account	1,200
Bonds	15,000
Cash	150
Mutual funds	7,000
Land	19,000

What is the value of their liquid assets? What is the value of their household assets? What is the value of their investments?

10. **Liability Levels.** Ryan and Nicole have the following liabilities:

Mortgage	$43,500
Car loan	2,750
Credit card balance	165
Student loans	15,000
Furniture loan (6 months)	1,200

What are their current liabilities? What are their long-term liabilities? What is their net worth?

11. **Impact on Net Worth.** Ryan and Nicole would like to trade in one of their cars with a fair market value of $7,000 for a new one with a fair market value of $21,500. The dealer will take their car and provide a $15,000 loan for the new car. If they make this deal, what will be the effect on their net worth?

12. **Liquidity and Debt.** What is Ryan and Nicole's liquidity ratio? What is their debt-to-asset ratio? Comment on each ratio.

13. **ETHICAL DILEMMA:** Jason and Mia are in their early 20s and have been married for three years. They are eager to purchase their first house, but they do not have sufficient money for a down payment. Mia's Uncle Chris has agreed to loan them the money to purchase a small house. Uncle Chris requests a personal balance sheet and cash flow statement as well as tax returns for the last two years to verify their income and their ability to make monthly payments.

For the past two years, Chris has been working substantial overtime, which has increased his income by over 25 percent. The cash flow statements for the last two years show that Mia and Jason will have no difficulty making the payments Uncle Chris requires. However, Jason's company has informed their employees that the overtime will not continue in the coming year. Mia and Jason are concerned that if they prepare their personal cash flow statement based on Jason's base salary that Uncle Chris will not loan them the money because it will show the loan payments can only be made with very strict cost cutting and financial discipline. Therefore they elect to present just what Uncle Chris requested, which are the last two years' personal cash flow statements and tax returns. They decide not to provide any additional information unless he asks.

a. Comment on Mia and Jason's decision not to provide the information underlying their cash flow statement. What potential problems could result from their decision?

b. Discuss in general the disadvantages of borrowing money from relatives.

FINANCIAL PLANNING ONLINE EXERCISES

1. After reading the information contained on the Web site www.moneycrashers.com/five-steps -to-effective-budgeting/, answer the following questions:

   a. What are three good sources of information that can be accessed to begin the budgeting process?

   b. How important is it to write out your budget? What is a good software you can use that provides a template should you wish to write out your budget?

   c. Explain what is meant by "looking ahead budgeting."

   d. Explain one effective method discussed in the Web site for organizing your budget.

2. Go to calculators.aol.com/tools/aol/savings13/tool.fcs and go to "What's it worth to reduce my spending?"

   You can input various expenses that can be reduced and determine the savings that will accrue over time. Input your age, your age at retirement, 2 percent for the rate you can earn on savings, and 25 percent and 6 percent for the federal and state tax rates, respectively.

   a. If you waited to buy a car, you could, perhaps, save $220 monthly. Enter this information and go to the Results page to find out what this savings would amount to at retirement.

   b. If you ate out less, you could save, say, $150 monthly. Enter this information and go to the Results page to find out what this adds up to by retirement.

   c. If you went to fewer movies and reduced expenses by $50 monthly, how much extra could you save by retirement? Enter this information and go to the Results page to find out the impact.

   d. If you paid off credit card balances and reduced interest costs by $100 monthly, how much could you accumulate by retirement? Enter this information and go to the Results page to find out.

   e. If you took all these measures to reduce your spending, what is the total savings you could accrue at retirement? To find out, look at the bottom section on the Results page.

3. Go to calculators.aol.com/tools/aol/budget03/tool.fcs and go to "How much am I spending?"

   Do you want to know how your spending habits affect your future wealth? Using this information, you can fine-tune your budget.

   a. Enter an actual home payment or rent of $600 per month and a desired amount of $550. Determine the impact of only this difference on future wealth. You can also view the impact graphically by clicking on the Graph tab.

b. Enter an actual expense for utilities of $350 per month and your desired amount of $250. Calculate the effect of only this change on future wealth. You can also view the impact graphically by clicking on the Graph tab.

c. Enter an actual expense for food of $600 monthly and a desired amount of $500. Determine the financial consequences of only this change in figures. You can also view the results graphically by clicking on the Graph tab.

d. Enter actual entertainment expenses of $250 monthly and a desired amount of $175. Determine the financial impact of only this change on future wealth. You can also view

the results graphically by clicking on the Graph tab.

VIDEO EXERCISE: Budgeting

Go to one of the Web sites that contain video clips (such as www.youtube.com) and view some video clips about budgeting. You can use search phrases such as "budgeting tips." Select one video clip on this topic that you would recommend for the other students in your class.

1. Provide the Web link for the video clip.
2. What do you think is the main point of this video clip?
3. How might you change your budgeting as a result of watching this clip?

BUILDING YOUR OWN FINANCIAL PLAN

Two major components of any good personal financial plan are a personal cash flow statement and a balance sheet. If you are a full-time student, prepare your cash flow statement based upon your anticipated cash flow at graduation.

To prepare your personal balance sheet and cash flow statement, turn to the worksheets at the end of this chapter and to the CD-ROM accompanying this text. In most cases, you will not have all of the cash inflows and outflows or assets and liabilities listed on the worksheet.

When listing your liabilities, be sure to include any educational loans even if they are not payable until after graduation.

When preparing your personal cash flow statement, break down all expenses into the frequency in which you are/will be paid. For example, if your car insurance is $700 per year and you are paid monthly, divide the $700 by 12. If you are paid biweekly, divide the $700 by 26. Personal cash flow statements should be set up based upon the frequency of your pay. This way, each time you are paid, you can distribute your paycheck to the appropriate cash outflow categories.

If, after preparing your personal cash flow statement, you have an excess of cash outflows over cash inflows, you should review in detail each cash outflow to determine its necessity and whether it can realistically be reduced in order to balance your cash inflows and outflows. Using Web sites like www.firsttechcu.com/Calculators/budget/calculators_budget.html (click "What's it worth to reduce my spending?"), you can also estimate the savings that you can accumulate over time by reducing your cash outflows.

Personal financial statements should be reviewed annually or whenever you experience a change that affects your cash inflows such as getting a raise, obtaining a new job, marrying, or getting divorced.

Your Money Beyond Graduation

BEFORE YOU KNOW IT, college will be over. You'll graduate, and with luck, be starting a career and managing a full-time paycheck. There's no manual for the Real World, no set of instructions. You have to find your own path. That said, there's a great deal you can prepare for, at least mentally. Here's what you ought to know.

The Anatomy of a Real-World Budget

You gross income may be $45,000 a year during your first year out of school, but your take-home pay will usually be 25% to 30% less. That's because after state and federal taxes, social security, and possibly any monthly contributions you make to your company's health care and retirement plans, you end up with much less to budget with at the end of the month. $45,000 a year actually comes out to be more like $31,500 a year, or $2,625 a month. **Wondering how to allocate your paycheck?** Here's my general budget breakdown for young professionals.

Retirement – 10%

We often neglect to properly save for retirement because it feels like there's plenty of time to save later, especially when you're living paycheck to paycheck now. Remember: Social Security is not all it was cut out to be. The younger you are, the less likely it is you'll receive much, if any, money from the government. Begin by automatically investing at least up to 10% in your company's 401k program, a retirement savings account established by employers. Make sure you take advantage of any matching program your company provides. For example, if the company offers to invest 50 cents for every dollar you invest up to 6% of your income, invest at least 6% of your income. That's free money on the table! Additionally, consider opening an individual retirement account or IRA at your local bank—either a ROTH or a traditional plan. Which one you choose depends on your income level and what tax benefits you'd prefer. A ROTH has income limitations, but allows your investments to grow tax-free. A traditional IRA has no income limitations, but you can use your annual contributions to lower your taxable income.

Personal Savings – 10%

Having at least six months of your take-home pay in a liquid savings account for a rainy day or cash emergency is a true measure of financial freedom. Remember: Online bank accounts offer some of the highest interest rates.

Loans, Including Credit Card Debt – 20%

Attack your credit card debt by reducing your balance on your highest interest rate credit card first, since that's your most expensive debt. If your debt is far too difficult to manage, consult a credit counselor. Search for a certified counselor in your area at the Web site for the National Foundation for Credit Counseling, www.nfcc.org.

Housing and Utilities – 35%

Depending on where you live—say, New York or San Francisco—you may feel pressure to spend 50% or more of your paycheck on rent. This is one of the biggest financial setbacks young adults make. By the time the end of the month rolls around, you may not have enough money to address your other needs. Be smart about your housing costs. Sometimes living an extra 15 minutes away from work or getting an extra roommate can save you hundreds of dollars a month.

Car Payments, Gas, and Insurance – 15%

One way to reduce your car payment is to refinance to a better loan with a lower rate. Check out Edmunds.com, a Web site dedicated to all-things cars, for expert advice on leasing or buying a vehicle. Or instead of buying a car, you may decide it's more worthwhile to join a car-sharing plan like Zipcar or Connect By Hertz. To save on gas, carpooling is an obvious answer, but little things like emptying your trunk, inflating your tires, and driving five miles below speed limit can help boost your car's fuel efficiency.

Groceries – 5–10%

Buying generic brand grocery items instead of upscale labels can help save up to 50% on everyday food and household products. Many neighborhoods have food coops that, in return for a membership fee or volunteer shift, give members access to discounted fresh fruits, vegetables, and meat. Find a coop near your campus via the Coop Directory (www.coopdirectory.org).

Miscellaneous: Entertainment, Travel, Dining Out, Shopping – 5%

Now that you've covered your needs, you can spring for your wants. At this point, you're probably left with somewhere between 5% and 10% of your disposable income (and that might be generous). This includes clothing, concert tickets, etc. As an incentive to paying off your debt, you'll be left with more money for this category.

Don't Forget Savings and Debt Repayment

We often address these two categories at the very end of the month, only to realize we have very little money left. As soon as you receive your first two-week paycheck, automatically deposit 10% into a rainy day savings account. Then, if you have any credit card debt, apply your paycheck toward that. Remember to pay far more than the minimum. Ideally you want to pay off your credit card debt in full every month. While you're at it, pay down your student loan by contributing at least the minimum amount due. Don't fall behind. As you've learned, student loan delinquency is one of the fastest ways to reach financial ruin.

THE SAMPSONS—A CONTINUING CASE

The Sampsons realize that the first step toward achieving their financial goals is to create a budget capturing their monthly cash inflows and outflows. Dave and Sharon's combined income is now about $4,000 per month after taxes. With the new cash inflows from Sharon's paycheck, the Sampsons have started spending more on various after-school programs for their children, such as soccer leagues and tennis lessons. In Chapter 8, they resolved to save a total of $800 per month for a new car and for their children's education.

Reviewing their checking account statement from last month, Dave and Sharon identify the following monthly household payments:

- $900 for the mortgage payment ($700 loan payment plus home insurance and property taxes)
- $60 for cable TV
- $80 for electricity and water
- $70 for telephone expenses
- $500 for groceries
- $160 for a health care plan provided by Dave's employer (this expense is deducted directly from Dave's salary)

The Sampsons also review several credit card bills to estimate their other typical monthly expenses:

- About $180 for clothing
- About $300 for car expenses (insurance, maintenance, and gas)
- About $100 for school expenses
- About $1,000 for recreation and programs for the children
- About $20 as a minimum payment on their existing credit card balance

To determine their net worth, the Sampsons also assess their assets and liabilities, which include the following:

- $300 in cash
- $1,700 in their checking account
- Home valued at $100,000
- Furniture worth about $3,000
- Sharon's car, which needs to be replaced soon, is worth about $1,000; Dave's car is worth approximately $8,000
- They owe $90,000 on their home mortgage and about $2,000 on their credit cards

Go to the worksheets at the end of this chapter, and to the CD-ROM accompanying this text, to continue this case.

Chapter 9: Building Your Own Financial Plan

GOALS

1. Determine how to increase net cash flows in the near future.
2. Determine how to increase net cash flows in the distant future.

ANALYSIS

1. Prepare your personal cash flow statement.

Personal Cash Flow Statement

Cash Inflows	This Month
Disposable (after-tax) income	
Interest on deposits	
Dividend payments	
Other	
Total Cash Inflows	
Cash Outflows	
Rent/Mortgage	
Cable TV	
Electricity and water	
Telephone	
Groceries	
Health care insurance and expenses	
Clothing	
Car expenses (insurance, maintenance, and gas)	
Recreation	
Other	
Total Cash Outflows	
Net Cash Flows	

If you enter your cash flow information in the Excel worksheet, the software will create a pie chart of your cash outflows.

2. Prepare your personal balance sheet.

Personal Balance Sheet

Assets

Liquid Assets

Cash

Checking account

Savings account

Other liquid assets

Total liquid assets

Household Assets

Home

Car

Furniture

Other household assets

Total household assets

Investment Assets

Stocks

Bonds

Mutual Funds

Other investments

Total investment assets

Real Estate

Residence

Vacation home

Other

Total real estate

Total Assets

Liabilities and Net Worth

Current Liabilities

Loans	
Credit card balance	
Other current liabilities	
Total current liabilities	

Long-Term Liabilities

Mortgage	
Car loan	
Other long-term liabilities	
Total long-term liabilities	
Total Liabilities	
Net Worth	

3. Reevaluate the goals you set in Chapter 8. Based on your personal cash flow statement, indicate how much you can save each year to reach your goals.

Personal Financial Goals

Financial Goal	Dollar Amount	Savings per Year	Number of Years
Short-Term Goals			
1.			
2.			
3.			
Intermediate-Term Goals			
1.			
2.			
3.			
Long-Term Goals			
1.			
2.			
3.			

DECISIONS

1. Describe the actions you will take to increase your net cash flows in the near future.

_____

_____

_____

_____

_____

_____

_____

_____

_____

_____

2. Detail your plans to increase your net cash flows in the distant future.

_____

_____

_____

_____

_____

_____

_____

_____

_____

_____

_____

Chapter 9: The Sampsons—A Continuing Case

CASE QUESTIONS

1. Using the information in the case, prepare a personal cash flow statement for the Sampsons.

Personal Cash Flow Statement

Cash Inflows   This Month

Total Cash Inflows	

Cash Outflows

Include categories for cash outflows as follows:

Rent/Mortgage	
Cable TV	
Electricity and water	
Telephone	
Groceries	
Health care insurance and expenses	
Clothing	
Car expenses (insurance, maintenance, and gas)	
School expenses	
Recreation	
Credit card minimum payments	
Other	
Total Cash Outflows	
Net Cash Flows	

2. Based on their personal cash flow statement, will the Sampsons be able to meet their savings goals? If not, how do you recommend that they revise their personal cash flow statement in order to achieve their savings goals?

_____

_____

_____

_____

_____

_____

3. Prepare a personal balance sheet for the Sampsons.

Personal Balance Sheet

Assets

Liquid Assets

Cash	
Checking account	
Savings account	
Total liquid assets	

Household Assets

Home	
Car	
Furniture	
Total household assets	

Investment Assets

Stocks	
Bonds	
Mutual Funds	
Total investment assets	
Total Assets	

Liabilities and Net Worth

Current Liabilities

Loans	
Credit card balance	
Total current liabilities	

Long-Term Liabilities

Mortgage	
Car loan	
Total long-term liabilities	
Total Liabilities	
Net Worth	

4. What is the Sampsons' net worth? Based on the personal cash flow statement that you prepared in question 2, do you expect that their net worth will increase or decrease in the future? Why?

_____

_____

_____

_____

_____

_____

_____

_____

_____

_____

_____

Applying Time Value Concepts

Scott Pilar has been smoking two packs of cigarettes a day. Today, on his 18th birthday, he decided to give up smoking for health reasons. He does not realize that this is an important financial decision as well. If Scott invests the money that he would have spent on smoking over the next 50 years, he will become a millionaire.

Let's assume that a pack of cigarettes is priced at $8. Scott will save $16 per day (2 packs × $8 per pack), or $5,840 per year ($16 × 365 days). If Scott could invest that money in a bank deposit account and earn 5 percent per year, his investment would accumulate to be worth $1,222,551 in 50 years. The specific method to estimate this amount of accumulated funds can be done in less than one minute, as explained in this chapter.

Cash accumulates when it is invested and earns interest because of the time value of money. Over a long period of time, money can grow substantially because interest is earned both on the deposited funds and on the interest that has already accumulated. The lesson is that saving even a small amount per month or year at an early age can enhance your wealth over time.

The concepts in this chapter can help you determine how much you may save over time based on a particular savings level per month or year. You can also determine how much money you need to save per month or year in order to achieve a specific savings goal in the future. Thus, you'll be able to calculate how much monthly or annual savings you will need to make a down payment on a new car or home, or to make other types of purchases at a future point in time.

The objectives of this chapter are to:

- Calculate the future value of a dollar amount that you save today
- Calculate the present value of a dollar amount that will be received in the future
- Calculate the future value of an annuity
- Calculate the present value of an annuity

■ THE IMPORTANCE OF THE TIME VALUE OF MONEY

The value of money is affected by the point in time it is received. Would you rather receive $1,000 five years from now or one year from now? It is better to receive the money one year from now because its value is higher if received in one year than in five years. If you wanted to spend the money, you could buy more with the money today than if you waited for five years. In general, prices of the products you might purchase rise over time due to inflation. Therefore, you can buy more products with $1,000 in one year than in five years.

If you wanted to save the money that you receive, you could earn interest on it if you deposited the money in an account with a financial institution. If you receive the money in one year, you would be able to earn interest on that money over the following four years. Its value would accumulate and would be worth more than the money received four years later. Thus, the value of money received in one year would be greater than the value of money received in five years.

Would you rather receive $1,000 now or $1,000 at the end of one year from now? As with the example above, it's better to receive the money now because its value is higher now than it will be in one year. If you wanted to spend the money, you could buy more with the money today than if you waited for a year. If you wanted to save the money, you could earn interest on money received today over the next year. Thus, the value of money received today would be greater than the value of money received in one year.

In general, the value of a given amount of money is greater the earlier that it is received. A dollar today has more value than a dollar received in one year. A dollar received in one year has more value than a dollar received in five years. A dollar received in five years has more value than a dollar received in ten years.

The time value of money is especially important when considering how much money you may have at a specific point in the future. The earlier that you start saving, the more quickly your money can earn interest and grow, and the greater the amount of money you can accumulate by a given future point in time.

The time value of money is most commonly applied to two types of cash flows: a single dollar amount (also referred to as a lump sum) and an annuity. An **annuity** is a stream of equal payments that are received or paid at equal intervals in time. For example, a monthly deposit of $50 as new savings in a bank account at the end of every month is an annuity. Your telephone bill is not an annuity, as the payments are not the same each month. This chapter will discuss time value of money computations related to the future and present value of both lump-sum and annuity cash flows. Calculations are illustrated using both time value tables and a financial calculator.

annuity (or ordinary annuity)
A series of equal cash flow payments that are received or paid at equal intervals in time.

■ FUTURE VALUE OF A SINGLE DOLLAR AMOUNT

When you deposit money in a bank savings account, your money grows because the bank pays interest on your deposit. The interest is a reward to you for depositing your money in the account, and is normally expressed as a percentage of the deposit amount and is paid annually.

You may want to know how your money will grow to determine whether you can afford specific purchases in the future. For example, you may want to estimate how your existing bank balance will accumulate in six months, when you will need to make a tuition payment. Alternatively, you may want to estimate how that money will accumulate in one year, when you hope to make a down payment on a new car. To do this, you can apply the interest rate that you expect to earn on your deposit to the deposit amount.

To determine the future value of an amount of money you deposit today, you need to know:

- The amount of your deposit (or other investment) today
- The interest rate to be earned on your deposit
- The number of years the money will be invested

EXAMPLE

compounding
The process of earning interest on interest.

If you created a bank deposit of $1,000 that earned 4 percent annually, the deposit will earn an annual interest of:

Interest rate times deposit

4 percent × $1,000 = $40

Thus, your deposit will accumulate to be worth $1,040 by the end of one year.

In the next year, the interest rate of 4 percent will be applied not only to your original $1,000 deposit, but also to the interest that you earned in the previous year. The process of earning interest on interest is called **compounding**.

Assuming that the interest rate is 4 percent in the second year, it will be applied to your deposit balance of $1,040, which results in interest of $41.60 (4 percent × $1,040). Thus, your balance by the end of the second year will be $1,081.60.

Notice that the interest of $41.60 paid in the second year is more than the interest paid in the first year, even though the interest rate is the same. This is because the interest rate was applied to a larger deposit balance.

In the third year, a 4 percent interest rate would result in interest of $43.26 (4 percent of $1,081.60). Your deposit balance will be $1,124.86 by the end of the third year.

future value interest factor(*FVIF*)
A factor multiplied by today's savings to determine how the savings will accumulate over time.

In some cases, you may want to know how your deposit will accumulate over a long period of time, such as 20 or 30 years. You can quickly determine the future value for any period of time by using the **future value interest factor** (*FVIF*), which is a factor multiplied by today's savings to determine how the savings will accumulate over time. It is dependent on the interest rate and the number of years the money is invested. Your deposit today is multiplied by the *FVIF* to determine the future value of the deposit.

Using the Future Value Table

Appendix B shows the *FVIF* for various interest rates (*i*) and time periods (*n*). Each column lists an interest rate and each row lists a possible time period.

EXAMPLE

Suppose you want to know how much money you will have in five years if you invest $5,000 now and earn an annual return of 4 percent. The present value of money (*PV*) is the amount invested, or $5,000. The *FVIF* for an interest rate of 4 percent and a time period of five years is 1.217 (look down the 4% column and across the row for year 5). Thus, the future value (*FV*) of the $5,000 in five years will be:

$$FV = PV \times FVIF_{i,n}$$

$$FV = PV \times FVIF_{4\%,5}$$

$$= \$5,000 \times 1.217$$

$$= \$6,085$$

Impact of a Longer Period

By reviewing any column of the *FVIF* table in Appendix B, you will notice that as the number of years increases, the *FVIF* increases. This means that the longer the time period in which your money is invested at a particular interest rate, the more your money will grow. This relationship is illustrated in the following example.

> **EXAMPLE**
>
> What if you invested your $5,000 for 20 years instead of five years? Assuming that the interest rate is still 4 percent, the future value (*FV*) will be:
>
> $$FV = PV \times FVIF_{i,n}$$
>
> $$FV = PV \times FVIF_{4\%,20}$$
>
> $$= \$5,000 \times 2.191$$
>
> $$= \$10,955$$
>
> This result shows how your $5,000 grows if you invest it for a longer period of time.

Impact of a Higher Interest Rate

By reviewing any row of the *FVIF* table in Appendix B, you will notice that as the interest rate increases, the *FVIF* increases. This means that the higher the interest rate at which your money is invested for a particular number of years, the more your money will grow. This relationship is illustrated in the following example.

> **EXAMPLE**
>
> What if you could invest your $5,000 at an interest rate of 9 percent instead of 4 percent? Assuming a period of 20 years (like in the previous example), the future value (*FV*) will be:
>
> $$FV = PV \times FVIF_{i,n}$$
>
> $$FV = PV \times FVIF_{9\%,20}$$
>
> $$= \$5,000 \times 5.604$$
>
> $$= \$28,020$$
>
> Thus, your $5,000 will be worth $28,020 in 20 years if you can earn 9 percent interest, versus only $10,955 in 20 years if you only earn 4 percent interest. This comparison illustrates the benefit of investing your money at a higher interest rate.

Using a Financial Calculator

There are a variety of financial calculators available for purchase that greatly simplify time value calculations. The typical financial calculator allows you easily to estimate the future value that you would accumulate at a specific point in time as a result of an initial deposit today. The main function keys on the calculator for this purpose are:

N = number of periods in which your deposit will be invested

I = interest rate per period

PV = present value (the initial amount deposited)

FV = future value of your initial deposit

CPT = the compute function, which you press just before the function you want the calculator to compute

EXAMPLE

Repeat the previous problem using the financial calculator instead of the future value table, and follow these steps:

- Press 5 and then press *N* (number of periods).
- Press 9 and then press *I* (interest rate).
- Press −5000 and then press *PV* (present value of the money you invest); the negative sign is used to represent your deposit.
- Press *CPT* (the compute function) and then press *FV* (future value).

Your calculator should display the computed future value, $7,693.12.

EXAMPLE

Suppose you have $5,687 to invest in the stock market today. You like to invest for the long term and plan to choose your stocks carefully. You will invest your money for 12 years in certain stocks on which you expect a return of 10 percent annually. Although financial calculators can vary slightly in their setup, most would require inputs as shown at left.

Using the calculator, follow these steps:

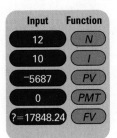

Input	Function
12	N
10	I
−5687	PV
0	PMT
?=17848.24	FV

- Press 12 and then press *N* (number of periods).
- Press 10 and then press *I* (interest rate).
- Press −5687 and then press *PV* (present value, which represents the value of today's investment).
- Press the *CPT* function and then *FV* (future value), and the computer will display the future value answer.

The *PV* is a negative number here, reflecting the outflow of cash to make the investment. The calculator computes the future value to be $17,848.24, which indicates that you will have $17,848.24 in your brokerage account in 12 years if you achieve a return of 10 percent annually on your $5,687 investment.

Use a financial calculator to determine the future value of $5,000 invested at 9 percent for 20 years. (This is the previous example used for the *FVIF* table.) Your answer should be $28,020. Any difference in answers using the *FVIF* table versus using a financial calculator is due to rounding.

The Power of Compounding

As a result of compounding, an amount of savings can grow substantially. Exhibit 10.1 illustrates how a deposit of $1,000 grows over time. Notice that your initial $1,000 deposit almost doubles in seven years when considering the compounding effect (you earn interest on your initial deposit and on any interest that has already accumulated). With the assumed interest rate of 10 percent, it would take 10 years for your deposit to double if you only earned interest on the initial deposit and not on the accumulated interest as well.

Just as compounding can expand your savings, it can also expand your debt. For example, if you had debt today of $1,000 and were charged 10 percent on the debt per year, and you did not pay off any of your debt, Exhibit 10.1 shows how your debt would grow over time. Notice how the debt would grow because you would pay interest not only on your initial debt amount but also on the interest that accumulates over time.

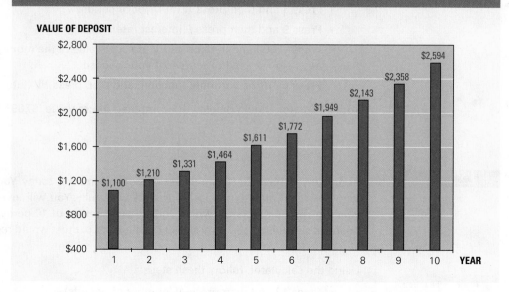

Exhibit 10.1   How an Initial Deposit of $1,000 Grows Over Time Due to Compounding (assume annual interest rate = 10 percent)

FOCUS ON ETHICS: **Delaying Payments**

Based on the time value of money, it seems rational to delay payment obligations. If you invest your money while delaying a payment, you can earn interest on your funds. You might be tempted to invest money before making your rent payment at the beginning of each month, or before making a car payment each month. However, delaying your payments too long can lead to late fees and penalties that could damage your credit rating. You might also risk being evicted from your apartment or having your car repossessed.

What alternative will still allow you to take advantage of the time value of money? You should invest your money in an interest-bearing account before you need to make payments. By paying bills electronically you can delay payments and still ensure that they will be paid on time. You can even use settings on many bill-paying Web sites that allow you to set a future date for a payment once you receive a bill. Make use of your money while you have it, but always make payments by the obligation dates.

■ PRESENT VALUE OF A DOLLAR AMOUNT

discounting
The process of obtaining present values.

In many situations, you will want to know how much money you must deposit or invest today to accumulate a specified amount of money at a future point in time. The process of obtaining present values is referred to as **discounting**. Suppose that you want to have $20,000 for a down payment on a house in three years. You want to know how much money you need to invest today to reach a total of $20,000 in three years. That is, you want to know the present value of $20,000 that will be needed in three years, based on an interest rate that you could earn over that period.

To determine the present value of an amount of money expected in the future, you need to know:

- The future amount of money
- The interest rate to be earned on your deposit
- The number of years the money will be invested

Financial Planning Online 10.1: **Paying Your Bills Online**

Go to
banking.about.com/od/
bankonline/f/setupbillpay
.htm

This Web site provides
information on how to pay
bills online.

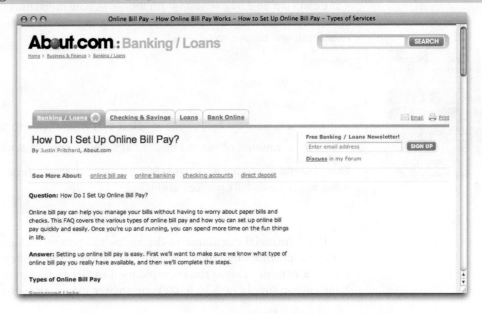

present value interest factor (*PVIF*)
A factor multiplied by a future value to determine the present value of that amount.

The present value can be calculated by using a **present value interest factor (*PVIF*)**, which is a factor multiplied by the future value to determine the present value of that amount. It is dependent on the interest rate and the number of years the money is invested.

Using the Present Value Table

Appendix B shows the *PVIF* for various interest rates (*i*) and time periods (*n*). Each column lists an interest rate, while each row lists a time period.

You will notice that in any column of the table the *PVIF* is lower as the number of years increases. This means that less money is needed to achieve a specific future value when the money is invested for a greater number of years.

Similarly, an inspection of any row reveals that less money is needed to achieve a specific future value when the money is invested at a higher rate of return.

EXAMPLE

You would like to accumulate $50,000 in five years by making a single investment today. You believe you can achieve a return from your investment of 7 percent annually. What is the dollar amount that you need to invest today to achieve your goal?

The *PVIF* in this example is .713 (look down the 7% column and across the row for year 5). Using the present value table, the present value (*PV*) is:

$$PV = FV \times PVIF_{i,n}$$

$$PV = FV \times PVIF_{7\%,5}$$

$$= \$50,000 \times 0.713$$

$$= \$35,650$$

Thus, you need to invest $35,650 today to have $50,000 in five years if you expect an annual return of 7 percent.

Using a Financial Calculator

Using a financial calculator, present values can be obtained quickly by inputting all known variables and solving for the one unknown variable.

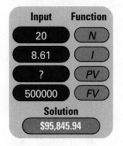

EXAMPLE

Loretta Callahan would like to accumulate $500,000 by the time she retires in 20 years. If she can earn an 8.61 percent return annually, how much must she invest today to have $500,000 in 20 years? Since the unknown variable is the present value (*PV*), the calculator input will be as shown at left.

Input	Function
20	N
8.61	I
?	PV
500000	FV
Solution	
$95,845.94	

Where:

N	=	20 years
I	=	8.61%
PV	=	present value, or the amount that would have to be deposited today
FV	=	amount of money desired at a future point in time

Thus, Loretta would have to invest $95,845.94 today to accumulate $500,000 in 20 years if she really earns 8.61 percent annually.

Use a financial calculator to determine the present value of a single sum by calculating the present value of $50,000 in five years if the money is invested at an interest rate of 8 percent. This is the example used earlier to illustrate the present value tables. Your answer should be $34,050. Your answer may vary slightly due to rounding.

Impact of Economic Conditions on the Time Value of Money

In reality, the return that you will earn on your money over time is often subject to uncertainty. When economic conditions change, the returns that you earn on your savings and investments change as well. During the financial crisis in 2008–2009, the returns on interest-bearing accounts were very low, as interest rates declined substantially. In addition, the market value of most stocks declined, reflecting negative returns for individual investors. Conversely, when economic conditions are more favorable, investments tend to grow at a higher level, which results in a higher future value. Given the uncertainty surrounding the returns on investments, you may want to estimate a future value of your investments for alternative possible rates of return. This allows you to estimate the future value of an investment if less favorable conditions occur that cause your return to be less than you expected.

■ FUTURE VALUE OF AN ANNUITY

Earlier in the chapter, you saw how your money can grow from a single deposit. An alternative way to accumulate funds over time is through an ordinary annuity, which represents a stream of equal payments (or investments) that occur at the end of each period. For example, if you make a $30 deposit at the end of each month for 100 months, this is an ordinary annuity. As another example, you may invest $1,000 at the end of each year for 10 years. There is a simple and quick method to determine the future value of an annuity. If the payment changes over time, the payment stream does not reflect an annuity. You can still determine the future value of a payment stream that does not reflect an annuity, but the computation process is more complicated.

annuity due
A series of equal cash flow payments that occur at the beginning of each period.

timelines
Diagrams that show payments received or paid over time.

An alternative to an ordinary annuity is an **annuity due**, which is a series of equal cash flow payments that occur at the beginning of each period. Thus, an annuity due differs from an ordinary annuity in that the payments occur at the beginning instead of the end of the period.

The best way to illustrate the future value of an ordinary annuity is through the use of **timelines**, which show the payments received or paid over time.

EXAMPLE

You plan to invest $100 at the end of every year for the next three years. You expect to earn an annual interest rate of 10 percent on the funds that you invest. Using a timeline, the cash flows from this annuity can be represented as follows:

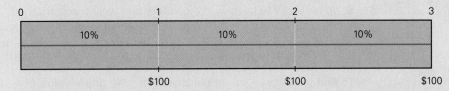

You would like to know how much money will be in your investment account at the end of the third year. This amount is the future value of the annuity. The first step in calculating the future value of the annuity is to treat each payment as a single sum and determine the future value of each payment individually. Next, add up the individual future values to obtain the future value of the annuity.

Since the first payment will be invested from the end of year 1 to the end of year 3, it will be invested for two years. Since the second payment will be invested from the end of year 2 to the end of year 3, it will be invested for one year. The third payment is made at the end of year 3, the point in time at which we want to determine the future value of the annuity. Hence, the third-year payment will not accumulate any interest. Using the future value in Appendix B to obtain the future value interest factor for two years and 10 percent ($FVIF_{10\%,2} = 1.21$) and the future value interest factor for one year and 10 percent ($FVIF_{10\%,1} = 1.10$), the future value of your annuity can be determined as follows:

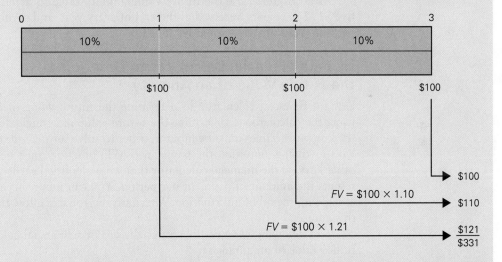

Adding up the individual future values shows that the future value of this annuity is $331 (i.e., you will have $331 in your account at the end of the third year). Notice that $300 of the $331 represents the three $100 payments. Thus, the remaining $31 of the $331 is the combined interest you earned on the three payments.

future value interest factor for an annuity (*FVIFA*)
A factor multiplied by the periodic savings level (annuity) to determine how the savings will accumulate over time.

Using the Future Value Annuity Table

Computing the future value of an annuity by looking up each individual single-sum future value interest factor (*FVIF*) is rather tedious. Consequently, Appendix B lists the factors for various interest rates and periods (years). These factors are referred to as **future value interest factors for an annuity (*FVIFA*$_{i,n}$)**, where i is the periodic interest rate and n is the number of payments in the annuity. The annuity payment (*PMT*) can be multiplied by the *FVIFA* to determine the future value of the annuity (*FVA* = *PMT* × *FVIFA*). Each column in the table lists an interest rate, while each row lists the period of concern.

EXAMPLE

Suppose that you have won the lottery and will receive $150,000 at the end of every year for the next 20 years. As soon as you receive the payments, you will invest them at your bank at an interest rate of 7 percent annually. How much will be in your account at the end of 20 years (assuming you do not make any withdrawals)?

To find the answer, you must determine the future value of an annuity. (The stream of cash flows is in the form of an annuity since the payments are equal and equally spaced in time.) Using the future value annuity table to determine the factor, look in the $i = 7\%$ column and the $n = 20$ periods row. The table shows that this factor is 40.995.

The next step is to determine the future value of your lottery annuity:

$$
\begin{aligned}
FVA &= PMT \times FVIFA_{i,n} \\
&= PMT \times FVIFA_{7,20} \\
&= \$150{,}000 \times 40.995 \\
&= \$6{,}149{,}250
\end{aligned}
$$

Thus, after 20 years, you will have $6,149,250 if you invest all your lottery payments in an account earning an interest rate of 7 percent.

As an exercise, use the future value annuity table to determine the future value of five $172 payments, received at the end of every year, and earning an interest rate of 14 percent. Your answer should be $1,137.

Using a Financial Calculator to Determine the Future Value of an Annuity

Using a financial calculator to determine the future value of an annuity is similar to using the calculator to determine the future value of a single dollar amount. As before, the known variables must be input in order to solve for the unknown variable. For problems involving annuities, the payment (PMT) function must be used in addition to the other keys on the financial calculator that were identified earlier. The PMT function represents the amount of payment per period. You can input this amount in the calculator along with the other information. Alternatively, you can allow the calculator to compute this amount.

The following example illustrates the use of a financial calculator to determine the future value of an annuity.

EXAMPLE

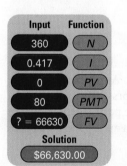

You have $80 of your paycheck invested in a retirement account. You expect to earn 5 percent annually on this account. How much will be in the account in 30 years?

This problem differs from the problems we have seen so far, in that the payments are received on a monthly (not annual) basis. You would like to obtain the future value of the annuity and consequently need the number of periods, the periodic interest rate, the present value, and the payment. Because there are 12 months in a year, there are 30 × 12 = 360 periods. Furthermore, since the annual interest rate is 5 percent, the monthly interest rate is 5/12 = 0.417 percent. Also, note that to determine the future value of an annuity, most financial calculators require an input of 0 for the present value. The payment in this problem is 80.

The input for the financial calculator would be as shown at left.

Thus, you will have $66,630 when you retire in 30 years as a result of your monthly investment.

Financial Planning Online 10.2: **Estimating the Future Value of Your Savings**

Go to
moneycentral.msn.com/
personal-finance/
calculators/
aim_to_save_calculator/
home.aspx#Results

This Web site provides
an estimate of the future
value of your savings, based
on your initial balance, the
amount saved per period,
the interest rate, and the
number of periods.

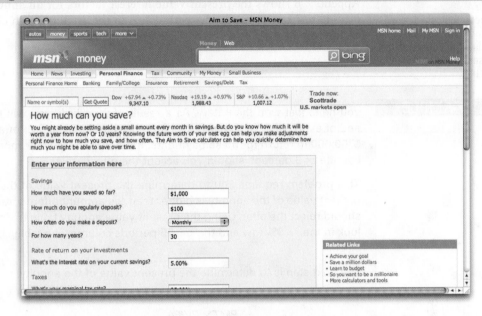

PRESENT VALUE OF AN ANNUITY

Just as the future value of an annuity can be obtained by compounding the individual cash flows of the annuity and then adding them up, the present value of an annuity can be obtained by discounting the individual cash flows of the annuity and adding them up.

Referring to our earlier example of an ordinary annuity with three $100 payments and an interest rate of 10 percent, we can graphically illustrate the process as follows:

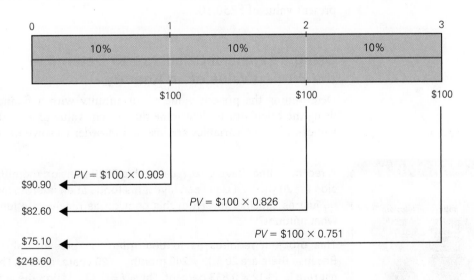

Adding up the individual present values leads to the conclusion that the present value of this annuity is $248.60. Therefore, three $100 payments received at the end of each of the next three years are worth $248.60 to you today if you can invest your money at an interest rate of 10 percent.

present value interest factor for an annuity (*PVIFA*)
A factor multiplied by a periodic savings level (annuity) to determine the present value of the annuity.

Using the Present Value Annuity Table

Appendix B shows the **present value interest factors for an annuity (*PVIFA$_{i,n}$*)** for various interest rates (*i*) and time periods (*n*) in the annuity. Each column in the table lists an interest rate, while each row lists a time period.

EXAMPLE

You have just won the lottery. As a result of your luck, you will receive $82,000 at the end of every year for the next 25 years. Now, a financial firm offers you a lump sum of $700,000 in return for these payments. If you can invest your money at an annual interest rate of 9 percent, should you accept the offer?

This problem requires you to determine the present value of the lottery annuity. If the present value of the annuity is higher than the amount offered by the financial firm, you should reject the offer. Using the present value annuity table to determine the factor, we look in the *i* = 9% row and the *n* = 25 periods column. The table shows that this factor is 9.823.

The next step is to determine the present value of the annuity:

$$PVA = PMT \times PVIFA_{i,n}$$
$$= PMT \times PVIFA_{9,25}$$
$$= \$82,000 \times 9.823$$
$$= \$805,486$$

Thus, the 25 payments of $82,000 each are worth $805,486 to you today if you can invest your money at an interest rate of 9 percent. Consequently, you should reject the financial firm's offer to purchase your future lottery payments for $700,000.

As an exercise, use the present value annuity table to determine the present value of eight $54 payments, received at the end of every year and earning an interest rate of 14 percent. Your answer should be $250.50, which means that the eight payments have a present value of $250.50.

Using a Financial Calculator to Determine the Present Value of an Annuity

Determining the present value of an annuity with a financial calculator is similar to using the calculator to determine the present value of a single-sum payment. Again, the values of known variables are inserted in order to solve for the unknown variable.

EXAMPLE

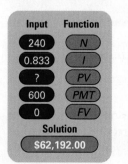

Input	Function
240	N
0.833	I
?	PV
600	PMT
0	FV
Solution	
$62,192.00	

A recent retiree, Dave Buzz receives his $600 pension monthly. He will receive this pension for 20 years. If Dave can invest his funds at an interest rate of 10 percent, he should be just as satisfied receiving this pension as receiving a lump-sum payment today of what amount?

This problem requires us to determine the present value of the pension annuity. Because there are 20 × 12 = 240 months in 20 years, *n* = 240. The monthly (periodic) interest rate is 10/12 = 0.833 percent. Thus, *i* = 0.833. Using these inputs with a financial calculator, we obtain the inputs shown to the left.

The present value is $62,192. If Dave is offered a lump sum of $62,192 today, he should accept it if he can invest his funds at an interest rate of 10 percent.

USING TIME VALUE TO ESTIMATE SAVINGS

Now that you understand the various time value calculations, you can apply them to financial planning. The key time value tools for building your financial plan are estimating the future value of annual savings and determining the amount of annual savings necessary to achieve a specific amount of savings in the future. Recognizing how much savings you can accumulate over time can motivate you to save money every month.

Estimating the Future Value from Savings

The future value of an annuity is especially useful when determining how much money you will have saved by a future point in time if you periodically save a specific amount of money every year. You can apply this process when you are saving for a large purchase (such as a down payment on a home) in the near future or even for your retirement in the distant future.

EXAMPLE

Stephanie Spratt believes that she may be able to save about $5,000 per year. She wants to know how much she will have in 30 years if she earns 6 percent annual interest on her investment. The annuity in this example is $5,000. The future value annuity factor based on a 30-year period and a 6 percent interest rate is 79.058. Thus, the future value is:

$$\$5,000 \times 79.058 = \$395,290$$

If she could earn 7 percent instead of 6 percent on her savings, the future value annuity factor would be 94.461, and the future value would be:

$$\$5,000 \times 94.461 = \$472,305$$

Estimating the Annual Savings That Will Achieve a Future Amount

The future value of annuity tables are also useful for determining how much money you need to save each year to achieve a specific amount of savings at a designated future point in time. Thus, you can estimate the size of the annuity that is necessary to achieve a specific future value of savings that you desire. Because $FVA = PMT \times FVIFA$, the terms can be rearranged to solve for the annuity:

$$FVA/FVIFA = PMT$$

Exhibit 10.2 shows how Stephanie Spratt uses the time value tools to develop a financial plan. Stephanie developed a tentative plan to save $5,000 per year. After applying the time value tools, however, she recognizes that she could accumulate $600,000 in 30 years by saving $6,352 per year. She decides to strive for this higher level of annual savings. Because she realizes that this goal is ambitious, she sets a minimum goal of saving $5,000 per year.

EXAMPLE

Stephanie Spratt now wants to know how much money she must save every year to achieve $600,000 in 30 years, based on a 7 percent interest rate. In this example, the future value is $600,000, and the future value interest factor is 94.461. The unknown variable is the annuity.

PMT	=	$FVA/FVIFA$
	=	$600,000/94.461
	=	$6,352

Thus, Stephanie would need to invest $6,352 each year to accumulate $600,000 in 30 years.

Exhibit 10.2   How Time Value of Money Decisions Fit Within Stephanie Spratt's Financial Plan

GOALS FOR A SAVINGS PLAN

1. *Calculate how much savings I will accumulate by various future points in time.*
2. *Determine how much I need to save each year to ensure a comfortable living upon retirement.*

ANALYSIS

Present Situation:

Expected Savings per Year = *$5,000*

Expected Annual Rate of Return = *6% or 7%*

Estimated Amount of Savings to Be Accumulated:

Savings Accumulated over:	Assume Annual Return = 6%	Assume Annual Return = 7%
5 years	$28,185	$28,753
10 years	65,905	69,080
15 years	116,380	125,645
20 years	183,930	204,975
25 years	274,325	316,245
30 years	395,290	472,305

Annual Savings Needed to Achieve a Specific Savings Goal:

Savings Goal = *$80,000 in 10 years, $200,000 in 20 years, $500,000 in 30 years*

Expected Annual Rate of Return = *6% or 7%*

Savings Goal	Assume Annual Return = 6%	Assume Annual Return = 7%
$80,000 in 10 years	$6,069	$5,790
$200,000 in 20 years	5,437	4,879
$500,000 in 30 years	6,324	5,293

To achieve a savings goal of $80,000 in 10 years, I would need to save $6,069 per year (assuming an annual return of 6 percent on my money). To achieve a goal of $200,000 in 20 years, I would need to save $5,437 per year (assuming a 6 percent annual return).

DECISIONS

Decision on My Savings Goal in the Future:

If I can save $5,000 a year, I should accumulate $28,185 in 5 years and $65,905 in 10 years. These estimates are based on an assumed annual return of 6 percent. If my annual return is higher, I should accumulate even more than that. The estimated savings for longer time periods are much higher.

A comparison of the third column with the second column in the table shows how much more savings I could accumulate if I can earn an annual return of 7 percent instead of 6 percent.

Decision on My Savings Goal per Year:

Although my initial plan was to develop a budget for saving about $5,000 a year, I will try to save more so that I can achieve my savings goals. I will use a minimum savings goal of $5,000, but will try to save about $6,000 per year.

■ HOW A SAVINGS PLAN FITS WITHIN YOUR FINANCIAL PLAN

The key savings decisions for building your financial plan are:

- How much should I attempt to accumulate in savings for a future point in time?
- How much should I attempt to save every month or every year?

These decisions require an understanding of the time value of money. Exhibit 10.2 shows how these savings decisions apply to Stephanie Spratt's financial plan.

DISCUSSION QUESTIONS

1. How would Stephanie's savings decisions be different if she were a single mother of two children?

2. How would Stephanie's savings decisions be affected if she were 35 years old? If she were 50 years old?

SUMMARY

- You can estimate the future value of a single dollar amount to determine the future value of a bank deposit or a fund established for retirement. It is determined by estimating the compounded interest that is generated by the initial amount. The future value can be determined by using a future value table or a financial calculator.

- You can estimate the present value of a single dollar amount so that you know what a future payment would be worth if you had it today. The present value of a single dollar amount to be received in the future is determined by discounting the future value. The present value of a future amount to be received can be determined by using a present value table or a financial calculator.

- You can estimate the future value of an annuity so that you can determine how much a stream of payments will be worth at a specific time in the future. This involves determining the future value of every single dollar amount contained within the annuity, which is easily estimated by using a future value annuity table or a financial calculator.

- You can estimate the present value of an annuity so that you can determine how much a stream of future payments is worth today. This involves determining the present value of every single dollar amount contained within the annuity, which is easily estimated by using a present value annuity table or a financial calculator.

REVIEW QUESTIONS

1. **Time Value of Money.** What is the time value of money? How is it related to opportunity costs?

2. **Time Value of Cash Flows.** To what types of cash flows is the time value of money concept most commonly applied?

3. **Annuity.** What is an annuity?

4. **Compounding.** Define compounding. How is it used in financial planning?

5. **Calculating Future Values.** What two methods can be used to calculate future values?

6. **Future Value Formula.** What is the formula for determining the future value of a single sum when using the future value interest factor table? What information must be known in order to find the correct future value interest factor?

7. **Discounting.** What is discounting?

8. **Present Value.** Describe some instances when determining the present value of an amount is useful.

In questions 9 through 12, indicate whether you would use the table for determining the future value of a single sum (FVIF), the present value of a single sum (PVIF), the future value of an annuity (FVIFA), or the present value of an annuity (PVIFA).

9. **Present Value.** You want to know how much you must deposit today to have $5,000 in five years.

10. **Future Value.** You plan to contribute $300 per month to your company's retirement plan and want to know how much you will have at retirement.

11. **Future Value.** You received $500 as a gift for graduation, and you want to know how much it will be worth in three years if you deposit it in a savings account.

12. **Future Value.** You must decide between accepting a lump-sum settlement and annual payments.

13. **Present Value of Annuity.** What formula is used to determine the present value of an annuity? What does the present value of an annuity indicate?

14. **Future Value of Annuity.** How would you modify the FVA equation to determine how much you would need to save each month to have a specific amount at a specific time in the future?

15. **Number of Periods.** In determining the future value of an annuity to be invested monthly over a five-year period, what number of periods should you use?

FINANCIAL PLANNING PROBLEMS

Problems 2, 5, 6, 7, 13, 14, and 15 require a financial calculator.

1. **Future Value.** Kyle has $1,000 in cash received in graduation gifts from various relatives. He wants to invest it in a certificate of deposit (CD) so that he will have a down payment on a car when he graduates from college in five years. His bank will pay 6 percent for the five-year CD. How much will Kyle have in five years to put down on his car?

2. **Future Value.** Sandra wants to deposit $100 each year for her son. If she places it in a savings account that pays 5 percent, what amount will be in the account in 20 years?

3. **Future Value.** Luis wants to know how much he will have available to spend on his trip to Belize in three years if he deposits $3,000 today at an interest rate of 9 percent.

4. **Future Value.** How much will you have in 36 months if you invest $75 a month at 10 percent interest?

5. **Present Value.** Cheryl wants to have $2,000 in spending money to take on a trip to Disney World in three years. How much must she deposit now in a savings account that pays 5 percent to have the money she needs in three years?

6. **Present Value.** Juan would like to give his newly born grandson a gift of $10,000 on his 18th birthday. Juan can earn 7 percent interest on a certificate of deposit. How much must he deposit now in order to achieve his goal?

7. **Present Value.** Winners of the Georgia Lotto drawing are given the choice of receiving the winning amount divided equally over 20 years or as a lump-sum cash option amount. The cash option amount is determined by discounting the winning amount at 7 percent over 20 years. This week the lottery is worth $6 million to a single winner. What would the cash option payout be?

8. **Future Value of Annuity.** Michelle is attending college and has a part-time job. Once she finishes college, Michelle would like to relocate to a metropolitan area. She wants to build her savings so that she will have a "nest egg" to start her off. Michelle works out her budget and decides she can afford to set aside $50 per month for savings. Her bank will pay her 3 percent on her savings account. What will Michelle's balance be in five years?

9. **Future Value of Annuity.** Twins Jessica and Joshua, both 25, graduated from college and began working in the family restaurant business. The first year, Jessica began putting $2,000 per year in an individual retirement account and contributed to it for a total of 10 years. After 10 years she made no further contributions until she retired at age 65. Joshua did not start making contributions to his individual retirement account until he was 35, but he continued making contributions of $2,000 each year until he retired at age 65. Assuming that both Jessica and Joshua receive 10 percent interest per year, how much will Jessica have at retirement? How much did she contribute in total? How much will Joshua have at retirement? How much did he contribute in total?

10. **Estimating the Annuity Amount.** Amy and Vince want to save $7,000 so that they can take a trip

to Europe in four years. How much must they save each month to have the money they need if they can get 8 percent on their savings?

11. **Future Value of Annuity.** Lena has just become eligible to participate in her company's retirement plan. Her company does not match contributions, but the plan does average an annual return of 12 percent. Lena is 40 and plans to work to age 65. If she contributes $200 per month, how much will she have in her plan at retirement?

12. **Future Value of Annuity.** Stacey would like to have $1 million available to her at retirement. Her investments have an average annual return of 11 percent. If she makes contributions of $300 per month, will she reach her goal when she retires in 30 years?

13. **Future Value of Annuity.** Jesse has just learned that she won $1 million in her state lottery. She has the choice of receiving a lump-sum payment of $312,950 or $50,000 per year for the next 20 years. Jesse can invest the lump sum at 8 percent, or she can invest the annual payments at 6 percent. Which should she choose for the greatest return after 20 years?

14. **Future Value of Annuity.** Jen spends $10 per week on lottery tickets. If she takes the same amount that she spends on lottery tickets and invests it each week for the next five years at 10 percent, how much will she have in five years?

15. **Future Value of Annuity.** Kirk can take his $1,000 income tax refund and invest it in a 36-month certificate of deposit at 7 percent, or he can use the money to purchase a stereo system and put $30 a month in a bank savings account that will pay him 7 percent interest. Which choice will give him more money at the end of three years?

16. **ETHICAL DILEMMA:** Cindy and Jack have always practiced good financial habits, in particular, developing and living by a budget. They are currently in the market to purchase a new car and have budgeted $300 per month for car payments.

While visiting a local dealership, a salesman, Scott, shows them a car that meets their financial requirements. Then he insists that they look at a much more expensive car that he knows they would prefer. The more expensive car would result in payments of $500 per month.

In discussing the two cars, Cindy and Jack tell Scott that the only way they can afford a more expensive car would be to discontinue making a $200 monthly contribution to their retirement plan, which they have just begun. They plan to retire in 30 years. Scott explains that they would only need to discontinue the $200 monthly payments for five years, i.e., the length of the car loan. Scott calculates that the $12,000 in lost contributions over the next five years could be made up over the remaining 25 years by increasing their monthly contribution by only $40 per month, and they would still be able to achieve their goal.

a. Comment on the ethics of a salesperson who attempts to talk customers into spending more than they had originally planned and budgeted.

b. Is Scott correct in his calculation that Cindy and Jack can make up the difference in their retirement by increasing their monthly contributions by only $40 per month for the remaining 25 years? (Note: Assume a rate of return of 6 percent on Cindy and Jack's investment and assume that they make the investments annually.)

FINANCIAL PLANNING ONLINE EXERCISES

1. After reading "How Do I Set Up Online Bill Pay" at banking.about.com/od/bankonline/f/setupbillpay.htm, answer the following questions:

a. Is setting up online bill pay a difficult process? Explain fully.

b. What are the two basic types of online bill pay and what information is needed to utilize each?

c. If your mortgage is $835 per month, will you need to remember to enter this data monthly? Explain in detail.

2. Go to moneycentral.msn.com/personal-finance/calculators/aim_to_save_calculator/home.aspx#Results

a. Using the calculator "How Much Can You Save?," determine how much money you will have if you currently have nothing saved and you deposit $500 quarterly for the next 20 years at a 10 percent rate of return and a 28 percent marginal tax rate.

b. Use the same data as in "a" except that you will only save the money for 18 years. Is the difference significantly greater than the $4,000 that you did not save over the last two years?

c. Use the same data as in "a" except that you will make a deposit of $167 per month. $167 per month is approximately equal to $500 per quarter. Does depositing the money monthly result in a greater total savings at the end of the 20 years?

d. Use the same data as in "a" except that you will make the deposits in an account that will grow tax-free. Does investing in a tax-free account result in a significant increase in the total amount saved?

VIDEO EXERCISE: How Your Savings Grows

Go to one of the Web sites that contain video clips (such as www.youtube.com) and view some video clips about how savings grows. You can use search phrases such as "future value of savings." Select one video clip on this topic that you would recommend for the other students in your class.

1. Provide the Web link for the video clip.

2. What do you think is the main point of this video clip?

3. How might you change your savings plans as a result of watching this video clip?

BUILDING YOUR OWN FINANCIAL PLAN

Based on the goals that you established in Chapter 8 and the personal cash flow statement that you created in Chapter 9, you are now ready to begin determining how to go about achieving many of your goals. Most financial goals are achieved by some sort of savings/investment plan.

Go to the worksheets at the end of this chapter, and to the CD-ROM accompanying this text, to continue building your financial plan.

THE SAMPSONS—A CONTINUING CASE

Recall that Dave and Sharon Sampson established a plan to save $300 per month (or $3,600 per year) for their children's education. Their oldest child is six years old and will begin college in 12 years. They will invest the $300 in a savings account that they expect will earn interest of about 5 percent a year over the next 12 years. The Sampsons wonder how much additional money they would accumulate if they could earn 7 percent a year on the savings account instead of 5 percent. Finally, they wonder how their savings would accumulate if they could save $400 per month (or $4,800 per year) instead of $300 per month.

Go to the worksheets at the end of this chapter, and to the CD-ROM accompanying this text, to continue this case.

Chapter 10: Building Your Own Financial Plan

GOALS

1. Determine how much savings you plan to accumulate by various future points in time.

2. Estimate how much you will need to save each year in order to achieve your goals.

ANALYSIS

1. For each goal you set in Chapter 8, make the calculations using an interest rate that you believe you can earn on your invested savings. Then recalculate the amount you will need for each goal based on a rate that is one point higher and a rate that is one point lower than your original rate. (The Excel worksheet will perform the calculations based on your input.)

Time Value of Money

Future Value of a Present Amount

Present Value	
Number of Periods	
Interest Rate per Period	
Future Value	

Future Value of an Annuity

Payment per Period	
Number of Periods	
Interest Rate per Period	
Future Value	

Present Value of a Future Amount

Future Amount	
Number of Periods	
Interest Rate per Period	
Present Value	

Present Value of an Annuity

Payment per Period	
Number of Periods	
Interest Rate per Period	
Present Value	

Personal Financial Goals

Financial Goal	Dollar Amount	Rate of Return	Priority (Low, Medium, High)
Short-Term Goals			
1.			
2.			
3.			
Intermediate-Term Goals			
1.			
2.			
3.			
Long-Term Goals			
1.			
2.			
3.			

2. Revise the cash flow statement you created in Chapter 9 as necessary to enable you to achieve your goals.

Personal Cash Flow Statement

Cash Inflows	This Month
Disposable (after-tax) income	
Interest on deposits	
Dividend payments	
Other	
Total Cash Inflows	

Cash Outflows	
Rent/Mortgage	
Cable TV	
Electricity and water	
Telephone	
Groceries	

Cash Outflows (continued)   **This Month**

Health care insurance and expenses	
Clothing	
Car expenses (insurance, maintenance, and gas)	
Recreation	
Other	
Total Cash Outflows	
Net Cash Flows	

DECISIONS

1. Report on how much you must save per year and the return you must earn to meet your goals.

Chapter 10: The Sampsons—A Continuing Case

CASE QUESTIONS

1. Help the Sampsons determine how much they will have for their children's education by calculating how much $3,600 in annual savings will accumulate if they earn interest of (a) 5 percent and (b) 7 percent. Next, determine how much $4,800 in annual savings will accumulate if they earn interest of (a) 5 percent and (b) 7 percent.

Savings Accumulated over the Next 12 Years
(Based on Plan to Save $3,600 per Year)

Amount Saved per Year	$3,600	$3,600
Interest Rate	5%	7%
Years	12	12
Future Value of Savings		

Savings Accumulated over the Next 12 Years
(Based on Plan to Save $4,800 per Year)

Amount Saved per Year	$4,800	$4,800
Interest Rate	5%	7%
Years	12	12
Future Value of Savings		

2. What is the impact of the higher interest rate of 7 percent on the Sampsons' accumulated savings?

_____

_____

_____

_____

3. What is the impact of the higher savings of $4,800 on their accumulated savings?

_____

_____

_____

_____

_____

4. If the Sampsons set a goal to save $70,000 for their children's college education in 12 years, how would you determine the yearly savings necessary to achieve this goal? How much would they have to save by the end of each year to achieve this goal, assuming a 5 percent annual interest rate?

Calculator: Savings Needed Each Year

Future Value	$70,000
Interest Rate	5%
Years	12
Savings Needed Each Year	

Managing Your Money

Jared lives from paycheck to paycheck. His checkbook register showed that he had a balance of $110, so he wrote seven checks totaling $90. Unfortunately, Jared made a math error when entering one of the checks into his checkbook register. Instead of there being $110 available, his real balance was $10. As a result, seven checks bounced. In addition, Jared was charged $15 for each bounced check, which resulted in penalty fees of $105.

This expensive lesson for Jared could have been avoided if he had requested overdraft protection on his account. The overdraft protection would have saved him from penalty fees, albeit at the cost of interest charged on the overdraft loan. Some people write checks without keeping track of their balances, and therefore may have insufficient funds to support the checks that they write. Consequently, they are charged penalty fees by their banks.

This chapter describes techniques for managing your checking account. It also identifies various types of money market investments and explains how the use of cash management can lead to increased liquidity within your financial plan.

The objectives of this chapter are to:

- Provide a background on money management
- Describe the most popular money market investments
- Identify the risk associated with money market investments
- Explain how to manage the risk of your money market investments

BACKGROUND ON MONEY MANAGEMENT

money management
A series of decisions made over a short-term period regarding cash inflows and outflows.

Money management describes the decisions you make over a short-term period regarding your cash inflows and outflows. It is separate from decisions about investing funds for a long-term period (such as several years) or borrowing funds for a long-term period. Instead, it focuses on maintaining short-term investments to achieve both liquidity and an adequate return on your investments, as explained next.

Liquidity

liquidity
Your ability to cover any cash deficiencies that you may experience.

As discussed in Chapter 8, **liquidity** refers to your ability to cover any short-term cash deficiencies. Recall that the personal cash flow statement determines the amount of excess or deficient funds that you have at the end of a period, such as one month from now. Money management is related to the personal cash flow statement because it determines how to use excess funds, or how to obtain funds if your cash inflows are insufficient. You should strive to maintain a sufficient amount of funds in liquid assets such as a checking account or savings account to draw on when your cash outflows exceed your cash inflows. In this way, you maintain adequate liquidity.

Some individuals rely on a credit card as a source of liquidity rather than maintaining liquid investments. Many credit cards provide temporary free financing from the time you make purchases until the date when your payment is due. If you have insufficient funds to pay the entire credit card balance when the bill is due, you may pay only a portion of your balance and finance the rest of the payment. The interest rate is usually quite high, commonly ranging from 8 to 20 percent. Maintaining liquid assets that you can easily access when you need funds allows you to avoid using credit and paying high finance charges.

Liquidity is necessary because there will be periods when your cash inflows are not adequate to cover your cash outflows. But there are opportunity costs when you maintain an excessive amount of liquid funds. A portion of those funds could have been invested in less liquid assets that could earn a higher return than, say, a savings account. In general, the more liquid an investment, the lower its return, so you forego higher returns when maintaining a high degree of liquidity.

EXAMPLE   Stephanie Spratt's cash inflows are $2,500 per month after taxes. Her cash outflows are normally about $2,100 per month, leaving her with $400 in cash each month. This month she expects that she will have an extra expense of $600; therefore, her cash outflows will exceed her cash inflows by $200. She needs a convenient source of funds to cover the extra expense.

Adequate Return

When you maintain short-term investments, you should strive to achieve the highest possible return. The return on your short-term investments is dependent on the prevailing risk-free rate and the level of risk you are willing to tolerate. Some assets that satisfy your liquidity needs may not necessarily achieve the return that you expect. For example, you could maintain a large amount of cash in your wallet as a source of liquidity, but it would earn a zero rate of return. Other investments may provide an adequate return, but are not liquid. To achieve both liquidity and an adequate return, you should consider investing in multiple money market investments with varied returns and levels of liquidity.

■ MONEY MARKET INVESTMENTS

Common investments for short-term funds include the following money market investments:

- Checking account
- NOW account
- Savings deposit
- Certificate of deposit
- Money market deposit account (MMDA)
- Treasury bills
- Money market fund
- Asset management account

All of these investments except Treasury bills and money market funds are offered by depository institutions and are insured for up to $100,000 in the event of default by the institution. In this section, we'll examine each of these investments in turn, and focus on their liquidity and typical return.

Checking Account

Individuals deposit funds in a checking account at a depository institution to write checks or use their debit card to pay for various products and services. A checking account is a very liquid investment because you can access the funds (by withdrawing funds or writing checks) at any time.

overdraft protection
An arrangement that protects a customer who writes a check for an amount that exceeds the checking account balance; it is a short-term loan from the depository institution where the checking account is maintained.

Overdraft Protection. Some depository institutions offer **overdraft protection**, which protects a customer who writes a check for an amount that exceeds the checking account balance. The protection is essentially a short-term loan. For example, if you write a check for $300 but have a checking account balance of only $100, the depository institution will provide overdraft protection by making a loan of $200 to make up the difference. Without overdraft protection, checks written against an insufficient account balance bounce, meaning that they are not honored by the depository institution. In addition, a customer who writes a check that bounces may be charged a penalty fee by the financial institution. Overdraft protection's cost is the high interest rate charged on the loan.

stop payment
A financial institution's notice that it will not honor a check if someone tries to cash it; usually occurs in response to a request by the writer of the check.

Stop Payment. If you write a check but believe that it was lost and never received by the payee, you may request that the financial institution **stop payment**, which means that the institution will not honor the check if someone tries to cash it. In some cases, a customer may even stop payment to prevent the recipient from cashing a check. For example, if you write a check to pay for home repairs, but the job is not completed, you may decide to stop payment on the check. Normally, a fee is charged for a stop payment service.

Fees. Depository institutions may charge a monthly fee such as $15 per month for providing checking services unless the depositor maintains a minimum balance in the checking account or a minimum aggregate balance in other accounts at that institution. Some financial institutions charge a fee per check written instead of a monthly fee. The specific fee structure and the rules for waiving the fee vary among financial institutions, so you should compare fees before you decide where to set up your checking account.

No Interest. A disadvantage of investing funds in a checking account is that the funds do not earn any interest. For this reason, you should keep only enough funds in your checking account to cover anticipated expenses and a small excess amount in case unanticipated expenses arise. You should not deposit more funds in your checking account than you think you may need because you can earn interest by investing in other money market investments.

NOW Account

NOW (negotiable order of withdrawal) account
A type of deposit offered by depository institutions that provides checking services and pays interest.

Another deposit offered by depository institutions is a **negotiable order of withdrawal (NOW) account.** An advantage of a NOW account over a traditional checking account is that it pays interest, although the interest is relatively low compared with many other bank deposits. The depositor is required to maintain a minimum balance in a NOW account, so the account is not as liquid as a traditional checking account.

EXAMPLE

Stephanie Spratt has a checking account with no minimum balance. She is considering opening a NOW account that requires a minimum balance of $500 and offers an interest rate of 3 percent. She has an extra $800 in her checking account that she could transfer to the NOW account. How much interest would she earn over one year in the NOW account?

Interest Earned	= Deposit Amount × Interest Rate
	= $800 × .03
	= $24

Stephanie would earn $24 in annual interest from the NOW account, versus zero interest from her traditional checking account. She would need to maintain the $500 minimum balance in the NOW account, whereas she has the use of all of the funds in her checking account. She decides to leave the funds in the checking account, as the extra liquidity is worth more to her than the $24 she could earn from the NOW account.

Savings Deposit

Traditional savings accounts offered by a depository institution pay a higher interest rate on deposits than offered on a NOW account. In addition, funds can normally be withdrawn from a savings account at any time. A savings account does not provide checking services. It is less liquid than a checking account or a NOW account because you have to go to the institution or to an ATM to access funds, which is less convenient than writing a check. The interest rate offered on savings deposits varies among depository institutions. Many institutions quote their rates on their Web sites.

EXAMPLE

Stephanie Spratt wants to determine the amount of interest that she would earn over one year if she deposits $1,000 in a savings account that pays 4 percent interest.

Interest Earned	= Deposit Amount × Interest Rate
	= $1,000 × .04
	= $40

Although the interest income is attractive, she cannot write checks on a savings account. As she expects to need the funds in her checking account to pay bills in the near future, she decides not to switch those funds to a savings account at this time.

"Your pot o' gold is doing nothing for you sitting at the end of the rainbow. At the very least, you should put it in a no—risk interest-bearing account."

retail CDs
Certificates of deposit that have small denominations (such as $5,000 or $10,000).

Certificate of Deposit

A certificate of deposit (CD) offered by a depository institution specifies a minimum amount that must be invested, a maturity date on which the deposit matures, and an annualized interest rate. Common maturity dates of CDs are one month, three months, six months, one year, three years, and five years. CDs can be purchased by both firms and individuals. CDs that have smaller denominations (such as $5,000 or $10,000) are sometimes referred to as **retail CDs** because they are more attractive to individuals than to firms.

Return. Depository institutions offer higher interest rates on CDs than on savings deposits. The higher return is compensation for being willing to maintain the investment until maturity. Interest rates are quoted on an annualized (yearly) basis. The interest to be generated by your investment in a CD is based on the annualized interest rate and the amount of time until maturity. The interest rates offered on CDs vary among depository institutions.

EXAMPLE	

A three-month (90-day) CD offers an annualized interest rate of 6 percent and requires a $5,000 minimum deposit. You want to determine the amount of interest you would earn if you invested $5,000 in the CD. Since the interest rate is annualized, you will receive only a fraction of the 6 percent rate because your investment is for a fraction of the year:

Interest Earned   = Deposit Amount × Interest Rate

               × Adjustment for Investment Period

              = $5,000 × .06 × 90/365

This process can be more easily understood by noting that the interest rate is applied for only 90 days, whereas the annual interest rate reflects 365 days. The interest rate that applies to your 90-day investment is for about one-fourth (90/365) of the year, so the applicable interest rate is:

Interest Rate   = .06 × 90/365

           = .0148 or 1.48%

The 1.48 percent represents the actual return on your investment.

Now the interest can be determined by simply applying this return to the deposit amount:

Interest Earned   = Deposit Amount × Interest Rate

               = $5,000 × .0148

               = $73.97

Liquidity. A penalty is imposed for early withdrawal from CDs, so these deposits are less liquid than funds deposited in a savings account. You should consider a CD only if you are certain that you will not need the funds until after it matures. You may decide to invest some of your funds in a CD and other funds in more liquid assets.

Choice among CD Maturities. CDs with longer terms to maturity typically offer higher annualized interest rates. However, CDs with longer maturities tie up your funds for a longer period of time and are therefore less liquid. Your choice of a maturity for a CD may depend on your need for liquidity. For example, if you know that you may need your funds in four months, you could invest in a three-month CD and then place the funds in a more liquid asset (such as your checking account or savings account) when the CD matures. If you do not expect to need the funds for one year, you may consider a one-year CD.

FOCUS ON ETHICS: Risky Deposits

Consider the case of a financial institution that promises an annual rate of interest to depositors that is 4 percent higher than the certificate of deposit rates offered by local banks. While this certificate sounds appealing, it is probably much riskier than you think.

A firm is not going to offer an interest rate of 4 percent more than other interest-bearing investments unless it needs to pay such a high return in order to compensate for risk. Inquire if the deposit is insured by the FDIC. While you might possibly earn 4 percent more on this investment than by depositing the funds at a bank, you might also lose 100 percent of your money if the financial institution goes bankrupt. There are many investment companies that prey on individuals (especially the elderly) who presume that because an investment sounds like a bank deposit, it is insured and safe. If an investment sounds too good to be true, it probably is.

Money Market Deposit Account (MMDA)

money market deposit account (MMDA)
A deposit offered by a depository institution that requires a minimum balance, has no maturity date, pays interest, and allows a limited number of checks to be written each month.

A **money market deposit account (MMDA)** is a deposit account offered by a depository institution that requires a minimum balance to be maintained, has no maturity date, pays interest, and allows a limited number of checks to be written each month. The specific details vary among financial institutions. For example, an account might require that a minimum balance of $2,500 be maintained over the month and charge a $15 per month fee in any month when the minimum balance falls below that level.

An MMDA differs from a NOW account in that it provides only limited checking services while paying a higher interest rate than that offered on NOW accounts. Many individuals maintain a checking account or NOW account to cover most of their day-to-day transactions and an MMDA to capitalize on the higher interest rate. Thus, they may maintain a larger amount of funds in the MMDA and use this account to write a large check for an unexpected expense. The MMDA is not as liquid as a checking account because it limits the amount of checks that can be written.

Treasury Bills

Treasury securities
Debt securities issued by the U.S. Treasury.

Treasury securities are debt securities issued by the U.S. Treasury. When the U.S. government needs to spend more money than it has received in taxes, it borrows funds by issuing Treasury securities. Individuals can purchase Treasury securities through a brokerage firm. Treasury securities are offered with various maturities, such as three months, six months, one year, 10 years, and 30 years. For money management purposes, individuals tend to focus on **Treasury bills (T-bills)**, which are Treasury securities that will mature in one year or less. T-bills are available with a minimum value at maturity (called the par value) of $10,000 and are denominated in multiples of $5,000 above that minimum.

Treasury bills (T-bills)
Treasury securities with maturities of one year or less.

Return. Treasury bills are purchased at a discount from par value. If you invest in a T-bill and hold it until maturity, you earn a capital gain, which is the difference between the par value of the T-bill at maturity and the amount you paid for the T-bill. Your return on the T-bill is the capital gain as a percentage of your initial investment.

When measuring returns on investments, you should annualize the returns so that you can compare returns on various investments with different maturities. An investment over a one-month period will likely generate a smaller dollar amount of return than a one-year investment. To compare the one-month and one-year investments, you need to determine the annualized yield (or percentage return) on each investment.

EXAMPLE

An investor pays $9,400 to purchase a T-bill that has a par value of $10,000 and a one-year maturity. When the T-bill matures, she receives $10,000. The return from investing in the T-bill is:

$$\text{Return on T-Bill} = \frac{\$10,000 - \$9,400}{\$9,400}$$

$$= 6.38\%$$

For an investment that lasts three months (one-fourth of a year), multiply by four to determine the annualized return. For an investment that lasts six months (one-half of a year), multiply by two to determine the annualized return. The most precise method of annualizing a return is to multiply the return by 365/N, where N is the number of days the investment existed.

EXAMPLE

An investor pays $9,700 to purchase a T-bill with a par value of $10,000 and a maturity of 182 days. The annualized return from investing in the T-bill is:

$$\text{Return on T-Bill} = \frac{\$10,000 - \$9,700}{\$9,700} \times \frac{365}{182}$$

$$= 6.20\%$$

secondary market
A market where existing securities such as Treasury bills can be purchased or sold.

Secondary Market. There is a **secondary market** for T-bills where they can be sold before their maturity with the help of a brokerage firm. This secondary market also allows individuals to purchase T-bills that were previously owned by someone else. The return on a T-bill is usually slightly lower than the return on a CD with the same maturity, but T-bills are more liquid because they have a secondary market, whereas CDs must be held until maturity. If you sell a T-bill in the secondary market, your capital gain is the difference between what you sold the T-bill for and what you paid for the T-bill. Your return is this capital gain as a percentage of your initial investment.

Quotations. The prices of various T-bills and the returns they offer for holding them until maturity are quoted in financial newspapers and online sites.

Financial Planning Online 11.1: **Interest Rate Data**

Go to
www.federalreserve.gov/
econresdata/releases/
statisticsdata.htm

This Web site provides historical interest rate data.

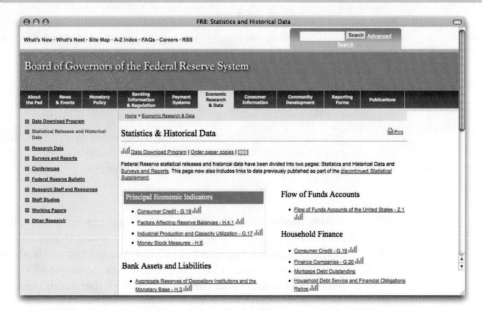

An investor purchases a T-bill for $9,700 and sells the T-bill in the secondary market 60 days later for a price of $9,820. The annualized return is:

$$\text{Return on T-Bill} = \frac{\$9,820 - \$9,700}{\$9,700} \times \frac{365}{60}$$

$$= \ 7.53\%$$

Money Market Funds (MMFs)

money market funds (MMFs)
Accounts that pool money from individuals and invest in securities that have a short-term maturity, such as one year or less.

commercial paper
Short-term debt securities issued by large corporations that typically offer a slightly higher return than Treasury bills.

Money market funds (MMFs) pool money from individuals to invest in securities that have a short-term maturity, such as one year or less. In fact, the average time remaining to maturity of debt securities held in an MMF is typically less than 90 days. Many MMFs invest in short-term Treasury securities or in wholesale CDs (in denominations of $100,000 or more). Investors can invest in MMFs by sending a check for the amount they wish to have invested for them. Some MMFs invest mainly in **commercial paper,** which consists of short-term debt securities issued by large corporations. Commercial paper typically generates a slightly higher interest rate than T-bills. Money market funds are not insured, but most of them invest in very safe investments and have a very low risk of default.

MMFs offer some liquidity in that individuals can write a limited number of checks on their accounts each month. Often the checks must exceed a minimum amount (such as $250). Individuals may use the checking account associated with an MMF to cover large expenditures, while maintaining a regular checking account to cover smaller purchases. Many individuals invest in an MMF so that they can earn interest until the money is needed. Some MMFs are linked with other accounts so that the money can earn interest until it is transferred to another account. For example, many brokerage accounts allow investors to place any unused funds in an MMF until the funds are used to purchase stock.

Assume that you set up an account with $9,000 to purchase stock at a brokerage firm on May 1. On that day, you purchase 100 shares of a stock priced at $50. To cover the purchase, the brokerage firm withdraws $5,000 ($50 × 100 shares) from your account. You still have $4,000 that you have not used, which is placed in a specific MMF account at the brokerage firm. This MMF offers the same limited check-writing services as other MMFs. The money will sit in that account until you use it to purchase stock or write checks against the account.

Assuming that the interest rate earned on the MMF is 6 percent annually (.5 percent per month), and you do not purchase any more stock until June 1, you will earn interest on that account over the month when the funds are not used:

Amount Invested in MMF × Interest Rate per Month = Interest Earned in 1 Month

$4,000 × .005 = $20

Therefore, the MMF account balance increases by $20 to $4,020 because the funds have earned interest. Any unused balance will continue to earn interest until you use it to purchase stock or write checks against the account.

Money Market Fund Quotations. Financial newspapers such as *The Wall Street Journal* commonly publish the yields provided by numerous money market funds. An example of the typical information provided in the quotations is shown in Exhibit 11.1 for one money market fund. The first column lists the name of the MMF; the second column, the average maturity of the investments of that fund; the third column, the annualized

Exhibit 11.1	Weekly Money Market Fund Yields		
Fund	**Average Maturity**	**7-Day Yield**	**Assets (millions of $)**
Star Fund	43	3.28%	496

yield generated by the fund; and the fourth column, the size of the fund (measured in millions of dollars). Review the quotation for Star Fund in Exhibit 11.1, which invests in government securities that have a short term remaining until maturity. This fund's investments have an average time to maturity of 43 days. It generated an annual yield of 3.28 percent for its investors over the last seven days. The fund presently manages $496 million in assets.

Asset Management Account

asset management account
An account that combines deposit accounts with a brokerage account and provides a single consolidated statement.

An **asset management account** combines deposit accounts with a brokerage account that is used to buy or sell stocks. The advantage of an asset management account is that it provides a single consolidated statement showing the ending balances and activity of all the accounts. Asset management accounts are available at some depository institutions and brokerage services. The financial institutions that offer these accounts require that the sum of all the accounts in the asset management account exceed some minimum amount, such as $15,000. A special type of asset management account is the **sweep account**, which sweeps any unused balance in the brokerage account into a money market investment at the end of each business day. The unused balance earns interest and remains available for writing checks.

sweep account
An asset management account that sweeps any unused balance in the brokerage account into a money market investment at the end of each business day.

Comparison of Money Market Investments

The various types of money market investments are compared in Exhibit 11.2. Notice that money market investments that offer a higher return tend to have less liquidity.

The relationship between the returns and the liquidity of money market investments is illustrated graphically in Exhibit 11.3. Checking accounts offer the most liquidity but provide no return. At the other extreme, a one-year CD provides the highest return but has less liquidity than the other money market instruments.

Exhibit 11.2	Comparison of Money Market Investments	
Money Market Investment	**Advantages**	**Disadvantages**
Checking account	Very liquid	No interest
NOW account	Very liquid	Low interest rate; minimum balance required
MMDA	Liquid	Low interest rate
Savings account	Liquid	Low interest rate
Certificate of deposit (CD)	Relatively high interest rate	Less liquid
Treasury bill	Relatively high interest rate	High minimum purchase
Money market fund (MMF)	Liquid	Not as liquid as checking or NOW accounts
Asset management account	Convenient	High minimum balance required

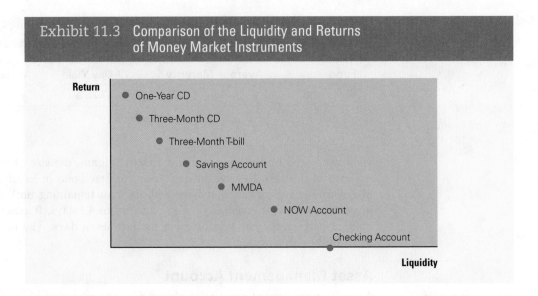

Exhibit 11.3 Comparison of the Liquidity and Returns of Money Market Instruments

■ RISK OF MONEY MARKET INVESTMENTS

Before you consider investing short-term funds in various money market instruments, you must factor in your exposure to risk, or the uncertainty surrounding the potential return. Money market investments are vulnerable to three types of risk: (1) credit risk, (2) interest rate risk, and (3) liquidity risk.

Credit Risk

credit risk
(or default risk)
The risk that a borrower may not repay on a timely basis.

When you invest in money market securities, you may be exposed to **credit risk** (also referred to as **default risk**), which is the risk that the borrower will not repay on a timely basis. The borrower may make late payments or even default on the credit. In that event, you will receive only a portion (or none) of the money you invested. MMFs that invest in large deposits of financial institutions that are insured only up to $250,000 by the Federal Deposit Insurance Corporation (FDIC). Treasury securities are backed by the federal government, but most other types of money market securities are subject to

---

Financial Planning Online 11.2: Impact of Different Deposit Rates on Your Wealth

Go to
cgi.money.cnn.com/tools/
savingscalc/savingscalc
.html

This Web site provides
estimates of future savings
that you will accumulate
over time at different interest rates in taxable or non-
taxable accounts adjusted
for inflation.

Retirement Savings: How fast will it grow? - Calculator - CNNMoney.com

CNNMoney.com
A Service of CNN, Fortune & Money

| Symbol | Get Quote | Keyword | Search |

• Subscribe to Fortune
• Free Trial
• Magazine Customer Service

Home   Business News   Markets   Personal Finance   Retirement   Technology   Luxury   Small Business   Fortune   Video   My Portfolio   CNN.co

How fast will my savings grow

From the editors of:
Money MAGAZINE

| Most Popular Questions | Top News From CNNMoney.com | Most Popular Videos |

① Taxable accounts

How much you have: _____

How much you will save: _____

per year ▼

Your federal rate: 28% ▼

Your state rate: 6% ▼

② Tax-deferred accounts

How much you have: _____

How much you will save: _____

per year ▼

Retirement calculators

• What you need to save
• How much will you need?
• Can you retire early?
• How does your net worth compare?
• When will you be a millionaire?
• Get income for life
• Compare cost of living in 2 cities
• Get the right asset allocation

1. How much money do I need?

2. Is a Roth 401(k) for me?

3. How does Social Security work?

4. What is an annuity?

5. When can I access my IRA?

the possibility of default. However, the potential for default is very low for some types of money market securities, but it is important that you assess this risk before you invest money in money market securities.

Interest Rate Risk

interest rate risk
The risk that the value of an investment could decline as a result of a change in interest rates.

Interest rate risk is the risk that the value of an investment could decline as a result of a change in interest rates. Investors who wish to limit their exposure to interest rate risk can invest in debt securities that fit the time frame in which they will need funds. That is, if you need funds in three months, you should consider an investment that has a maturity of three months, so that you do not have to worry about changes in interest rates. The following example illustrates how the value of an investment can be affected by interest rate movements.

EXAMPLE

Suppose that three months ago you purchased a one-year T-bill that offered a return of 5 percent. Interest rates have recently risen and you are disappointed that you locked in your investment at 5 percent while more recently issued investments (including one-year T-bills) are now offering an annualized return of about 6 percent. You can sell your T-bill in the secondary market, but investors will pay a relatively low price for it because they can buy new securities that offer an annualized return of 6 percent. This explains why the value of a debt security decreases in response to an increase in interest rates.

Rather than selling your T-bill at a discounted price, you can simply hold it to maturity. However, the return on your investment over the entire one-year period will be only 5 percent, even though recently issued T-bills are offering higher returns. Neither of your two options is desirable.

Liquidity Risk

liquidity risk
The potential loss that could occur as a result of converting an investment into cash.

Recall that liquidity represents your ability to cover any short-term cash deficiencies. To be liquid, an investment should be easily converted to cash. **Liquidity risk** is the potential loss that could occur as a result of converting an investment to cash. For example, a retail CD has liquidity risk because it cannot be sold in the secondary market. You would suffer a penalty if you tried to redeem it before maturity at the financial institution where you invested in the CD.

The liquidity risk of an investment is influenced by its secondary market. If a particular debt security has a strong secondary market, it can usually be sold quickly and at less of a discount than a debt security with an inactive secondary market. For example, you can easily sell a T-bill in a secondary market, which is why T-bills are more liquid than CDs.

FINANCIAL IMPACT

Impact of Expected Economic Conditions on Liquidity Needs

When economic conditions weaken, it can create some liquidity problems, as shown in Exhibit 11.4. For example, during the financial crisis in 2008–2009, some individuals lost their jobs. Other individuals who retained their jobs did not work as much as expected, and therefore earned less income than they anticipated. Many retired individuals relied on their investments for income, but their investments generated very poor returns over this period, which resulted in lower income than expected. As a result, their cash inflows were not always large enough to cover their cash outflows.

If you suspect that economic conditions may weaken and may possibly result in lower income from your employer or your investments, you may wish to ensure that you maintain a greater degree of liquidity. You could allocate more funds to liquid money market securities and less to other types of investments. In this way, if economic conditions weaken and reduce your cash inflows, you can rely on your money market securities as a source of liquidity.

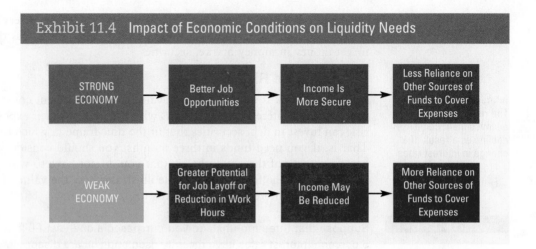

Exhibit 11.4   Impact of Economic Conditions on Liquidity Needs

QUESTIONS

a. **Economic Impact on Liquidity Needs.** Assume that your monthly expenses will not change over the next three years, but you expect that the economy will be much weaker in about a year. Explain why you may need more liquidity even if your expenses do not change.

b. **Cost of Maintaining More Liquidity.** Explain why maintaining more liquidity during a weak economy is costly. What is the disadvantage of keeping most of your assets in a very liquid form?

■ RISK MANAGEMENT OF MONEY MARKET INVESTMENTS

Risk management of money market investments involves (1) assessing the risk exhibited by the investments and (2) using your assessment of risk and your unique financial situation to determine the optimal allocation of your short-term funds among money market investments.

Financial Planning Online 11.3: **Identifying Insured Investments**

Go to
www.fdic.gov/consumers/
consumer/information/
fdiciorn.html

This Web site provides
information about what
types of investments are
insured and what types are
not.

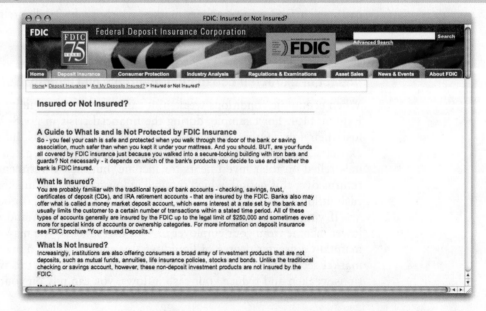

Risk Assessment of Money Market Investments

You must consider the risk-return trade-off before making investment decisions. The money market securities described in this chapter tend to be insulated from credit risk because they are insured or backed by the government. Treasury securities and small bank deposits are largely free from credit risk. One exception is MMFs that invest in commercial paper. If the commercial paper held by a particular MMF defaults, the return generated by the MMF will be adversely affected, and so will the return to investors who invested in that MMF.

As mentioned earlier, money market investments that have shorter maturities have less interest rate risk. In addition, investments in MMFs tend to have the least liquidity risk, especially when their investments focus on securities that will mature within the next month. Treasury securities that will mature in the next month or so also have very little liquidity risk.

Would you invest in a high-risk security if a lower-risk security offered the same yield? Probably not. Securities that are exposed to risk have to offer higher yields than less risky investments to attract funds from investors. The prospect of a higher return compensates investors for taking on a higher level of risk. Investors can earn a higher return by investing in MMFs that hold investments subject to credit risk and for securities that are particularly vulnerable to interest rate risk. Recall that debt securities with shorter maturities offer lower annualized yields. A three-month debt security typically offers a slightly lower annualized yield than a one-year security. However, the debt securities with longer maturities are more exposed to interest rate movements.

Yields are also higher for securities that are more exposed to liquidity risk. A retail CD must offer a slightly higher yield than a Treasury security with the same maturity because the Treasury security is more liquid.

Determining the Optimal Allocation of Money Market Investments

In general, your money management should be guided by the following steps:

1. Anticipate your upcoming bills and ensure that you have sufficient funds in your checking account.
2. Estimate the additional funds that you might need in the near future and consider investing them in an investment that offers sufficient liquidity (such as an MMF). You may even keep a little extra in reserve here for unanticipated expenses.
3. Use the remaining funds in a manner that will earn you a higher return, within your level of risk tolerance.

The optimal allocation for you will likely be different from the optimal allocation for another individual. If your future net cash flows will be far short of upcoming expenses, you will need to keep a relatively large proportion of funds in a liquid investment (such as a checking account or a NOW account). Another person who has sufficient cash flows to cover expenses will not need much liquidity. The difference is illustrated in Exhibit 11.5. Even though the two individuals have the same level of net cash flows, one person must maintain more liquidity than the other.

Your decision on how to invest your short-term funds (after determining how much money to maintain in your checking account) should account for your willingness to tolerate risk. If you want to minimize all forms of risk, you may simply consider investing all of your funds in an MMF that always focuses on Treasury securities maturing within a month or less. However, you will likely improve on the yield if you are willing to accept some degree of risk.

For example, if you know that you will not need your funds for at least six months and do not expect interest rates to rise substantially over that period, you might consider investing your funds in a six-month retail CD. A compromise would be to invest a portion of your short-term funds in the six-month retail CD and the remaining funds in

Exhibit 11.5   How Liquidity Is Affected by Anticipated Expenses

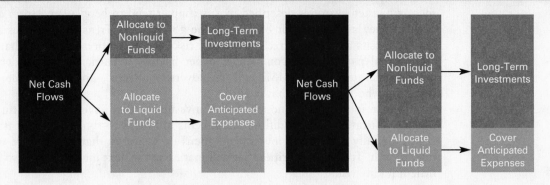

the MMF that focuses on Treasury securities. The CD offers you a higher expected return (although less liquidity), while the MMF offers you liquidity in case you need funds immediately.

EXAMPLE

Stephanie Spratt has $2,000 available to allocate to money market investments. She knows that she will need $400 to cover several small bills in the next week and may also need $600 in a month or so to pay for repairs on her car engine. She does not expect to need the other funds for at least six months. Her financial institution offers the following annualized yields on various money market instruments:

	Annualized Yield (%)
Checking account	0
NOW account ($500 minimum balance)	2.0
Savings deposit	3.0
MMDA ($2,500 minimum balance)	4.0
MMF ($300 minimum balance)	4.0
Three-month CD	4.5
Six-month CD	5.2
One-year CD	6.0

Stephanie's existing checking account has a balance close to zero. She also has an MMF with a balance of $300, which she must maintain to meet the minimum balance. She will first focus on meeting her liquidity needs and then decide how to invest the remaining funds that are not needed to cover possible expenses. She decides to allocate $400 to her checking account so that she can write several checks to cover her upcoming bills. It is not worthwhile to invest these funds elsewhere as she will need the funds soon, and the checking account is the only investment that will allow her to write several small checks.

She knows that she might need another $600 in the near future for car repairs, but wants to earn as high a return as possible until she needs the money. She immediately eliminates the MMDA from consideration because it would require a minimum balance of $2,500. She decides to invest the $600 in her MMF. She can write a check from this account to cover the car repairs; meanwhile, the funds invested in the MMF will earn 4 percent interest on an annualized basis.

Stephanie now has $1,000 remaining to allocate and anticipates that she will not need the money for at least six months. She does not consider investing the $1,000 in a one-year CD, even though it offers a relatively high interest rate, because she may need the funds in six months. She decides to invest the $1,000 in a six-month CD, so that she can increase liquidity while still earning a relatively high return.

If Stephanie had excess funds that she would not need for a few years, she would consider investing the residual in other investments (such as stocks) that offer a higher potential return. The potential return and risk on these other investments are discussed in Part 5.

■ HOW MONEY MANAGEMENT FITS WITHIN YOUR FINANCIAL PLAN

The following are the key money management decisions that you should include in your financial plan:

- How can you ensure that you can pay your anticipated bills on time?
- How can you maintain adequate liquidity in case you incur unanticipated expenses?
- How should you invest any remaining funds among money market investments?

By making proper decisions, you can minimize your use of credit and maximize the return on your liquid assets. As an example, Exhibit 11.6 shows how money market decisions apply to Stephanie Spratt's financial plan.

Exhibit 11.6 How Money Management Fits Within Stephanie Spratt's Financial Plan

GOALS FOR MONEY MANAGEMENT

1. Maintain sufficient liquidity to ensure that all anticipated bills are paid on time.
2. Maintain sufficient liquidity in case I incur unanticipated expenses.
3. Invest any excess funds in deposits that offer the highest return while ensuring adequate liquidity.

ANALYSIS

	Amount	Payment Method
Monthly cash inflows	$2,500	Direct deposited into checking account.
Typical monthly expenses	1,400	Write checks to pay these bills.
Other expenses for clothing or recreation	700	Use credit cards and then pay the credit card balance by check once a month.

DECISIONS

**Decision on How to Ensure Adequate Liquidity
to Cover Anticipated Expenses:**

The two paychecks I receive each month amounting to $2,500 after taxes are direct deposited into my checking account. I can use this account to cover the $1,400 in anticipated bills each month. I can also use this account to write a check for the monthly credit card bill. I will attempt to leave about $400 extra in the checking account because my expenses may vary from month to month.

**Decision on How to Ensure Liquidity
to Cover Unanticipated Expenses:**

I will also attempt to maintain about $2,500 in a money market fund or a money market deposit account in case I need additional funds. I can earn interest on this money while ensuring liquidity.

(continues)

Exhibit 11.6   How Money Management Fits Within Stephanie Spratt's Financial Plan (continued)

**Decision on How to Invest Remaining Funds
to Achieve the Highest Return While Enhancing Liquidity:**

As I accumulate additional savings, I will invest in certificates of deposit with short terms to maturity (such as one month). This money will not be as liquid as the MMF or MMDA, but it will be accessible when the CD matures. The interest rate on the CD will be higher than the interest I can earn on my MMF or MMDA.

DISCUSSION QUESTIONS

1. How would Stephanie's money management decisions be different if she were a single mother of two children?

2. How would Stephanie's money management decisions be affected if she were 35 years old? If she were 50 years old?

SUMMARY

▪ Money management involves the selection of short-term investments that satisfy your liquidity needs and also provide you with an adequate return on your investment. It is challenging because the short-term investments that offer relatively high returns tend to have less liquidity.

▪ Popular short-term investments considered for money management include checking accounts, NOW accounts, savings accounts, CDs, MMDAs, Treasury bills, money market funds, and asset management accounts. Checking accounts and NOW accounts offer the most liquidity. CDs and T-bills offer the highest return.

▪ The risks related to money market investments are credit (default) risk, interest rate risk, and liquidity risk. The money market investments offered by depository institutions are insured and insulate you from the risk that the institution

could default. Investments in T-bills have no default risk because they are backed by the federal government. Money market securities tend to have a low level of interest rate risk because they have short-term maturities. They also have relatively low liquidity risk because of the short-term maturities of their assets.

▪ When applying money management, you should first anticipate your expenses in the next month and maintain enough funds in your checking account to cover those expenses. In addition, you should estimate the potential level of unanticipated expenses (such as possible car repairs) and maintain enough funds in a short-term investment such as a money market fund to cover these expenses. Finally, invest the remaining funds to earn a high return within your level of risk tolerance.

REVIEW QUESTIONS

1. **Money Management.** Define money management. How does it differ from long-term investment or long-term borrowing decisions?

2. **Liquidity.** What is liquidity? How is your personal cash flow statement used to help manage your liquidity? How does money management relate to the cash flow statement?

3. **Cash Flow Deficiency.** Name some ways an individual might handle a cash flow deficiency. Which way would be preferable? Why?

4. **Opportunity Cost of Liquid Funds.** What is the opportunity cost of having excessive amounts of liquid funds?

5. **Liquid Investments.** What two factors affect the return on short-term investments? What investments should you consider to achieve liquidity and an adequate return?

6. **Checking Accounts.** Why do individuals use checking accounts? What is the disadvantage of having funds in a checking account? Explain overdraft protection and stop payment orders. Are all bank fee structures the same?

7. **Now Account.** What is a NOW account? How is it different from a regular checking account? How does a savings account compare with a NOW account?

8. **CDs.** What terms does a financial institution specify for certificates of deposit? Why are rates

on CDs higher than those on savings accounts? What factor would most affect your choice of maturity date on a CD?

9. **MMDAs.** How does a money market deposit account (MMDA) differ from a NOW account? When might a depositor use an MMDA?

10. **Treasury Securities.** What are Treasury securities? What is a T-bill? How is it denominated? How do you earn a return on a T-bill? How is the return calculated?

11. **T-bills Versus CDs.** Compare the interest rates offered on T-bills and CDs. Which type of investment is more liquid? Why?

12. **MMFs.** What are money market funds (MMFs)? What types of securities do they invest in? What is commercial paper? Are MMFs risky investments? Are MMFs liquid?

13. **Asset Management Account.** What is an asset management account? Discuss the advantages of such an account as well as its requirements.

14. **Money Market Investments.** Compare the return and liquidity of the various money market investments. Give specific examples.

15. **Risk of Money Market Investments.** What are the three types of risk that affect money market investments?

16. **Risk of Money Market Investments.** Generally compare the money market investments described in this chapter in terms of their vulnerability to credit risk, interest rate risk, and liquidity risk. Provide some examples of specific securities. What is the risk-return tradeoff for these investments?

17. **Money Market Investments.** What steps should you take to determine the best allocation of your money market investments? What factors should you consider in determining your allocation?

FINANCIAL PLANNING PROBLEMS

1. **Interest Earned.** Teresa has just opened a NOW account that pays 3.5 percent interest. If she maintains a minimum balance of $500 for the next 12 months, how much interest will she earn?

2. **Interest Earned.** Lisa is depositing $2,500 in a six-month CD that pays 4.25 percent interest.

How much interest will she accrue if she holds the CD until maturity?

3. **Value of CD.** Travis has invested $3,000 in a three-month CD at 4 percent. How much will Travis have when the CD matures?

4. **Interest Earned.** Claire has invested $10,000 in an 18-month CD that pays 6.25 percent. How much interest will Claire receive at maturity?

5. **T-bill Return.** Troy paid $9,600 for a T-bill with a face value of $10,000. What is Troy's return if he holds the T-bill to maturity?

6. **MMF Value.** Bart is a college student who has never invested his funds. He has saved $1,000 and has decided to invest it in a money market fund with an expected return of 2.0 percent. Bart will need the money in one year. The MMF imposes fees that will cost Bart $20 at the time he withdraws his funds. How much money will Bart have in one year as a result of this investment?

7. **Return on T-bills.** Dave has $20,000 excess cash to invest. He can purchase a $20,000 T-bill for $19,400 or two $10,000 T-bills for $9,600 each. Which will give him the better return?

8. **Return on T-bills.** Stacy purchased a $40,000 T-bill for $38,400. A few months later, Lauren sold the T-bill for $39,000. What was Lauren's return on the T-bill?

9. **Annualized T-bill Rate.** Brenda purchased a $30,000, 90-day T-bill for $29,550. What will Brenda's return be when the T-bill matures? What will her annualized rate be?

10. **Interest Earned.** On June 1, Mia deposited $4,000 in an MMDA that pays 5 percent interest. On October 31, Mia invested $2,000 in a three-month CD that pays 6 percent. At the end of the year, how much interest will Mia have earned, assuming she hasn't taken anything out of the money market deposit account?

11. **Investment Return.** Thomas can invest $10,000 by purchasing a 1-year T-bill for $9,275, or he can place the $10,000 in a 12-month CD paying 8 percent. Which investment will provide a higher return? In addition to return, what else should Thomas consider when making his investment decision?

12. **ETHICAL DILEMMA:** Jason is in his mid-50s and was raised by parents of the Depression era. As a result, he is very risk adverse. He recently

came into a very large amount of money and he wants to put it where it will be safe, but where it will earn him some return. His banker tells him that he should put the money in a five-year CD. Jason asks if there is any way he can lose his money and he is told that the federal government insures the deposit and will give him a higher return than a passbook savings account. Jason purchases a CD and goes home happy knowing that his money is safe and available whenever he needs it.

Four months later, the roof on Jason's barn collapses and he needs the money to make repairs, but finds that he can only withdraw it at a substantial penalty.

a. Comment on the ethics of the banker in not fully discussing all the risks of money market investments.

b. Is Jason correct in his thinking that he can find a totally risk-free investment?

FINANCIAL PLANNING ONLINE EXERCISES

1. Go to www.bankrate.com/checking.aspx and answer the following questions:

a. What bank in what city, nationally, will give you the highest rate on an MMA?

b. What bank in what city, locally, will give you the highest rate on an MMA?

c. Locate "CDs and Investments" and find what bank in what city, nationally, will pay you the highest rate on a one-year CD.

d. Locate "CDs and Investments" and find what bank in what city, locally, will pay you the highest rate on a one-year CD.

2. Go to www.bankrate.com/calculators/savings/simple-savings-calculator.aspx. Using this site, you can estimate how your savings will grow.

a. By inputting an investment amount, the monthly deposit, the return, and the period of investment, you can calculate the value of your investment. Input $5,000 as the initial investment, $100 for the monthly deposit, and 6 percent for the return. How much will your investment be worth in 20 years? Click on the Graphs option to view the results graphically.

b. Now change the monthly deposit to $300. How much will your investment be worth in 20 years?

c. Now change the period of investment to 30 years. How much more money will you be able to accumulate in 30 years as opposed to 20, using the original $100 monthly deposit amount?

d. Now change the rate you can earn on your investment from 6 to 8 percent and evaluate the results and graph using the original inputs.

3. Go to www.fdic.gov/consumers/consumer/information/fdiciorn.html and answer the following questions:

a. List at least three types of bank accounts that are insured by the FDIC. Are money market deposit accounts insured and, if so, to what limit?

b. List three types of consumer investment products that are not insured.

c. Are Treasury Securities insured by the FDIC? If Treasury Securities payments of interest and principal are deposited to your checking account are they FDIC insured? Explain.

d. If you have a safety deposit box at an FDIC-insured bank, are the contents of the box insured by the FDIC? Explain fully.

VIDEO EXERCISE: Investing in Money Markets

Go to one of the Web sites that contain video clips (such as www.youtube.com) and view some video clips about investing in money market securities. You can use search phrases such as "investing in money markets." Select one video clip on this topic that you would recommend for the other students in your class.

1. Provide the Web link for the video clip.

2. What do you think is the main point of this video clip?

3. How might you change your investment in money market securities as a result of watching this video clip?

BUILDING YOUR OWN FINANCIAL PLAN

Money market investments provide vehicles to assist you in accomplishing your short-term financial goals. Refer to the three short-term goals you established in Chapter 8. Then turn to the worksheets at the end of this chapter, and to the CD-ROM accompanying this text, to continue building your financial plan.

Note: You may find it necessary to revisit some of the financial institutions involved in your analysis to gather the information necessary to select the most appropriate money market investment for each short-term goal.

THE SAMPSONS—A CONTINUING CASE

Recall from Chapter 9 that the Sampsons currently have about $300 in cash and $1,700 in their checking account. This amount should be enough to cover upcoming bills. The Sampsons have just started saving $800 per month. This money will be placed in CDs every month. These funds, earmarked for a down payment on a car and their children's college education, are not available to the Sampsons for the maturity of the CD. Review the Sampsons' recent cash flow statement and personal balance sheet. The monthly savings of $800 are not included in the cash flow statement.

The Sampsons' Personal Cash Flow Statement

Cash Inflows (Monthly)	**$4,000**
Cash Outflows (Monthly)	
Mortgage payment	$900
Cable TV	60
Electricity and water	80
Telephone	70
Groceries	500
Health care insurance and expenses	160
Clothing	280
Car expenses (insurance, maintenance, and gas)	400
School expenses	100
Partial payment of credit card balance	20
Recreation	700
Total Cash Outflows	**$3,270**
Net Cash Flows (Monthly)	**+ $730**

The Sampsons' Personal Balance Sheet

Assets	
Liquid Assets	
Cash	$300
Checking account	1,700
Savings account	0
Total liquid assets	**$2,000**
Household Assets	
Home	$130,000
Cars	9,000
Furniture	3,000
Total household assets	**$142,000**
Investment Assets	
Stocks	0
Total investment assets	**0**
Total Assets	**$144,000**
Liabilities and Net Worth	
Current Liabilities	
Credit card balance	$2,000
Total current liabilities	$2,000
Long-Term Liabilities	
Mortgage	$100,000
Car loan	0
Total long-term liabilities	$100,000
Total Liabilities	$102,000
Net Worth	**$42,000**

Go to the worksheets at the end of this chapter, and to the CD-ROM accompanying this text, to continue this case.

Chapter 11: Building Your Own Financial Plan

GOALS

1. Maintain sufficient liquidity to ensure that all your anticipated bills are paid on time.

2. Maintain sufficient liquidity so that you can cover unanticipated expenses.

3. Invest any excess funds in deposits that offer the highest return while ensuring liquidity.

ANALYSIS

1. Review the cash flow statement you prepared in Chapter 10 and assess your liquidity.

2. Evaluate the short-term goals you created in Chapter 9 as high, medium, or low with respect to liquidity, risk, fees/minimum balance, and return.

Short-Term Goal Prioritization of Factors

Short-Term Goal	Liquidity	Risk	Fees/Minimum Balance	Return

3. Rank each of the money market investments as good, fair, or poor with respect to liquidity, risk, fees/minimum balance, and return.

Money Market Investment	Liquidity	Risk	Fees/Minimum Balance	Return
Checking Account				
NOW Account				
Savings Account				
Money Market Deposit Account (MMDA)				
Certificate of Deposit				
Treasury Bill				
Money Market Fund				
Asset Management Account				

DECISIONS

1. Describe how you will ensure adequate liquidity to cover anticipated expenses.

_____

_____

_____

_____

_____

_____

_____

2. Detail how you will ensure liquidity to meet unanticipated expenses.

_____

_____

_____

_____

_____

_____

_____

_____

3. Explain which money market investments will be most effective in reaching your short-term goals.

_____

_____

_____

_____

_____

_____

_____

Chapter 11: The Sampsons—A Continuing Case

CASE QUESTIONS

1. Based on the cash flow statement and personal balance sheet, do the Sampsons have adequate liquidity to cover their recurring cash flows and planned monthly savings in the long-run? If not, what level of savings should they maintain for liquidity purposes?

_____

_____

_____

_____

_____

_____

_____

_____

_____

_____

2. Advise the Sampsons on money market investments they should consider to provide them with adequate liquidity.

_____

_____

_____

_____

_____

_____

_____

_____

_____

_____

_____

_____

Chapter 12
Your Credit Score

YOU KNOW YOUR SHOE SIZE, YOUR BIRTHDAY, and how many siblings you have, but did you know there is one number that could affect how much you pay for a car or a house, or what kind of job you can get? It is your credit score, and knowing how to build and protect it will save you thousands of dollars over a lifetime.

Credit Reports

Your **credit report** is a collection of information about you and your credit history.

Every time you fill out a credit application, whether it is for a credit card, a car loan, or to rent an apartment, you are providing information. Using the example of applying for a store credit card, once you have filled out the application at the Gems and Junk Store, the store starts a process to "check you out."

First, it will use one of the three credit reporting agencies: Experian, Equifax, or TransUnion, to order your credit report. When it requests your report, it will type in the current information you just supplied. This happens every time you apply for credit, and it becomes part of the information that will be provided to the next company that pulls your credit report.

These three agencies do not give an opinion of you or provide a recommendation as to whether or not you should be given the credit; they simply take the information that is supplied to them and produce what is commonly known as a credit report.

On the following pages, you will get an idea of what a credit report may look like.

This sample credit report is divided into these sections:

Personal Information – including your name, current and past addresses, telephone number(s), date of birth, Social Security number, marital status, number of dependents, whether you own or rent your property, and how long you have lived there. It will also include your current and past employers, your positions, and your dates of employment.

Account Information – this is where every account you currently have, or have had in the past, is listed. Each account, or line of trade (you are trading money for a product or service), will show when the account was opened, if there is a balance owing, and how many times you have been 30, 60, or 90 days late in the past. There may also be notes showing whether the account is open in good standing or has been closed, either by you or by the creditor. If you are an authorized user on someone else's account, such as that of your spouse or parents, this will also be reflected in this section.

Public Record Information – matters of public record obtained from government sources such as courts of law—including liens, bankruptcies, and overdue child support — may appear on your credit report. Most public record information stays on your credit report for seven years. It is your responsibility at the end of that time to request that the information

FIGURE **15** | Sample Credit Report

> ▶ Print This Page   ▶ Close Window

3-in-1 Credit Report as of June 6, 2011

Name:	MELISSA CARSON

This credit report is available for you to view until date. This report will not update. If you would like a credit report as of a later date, you may order another one in the Member Center.

Section Title	Section Description
1. Personal Information	Personal data, addresses, employment history
2. Account Information	Detailed account information
3. Inquiries	Companies that have requested or viewed your credit information
4. Collections	Accounts turned over to collection agencies
5. Public Records	Bankruptcies, lines, garnishments, and other judgment
6. Consumer Statement	Letter added to credit file written by consumer
7. Dispute File Information	How to dispute information found on this credit report

Personal Information

This 3-in-1 Credit Report is available for you to view until date. This report will not update. If you would like a current 3-in-1 Credit Report, you may order another by clicking Order New Report above.

Registration Information

Name: MELISSA CARSON
Address: 123 Peachtree Circle Atlanta, GA 30303
Social Security Number: 123-45-6789

The following information is from the three nationwide credit reporting agencies.

Identification Information

	Equifax	Experian	TransUnion
	Reported	Reported	Reported
Name:	MELISSA CARSON	MELISSA CARSON	MELISSA J CARSON
Social Security Number:	123456789	123456789	123456789
Age or Date of Birth:	03/1958	03/1958	03/1958

Address Information

	Equifax	Experian	TransUnion
	Reported	Reported	Reported
Address:	123 Peachtree Circle Atlanta GA 30303	123 Peachtree Circle 123456789	123 Peachtree Circle 123456789
Date Reported:	07/2011	09/2011	07/2011
	Reported	Reported	Reported
Address:	123 Wyndham Ct BIRMINGHAM AL 35226	123 Wyndham Ct BIRMINGHAM AL 35226	123 Wyndham Ct BIRMINGHAM AL 35226
Date Reported:	05/2010	06/2010	06/2010

Please note: All references to consumers, creditors, account numbers, and credit reporting agencies are for illustration purposes only and are not intended to be actual or legitimate.

FIGURE **15** | **Continued**

Employment Information

	Equifax Reported	Experian Reported	TransUnion Reported
Employer:	ABC CORP		ABC CORP
Address:			
Date Reported:	02/2005		

⬆ Back to Top

Account Information

Key

KEY: Meaning	Pays or Paid as Agreed	30 Days Past Due	60 Days Past Due	90 Days Past Due	120+ Days Past Due/ Collection Account	Payment Plan	Repossession or Foreclosure	Charged Off to bad debt	Not Reported
Symbol	*	30	60	90	120	PP	RF	CO	NR

123 CREDIT CO

	Equifax Reported	Experian Reported	TransUnion Reported
Account Type:	Revolving	Revolving	Revolving
Account Number:	533696884221XXXX	533696884221XXXX	533696884221XXXX
Payment Responsibility:	Individual	Individual	Individual
Date Opened:	02/2005	02/2005	02/2005
Balance Date :	06/2011	06/2011	06/2011
Balance Amount :	$0	$0	$0
Monthly Payment:			
High/Limit:	$3,200	$3,200	$3,200
Account Status:	As Agreed	As Agreed	As Agreed
Past Due Amount:	$0	$0	$0
Comments:	ACCOUNT PAID ACCOUNT CLOSED BY CONSUMER	ACCOUNT PAID SATISFACTORILY ACCOUNT CLOSED BY CONSUMER	ACCOUNT CLOSED BY CONSUMER

123 CREDIT CO

123 Allyson Rd
Tucson, AZ 19019
(215) 555-8863

(Continued)

FIGURE **15** | **Continued**

Inquiries

Equifax

Name of Company	Date of Inquiry	Type of Business
ABC LENDING CO	04/06/11	Finance
123 UTILITY	04/06/11	Utilites and Fuel
321 LOANS	02/21/10	Finance
XYZ CREDIT	01/29/12	Miscellaneous and Public Record

Experian

Name of Company	Date of Inquiry	Type of Business
789 MOBILE	02/19/11	Utilites and Fuel

TransUnion

Name of Company	Date of Inquiry	Type of Business
XYZ INSTALLMENT LOANS	04/08/11	Finance
AAA MORTGAGE	11/10/10	Finance

⬆ Back to Top

Collections

	Equifax	Experian	TransUnion
	Reported	**Reported**	**Reported**
Collector:	321 INSTALLMENT LOANS	321 INSTALLMENT LOANS	321 INSTALLMENT LOANS
Account Number:	25XXXX	25XXXX	25XXXX
Date Opened:			
Balance Date:	10/2011	10/2011	10/2011
Balance Amount:	$35	$35	$35
Date of Status:	10/2011	10/2011	10/2011
Status:	Unpaid	Unpaid	Unpaid

321 INSTALLMENT LOANS

7754 W 84th St

Chicago, IL 60601
(770) 740-7400

be removed from your report. If you are ever sued in court over a debt, such as back child support or failure to pay your rent or house payment, and you lose the lawsuit, there will be a **judgment** against you. The person or company to whom you owe the money can take this judgment to your employer and have money taken out of your paychecks to pay back what you owe. This is commonly called "attaching your wages," or a **wage garnishment**. Or, when you become excessively behind on your house payments, the mortgage company can get a judgment against you, and they will put a **lien** against your house. A lien means that when the house is sold, the money you owe has to be paid before you get paid. These are the types of information that would show up in the Public Record Information section.

Inquiries – an **inquiry** is like an investigation, and in this case, it means that someone is investigating your credit history. That someone could be you, checking to make sure everything is true and accurate on your credit report, or it could be someone else who is considering granting you credit, and your credit history will help make that decision. There are two ways others can check your credit history. When you fill out a credit, employment, or housing application, you usually give permission for them to run a credit check, which is mentioned in the small print of the application. Companies can also look at your credit history to see if they want to extend an offer of pre-approved credit to you.

Creditor Information List – in this area of your credit report, you will see the contact information for all the creditors listed in the Trade Information section. If you see a mistake in the information a creditor may have reported about you, the address or phone number is listed so that you can contact the credit grantor directly to ask that the information be corrected.

How to Obtain Your Free Credit Report

Every consumer in the United States is entitled to receive one free credit report per year from EACH of the three credit reporting agencies. Unfortunately, there are several businesses that advertise free credit reports, but these "free" credit reports come with strings attached. Usually, when you request your credit report from them, you are signing up for a credit monitoring service, which you pay for every month. That is not what was intended by the Fair and Accurate Credit Transactions Act of 2003 (FACTA).

FACTA was signed into law primarily to help consumers fight the growing crime of identity theft. Consumer advocates have long encouraged individuals to monitor their credit reports as a way to detect identity theft. Until FACTA was passed, consumers usually had to pay for their credit reports. We will discuss identity theft in more detail later in this chapter.

The three credit reporting agencies collaborated to create one central clearinghouse to provide consumers with their free annual credit report. This clearinghouse can be accessed at www.annualcreditreport.com, or by calling 1-877-322-8228.

When you order your report, you can either order one report from each of the three agencies or stagger the reports every few months. For example, you could order your TransUnion report first, then a few months later order your Experian report, then later on order your Equifax report. The advantage to this method is that you can see if there are any fraudulent charges or accounts that have shown up since the last time you requested a report, which is an important tool in preventing identity theft.

If you are turned down for credit due to the information contained in your credit report, you are entitled to receive a free credit report directly from the credit reporting agency that supplied the information. Also, if you are receiving unemployment payments, you are entitled to receive a free credit report directly from a credit reporting agency. And, if you are the victim of identity theft, you can request a complimentary credit report directly from one of the credit

····● QUICK TIPS ●····

Free Credit Report

Financial advisors recommend you check your credit report for accuracy every six months.

You can do so for FREE by visiting www.annualcreditreport.com or by calling 1-877-322-8228

QUICK FACTS

▼

Judgment: a court act affirming an obligation, such as a debt.

Wage Garnishment: money automatically taken out of your paycheck to satisfy a debt.

Lien: a court order placing a claim on property of a debtor, making the property security for payment of the debt.

Inquiry: you or someone else looks at your credit report.

reporting agencies. You may need to provide them with a case number from the local law enforcement agency. It is imperative that you report any incidents of identity theft immediately; this will help you in proving that it was not you who made the purchases. In any of the situations listed in this paragraph, obtaining a copy of your credit report will not count as your free credit report.

When you qualify for a free credit report due to the circumstances mentioned above, you request it directly from the credit reporting agency: Equifax, Experian, or TransUnion. If you are not eligible, and just want to receive the free credit reports you are entitled to, contact www.annualcreditreport.com.

Credit Scores

All three of the credit reporting agencies take the information that is supplied to them and apply a scoring model to arrive at a credit score. The purpose of this score is to rate the likelihood that you will responsibly handle any credit that is granted to you. The most widely recognized score is the **FICO score**, named for the company that created it, the **Fair Isaac Corporation**. This company, founded in 1956, created this standard measure of credit risk to help consumers and businesses manage their financial health.

If you have ever competed in certain types of athletic events, such as gymnastics, or watched them during the Olympics, you are familiar with a similar scoring model. In gymnastics, each element of the performance is assigned a point value, based on the contribution to the overall performance. There is usually a maximum number of points available, and each person is striving to get the most points possible. When judges apply the exact same scoring model to each competitor, it is a fair way to judge each performance, and the scores can then be compared to the others to determine the winner.

In the credit scoring scenario, there is a range of points available. For example, FICO scores range from 300-850, and the other scoring models are similar. We will use the FICO model for our example. Let's look at how the information in your credit report is translated into a credit score, and what you can do now to start increasing your score.

There are generally five factors that make up your credit score. Here are the factors, along with the weight each has on your score:

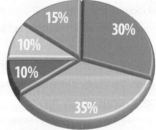

35% Payment History
30% Amount Owed
15% Length of Credit History
10% New Credit
10% Types of Credit

Let's now explore each of these areas in detail so that you will understand how your actions affect your credit and your future.

Payment History carries the most weight, so it is obviously the most important. This is simply a record of whether you have paid your bills on time. If you make it a habit to *always* pay your bills *on time,* your payment history will reflect that and so will your score. If you are late by even one day, it can become part of your record for up to seven years. That is a long time to pay for being tardy!

Amount Owed is the total amount of your available credit compared to how much credit you have used. For example, if your VISA card allows you a $1,000 line of credit, and you cur-

rently have a balance of $300, then you are using 30% of your available credit. Keep in mind that your score will reflect all of your available credit combined, along with the amount used from all accounts combined. The ratio of the amount owed to the available balance is called the **utilization ratio**, and experts recommend keeping this at or below 20% to positively impact your credit score.

Length of Credit History reflects how long you have had credit. The longer you have had an account in good standing, the better. At the same time, any account in bad standing will also follow you for up to seven years. Choose your new accounts carefully and continue to use them rather than opening a lot of other accounts.

New Credit takes into consideration both the number of new accounts you have opened and the number of inquiries on your account. If the inquiries are from potential creditors and you have initiated them, it will look like you are getting ready to go on a major spending spree, which will hurt your credit score. If you are car shopping, though, and go to several dealerships within a 45-day period, and several of these dealerships run your credit report as you shop for the best car and loan, these inquiries will be counted as one inquiry since they are all from the same type of creditor. They must be made within that time frame, however. If you also apply for a store charge card during that time, it will still count as an additional inquiry. *Obtaining your own credit report does not create an inquiry or count against your score.*

Types of Credit is a way of looking at the mix of accounts on your credit report. For example, it is considered good to have a variety of accounts, such as a mortgage, a car loan, and a few revolving accounts. A mortgage represents long-term stability, which is of course desirable, and even a car loan symbolizes a moderate amount of stability. The more diverse your credit mix, the higher this portion of your score will be.

In 2006, Experian, Equifax, and TransUnion collaborated to create a new credit scoring model called **VantageScore**. This score is designed to be more objective, predictable, and easy to understand than the popular FICO score since it is used by all three credit reporting agencies. The VantageScore system uses a scale that ranges from 501 to 990, which is slightly different from FICO's range of 300-850. In 2009, Experian discontinued participation in the FICO scoring system in favor of their proprietary scoring system that is not available to consumers.

Whether your credit score is generated by FICO or VantageScore, a central truth remains: Your score will only be as good as the information in your credit file. And you are the only person who can make sure that this information is positive and worthy of a high score.

The First Signs of Trouble

With every new account that you open, a statement will eventually follow and, as you use this credit, these statements will require that you make a payment on your account. If it is a **revolving account** (which does not have a fixed number of payments), like a credit card, and you can pay the bill in full each month, you are doing great. Even if you pay way more than the minimum and can pay it off in a few months, that may still be okay. The problem comes when you are having a hard time even making the minimum payment each month. Generally that happens when you have overextended yourself and taken on too much credit. Combine that with a change in your income, like losing your job or not being able to work for a while due to an illness, accident, or emergency, and you have a recipe for financial disaster.

What follows is a list of signs that you may be in over your head. If you can say "yes" to two or more of these questions, you may need to seek some help:

- Are you forced to choose which bills you will pay each month?
- Are you having a hard time just paying the minimum payment on your accounts?
- Are you bouncing checks?

QUICK FACTS

Utilization Ratio: the relationship between the amount owed and the available balance.

Revolving Account: a credit account that requires at least a minimum payment each month, and as the balance declines, more credit becomes available.

- Are you getting calls from bill collectors or collection agencies?
- Have you given up on budgeting because you are so far behind on all your bills?
- Have you lost track of the total amount you owe?
- Are you feeling overwhelmed and hopeless over the state of your finances?

Where to Get Help

There is good news: Plenty of ethical, trustworthy help is available. Much of this assistance may come from nonprofit organizations that have a mission to help people who are experiencing financial difficulties.

Before you look for outside help, you may want to start by talking to your family. Even though you don't want to hear "I told you so," if you approach family members with a responsible, mature attitude that you recognize you made a mistake and need help correcting it, you might be surprised at their response. They probably won't offer to just pay off everything for you, but you are not asking for that. Perhaps you could ask for some assistance until you get things stable again. This could mean giving you a small loan, or helping with your budget or giving you opportunities to make extra money to get caught up. Just remember—it is incredibly risky to get out of debt by borrowing more money so, if you resort to that, make sure you have a plan to get out, and STAY OUT of debt thereafter.

If your problem has escalated past a point where your family can help, you may want to find a reputable organization for credit and debt counseling.

Look for nonprofit organizations that are **accredited**, meaning they uphold a national standard for excellence in their industry. Their counselors should be certified by an organization with nationally recognized standards for credit counseling, such as the **National Foundation for Credit Counseling (NFCC)**. The fees they charge should be clearly explained to you up front and in writing and should not exceed what their state permits them to charge. Since you probably won't know what the state allows, ask them to clarify it for you.

Other types of help are also available. There are, for instance, church-based financial education programs. Some of these programs utilize well-trained community volunteers who can meet with you and help you establish a new plan to get back on your feet. There are also small groups that meet weekly to discuss the various aspects of money management, including why we sometimes feel compelled to spend money when we know we shouldn't. Look in bookstores and at the library for some of the excellent books that have been written on the subjects of personal finance and getting out of debt.

The important thing is to start small with your credit usage and make sure you handle that well. From there, you can add credit as the need arises and as your financial picture improves. Keep a close eye on your finances and, if you should see things starting to get away from you, get help as soon as possible. Credit is an incredibly important tool for your future, so you will want to handle it correctly!

Another Kind of Credit Problem: Identity Theft

There is a lot of talk lately about **identity theft**, which is what happens when someone steals your identity and obtains or uses credit under your name. It has been reported that 29% of all identity theft victims are 18–29 years of age. This is the highest category reported and is growing. So how can you protect yourself from becoming a victim, and what should you do if you discover someone has used your personal information to obtain credit?

QUICK TIPS

Remember:

Your credit history is a snapshot of how you handle money. Make sure it is a flattering picture!

QUICK FACTS

Accredited: recognized as maintaining high quality standards by an independent agency.

Identity Theft: someone steals your identity and obtains or uses credit under your name.

While there is no foolproof method to ensure you will never become a victim, there are many strategies that you can employ that will minimize the likelihood of this problem:

- Shred any credit card offers or preapproval letters, receipts, bank or account statements, or any other information with your account number printed on it that you have finished using.

- Do not carry your Social Security card with you. Memorize the number; then store the card in a safe place. Do not give the card or number to anyone who does not absolutely need to use it. Question why someone wants to use it.

- Guard your wallet and purse very carefully. It only takes a second for a thief to steal your purse or wallet from your car, shopping cart, apartment, or backpack.

- Do not mail checks from your home. Drop off envelopes that contain your personal checks at the post office. Some thieves like to steal mail from the mailbox and then cash the checks or use them to create more checks.

- Make sure your incoming mail is not left unattended for hours every day. If you do not have a locked mailbox, consider getting one or using a post office box. If your incoming mail is stolen, the thief may have access to any checks that were sent to you as well as credit card offers and account statements. You do not want any of these things to get into the wrong hands.

- Do not leave any of your personal identification numbers (PIN) where other people would find them. This goes for your bank account PIN as well as the user name and password for any of your other accounts. When choosing your PIN or password, do not choose a word or date that is easy to guess, like your birthdate or phone number. Use a combination of letters, numbers, and symbols whenever possible. If someone visiting your roommate happened to find a notebook with the log-in information to get into your favorite book and music Web site, that person could charge hundreds or even thousands of dollars on your account before you would know what happened. Keep all that information under lock and key.

- Be very suspicious of emails or phone calls from companies asking you to confirm your account information. Legitimate companies will almost never call or email you asking you to provide sensitive account information. This practice is known as **phishing**, and you may be told that this information is necessary to keep your account open or to reverse an unauthorized charge on your account. Chances are, there has not really been an unauthorized purchase made on your account, but when you provide the information, the thieves then use it to go on a shopping spree at your expense.

- When shopping on the Internet, choose companies that offer a secure site. Here are some tips from the **Federal Trade Commission (FTC)** to ensure a safe online experience:

  - **Use a secure browser.** This is the software you use to navigate the Internet. Your browser should comply with industry security standards, such as Secure Sockets Layer (SSL). These standards scramble the purchase information you send over the Internet, helping to secure your transaction. Most computers come with a browser installed. You also can download some browsers for free over the Internet.

  - **Shop with companies you know.** Anyone can set up shop online under almost any name. If you're not familiar with a merchant, ask for a paper catalog or brochure to get a better idea of its merchandise and services. Also, determine the company's refund and return policies before you place your order. These should be posted on the company's Web site.

- **Pay by credit or charge card instead of the debit card from your checking account.** If you pay by credit or charge card online, your transaction will be protected by the Fair Credit Billing Act. Under this law, you have the right to dispute charges under certain circumstances and temporarily withhold payment while the creditor is investigating your claims. In the event of unauthorized use of your credit or charge card, you generally would be held liable only for the first $50 in charges. Some companies offer an online shopping guarantee that ensures you will not be held responsible for any unauthorized charges made online, and some cards may provide additional warranty, return, and/or purchase protection benefits.
- **Keep a record.** Be sure to print a copy of your purchase order and confirmation number for your records. Also, you should know that the Mail and Telephone Order Merchandise Rule covers online orders. This means that unless the company states otherwise, your merchandise must be delivered within 30 days; and, if there are delays, the company must notify you.

Resolving an Identity Theft Crisis

If you discover that you have been the victim of identity theft, there is no magic wand to make all your problems disappear. It takes time and energy to follow the necessary steps to clear your name. You will discover that you have three options when faced with this situation: You can ignore it, pretend it doesn't exist, and hope it goes away on its own (which it won't—so we highly discourage this option); you can fight it yourself; or you can enlist the services of a company that can do all the unpleasant work for you.

We have established that the first option is a very bad idea, since the problem will only get worse instead of better, so let's focus on the other two options. What does it take to begin the process to resolve this situation? There are five critical steps to take if you have been the victim of identity theft:

1. **Place a fraud alert on your credit report by contacting one of the major credit reporting agencies. Attempt to immediately close any open fraudulent accounts.** A fraud alert helps prevent an identity thief from opening additional accounts in your name by requiring creditors to contact you before opening any new accounts. By placing a fraud alert with any one of the agencies, the other two will be notified automatically and you will be provided with a copy of your credit report from all three credit reporting agencies. The process is automated if you call Equifax at 1-800-525-6285, Experian at 1-888-397-3742, or TransUnion at 1-800-680-7289.

2. **File a police report with your local law enforcement agency, such as the police or sheriff's department.** Provide as much documentation as you can including names and telephone numbers of collectors calling you on **fraudulent** debt or debt collection letters. Also be sure to explain, if known, how you believe the thief obtained your personal information. You should receive a copy of this report at the time of filing.

3. **File a complaint with the Federal Trade Commission (FTC) and complete an ID Theft Affidavit.** The FTC can be reached as follows:

   a. Email: www.consumer.gov/idtheft
   b. Telephone: 1-877-ID THEFT (877-438-4338)
   c. TDD: 202-326-2502
   d. U.S. Mail: Consumer Response Center, FTC 600 Pennsylvania Avenue, N.W. Washington, DC 20580

4. **Send dispute letters to each credit reporting agency.*** To simplify the process, write one detailed letter and make copies for each credit reporting agency. Decide which agency you are going to contact first and add your personal information in the appropriate areas of the letter. Be sure to review your credit report so that you include all items that need to be disputed in the letter. Once you have finished the first detailed letter, create the same letter with the appropriate address for each of the other two credit reporting agencies. When the three letters are ready, sign them, make copies for your records, include copies (never originals) of the police report and ID Theft Affidavit (required for the dispute to be investigated as identity theft), and mail them by certified mail, return-receipt requested.

5. **Send dispute letters to creditors that are reporting fraudulent charges on your legitimate accounts.** Send a dispute letter for each account showing a fraudulent charge and mail them by certified mail, return-receipt-requested. Include with your letters a copy of each statement showing fraudulent charges. Also include a copy of the police report and the ID Theft Affidavit.

   *Before continuing with steps four and five, carefully review your credit reports. Check to see what fraudulent accounts, if any, have been opened in your name, and review each credit account for any unusual balances or unauthorized charges.

You can use the sample letters on the following pages to dispute fraudulent charges and put a block on your credit report. The FTC also has information on identity theft that is available on its Web site at www.consumer.gov/idtheft.

As you get older and become more established in the credit world, you face more responsibilities, more challenges, and yet have many more opportunities available to you. When you make wise choices and keep a close watch on your spending and your credit report, you will be building a firm financial foundation to last a lifetime.

FIGURE **16** | **Sample Blocking Letter - Consumer Reporting Agency**

Date
Your Name
Your Address
Your City, State, Zip Code

Complaint Department
Name of Consumer Reporting Company
Address
City, State, Zip Code

Dear Sir or Madam:

I am a victim of identity theft. I am writing to request that you block the following fraudulent information in my file. This information does not relate to any transaction that I have made. The items also are circled on the attached copy of the report I received. (Identify item(s) to be blocked by name of source, such as creditors or tax court, and identify type of item, such as credit account, judgment, etc.)

Enclosed is a copy of the law enforcement report regarding my identity theft. Please let me know if you need any other information from me to block this information on my credit report.

Sincerely,
Your name

Enclosures: (List what you are enclosing.)

FIGURE **17** | **Sample Dispute Letter - For Existing Accounts**

Date
Your Name
Your Address
Your City, State, Zip Code

Your Account Number
Name of Creditor
Billing Inquiries
Address
City, State, Zip Code

Dear Sir or Madam:

I am writing to dispute a fraudulent (charge or debit) on my account in the amount of $_____. I am a victim of identity theft, and I did not make this (charge or debit). I am requesting that the (charge be removed or the debit reinstated), that any finance and other charges related to the fraudulent amount be credited, as well, and that I receive an accurate statement.

Enclosed are copies of (use this sentence to describe any enclosed information, such as a police report) supporting my position. Please investigate this matter and correct the fraudulent (charge or debit) as soon as possible.

Sincerely,
Your name

Enclosures: (List what you are enclosing.)

Chapter 13
Your Debt Management

EVERYONE HAS DEBT IN SOME FORM OR ANOTHER: A MORTGAGE, A CAR PAYMENT, OR A STUDENT LOAN. The key is knowing how to manage your debt wisely. This chapter will show you how to reduce the overall cost of your debt and prioritize your financial life.

We have all heard the expression, "don't buy what you can't afford to pay for with cash." If we all followed that advice, we would have to wait years to buy a car or attend college. Only the rich would be able to afford a home. Borrowing money allows us to have those things sooner, with the understanding that we will be able to repay our debts over time. There are other reasons we might need to borrow money, and there are many different types of credit to match those needs.

Credit is not always necessary, but it helps us obtain some of life's essentials, such as transportation and shelter. Each of us has different priorities in the way that we manage our budget, but the decision to borrow should be based on two simple questions. (1) "Is this something I need, or want?" If the credit is being used to meet an important need such as a car or house, then it may be a good idea to borrow. (2) "Will I be able to afford the loan?" This question has to do with your budget, and your ability to maintain one that is balanced as you repay the money you borrow. Check the terms such as interest rate, payment, and other fees before borrowing.

Credit has been around in the United States for a long time. In fact, credit cards have been used since the late 1920s when Diners Club offered a system of charging on a single account at multiple unrelated merchant locations. There was no plastic card, but the concept was the beginning of credit as we know it today. After the end of World War II retail credit began to grow as the baby boom spurred a spending spree. Retailers such as Sears and Roebuck used plastic "charger plates" that displayed the consumer's account information and could be taken from store to store. Other financing options, like American Express, became more widely accepted and more readily available to more consumers. Banks started getting into the credit card business in the 1960s and 1970s with the launch of Bank Americard (now Visa) and Master Charge (now MasterCard). By the 1980s, America was right in the middle of a consumer credit boom. Today, there are many credit options offered by banks and retailers. The choices can be overwhelming at times, but informed consumers can quickly sort out the confusion and make smart credit choices.

Types of Credit

There are four basic types of credit available to consumers. Selecting among these credit types will determine how you use the account and how you repay the debt you owe. The first two types of credit are related to how often you will need to borrow.

Revolving credit is widely used, and is attractive to consumers for its convenience and ease of use. This type of credit allows you to have an available pool of money (credit line) that you can borrow from. A limit is set on the amount of money available to you, and this is called your *credit limit*. As you pay down the balances you owe, it will increase the amount that you could potentially borrow up to your credit limit. Revolving accounts are most commonly known as credit cards, but also can be found as retail signature accounts and home equity loans (second mortgages).

Fixed (or Closed-End) credit is the opposite of revolving because it only allows consumers to borrow a lump-sum of money with a single payout to the borrower. In other words, the borrower who is approved for $1,000 will receive that entire amount when the loan becomes official. The credit limit is whatever the balance of the loan is at a given time. There is no access to any available credit, and the loan is set to pay off over a specific period of time. The time in which the loan is set to pay off is referred to as the *term*. These loans are typically used to satisfy a single purchase such as a car, furniture, debt consolidation loan, or even a house.

A lender takes a risk when it offers consumers the use of its money. In some cases, for large purchases or in situations where the borrower is a credit risk, the bank may require that an item of equal value is offered as a guarantee that the loan will be repaid. The item of value is usually the item being purchased with the borrowed money, and is referred to as *collateral*. Timely repayment of secured loans is doubly important since the lender has the right to take possession of the collateral if the borrower doesn't honor the terms of the loan contract. Car loans, mortgages, and furniture loans are all examples of secured loans.

On the other end of the scale is **unsecured credit**. These accounts are called *signature loans* or *credit cards*. The only collateral involved with these accounts is the signature of the borrower and their promise to honor the terms of repayment. Unsecured credit offers a high risk to the lender and the greatest convenience to the consumer. Because of the increased risk, unsecured accounts typically carry a higher cost of borrowing (interest rate) than secured loans. It is also true that the consumer's credit history plays a greater role in determining approval for these accounts.

Sources of Credit

Where you get your credit is largely determined by your creditworthiness. We will look at sources of credit as they relate to that as well as ease of access. When reviewing this section, keep in mind that convenience usually carries a higher price. This is true with almost everything, and is especially true when it comes to credit.

Credit for those with a healthy credit history comes from the prime lenders. This is also referred to as the "A Credit" and "B Credit" tier of lending. Just as is the case with your semester report card, credit carries a letter grade scale as well. The prime lenders offer their "A Credit" with the lowest interest rates and the most flexible terms. You could imagine that this is reserved only for those with very healthy credit histories and ability to repay. Some of these lenders will also offer a "B Credit" product that is tailored to suit the needs of consumers with nearly perfect credit. Ultimately, lower risk to the lender translates into a lower cost of borrowing. Most major banks and credit unions are considered to be in this lending category.

For those who fall short of the perfect or nearly perfect credit history, there are the subprime lenders. These lenders fulfill an important need for those with damaged credit (FICO of 620 or lower), but at a greater cost. In fact, were it not for subprime lenders, nearly 25% of Americans would not have any access to credit. The interest rates are much higher than prime credit, and in some cases there are service fees charged in addition to the higher interest in order to offset the borrower's risk. These loans are referred to as "C Credit" and "D Credit." Consumers should use caution when conducting business with these lenders, and should

---

always attempt to obtain financing from a prime lender first in order to secure better terms. In 2006, *The Wall Street Journal* reported that 61% of all subprime borrowers had credit scores that would have made them eligible for prime credit.

Somewhere in the midst of these lenders are ones who are looking to take advantage of vulnerable consumers. **Predatory lenders** take advantage of uninformed or desperate consumers using slick sales techniques or very low teaser rates. They often misrepresent loan terms. While states are becoming more aggressive in finding and prosecuting these unscrupulous practitioners, consumers must be diligent in reading documents for their own protection. The Better Business Bureau and state banking commissions are valuable sources of background information on many companies. One universal rule of caution applies in these situations: If something sounds too good to be true, it probably is.

Run away from anyone who asks you for cash up front. These are called prepaid loan scams: The lender offers you a loan, but asks you to give them a payment upfront as security. By the time many consumers realize they have been had, the "lender" has already moved on to another location and another victim.

Lending has taken other, nontraditional forms in recent years as the economy has changed. Nontraditional borrowing is simply a way to access money from sources other than a bank or finance company. If borrowing from a bank is difficult because a consumer does not have a long enough credit history to qualify, they may turn to sources like family or a retirement account. Borrowing from family can be easy, and it may even come with the benefit of low or no interest, but it may also place a strain on relationships if terms of repayment are not kept, or when the lending family member becomes aggressive about collecting the balance. Borrowing against a retirement fund, such as a 401K, can also make funds easily accessible in an emergency. Use caution, since there are both tax implications and early withdrawal penalty fees.

Terms of Borrowing

Terms of borrowing include much more than the just the amount of time you are given to repay the debt.

An interest rate is the price the borrowers pay for the use of money they do not own. For instance, a small company might borrow from a bank to kick-start its business. It is also the return a lender receives for deferring the use of funds, by lending it to the borrower. Interest rates are normally expressed as a percentage rate over the period of one year.

PENALTY CLAUSES

Some loans and lines of credit may include penalty clauses that assign additional fees or interest when specific terms are broken. These include late fees, over-limit fees, and even early payout fees. Some penalty interest rates can exceed 35% and some monthly late fees can exceed $40. Always read your credit contract to be aware of these before you open an account.

The length of time you are given to pay off your credit is also a part of the terms of borrowing. This is most common with closed-end loans; however, it can also be a factor in revolving lines of credit. Some revolving lines of credit contain a clause that imposes a term on paying off a balance if the account is not renewed, or the account may expire if it remains unused for a period of time. Always be aware of the length of time you have to repay your debt, and make every effort to pay it off before the end of the term you are given.

Minimum payments are designed to allow you to pay a portion of your balance and all of the interest charged during a billing period. Most minimum payments on revolving debt are calculated at 2% or 3% of your average daily balance. This doesn't give you much room for progress in paying down your balance. Let's take the example of $1,000 of debt borrowed at a rate of 12% APR. The monthly interest rate can be calculated by dividing the APR by 12. In this case, the monthly rate is 1% of the average daily balance during the monthly billing period. If the minimum payment is 2% of the balance and the interest rate is 1%, you don't have to be a math genius to figure out that half of your minimum payment is allocated to interest. This underscores the importance of paying more than the minimum in order to get out of debt faster and avoid letting interest slow you down.

When you open a credit account or borrow any amount of money, it is likely to involve a legally binding contract between you and the lender. Each party has qualifications that it is expected to meet in order for the contract to remain valid. Any violation by the borrower of the terms of a lending contract could mean the cancellation of access to available credit and a whole host of penalty fees, collection activities, and even the possibility of legal action in order to recover the debt. This simply demonstrates the fact that borrowing any amount of money is serious business. No loan contract should be entered into with haste or without serious consideration of the obligation a borrower has to the lender.

Managing Credit within Your Budget

Make a list of your debt obligations, including the balance, interest, and monthly payment amounts. Develop a plan to pay off the debts in a way that makes the most progress and saves the most money over time. The most widely recommended method is to attack the account carrying the highest APR with any extra money you have. This allows you to pay the account off faster and save money on interest you would have paid had the loan gone to full term on minimum payments. This method is mathematically proven to save consumers hundreds and in some cases thousands of dollars. Other financial experts have insisted that it helps to pay off the lower balances first. This method, known as "snowballing," has more psychological benefits than real monetary savings, because it gives one an immediate sense of fast progress and success.

Be sure to track your balances as you pay down your debt. Do this by opening your statements and reviewing the balance and payments made. Look closely at when your payment is posted, how much is going to interest, how much is going to principal, and what other fees are being applied. Don't take the lenders' word for everything you see on a statement. Get a calculator and check their math. Using the method in the previous example, you can check the way that they calculate your interest rate. Looking closely at your statements and checking them for accuracy can save you a lot of money by allowing you to address potentially costly mistakes.

One of the most common areas where consumers fall short is that they are reluctant to communicate with their lenders. Some are afraid of calling a bank or credit card company because they are not sure what questions to ask. Most people wait until a crisis, or worse, until they have a missed payment. Don't put off calling your lender if you have questions or need to discuss changes in your financial situation. Most will appreciate your honesty and initiative. Keeping the lines of communication open will make it easier to resolve issues and avoid problems.

An example of a time when you may need to communicate with a lender is to dispute information on your billing statement. Most creditors can resolve these issues with a simple phone call, while some may require you to register your dispute in writing either by postal mail or on a Web site.

Always include your debt in your regular budget review, and be mindful of how much debt you are carrying and how much you can afford. A good way to control debt is to live within the 20% rule. This means that your monthly debt payments should not exceed 20% of your net monthly income.

Resolving Credit Problems

We all seek financial success in life, but we must prepare for the possibility there will be tough times along the road. Take good care of your credit score by making payments on time, or by talking to your lenders before a problem escalates. Tracking your spending and keeping to a budget will help you identify potential trouble spots.

In situations where you must talk to your lender, always be honest about your circumstances. Avoid making the situation sound better or worse than it actually is. This will allow your creditor to help you find options that are appropriate to your financial situation. You also want to include everyone in the household in discussions about where things stand and what is being done to get back on track. Let everyone have a say, and encourage an open conversation to allow inclusion and creativity.

Sometimes communication is not enough to get you through a financial rough patch. This is when it is important to consider reaching out to someone who can provide objective, confidential, and professional help with your budget and creditors. Nonprofit credit counselors offer these services for low or no cost to consumers. Be careful in selecting an agency to assist you, and do some research by looking them up with the **Better Business Bureau**. Most reputable nonprofit credit counseling agencies are affiliated with the **National Foundation for Credit Counseling,** which ensures that they are performing to a set of standards that promote quality and adherence to a nonprofit business model. There is no shame in seeking help from these agencies, and it is best to get help from a credit counselor early in the process rather than later. Those who wait until repossession or court action from their creditors is on the horizon will find that their options are few.

There are other remedies for resolving a debt crisis, but each should be considered carefully before any decision is made. Among these options are debt settlement, deferment plans, and bankruptcy.

Personal Loans

Karen realized that her car was facing some serious maintenance issues, and decided to lease a new car. The monthly lease was $499.35 and she was allowed to drive 15,000 miles per year with extra miles charged at $0.25 per mile. After 18 months, however, Karen began to tire of the large monthly payments. She went back to the auto dealer to explore ending the lease early. The dealership told her that in order to end the lease, she must pay $7,350. Karen only had two real choices: to buy the car outright or to continue the lease to its three-year term. Ending the lease was not a financially attractive option.

You may be faced with a similar decision in your future. The time to make a "lease versus buy" decision is before the lease is signed or before the car is purchased. Once committed to either action, you most likely will need to remain committed to your course.

This chapter focuses on your use of personal loans to finance large purchases. Proper decisions on whether to obtain a personal loan, which source to use for a personal loan, how much to borrow, and what terms to arrange can have a significant impact on your financial situation.

The objectives of this chapter are to:

- Provide a background on personal loans
- Outline the types of interest rates that are charged on personal loans
- Discuss car loans
- Explain how to decide between financing the purchase of a car and leasing a car
- Describe the key features of student loans
- Describe home equity loans

■ BACKGROUND ON PERSONAL LOANS

Consumers commonly obtain a personal loan to finance a large purchase such as a car. A personal loan is different from access to credit (from a credit card) in that it is normally used to finance one large purchase and has a specific repayment schedule. The loan is provided at the time of your purchase and is used along with your cash down payment to cover the entire purchase price. You can pay off the personal loan on an installment basis, for example, by making a payment each month for the next 48 months.

Determining Whether a Loan Is Sensible

Before pursuing a loan, first you should decide if a loan is sensible. Just because you think you can obtain a loan, a loan may not be a good idea. The loan will require you to make periodic payments over time. Consider the sacrifice you may have to make over time as you use a portion of your monthly income to pay off the loan rather than use the money for some other purpose. For example, a loan of $2,000 to buy a used car so that you can commute to your workplace and to school may be sensible. However, a loan of $30,000 so that you can purchase a new car with a big engine is questionable. Such a large loan will require very large monthly payments, and might leave you with very little income left to cover necessities such as food or rent.

Financial Planning Online 14.1: **Loan Information**

Go to
www.helpwithmybank.gov/
faqs/loan_general.html

This Web site provides
background information on
personal loans.

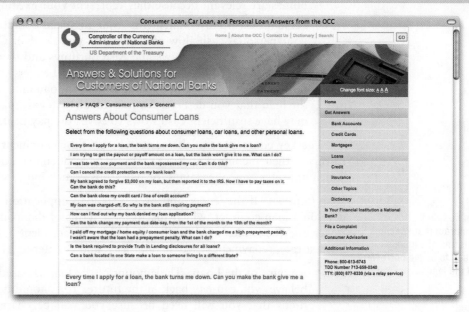

You should avoid a loan if your source of income to repay the loan is questionable. When economic conditions are weak, job layoffs are common. Consider the consequences of having a personal loan if there are no job opportunities. How would you repay the loan? Do you have alternative sources of funds to repay the loan?

Sources of Loans

The first step in obtaining a personal loan is to identify possible sources of financing and evaluate the possible loan terms. The most common source of financing is a personal loan from a financial institution. Commercial banks, savings institutions, finance companies, and credit unions all provide personal loans. Some finance companies are subsidiaries of automobile manufacturers that finance car purchases. For example, GMAC Financial Services is a finance company that is owned by General Motors. Savings institutions are the primary lenders to individuals who need mortgage loans, the subject of Chapter 15.

An alternative source of financing is one or more family members or friends. If they trust that you will repay the loan on time and in full, they may be willing to provide you with a loan that earns the same interest rate as their savings account. You could also offer to pay an interest rate on the loan that is a few percentage points above the savings rate. By borrowing funds from family and friends, you can often get a more favorable rate than financial institutions offer. The loan agreement should be in writing and signed by all parties to avoid any possible misinterpretations.

The Personal Loan Process

The process of applying for a personal loan from a financial institution involves filling out the application, negotiating the loan contract, and negotiating the interest rate. A sample loan application is shown in Exhibit 14.1.

Application Process. When applying for a loan, you need to provide information from your personal balance sheet and personal cash flow statement to document your ability to repay the loan.

- **Personal Balance Sheet.** Recall from Chapter 9 that your financial condition is partially measured by a personal balance sheet. The personal balance sheet indicates your assets, liabilities, and net worth at a specific point in time. The assets are relevant because they may serve as possible collateral to back a loan. The liabilities are relevant because they represent your existing debts.

- **Personal Cash Flow Statement.** Your financial condition is also represented by your personal cash flow statement, as discussed in Chapter 9. This statement indicates your cash inflows and cash outflows and therefore suggests how much free cash flow you have on a periodic basis. Lenders use this cash flow information to determine whether you qualify for a loan and, if so, the maximum size of the loan that you deserve. An individual with existing loans or credit card debt may have insufficient cash flows to cover the payments on any additional loans.

The key component of the personal cash flow statement of most prospective borrowers is their income. Lenders require income documentation, such as a Form W-2, which indicates annual earnings, or pay stubs, which indicate recent salary.

Loan Contract. If the lender approves your loan application, it will work with you to develop a **loan contract**, which specifies the terms of the loan, as agreed to by the borrower and the lender. Specifically, the loan contract identifies the amount of the loan, interest rate, repayment schedule, maturity, and collateral.

loan contract
A contract that specifies the terms of a loan, as agreed to by the borrower and the lender.

- **Amount of the Loan.** The amount of the loan is based on how much the lender believes you can pay back in the future. You should borrow only the amount of funds that you will need because you will be charged interest on the entire amount that you borrow.

Exhibit 14.1 An Example of a Loan Application

DCU Digital Federal Credit Union

141 PARKER STREET • PO BOX [illegible] • MAYNARD, MA [illegible]
[illegible] • WEB SITE: www.dcu.org • E-MAIL: [illegible]

Loan application Vehicle: ❑ Purchasing ❑ Refinance ❑ RV/Boat ❑ Motorcycle

Loan Amount or monthly payment amount $__________ Loan Term__________ months

BORROWER

Member #	SS#
Name	Date of Birth
Home Address	
City State Zip	
Home Phone #	Work Phone #
# of Dependents/Ages	
Own / Rent / Board (circle one)	Payment Amount / How Long?
Mortgage/Landlord Name	
Employer Name	Date of Hire
Previous Employer	From / To
Checking Account Institution	

CO-BORROWER/COSIGNER

Member #	SS#
Name	Date of Birth
Home Address	
City	State Zip
Home Phone #	Work Phone #
# of Dependents/Ages	
Employer Name	Date of Hire

M730A (3/2000)

Monthly Gross Income (please attach verification of income). Alimony, child support, or separate maintenance income need not be revealed if you do not wish to have it considered as a basis for repaying this obligation.

	Gross Income	Overtime	Other
Borrower	$	$	$
Co-Borrower	$	$	$

Are you obligated to pay alimony, child support, separate maintenance? If yes, amount $__________per__________

SIGNATURES REQUIRED BELOW

Subject to Digital Federal Credit Union (DCU) Loan Underwriting Guidelines.

BY SIGNING THIS APPLICATION YOU AGREE TO THE FOLLOWING: You agree that we may obtain and use consumer credit reports and exchange credit and employment information in connection with this application and any update, renewal, or extension of credit we may extend to you. You agree, upon approval of this loan, that you will ensure DCU is properly listed as lienholder on the vehicle title as: Digital Federal Credit Union, 141 Parker Street, Maynard, MA 01754. You agree that your account will be subject to the terms and conditions of all applicable Loan Agreements and Disclosure Statements. You agree that a photocopy or facsimile of this application shall be as binding as the original. You understand that we will retain this application whether or not it is approved. Everything you have stated in this application is correct.

Borrower's Signature **Date**

Co-Borrower's/Cosigner's Signature **Date**

CREDIT LIFE/DISABILITY INSURANCE

❑ I am interested in obtaining Credit Life and/or Disability Insurance. Please send me more information.

ELECTRONIC PAYMENT METHOD

By selecting one of the two electronic payment methods below, you agree to the following as applicable:

DCU Initiated Automatic Transfer: You authorize us to initiate a transfer of sufficient funds from the DCU account indicated to pay all amounts due monthly. The transfers will be made as indicated below. You agree you are responsible for maintaining a sufficient balance to cover the amount of the payment and that the funds will be available to transfer as of the start of business on the scheduled transfer date. We will only transfer from the available balance in the account you have designated. If there are insufficient funds, the available funds will be transferred but your payment may be considered late.

Member Initiated Loan Payment Via PC Branch or Easy Touch Telephone Teller: You agree to initiate and complete one or more loan payment transactions via either the "Account Transfer" or "Automatic Transfer" PC Branch option or the "Loan Payment Transaction" Easy Touch Telephone Teller option each month on or before the loan payment due date. You understand that you will not receive a coupon book or monthly bill. You accept responsibility and agree that you will have paid no less than the Monthly Payment Due to your loan by 5:00 p.m. on the payment due date each month.

PLEASE SELECT ONE OF THE FOLLOWING:

❑ **DCU Initiated Automatic Transfer**
Frequency:
☐ Weekly (Friday) ☐ Monthly (On the payment due date or business day closest to but not before)
Transfer From:
☐ DCU Primary Savings ☐ DCU Checking
Member #__________, Account #__________

❑ **Member Initiated PC Branch or Easy Touch Telephone Teller**

❑ **Coupon Book**(non-Electronic)

You understand that direct deposit and use of an Electronic Payment Method is voluntary and is not a factor in whether the loan will be granted. However, both are required to obtain the reduced interest rate.

We reserve the right to terminate this payment method and adjust the annual percentage rate if the privilege is abused. Termination will not affect prior transactions nor your responsibility to repay the entire amount.

Borrower's Signature **Date**

Co-Borrower's/Cosigner's Signature **Date**

Internal Use Only
Member #__________, Loan#__________
Processed By #__________, Date____/____/____

- **Interest Rate.** The interest rate is critical because it determines the cost incurred on a personal loan. It must be specified in a loan contract. More information about interest rates is provided in a later section.
- **Loan Repayment Schedule.** Personal loans are usually **amortized,** which means that the principal (original amount loaned out) is repaid through a series of equal payments. Each loan repayment includes both interest owed and a portion of the principal. As more of the principal is paid down, the amount of interest is reduced, and a larger portion of the payment is used to repay principal.
- **Maturity.** A loan contract specifies the **maturity,** or life of the loan. A longer maturity for a loan results in lower monthly payments and therefore makes it easier to cover the payments each month. For example, the monthly payment on a five-year loan for $16,000 may be $100 less than the payment on a four-year loan for the same amount. With the five-year loan, however, you are in debt for an additional year, and you pay more interest over the life of the loan than you would on the four-year loan. In general, you should select a maturity on personal loans that is as short as possible, as long as you allow yourself sufficient liquidity. If you have extra funds during the time you have a loan, you should consider paying off the loan early for two reasons. First, you can reduce the total amount of interest by paying off the loan early. Second, you will be able to save the money that you would otherwise have used to make the loan payments.

amortize
To repay the principal of a loan (the original amount loaned out) through a series of equal payments. A loan repaid in this manner is said to be amortized.

maturity
With respect to a loan, the life or duration of the loan.

- **Collateral.** A loan agreement also describes the **collateral**, or assets of the borrower (if any) that back the loan in the event that the borrower defaults. When a loan is used to purchase a specific asset, that asset is commonly used as collateral. For example, if your purchase of a boat is partly financed, the boat would serve as collateral. That is, the lender could repossess the boat if you were unable to make the loan payments. Some loans are backed by assets other than those purchased with the loan. For example, a boat loan could be backed by stocks that you own.

A loan that is backed or secured by collateral is referred to as a **secured loan**; a loan that is not backed by collateral is an **unsecured loan**. In general, you will receive more favorable terms (such as a lower interest rate) on a secured loan because the lender has less to lose in the event that the loan is not repaid.

A **payday loan** is a short-term loan provided to you if you need funds in advance of receiving your paycheck. To obtain a payday loan, you write a check to the lender for the amount of the loan plus the interest. You date the check for the date in the future when you will receive your paycheck. The payday loan firm will hold the check until that time and will cash it then because your checking account will have sufficient funds. After you provide this check to the payday loan firm, it provides you with your loan in cash or by transmitting funds into your checking account.

As an example, assume that you need $400 for some immediate purpose, but will not have any money until you receive your paycheck one week from today. You provide the payday loan firm a check dated one week from today. Be aware that firms such as Cash King, Cash One, CheckMate, and EZLoans, which provide payday loans, charge a high rate of interest on these short-term loans. The payday loan firm may request that your payment be $440, which reflects the loan of $400 and $40 interest and/or fees. You are paying $40 more than the loan you received, which reflects 10 percent of the loan amount. The cost of financing a payday loan follows:

$$\text{Cost of Financing} = 10 \text{ percent} \times (\text{number of days in a year/number of days in which you have the loan})$$
$$= 10\% \times (365/7)$$
$$= 521\%$$

This is not a misprint. It is within the typical range of the cost of financing charged for payday loans.

While states have usury laws that place a limit on the maximum interest rate that can be charged, the payday loan firms have circumvented that limit by referring to the interest as fees. Some states recognize that the fees are really interest payments and prevent payday firms from establishing businesses. However, payday loan firms can reside in the states that allow them and still reach residents in any state via the Internet.

You should avoid payday loans for the following reasons. First, by using your next paycheck to cover a loan payment, you may not have sufficient cash available to make normal purchases after covering the loan. Thus, you may need another loan to cover your purchases in that period, and this can create a continual cycle in which your paycheck is always needed to repay short-term loans.

Second, as we have seen, the cost of financing with a payday loan is outrageous. Consider how much you would have paid in interest on $400 if you were able to get a loan that charged you a more reasonable rate such as 10 percent annually.

$$\text{Interest rate for a 7-day period} = 10\% \times (7/365)$$
$$= .192\%$$

The interest to be paid = $400 \times .192$ percent = $0.76. Thus, you would pay less than $1 interest on a seven-day loan if you were charged a 10 percent annualized interest rate. This is substantially less than the interest you would be charged by a payday loan firm. The payday loan firms are able to charge excessive rates because some people who need money quickly may not be creditworthy and therefore have difficulty obtaining funds

"A high-five isn't binding, sir. You still have to sign a loan agreement."

from other sources. Alternatively, some borrowers do not realize how high the cost of financing is when they borrow money from a payday loan firm.

The simple solution is to avoid borrowing money until you have the funds to spend. But if you have to borrow, there are alternative ways of financing that are not as expensive. For example, perhaps you can borrow funds from a friend or family member for a week. Or you may be able to obtain credit through your credit card. While relying on credit card financing is not recommended, it is substantially wiser than financing through a payday loan. To illustrate, assume that you could have used a credit card to make your $400 purchase. Also assume that the rate on your credit card is 18 percent annually, or 1.5 percent over one month. In this case, your cost of financing would be $400 × 1.5 percent = $6. This financing cost for one month is much lower than the cost of financing when using a payday loan, and in this example the credit card financing lasts three weeks longer than the payday financing period.

Cosigning. Some borrowers are only able to obtain a personal loan if someone with a stronger credit history cosigns. The cosigner is responsible for any unpaid balance if the borrower does not repay the loan. If the borrower defaults and the cosigner does not repay the loan, the lender has the right to sue the cosigner or to try to seize his assets, just as if he were the borrower. In addition, cosigning on a loan can restrict the amount that the cosigner is able to borrow. Therefore, you should only be willing to cosign a loan if you trust the borrower and will not need to borrow funds for yourself in the near future.

FOCUS ON ETHICS: **Predatory Lending**

Watch out for dishonest predatory lenders who use illegal practices. Several of the more common predatory lending practices are listed here:

- A lender charges high loan fees, which cause the financing cost to be much higher than the quoted interest rate.

- A lender provides a home equity loan with the expectation that the loan will not be repaid because the lender wants to take ownership of the collateral backing the loan.

- A lender stipulates that a loan will only be provided if the borrower purchases insurance or other financial services.

- A lender includes a large balloon payment at the end of a loan that will require additional financing to pay off.

- A loan agreement includes confusing information that does not clearly disclose the borrower's obligations.

Borrowers who accept these kinds of terms often think they have no alternative, but shopping around for the best loan terms and interest rates is always the best option.

ECONOMIC IMPACT

Impact of the Economy on the Credit Limit

As economic conditions change, so does the value of a home, and therefore the credit limit on a home equity loan. During the financial crisis in 2008–2009, the market values of homes declined substantially. In many cases, the market value of the home declined below the mortgage balance, which meant that there was no equity in the home. Many homeowners needed funding during this period because they lost their jobs or their work hours were reduced, and therefore their income was reduced. In addition, their investments that declined in value were generating less income during this period. Some of these homeowners could not rely on home equity loans because of the decline in the market value of their home.

QUESTIONS

a. **Impact of Weak Economy on Home Equity.** Explain why home equity loans may not offer much access to credit in periods when the economy is weak and home prices decline.

b. **Impact of Strong Economy on Home Equity.** Explain how the estimated home equity increases as economic conditions improve.

There are several other steps you can take to protect yourself. Be wary of any lenders who pursue you with high-pressure tactics. Short-term offers and up-front application fees also indicate a disreputable lender. Always make sure you understand the loan terms before signing a loan agreement. If you cannot obtain reasonable loan terms, reconsider whether you truly need a loan at this time.

■ INTEREST RATES ON PERSONAL LOANS

The three most common types of interest rates financial institutions use to measure the interest due on personal loans are the annual percentage rate, simple interest, and add-on interest.

Annual Percentage Rate

annual percentage rate
A rate that measures the finance expenses (including interest and other expenses) on a loan annually.

As a result of the Truth-in-Lending Act (1969), lenders are required to disclose a standardized loan rate with directly comparable interest expenses over the life of the loan. This makes it easier for you to compare loans offered by different lenders and select the best loan. The **annual percentage rate (APR)** measures the finance expenses (including interest and all other expenses) on a loan annually.

EXAMPLE

Suppose that you have a choice of borrowing $2,000 over the next year from Bank A, Bank B, or Bank C. Bank A offers an interest rate of 10 percent on its loan. Bank B offers an interest rate of 8 percent, but also charges a fee of $100 at the time the loan is granted. Bank C offers an interest rate of 6 percent, but charges a loan fee of $200 at the time the loan is granted. Exhibit 14.2 shows the APRs.

In this example, Bank A offers the lowest APR for a one-year loan. Even though its interest rate is higher, its total financing costs are lower than those charged by the other banks because it does not have any fees. Thus, the APR on its loan is equal to the interest rate charged on the loan. In contrast, the APRs on the loans provided by Banks B and C are much higher than the interest rate charged on their loans because of the fees.

Simple Interest

simple interest
Interest on a loan computed as a percentage of the existing loan amount (or principal).

Simple interest is the interest computed as a percentage of the existing loan amount (or principal). It is measured using the principal, the interest rate applied to the principal, and the loan's time to maturity (in years). The loan repayment schedule is easily determined by a computer or a calculator or even on various Web sites. If you input the loan

Exhibit 14.2 Measurement of the Annual Percentage Rate

	Interest Expenses	Other Finance Expenses	Total Finance Expenses	Number of Years	Average Annual Finance Expenses	Annual Percentage Rate (APR)*
Bank A	$200	0	$200	1	$200	$200/$2,000 = 10%
Bank B	160	$100	260	1	260	$260/$2,000 = 13%
Bank C	120	200	320	1	320	$320/$2,000 = 16%

*The APR is calculated by dividing the average annual finance expenses by the average annual loan balance.

amount, the interest rate, and the loan maturity, the loan repayment schedule will provide you with the following information:

- The monthly payment
- The amount of each monthly payment applied to pay interest
- The amount of each monthly payment applied to pay down the loan principal
- The outstanding loan balance that remains after each monthly payment

The size of the monthly payment is dependent on the size of the loan, the interest rate, and the maturity. The larger the loan amount, the larger the monthly payment. The higher the interest rate, the larger the monthly payment. For a given loan amount and interest rate, the longer the period over which the loan is repaid (e.g., 36 months versus 24 months), the smaller the monthly payment. As mentioned earlier, however, the longer the maturity, the more you will pay in interest expenses.

EXAMPLE

You obtain a loan of $2,000 that is based on the simple interest method with an annual interest rate of 12 percent (1 percent per month) and 12 equal monthly payments. Given this information, a computer generates the loan repayment schedule in Exhibit 14.3. Notice at the top of the exhibit that each monthly payment is $177.70. Each payment consists of an interest payment and a portion that goes to repay the loan principal. At the end of the first month, the interest owed on $2,000 based on a monthly interest rate of 1 percent is:

$$\text{Interest Owed} = \text{Outstanding Loan Balance} \times \text{Interest Rate}$$
$$= \$2,000 \times .01$$
$$= \$20$$

Since the total payment is $177.70, and the interest payment is $20, the remainder ($157.70) is applied to pay down the principal. The outstanding loan balance after one month is:

$$\text{Outstanding Loan Balance} = \text{Previous Balance} - \text{Principal Payment}$$
$$= \$2,000 - \$157.70$$
$$= \$1,842.30$$

At the end of the second month, the interest rate of 1 percent is applied to the outstanding balance to determine the interest payment:

$$\text{Interest Owed} = \$1,842.30 \times .01$$
$$= \$18.42$$

Exhibit 14.3   Example of Loan Repayment Schedule: One-Year Loan, 12 Percent Interest Rate (Monthly Payment = $177.70)

Month	Interest Payment	Payment of Principal	Outstanding Loan Balance
			$2,000.00
1	$20.00	$157.70	1,842.30
2	18.42	159.28	1,683.02
3	16.83	160.87	1,522.16
4	15.22	162.48	1,359.68
5	13.60	164.10	1,195.58
6	11.96	165.74	1,029.84
7	10.30	167.40	862.44
8	8.63	169.07	693.37
9	6.94	170.76	522.61
10	5.23	172.47	350.13
11	3.50	174.20	175.94
12	1.76	175.94	0

This same process is followed to determine the amount of interest that is paid each month. The remainder of each payment is applied to pay off the principal. As each month passes, the outstanding loan balance is reduced, so the interest payment in the following month is reduced. The total monthly payment remains the same for all months, so the principal payment increases over time.

add-on interest method
A method of determining the monthly payment on a loan; involves calculating interest that must be paid on the loan amount, adding together interest and loan principal, and dividing by the number of payments.

Add-On Interest

With the **add-on interest method,** the amount of the monthly payment is determined by calculating the interest that must be paid on the loan amount, adding the interest and loan principal together, and dividing by the number of payments.

EXAMPLE

Reconsider the example in which you receive a loan of $2,000 to be repaid over one year, but assume that you are charged 12 percent interest based on the add-on method. You would first determine the amount of interest that is owed by applying the annual interest rate to the loan amount:

Interest Owed   = $2,000 × .12

= $240

Next, determine the total payment owed by adding the interest to the loan amount:

Total Payment   = $2,000 + $240

= $2,240

Finally, divide the total payment by the number of monthly payments:

Monthly payment   = $2,240/12

= $186.67

Notice that your monthly payment with the add-on method is about $9 per month more than your payment with the simple interest method. Even though the same interest rate is used for both methods, the add-on method is more costly. The reason is that the interest payment is not reduced over time as you pay off the loan.

■ CAR LOANS

A common type of personal loan is a car loan. When you decide to buy a car, you must select the car, negotiate the price, and determine whether to finance the purchase of the car or lease the car.

Selecting the Car

Before making any car-buying decisions, you should take into account the following points.

Personal Preferences. First, determine the type of car that you need. Keep in mind that the car that you want can be different from the car that you need. Reduce the list of available cars by deciding on the size of the car that you need. Do you want a small car that is easy to park and gets good gas mileage? Or do you need a minivan to fit your children and their sports equipment? You can always screen the cars on your list further by deciding on the size of the engine. Do you want a car with a large engine that has fast acceleration or a car with a small engine that is less expensive?

Price. Stay within your budget. Avoid purchasing a car that will require you to obtain a second job or establish an unrealistic monthly budget to afford the car payments.

Some college students are on a tight budget, and would only have sufficient funds to purchase a very inexpensive car that is likely to require more maintenance in the near future. Newer cars require less maintenance but are much more expensive. A compromise is a car that is a few years old. While its price may exceed the amount of cash that many college students have, financing can be arranged. No matter what your budget is, you should not consider purchasing the most expensive car that financing will allow because the finance payments will absorb much of your income for the next several years.

Financial Planning Online 14.2: **Prices of New Cars**

Go to
autos.yahoo.com

Click
"New Cars"

This Web site provides estimates of what you should pay for any new car based on the car's features and options that you specify.

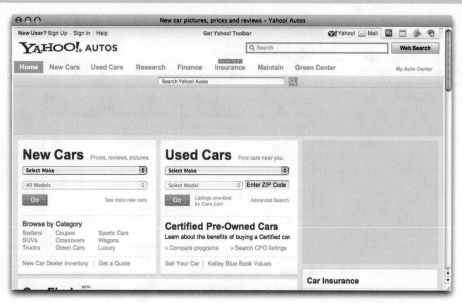

Condition. When buying a used car, be sure to assess the condition of your car beginning with the exterior. Has some of the paint worn off? Is there rust? Are the tires in good shape? Are the tires worn on one side (which may indicate that a wheel alignment is needed)? Next, check the interior. Are the seats worn? Do the electric devices work? Now look under the hood. Is there any sign of leaks? If you are still seriously considering the vehicle, ask the car owner for repair and maintenance records. Has the car been properly maintained and serviced over time? Has the oil been changed periodically?

All of these checks can help you assess a car's condition, but none replaces the expertise of a qualified mechanic. The cost of having a mechanic evaluate the car is worthwhile, because it may enable you to avoid buying a car that will ultimately result in large repair expenses.

Insurance. Some cars are subject to significantly higher insurance costs because they are more difficult to repair after accidents, are higher priced, or are common theft targets. Obtain insurance estimates on any car before making the purchase.

Resale Value. Some cars have a much higher resale value than others. For example, you can expect that an Acura will have a higher resale value than a Hyundai. Although you cannot perfectly predict the future resale value of a car, you can look at today's resale value of similar cars that were sold years ago. Numerous sites on the Internet, such as www.edmunds.com, provide the market values of used cars, which you can use to determine the resale value as a proportion of the original sales price.

Repair Expenses. Some cars are subject to much higher repair bills than others. To compare potential repair expenses, review *Consumer Reports* magazine, which commonly estimates the typical repair expenses for various cars.

Financing Rate. If you plan to finance your car purchase through the car dealer, you should compare financing rates among dealers. One dealer may charge a lower price for the car but charge higher financing costs for the loan. Other dealers may offer an unusually low financing rate, but charge a higher price on the car. When financing through a car dealer, beware of a dealer markup, in which the dealer arranges the loan and then marks up the lender's interest rate without disclosing the markup to the customer. For example, a dealer may obtain financing for your car at 10 percent, but charge you 12 percent. If you obtain financing from a financial institution rather than the dealer, you can easily compare financing rates of various financial institutions on the Internet.

Financial Planning Online 14.3: **Trade-in and Retail Values of Used Cars**

Go to
www.kbb.com/

This Web site provides trade-in and retail values for a used car, based on the condition of the car, its age, and other characteristics that you specify.

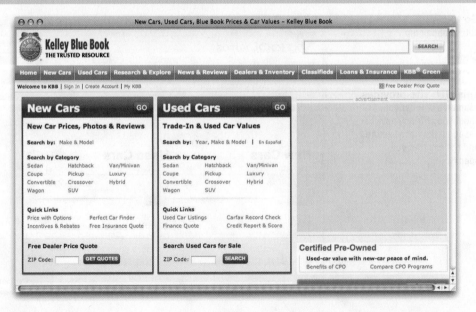

Financial Planning Online 14.4: **Car Loan Interest Rate Quotations**

Go to
www.ftc.gov/bcp/edu/pubs/
consumer/autos/aut05.shtm

This Web site suggests
questions that you should
ask when you are offered
unusually low financing
rates.

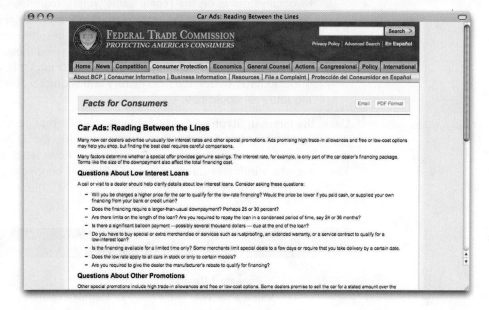

In some cases, you may wish to determine how much you can borrow before you decide which car to purchase. You can use auto loan Internet sites to estimate the maximum amount you can borrow, based on financial information you provide.

Revised Car Loan Contracts. Some car dealers will allow a car buyer to write a check for the down payment, fill out a car loan application, and drive the car home. If the application is not approved, the car buyer may have to reapply for a car loan that is set at a higher rate. At this point, the buyer may not have much choice except to accept the less favorable terms set by the lender. This situation is referred to as yo-yo financing. The consumer group Public Citizen received more than 1,000 complaints about this type of lending practice in 2004.

EXAMPLE

Stephanie Spratt has been working full-time for about a year and has saved enough money to afford a down payment on a new car. She considers which car to buy based on the following criteria:

- **Price.** Stephanie's favorite cars are priced in the $35,000 to $45,000 range, but she does not want to borrow such a large amount of money. She hopes to buy a home within a few years (which will require another loan) and therefore wants to limit the amount she borrows now.

  Next, Stephanie reviews her current assets to determine her down payment amount. She can sell her existing car for $1,000. She has accumulated about $4,000 in savings, which she would like to maintain for liquidity. She also still has her stock, which is worth about $3,000 at this time. She would prefer to keep her stock rather than sell it. She decides to use the $1,000 from the sale of her used car to make the down payment.

  Stephanie wants to borrow no more than $17,000 to buy a car, so she considers cars in the $16,000 to $20,000 price range. She identifies eight cars that are within that range, but she does not like three of them and therefore focuses on the remaining five cars. Next, she obtains more detailed information on the prices of the five cars online.

- **Resale Value, Repair Expenses, and Insurance.** Stephanie also uses the Internet to obtain ratings on the resale value, repair expenses, and insurance rates for each of the five cars. She recognizes that some dealers attempt to attract customers by offering unusually low financing rates, but then price the car higher to offset the low financing rate. She prefers to avoid these types of dealers, so she plans to obtain her financing from a car-financing Web site. She inputs information about her salary and loan history and is quickly able to determine the financing rate she would pay.

Using the Internet, Stephanie easily obtains the information shown in Exhibit 14.4. Car A has a relatively low resale value after two years. Car D has relatively high repair expenses and service maintenance. Cars A and C have relatively high insurance rates. Therefore, she eliminates Cars A, C, and D. She will choose between Cars B and E.

Exhibit 14.4   Stephanie Spratt's Car Analysis

Car	Expected Resale Value after Two Years (as a proportion of original sales price)	Repair Expenses and Service Maintenance	Insurance
A	Low	Moderate	High
B	Moderate	Low	Low
C	Moderate	Moderate	High
D	Moderate	High	Moderate
E	Moderate	Low	Moderate

Negotiating the Price

When shopping for a car, you have a choice between dealers that negotiate and dealers that offer one set price for a specific car to all customers. Any dealer that negotiates will purposely price its cars well above the price for which it is willing to sell the car. For example, the dealer may initially quote a price that represents the manufacturer's suggested retail price (MSRP). This price is also referred to as the sticker price. The strategy of some dealers is to make you think that you are getting a great deal as a result of the negotiations. If any customer is naïve enough to pay the full price, the car dealer earns a much larger profit at the customer's expense.

The salespeople are trained to act as if they are almost giving the car away to the customer by reducing the price by 5 to 20 percent. During the negotiations, they will say that they must discuss the price you offer with the sales manager. They already know the price at which they can sell the car to you, but this creates the appearance that they are pleading with the sales manager. During the negotiations, the dealer may offer you "free" rustproofing, a CD system, floor mats, or other features. These features are usually priced very high to make you believe that you are getting a good deal.

Negotiating by Phone. When purchasing a new car, it may be beneficial to negotiate by phone. After deciding on the type of car that you want, call a dealer and describe the car and options you desire. Explain that you plan to call other local car dealers, and that you will select the dealer that offers the lowest price. You may also want to emphasize that you will only call each dealer once.

Some dealers may not have the exact car that you want, so you may still have to compare features. For example, one dealer may quote a price that is $200 lower than the next-lowest quote, but the car may not be the specific color you requested. Nevertheless, the process described here can at least minimize the negotiation process.

Trade-In Tactics. If you are trading a car in, some dealers will pay a relatively high price for your trade-in, but charge a high price for the new car. For example, they may pay you $500 more than your used car is worth, but then charge you at least $500 more than they would have charged for the new car if you did not have a car to trade in. Attempt to negotiate the price on the new car first, before even mentioning that you have a car to trade in.

If you purchase a car from a typical dealer, many of the salespeople will congratulate you as if you had just won the lottery. This is also part of their strategy to make you feel that you got a great deal.

No-Haggle Dealers. Recently, many car dealerships have been created that do not haggle on the price. Buying a car from these dealers is not only less stressful but far less time-consuming. They set one price for a car, so you do not have to prepare for a negotiating battle. Some of these car dealerships still negotiate, however, so before you buy the car, you should make sure the price is no higher than that quoted by other dealers.

The Value of Information. Some car dealers attempt to make a higher profit from customers who are not well informed about the price that they should pay for a car. One way to avoid being taken advantage of when purchasing a car is to be informed. Shop around and make sure that you know the typical sales price for your car. You can obtain this information from *Consumer Reports* and other consumer magazines. Some Web sites will provide you with a quote based on the car model and features you want. You can do all of your shopping from your computer. For example, you may be able to obtain the dealer invoice price, which represents the price that the dealer pays the manufacturer for the car. The difference between the price quoted by the dealer and the invoice price represents the dealer markup. Be aware that manufacturers commonly provide dealers a rebate (referred to as a hold back), but dealers do not normally provide this information to their customers. A dealer could possibly charge a price that is only $200 above its dealer invoice, but if it received an $800 rebate from the manufacturer, the price is really marked up $1,000.

Financial Planning Online 14.5: **Prevailing Car Loan Interest Rates**

Go to
finance.yahoo.com/rates/
query?t=a

This Web site provides average car loan interest rates across regions of the U.S. and in specific states, which provide a useful benchmark for you to consider before obtaining a car loan.

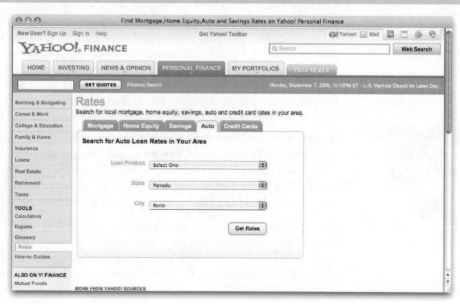

Purchasing a Car Online. You can buy a car online directly from some car manufacturers or from car referral services such as Autobytel Inc. or Carpoint. Car referral services forward your price quotation request to specific dealerships, which then respond by sending you a quote. www.carsdirect.com provides you with quotes based on deals it has made with various dealerships. That is, it receives guarantees from some dealerships on the prices for various types of cars. When a customer requests a quote, the car-buying service provides quotations that include a markup for its service. In other words, it is serving as the middleman between you and the dealership. If a customer agrees to the price, the car-buying service informs one of its dealerships to deliver the car.

Buying a new car online is not as efficient as buying an airline ticket or a book online. A car is not as standardized as a book, and the personal options can make the online correspondence more difficult. At a dealership, a customer can see the actual difference in the design of the two models of a particular car. It is not as easy to detect the differences on a Web site. Unlike a Web site, a dealership can anticipate your questions and arrange for a test drive. It is also more difficult to force an online service to meet its delivery promise to you. For example, an online car seller may guarantee you a price for a specific car, but not necessarily meet the delivery date. You have limited ability to enforce the deal because you may only be able to reach them by e-mail or voice mail. You can place more pressure on a local dealership to meet its promise by showing up at the dealership and expressing your concerns.

You can also buy used cars online, through eBay. However, the purchase of a used car online is subject to the same limitations as the purchase of a new car online. Given the limitations of buying a car online, many customers still prefer to buy a car at a dealership.

EXAMPLE

Stephanie Spratt has decided to use the Internet to shop for her car. Several Web sites state the price for each of the two new cars she is considering (Cars B and E from the previous example). She reviews specific details about each car, including which car has more value relative to its price, the options, available colors, and the delivery dates. She believes that while Car B is cheaper, its value will depreciate more quickly than Car E's. In addition, she can get the exact options and color she desires for Car E, and it can be delivered soon. She is almost ready to purchase Car E, which is priced at $18,000 including taxes. But first, she wants to consider the financing costs per month and whether to lease the car or purchase it.

Financing Decisions

If you consider purchasing a new car and plan to finance the purchase, you should estimate the dollar amount of the monthly payment. By evaluating your typical monthly cash inflows and outflows, you can determine whether you can afford to make the required payments to finance the car. You should conduct the estimate before shopping for a car so that you know how much you can afford. The more money needed to cover the car payments, the less you can add to your savings or other investments.

EXAMPLE

Stephanie Spratt wants to compare her monthly car payments if she borrows $15,000 versus $17,000 to buy a car. She must also decide whether to repay the loan over three years, four years, or five years. The larger the down payment she makes, the less she will need to borrow. However, she wants to retain some of her savings to maintain liquidity and to use for a future down payment on a house.

Stephanie goes to a car-financing Web site where she is asked to input the approximate amount she will borrow. The Web site then provides the available interest rate and shows the payments for each alternative loan amount and repayment period, as shown in Exhibit 14.5. The interest rate of 7.6 percent at the top of the exhibit is a fixed rate that

Exhibit 14.5 Stephanie's Possible Monthly Loan Payments (7.6 percent interest rate)		
	Loan Amount	
Loan Maturity	**$15,000**	**$17,000**
36 months (3 years)	$467	$530
48 months (4 years)	363	412
60 months (5 years)	301	341

Stephanie can lock in for the loan period. The possible loan amounts are shown at the top of the columns and each row shows a different loan repayment period.

Notice how the payment decreases if Stephanie extends the loan period. If she borrows $17,000, her payment would be $530 for a three-year loan, $412 for a four-year loan, or $341 for a five-year loan. Alternatively, she can lower her monthly payments by reducing her loan amount from $17,000 to $15,000. Notice that if she takes out a four-year loan for $15,000, her monthly payment is less than if she borrows $17,000.

Stephanie selects the $17,000 loan with a four-year term and a $412 monthly payment. The four-year term is preferable because the monthly loan payment for a three-year term is higher than she wants to pay. Since the purchase price of the car is $18,000, she will use the proceeds from selling her old car to cover the $1,000 down payment.

Some auto dealerships provide financing for up to seven years. The advantage of such a long period to repay the loan is that for a given loan amount, your monthly payment will be lower. However, the disadvantage of such a long period is that by the time you pay off the loan, the car may be worthless. Even if you sell the car after a few years, the car is likely to be worth less than the amount you still owe on the car. Conversely, if you pay off a car loan in a short amount of time, you are relieved of car payments until you purchase another car.

■ PURCHASE VERSUS LEASE DECISION

A popular alternative to buying a car is leasing one. An advantage of leasing is that you do not need a substantial down payment. In addition, you return the car to the car dealer at the end of the lease period, so you do not need to worry about finding a buyer for the car.

Leasing a car also has disadvantages. Since you do not own the car, you have no equity investment in it, even though the car still has value. You are also responsible for maintenance costs while you are leasing it. Keep in mind that you will be charged for any damage to the car over the lease period.

Some car dealers impose additional charges beyond the monthly lease payments. You will be charged if you drive more than the maximum number of miles specified in the lease agreement. You may be assessed a fee if you end the lease before the period specified in the contract. You may also have to purchase more car insurance than you already have. Some of these charges may be hidden within the lease agreement. Thousands of customers have filed legal claims, alleging that they were not informed of all possible charges when they leased a car. If you ever seriously consider leasing, make sure that you read and understand the entire lease agreement.

Financial Planning Online 14.6: **Should You Lease or Buy?**

Go to
www.bloomberg.com/
invest/calculators/leasebuy
.html

This Web site provides
a comparison of the cost of
leasing versus purchasing a
car.

EXAMPLE

Stephanie Spratt now wonders if she should lease the car she selected, rather than purchasing it for $18,000. If she purchases the car, she can invest $1,000 as a down payment today, and the remaining $17,000 will be financed by a car loan. She will pay $412 per month over four years to cover the financing. She expects that the car will be worth $10,000 at the end of four years. By purchasing instead of leasing, she foregoes interest that she could have earned from investing the $1,000 down payment over the next four years. If she invests the funds in a bank, she would earn 4 percent annually after considering taxes paid on the interest.

Alternatively, she could lease the same car for $300 per month over the four-year period. The lease would require an $800 security deposit, which she would receive back at the end of the four-year period. However, she would forego interest she could have earned if she had invested the $800 instead. And, at the end of a lease, she would have no equity and no car.

Stephanie's comparison of the cost of purchasing versus leasing is shown in Exhibit 14.6. Stephanie estimates the total cost of purchasing the car to be $10,936 while the total cost of leasing is $14,528. Therefore, she decides to purchase the car.

The decision to purchase versus lease a car is highly dependent on the estimated market value of the car at the end of the lease period. If the expected value of the car in the previous example were $6,000 instead of $10,000 after four years, the total cost of purchasing the car would have been $4,000 more. Substitute $6,000 for $10,000 in Exhibit 14.6 and recalculate the cost of purchasing to verify this. With an expected market value of $6,000, the total cost of purchasing the car would have been higher than the total cost of leasing, so leasing would have been preferable. Remember that some dealers may impose additional charges for leasing, such as a charge for driving more than the maximum miles allowed. Include any of these expenses in your estimate of the leasing expenses.

student loan
A loan provided to finance
part of the expenses a
student incurs while
pursuing a degree.

■ STUDENT LOANS

Another popular type of personal loan is a **student loan,** which is a loan to finance a portion of a student's expenses while pursuing an undergraduate or graduate degree.

Exhibit 14.6 Stephanie's Comparison of the Cost of Purchasing versus Leasing

Cost of Purchasing the Car

	Cost
1. Down payment	$1,000
2. Down payment of $1,000 results in foregone interest income:	
Foregone Interest	
Income per Year = Down Payment × Annual Interest Rate	
= $1,000 × .04	
= $40	
Foregone Interest over Four Years = $40 × 4	
= $160	160
3. Total monthly payments are:	
Total Monthly Payments = Monthly Payment × Number of Months	
= $412 × 48	
= $19,776	$19,776
Total	$20,936
Minus: Expected amount to be received when car is sold in four years	10,000
Total cost	$10,936

Cost of Leasing the Car for Four Years

	Cost
1. Security deposit of $800 results in foregone interest income (although she will receive her deposit back in four years):	
Foregone Interest	
Income per Year = Down Payment × Annual Interest Rate	
= $800 × .04	
= $320	
Foregone Interest over Four Years = $32 × 4	
= $128	$128
2. Total monthly payments are:	
Total Monthly Payments = Monthly Payment × Number of Months	
= $300 × 48	
= $14,400	14,400
Total cost	$14,528

One of the best sources of information about student loans is your school's financial aid office. Some student loans are provided directly to the student, while others are provided to the student's parents.

The lender may be the federal government or one of many financial institutions that participate in student loan programs. For example, the Federal Direct Loan Program provides government loans to students through schools' financial aid offices. In addition, the Stafford loan program extends loans from financial institutions directly to students. There are set limits on how much a student can borrow each year that increase as the student progresses. Loan limits are lower for students who are dependents. The repayment schedule is deferred, so students do not begin to repay the loans until they have completed their degrees and entered the workforce.

Even if you don't complete your education, you still have to pay back your student loans. Failure to do so will damage your credit history. The interest is tax-deductible up to a maximum of $2,500, which reduces the financing costs even more. The tax benefits are phased out for individuals who are in high tax brackets.

■ HOME EQUITY LOAN

home equity loan
A loan where the equity in a home serves as collateral for the loan.

One of the most popular types of personal loans is a **home equity loan**, which allows homeowners to borrow against the equity in their home. The home serves as collateral to back the loan. The borrowed funds can be used for any purpose, including a vacation, tuition payments, or health care expenses.

equity of a home
The market value of a home minus the debt owed on the home.

The **equity of a home** is determined by subtracting the amount owed on the home from its market value. If a home has a market value of $100,000 and the homeowner has a mortgage loan (discussed in the next chapter) with a balance of $60,000, the equity value is $40,000. A home equity loan essentially provides you with a line of credit. That is, it allows you to borrow the amount that you need up to a specific credit limit. You pay interest only on the amount of funds that you borrow. You can typically pay the interest owed per month on the amount you borrow and then pay the principal at a specified maturity date. You may also be allowed to pay off the principal at any point prior to maturity and still have access to the funds if you need them in the future.

Credit Limit on a Home Equity Loan

Financial institutions provide home equity loans of up to 80 percent (or more in some cases) of the value of the equity in a home.

Financial institutions define the market value of your equity as the market value of your home minus the mortgage balance (amount still owed on the home). When the

---

Financial Planning Online 14.7: Applying for a Home Equity Loan

Go to
www.federalreserve.gov/
Pubs/equity/
equity_english.htm

This Web site provides more information on home equity loans.

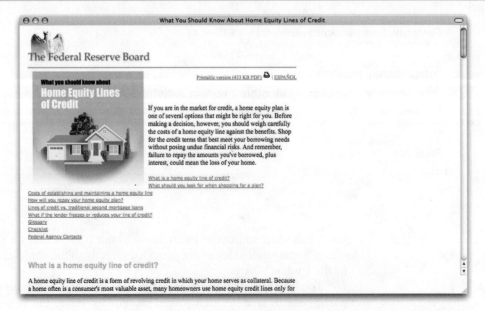

market value of a home rises, they are willing to provide more credit than if the market value remains the same.

If you default on a home equity loan, the lender can claim your home, use a portion of the proceeds to pay off the mortgage, and use the remainder to cover your home equity loan. If the market price of the home declines, the equity that you invested is reduced. For this reason, lenders do not like to lend the full amount of the equity when extending a home equity loan.

The following example illustrates how to determine the maximum amount of credit that can be provided on a home equity loan.

EXAMPLE

Suppose that you own a home worth $100,000 that you purchased four years ago. You initially made a down payment of $20,000 and took out an $80,000 mortgage. Over the last four years, your mortgage payments have added $10,000 in equity. Thus, you have invested $30,000 in the home, including your $20,000 down payment. Assume that the home's market value has not changed. Also, assume that a creditor is willing to provide you with a home equity loan of 70 percent based on the market value of equity in the home. In this example, the market value of equity is equal to the amount of equity you invested in the home.

$$\text{Maximum Amount of Credit Provided} = \text{Market Value of Equity in Home} \times .70$$
$$= \$30,000 \times .70$$
$$= \$21,000$$

EXAMPLE

Use the information in the previous example, except now assume that the market value of your home has risen from $100,000 to $120,000 since you purchased it. Recall that you paid off $10,000 of the $80,000 mortgage loan, so your mortgage balance is $70,000. The market value of the equity in the home is:

$$\text{Market Value of Equity in Home} = \text{Market Value of Home} - \text{Mortgage Balance}$$
$$= \$120,000 - \$70,000$$
$$= \$50,000$$

The market value of the equity is $50,000, while the amount of equity that you invested in the home is $30,000. The difference between these two amounts is the $20,000 increase in the value of the home since you purchased it. The credit limit based on the market value of the equity is:

$$\text{Maximum Amount of Credit Provided} = \text{Market Value of Equity in Home} \times .70$$
$$= \$50,000 \times .70$$
$$= \$35,000$$

Interest Rate

A home equity loan typically uses a variable interest rate that is tied to a specified interest rate index that changes periodically (such as every six months). The loan contract specifies how the interest rate will be determined. For example, it may be set equal to the average deposit rates across financial institutions within a particular district plus three percentage points. Because the home serves as collateral for a home equity loan, the lender faces less risk than with an unsecured loan and the interest rate is lower.

You borrow $10,000 with a home equity loan and pay $1,000 in interest on the home equity loan in a particular year. Assuming that you can deduct this amount from your taxable income and that your marginal income tax rate is 25 percent, your tax savings in that year are:

$$\text{Tax Savings in One Year from Home Equity Loan} = \text{Amount of Interest Paid} \times \text{Marginal Tax Rate}$$
$$= \$1,000 \times .25$$
$$= \$250$$

Tax-Deductible Interest. Interest that is paid on a home equity loan of up to $100,000 is tax-deductible. Borrowers can therefore reduce their taxes by using a home equity loan instead of other types of loans or credit cards.

Thus, when you use a home equity loan, not only do you benefit from a relatively low interest rate, but also you generate tax savings.

HOW PERSONAL LOANS FIT WITHIN YOUR FINANCIAL PLAN

The following are the key personal loan decisions that should be included within your financial plan:

1. How much money can you afford to borrow on a personal loan?
2. If you obtain a personal loan, should you pay it off early?

By making sound decisions, you can avoid accumulating an excessive amount of debt. Exhibit 14.7 provides an example of how personal loan decisions apply to Stephanie Spratt's financial plan. The exhibit shows how Stephanie reviews her typical monthly cash flows to determine whether she can cover her monthly loan payments.

Financial Planning Online 14.8: **Personal Loan Scams**

Go to
www.ftc.gov/bcp/edu/pubs/
consumer/telemarketing/
tel16.shtm

This Web site expains
some personal loan scams
of which you should be
aware.

Exhibit 14.7 How Personal Loan Management Fits within Stephanie Spratt's Financial Plan

GOALS FOR PERSONAL FINANCING

1. Limit the amount of financing to a level and maturity that I can pay back on a timely basis.
2. For any personal loan, I will consider paying off the loan balance as soon as possible.

ANALYSIS

Monthly Cash Inflows	$2,500
− Typical Monthly Expenses	1,400
− Monthly Car Loan Payment	412
= Amount of Funds Available	**$688**

DECISIONS

Decision on Affording a Personal Loan:

The financing of my new car requires a payment of $412 per month. This leaves me with $688 per month after paying typical monthly expenses. I can afford to make the payments. I will not need additional personal loans for any other purpose.

Decision on Paying Off Personal Loan Balances:

The car loan has an interest rate of 7.6 percent. I expect that my stock investment will earn a higher rate of return than this interest rate. Once I have accumulated more savings, however, I will seriously consider using my savings and invested funds to pay off the balance of the loan early.

DISCUSSION QUESTIONS

1. How would Stephanie's personal loan decisions be different if she were a single mother of two children?

2. How would Stephanie's personal loan decisions be affected if she were 35 years old? If she were 50 years old?

SUMMARY

- When applying for a personal loan, you need to disclose your personal balance sheet and cash flow statement so that the lender can evaluate your ability to repay a loan. A loan contract specifies the amount of the loan, interest rate, maturity, and collateral.

- The common types of interest rates charged on personal loans are the annual percentage rate (APR), simple interest, and add-on interest. The APR measures the interest and other expenses as a percentage of the loan amount on an annualized basis. Simple interest measures the interest as a percentage of the existing loan amount. Add-on interest calculates interest on the loan amount, adds the interest and principal, and divides by the number of payments.

- Your decision to purchase a car may require financing. You can reduce your monthly payments on the car loan if you make a higher down payment, but doing this may reduce your liquidity. Alternatively, you can reduce your monthly payments by extending the loan period.

- The decision of whether to purchase a car with a car loan or lease a car requires an estimation of the total cost of each alternative. The total cost of purchasing a car consists of the down payment, the foregone interest income from the down payment, and the total monthly loan payments. The total cost of leasing consists of the foregone interest income from the security deposit and the total monthly lease payments.

- Student loans are provided by the federal government and by financial institutions that participate in student loan programs.

- A home equity loan commonly has more favorable terms than other personal loans. It has a relatively low interest rate because of the collateral (the home) that backs the loan. In addition, the interest paid on a home equity loan is tax-deductible up to a limit.

REVIEW QUESTIONS

1. **Sources of Personal Loans.** List some possible sources of personal loans. What precautions should be taken with loans from family members or friends?

2. **Personal Loan Process.** What does the personal loan process involve?

3. **Loan Amortization.** What does it mean if a loan is amortized? What do the loan payments represent?

4. **Loan Application Process.** What information must borrowers supply to lenders in the loan application process? Why is this information important to lenders?

5. **Loan Contract.** What information is included in a loan contract? How is the amount of the loan determined?

6. **Collateral.** Explain how collateral works. Do all loans have collateral? What is the relationship between collateral and interest rates?

7. **Loans Maturity.** How does the maturity of a loan affect the monthly payments? What should you consider when selecting the maturity?

8. **Payday Loan.** Explain the difference between a 10% rate charged on a payday loan and a 10% rate charged by a bank on a personal loan.

9. **Cosigning a Loan.** What are your responsibilities if you cosign a loan? What are the potential consequences of failing to live up to your responsibilities as a cosigner?

10. **APR.** What is the purpose of the annual percentage rate measurement? Could lenders with the same interest rates report different APRs?

11. **Simple Interest.** What is simple interest? What information is needed to compute it? What information is contained in a loan repayment schedule?

12. **Add-On Interest.** How are payments calculated under the add-on interest method?

13. **Simple versus Add-On Interest.** Why are loan payments under the simple interest method usually lower than loan payments under the add-on interest method?

14. **Buying a Car.** List the steps in buying a car. What financial criteria should be considered? Discuss each briefly.

15. **Buying a Car Online.** Why is purchasing a new car online not as efficient as buying a new car at a dealership?

16. **Car Sales Tactics.** Describe some techniques that car salespeople might use in negotiating the price of the car. What should you be aware of at "no-haggle" dealerships?

17. **Financing.** What should be the first step in financing a purchase of a car? Aside from the interest rate, what two factors will have the largest impact on the size of your monthly payment?

18. **Leasing a Car.** What are the advantages and disadvantages of leasing a car? Give some advice for someone considering leasing.

19. **Student Loan.** Who extends student loans? What are the characteristics of student loans?

20. **Home Equity.** What is home equity? Describe how a home equity loan works.

21. **Credit Limits.** Discuss the two ways financial institutions might define equity to set credit limits. What happens if you default on a home equity loan?

22. **Home Equity Loan.** How are interest rates calculated for home equity loans? Why do borrowers prefer home equity loans to other loans?

23. **Home Equity Loan.** How can borrowers enjoy tax savings by using a home equity loan? How are these tax savings computed?

FINANCIAL PLANNING PROBLEMS

1. **Origination Fees.** Jack needs to borrow $1,000 for the next year. Bank South will give him the loan at 9 percent. SunCoast Bank will give him the loan at 7 percent with a $50 loan origination fee. First National will give him the loan at 6 percent with a $25 loan origination fee. Determine the total interest and fees Jack will be charged in each case. Which loan should Jack choose?

2. **Amortization.** Beth has just borrowed $5,000 on a four-year loan at 8 percent simple interest. Complete the amortization table below for the first five months of the loan.

3. **Add-On Interest Loan.** What if Beth had made the same loan as an add-on interest loan? How would her payments differ? Why is there a difference?

4. **Loan Payments.** Tracy is borrowing $8,000 on a six-year, 11 percent, add-on interest loan. What will Tracy's payments be?

5. **Loan Interest.** Sharon is considering the purchase of a car. After making the down payment, she will finance $15,500. Sharon is offered three maturities. On a four-year loan, Sharon will pay $371.17 per month. On a five-year loan, Sharon's monthly payments will be $306.99. On a six-year loan, they will be $264.26. Sharon rejects the four-year loan, as it is not within her budget. How much interest will Sharon pay over the life of the loan on the five-year loan? On the six-year loan? Which should she choose if she bases her decision solely on total interest paid?

6. **Loan Interest.** Refer to question 5. If Sharon had been able to afford the four-year loan, how much interest would she have saved compared to the five-year loan?

7. **Finance Charges.** Bill wants to purchase a new car for $45,000. Bill has no savings, so he needs to finance the entire purchase amount. With no down payment, the interest rate on the loan is 13 percent and the maturity of the loan is six years. His monthly payments will be $903.33. Bill's monthly net cash flows are $583.00. Bill also has a credit card with a $10,000 limit and an interest rate of 18 percent. If Bill uses all of his net cash flows to make the monthly payments on the car, how much will he add each month to his credit card balance if he uses it to finance the remainder of the car? What will the finance charges be on his credit card for the first two months that finance charges apply? (Assume that Bill makes no payments on his credit card.)

8. **Credit Limit.** Mary and Marty are interested in obtaining a home equity loan. They purchased their house five years ago for $125,000 and it now has a market value of $156,000. Originally, Mary and Marty paid $25,000 down on the house and took out a $100,000 mortgage. The current balance on their mortgage is $72,000. The bank uses 70 percent of equity in determining the credit limit. What will their credit limit be if the bank bases their credit limit on equity invested and will loan them 70 percent of the equity?

9. **Credit Limit.** Refer to question 8. What will Mary and Marty's credit limit be if the bank uses the market value of equity to determine their credit limit and will loan them 70 percent of the equity?

10. **Tax Savings.** John and Cheryl just borrowed $30,000 on a home equity line of credit. The interest rate for the loan is 6.75 percent for the entire year, and they took out the loan on May 1. John and Cheryl are in the 28 percent tax bracket. What will be their tax savings for the first year ending December 31st?

Payment Number	Beginning Balance	Payment Amount	Applied to Interest	Applied to Principal	New Balance
1	$5,000.00	$122	$33.33	$88.67	$4,911.33
2	a	122	32.74	b	4,822.07
3	4,822.07	c	d	89.85	4,732.22
4	4,732.22	122	e	90.45	f
5	4,641.77	122	30.95	g	h

11. **Tax Savings.** Noel has a 15 percent marginal tax rate. If he pays $1,400 in interest on a home equity loan in the first year, what will his tax savings be?

12. ETHICAL DILEMMA: Fritz and Helga work for a local manufacturing company. Since their marriage five years ago, they have been working extensive overtime, including Sundays and holidays. Fritz and Helga have established a lifestyle based on their overtime earnings. Recently, the company lost two major contracts and all overtime has been eliminated. As a result, Fritz and Helga are having difficulty paying their bills. Several months ago they began using a local payday loan company to pay their bills on time. The first week they borrowed only a small amount to cover some past due bills. The next week, however, in order to pay back the loan plus interest, they were left with an even smaller amount to pay bills resulting in a higher payday loan the second week. In paying back the second week's loan, their remaining available funds were further reduced. This cycle continued until they were no longer able to borrow because the repayment plus interest would have exceeded their paychecks. Fritz and Helga have had their cars repossessed, their home foreclosed on, and they are preparing to file for bankruptcy.

   a. Is the payday loan company being ethical in continuing to loan more and more to Fritz and Helga each week?

   b. What could Fritz and Helga have done to avoid ultimate financial ruin?

FINANCIAL PLANNING ONLINE EXERCISES

1. On www.lendingtree.com/ click "FHA Loans" and answer the following questions:

   a. What is an FHA loan and how long have they been in existence?

   b. What are the key components of an FHA loan?

   c. What are the five eligibility requirements?

2. Go to www.ditech.com/ and click "Calculators."

   a. Using the calculator, "How Much Will My Payments Be?" compute your monthly payments assuming a $100,000 loan at 6% for 30 years.

   b. Use the same information in "a" except compute the payments for a 15-year loan.

   c. Using the calculator, "How Much Home Can I Afford?" input your current monthly income or estimated monthly income after graduating, your other monthly debt payment including credit cards, and an interest rate of 6%. How large a mortgage do you qualify for assuming a 15-year loan? Assuming a 30-year loan?

3. Using the "New Car Calculator" on autos.yahoo.com/, enter the information identifying the make, model, and features of your dream car. Are there any available in your area? What are the price ranges?

4. Go to www.kbb.com.

   a. Click "Used Car Values By Make & Model." In the fields provided, select "2005" for year, "Ford" for make, and "Taurus" for model. Click "Go," then click "Retail Value." Click "GL Sedan 4D." Assume a 3.0 liter V6 engine, mileage of 85,000, standard equipment, and enter your Zip code. Click "Continue." What is the retail value if the car is in excellent condition?

   b. Click "Trade-In value." What is the trade-in price? How does it differ from the retail price?

   c. Click the "Reviews & Ratings" tab, then click "Previews: Check Out New and Future Models" and "Auto Show Coverage." Look for information on a car that has had major revisions.

   d. Click the "New Cars" tab. Select a make and model that interests you. You will find useful information about the new model.

5. In the box "Compare Local Auto Loan Rates" on the Web site www.bankrate.com/auto.aspx, click "Zip Code," enter your Zip code, and after clicking "36 month new car loan" hit search and answer the following questions:

   a. Which lender offers the best rate?

   b. What fees and conditions are attached to this rate?

   c. Do the same search, only this time for a 36-month used car loan. Who has the lowest rate?

   d. What are the conditions attached to the rate in "c" above?

e. Why do you think the rates are different on a new car versus a used car loan for the same period of time?

6. Using the Web site finance.yahoo.com/rates/query?t=a, find the following:

   a. What is the best rate that you could obtain for a 36-month new car loan in Poughkeepsie, NY?

   b. Find the same information for Rapid City, SD.

   c. Locate the same information for San Francisco, CA.

   d. Based on the results in "a" through "c," what would be the best city in which to finance a new car purchase? Briefly discuss why there are differences in auto loan rates between Poughkeepsie, Rapid City, and San Francisco.

7. Using the Web site www.bankrate.com/calculators/auto/auto-loan-calculator.aspx, compute the following information:

   a. Assume you purchase an automobile requiring a $30,000 loan at 7% for 48 months. What will be the monthly payment? What will be the total amount that you will pay over the 48 months?

   b. Assume the same data as in "a" except for a 60-month loan. What is your monthly payment? What is the total amount that you will pay over the 60 months?

   c. Using the same data as in "a," compute the monthly payment assuming a 36-month loan. What is the total amount that you will pay over the 36 months?

   d. Which of the three loan periods used in "a," "b," and "c" will result in the lowest monthly payment? Which of the three will result in the lowest total amount paid over the term of the loan?

8. Using the calculator at www.bloomberg.com/invest/calculators/leasebuy.html, determine whether it is better to lease or buy a vehicle. Assume the purchase price of the car is $30,000, you will make a $2,000 down payment, the sales tax rate in your state is 6%, and your investment rate of return is 10%. The term of the loan will be 60 months with an interest rate of 7%, no other fees, and an annual depreciation rate of 20%. The term of the lease will be 24 months with an interest rate of 7%, other fees totaling $150, a residual percentage of 50%, and a security deposit of $1,000. Based strictly on the monthly payments, is it better to buy or lease? What is the monthly difference in cost between the two?

VIDEO EXERCISE:
Applying for a Personal Loan

Go to one of the Web sites that contain video clips (such as www.youtube.com) and view some video clips about banking tips. You can use search phrases such as "banking tips." Select one video clip on this topic that you would recommend for the other students in your class.

1. Provide the Web link for the video clip.

2. What do you think is the main point of this video clip?

3. How might you change your personal loan application process as a result of watching this video clip?

BUILDING YOUR OWN FINANCIAL PLAN

Loans to finance purchases such as automobiles and homes may be obtained from a variety of sources, each of which has advantages and disadvantages. For example, automobile purchases may be financed through the dealer, a local bank, a credit union, or a finance company. Review all loans that you currently have or anticipate having upon graduation and identify as many sources of these loans as possible. Evaluate the advantages and disadvantages of each source to assist you in determining where to best meet your various borrowing needs.

Go to the worksheets at the end of this chapter, and to the CD-ROM accompanying this text, to continue building your financial plan.

THE SAMPSONS—A CONTINUING CASE

After about 10 months of saving $500 a month, the Sampsons have achieved their goal of saving $5,000 that they will use as a down payment on a new car. (They have also been saving an additional $300 per month over the last year for their children's college education.) Sharon's new car is priced at $25,000 plus 5 percent sales tax. She will receive a $1,000 trade-in credit on her existing car and will make a $5,000 down payment on the new car. The Sampsons would like to allocate a maximum of $500 per month to the loan payments on Sharon's new car. The annual interest rate on a car loan is currently 7 percent. They would prefer to have a relatively short loan maturity, but cannot afford a monthly payment higher than $500.

Go to the worksheets at the end of this chapter, and to the CD-ROM accompanying this text, to continue this case.

Chapter 14: Building Your Own Financial Plan

GOALS

1. Limit your personal financing to a level and maturity that you can pay back on time.

2. For loans you anticipate needing in the future, evaluate the advantages and disadvantages of lenders.

3. Compare the cost of buying and leasing a car.

ANALYSIS

1. Review your personal cash flow statement. How much can you afford to pay each month for personal loans?

2. Identify several prospective lenders for personal loans you may need in the future. What are the advantages and disadvantages of each source with respect to the interest rates offered, method of calculating interest, and other criteria of importance to you?

Loan Evaluation

Loan One:

Description of Loan	Sources for Loan	Advantages of Source	Disadvantages of Source
	1.		
	2.		
	3.		

Loan Two:

Description of Loan	Sources for Loan	Advantages of Source	Disadvantages of Source
	1.		
	2.		
	3.		

Loan Three:

Description of Loan	Sources for Loan	Advantages of Source	Disadvantages of Source
	1.		
	2.		
	3.		

3. Compare the cost of purchasing a car versus leasing a car over a four-year period.

Cost of Purchasing versus Leasing a Car

Cost of Purchasing a Car

Down payment	
Interest rate	
Number of months	
Annual foregone interest on down payment	
Monthly payment on car loan	
Total monthly payments	
Total cost of purchasing	
Expected amount to be received when car is sold	
Total cost of purchasing	

Cost of Leasing a Car

Security deposit	
Foregone interest	
Monthly lease payments	
Total monthly payments	
Total cost of leasing	

If you enter this information in the Excel worksheet, the software will create a graphical comparison of purchasing versus leasing.

DECISIONS

1. Report how much you can afford to spend each month on personal loans.

_____

_____

_____

_____

_____

_____

_____

2. Report which lenders you may consider using in the future and why.

_____

_____

_____

_____

_____

_____

3. Is purchasing or leasing a vehicle a better choice for your needs?

_____

_____

_____

_____

_____

_____

_____

_____

Chapter 14: The Sampsons—A Continuing Case

CASE QUESTIONS

1. Advise the Sampsons on possible loan maturities. Go to loan.yahoo.com/a/autocalc.html and click "Loan Payment Calculator." Input information to determine the possible monthly car payments for a three-year (36-month) payment period, a four-year (48-month) payment period, and a five-year (60-month) period. Enter the results in the following table:

	Three-Year (36-month) Periods	Four-Year (48-month) Periods	Five-Year (60-month) Periods
Interest rate	7%	7%	7%
Monthly payment			
Total finance payments			
Total payments including the down payment and the trade-in			

2. What are the trade-offs among the three alternative loan maturities?

_____

_____

_____

_____

_____

_____

_____

3. Based on the information on finance payments that you retrieved from the loan payment Web site, advise the Sampsons on the best loan maturity for their needs.

_____

_____

_____

_____

_____

_____

_____

Purchasing and Financing a Home

Two years ago, Brian Menke purchased a small home that he could easily afford near the firm where he works. His co-worker, Tim Remington, also bought a home. Unlike Brian, Tim would need most of his paycheck to cover the mortgage and expenses of his home, but he thought the purchase would be a good investment.

Because his mortgage payment was relatively low, Brian was able to save money during the next year. Tim, however, was unable to save any money, and when interest rates increased, his mortgage payment increased. Tim suddenly realized he could not afford his home. Because the demand for homes had weakened, housing prices had declined since Tim purchased his home. Tim sold his home, but for $20,000 less than he paid for it. He also had to pay the real estate broker a commission of $16,000. Thus, Tim received $36,000 less from the sale of his home than his purchase price in the previous year.

During the following year, the economy improved and home prices increased. Brian's home was now worth $12,000 more than he paid for it. But the improved economy did not help Tim, who no longer owned a home.

Financial planning made the difference. Brian's strategy was more conservative, which allowed for the possibility that the economy and market conditions could weaken temporarily. Conversely, Tim did not consider that his mortgage payment could increase and also wrongly assumed that home prices would never decline.

Buying your first home is an important personal financial decision due to the long-term and costly nature of the investment. Your decision on how much to spend and how much to finance will affect your cash flows for years. This chapter describes the fundamentals of purchasing a home and will help you evaluate your first home purchase.

The objectives of this chapter are to:

- Explain how to select a home to purchase

- Explain how to conduct a valuation of a home

- Describe the transaction costs of purchasing a home

- Describe the characteristics of a fixed-rate mortgage

- Describe the characteristics of an adjustable-rate mortgage

- Show how to compare the costs of purchasing versus renting a home

- Explain the mortgage refinancing decision

■ SELECTING A HOME

Buying a home may be the single biggest investment you will ever make, so the decision should be taken very seriously. You should carefully consider several factors. Evaluate the homes for sale in your target area to determine the typical price range and features. Once you decide on a realistic price range, identify a specific home that you desire. You can compare the cost of buying that home to the cost of renting. This way, you can weigh the extra costs against the benefits of home ownership.

An alternative to purchasing a house is to purchase a condominium. In a condominium, individuals own units of a housing complex, but jointly own the surrounding land and common areas (such as parking lots) and amenities (such as a swimming pool). The benefits of a condominium are somewhat different from those of a house. Whereas a house is detached, units in a condominium are typically attached, so there is less privacy. Condominium expenses are shared among unit owners, while the owners of a house pay for expenses on their own. Nevertheless, the factors to be considered when selecting or financing a house are also relevant when purchasing a condominium. Thus, the following discussion will use *home* rather than *house* to indicate that it also applies to a condominium.

Relying on a Realtor

You may consider advice from a real estate broker when you assess homes, decide whether to buy a home, or determine which home to purchase. Yet you should not rely completely on the advice of real estate brokers because they have a vested interest: they earn a commission only if you purchase a home through them. You should consider their input, but make decisions that meet your needs and preferences. A good real estate broker will ask you about your preferences and suggest appropriate homes.

Using Online Realtor Services

Increasingly, online services are being used to facilitate home purchases. Web sites such as www.ziprealty.com allow sellers to present detailed information about their home in a database that is made accessible to potential home buyers. These types of Web sites are sometimes limited to particular cities. The realty company sponsoring the Web site may provide services to complete a contract, and the commission for using the online service is less than the traditional commission charged by real estate agents.

Other online services allow sellers to list their home in a database, without providing other real estate-related services. The contract would have to be completed by the buyer and seller without the help of a realtor. The advantage of this type of service is that it charges lower commissions than a traditional full-service real estate company. Some of these online services are actually subsidiaries of the traditional full-service real estate companies. For example, Blue Edge Realty (blueedge.com) is a subsidiary of Coldwell Banker Real Estate Corporation. Customers who want full-service real estate

"You see that dark, spooky image on the screen? That's your credit history coming back to haunt you."

services can rely on Coldwell Banker, while customers who primarily want to list their home for potential buyers can use Blue Edge Realty.

■ HOW MUCH CAN YOU AFFORD?

When selecting a home, first, you should determine how much money you can afford to pay per month for a mortgage based on your budget. Once you remove homes from consideration that are too expensive, you should use various criteria to evaluate the homes that you are still considering.

Most individuals pay for a home with a down payment (perhaps 10 to 20 percent of the purchase price) and obtain a mortgage loan to finance the rest. You will pay monthly mortgage payments over the life of the loan. Mortgage loan lenders determine how much money they will lend you based on your financial situation and credit history. Various Web sites can estimate the maximum value of a home you can afford based on your financial situation (such as your income and your net worth).

Financial planners suggest that a home price should be no more than two times the total gross annual household income and that all of the monthly household debt payments (including the mortgage loan) should be no more than about 40 percent of the total monthly gross income. However, these generalizations do not apply to everyone, as other financial information and spending habits of the homeowners should also be considered.

Affordable Down Payment

You can determine your maximum down payment by estimating the market value of the assets that you are willing to convert to cash for a down payment and for transaction costs (such as closing costs) when obtaining a mortgage. Be sure to maintain some funds for liquidity purposes to cover unanticipated bills.

Affordable Monthly Mortgage Payments

How large a mortgage payment can you afford? Refer to your cash flow statement to determine how much net cash flow you have to make a mortgage payment. If you purchase a home, you will no longer have a rent payment, so that money can be used as part of the mortgage payment. You should also be aware, however, that owning a home entails some periodic expenses (such as property taxes, homeowner's insurance, and home repairs). You should not plan to purchase a home that will absorb all your current rent excess cash inflows. The larger your mortgage payments, the less you can add to your savings or other investments.

EXAMPLE

Stephanie Spratt just received an unexpected bonus and a promotion from her employer. After assessing her financial situation, she decides that she may want to purchase a home in the near future. She has about $15,000 in liquid assets for use toward a down payment and transaction costs. She evaluates her personal cash flows. Since she would no longer need to pay rent for her apartment, she can afford to allocate $900 a month to monthly mortgage payments. She begins to look at homes for sale in the range of $70,000 to $85,000. Once she identifies a home that she may want to purchase, she will obtain estimates of the required down payment, the transaction costs, and the mortgage payment.

When you consider how much you can afford, consider the economic conditions and stability of your job situation. If economic conditions weaken, will your job be affected? Your mortgage payments extend for a long period of time, so you should assess the likelihood that you will continue to earn income over the life of the mortgage that would be sufficient to make mortgage payments. While you could obtain another job if you are laid off, you might not be able to earn the same level of income. Thus, you may want to use a conservative estimate of your future income when determining the mortgage payment you can afford, just to make sure that you can afford the home even if economic conditions deteriorate.

Criteria Used to Select a Home

The most important factors to consider when selecting a home are identified here:

- **Price.** Stay within your budget. Avoid purchasing a home that you cannot afford. Although your favorite home may have ample space and a large yard, it may not be worth the stress of struggling to make the mortgage payments.

- **Convenient Location.** Focus on homes in a convenient area so that you can minimize commuting time to work or travel time to other activities. You may save 10 or more hours of travel time a week.

- **Maintenance.** Some homes built by well-known construction companies have lower repair bills than others. In addition, newer homes tend to need fewer repairs than older homes. A home with a large yard requires more maintenance.

    In condominiums, residents share common areas, such as a swimming pool or tennis court. Normally, the residents pay a fixed monthly fee to cover the costs of maintaining the common areas. In addition, they may be assessed an extra fee to maintain the structure of the condominium, such as a new roof or other repairs.

- **School System.** If you have children, the reputation of the school system is very important. Even if you do not have children, the resale value of your house benefits from a good school system.

- **Insurance.** When you own a home, you need to purchase homeowner's insurance, which covers the home in case of burglary or damage. The cost of insurance varies among homes. It is higher for more expensive homes and for homes

Financial Planning Online 15.1: **How Much Money Can You Borrow?**

Go to
www.calculatorweb.com/
calculators/
borrowcalc.shtml

This Web site provides
an estimate of how much
money you could borrow to
finance a home, based on
your income and other
financial information.

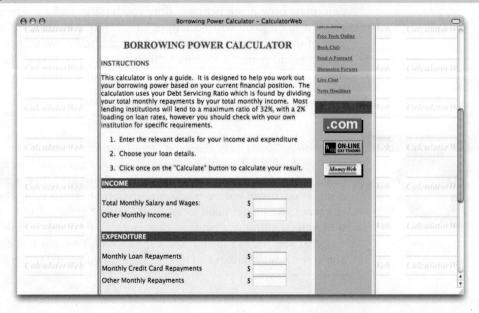

in high-risk areas (such as flood zones) because it costs the insurer more to replace parts of the home that are damaged.

- **Taxes.** Taxes are imposed on homes to pay for local services, such as the local school system and the local park system. Taxes vary substantially among locations. Annual property taxes are often between 1 and 2 percent of the market value of the home. Thus, the tax on a $100,000 home is typically between $1,000 and $2,000 per year. Property taxes are tax-deductible if you itemize deductions on your income tax return. You can deduct them from your income when determining your federal income tax.

- **Homeowner's Association.** Some homes are connected with homeowner's associations, which set guidelines for the homes and may even assess fees that are used to hire security guards or to maintain common grounds within the area. The monthly fees charged by some homeowner's associations are very high and should be considered when buying a home.

- **Resale Value.** The resale value of a home is highly dependent on its location. Most homes with similar features within a specific subdivision or neighborhood are in the same range. Although home prices in a given subdivision tend to move in the same direction, the price movements can vary substantially among homes. For example, homes in a subdivision that are within walking distance of a school may be worth more than comparable houses several miles from the school.

  You cannot perfectly predict the future resale value of a home, but you can evaluate today's resale value of similar homes in that location that were sold years ago. Information about home prices is provided on numerous Web sites. Be aware, however, that the rate of increase in home prices in previous years does not necessarily serve as a good predictor of the future.

  Keep in mind that when you use a realtor to sell a home (as most people do), you will pay the realtor a commission that is usually about 6 percent of the selling price. Thus, if you resell your home for $100,000, you will probably pay a commission of about $6,000 and therefore receive $94,000. The buyer of a home does not pay a commission.

- **Personal Preferences.** In addition to the general criteria described above, you will have your own personal preferences regarding features such as the number of bedrooms, size of the kitchen, and size of the yard.

Financial Planning Online 15.2: **Recent Sales Prices of Nearby Homes**

Go to
realestate.yahoo.com/
Homevalues

This Web site provides sales prices of homes on a street in a city that you specify over a recent period. It can also provide a list of homes in the city you specify that sold within a certain price range.

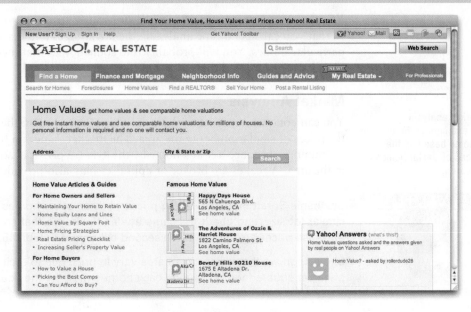

Financial Planning Online 15.3: **Listing of Homes Nearby for Sale**

Go to
www.realtor.com/

This Web site provides
a listing of homes for sale in
an area that you specify
and homes in the price and
size range that you specify.

FOCUS ON ETHICS: **Disclosing Defects**

For both the buyer and seller, the sale of a home is stressful due to the large amount of money involved. Concerns about unethical behavior only add to the tension. For example, there are many cases of sellers of homes who did not disclose problems (such as a leaky roof or cracked foundation).

As a seller, by law most states require that you fully disclose any defect that may affect the value of the home. In addition to being the legal thing to do, disclosure is the moral thing to do. You would hope that a seller would be completely honest with you, so you should treat the potential buyer in the manner that you wish to be treated. And if any problem arises shortly after you sell a house, the buyer can sue you for any misrepresentations.

▇ VALUATION OF A HOME

You should use the criteria described previously to screen your list of desirable homes so that you can spend time analyzing the advantages and disadvantages of three or four particular homes. You will probably find some homes that meet all your criteria, but are simply overpriced and therefore should not be considered.

Market Analysis

market analysis
An estimate of the price of
a home based on the
prices of similar homes in
the area.

You can conduct a **market analysis**, in which you estimate the price of a home based on the prices of similar homes in the area. The market value can be estimated by multiplying the number of square feet in a home by the average price per square foot of similar homes in the area. A real estate broker or appraiser may also provide you with a valuation.

EXAMPLE

Stephanie Spratt finds the selling prices of three other homes in the same area, with a similar lot size, and about the same age as the home that she wants to purchase. The purchase prices are shown in the second column of Exhibit 15.1.

She recognizes that homes in an area vary in price due to their size. She determines the price per square foot by dividing each home's price by the square feet, as shown in the

Exhibit 15.1   Using a Market Analysis to Purchase a Home

House Size	Price	Price per Square Foot
1,200 square feet	$78,000	$78,000/1,200 = $65
1,300 square feet	$87,100	$87,100/1,300 = $67
1,100 square feet	$66,000	$66,000/1,100 = $60

Average price per square foot = ($65 + $67 + $60)/3 = $64

third column. Then she determines that the average price per square foot of the three homes is $64, as shown at the bottom of the exhibit.

Since the home that Stephanie wants to purchase has 1,300 square feet, she estimates its market value to be:

Market Value of Home = Average Price per Square Foot × Square Feet of Home

= $64 × 1,300

= $83,200

She estimates the price of this home at $83,200. Although she will consider other factors, this initial analysis gives her some insight into what the home is worth. For example, the real estate broker told her that the owner of the home has already moved and wants to sell it quickly. Stephanie considers making an offer of $80,000, but first, she needs to determine the costs that she will incur as a result of purchasing the home.

Economic Impact on Market Prices

Economic conditions affect the valuations of homes that are estimated by market valuations. When economic conditions improve, people are more confident that their income will be stable or may even grow over time, and they are more willing to purchase homes. As the demand for homes increases, the prices of homes rise. The average price per square foot of homes rises, and so the market analysis of a home results in higher valuations. Conversely, when economic conditions weaken, people become more concerned that their income might be eliminated (due to layoffs) or reduced over time. They are less willing to purchase homes, and the decline in demand for homes causes the prices of homes to decline. The average price per square foot of homes declines, and so the market analysis of a home results in lower valuations.

Effects of Business Activity and Zoning Laws

The value of a home is also dependent on the demand for homes in that area or subdivision, which can vary in response to business activity or zoning laws.

Business Activity Nearby. When a large firm moves into an area, people hired for jobs at that firm search for homes nearby. As a result, demand for homes in the area increases, and home prices may rise as well. Conversely, when a large firm closes its facilities, home prices in that area may decline as homeowners who worked there attempt to sell their homes. The large supply of homes for sale relative to demand may cause homeowners to lower their price in order to find a willing buyer.

Zoning Laws. Locations are zoned for industrial use or residential use. When zoning laws for a location change, its desirability may be affected. Homes near areas that have just been zoned for industrial use become less desirable. Therefore, the demand for homes in these areas may decline, causing prices of homes to decline as well.

Zoning laws also change for school systems. The value of a subdivision can change substantially in response to a change in the public schools that the resident children would attend. Proximity to schools can increase home values, while increased distance from schools often lowers home values.

Obtaining a Second Opinion on Your Valuation

If your valuation leads you to believe that a particular home is undervalued, you may want to get a second opinion before you try to purchase that home. If you are using a real estate broker to help you find a home, that broker may conduct a valuation of the home and offer suggestions about the price that you should be willing to offer. Be aware, however, although brokers are experienced at valuing homes, some brokers provide a valuation that is intended to serve the seller rather than the buyer. That is, they may overestimate the value so that potential buyers are convinced that the home is worth buying. In this way, the brokers can ensure that a home will sell and that they will receive a commission. Although many real estate brokers are honest and will provide an unbiased estimate, you should always conduct your own valuation and carefully assess the broker's valuation.

Negotiating a Price

Once you have finished your valuation and are convinced that you should buy a particular home, you need to negotiate a price with the seller of the home by making an offer. Some homes are initially priced above the price that the seller will accept. As with any investment, you want to make sure that you do not pay more than you have to for a home.

You may consider the advice of your real estate broker on the offer that you should make. Most sellers are willing to accept less than their original asking price. Once you decide on an offering price, you can submit an offer in the form of a contract to buy the home, which must be approved by the seller. Your real estate broker takes the contract to the seller and serves as the intermediary between you and the seller during the negotiation process.

The seller may accept your offer, reject it, or suggest that you revise it. If the asking price is $100,000, and you offer $90,000, the seller may reject that offer but indicate a willingness to accept an offer of, say, $96,000. Then the decision reverts to you. You can agree, reject that offer, or revise the contract again. For example, you may counter by offering $94,000. The contract can go back and forth until the buyer and seller either come to an agreement or decide that it is no longer worthwhile to pursue a possible agreement. The contract stipulates not only the price, but also other conditions that are requested by the buyer, such as repairs to be completed by the seller and the date when the buyer will be able to move into the home.

■ TRANSACTION COSTS OF PURCHASING A HOME

Once you have started the offer process, you should begin applying for a mortgage from a financial institution. The loan application process requires that you summarize your financial condition, including your income, your assets, and your liabilities. You will need to provide proof of income, such as recent paycheck stubs and bank statements. The lender will check your financial condition by contacting your employer to verify your employment and to learn your present salary.

In addition to applying for a mortgage, you will need to plan to cover the transaction costs of purchasing the home. These include the down payment and closing costs.

Down Payment

When you purchase a home, you use your money to make a down payment and pay the remaining amount owed with financing. Your down payment represents your equity investment in the home.

Financial Planning Online 15.4: **Applying for a Mortgage**

Go to
www.mortgageloan.com/
refinance-mortgage

This Web site provides information on refinancing loans and a mortgage calculator.

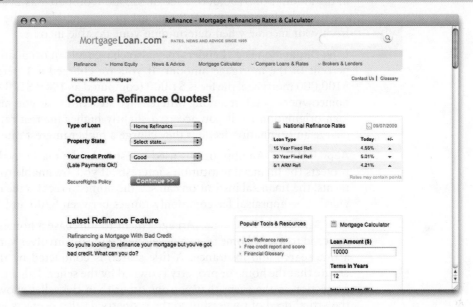

For a conventional mortgage, a lender typically requires a down payment of 10 to 20 percent of the home's selling price. The lender expects you to cover a portion of the purchase price with your own money because the home serves as collateral to back the loan. The lending institution bears the risk that you may possibly default on the loan. If you are unable to make your mortgage payments, the lender can take ownership of the home and sell it to obtain the funds that you owe.

If the home's value declines over time, however, a creditor may not obtain all the funds that it initially lent. Your down payment provides a cushion in case the value of the home declines. The lender could sell the home for less than the original purchase price and still recover the entire mortgage loan.

With government-backed loans, a traditional lender extends the loan, but the government insures it in the event of default. Government-backed mortgages may require lower down payments and may even specify lower interest rates than conventional mortgages. Government-backed mortgages are often backed by the Federal Housing Administration (FHA) or the Veterans Administration (VA). To qualify for federally insured mortgages, borrowers must satisfy various requirements imposed by the guarantors. The FHA loans enable low- or middle-income individuals to obtain mortgage financing. The VA loans are extended to military veterans. Both FHA and VA loans are assumable in the event that the homeowner who initially qualified for the mortgage loan decides to sell the home.

If you obtain an FHA or VA loan, you will need to maintain an escrow account. Your monthly mortgage payment will include an additional payment for your home insurance and your property taxes. The mortgage lender that receives your monthly mortgage payment will place these extra additional payments in your escrow account so that it can pay for your insurance and property taxes on an annual basis.

Closing Costs

A borrower incurs various fees in the mortgage loan application process. These fees are often referred to as closing costs. The most important fees are identified here.

Loan Application Fee. When applying for a mortgage loan, you may be charged an application fee by the lender. The fee typically ranges from $100 to $500.

Points. Lenders often charge a fee that is commonly referred to as **points**. Points are stated as a percentage of the loan amount. Many lenders charge between 1 and 2

points
A fee charged by the lender when a mortgage loan is provided; stated as a percentage of the mortgage loan amount.

percent of the mortgage loan. If you are charged 2 points when you obtain a mortgage in the amount of $100,000, a fee of $2,000 (computed as 2% × 100,000) is charged at the time the loan is granted. Points are tax-deductible, so the expense can be deducted from your income when determining your taxable income.

Loan Origination Fee. Lenders may also charge a loan origination fee, which is usually 1 percent of the mortgage amount. If you are charged a 1 percent origination fee on a $100,000 mortgage, the fee is $1,000 (computed as 1% × $100,000). Many lenders allow homeowners to select among different fee structures, so you may be able to pay a lower loan origination fee if you accept a slightly higher interest rate. Some lenders may not charge an origination fee, but they charge a higher interest rate on the mortgage instead.

Appraisal Fee. An appraisal is used to estimate the market value of the home and thus protects the financial institution's interests. If you are unable to make your monthly payments, the financial institution can sell the home to recoup the mortgage loan that it provided. The appraisal fee commonly ranges between $200 and $500.

Title Search and Insurance. An agreement to purchase a home from a current owner (as opposed to a new home from a developer) typically involves various transaction costs for a title search and insurance. A title search is conducted by the mortgage company to ensure that the home or property is owned by the seller. Title insurance provides you with protection in the event that persons other than the seller show evidence that they hold the actual deed of ownership to the property. It also protects you in the event that there are other liabilities attached to the home that were not discovered during the title search.

Both the closing costs and the down payment are due after the offer for the home has been accepted at the time of the closing. During the closing, the title for the home is transferred to the buyer, the seller is paid in full, and the buyer takes possession of the home.

EXAMPLE

Recall that Stephanie Spratt is considering making an offer of $80,000 on a house. She wants to determine the transaction costs. She is planning to make a down payment of $8,000 and borrow $72,000. She called York Financial Institution for information about obtaining a mortgage loan. She learned that if she applied for a $72,000 mortgage, York would charge the following:

- 1 point
- 1 percent origination fee
- $300 for an appraisal
- $200 application fee
- $400 for a title search and title insurance
- $200 for other fees

Thus, the total closing costs would be:

Points	(1% × $72,000)	$720
Origination Fee	(1% × $72,000)	720
Appraisal Fee		300
Application Fee		200
Title Search and Insurance		400
Other Fees		200
Total		**$2,540**

Stephanie will need a down payment of $8,000 and $2,540 in closing costs to purchase the home.

Financial Planning Online 15.5: **Mortgage Rates**

Go to
www.finance.yahoo.com/
loans

This Web site provides
national averages for mortgage rates, as well as average mortgage rates for specific regions and states.

■ CHARACTERISTICS OF A FIXED-RATE MORTGAGE

fixed-rate mortgage
A mortgage in which a fixed interest rate is specified until maturity.

A mortgage loan is most likely the biggest loan you will ever obtain in your lifetime. The terms for mortgages vary. You will need to decide whether to obtain a fixed-rate or adjustable-rate mortgage and what the maturity of the mortgage should be. Traditionally, mortgages had a fixed interest rate and a maturity of 30 years. A **fixed-rate mortgage** specifies a fixed interest rate that is constant for the life of the mortgage. When homeowners expect that interest rates will rise, they tend to prefer fixed-rate mortgages because their mortgage payments will be sheltered from the rising market interest rates. Many other types of mortgages are available, but the traditional fixed-rate 30-year mortgage is still popular. You can access various Web sites to obtain a general summary of prevailing mortgage rates, but rates vary among financial institutions. If you sell a home before the mortgage is paid off, you can use a portion of the proceeds from selling the home to pay off the mortgage. Alternatively, it may be possible for the buyer to assume your mortgage under some conditions.

Amortization Table

Your monthly mortgage payment for a fixed-rate mortgage is based on an amortization schedule. This schedule discloses the monthly payment that you will make, based on a specific mortgage amount, a fixed interest rate level, and a maturity.

Allocation of the Mortgage Payment. Each monthly mortgage payment represents a partial equity payment that pays a portion of the principal of the loan and an interest payment.

EXAMPLE

Stephanie Spratt decides to review mortgage Web sites to estimate her monthly mortgage payments. One Web site asks her to input the mortgage amount she desires and the interest rate that she expects to pay on a 30-year mortgage. She inputs $72,000 as the amount and 8 percent as the interest rate. The Web site then provides her with an amortization schedule, which is summarized in Exhibit 15.2. This exhibit shows how her mortgage payments would be allocated to paying off principal versus interest. Notice

	Exhibit 15.2	Amortization Schedule for a 30-Year (360-Month) Fixed-Rate Mortgage for $72,000 at an 8 Percent Interest Rate		
Month	**Payment**	**Principal**	**Interest**	**Balance**
1	$528	$48	$480	$71,952
2	528	49	479	71,903
10	528	51	477	71,502
•••				
25	528	57	472	70,691
•••				
49	528	66	462	69,211
•••				
100	528	93	435	65,163
•••				
200	528	181	347	51,877
•••				
360	528	525	3	0

Note: Numbers are rounded to the nearest dollar.

how the initial payments are allocated mostly to interest, with a relatively small amount used to pay off the principal. For example, for month 2, $49 of her payment is applied to the principal, while $479 goes to pay the interest expense. Initially, when the amount of principal is large, most of her payment is needed to cover the interest owed. As time passes, the proportion of the payment allocated to equity increases. Notice that by month 360, $525 of the payment is applied to principal and $3 to interest.

Notice, too, that her balance after 100 months is $65,163. This means that over a period of more than eight years, Stephanie would pay off less than $7,000 of the equity in her home, or less than 10 percent of the original mortgage amount. After 200 months (two-thirds of the life of the 30-year mortgage), her mortgage balance would be almost $52,000, which means she would have paid off about $20,000 of the $72,000 mortgage.

The amount of Stephanie's annual mortgage payments that would be allocated to paying off the principal is shown in Exhibit 15.3. In the first year, she would pay off only $601 of the principal, while the rest of her mortgage payments ($5,738) in the first year would be used to pay interest. This information is very surprising to Stephanie, so she reviews the mortgage situation further to determine if it is possible to build equity more quickly.

Impact of the Mortgage Amount on the Monthly Payment

The larger the mortgage amount, the larger your monthly payments will be for a given interest rate and maturity. Exhibit 15.4 shows the monthly payment based on a 30-year mortgage and an 8 percent interest rate for different mortgage amounts. Notice the

Exhibit 15.3 Allocation of Principal versus Interest Paid per Year on a $72,000 Mortgage

Year	Principal Paid in That Year	Interest Paid in That Year
1	$601	$5,738
2	651	5,688
3	705	5,634
4	764	5,576
6	896	5,444
8	1,051	5,289
10	1,233	5,107
12	1,446	4,894
15	1,836	4,503
17	2,154	4,186
20	2,736	3,603
22	3,209	3,131
24	3,764	2,576
26	4,415	1,925
28	5,178	1,161
30	6,073	266

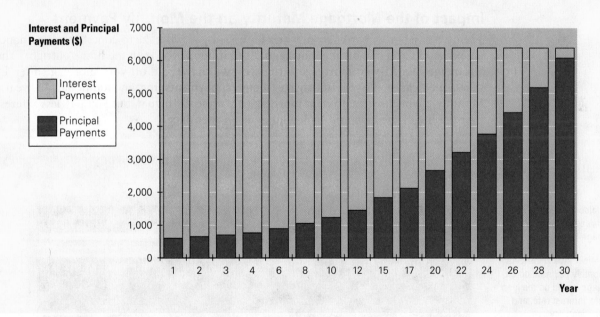

change in the mortgage payment for larger mortgage amounts. For example, the monthly mortgage payment for a $90,000 mortgage is $660, while the monthly payment for a $100,000 mortgage is $734.

Impact of the Interest Rate on the Monthly Payment

Given the large amount of funds that you may borrow to finance a home, you should make every effort to obtain a mortgage loan that has a low interest rate. The lower the

Exhibit 15.4   Monthly Mortgage Payments Based on Different Mortgage Amounts (30-Year Fixed-Rate Mortgage; 8 Percent Interest Rate)

Mortgage Amount	Monthly Mortgage Payment
$60,000	$440
70,000	513
80,000	587
90,000	660
100,000	734
110,000	807
120,000	880

interest rate on the mortgage, the smaller the monthly mortgage payment. Even a slight increase (such as 0.5 percent) in the interest rate increases your monthly mortgage payment.

In the last decade, the 15-year mortgage has become very popular as an alternative to the 30-year mortgage. The interest rate charged on 15-year and 30-year fixed-rate mortgages is typically related to other long-term interest rates (such as the 30-year Treasury bond rate) at the time that the mortgage is created. For this reason, home-owners seek a fixed-rate mortgage when they believe that interest rates will rise in the future.

Impact of the Mortgage Maturity on the Monthly Payment

The maturity of the mortgage indicates how long you will take to complete your financing payments and pay off the mortgage. At that point, you own the home outright. The advantage of a 15-year mortgage is that you will have paid off your mortgage after 15 years, whereas a 30-year mortgage requires payments for an additional 15 years. Monthly payments on a 15-year mortgage are typically higher, but you pay less interest over the life of the loan and build equity at a faster pace.

Financial Planning Online 15.6: **Estimating Mortgage Payments**

Go to
www.bloomberg.com/
invest//calculators/
mortgage.html

This Web site provides
the monthly payment on a
mortgage based on the loan
amount, interest rate, and
the loan maturity.

The advantage of a 30-year mortgage is that you have smaller monthly payments for a given mortgage loan amount than you would for a 15-year mortgage. The monthly payments may be more affordable, and you may have more liquidity.

Some financial institutions now offer 40-year and 50-year maturities on mortgage loans. The obvious advantage on mortgages with long maturities is that it makes the mortgage more affordable because monthly payments are lower. However, you build equity in the home more slowly. In general, homeowners prefer shorter maturities as long as they can afford the monthly payments.

Estimating the Monthly Mortgage Payment

You can use mortgage loan Web sites to obtain estimates of your monthly payments based on a specific mortgage amount and maturity.

EXAMPLE

Stephanie Spratt wants to estimate her monthly mortgage payment on a $72,000 fixed-rate mortgage, based on several interest rate scenarios for 15- and 30-year maturities, as shown in Exhibit 15.5. At an interest rate of 7 percent, the monthly payment on the 30-year mortgage would be $479. At an interest rate of 9 percent, the monthly payment on the 30-year mortgage would be $579, or $100 more. Next, Stephanie evaluates the payments for a 15-year term. She believes she can obtain a loan at an 8 percent interest rate on either maturity, so she focuses on the difference in monthly payments pertaining to that rate.

Although the monthly payment is more for the 15-year mortgage, the difference is not as large as Stephanie expected. Given the interest rate of 8 percent, the 15-year mortgage requires a monthly payment of $688, which is $160 more than the $528 payment on the 30-year mortgage. This is the obvious disadvantage of a 15-year mortgage.

The advantage is that she would pay down the mortgage sooner, meaning that she would accumulate a larger equity investment in the home more quickly. To gain more insight on this advantage, she reviews a Web site to compare the remaining loan balance for each of the two mortgage maturities on a year-by-year basis. This comparison is summarized in Exhibit 15.6. Notice that after six years, she would still owe $67,554 on the 30-year mortgage, versus $52,852 (almost $15,000 less) on the 15-year mortgage. After 10 years, she would owe almost $30,000 more on the 30-year mortgage than on the 15-year mortgage. After 15 years, she would still owe about $55,000 on the 30-year mortgage, while the 15-year mortgage would be paid off.

The Web site also shows the total payments over the life of the mortgage for both types of mortgages if the mortgage is not paid off until maturity.

	30-Year Mortgage	15-Year Mortgage
Total Principal Payments	$72,000	$72,000
Total Interest Payments	118,192	51,852
Total Payments	$190,192	$123,852

Stephanie would pay about $66,000 more in interest with the 30-year mortgage than with the 15-year mortgage. The total interest payments on the 30-year mortgage are much larger than the total principal payments that would be made over the life of the 15-year mortgage.

Weighing the advantages of the 15-year mortgage against the disadvantage of paying the extra $160 per month, Stephanie decides she prefers the 15-year mortgage. Even if she decides to sell this home before she pays off the 15-year mortgage, she will have paid down a larger amount of the mortgage. Since she will have a larger equity investment (from paying off more of the principal) with the 15-year mortgage, she will increase her net worth to a greater degree.

Exhibit 15.5 Comparison of Monthly Payments for a 30-Year versus a 15-Year Mortgage of $72,000 Based on Different Interest Rates

	Monthly Payment on a:	
Interest Rate	30-Year Mortgage	15-Year Mortgage
7.0%	$479	$647
7.5	503	667
8.0	528	688
8.5	554	709
9.0	579	730
9.5	605	752
10.0	632	774

Note: Payments are rounded to the nearest dollar.

Exhibit 15.6 Comparison of Mortgage Balance for a 30-Year versus a 15-Year Mortgage ($72,000 Initial Mortgage Amount; 8 Percent Interest Rate)

End of Year	Balance on 30-Year Mortgage	Balance on 15-Year Mortgage
1	$71,399	$69,410
2	70,747	66,604
3	70,042	63,566
4	69,278	60,275
5	68,450	56,712
6	67,554	52,852
7	66,583	48,672
8	65,533	44,146
9	64,395	39,244
10	63,162	33,934
11	61,826	28,185
12	60,381	21,957
13	58,815	15,213
14	57,119	7,910
15	55,283	0

Note: Balances are rounded to the nearest dollar.

■ CHARACTERISTICS OF AN ADJUSTABLE-RATE MORTGAGE

adjustable-rate mortgage (ARM)
A mortgage where the interest owed changes in response to movements in a specific market-determined interest rate.

An alternative to a fixed-rate mortgage is an **adjustable-rate mortgage (ARM)**, in which the interest owed changes in response to movements in a specific market-determined interest rate. An ARM is sometimes referred to as a variable-rate mortgage. ARMs should definitely be considered along with fixed-rate mortgages. Like a fixed-rate mortgage, an

ARM can be obtained for a 15-year or a 30-year maturity. ARMs have various characteristics that must be stated in the mortgage contract.

The advantage of an adjustable-rate mortgage is that the interest rate you pay on your mortgage declines when market interest rates decline. This reduces your monthly mortgage payment, so that you have more money to spend or to invest. The disadvantage of an adjustable-rate mortgage is that the interest rate you pay on your mortgage increases when market interest rates increase. This increases your monthly mortgage payment, so that you have less money to spend or invest. In fact, some homeowners have defaulted on their loans when interest rates increased because they could not afford to pay the higher monthly payment.

Initial Rate

Many ARMs specify a relatively low initial mortgage rate over the first year or so. This initial rate is beneficial to homeowners in that it results in a low monthly mortgage payment over the first year. Recognize, however, that this rate is only temporary, as the mortgage rate will be adjusted.

Interest Rate Index

The initial mortgage rate will be adjusted after a period (such as one year) in line with a specified interest rate index. The interest rate index to which the mortgage rate is tied must be included in the mortgage contract. Many ARMs use a rate that is tied to the average cost of deposits of financial institutions. For example, the interest rate charged on an ARM might be set at 3 percentage points above that benchmark. Thus, if the benchmark is 4 percent in a given year, the ARM will apply an interest rate of 7 percent (computed as 4% + 3%). If the interest rate index has risen to 5 percent by the time of the next mortgage rate adjustment, the new mortgage rate will be 8 percent (computed as 5% + 3%).

Frequency of Rate Adjustments

The mortgage contract also specifies how frequently the mortgage rate will be adjusted. Many ARMs specify that the rate will be adjusted once a year. Thus, the mortgage rate is set based on the specified interest rate index and then remains the same for the next 12 months. This means that the monthly payments will be constant for the next 12 months. At the end of the 12-month period, the mortgage rate is revised based on the prevailing interest rate index and is held constant for the following 12 months.

Financial Planning Online 15.7: **Should You Obtain a Fixed- or an Adjustable-Rate Mortgage?**

Go to
www.federalreserve.gov/
pubs/arms/arms_english
.htm

This Web site provides valuable information regarding adjustable-rate mortgages that may be useful when deciding whether to finance your home with a fixed- or adjustable-rate mortgage.

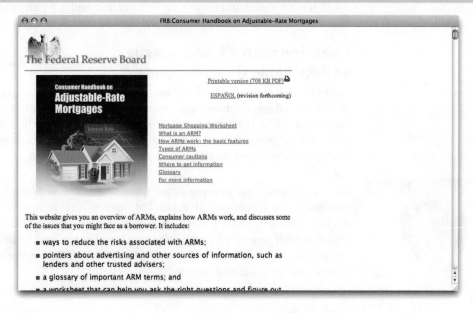

Some mortgages allow for less frequent adjustments, such as every three years or every five years. Others allow a single adjustment at the end of the fifth year, and the adjusted rate is then held constant over the next 25 years of a 30-year mortgage.

Other ARMs offer the following alternatives:

- An interest rate that adjusts every five years
- An interest rate that is fixed for the first three years, but converts to an ARM (and adjusts annually) after three years
- An interest rate that is fixed for the first five years, but converts to an ARM (and adjusts annually) after five years
- An interest rate that adjusts for the first five years and then is fixed (based on an interest rate index at that time) for the next 25 years

With so many alternatives available, you can easily find a mortgage that fits your preferences. For example, if you expect that interest rates will decline consistently over time, you may prefer an ARM that is adjusted every year. If your expectations are correct, your mortgage rate will decline over time with the decline in market interest rates. It is difficult to forecast the direction of interest rates accurately, however, which means that your future mortgage payments are uncertain. When considering a particular adjustable-rate mortgage, you should estimate what the monthly payments would be under the adverse conditions in which market rates rise substantially over time. Make sure that you can afford the monthly payments if interest rates increase.

■ CAPS ON ADJUSTABLE-RATE MORTGAGES

caps
Maximum and minimum fluctuations in the interest rate on an adjustable-rate mortgage.

The mortgage contract also typically specifies **caps**, or a maximum and minimum fluctuation in the interest rate. For example, an ARM may have a cap of 2 percent per year, which prevents the mortgage rate from being adjusted upward by more than 2 percentage points from its existing level in each year. Assume the market interest rate increases by 3 percentage points from one year to the next. Without a cap, the mortgage rate on the ARM would increase by 3 percentage points. With a 2 percent cap, however, only an increase of 2 percentage points is allowed in that year. This cap is useful because it limits the potential increase in the mortgage payments that may result from an increase in interest rates.

In addition to a cap on the annual increase in the mortgage rate, there is usually a lifetime cap, which represents the maximum amount of the increase in the mortgage rate over the life of the mortgage. A lifetime cap of 5 percent is commonly used. Thus, if an ARM has an initial mortgage rate of 7 percent and a 5 percent cap, the maximum mortgage rate over the life of the mortgage would be 12 percent.

Financing with a Fixed- versus an Adjustable-Rate Mortgage

Your decision to use a fixed- versus an adjustable-rate mortgage to finance the purchase of a home is dependent on your expectations of future interest rates. The primary advantage of an ARM is that the initial interest rate is lower than that of a fixed-rate mortgage. Yet, if interest rates rise, you may end up paying a higher interest rate on your mortgage than if you had obtained a fixed-rate mortgage.

EXAMPLE

Stephanie Spratt has already determined that if she finances with a 15-year fixed-rate mortgage, she would pay an 8 percent interest rate. Alternatively, she could obtain an adjustable-rate mortgage that specifies an initial rate of 6 percent, with the interest rate adjusted each year to an index reflecting the average cost of bank funds plus 3 percentage points. Assuming the index rate is 5 percent next year, the rate applied to her mortgage would be 8 percent for the following year.

Stephanie notices that financial experts have predicted an increase in interest rates in the near future. She is uncomfortable with the uncertainty surrounding her mortgage rate and therefore surrounding her mortgage payment. Although an ARM would result in a lower mortgage payment in the first year, it would result in a higher mortgage payment in the following years if interest rates increase. Thus, Stephanie decides to choose a fixed-rate mortgage instead of an ARM.

FINANCIAL CRISIS

Subprime Mortgage Crisis

During 2003–2006, economic conditions were favorable and home builders were building many new homes. Mortgage lenders were aggressively attempting to find buyers for these homes because not only could they earn interest on the loans provided, but also they could earn fees from the mortgage application process. Some mortgage lenders were providing subprime mortgages, which represent mortgage loans to borrowers without sufficient income or a down payment to qualify for prime mortgages. Mortgage lenders were willing to provide these mortgages because they could charge a higher interest rate and additional upfront fees to compensate for the higher level of risk. If the borrowers defaulted on the mortgage loans, the mortgage lender could take ownership of the homes. Mortgage lenders were optimistic that home prices would rise or at least not decline, and therefore would serve as effective collateral in the event that a borrower defaulted on the loan. Thus, they were willing to take the risk of extending subprime loans.

As interest rates increased in 2006, some home buyers could no longer afford their payments. Many others defaulted on their subprime mortgages because they could not afford the homes, and should not have qualified for a mortgage in the first place. Some mortgages that were insured against default by a private insurer defaulted because some insurance companies that insured mortgages did not have sufficient funds to cover their obligations. By January 2009, about 10 percent of all homeowners were late on their mortgage payments or defaulted on their loans. About 25 percent of all outstanding subprime mortgages had late payments of at least 30 days. Many financial institutions were involved in provided mortgage loans and therefore experienced large losses or even bankruptcy.

In an effort to stimulate the market for homes and mortgages, the Housing and Economic Recovery Act of 2008, passed in July 2008, allowed some homeowners to avoid foreclosure. Some financial institutions participated in a voluntary program in which they worked with the homeowners who were at risk of foreclosure. They refinanced the mortgages in a manner that made the payments more affordable to homeowners. While this was costly to the financial institutions, it was less costly than if foreclosure occurred and they were stuck with the homes that lost much of their value.

The U.S. government also created several programs to help financial institutions that suffered major losses because of a large number of defaults on their mortgage loans.

QUESTIONS

a. **Economic Impact on Subprime Mortgage Defaults.** Explain why subprime mortgages seemed safe in 2006 but experienced major defaults in 2009. What changed?

b. **Economic Impact on Access to Credit.** As the economy weakened in 2009, it was more difficult for prospective homeowners to obtain a mortgage. Explain why credit became less accessible.

■ DECISION TO OWN VERSUS RENT A HOME

When considering the purchase (and therefore ownership) of a home, you should compare the cost of purchasing a home with the cost of renting. People attribute different advantages and disadvantages to owning a home versus renting because preferences are subjective. Some individuals value the privacy of a home, while others value the flexibility of an apartment, which allows them to move without much cost or difficulty. The financial assessment of owning a home versus renting can be performed objectively. Once the financial assessment is conducted, personal preferences can also be considered.

Estimating the Total Cost of Renting and Owning

The main cost of renting a home is the monthly rent payment. There is also an opportunity cost of tying up funds in a security deposit. Those funds could have been invested if you did not need to provide the security deposit. Another possible cost of renting is the purchase of renter's insurance.

The primary costs of purchasing a home are the down payment and the monthly mortgage payment. The down payment has an opportunity cost because the funds could have been invested to earn interest if they were not tied up in the purchase of the home. Closing costs are incurred at the time the home is purchased, although a portion of these costs is tax-deductible. Owning a home also involves some additional costs, such as maintenance and repair. Property taxes are assessed annually as a percentage of the home's value. Homeowner's insurance is paid annually and is primarily based on the value of the home.

EXAMPLE

Stephanie Spratt has found a home she desires and has obtained financing. Before making a final decision, she wants to compare the cost of the home to the cost of remaining in her apartment. Although she would prefer a home, she wants to determine how much more expensive the home is compared to the apartment. If she purchases the home, she expects to live in it for at least three years. Therefore, she decides to compare the cost of owning a home to the cost of renting over the next three years. First, Stephanie calculates the cost of renting:

- **Cost of Rent.** Her estimated cost of renting is shown in the top panel of Exhibit 15.7. Her rent is currently $600 per month, so her annual rent is $7,200 (computed as $600 × 12). She does not expect a rent increase over the next three years and therefore estimates her cost of renting over this period to be $7,200 × 3 = $21,600. (If she had expected an increase in rent, she would have simply added the extra cost to the estimated rent over the next three years.)

- **Cost of Renter's Insurance.** She does not have renter's insurance at this time, as the value of her household assets is low.

- **Opportunity Cost of Security Deposit.** She provided a security deposit of $1,000 to the apartment complex. While she expects to get this deposit back when she stops renting, there is an opportunity cost associated with it. She could have invested those funds in a tax-free money market fund earning 4 percent annually, which would have generated annual interest of $40 (computed as $1,000 × .04). The opportunity cost over three years is three times the annual cost, or $120.

- **Total Cost of Renting.** Stephanie estimates the total cost of renting as $7,240 per year and $21,720 over the next three years, as shown in Exhibit 15.7.

Stephanie determines the total cost of purchasing a home by adding up expenses, subtracting any tax savings, and subtracting the value of the equity:

- **Mortgage Payment.** The primary cost of buying a home is the mortgage payment, which she expects to be $688 per month or $8,256 per year (not including payments for property taxes or house insurance).

- **Down Payment.** Stephanie would make a down payment of $8,000 to buy the home.

Exhibit 15.7   Comparing the Total Cost of Renting versus Buying a Home over a Three-Year Period

Cost of Renting	Amount per Year	Total over Next Three Years
Rent ($600 per month)	$7,200	$21,600
Renter's insurance	0	0
Opportunity cost of security deposit	40	120
Total cost of renting	$7,240	$21,720

Cost of Purchasing	Amount per Year	Total over Next Three Years
Mortgage payment ($688 per month)	$8,256	$24,768
Down payment	8,000	8,000 (first year only)
Opportunity cost of down payment	320	960
Property taxes	1,000	3,000
Home insurance	600	1,800
Closing costs	2,540	2,540 (first year only)
Maintenance costs	1,000	3,000
Total costs before tax benefits		**$44,068**
Total tax savings		$1,180
Equity investment		$16,434
Increase in home value		0
Value of equity		$16,434
Cost of purchasing home over three years		**$26,454**

- **Opportunity Cost of the Down Payment.** If Stephanie did not buy a house, she could have invested the $8,000 in a tax-free security and earned 4 percent per year. Therefore, the annual opportunity cost (what she could have earned if she invested the funds) is $320 (computed as $8,000 × .04).

- **Property Taxes.** Stephanie assumes that the annual property tax will be $1,000 based on last year's property tax paid by the current owner of the home.

- **Home Insurance.** Insurance on this home will cost $600 per year (this estimate is based on the home insurance premium paid by the current owner of the home).

- **Closing Costs.** Closing costs (transaction costs) associated with buying a home must be included, although those costs are incurred only in the first year for a mortgage. The closing costs are estimated to be $2,540, as shown earlier.

- **Maintenance Costs.** Stephanie expects maintenance costs on the home to be $1,000 per year.

- **Utilities.** She will pay for utilities such as water and electricity and will incur a cable TV bill if she buys the home. She already incurs those costs while renting an apartment, so she does not need to include them in her analysis.

- **Tax Savings.** Stephanie must also consider the tax savings that a home provides. Since the home mortgage interest is tax-deductible, she estimates that her taxes will be reduced by 25 percent of the amount by which her taxable income is reduced. The amount of mortgage interest changes every year, and therefore so does her tax savings from interest expenses. She can estimate her interest expenses over three years by using an amortization table based on her mortgage amount, mortgage maturity, and mortgage rate. She estimates that her interest expense over the next three years will be about $16,000.

Note that Stephanie will generate tax savings from property taxes because they are tax-deductible. Given an annual property tax of $1,000, she will have a $3,000 tax deduction over the next three years. Stephanie will also generate tax savings from the points that she would pay (a one-time fee of $720) as part of the closing costs, because the points are tax-deductible.

The total itemized deductions resulting from the purchase of the house over the next three years are:

	Deduction
Interest	$16,000
Property Taxes	$3,000
Points	$720
Total	$19,720

However, keep in mind that individuals without significant tax deductions can receive their standard deduction. That Stephanie can take a standard deduction of $5,000 each year if she does not itemize her deductions. If she does not buy the home, she would take the standard deduction each year, which would be worth $15,000 over three years ($5,000 × 3 years).

The tax savings from buying the home occur because the value of itemized deductions exceeds the value of standard deductions by $4,720 ($19,720 − $15,000) over the three-year period. When considering Stephanie's marginal tax rate, extra deductions result in a tax savings of:

Tax Savings = Value of Extra Deductions × Marginal Tax Rate

= $4,720 × .25

= $1,180

- **Value of the Equity Investment.** Another advantage of owning a home is that Stephanie will have an equity investment in it. Her down payment will be $8,000, and she will pay about $8,434 in principal on her mortgage over the three-year period. The value of this equity investment could be higher in three years if the market value of the home increases. If Stephanie assumes that the home's value will not change, the value of the equity investment will be $16,434 (computed as $8,000 + $8,434).

- **Total Cost of Purchasing a Home.** The total cost of purchasing a home is determined by adding all the expenses, subtracting the tax savings, and then subtracting the equity investment. As shown in Exhibit 15.7, Stephanie estimates that the total cost of purchasing the home over the three-year period will be $26,454.

The total cost of purchasing a home over three years is about $4,734 more than the cost of renting. Stephanie decides that she wants to buy the home, mainly because she would rather live in a home than an apartment. She also believes that the home's value may rise over time, a factor that was not part of her analysis. If the value of the home increased by 2 percent per year, the market value of her equity in the home would increase by about $5,000.

Now that Stephanie has decided that she wants to purchase a home and can afford it, she submits her offer of $80,000, which is accepted by the seller.

■ SPECIAL TYPES OF MORTGAGES

In some cases, prospective buyers do not qualify for a traditional fixed-rate mortgage or an adjustable-rate mortgage. Some special types of mortgages are available that can make a home more affordable.

Graduated Payment Mortgage

A **graduated payment mortgage** sets relatively low monthly mortgage payments when the mortgage is first created and then gradually increases the payments over the first five or so years. The payments level off after that time. This type of mortgage may be useful for someone whose income will increase over time, since the mortgage payments will increase as the homeowner's income increases. A graduated payment mortgage would not be desirable for people who are not certain that their income will rise.

Balloon Payment Mortgage

A **balloon payment mortgage** sets relatively low monthly payments and then requires one large payment (called a balloon payment) after a specified period (such as five years) to pay off the remainder of the mortgage loan. A balloon payment mortgage is sometimes offered by the seller of a home to the buyer, especially when the buyer cannot afford to make large monthly payments and does not qualify for a more traditional mortgage. In this situation, the seller might provide a mortgage for five years. The expectation is that the buyer's income will rise, enabling the buyer to obtain a traditional mortgage from a financial institution before the end of the five-year period. Then, the buyer will have enough cash to make the balloon payment to the seller.

Interest-Only Mortgage

Interest-only mortgages are adjustable-rate mortgages that allow home buyers to pay only interest on the mortgage during the first few years. These mortgages have become very popular in recent years because no principal is paid in this period and mortgage payments are more affordable. However, the disadvantage is that the mortgage payment increases abruptly at the time that the homeowner must begin to make principal payments. The mortgage payment may be 30 percent higher at this point, and some homeowners may not be able to make a mortgage payment that is substantially higher than their previous payments.

■ MORTGAGE REFINANCING

Mortgage refinancing involves paying off an existing mortgage with a new mortgage that has a lower interest rate. You may use mortgage refinancing to obtain a new mortgage if market interest rates (and therefore mortgage rates) decline. One disadvantage of mortgage refinancing is that you will incur closing costs again. Nevertheless, it may still be advantageous to refinance because the savings on your monthly mortgage payments (even after considering tax effects) may exceed the new closing costs. Mortgage refinancing is more likely to be worthwhile when the prevailing mortgage interest rate is substantially below the interest rate on your existing mortgage. It is also more likely to be worthwhile when you expect to be living in the home for a long time because you will reap greater benefits from the lower monthly mortgage payments that result from refinancing.

Rate Modification

When interest rates decline, some mortgage lenders may be willing to allow a "rate modification" to existing mortgage holders with a fixed-rate mortgage. They may charge a one-time fee that is typically between $500 and $1,500. Your fixed-rate mortgage may be revised to reflect the prevailing mortgage rate. You can benefit because you receive the

Financial Planning Online 15.8: **Should You Rent or Buy?**

Go to
realestate.yahoo.com/
calculators/rent_vs_own
.html

This Web site provides a recommendation on whether you should buy a home, based on your rent versus the expenses of the home you are considering.

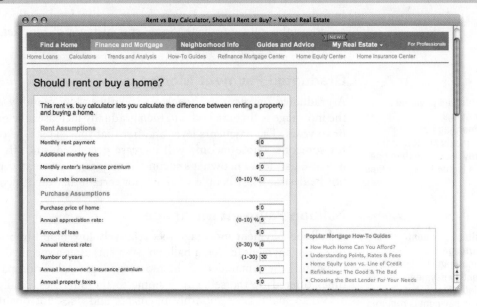

lower interest rate. You would not need to go through the process of refinancing through another mortgage lender, or incur costs associated with a new mortgage application. Some mortgage lenders are willing to allow rate modifications because they realize that if they do not provide you with an opportunity to pay the lower interest rate, you will likely obtain a new mortgage from another lender and will pay off your existing mortgage. In this case, you will no longer make payments at the high interest rate and your existing mortgage lender will lose you as a customer. By allowing a rate modification, your existing mortgage lender retains you as a customer by offering you a mortgage that is similar to what it is presently offering to other new customers, and it earns a one-time fee from you for modifying the mortgage rate that you are charged.

Refinancing Analysis

To determine whether you should refinance, you can compare the advantage of monthly savings of interest expenses to the cost of refinancing. If the benefits from reducing your interest expenses exceed the closing costs incurred from refinancing, the refinancing is feasible.

The advantages of refinancing (lower interest payments) occur each year, while the disadvantage (closing costs) occurs only at the time of refinancing. Therefore, refinancing tends to be more beneficial when a homeowner plans to own the home for a longer period. The savings from a lower interest payment can accumulate over each additional year the mortgage exists.

EXAMPLE

Stephanie Spratt decides that if interest rates decline in the future, she may refinance. If interest rates decline to 7 percent a year from now, Stephanie would save about $40 on her monthly mortgage payment by refinancing. Stephanie needs to determine the potential savings in the monthly interest payments over the time that she expects to remain in the home.

A monthly reduction in interest payments of $40 reflects an annual reduction of $480 (computed as $40 × 12). But because interest on the mortgage is tax-deductible, the reduction in interest payments by $480 interest means that her taxable income would be $480 higher. Since her marginal tax rate is 25 percent, her taxes would increase:

$$\text{Annual Increase in Taxes} = \text{Annual Increase in Taxable Income} \times \text{Marginal Tax Rate}$$
$$= \$480 \times .25$$
$$= \$120$$

Her annual savings due to refinancing at a lower interest rate would be:

$$\$480 - \$120 = \$360.$$

Assuming that she plans to remain in the home for two more years from the time of refinancing, her total savings would be:

$$\$360 \times 2 = \$720.$$

The disadvantage of refinancing is that Stephanie may once again incur the same closing costs ($2,540). Before comparing this cost to the benefits of refinancing, she accounts for the tax savings. Since the points are tax-deductible, she determines the tax savings from these costs:

$$\text{Tax Savings on Points} = \text{Cost of Points} \times \text{Marginal Tax Rate}$$
$$= \$720 \times .25$$
$$= \$180$$
$$\text{After-tax Closing Costs} = \text{Closing Costs} - \text{Tax Savings}$$
$$= \$2,540 - \$180$$
$$= \$2,360$$

The after-tax closing costs ($2,360) due to refinancing would exceed the savings on the interest payments ($720) over the next two years. Stephanie is now aware that if interest rates decrease by 1 percent over the next year, it would not be worthwhile for her to refinance her home.

■ HOW A MORTGAGE FITS WITHIN YOUR FINANCIAL PLAN

The following are the key mortgage loan decisions that should be included within your financial plan:

- What mortgage amount can you afford?
- What maturity should you select?
- Should you consider a fixed-rate or an adjustable-rate mortgage?

By making informed decisions, you can avoid accumulating an excessive amount of debt. Exhibit 15.8 provides a summary of how Stephanie Spratt's mortgage loan decisions apply to her financial plan.

Exhibit 15.8 How Mortgage Financing Fits Within Stephanie's Financial Plan

GOALS FOR MORTGAGE FINANCING

1. Limit the amount of mortgage financing to a level that is affordable.
2. Select a short loan maturity if possible, assuming that the payments are affordable.
3. Select the type of mortgage loan (fixed- or adjustable-rate) that is more likely to result in lower interest expenses.

(continues)

Exhibit 15.8	How Mortgage Financing Fits Within Stephanie's Financial Plan (continued)

ANALYSIS

	15-Year Mortgage (8% interest rate)	30-Year Mortgage (8% interest rate)
Monthly payment	$688	$528
Total interest payments	$51,852	$118,192
Advantages	Pay off mortgage in half the time of a 30-year mortgage; pay lower interest expenses on the loan	Smaller monthly payment
Difference between mortgage payment and rent payment	$688 – $600 = $88	$528 – $600 = –$72

DECISIONS

Decision on Affording a Mortgage:

The monthly interest payment on a $72,000 mortgage loan with a 15-year maturity is $688. My rent is $600 per month, so the difference is $88 per month. Since my monthly cash flows (from my salary) exceed my typical monthly expenses (including my car loan payment) and my purchases of clothes by almost $600, I can afford that difference. I will not save as much money as I planned if I buy a home, but I will be building equity.

Decision on the Mortgage Maturity:

I prefer the 15-year mortgage because I will pay off a larger portion of the principal each year.

Decision on the Type of Mortgage Loan:

I prefer the fixed-rate mortgage because I know with certainty that the monthly payments will not increase. I am worried that interest rates may increase in the future, which would cause interest expenses to be higher on the adjustable-rate mortgage.

DISCUSSION QUESTIONS

1. How would Stephanie's mortgage financing decisions be different if she were a single mother of two children?

2. How would Stephanie's mortgage financing decisions be affected if she were 35 years old? If she were 50 years old?

SUMMARY

- When considering the purchase of a home, you should evaluate your financial situation to determine how much you can afford. Some of the key criteria used in the selection process are price, convenience of the location, quality, the school system, and the potential resale value.

- You can conduct a valuation of a home with a market analysis. Homes in the same area that were recently sold can be used to determine the average price per square foot. Then, this price per square foot can be applied to the square footage of the home you wish to value.

- The transaction costs of purchasing a home include the down payment and closing costs. The key closing costs are points and the origination fee.

- A fixed-rate mortgage specifies a fixed interest rate to be paid over the life of the mortgage. Since most of the monthly mortgage payment on a 30-year mortgage is allocated to cover the interest expense in the early years, a relatively small amount of principal is paid off in those years. A 15-year fixed-rate mortgage is a popular alternative to the 30-year mortgage. It requires a larger monthly payment, but a larger proportion of the payment is allocated to principal in the early years.

- An adjustable-rate mortgage (ARM) ties the interest rate to an interest rate index, so the mortgage interest rate changes over time with the index. Homeowners who expect interest rates to decline in the future are especially likely to choose ARMs.

- Before making a final decision to buy a home, you can compare the total cost of owning a home versus renting over a particular period to determine which choice will enhance your financial position more. The total cost of owning a home is estimated by adding up the expenses associated with the home, subtracting the tax savings from owning the home, and subtracting the expected value of the equity of the home at the end of the period.

- You may consider mortgage refinancing when quoted interest rates on new mortgages decline. When refinancing, you will incur closing costs. Thus, you should consider refinancing only if the benefits (expected reduction in interest expenses over time) exceed the closing costs.

REVIEW QUESTIONS

1. **Steps in Buying a Home.** What is your first task when considering buying a home? Why is this step important? How can a real estate broker help you?

2. **Purchasing a Home.** What are the two financial components you must consider before purchasing a home? Why should you consider them?

3. **Affordable Payments.** What should you consider when determining an affordable down payment and monthly mortgage payments?

4. **Selection Criteria.** List the criteria you should use when selecting a home.

5. **Selection Criteria.** How do price, convenience of the location, and maintenance affect your home-buying decisions?

6. **School System Influence.** Why is the reputation of the school system in the area of the home you are buying important?

7. **Home Insurance and Taxes.** Why do insurance costs and taxes vary among homes?

8. **Home Resale Value.** What is the main factor in determining a home's resale value? How can you predict a home's resale value? Who pays commissions when a home is sold?

9. **Market Analysis.** Once you have reduced your list of three or four homes down to one home, what is your next step? Should you offer the price the seller is asking? Describe how you would conduct a market analysis of the home.

10. **Demand for Homes.** Why does the value of a home depend on the demand for homes? What factors influence the demand for homes?

11. **Loan Programs.** How do lenders protect their interest in a home? Describe two government-backed home loan programs.

12. **Closing Costs.** What are closing costs? List and briefly describe the different closing costs you might incur when applying for a mortgage.

13. **Fixed-Rate Mortgage.** Describe the characteristics of a fixed-rate mortgage. Why do certain homeowners prefer a fixed-rate mortgage to an adjustable-rate mortgage?

14. **Amortization Table.** What is an amortization table? What does each mortgage payment represent?

15. **Monthly Mortgage Payments.** List the three things that determine the amount of the monthly mortgage payment. Explain how each affects the payment.

16. **Adjustable-Rate Mortgage.** Discuss the characteristics of an adjustable-rate mortgage. What influences your choice of a fixed- or adjustable-rate mortgage?

17. **Costs of Renting.** What are the costs of renting a home?

18. **Costs of Buying a Home.** Describe some of the costs of buying a home. Are there potential tax savings associated with buying a home?

19. **Features of Graduated Payment.** Describe the features of graduated payment and balloon payment mortgages.

20. **Mortgage Refinancing.** What is mortgage refinancing? Are there any disadvantages to refinancing?

FINANCIAL PLANNING PROBLEMS

1. **Mortgage Payment.** Dorothy and Matt are ready to purchase their first home. Their current monthly cash inflows are $4,900, and their current monthly cash outflows are $3,650. Their rent makes up $650 of their cash flows. They would like to put 10 percent of their cash inflows in savings and leave another $200 in their checking account for emergencies. How much of a mortgage payment can they manage under these conditions?

2. **Home Price Offer.** Denise and Kenny are ready to make an offer on an 1,800-square-foot home that is priced at $135,000. They investigate other homes on lots of similar size and find the following information:

   ▪ A 2,400-square-foot home sold for $168,000.

   ▪ A 1,500-square-foot home sold for $106,500.

   ▪ A 1,100-square-foot home sold for $79,000.

   What offer should they make on the home?

3. **Closing Costs.** Larry and Laurie have found a home and made a $125,000 offer that has been accepted. They make a down payment of 10 percent. Their bank charges a loan origination fee of 1 percent of the loan and points of 1.5 percent (both are applied to the loan amount). Other fees include a $25 loan application fee, a $250 appraisal fee, and $350 for title search and insurance. How much cash will Larry and Laurie need at closing?

4. **Total Interest Paid.** Lloyd and Jean are considering purchasing a home requiring a $75,000 mortgage. The payment on a 30-year mortgage for this amount is $498.97. The payment for a 15-year maturity is $674.12. What is the difference in the total interest paid between the two different maturities?

5. **Tax Savings.** This month you made a mortgage payment of $700, of which $600 was an interest payment and $100 is a payment of the loan principal. You are in the 25 percent marginal tax bracket. What is the tax savings as a result of this payment?

6. **Annual Costs of Renting.** Teresa rents her apartment for $650 per month, utilities not included. When she moved in, she paid a $700 security deposit using money from her savings account that was paying 3 percent interest. Her renter's insurance costs her $60

per year. What are Teresa's total annual costs of renting?

7. **Cost of Condo.** Matt has found a condominium in an area where he would enjoy living. He would need a $5,000 down payment from his savings and would have to pay closing costs of $2,500 to purchase the condo. His monthly mortgage payments would be $520 including property taxes and insurance. The condominium's homeowner's association charges maintenance fees of $400 per year. Calculate the cost of Matt's condo during the first year if he currently has the $5,000 down payment invested in an account earning 5 percent interest.

8. **Tax Savings.** Matt (from problem 7) paid mortgage interest of $4,330 during his first year in the condo. His property taxes were $600, and his homeowner's insurance was $460. If Matt is in a 25 percent marginal tax rate bracket, what were his tax savings for his first year?

9. **Refinancing.** Doug and Lynn bought their home three years ago. They have a mortgage payment of $601.69. Interest rates have recently fallen, and they can lower their mortgage payments to $491.31 if they refinance. What would their annual savings be if they refinance? They are in a 15 percent marginal tax rate bracket. (Hint: Consider the reduction in tax savings.)

10. **Refinancing.** If the cost of refinancing their house is $3,860, how long would Doug and Lynn (from problem 9) have to remain in their home in order to recover the cost? (Ignore any interest on the savings in answering this question.)

Questions 11 and 12 require a financial calculator.

11. **Accumulating the Down Payment.** Paul wants to purchase his own home. He currently lives in an apartment, and his rent is being paid by his parents. Paul's parents have informed him that they would not pay his mortgage payments. Paul has no savings, but can save $400 per month. The home he desires costs $100,000, and his real estate broker informs him that a down payment of 20 percent would be required. If Paul can earn 8 percent on his savings, how long will it take him to accumulate the required down payment?

12. **Mortgage Affordability.** Paul (from problem 11) will be able to save $400 per month (which can be used for mortgage payments) for the indefi-

nite future. If Paul finances the remaining cost of the home (after making the $20,000 down payment) at a rate of 9 percent over 30 years, what are his resulting monthly mortgage payments? Can he afford the mortgage?

13. **ETHICAL DILEMMA:** Sarah and Joe own a small home that they would like to sell in order to build their dream home. Their current home has a mortgage and needs extensive repairs to make it marketable. A local loan company is offering home equity loans equal to 125% of the home's value. Since Sarah and Joe have good jobs and can make the additional home equity loan payments, they easily qualify for the 125% equity home loan. It takes the entire home equity loan to complete the repairs and upgrades to the home.

They are shocked to find that even after the upgrades they are unable to sell their home for enough to repay the mortgage and the home equity loan. In other words, they have negative equity in the home.

a. Comment on the finance company's ethics in making loans in excess of a home's appraised value.

b. What are Sarah and Joe's options in their current situation? Is there a way they can proceed with building their dream home?

FINANCIAL PLANNING ONLINE EXERCISES

1. Go to calculators.aol.com/tools/aol/home01/tool.fcs and click "How much can I borrow?"

   a. Input $3,000 wages, $500 in other income, $300 in auto loans, $100 for student loans, $125 for other loans, a desired interest rate of 9 percent, a 15-year loan term, a 5 percent down payment, no other debts, a $200 monthly credit card payment, $1,500 property tax, and $300 property insurance. What are the conservative estimates and aggressive estimates of what you can afford to borrow to finance the purchase of a home?

   b. Now change the interest rate to 10 percent. What is the difference in monthly payments on the loan?

   c. Now change the loan term to 30 years. What is the difference in monthly payments on the loan?

2. Go to realestate.yahoo.com/Homevalues and enter your address and Zip code in the appropriate boxes. After clicking "Search," answer the following questions:

   a. What is the range of values for homes in your area?

   b. What has been the general price trend of home values in your area?

   c. What is the estimated value of your home?

   d. What is the tax assessed value?

3. Go to www.realtor.com/. Enter the Zip code of your current home or the Zip code of where you plan to live after graduation, the price range of houses you are interested in, the number of bedrooms and baths, and hit "Search."

   a. How many houses meet your criteria in the designated area?

   b. What is the range of prices, highest to lowest?

   c. Of the houses listed, identify the one that you are most interested in and explain why.

4. Go to www.mortgageloan.com/refinance-mortgage.

   a. What are the current national refinance rates for a 30-year fixed? For a 15-year fixed?

   b. Discuss the benefits of home refinancing.

5. Go to www.finance.yahoo.com/loans. When answering "b" and "c," click "View rates in your area" under the rates table.

   a. What are the average national mortgage rates for 30-year fixed, 15-year fixed, and adjustable-rate mortgages?

   b. What mortgage rates are available in your nearest metro region? What mortgage rates are available in your state?

   c. Compare the mortgage rates available in New York and in Utah. Which is higher? Why?

6. Go to www.bloomberg.com/invest//calculators/mortgage.html and using the "Fixed Mortgage Loan Calculator," answer the following questions:

   a. Assume you have a mortgage of $150,000 for 30 years at 5%, what are: 1) the monthly payment; 2) the total payments; and 3) the total interest payment?

   b. Assume the same data as in "a" except for a term of 15 years, what are: 1) the monthly payment; 2) the total payments; and 3) the total interest payment?

c. Assume the same facts as in "a" except the interest rate is 6%, what are: 1) the monthly payment; 2) the total payments; and 3) the total interest payment?

7. Use the Web site www.federalreserve.gov/pubs/arms/arms_english.htm to answer the following questions:

a. Click "Your monthly payments could change." If your initial rate is 4%, by how much would your monthly payment increase in year two if the rate rises to 6%? To 7%?

b. Discuss how you could end up owing more money than you borrowed.

c. What could happen if you want to pay off your ARM early to avoid higher payments?

8. Using the calculator at realestate.yahoo.com/calculators/rent_vs_own.html, use the following data to compute "Should I Rent or Buy a Home": Your rent is $650 per month, you pay your own electric bill which averages $100 per month, your renter's insurance premium is $125 per year, and rent payments have increased at an annual rate of 3%. You can buy a home for $85,000 in an area that has shown an annual appreciation of 3%. You have enough cash to make a down payment of $20,000, which will allow you to get an interest rate of 5.5% for 30 years. Your annual homeowner's insurance premium will be $750 and your property taxes will be $1,500 per year. You estimate annual maintenance costs on the home at $350 per year. You will base your comparison on 30 years assuming your marginal tax bracket is 25%, your opportunity cost is 8%, and the anticipated annual inflation rate is 3%. Will you be better off buying or renting and by how much?

VIDEO EXERCISE: Purchasing a Home

Go to one of the Web sites that contain video clips (such as www.youtube.com) and view some video clips about banking tips. You can use search phrases such as "banking tips." Select one video clip on this topic that you would recommend for the other students in your class.

1. Provide the Web link for the video clip.

2. What do you think is the main point of this video clip?

3. How might you change your process of purchasing a home as a result of watching this video clip?

BUILDING YOUR OWN FINANCIAL PLAN

The purchase of a home is the largest expenditure that most individuals will make in their lifetime. For this reason, you should approach this decision with as much information as possible. This exercise will familiarize you with various information sources and will alert you to what you can and cannot expect from a realtor.

Go to the worksheets at the end of this chapter, and to the CD-ROM accompanying this text, to continue to build your financial plan.

THE SAMPSONS—A CONTINUING CASE

The Sampsons purchased a home last year. They have a 30-year mortgage with a fixed interest rate of 8.6 percent. Their monthly mortgage payment (excluding property taxes and insurance) is about $700 per month. In the last year, interest rates have declined. A 30-year mortgage now has an interest rate of 8 percent. Dave and Sharon want to determine how much they can lower their monthly payments by refinancing. By refinancing, they would incur transaction fees of $1,400 after considering any tax effects. The Sampsons are in the 25 percent tax bracket.

Go to the worksheets at the end of this chapter, and to the CD-ROM accompanying this text, to continue this case.

PART 3: BRAD BROOKS—A CONTINUING CASE

Brad Brooks decides it is time to upgrade his car and housing situations. Brad has more closely monitored his entertainment expenses, reducing them by $207. As a result, his monthly cash inflows now exceed his outflows by approximately $350 per month. Brad is interested in purchasing an SUV for $35,000. He still owes $10,000 on his two-year-old sedan (which has 57,000 miles) and has found a buyer who will pay him $15,000 cash. This would enable him to pay off his current car loan and still have $5,000 for a down payment on the SUV. He would finance the remainder of the purchase price for four years at 8 percent. Anticipating your objections to purchasing the SUV, Brad has an alternative plan to lease the SUV for three years. The terms of the lease are $600 per month, a $0.20 charge per mile over 15,000 miles annually, and $1,200 due upon signing for the first month's lease payment and security deposit.

Brad would also like to purchase his condo. He knows that he will enjoy tax advantages with ownership and is eager to reduce his tax burden. He can make the purchase with 10 percent down; the total purchase price is $90,000. A 30-year mortgage is available with an 8 percent rate. Closing costs due at signing will total $3,100. The property taxes on his condo will be $1,800 per year, his Property Owners' Association (POA) fee is $70 per month, and his household insurance will increase by $240 a year if he buys the condo.

Turn to the worksheets at the end of this chapter, and to the CD-ROM accompanying this text, to continue this case.

Chapter 15: Building Your Own Financial Plan

GOALS

1. Limit the amount of mortgage financing to an affordable level; determine if homeownership or renting is better financially.

2. Select the shortest loan maturity with affordable monthly payments.

3. Select the mortgage loan type (fixed or adjustable rate) that is most likely to result in the lowest interest expenses.

ANALYSIS

1. The amount of home that a person can afford is affected by many factors. The following worksheets will help you to determine the impact of interest rates, term of loan, and loan type (i.e., fixed or adjustable rate) on this process. Go to www.lendingtree.com. Click "Knowledge Center," then click "Calculators." Referring to the personal cash flow statement developed in Chapter 9, use the amount that you determined is available for rent as the basis for the amount of home payment that you can afford each month. By using trial and error on the adjustable and fixed mortgage loan calculators, adjust the amount of mortgage either up or down until the "monthly payment" approximately equals the amount you determined for rent in your cash flow statement. Enter the amount of the mortgage that you can afford in the worksheets below as well as the amount of the down payment that you have or expect to have when you purchase a home. Repeat the process using the other interest rates and mortgage terms indicated in the worksheets. Remember: Maintain the same "number of months between adjustments," "expected adjustments," and "interest rate cap" for each of the adjustable-rate calculations.

Fixed Rate

Interest Rate	6%
Term	30 Years
Amount of Down Payment	$
Amount of Mortgage	$
Total Price of Home (Down Payment Plus Mortgage)	$

Interest Rate	8%
Term	30 Years
Amount of Down Payment	$
Amount of Mortgage	$
Total Price of Home (Down Payment Plus Mortgage)	$

Interest Rate	6%
Term	15 Years
Amount of Down Payment	$
Amount of Mortgage	$
Total Price of Home (Down Payment Plus Mortgage)	$

Interest Rate	8%
Term	15 Years
Amount of Down Payment	$
Amount of Mortgage	$
Total Price of Home (Down Payment Plus Mortgage)	$

Adjustable Rate

Starting Interest Rate	6%
Term	15 Years
Months between Adjustments (not to exceed 12 months)	
Expected Adjustment	
Interest Rate Cap	
Amount of Down Payment	$
Amount of Mortgage	$
Total Price of Home (Down Payment Plus Mortgage)	$

Starting Interest Rate	8%
Term	15 Years
Months between Adjustments (not to exceed 12 months)	
Expected Adjustment	
Interest Rate Cap	
Amount of Down Payment	$
Amount of Mortgage	$
Total Price of Home (Down Payment Plus Mortgage)	$

Starting Interest Rate	6%
Term	30 Years
Months between Adjustments (not to exceed 12 months)	
Expected Adjustment	
Interest Rate Cap	
Amount of Down Payment	$
Amount of Mortgage	$
Total Price of Home (Down Payment Plus Mortgage)	$

Starting Interest Rate	8%
Term	30 Years
Months between Adjustments (not to exceed 12 months)	
Expected Adjustment	
Interest Rate Cap	
Amount of Down Payment	$
Amount of Mortgage	$
Total Price of Home (Down Payment Plus Mortgage)	$

2. At www.msn.com, search listings of homes for sale in your price range by clicking "Shop," then "Buying a House." Complete the information requested under "Compare and Find Homes" to research cities and neighborhoods that you are interested in. Record information on homes of interest below.

	From	To
Price Range:		
Zip Code:		

Potential Homes

Address	List Price	MSN Price Estimate	Monthly Payment	Realtor

3. Referring to your cash flow statement and personal balance sheet, compare the monthly payment estimates to the rent you are currently paying. Determine the amount of a down payment you can afford to make.

   Down payment $ _____

4. At www.msn.com, click "House and Home," then click "Loans and Financing." Gather current information on loan rates and record it below.

Mortgage Type	Rate

5. Create an amortization table for the fixed-rate mortgage that is most affordable. (The Excel worksheet will calculate the monthly payment based on your input and create the amortization table.)

   Loan Amount   _____

   Number of Years   _____

   Annual Interest Rate _____

   Monthly Payment   _____

Amortization Schedule for Year 1

Monthly Payment	Payment	Principal	Interest	Balance

Compare the allocation of principal versus interest paid per year on the loan. (The Excel worksheet will create a bar graph based on your input.)

Amortization Schedule (Annual Totals)

Year	Annual Payments	Principal	Interest	Balance
1				
2				
3				
4				
5				
6				
7				
8				
9				
10				
11				
12				
13				
14				
15				
16				
17				
18				
19				
20				
21				
22				
23				
24				
25				
26				
27				
28				
29				
30				

6. Select the mortgage with the best terms. Compare the cost of purchasing a home with these mortgage terms to renting over a three-year period.

Renting versus Owning a Home

Cost of Renting	Per Month	Amount per Year	Total over Three Years
Rent			
Renter's Insurance			
Opportunity cost of security deposit			
Total cost of renting			

Cost of Purchasing	Per Month	Amount per Year	Total over Three Years
Mortgage payment			
Down payment			
Opportunity cost of down payment			
Property taxes			
Home insurance			
Closing costs			
Maintenance costs			
Total costs before tax benefits			
Total tax savings			
Equity investment			
Increase in home value			
Value of equity			
Cost of purchasing home over three years			

If you enter this information on the Excel worksheet, the software will create a chart comparing the cost of renting versus purchasing.

DECISIONS

1. What is the mortgage amount and down payment that you can afford?

_____

_____

_____

_____

_____

_____

_____

2. Is a fixed-rate or adjustable-rate mortgage better suited to your financial situation? What maturity, interest rate, and monthly payment can you afford?

_____

_____

_____

_____

_____

_____

_____

3. Describe whether buying or renting a home is preferable for you.

_____

_____

_____

_____

_____

_____

_____

Chapter 15: The Sampsons—A Continuing Case

CASE QUESTIONS

1. Use a Web site or a financial calculator to determine the monthly mortgage payment (excluding property taxes and insurance) on a $90,000 mortgage if the Sampsons obtain a new 30-year mortgage at the 8 percent interest rate (for example, loan.yahoo.com/m/mortcalc.html.)

Mortgage loan	$90,000
Interest rate	8%
Years	30
Loan payment	

2. The Sampsons expect that they will not move for at least three years. Advise the Sampsons on whether they should refinance their mortgage by comparing the savings of refinancing with the costs.

Current mortgage payment	
New mortgage payment	
Monthly savings	
Annual savings	
Marginal tax rate	
Increase in taxes	
Annual savings after tax	
Years in house after refinancing	
Total savings	

3. Why might your advice about refinancing change in the future?

_____

_____

_____

_____

_____

_____

_____

Part 3: Brad Brooks—A Continuing Case

CASE QUESTIONS

1. Refer to Brad's personal cash flow statement that you developed in Part 1. Recompute his expenses to determine if Brad can afford to

   a. Purchase the new car

   b. Lease the new car

   c. Purchase the condo

   d. Purchase the car and the condo

   e. Lease the car and purchase the condo

Personal Cash Flow Statement

Cash Inflows	This Month
Total Cash Inflows	

Cash Outflows	
Total Cash Outflows	
Net Cash Flows	

2. Brad's uncle has offered to provide him with a loan for the closing costs and the down payment needed to purchase the condo. Brad exclaims, "This is great. I don't even need a loan contract!" Advise Brad on the situation.

_____

_____

_____

_____

3. What are the advantages and disadvantages to Brad of leasing rather than purchasing the car?

_____

_____

_____

_____

_____

_____

4. Based on the information you provided, Brad decides not to buy the condo at this time. How can he save the necessary funds to purchase a condo or house in the future? Be specific in your recommendations.

Future Value of an Annuity

Payment per Period	
Number of Periods	
Interest Rate per Period	
Future Value	

_____

_____

_____

_____

_____

_____

5. How would your advice to Brad differ if he were

   a. 45 years old?

_____

_____

_____

   b. 60 years old?

_____

_____

_____

6. Prepare a written or oral report on your findings and recommendations to Brad.

_____

_____

_____

_____

_____

_____

_____

_____

_____

_____

_____

_____

_____

_____

_____

_____

_____

_____

_____

_____

_____

_____

_____

_____

_____

CHAPTER 16

Investing Fundamentals

A nita is a patient investor. In 2002 she invested $3,000 in stocks of well-known companies. By 2010, her original investment was worth $8,000.

Meanwhile, Lisa invested $3,000 in stock of Zyko Co. because Zyko suggested its technology would change the world. Lisa wanted to earn higher returns on her investment than she might earn on stock of well-established firms. Zyko's technology failed, and in 2010, Zyko went bankrupt. Consequently, Lisa's stock was worthless.

These examples demonstrate that the same type of investment can have entirely different outcomes. As you will learn in this chapter, there are a variety of types of investments, and the risk and return of these different investments vary widely. Your ability to analyze investments can enhance your investment income and increase your net worth.

The objectives of this chapter are to:

- Describe the common types of investments
- Explain how to measure the return on investments
- Identify the risks of investments
- Explain the trade-off between the return and risk of investments
- Describe common investment mistakes that should be avoided

■ TYPES OF INVESTMENTS

If you have money to invest, your first priority should be to ensure adequate liquidity. You can satisfy your liquidity needs by placing deposits in financial institutions or by investing in money market securities such as certificates of deposit. Since these types of investments are primarily focused on providing liquidity, they offer a relatively low return. If you have additional funds beyond your liquidity needs, you have a wide variety of investments to consider.

Money Market Securities

Recall from Chapter 11 that there are several different money market securities available, including certificates of deposit, money market deposit accounts, and money market funds. Most money market securities provide interest income. Even if your liquidity needs are covered, you may invest in these securities to maintain a low level of risk. However, you can also consider some alternative securities that typically provide a higher rate of return but are more risky.

Stocks

As defined in Chapter 9, stocks are certificates representing partial ownership of a firm. Stock investors become shareholders of the firm. Firms issue stocks to obtain funds to expand their business operations. Investors invest in stock when they believe that they may earn a higher return than alternative investments offer. Since stocks are a popular type of investment for individuals.

primary market
A market in which newly issued securities are traded.

Primary and Secondary Stock Markets. Stocks can be traded in a primary or a secondary market. The **primary market** is a market in which newly issued securities are traded. Firms can raise funds by issuing new stock in the primary market. The first offering of a firm's stock to the public is referred to as an **initial public offering (IPO)**. A **secondary market** facilitates the trading of existing securities by enabling investors to sell their shares at any time. These shares are purchased by other investors who wish to invest in that stock. Thus, even if a firm is not issuing new shares of stock, investors can easily obtain shares of that firm's stock by purchasing them in the secondary market. On a typical day, more than 1 million shares of any large firm's stock are traded in the secondary market. The price of the stock changes each day in response to changes in supply and demand.

initial public offering (IPO)
The first offering of a firm's stock to the public.

secondary market
A market in which existing securities are traded.

Types of Stock Investors. Stock investors can be classified as institutional investors or individual investors. **Institutional investors** are professionals employed by a financial institution who are responsible for managing money on behalf of the clients they serve. They attempt to select stocks or other securities that will provide a reasonable return on investment. The employees of financial institutions who make investment decisions are referred to as **portfolio managers** because they manage a portfolio of securities (including stocks). More than half of all trading in financial markets is attributable to institutional investors.

institutional investors
Professionals responsible for managing money on behalf of the clients they serve.

portfolio managers
Employees of financial institutions who make investment decisions.

individual investors
Individuals who invest funds in securities.

Individual investors commonly invest a portion of the money earned from their jobs. Like institutional investors, they invest in stocks to earn a reasonable return on their investment. In this way, their money can grow by the time they wish to use it to make purchases. The number of individual investors has increased substantially in the last 20 years.

day traders
Investors who buy stocks and then sell them on the same day.

Many individual investors hold their stocks for periods beyond one year. In contrast, some individual investors called **day traders** buy stocks and then sell them on the same day. They hope to capitalize on very short-term movements in security prices. In many cases, their investments last for only a few minutes. Many day traders conduct their investing as a career, relying on their returns from investing as their main source of income. This type of investing is very risky because the stock prices of even the best-managed firms periodically decline. Day trading is not recommended for most investors.

Return from Investing in Stock. Stocks can offer a return on investment through dividends and stock price appreciation. Some firms distribute quarterly income to their shareholders in the form of dividends rather than reinvest the earnings in the firm's operations. They tend to keep the dollar amount of the dividends per share fixed from one quarter to the next, but may periodically increase the amount. They rarely reduce the dividend amount unless they experience relatively weak performance and cannot afford to make their dividend payment. The amount of dividends paid out per year is usually between 1 and 3 percent of the stock's price.

growth stocks
Stocks of firms with substantial growth opportunities.

A firm's decision to distribute earnings as dividends, rather than reinvesting all of its earnings to support future growth, may depend on the opportunities that are available to the firm. In general, firms that pay high dividends tend to be older, established firms that have less chance for substantial growth. Conversely, firms that pay low dividends tend to be younger firms that have more growth opportunities. The stocks of firms with substantial growth opportunities are often referred to as **growth stocks**. An investment in these younger firms offers the prospect of a very large return because they have not reached their full potential. At the same time, an investment in these firms is exposed to much higher uncertainty because young firms are more likely to fail or experience very weak performance than mature firms.

income stocks
Stocks that provide investors with periodic income in the form of large dividends.

The higher the dividend paid by a firm, the lower its potential stock price appreciation. When a firm distributes a large proportion of its earnings to investors as dividends, it limits its potential growth and the potential degree to which its value (and stock price) may increase. Stocks that provide investors with periodic income in the form of large dividends are referred to as **income stocks**.

Financial Planning Online 16.1: **IPOs**

Go to
www.renaissancecapital
.com/IPOHome/
Marketwatch.aspx

This Web site provides information about firms that are about to engage in an IPO and also summarizes the performance of recent IPOs.

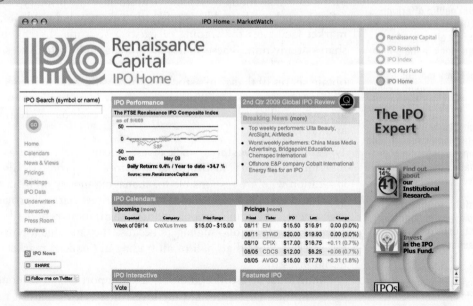

Shareholders can also earn a return if the price of the stock increases by the time they sell it. The market value of a firm is based on the number of shares of stock outstanding multiplied by the price of the stock. The price of a share of stock is determined by dividing the market value of the firm by the number of shares of stock outstanding. Thus, a firm that has a market value of $600 million and 10 million shares of stock outstanding has a value per share of:

$$\text{Value of Stock per Share} = \text{Market Value of Firm/Number of Shares Outstanding}$$
$$= \$600,000,000/10,000,000$$
$$= \$60$$

The market price of a stock is dependent on the number of investors who are willing to purchase the stock (the demand for the stock) and the number of investors who wish to sell their holdings of the stock (the supply of stock for sale). There is no limit to how high a stock's price can rise. The demand for the stock and the supply of stock for sale are influenced by the respective firm's business performance, as measured by its earnings and other characteristics. When the firm performs well, its stock becomes more desirable to investors, who demand more shares of that stock. In addition, investors holding shares of this stock are less willing to sell it. The increase in the demand for the stock and the reduction in the number of shares of stock for sale by investors results in a higher stock price.

Conversely, when a firm performs poorly (has low or negative earnings), its market value declines. The demand for shares of its stock also declines. In addition, some investors who had been holding the stock will decide to sell their shares, thereby increasing the supply of stock for sale and resulting in a lower stock price. The performance of the firm depends on how well it is managed.

Investors benefit when they invest in a well-managed firm because the firm's earnings usually will increase, and so will its stock price. Under these conditions, investors may generate a capital gain, which represents the difference between their selling price and purchase price. In contrast, a poorly managed firm may have lower earnings than expected, which could cause its stock price to decline.

common stock
A certificate issued by a firm to raise funds that represents partial ownership in the firm.

Common versus Preferred Stock. Stock can be classified as common stock or preferred stock. **Common stock** is a certificate issued by a firm to raise funds that represents

---

Financial Planning Online 16.2: **Price Trends of Your Stocks**

Go to
finance.yahoo.com

This Web site provides historical price movements for stock that you specify.

preferred stock
A certificate issued by a firm to raise funds that entitles shareholders to first priority to receive dividends.

partial ownership in the firm. Investors who hold common stock normally have the right to vote on key issues such as the sale of a company. They elect the board of directors, which is responsible for ensuring that the firm's managers serve the interests of its shareholders. **Preferred stock** is a certificate issued by a firm to raise funds that entitles shareholders to first priority (ahead of common stockholders) to receive dividends. Corporations issue common stock more frequently than preferred stock. The price of preferred stock is not as volatile as the price of common stock and does not have as much potential to increase substantially. For this reason, investors who strive for high returns typically invest in common stock.

Bonds

Recall that bonds are long-term debt securities issued by government agencies or corporations. Treasury bonds are issued by the Treasury and backed by the U.S. government. Corporate bonds are issued by corporations.

Return from Investing in Bonds. Bonds offer a return to investors in the form of coupon payments and bond price appreciation. They pay periodic interest (coupon) payments, and therefore can provide a fixed amount of interest income per year. Thus, they are desirable for investors who want to have their investments generate a specific amount of interest income each year.

A bond's price can increase over time and therefore may provide investors with a capital gain, representing the difference between the price at which it was sold by an investor versus the price at which it was purchased. However, a bond's price may decline, which could cause investors to experience a capital loss. Even the prices of Treasury bonds decline in some periods.

Mutual Funds

Recall that mutual funds sell shares to individuals and invest the proceeds in a portfolio of investments such as bonds or stocks. They are managed by experienced portfolio managers. They are attractive to investors who have limited funds and want to invest in a diversified portfolio. Because a stock mutual fund typically invests in numerous stocks, it enables investors to achieve broad diversification with an investment as low as $500. There are thousands of mutual funds from which to choose.

Return from Investing in Mutual Funds. The coupon or dividend payment generated by the mutual fund's portfolio of securities is passed on to the individual investor. Since a mutual fund represents a portfolio of securities, its value changes over time in response to changes in the values of those securities. Therefore, the price at which an investor purchases shares of a mutual fund changes over time. A mutual fund can generate a capital gain for individual investors, since the price at which investors sell their shares of the fund may be higher than the price at which they purchased the shares. However, the price of the mutual fund's shares may also decline over time, which would result in a capital loss.

publicly traded stock indexes
Securities whose values move in tandem with a particular stock index representing a set of stocks.

Publicly Traded Indexes. Another option for investors who want a diversified portfolio of stocks is to invest in **publicly traded stock indexes,** which are securities whose values move in tandem with a particular stock index representing a set of stocks.

Much research has shown that sophisticated investors (such as well-paid portfolio managers of financial institutions) are unable to outperform various stock indexes on average. Thus, by investing in an index, individual investors can ensure that their performance will match that index.

One of the most popular publicly traded indexes is the Standard & Poor's Depository Receipt (S.P.D.R., also called Spider), which is a basket of stocks that matches the S&P 500 index and is traded on the American Stock Exchange. You can buy Spiders through a broker, just like stocks. When investors expect that the large U.S. stocks represented by the S&P 500 will experience strong performance, they can capitalize on their expectations by purchasing shares of Spiders. Spiders provide investors with a return not only in the form of potential share price appreciation, but also dividends in the form of additional shares to the investors. Any expenses incurred by the Spiders from creating the index are deducted from the dividends.

Investors can also invest in specific sector indexes as well as in market indexes. There are publicly traded indexes that represent a variety of specific sectors, including the Internet, energy, technology, and financial sectors. Because an index represents several stocks, you can achieve some degree of diversification by investing in an index.

Real Estate

One way of investing in real estate is by buying a home. The value of a home changes over time, in response to supply and demand. When the demand for homes in your area increases, home values tend to rise. The return that you earn on your home is difficult to measure because you must take into account the financing, real estate agent commissions, and tax effects. However, a few generalizations are worth mentioning. For a given amount invested in the home, your return is dependent on how the value of your home changes over the time that you own it. Your return is also dependent on your original down payment on the home. The return will be higher if you made a smaller down payment when purchasing the home. Since the value of a home can decline over time, there is the risk of a loss (a negative return) on your investment. If you are in a hurry to sell your home, you may have to lower your selling price to attract potential buyers, which will result in a lower return on your investment.

You can also invest in real estate by purchasing rental property or land. The price of land is based on supply and demand. There is little open land, and with dense populations along the coasts of the United States, open land along the coasts typically has a high price.

Return from Investing in Real Estate. Real estate that can be rented (such as office buildings and apartments) generates income in the form of rent payments. In addition, investors may earn a capital gain if they sell the property for a higher price than they paid for it. Alternatively, they may sustain a capital loss if they sell the property for a lower price than they paid for it.

The price of land changes over time in response to real estate development. Many individuals may purchase land as an investment, hoping that they will be able to sell it in the future for a higher price than they paid for it.

■ INVESTMENT RETURN AND RISK

When individuals consider any particular investment, they typically attempt to assess two characteristics: (1) the potential return that will be earned on the investment, and (2) the risk of the investment.

Measuring the Return on Your Investment

For investments that do not provide any periodic income (such as dividends or coupon payments), the return can be measured as the percentage change in the price (P) from the time the investment was purchased (time $t-1$) until the time at which it is sold (time t):

$$R = \frac{P_t - P_{t-1}}{P_{t-1}}$$

For example, if you pay $1,000 to make an investment and receive $1,100 when you sell the investment in one year, you earn a return of:

$$R = \frac{\$1,100 - \$1,000}{\$1,000}$$

$$= .10, \text{ or } 10\%$$

Incorporating Dividend or Coupon Payments. If you also earned dividend or coupon payments over this period, your return will be even higher. For a short-term period such as one year or less, the return on a security that pays dividends or interest can be estimated by adjusting the equation above. Add the dividend or coupon amount to the numerator. The return on your investment in stocks accounts for any dividends or coupon payments you received as well as the change in the investment value over your investment period. For stocks that pay dividends, the return is:

$$R = \frac{(P_t - P_{t-1}) + D}{P_{t-1}}$$

where R is the return, P_{t-1} is the price of the stock at the time of the investment, P_t is the price of the stock at the end of the investment horizon, and D is the dividends earned over the investment horizon.

EXAMPLE

You purchased 100 shares of stock from Wax, Inc., for $50 per share one year ago. During the year, the firm experienced strong earnings. It paid dividends of $1 per share over the year, and you sold the stock for $58 at the end of the year. Your return on your investment was:

$$R = \frac{(P_t - P_{t-1}) + D}{P_{t-1}}$$

$$= \frac{(\$58 - \$50) + \$1}{\$50}$$

$$= .18, \text{ or } 18\%$$

Differing Tax Rates on Returns. Income received as a result of interest payments or bond coupon payments is classified as ordinary income for tax purposes. In addition, capital gains resulting from the sale of investments held for one year or less are classified as ordinary income. Capital gains resulting from the sale of investments held more than one year are subject to a long-term capital gains tax. Given the difference in tax rates applied to short- and long-term capital gains, some investors may achieve a higher after-tax return by holding on to investments for more than one year.

EXAMPLE

As in the previous example, you purchased 100 shares of Wax stock, except that instead of selling the stock after one year, you sell the stock after 366 days (one day over a year). Because you have held the stock for one more day, your capital gain shifts from a short-term gain to a long-term gain (taxed at 15 percent). Assume that your marginal tax rate (tax rate charged on any additional ordinary income) is 35 percent. The tax effects of the previous example involving a short-term capital gain are shown in the second column of Exhibit 16.1, while the tax effects of the long-term capital gain are shown in the third column. The taxes on dividends are as follows:

$$\text{Tax on Dividends Received} = \text{Amount of Dividend} \times \text{Dividend Tax Rate}$$

$$= \$100 \times .15$$

$$= \$15$$

Exhibit 16.1 Comparing the Tax Effects on Short- and Long-Term Capital Gains		
	If Stock Is Held for One Year	**If Stock Is Held for More Than One Year**
Dividends	$100	$100
Short-term capital gain	800	0
Long-term capital gain	0	800
Total income	$900	$900
Tax on dividends (15%)	$15	$15
Short-term capital gains tax (35%)	280	0
Long-term capital gains tax (15%)	0	120
Total taxes	$295	$135
After-tax income	$605	$765

The tax on capital gains depends on whether the gain is short term or long term. The short-term capital gains tax is:

Tax on Short-Term Capital Gain = Amount of Short-Term Capital Gain
× Marginal Income Tax Rate

= $800 × .35

= $280

The long-term capital gains tax is:

Tax on Long-Term Capital Gain = Amount of Long-Term Capital Gain
× Long-Term Capital Gain Tax Rate

= $800 × .15

= $120

The long-term capital gains tax is $160 lower than the short-term capital gains tax. Thus, your after-tax income from holding the stock one extra day is $160 higher.

How Wealth Is Influenced by Your Return on Investment

When an investment provides income to you, any portion of that income that you save will increase the value of your assets. For example, if you receive a coupon payment of $100 this month as a result of holding a bond and deposit the check in your savings account, your assets will increase by $100. If the value of your investments increases and your liabilities do not increase, your wealth increases.

The degree to which you can accumulate wealth is partially dependent on your investment decisions. You can estimate the amount by which your wealth will increase from an investment based on an assumed rate of return.

EXAMPLE

Stephanie Spratt hopes to invest $4,000 at the end of the year. If her investments appreciate by 6 percent annually, the value of her investment will be $7,163 in 10 years. If she earns an annual return of 10 percent, the value of those investments will be $10,375 in 10 years. If she can earn an annual return of 20 percent, the value of her investment will be $24,767 in 10 years. The higher the rate of return, the higher the future value interest factor (*FVIF*), and the larger the amount of funds that she will accumulate.

If you can invest a specific amount in the stock market every year, the future value of these annual investments can be estimated as an annuity.

EXAMPLE

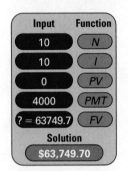

Input	Function
10	N
10	I
0	PV
4000	PMT
? = 63749.7	FV

Solution
$63,749.70

Stephanie Spratt believes that she can save $4,000 to invest in stocks at the end of each year for the next 10 years. If she expects the investment value to increase by 10 percent annually, she can use the future value interest factor of an annuity at 10 percent over 10 years, which is 15.937 (see Table C-3 in Appendix C). Based on her annual investment of $4,000 and the future value interest factor of an annuity (*FVIFA*), she will accumulate:

$$FV \text{ of Annual Stock Investments} = \text{Annual Investment} \times FVIFA_{i,n}$$
$$= \$4,000 \times 15.937$$
$$= \$63,748$$

The input for the financial calculator is shown at the left.

If Stephanie's investment value increases by 20 percent per year, the *FVIFA* is 25.959, and the value of her annual investments in 10 years will be:

$$FV \text{ of Annual Stock Investments} = \text{Annual Investment} \times FVIFA_{i,n}$$
$$= \$4,000 \times 25.959$$
$$= \$103,836$$

The input for the financial calculator is shown at the left.

Notice how the increase in Stephanie's wealth is sensitive to the rate of return earned on her annual investment. An annual increase in investment value of 20 percent would allow her to accumulate $40,088 more than if the annual increase is 10 percent.

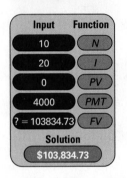

Input	Function
10	N
20	I
0	PV
4000	PMT
? = 103834.73	FV

Solution
$103,834.73

The example shows how your investment decisions and the performance of your investments can affect your future wealth.

Risk from Investing

The risk of an investment comes from the uncertainty surrounding its return. The return that you will earn on a specific stock is uncertain because its future dividend payments are not guaranteed, and its future price (when you sell the stock) is uncertain. The return that you will earn on a bond is uncertain because its coupon payments are not guaranteed, and its future price (when you sell the bond) is uncertain. The return that you will earn from investing in real estate is uncertain because its value when you sell it is uncertain.

Exposure to the Economy. The future values of investments are dependent on the demand by investors. When economic conditions are favorable, the income levels of investors are high, the earnings levels of firms are high, and there is a strong demand for most types of investments. When economic conditions are weak, the income levels of investors are low, the earnings levels of firms are low, and there is a weak demand for most types of investments. However, future economic conditions are uncertain, so it is difficult to predict the level of demand for various investments, and therefore the future values of these investments.

EXAMPLE

You are considering purchasing the stock of Cerro Inc. The future value of Cerro's stock is dependent on the future performance of Cerro Inc. If the economy strengthens, Cerro Inc. should perform well, and the value of its stock may increase by more than 9 percent. However, if the economy weakens, Cerro Inc. may perform poorly, and the stock could decline by 30 percent or more.

It is easy to find examples to illustrate the risk from investing. Many firms went bankrupt during the financial crisis in 2008–2009, including Circuit City and Lehman Brothers. Numerous investors who invested in these stocks lost 100 percent of their investment. Even firms that have normally performed well over time can experience weak performance in particular periods. Thus, it is not unusual for the stock or bond prices of even the most well-known firms to decline by more than 10 percent within a particular month or year. Many stocks of large well-known companies experienced price declines of 40 percent or more during the financial crisis.

Stocks and bonds of smaller firms tend to be even more risky, as they commonly experience pronounced fluctuations in their performance level. Some firms are more stable than others and are therefore less likely to experience a major decline in performance. Nevertheless, some investors prefer investments that have a higher growth potential, and they tolerate the higher level of risk. Before you select an investment, you should assess the risk.

Measuring an Investment's Risk. Investors measure the risk of investments to determine the degree of uncertainty surrounding their future returns. Two common measures of an investment's risk are its range of returns and the standard deviation of its returns. These measures can be applied to investments whose prices are frequently quoted over time.

range of returns
Returns of a specific investment over a given period.

Range of Returns. By reviewing the monthly returns of a specific investment over a given period, you can determine the **range of returns,** from the smallest (most negative) to the largest return. Compare an investment that has a range of monthly returns from .2 percent to 1.4 percent over the last year with another investment that has a range of −3.0 percent to 4.3 percent. The first investment is less risky because its range of returns is smaller and therefore it is more stable. Investments with a wide range have more risk because they have a higher probability of experiencing a large decline in price.

standard deviation
The degree of volatility in the stock's returns over time.

Standard Deviation of Returns. A second measure of risk is the **standard deviation** of a stock's monthly returns, which measures the degree of volatility in the stock's returns over time. A large standard deviation means that the returns deviate substantially from the mean over time. The more volatile the returns, the greater the chance that the stock could deviate far from its mean in a given period. Thus, an investment with a high standard deviation is more likely to experience a large gain or a large loss in a given period. The investment's return is subject to greater uncertainty, and for this reason, it is perceived as more risky.

Although these two measures differ, they tend to rank the risk levels of stocks rather consistently. That is, a very risky stock will normally have a relatively wide range of returns and a high standard deviation of returns.

Subjective Measures of Risk. The use of the range and standard deviation is limited because these measures of risk are not always accurate predictors of the future. For example, an investment that had stable returns in the past could experience a substantial decline in price in the future in response to poor economic conditions. Because of this limitation, the risk of some investments is commonly measured subjectively. For example, the risk of a bond may be measured by a subjective assessment of the issuing firm's ability to repay its debt. The assessment may include an estimate of the firm's future monthly revenue to determine whether the firm will have sufficient funds to cover its interest and other expenses. Investors may rely on experts to offer their risk assessment of a particular type of investment.

■ TRADE-OFF BETWEEN RETURN AND RISK

Every individual investor would like investments that offer a very high return and have no risk. However, such investments do not exist. Investors must weigh the trade-off between the potential return of an investment and the risk. If you want an investment that may generate a higher return, you have to tolerate the higher degree of uncertainty (risk) associated with that investment.

EXAMPLE

Stephanie Spratt has $1,000 that she could invest for the next three months in a three-month bank CD or in a stock. The bank CD offers a guaranteed return of 2 percent over the three-month period. Alternatively, she thinks the price of the stock will rise by 5 percent over the next three months. Yet, since the future price of the stock is uncertain, her return from investing in this stock is also uncertain. The return could be less than 5 percent, and might even be negative. Stephanie decides to invest in the CD rather than the stock.

The example above illustrates the trade-off between a risk-free investment and a risky investment. There are also trade-offs between assets with varying degrees of risk, as explained below for each type of investment.

Return-Risk Trade-Off among Stocks

Some firms have the potential to achieve a much higher performance level than others. But to do so, they take on more risk than other firms. That is, they may try to operate with less funding and pursue long-shot opportunities. Investors who invest in one of these firms may earn very high returns if the firm's strategies are successful. However, they could lose most or all of their investment if the firm's strategies fail.

In general, smaller firms have more potential for fast growth and their stocks have the potential to increase in value to greater degree. Yet, their stocks are risky because many small firms never reach their potential. The more mature firms that have already achieved high growth have less potential for future growth. However, these firms tend to be less risky because their business is more stable.

Initial public offerings (IPOs) are another stock investment option. You may have heard that IPO returns often exceed 20 percent over the first day. However, there is much risk to this type of investment. Individual investors rarely have access to these IPOs at the initial price. Institutional investors (such as mutual funds or insurance companies with large amounts of money to invest) normally have the first shot at purchasing shares of an IPO. Most individual investors can invest (if there are any shares left) only after the institutional investors have had a chance to purchase shares. By the time individual investors are able to invest in a newly issued stock, the price has already risen. Thus, individual investors commonly obtain the shares only after the price has reached its peak, and can incur large losses as the stock price declines over the following several months.

Many IPOs have performed poorly. On average, the long-term return on IPOs is weak compared to typical returns of other stocks in aggregate. Many firms (such as Pets.com) that engaged in IPOs failed within a few years, causing investors to lose all of their investments.

"Good news! I held my IPO at recess and now I'm the 12th richest man in America."

Return-Risk Trade-Off among Bonds

You may invest in a bond issued by a firm to earn the high coupon payment. The risk of your investment is that the firm may be unable to pay its coupon payment if its financial condition deteriorates. If you purchase a bond of a large, well-known, and successful firm, there is minimal risk that the firm will default on its payments. If you purchase a bond issued by a firm that is struggling financially, there is more risk that this firm will default on its payments. If this firm defaults on the bond, your return will be very poor. During the financial crisis in 2008–2009, many bonds defaulted.

High-risk bonds tend to offer higher coupon payments. Thus, you must weigh the trade-off between the potential return and the risk. If you are willing to tolerate the higher risk, you may consider investing in the bond issued by a weak firm. Alternatively, if you prefer less risk, you can purchase a bond issued by a successful and established firm, as long as you are willing to accept a lower return on your investment.

Return-Risk Trade-Off among Mutual Funds

When you invest in a mutual fund composed of stocks, you earn a return from the dividend payments and the increase in the prices of stocks held by the mutual fund. The risk of a stock mutual fund is that the prices of stocks can decline in any particular period. Since the mutual fund is composed of numerous stocks, the adverse impact caused by any single stock is reduced. However, when economic conditions weaken, most stocks tend to perform poorly. Just as smaller stocks tend to be more risky than larger stocks, mutual funds that contain mostly small stocks are more risky than mutual funds containing larger stocks. Yet, some investors still prefer mutual funds consisting of small stocks because they expect a higher return from these stocks.

When you invest in a mutual fund composed of bonds, your primary risk is that the bonds held by the mutual fund could default. Since a bond mutual fund contains numerous bonds, the adverse effect of a single bond default within a mutual fund is reduced. Yet, when economic conditions deteriorate, many firms that issued bonds can experience financial problems and have difficulty making their coupon payments. Some bond mutual funds are not highly exposed to risk because they invest only in corporate bonds issued by the most creditworthy corporations. Others are highly exposed because they invest in bonds issued by relatively weak corporations that pay high coupon rates. Investors who prefer risky bond mutual funds because of their potential to offer a high return must tolerate the high level of risk.

Return-Risk Trade-Off among Real Estate Investments

When you invest in real estate, your risk depends on your particular investment. If you buy rental property, it may not generate your anticipated periodic income if you cannot find renters or if your renters default on their rent payment. In addition, there is a risk that the property's value will decline over time. The degree of risk varies with the type of real estate investment. If you purchase an office building that is fully occupied, the risk is relatively low. Conversely, if you purchase a piece of open land in New Mexico because you hope that you will someday discover oil on the land, there is much risk in this investment.

Comparing Different Types of Investments

As a prudent investor, you must choose investments that suit your personal objectives. If you want to achieve a fixed return over a short-term period without any risk, you should consider investing in a certificate of deposit. The disadvantage of this investment is that it offers a relatively low return. If you want to achieve a stable return over a long-term period, you should consider Treasury bonds, or mutual funds that contain Treasury bonds. At the other extreme, if you desire a very high return, you could consider investing in land or in some small stocks.

Many investors fall in between these two extremes. They prefer a higher return than is offered by CDs or Treasury bonds but want to limit their risk. There is no formula that can determine your ideal investment because the choice depends on how much risk you want to take, and on your financial situation.

To illustrate, consider the following situations and the possible solutions shown in Exhibit 16.2. In general, you are in a better position to take some risk when you know that you will not need to sell the investment in the near future. Even if the value of the investment declines, you have the flexibility to hold on to the investment until the value increases. Conversely, individuals investing for the short term should play it safe. Since the prices of risky investments fluctuate substantially, it is dangerous to invest in a risky investment

Exhibit 16.2 How Investment Decisions Vary with Your Situation

Situation	Decision
You have $1,000 to invest but will need the funds in one month to pay bills.	You need liquidity. You should only consider money market securities.
You have $3,000 to invest but will need the funds in a year to make a tuition payment.	You should consider safe money market securities such as a one-year insured CD.
You have $5,000 to invest and will likely use the funds in about three years when you buy a home.	Consider a three-year insured CD or stocks of relatively stable firms that have relatively low risk.
You have $10,000 to invest and have no funds set aside for retirement in 20 years.	Consider investing in a diversified stock mutual fund.
You have $5,000 to invest. You expect that you will be laid off from your job within the next year.	You should probably invest the funds in money market securities so that you will have easy access to the funds if you lose your job.

when you know that you will be selling that investment in the near future. You could be forced to sell it when the investment has a low value. Investors who decide to pursue higher potential returns must be willing to accept the high risk associated with these investments.

By keeping a variety of investments, you can find a tolerable risk level. You can diversify your investments among many different stocks, thereby reducing your exposure to any particular investment. If you divide your money equally among five investments and one investment performs poorly, your exposure is limited.

Even if you diversify your portfolio among various investments, you are still exposed to general economic conditions, as the values of all investments can decline during periods in which economic conditions are weak. For this reason, you should consider diversifying among various types of investments that are not equally sensitive to economic conditions.

■ LEARNING FROM THE INVESTMENT MISTAKES OF OTHERS

Many individual investors learn from their own mistakes or the mistakes of others. Consider the following investment mistakes, so that you can avoid them.

Making Decisions Based on Unrealistic Goals

One of the most common mistakes is letting unrealistic goals dictate your investment decisions. These goals may force you to take more risk than you should, and can result in major losses.

EXAMPLE

Laurie Chen has $4,000, which should cover her school expenses next year. She is considering investing the money in a one-year CD that would earn about 6 percent, or about $240 in interest before next year. However, she would like to earn a higher return on her money within the next year, so that she can buy a used car. She decides to invest in a small stock that earned a return of 50 percent last year. If the stock's value increases by 50 percent again, her investment would generate a gain of $2,000, which would allow her to buy a used car. Unfortunately, the stock's value declines by 30 percent over the year. At the end of the year, her investment is worth $2,800, a $1,200 loss. She does not have sufficient funds to buy the car or cover her school expenses. She did not view her investment as a gamble, as the money was invested in the stock of a firm. However, her investment in one small stock was just as risky as gambling, especially since she had no information to support her decision except for the fact that the stock performed well in the previous year.

Borrowing to Invest

Another common mistake is to invest money that could have been used to pay off an existing loan. The potential to earn a high return on an investment can tempt individuals to take more risk than they should.

EXAMPLE

Charles Krenshaw recently took out a $5,000 loan to cover this year's college expenses. His parents gave him $5,000 so that he could pay off the loan. Rather than pay off the loan, Charles invested the $5,000 from his parents in a stock. He had hoped that he could earn a large return on the $5,000, so that he could sell the investment at the end of the year, pay off the loan, and have enough funds to travel through Europe during the summer. During the year, he had to make interest payments on the existing loan. The stock that he purchased declined in value by 90 percent, leaving him with just $500 at the end of the year. He now has insufficient funds to take a vacation, or to pay off the loan.

Taking Risks to Recover Losses from Previous Investments

Another common mistake is taking excessive risks to recover your losses. This can lead to additional losses, and may even push individuals toward bankruptcy.

EXAMPLE

Sarah Barnes lost 10 percent of her investment in the last year from investing in a diversified mutual fund. She needs the money before next winter to purchase a new furnace for her home. Yet she wants to make up for her loss, and has shifted her money into a risky mutual fund that will likely generate a higher return if economic conditions are favorable, but will perform poorly if economic conditions are unfavorable. She experiences a 20 percent loss on this investment because economic conditions weakened. She no longer has a sufficient amount of funds to pay for the furnace.

During the late 1990s, many investors bid up the prices of stocks because of their unrealistic expectations about how well these stocks would perform in the future. The media hype added to the investors' irrational exuberance. These actions created a so-called speculative bubble, meaning that once the prices are blown up to a certain level, the speculative bubble will burst, and stock prices will decline to where they should be. One reason for the generally poor stock performance in 2000–2002 was that the speculative bubble burst. In addition, economic conditions weakened. Stock prices of Motorola, Oracle, Cisco, and many other firms declined substantially in the 2000–2002 period.

While there may someday be another period in which stocks or other investments earn abnormally high returns, you should be realistic when making investment decisions. An investment that has the potential to rise substantially in value also has the potential to decline substantially in value. If you cannot afford the possible loss, you should not make that investment.

FOCUS ON ETHICS: Falling Prey to Online Investment Fraud

The Internet is a remarkably easy and inexpensive means of obtaining investment advice and researching investment opportunities. Hundreds of online newsletters recommend investments, such as specific stocks or bonds. Investors can use online bulletin boards to share information. Advice is also distributed in the form of spam, or junk e-mail.

With all of these sources at hand, it can be tough to tell the difference between legitimate and fraudulent opportunities. The recommendations could be provided by unqualified individuals or people paid by the companies to recommend their stocks or bonds. In some cases individuals send out millions of e-mails and set up Web sites to push a particular firm's stock. Others push specific investments that they already own, hoping to create more demand to drive the price higher. For some small stocks that have less than 1,000 shares traded per day, orders instigated by Internet rumors could easily push the stock price higher, at least temporarily.

To protect against this type of fraud, avoid making any investment decisions until you have the facts at hand. Obtain the annual report of the firm to review general background information. Check credible news sources such as *The Wall Street Journal*. If you would rather not wait a day to read a financial newspaper, use trustworthy online services such as Bloomberg.com (www.bloomberg.com). However, be careful how you interpret news about a rumor. The news source may repeat a rumor, but will not necessarily confirm that the rumor is true. Another option is to check with a trusted financial adviser. As a general rule, be wary about promises of quick profits, "guaranteed" or limited-time opportunities, or investments based in foreign countries.

■ HOW INVESTMENTS FIT WITHIN YOUR FINANCIAL PLAN

The following are the key investment decisions that should be included within your financial plan:

▯ What are your investment goals?

▯ Given your existing budget, should you make investments?

▯ Based on your risk tolerance, how should you invest funds?

Exhibit 16.3 provides an example of how these decisions apply to Stephanie Spratt's financial plan.

Exhibit 16.3 How Investments Fit Within Stephanie Spratt's Financial Plan

GOALS FOR INVESTING

1. Determine my investment goals.
2. Determine whether to make investments.
3. Determine the types of investments that would achieve my investment goals.

ANALYSIS OF FUNDING

Monthly Cash Inflows	$2,500
– Typical Monthly Expenses	1,488
– Monthly Car Loan Payment	412
= Amount of Funds Available	$600

ANALYSIS OF POSSIBLE INVESTMENTS

Type of Investment	Assessment
1. CDs and Other Money Market Securities	Many money market securities provide good liquidity and are safe, but they typically offer low returns.

2. Stocks	*Can provide high returns, but are risky given the limited amount of funds I anticipate I will have for investing.*
3. Bonds	*Some bonds have low risk, but they offer lower potential returns than stocks.*
4. Real Estate	*The value of my home may increase over time. Additional real estate investments can generate high returns but are usually risky.*
5. Stock Mutual Funds	*Can provide high returns, and offer more diversification than investing in individual stocks, but can generate losses if stock market conditions are weak.*
6. Bond Mutual Funds	*Offer more diversification than investing in individual bonds, but can generate losses if bond market conditions are weak.*

DECISION

My primary investment goal is to maintain sufficient liquidity in any funds that I invest to cover any unanticipated expenses. However, I would like to earn a return on any funds that I have until they are needed to cover expenses.

After paying for my typical monthly expenses (not including recreation), I have $600 left each month. I am not in a financial position to make long-term investments at this time because I will use some of these funds each month for recreation and will deposit the remaining funds in liquid accounts such as a money market fund. I need to increase my liquidity since I might incur unexpected home repair expenses periodically. Beyond maintaining liquidity, I hope to save enough money to pay off my car loan early. Once I pay off that loan, I will reconsider whether to invest in riskier investments that have the potential to offer a higher return. My salary should also increase over time, which will make investments more affordable.

When I start long-term investing, I will consider stock mutual funds and bond mutual funds rather than individual stocks or bonds. I can periodically invest in mutual funds with small amounts of money and achieve diversification benefits. Since I already own a home, I do not want to invest in additional real estate.

DISCUSSION QUESTIONS

1. How would Stephanie's investing decisions be different if she were a single mother of two children?

2. How would Stephanie's investing decisions be affected if she were 35 years old? If she were 50 years old?

SUMMARY

- Common types of investments include money market securities, stocks, bonds, mutual funds, and real estate. Each type of investment is unique in how it provides a return to its investors.

- The return on an investment is determined by the income that the investment generates and the capital gain of the investment over the investment horizon. Some stocks offer periodic income in the form of dividends, while bonds offer periodic income in the form of coupon payments.

- The risk from making an investment varies among types of investments. In particular,

money market securities tend to have lower risk, while many stocks and real estate investments have higher risk. However, the risk also varies within a particular type of investment. Some money market securities have more risk than others. Some stocks have more risk than others.

- Investors weigh the trade-off between return and risk when making investments. When they select investments that have the potential to offer high returns, they must accept a higher degree of risk. Alternatively, they can select investments with lower risk, but they must accept a relatively low return. The proper choice is dependent on the investor's willingness to accept risk, which is influenced by the investor's financial position. Some investors are not in a financial position in which they can afford to take much risk, and should therefore select investments with little or no risk.

- You can learn from investment mistakes made by others. In particular, do not make investments that are driven by unrealistic goals. Do not invest when the funds could be more properly used to pay off existing debt. Do not attempt high-risk investments as a means of recovering recent losses. Recognize the risk of making investments that may be experiencing a speculative bubble.

REVIEW QUESTIONS

1. **Investing Priorities.** What should your first priority of investing be? What is the disadvantage of investments that satisfy that priority?

2. **Stocks.** What are stocks? How are stocks beneficial to corporations? Why do investors invest in stocks?

3. **Secondary Markets.** Distinguish between the primary and secondary stock markets. Why does the price of a stock change each day in the secondary market?

4. **Types of Investors.** Classify and describe the two types of investors. What are day traders?

5. **Return on Stocks.** How do shareholders earn returns from investing in stocks? How is the market value of a firm determined? What determines the market price of a stock?

6. **Dividends.** What type of firm typically pays dividends? What are growth stocks? What are income stocks?

7. **Dividends.** What are dividends? Do all firms pay them?

8. **Preferred Stock.** Discuss the differences between common stock and preferred stock.

9. **Bonds.** What are bonds? How do bonds provide a return to investors?

10. **Mutual Funds.** How do mutual funds operate? Who manages mutual funds? How are coupon or dividend payments handled by the mutual fund? Can investors incur capital losses with mutual funds?

11. **Real Estate Investment.** In what geographic areas is the price of land relatively high? What components make up the return from investing in real estate?

12. **Dividend-Paying Stocks.** What is the formula for estimating returns on dividend-paying stocks? Describe each element of the formula. How do you calculate the dollar amount of your returns?

13. **Capital Gains Taxes.** What is the difference in tax rates on long-term versus short-term capital gains?

14. **Investments in Stocks.** How can investments in stock increase your wealth? How would you calculate the value of a stock investment of a single sum over time? How would you calculate the value of a stock investment of a specific amount over several periods?

15. **Risk of Investments.** Define the risk of an investment. What types of firms are particularly risky?

16. **Measuring Risk.** Why do investors measure risk? Describe the two common measures of risk.

17. **Return-Risk Trade-Off.** What is the return-risk trade-off? What types of stock investments are particularly tempting for stock investors? What other factors must individual investors consider before making this type of investment?

18. **Risk among Investments.** Describe the return-risk trade-offs among bonds, mutual funds, and real estate investments.

19. **Diversification.** How can you limit your risk through diversification?

20. **Investment Mistakes.** Describe common investment mistakes made by individuals.

FINANCIAL PLANNING PROBLEMS

1. **Return on Stock.** Joel purchased 100 shares of stock for $20 per share. During the year, he received dividend checks amounting to $150. Joel recently sold the stock for $32 per share. What was Joel's return on the stock?

2. **Dollar Amount of Return.** What is the dollar amount of Joel's return (see problem 1)?

3. **Capital Gains Tax.** Joel (from problem 1) is in a 25 percent tax bracket. What amount of taxes will he pay on his capital gain if he held the stock for less than a year?

4. **Capital Gains Tax.** How much would Joel (from problem 1) save in taxes if he held the stock for more than a year, assuming he sold it for the same amount?

5. **Return on Stock.** Emma bought a stock a year ago for $53 per share. She received no dividends on the stock and sold the stock today for $38 per share. What is Emma's return on the stock?

6. **Value of Investment.** Tammy has $3,500 that she wants to invest in stock. She believes she can earn a 12 percent annual return. What would be the value of Tammy's investment in 10 years if she is able to achieve her goal?

7. **Value of Investment.** Dawn decides to invest $2,000 each year in stock at the end of each of the next five years. She believes she can earn a 9 percent return over that time period. How much will Dawn's investment be worth at the end of five years?

8. **Value of Investment.** Bob purchased a dot-com stock, which was heavily advertised on the Internet for $40 per share shortly after the stock's IPO. Over the next three years, the stock price declined by 15 percent each year. What is the company's stock price after three years?

9. **Value of Investment.** Floyd wants to invest the $15,000 he received from his grandfather's estate. He wants to use the money to finance his education when he pursues his doctorate in five years. What amount will he have in five years if he earns a 9 percent return? If he receives a 10 percent return? A 12 percent return?

10. **Value of Investment.** Morris will start investing $1,500 a year in stocks. He feels he can average a 12 percent return. If he follows this plan, how much will he accumulate in 5 years? In 10 years? In 20 years?

11. **Capital Gains Tax.** Thomas purchased 400 shares of stock A for $23 a share and sold them more than a year later for $20 per share. He purchased 500 shares of stock B for $40 per share and sold them for $53 per share after holding them for more than a year. Both of the sales were in the same year. If Thomas is in a 25 percent tax bracket, what will his capital gains tax be for the year?

12. **Capital Loss.** Charles just sold 500 shares of stock A for $12,000. In addition, he just sold 600 shares of stock A for $6,000. Charles had paid $20 per share for all his shares of stock A. What amount of loss will he have, assuming both sales were on stocks held for more than one year?

13. **ETHICAL DILEMMA:** Carlo and Rita's daughter just celebrated her 16th birthday and Carlo and Rita realize they have accumulated only half the money they will need for their daughter's college education. With college just two years away, they are concerned about how they will save the remaining amount in such a short time.

    Carlo regularly has lunch with Sam, a co-worker. While discussing his dilemma of financing his daughter's education, Sam tells Carlo about an investment that he made based on a tip from his cousin Leo that doubled his money in just over one year. Sam tells Carlo that Leo assured him there was very little risk involved. Carlo asks Sam if he will contact Leo to see if he has any additional hot tips that could double his daughter's college savings in two years with virtually no risk.

    The next day at lunch Sam gives Carlo the name of a stock that Leo recommended. It is a small start-up company that Leo believes will double within the next 24 months with virtually no risk. Carlo immediately invests his daughter's college fund in the stock of the company. Six months later, Carlo receives a letter from the company announcing they are out of business and closing their doors. Upon calling his broker, Carlo finds the stock is now worthless.

    a. Comment on Leo's ethics when assuring his friends and relatives that the investments he recommends can produce major rewards with virtually no risk.

    b. What basic investing principle did Carlo forget in his desire to fund his daughter's college education?

FINANCIAL PLANNING ONLINE EXERCISES

1. After going to www.renaissancecapital.com/IPOHome/Marketwatch.aspx, click "IPO Index" and answer the following questions:

    a. What was the best performing IPO and by what percentage had it increased?

b. What was the worst performing IPO and by what percentage had it declined?

c. What was the best performing sector and by what percentage had it increased?

d. What was the worst performing sector and by what percentage had it declined?

2. Enter the symbol of a stock you are interested in researching in the box next to "GET QUOTES" on the Web site finance.yahoo.com/ and answer the following questions:

a. What was the last price of the stock you looked up?

b. What is the P/E ratio of the stock?

c. Does the stock pay a dividend? If so, how much?

d. Click on "Headlines" under "News & Info." What were the date, title, and source of the most recent article about your stock?

VIDEO EXERCISE: Investing

Go to one of the Web sites that contain video clips (such as www.youtube.com) and review some video clips about investing. You can use search phrases such as "tips on investing." Select one video clip on this topic that you would recommend for the other students in your class.

1. Provide the Web link for the video clip.

2. What do you think is the main point of this video clip?

3. How might you change your process of investing as a result of watching this video clip?

BUILDING YOUR OWN FINANCIAL PLAN

Very likely, some of the goals you established in Chapter 8 can best be met through investing. Before taking the plunge into investing, however, you need to address a few questions. The first of these is to determine your risk tolerance. Not all investors have the "stomach" for the uncertainty surrounding returns on investments.

The next issue to be addressed is how different investments are suited to different goals. For example, a growth stock might be desirable if your goal is to build savings for a retirement that is 30 years away, while a certificate of deposit might be better suited to provide the down payment for a house within the next five years.

The decision as to what kind of investment is right for a particular goal should be reviewed annually. The closer a goal comes to fulfillment, the more likely it is that a change in investing strategy will be necessary.

Go to the worksheets at the end of this chapter, and to the CD-ROM accompanying this text, to continue building your financial plan.

THE SAMPSONS—A CONTINUING CASE

Recall that the Sampsons recently started saving about $300 per month ($3,600 per year) for their children's college education. They are currently investing this amount in bank CDs each month, but they are now considering investing in stock instead. Dave and Sharon have never owned stock before.

The Sampsons are currently earning an interest rate of 5 percent on their CDs. If they invest in a specific stock from this point on, they will achieve an annual return ranging from 2 to 9 percent. The stock will generate an annual return of only 2 percent if stock market conditions are weak in the future, but it could generate an annual return of 9 percent if stock market conditions are strong. The Sampsons want to compare the potential returns of investing in stock to the CDs.

Go to the worksheets at the end of this chapter, and to the CD-ROM accompanying this text, to continue this case.

Chapter 14: Building Your Own Financial Plan

GOALS

1. Determine whether to invest, given your current cash flows.

2. Determine what kinds of investments you should purchase to meet your financial goals.

ANALYSIS

1. Review your cash flow statement to determine how much you can afford to invest in stocks each month.

2. Evaluate your risk tolerance to see if your temperament is suited to the uncertainty of stock investments.

Risk Tolerance Quiz

Answer True or False by entering an X in the appropriate box.
(The Excel worksheet will offer an assessment based on your input.)

		TRUE	FALSE
1.	If I own stock, I will check its price at least daily if not more often.	☐	☐
2.	When driving on an interstate, and traffic and weather permit, I never drive in excess of the posted speed limit.	☐	☐
3.	If the price of my stock declines, my first reaction is to sell.	☐	☐
4.	Another stock market crash similar to 1929 could occur very unexpectedly.	☐	☐
5.	When I fly in less than perfect weather, I tend to get nervous and concerned about my safety.	☐	☐
6.	If I sold a stock at a loss of more than 25 percent, it would greatly shake my confidence in my ability to invest.	☐	☐
7.	I intensely dislike blind dates.	☐	☐
8.	When I travel, I write down a packing list to be sure that I don't forget anything.	☐	☐
9.	When traveling with others, I prefer to do the driving.	☐	☐
10.	Before buying a bond I would want to talk to at least two other people to confirm my choice.	☐	☐

Results

0–3   True: You have the risk tolerance to invest in individual common stocks.

4–6   True: You would be a nervous investor, but with more knowledge and a few successes, you could probably raise your risk tolerance to a suitable level. Mutual funds might prove a good starting point for your level of risk tolerance.

7–10   True: You are probably a very conservative and risk-intolerant investor who is probably better suited to a bond portfolio.

3. Determine whether investments will help you achieve your short-, intermediate-, and long-term goals. Complete the worksheet below for the short-, intermediate-, and long-term goals that you have established and reviewed throughout the course. In determining whether investing is suitable for each goal, take into consideration the timeline for accomplishing the goal, the critical nature of the goal, and, of course, the results of your risk tolerance test. For those goals that you determine investments are not suitable, enter "No" in column two, and leave the rest of the line blank for that goal. If, however, you enter "Yes" in column two, think about the kind of investment that is appropriate and justify your selection of stocks as a risk-appropriate means to accomplish this goal.

Short-Term Goals	Suitable? Yes or No	Type of Investment	Justification
1.			
2.			
3.			

Intermediate-Term Goals	Suitable? Yes or No	Type of Investment	Justification
1.			
2.			
3.			

Long-Term Goals	Suitable? Yes or No	Type of Investment	Justification
1.			
2.			
3.			

DECISIONS

1. Summarize your reasoning for either investing or not investing to meet your goals.

_____

_____

_____

2. If you decide to invest, how much will you invest each month? What types of investments will you purchase? Why?

_____

_____

_____

Chapter 14: The Sampsons—A Continuing Case

CASE QUESTIONS

1. Compare the returns from investing in bank CDs to the possible returns from stock over the next 12 years by filling in the following worksheet.

Savings Accumulated over the Next 12 Years

	CD: Annual Return = 5%	Weak Stock Market Conditions	Strong Stock Market Conditions
Amount Invested per Year	$3,600	$3,600	$3,600
Annual Return	5%	2%	9%
FVIFA (n = 12 Years)			
Value of Investments in 12 Years			

2. Explain to the Sampsons why there is a trade-off when investing in bank CDs versus stock to support their children's future college education.

_____

_____

_____

_____

3. Advise the Sampsons on whether they should invest their money each month in bank CDs, in stocks, or in some combination of the two, to save for their children's college education.

_____

_____

_____

_____

4. The Sampsons are considering investing in an IPO of a high-tech firm, since they have heard that the return on IPOs can be very high. Advise the Sampsons on this course of action.

_____

_____

_____

_____

Part V: Work

Chapters taken from:
Cornerstones for Professionalism, Second Edition
by Robert M. Sherfield and Patricia G. Moody

chapter seventeen

PRIORITIZE

STRATEGIES FOR MANAGING PRIORITIES AND STRESS

*If you want to make good use of your time,
you've got to know what's most important
and then give it all you've got.
—Lee Iacocca*

Why read this chapter?

Because you'll learn...

- The relationship between time management, your value system, and self-discipline
- How you spend your time and develop a "to do" list based on your findings
- How to deal with the major stressors in your life

Because you'll be able to...

- Simplify your life
- Avoid distractions, interruptions, and procrastination in your daily life

PROFESSIONALS from the Field

Name: F. Javier Ortiz B.

Business: Assistant VP, Citigroup

I have 40 people who report to me. I am responsible for completing my own job duties, but I must also do a performance review on all 40 employees every month. If I do not manage my time to do this accurately and fairly, I am not meeting my own position requirements. Time management is extremely important—from showing up on time to being able to manage multiple projects at the same time. My advice to you would be to watch your deadlines carefully so that you do not get overwhelmed. If you get overwhelmed, your job performance will suffer and before long, you won't have a job. Time management is that important at work.

TIME—YOU HAVE ALL THERE IS

Can You Take Control of Your Life and Make the Most of Your Time?

You can definitely say four things about time: *It is fair. It does not discriminate. It treats everyone the same. Everyone has all there is.* No person has any more or less hours in a day than the next person. It may seem that Gary or Tamisha has more time than you do, but that's not the case. In a 24-hour span we all have 1440 minutes. No more. No less. There is one more thing you can definitely say about time, too: *It can be cruel and unrelenting*. It is one of the few things in our lives that we cannot stop. There are no time-out periods, no breaks, and try as we might, we can't turn it back, shut it down, or stop it. The good news, however, is that by learning how to manage our time more effectively, we don't need to slow it down or stop it. We can learn how to get things done and have more time for joy and fun.

So, how do you spend your time? Some people are very productive, whereas others scramble to find a few moments to enjoy life and have quality relationships. According to time management and personal productivity expert Donald Wetmore (2008), "The average working person spends less than two minutes per day in meaningful communication with their spouse or significant other and less than 30 seconds per day in meaningful communication with their children." Think about that for a moment. *Thirty seconds.* If you think that is amazing, consider the following list. As strange as it may seem, these figures are taken from the U.S. Bureau of Labor Statistics (2006). During your **working years** (age 20–65, a 45-year span) you spend an average of:

- 16 years sleeping
- 2.3 years eating
- 3.1 years doing housework
- 6 years watching TV
- 1.3 years on the telephone

This totals **28.7 years of your working life** doing things that you may not even consider in your time management plan. What happens to the remaining 16.3 years? Well, you will spend **14 of those years working**, which leaves you with 2.3 years, or only 20,000 hours during your working life, to embrace joy, spend time with your family, educate yourself, travel, and experience a host of other life-fulfilling activities. Dismal? Scary? It does not have to be. By learning how to manage your time, harness your energy and passion, and take control of your day-to-day activities, 2.3 years can be a long, exciting, productive time.

Why is it that some people seem to get so much more done than other people? They appear to always be calm and collected and have it together. Many people from this group work long hours in addition to going to school and taking care of a family. They never appear to be stressed out, and they seem to be able to do it all with grace and charm.

You are probably aware of others who are always late, never finish their projects on time, rarely seem to have time to get everything done, and appear to have no concrete goals for their lives. Sometimes, we get the idea that the first group accomplishes more because they have more time or because they don't have to work or they don't have children or they are smarter or have more help. Some of these reasons may be true, but in reality, many of them have learned how to so, you make time for them. Do you value your friends? If so, you make time for them. Think about these questions: How much do you value having a career that you find fulfilling and rewarding? If you value your career, you will find time to devote toward making it successful. *We spend time on what we value!*

TIME MANAGEMENT AND SELF-DISCIPLINE

Do You Have What It Takes to "Git 'er Done"?

> *Self-discipline is teaching ourselves to do the things necessary to reach our goals without becoming sidetracked by bad habits.*
>
> —Denis Waitley

Time management is actually about managing you! It is about taking control and assuming responsibility for the time you are given on this earth. The sooner you understand and get control of how you use your time, the quicker you will be on your way to becoming successful in your career and many other activities. Learning to manage your time is a lesson that you will use in all aspects of your life. *You can't control time*, but you can control yourself. Time management is basically self-discipline—and self-discipline involves self-motivation

The word *discipline* comes from the Latin word meaning "to teach." Therefore, *self-discipline* is really about "teaching ourselves" (Waitley, 1997). Self-discipline implies that you have the ability to teach yourself how to get more done when things are going well and when they are not going so well. If you have self-discipline, you have learned how to hold it all together when things get tough, when you feel beaten, and when defeat seems just around the corner. It also means that when you have important tasks to complete, you can temporarily pull yourself away from enjoyable situations and fun times until those tasks are completed. Consider the chart in Figure 17.1 regarding self-discipline. **Self-discipline is really about four things: making choices, making changes, using willpower, and taking responsibility.**

Once you have made the *choice* to engage wholeheartedly in your work, stop procrastinating, and mange your time more effectively, you have to make the *changes* in your thoughts and behaviors to bring those choices to fruition. Then, you have to *accept responsibility* for your actions and take control of your life. You have to call on your *inner strength or willpower*—and you *do* have willpower. It may just be hidden or forgotten, but you do have it. You have the ability to empower yourself to get things done. No one can do this for you. You are responsible for your life and your actions. Self-discipline and willpower help you move in the direction of your dreams.

Willpower and self-discipline are all about *re-training your mind* to do what *you* want it to do and not what *it* wants to do. It is about eliminating the negative self-talk that so often derails us and causes us to procrastinate and get stressed out. By re-training your mind and resisting the urge to simply "obey" your subconscious, you are basically re-training your life. Consider the following situations:

- You come home from work, tired and weary, and you still have to finish a report for your boss by 8:00 a.m. tomorrow. Your subconscious mind tells you to sit down, put your feet up, and watch TV for a while. You have to tell your mind, "NO! I am going to take a short walk around the block to get my adrenaline flowing and then I'm going to write that report."

- You look at your desk or study space and you see all of the books and papers you have gathered for writing your report. Your subconscious mind tells you to just ignore it

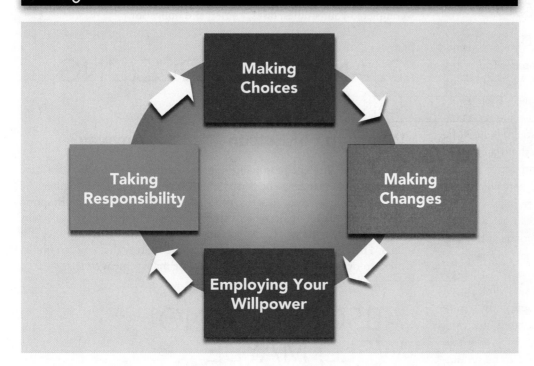

Figure 17.1 Components of Self-Discipline

for a while; there's still time to get it done! You have to tell your mind, "ABSOLUTELY NOT! I'm going to get those materials organized and finish this report before I do anything else so I can get it off my back."

By re-training your mind and paying attention to your subconscious, you can teach yourself to develop the self-discipline and willpower to get things done and avoid the stress caused by procrastination. Willpower gives you strength to stay on track and avoid the guilt associated with putting things off or not doing them at all. Guilt turns to frustration, frustration turns to anger, and before you know it, your negative self-talk and subconscious mind have "won" and nothing gets done. You have the power to change this.

> *Begin doing what you want to do now. We are not living in eternity. We have only this moment, sparkling like a star in our hand and melting like a snowflake.*
>
> —Marie B. Ray

I'LL DO IT WHEN I HAVE A LITTLE FREE TIME

Is Time Really "Free"?

What is "free time" and when does it happen? We've all used that expression at one time or another: "I'll do that when I get a little more free time," or "I'm going to wait until I find a little more time." Can time be found? Is time free? Do we ever have a moment to call our own? The answer is "maybe," but free time has to be created by you, and it can only be created by getting the things done that must be completed for your success.

Free time is *not* time that you simply create by putting off work that needs to be done. Free time is *not* time that is spent procrastinating. Free time is *not* time that you take away from your duties, chores, studies, family, and obligations. That is ***borrowed time,*** and if you know the rules of good behavior, you know that anything you borrow, you must repay. When are you going

BIGGEST INTERVIEW *Blunders*

Joaquim interviewed with a business owner of a large plumbing company. The owner interviewed him personally, explaining that he liked to know as much about every employee as possible. He gave Joaquim an intense interview. Joaquim thought he was doing very well until the owner asked him to take a pencil-and-paper test on managing priorities and handling stress. The test required him to prioritize 15 tasks and describe how he would get them accomplished in one day. Joaquim became very frustrated and stressed and finally told the owner that it was impossible to get the entire list done in one day. The owner responded, "This is a typical day's work for our associates; sometimes the work schedule is even heavier." The owner told Joaquim that he appeared to be an outstanding young man but recommended that he work as an apprentice until he learned to manage his time and priorities better.

LESSON: Try to be prepared for real-world activities that might be tested via simulations and other activities. Be sure to familiarize yourself with time and stress management techniques.

Time is the most valuable and most perishable of our possessions.

—John Randolph

to find the time to "repay" these blocks of time to yourself? Usually, you don't, and that is when and where you get into trouble and your stress level starts to rise. Free time *is* time that you reward yourself with when you have completed your studies, tasks, chores, and obligations.

PLANNING, DOODLING, OR BEGGING

What Type of Person Are You, Anyway?

We all have different personality types, but did you know we also have different time management personalities? Consider the list in Figure 17.2 explaining the different negative time management personalities. Respond YES or NO to each management style. Then, out to the side, explain why you think this type represents you and your daily thoughts on time, if it does. Then, in the last column, list at least one strategy that you can implement to overcome this type of negative time management style.

ABSOLUTELY NO . . . WELL, MAYBE

Do You Know How to Say No?

"No, I'm sorry, I can't do that," is perhaps one of the most difficult phrases you must learn to say when it comes to effective time management, but learning it is absolutely essential." If you continually say yes to everyone and every project, then quickly, you will have no time left for yourself, your family, your friends, and your projects. Many of us are taught from an early age that *no* is a bad word and that we should always try to avoid saying it to others. However, we are not taught that never saying "no" can cause us undue stress and feelings of guilt and frustration, as well as throw our time management plans into disarray. The word *no* needs to become a part of your everyday vocabulary. By learning to say "no" to a few things, you can begin to say "yes" to many other things—things that you want to do, things that you need to do, things that will help others in the long run, and goals and priorities at work that will help you get ahead. "No" is not rude; it is simply a way of managing your time so that you have more time to say "yes" to what is important and useful.

Learning to Say No: It's as Simple as Not Saying Yes

- Think before you answer out loud with an insincere or untrue "yes." Tell the person who is asking that you need time to think about it because you are already stretched pretty thin. Don't make an immediate decision. Buy yourself some time to think before you take on something that is going to stress you.

- Make sure you understand exactly what is being asked of you and what the project involves before you answer.

- Review your schedule to see if you really have the time to do a quality job. ("If you have to have an answer immediately, it is 'no.' If you can wait a few days for me to finish project X, and review my schedule, I'll take a careful look at it.")

Figure 17.2 Time Management Types

Type	Explanation	Do You Have Any of These Tendencies?	What Actions Make You Like This Type of Person?	What Can You Do to Begin Eliminating This Type of Behavior?
The Circler	Doing the same things over and over again and again and hoping for a different result; basically, going around in circles.	YES NO		
The Doodler	Not paying attention to details, doing things that do not really matter to the completion of your project.	YES NO		
The Squanderer	Wasting too much time trying to "get ready" to work and never really getting anything done until it is too late to do a good job.	YES NO		
The Beggar	Expecting time to stop for you after you've wasted time doing nothing or going in circles, then becoming frustrated when you don't have enough time.	YES NO		
The Planner	Planning out your project so carefully and meticulously that by the time you have everything you think you need, there is no time to really do the project.	YES NO		
The Hun	Waiting too late to plan or get things done and then stomping on anyone or anything to get the project done with no regard for others' feelings, time, or relationships.	YES NO		
The Passivist	Convincing yourself that you'll never get it all done and that there is no use to try anyway.	YES NO		

How can becoming a more organized person help you manage your time more effectively?

Shutterstock

- Learn the difference between assertiveness (politely declining) and rudeness ("Have you lost your mind?").

- Learn how to put yourself and your future first (for a change). By doing this, you can say "yes" more often later on.

- Inform others of your time management schedule so that they will have a better understanding of why you say "no."

- If you must say "yes" to an unwanted project (something at work, for example), try to negotiate a deadline that works for everyone—you first!

- Keep your "no" short. If you have to offer an explanation, be brief so that you don't talk yourself into doing something you can't do and to avoid giving false hope to the other person. If the answer is "no" right now and it will be "no" in the future, say so now. Don't smile, because that indicates "maybe."

- If you feel you simply have to say "yes," try to trade off with the other person and ask him or her to do something on your list.

- Put a time limit on your "yes." For example, you might agree to help someone but you could say, "I can give you 30 minutes and then I have to leave."

BEGINNING YOUR DAY WITH PEACE

Can You Start Your Day as a Blank Page and Simplify Your Life?

Imagine a day with nothing to do! That may be difficult, if not impossible, for you to conceive right now. But as an exercise in building your own day from scratch and simplifying your life, think about having a day where you build your schedule and where you do not have to be constrained by activities and projects that others have thrust on you. Think about a day where you are in charge. Crazy? Impossible? Outrageous? Maybe not as much as you think.

Yes, you will need to plot activities such as work, training, and family duties into your daily calendar, but you also need to learn how to schedule time for fun activities, time for silence and peace, and time to be alone with your thoughts. By learning how to build your schedule each evening from scratch, you have the opportunity to plan a day where you simplify your life. There is an old quote that states, "If you want to know what you value in your life, look at your checkbook and your calendar." Basically, this suggests that we spend our money and time on things we value.

12 Ways to Simplify Your Life

- Know what you value and work hard to eliminate activities that are not in conjunction with your core value system. This can be whittled down to one statement: "Identify what is important to you. Eliminate everything else." Match your priorities with your goals and values.

- Get away from technology for a few hours a day. Turn off your computer, cell phone, iPod, and other devices that can take time from what you value.

- Learn to delegate. You may say to yourself, "My family does not know how to use the washing machine." Guess what? When all of their underwear is dirty, they'll learn how to use it. Don't enable others to avoid activities that complicate your life.

- Make a list of everything you are doing. Prioritize this list into what you enjoy doing and what fits into your value system. If you can only feasibly do three or four of these activities per day, draw a line after number four and eliminate the rest of the list.

- Do what is essential for the well-being of you and your family and eliminate everything else. Delegate some things to family members of all ages that they can accomplish. Don't waste time saving money. This doesn't mean not to save money—it means not to be "penny wise and pound foolish." Spend money to save time. In other words, don't drive across town to save three cents per gallon on fuel or 10 cents for a gallon of milk. Pay the extra money and have more time to do what you like.

- Clean your home of clutter and mess. Make sure everything has a place. Do the same thing at work. Get rid of things you don't need.

What is most important in your life? Do you spend some of your time with the people and activities that you truly value?

Shutterstock

- Donate everything you don't need or use to charity. Simplifying your life may also mean simplifying your closets, drawers, cabinets, and garage. If we are not careful, we are soon possessed by our possessions.

- Go through your home or apartment and eliminate everything that does not bring you joy or have sentimental value. If you don't love it or need it or use it, ditch it.

- Clean up the files on your computer. Erase everything that you don't need or want so that you can find material more easily. If you have not used the file in a month, put it on a flash drive for later use.

- Live in the moment. Yes, it is important to plan for the future, but if you ignore "the moment," your future will not be as bright. Although it is important to plan for the future, it is equally important to live today!

- Spend a few moments each morning and afternoon reflecting on all of the abundance in your life. Learn to give thanks and learn to do nothing. Count your blessings. (Adapted from Zen Habits, 2008; and Baca, 2009)

In Figure 17.3, compile a list that can help you simplify your life in each category. Add only those things to the list that you can actually do on a daily basis.

THE DREADED "P" WORD

Why Is Procrastination So Easy to Do and How Can You Beat It Once and for All?

It's not just you! Almost all of us procrastinate, and then we worry and tell ourselves, "I'll never do it again if I can just get through this one project." We say things to ourselves like, "If I can just live through this project, I will never wait until the last minute again." But someone comes along with a great idea for fun, and off we go. Or there is a great movie on TV, the kids want to play a game of ball, you go to the refrigerator for snack, and before you know it, you reward yourself with free time before you have done your work. You have to work first; then reward yourself with play.

> *If you have to eat two frogs, eat the ugliest one first.*
> —Brian Tracy

The truth is simple: We tend to avoid the hard jobs in favor of the easy ones. Even many of the list makers fool themselves. They mark off a long list of easy tasks while the big ones still loom in front of them. Many of us put off unpleasant tasks until our back is against the

Figure 17.3 Ways to Simplify Your Life

| Two things I can do to simplify my life at home |
| Two things I can do to simplify my life at work |
| Two things I can do to simplify my life with technology (using cell phones, texting, etc.) |
| Two things I can do to simplify my life with my children, friends, or pets |
| Two things I can do to simplify my life with my spouse/partner/loved one |
| Two things I can do to simplify my financial matters |

> *Don't wait. The time will never be just right.*
> —*Napoleon Hill*

POSITIVE HABITS *at Work*

Make it a habit never to go home from work until you have made your to do list for the next day. Although you may be tired, you will be able to begin work immediately the next morning, and this will put you way ahead of the average employee, who leaves without thinking about the next day. Being prepared and organized is also a great stress reliever.

wall. So why do we procrastinate when we all know how unpleasant the results can be? Why aren't we disciplined, organized, and controlled so we can reap the rewards that come from being prepared? Why do we put ourselves through so much stress just by putting things off?

The biggest problem with procrastination, even beyond not getting the job, task, or paper completed, is *doing it poorly* and then suffering the stress caused by putting it off and not doing our best work. By putting the project off, you have cheated yourself of the time needed to bring your best to the table. Most likely, you are going to hand over a project, *with your name on it,* that is not even close to your potential. If you know your work is not good, so will your boss and your colleagues.

What has procrastination cost you? This is perhaps one of the most important questions that you can answer with regard to managing your time more effectively. Did it cost you an opportunity to look good in the eyes of your boss? Did it cost you money? Did it cost you your reputation? Did it cost you your dignity? Did it cost you your ability to do your best? Did it cost you a friend? **Procrastination is not free.** Every time you do it, it costs you something. You need to determine what it is worth.

In order to beat procrastination, you will also need to consider **what type** of procrastinator you are. Each type requires a different strategy and different energy to overcome, but make no mistake about it, success requires overcoming all degrees and types of procrastination. Which are you? Consider Figure 17.4.

Take a moment and complete the Time Management Assessment in Figure 17.5. Be honest and truthful with your responses. The results of your score are located after the assessment.

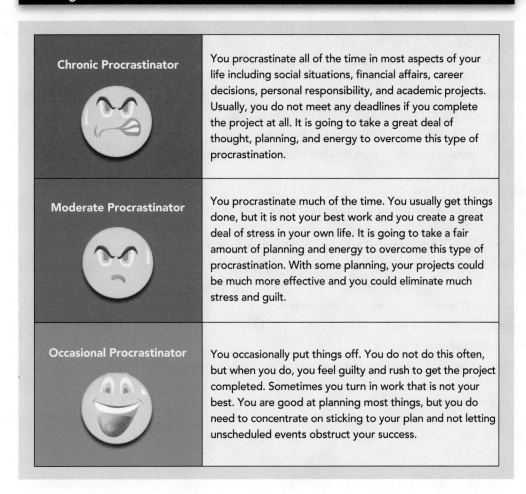

Figure 17.4 Procrastinator Types

Chronic Procrastinator	You procrastinate all of the time in most aspects of your life including social situations, financial affairs, career decisions, personal responsibility, and academic projects. Usually, you do not meet any deadlines if you complete the project at all. It is going to take a great deal of thought, planning, and energy to overcome this type of procrastination.
Moderate Procrastinator	You procrastinate much of the time. You usually get things done, but it is not your best work and you create a great deal of stress in your own life. It is going to take a fair amount of planning and energy to overcome this type of procrastination. With some planning, your projects could be much more effective and you could eliminate much stress and guilt.
Occasional Procrastinator	You occasionally put things off. You do not do this often, but when you do, you feel guilty and rush to get the project completed. Sometimes you turn in work that is not your best. You are good at planning most things, but you do need to concentrate on sticking to your plan and not letting unscheduled events obstruct your success.

GETTING THE MOST OUT OF THIS MOMENT

Do You Know the Causes of and Cures for Procrastination?

Below, you will find a list of the 10 most common causes of procrastination and some simple, doable, everyday strategies that you can employ to overcome each cause.

Superhuman Expectations and Trying to Be a Perfectionist

- Allow yourself more time than you think you need to complete a project.
- Allow enough time to do your very best and let that be that. If you plan and allow time for excellence, you can't do more.

Fear of Not Knowing How to Do the Task

- Ask for clarification from whomever asked you to do the project.
- Read as much as you can about the task at hand and ask for help.
- Break up big tasks into small ones.

Figure 17.5 Time Management Assessment

Answer the following questions with the following scale:

1 = Not at all   2 = Rarely   3 = Sometimes   4 = Often   5 = Very often

1.	I prioritize my tasks every day and work from my priority list.	1 2 3 4 5
2.	I work hard to complete tasks on time and not put them off until the last minute.	1 2 3 4 5
3.	I take time to plan and schedule the next day's activities the night before.	1 2 3 4 5
4.	I make time during my daily schedule to organize, plan, and get my projects completed so that I can have more quality time at home.	1 2 3 4 5
5.	I get my work done before I take fun breaks.	1 2 3 4 5
6.	I analyze my assignments to determine which ones are going to take the most time and then work on them first and most often.	1 2 3 4 5
7.	I have analyzed my daily activities and determined where I actually spend my time.	1 2 3 4 5
8.	I know how to say "no" and do so frequently.	1 2 3 4 5
9.	I know how to avoid distractions and how to work through unexpected interruptions.	1 2 3 4 5
10.	I do not let "fear of the unknown" keep me from working on a project.	1 2 3 4 5
11.	I know how to overcome apathy and/or laziness.	1 2 3 4 5
12.	I always tackle the difficult and most important jobs first.	1 2 3 4 5
13.	I know how to reframe a project that may not interest me so that I can see the benefit in it and learn from it.	1 2 3 4 5
14.	I know how to break down a major, complex, or overwhelming task to get it done in pieces and then put it all together.	1 2 3 4 5
15.	I build time into my schedule on a daily or weekly basis to deal with unexpected interruptions or distractions.	1 2 3 4 5

YOUR TOTAL SCORE: _____

RESULTS:		
	60–75	You manage your time well and you know how to build a schedule to get things done. Your productivity is high. You don't let procrastination rule your life.
	45–59	You are good at doing some things on time, but you tend to procrastinate too much. Learning how to build and work from a priority list may help you manage your time more effectively.
	30–44	You need to work hard to change your time management skills and learn how to set realistic goals. Procrastination is probably a major issue for you, causing you much stress and worry. Working from a priority list can help you greatly.
	29–below	Your time management skills are very weak and without improvement, your career could be in jeopardy. You could benefit from learning to set realistic goals, working from a priority list, and reframing your thought process toward tasks.

Lack of Motivation

- Reframe your attitude to find the benefit in any task.
- Consider how this task will help you reach your overall goals and dreams.
- Take time to do the things you love, creating a healthy balance in your life.

Fear of Failing or Fear of the Task Being Too Hard

- Start the project with positive, optimistic thoughts.
- Face your fears; look them right in the face and make a decision to defeat them.
- Visualize your successful completion of the project.

No Real Plan or Goal for Getting the Task Done

- Set reasonable, concrete goals that you can reach in about 20 to 25 minutes.
- Draw up an action plan the night before you begin the project.
- Look at completing the project in terms of your long-range goals and your overall life plan.

Considering the Task Too Unpleasant or Uninteresting

- Realize that most tasks are not as unpleasant as we've made them out to be.
- Do the hardest tasks first, and save the easiest for last.
- Schedule tasks that you consider unpleasant to be done during your peak hours.

Laziness and/or Apathy

- Concentrate on the rewards of managing yourself and your time more effectively.
- Give yourself a time limit to accomplish a task.

Distractions and/or Lack of Focus

- Close your door and make yourself get started. Turn your desk away from the door, and people are less likely to interrupt you.
- Start on the difficult, most boring tasks first.
- Weed out your personal belongings and living space. Organization helps you manage your time and get to work.

Choosing Fun Before Responsibility

- Reward yourself when you have accomplished an important body of work.
- Don't get involved in too many organizations, accept too many commitments, or overextend yourself. Allow enough time to concentrate on what needs to be done.
- Consider the consequences of not doing what you're responsible for doing.

Waiting for the "Right" Mood

- Avoid whining and complaining, and realize that the right mood can be created by you at any time.
- Just do it! Force yourself to jump into the task.
- Work during your peak hours of the day.

EVALUATING HOW YOU SPEND YOUR TIME

Do You Know Where Your Time Goes?

So how do you find out where your time goes? The same way that you find out where your money goes—you track it. Every 15 minutes for one week, you will record exactly how you spent that time. This exercise may seem a little tedious at first, but if you will complete the process over a period of a week, you will have a much better concept of where your time is being used. Yes, that's right—for a week, you need to keep a written record of how much time you spend sleeping, reading, eating, working, getting to class and back, cooking, caring for children, walking pets, watching television, doing yard work, going to movies, attending athletic events, hanging out, doing laundry, whatever. You will probably be surprised at where your time really goes.

Take your plan with you and keep track of your activities during the day. To make things simple, round off tasks to 15-minute intervals. For example, if you start walking to the cafeteria at 7:08, you might want to mark off the time block that begins with 7:00. If you finish eating

GRADUATE *Quote*

Christian Garcia
Graduate!
UEI College, Ontario, CA
Career: Associate Director of Education,
UEI College

My advice to anyone in college would be to love what you do. If you truly love what you do, then the old quote is true: "You'll never have to work a day in your life." This is how I feel every day. I actually tell my friends that I stopped working in 1999 because I found my joy—my passion. I would also say that you have to seek opportunities because they usually do not come to you; you have to go to them.

and return to your home at 7:49, you can mark off the next two blocks. You will also want to note the activity so you can evaluate how you spent your time later. Study the example that is provided for you in Figure 17.6.

In Figure 17.7 you will find a daily time log for you to use for this exercise. Remember to take these pages with you and record how you are spending your time during the day. As you progress through the week, try to improve the use of your time. When you finish this exercise, review how you spent your time.

Figure 17.6 How You Really Spend Your Time

7:00	get up	7:00			12:15
	& shower	7:15			12:30
	✕	7:30	Walked to Union		12:45
	Breakfast	7:45	1:00	Ate lunch	1:00
8:00		8:00			1:15
		8:15			1:30
	Read paper	8:30		Talked w/ Joe	1:45
	Walked to class	8:45	2:00		2:00
9:00	English 101	9:00		Went to book	2:15
		9:15		store	2:30
		9:30		Walked to	2:45
		9:45	3:00	my room	3:00
10:00		10:00		Called Ron	3:15
		10:15			3:30
		10:30			3:45
	Walked to class	10:45	4:00	Watched	4:00
11:00	History 210	11:00		TV	4:15
		11:15			4:30
		11:30		Walked to	4:45
		11:45	5:00	library	5:00
12:00		12:00			5:15

Figure 17.7 Daily Time Sheet

Monday		Tuesday		Wednesday	
6:00	6:00	6:00	6:00	6:00	6:00
	6:15		6:15		6:15
	6:30		6:30		6:30
	6:45		6:45		6:45
7:00	7:00	7:00	7:00	7:00	7:00
	7:15		7:15		7:15
	7:30		7:30		7:30
	7:45		7:45		7:45
8:00	8:00	8:00	8:00	8:00	8:00
	8:15		8:15		8:15
	8:30		8:30		8:30
	8:45		8:45		8:45
9:00	9:00	9:00	9:00	9:00	9:00
	9:15		9:15		9:15
	9:30		9:30		9:30
	9:45		9:45		9:45
10:00	10:00	10:00	10:00	10:00	10:00
	10:15		10:15		10:15
	10:30		10:30		10:30
	10:45		10:45		10:45
11:00	11:00	11:00	11:00	11:00	11:00
	11:15		11:15		11:15
	11:30		11:30		11:30
	11:45		11:45		11:45
12:00	12:00	12:00	12:00	12:00	12:00
	12:15		12:15		12:15
	12:30		12:30		12:30
	12:45		12:45		12:45
1:00	1:00	1:00	1:00	1:00	1:00
	1:15		1:15		1:15
	1:30		1:30		1:30
	1:45		1:45		1:45
2:00	2:00	2:00	2:00	2:00	2:00
	2:15		2:15		2:15
	2:30		2:30		2:30
	2:45		2:45		2:45
3:00	3:00	3:00	3:00	3:00	3:00
	3:15		3:15		3:15
	3:30		3:30		3:30
	3:45		3:45		3:45
4:00	4:00	4:00	4:00	4:00	4:00
	4:15		4:15		4:15
	4:30		4:30		4:30
	4:45		4:45		4:45
5:00	5:00	5:00	5:00	5:00	5:00
	5:15		5:15		5:15
	5:30		5:30		5:30
	5:45		5:45		5:45
6:00	6:00	6:00	6:00	6:00	6:00
	6:15		6:15		6:15
	6:30		6:30		6:30
	6:45		6:45		6:45
7:00	7:00	7:00	7:00	7:00	7:00
	7:15		7:15		7:15
	7:30		7:30		7:30
	7:45		7:45		7:45
8:00	8:00	8:00	8:00	8:00	8:00
	8:15		8:15		8:15
	8:30		8:30		8:30
	8:45		8:45		8:45
9:00	9:00	9:00	9:00	9:00	9:00
	9:15		9:15		9:15
	9:30		9:30		9:30
	9:45		9:45		9:45
10:00	10:00	10:00	10:00	10:00	10:00
	10:15		10:15		10:15
	10:30		10:30		10:30
	10:45		10:45		10:45
11:00	11:00	11:00	11:00	11:00	11:00
	11:15		11:15		11:15
	11:30		11:30		11:30
	11:45		11:45		11:45
12:00	12:00	12:00	12:00	12:00	12:00

(continued)

Figure 17.7 Daily Time Sheet (continued)

Thursday		Friday		Saturday		Sunday	
6:00	6:00	6:00	6:00	6:00	6:00	6:00	6:00
	6:15		6:15		6:15		6:15
	6:30		6:30		6:30		6:30
	6:45		6:45		6:45		6:45
7:00	7:00	7:00	7:00	7:00	7:00	7:00	7:00
	7:15		7:15		7:15		7:15
	7:30		7:30		7:30		7:30
	7:45		7:45		7:45		7:45
8:00	8:00	8:00	8:00	8:00	8:00	8:00	8:00
	8:15		8:15		8:15		8:15
	8:30		8:30		8:30		8:30
	8:45		8:45		8:45		8:45
9:00	9:00	9:00	9:00	9:00	9:00	9:00	9:00
	9:15		9:15		9:15		9:15
	9:30		9:30		9:30		9:30
	9:45		9:45		9:45		9:45
10:00	10:00	10:00	10:00	10:00	10:00	10:00	10:00
	10:15		10:15		10:15		10:15
	10:30		10:30		10:30		10:30
	10:45		10:45		10:45		10:45
11:00	11:00	11:00	11:00	11:00	11:00	11:00	11:00
	11:15		11:15		11:15		11:15
	11:30		11:30		11:30		11:30
	11:45		11:45		11:45		11:45
12:00	12:00	12:00	12:00	12:00	12:00	12:00	12:00
	12:15		12:15		12:15		12:15
	12:30		12:30		12:30		12:30
	12:45		12:45		12:45		12:45
1:00	1:00	1:00	1:00	1:00	1:00	1:00	1:00
	1:15		1:15		1:15		1:15
	1:30		1:30		1:30		1:30
	1:45		1:45		1:45		1:45
2:00	2:00	2:00	2:00	2:00	2:00	2:00	2:00
	2:15		2:15		2:15		2:15
	2:30		2:30		2:30		2:30
	2:45		2:45		2:45		2:45
3:00	3:00	3:00	3:00	3:00	3:00	3:00	3:00
	3:15		3:15		3:15		3:15
	3:30		3:30		3:30		3:30
	3:45		3:45		3:45		3:45
4:00	4:00	4:00	4:00	4:00	4:00	4:00	4:00
	4:15		4:15		4:15		4:15
	4:30		4:30		4:30		4:30
	4:45		4:45		4:45		4:45
5:00	5:00	5:00	5:00	5:00	5:00	5:00	5:00
	5:15		5:15		5:15		5:15
	5:30		5:30		5:30		5:30
	5:45		5:45		5:45		5:45
6:00	6:00	6:00	6:00	6:00	6:00	6:00	6:00
	6:15		6:15		6:15		6:15
	6:30		6:30		6:30		6:30
	6:45		6:45		6:45		6:45
7:00	7:00	7:00	7:00	7:00	7:00	7:00	7:00
	7:15		7:15		7:15		7:15
	7:30		7:30		7:30		7:30
	7:45		7:45		7:45		7:45
8:00	8:00	8:00	8:00	8:00	8:00	8:00	8:00
	8:15		8:15		8:15		8:15
	8:30		8:30		8:30		8:30
	8:45		8:45		8:45		8:45
9:00	9:00	9:00	9:00	9:00	9:00	9:00	9:00
	9:15		9:15		9:15		9:15
	9:30		9:30		9:30		9:30
	9:45		9:45		9:45		9:45
10:00	10:00	10:00	10:00	10:00	10:00	10:00	10:00
	10:15		10:15		10:15		10:15
	10:30		10:30		10:30		10:30
	10:45		10:45		10:45		10:45
11:00	11:00	11:00	11:00	11:00	11:00	11:00	11:00
	11:15		11:15		11:15		11:15
	11:30		11:30		11:30		11:30
	11:45		11:45		11:45		11:45
12:00	12:00	12:00	12:00	12:00	12:00	12:00	12:00

ELIMINATING DISTRACTIONS AND INTERRUPTIONS

When Is Enough Really Enough?

If you were diligent and kept an accurate account of all of your time, your evaluation will probably reveal that much of your time is spent dealing with distractions, getting side-tracked, and handling interruptions. These three things account for much of the time wasted within a 24-hour period. In Figure 17.8, you will find a list of some of the most common distractions

Figure 17.8 Common Distractions

Common Distractions	My Plan to Overcome These Distractions
Friends/family dropping by unexpectedly at home	
Colleagues stopping by your work space and talking when you are trying to work	
Working on small, unimportant tasks while the big, career-changing jobs go undone or get done poorly	
Spending too much time on breaks and at lunch when you should be working	
Taking time to read mindless e-mails and jokes sent by people who have nothing else to do	
Technology (playing on YouTube, Facebook, iTunes, Google, etc.)	
Constant phone calls that do not pertain to anything of importance	
Not setting aside any time during the day to deal with the unexpected	
Friends/family demanding things of you because they do not understand your schedule or commitments	
Not blocking private time in your daily schedule	
Being disorganized and spending hours piddling and calling it "work"	
Playing with your children or pets before your tasks are complete (and not scheduling time to be with them in the first place)	
Saying "yes" when you need to say "no"	
Other distractions faced by you	

faced by people who are pursuing a career. Consider how you might deal with these distractions in an effective, assertive manner.

PLANNING AND PREPARING

Is There a Secret to Time Management?

In the past, you may have said to yourself, "I don't have time to plan." "I don't like to be fenced in and tied to a rigid schedule." "I have so many duties that planning never works." Scheduling does not have to be a tedious chore or something you dread. Scheduling can be your lifeline to more free time. After all, if you build your own schedule, it is yours! As much as you are able, build your schedule the way you want and need it.

To manage your time successfully, you need to spend some time planning. To plan successfully, you need a calendar that has a week-at-a-glance or month-at-a-glance section as well as sections for daily notes and appointments. Most companies will furnish a calendar, but it they don't, you can download one from the Internet or create one using Word or another computer program.

Planning and Organizing for Work

Each evening, you should take a few minutes (and literally, that is all it will take) and sit in a quiet place and make a list of all that needs to be done tomorrow. Successful time management comes from **planning the night before!** Let's say your list looks like the one in Figure 17.9.

Next, separate this list into three categories, as shown in Figure 17.10.

Don't get too excited yet. Your time management plan is *not finished.* The most important part is still ahead of you. Now, you will need to rank the items in order of their importance. You will put a 1 by the most important tasks, a 2 by the next most important tasks, and so on in each category, as shown in Figure 17.11.

You have now created a plan to actually get these tasks done! Not only have you created your list, but now you have divided the tasks into important categories, ranked them, and made a written commitment to them.

Figure 17.9 To Do List

To Do List

Research procurement project	Exercise
Write report for supervisor— due next week	Go to movie
	Buy birthday card for Mom
Prepare for next training class two days from now	Wash the car
	Take shirts to dry cleaner
Schedule team mtg. at work	Buy groceries
Attend department meeting at 8:00 a.m.	Call Janice about weekend
Meet with supervisor at 10:00 a.m.	

Figure 17.10 Setting Priorities for To Do List

Must Do	Need to Do	Would Like to Do
Prepare for training class	Research procurement project	Wash the car
Exercise	Buy birthday card for Mom	Call Janice about weekend
Schedule team meeting at work	Take shirts to cleaner	Go to movie
Department meeting at 8:00 a.m.	Buy groceries	
Meeting with supervisor at 10:00 a.m.	Write report for supervisor	

Figure 17.11 Ranking Priorities for To Do List

Must Do	Need to Do	Would Like to Do
4 Prepare for training class	1 Research procurement project	3 Wash the car
5 Exercise	5 Buy birthday card for Mom	1 Call Janice about weekend
3 Schedule team meeting at work	4 Take shirts to cleaner	2 Go to movie
1 Department meeting at 8:00 a.m.	3 Buy groceries	
2 Meeting with supervisor at 10:00 a.m.	2 Write report for supervisor	

If these were real tasks, you would now schedule them into your daily calendar (see Figure 17.12). You would schedule category 1 (MUST DO) first, category 2 (NEED TO DO) next, and category 3 (WOULD LIKE TO DO) last. Remember, never keep more than one calendar. Always carry it with you and always schedule your tasks immediately so that you won't forget them.

Great Tips for New Employees

Good time management often boils down to doing a few things extremely well and doing them over and over. When you go to work, the big things count—but so do the little ones! If you have a family, you will need to be highly organized so you can spend quality time with them.

- Break up big jobs into little ones so they don't overwhelm you.
- Allow yourself enough time to complete a task with a few extra minutes, in case there is a glitch. Work expands to fill up whatever amount of time you have, so push yourself to complete the job in a reasonable time frame.

Figure 17.12　Daily Calendar

DAY	Monday		Priority	Complete?
Time	**Task**			
6:00				__Yes__No
6:30				__Yes__No
7:00	Study for finance			__Yes__No
7:30	↓			__Yes__No
8:00	English 101			__Yes__No
8:30				__Yes__No
9:00	↓			__Yes__No
9:30	Read Pg. 1–10 of Chem. Chapter			__Yes__No
10:00	Management 210			__Yes__No
10:30				__Yes__No
11:00	↓			__Yes__No
11:30	Finish Reading Chem. Chapter			__Yes__No
12:00				__Yes__No
12:30	↓			__Yes__No
1:00	Meet w/Chemistry group (take lunch)			__Yes__No
1:30	↓			__Yes__No
2:00	Work			__Yes__No
2:30				__Yes__No
3:00				__Yes__No
3:30				__Yes__No
4:00				__Yes__No
4:30				__Yes__No
5:00				__Yes__No
5:30				__Yes__No
6:00	↓			__Yes__No
6:30	Dinner/run by grocery store			__Yes__No
7:00	↓			__Yes__No
7:30	Internet Research for speech			__Yes__No
8:00				__Yes__No
8:30	↓			__Yes__No
9:00	call Janice @ w/end			__Yes__No
9:30				__Yes__No

- If you are still taking courses or working on another degree, set up a regular time to study and stick to it.
- When you have a project, set reasonable goals that you can meet in 20- to 25-minute blocks.
- Take short breaks; get up from your computer and move around. Leave your desk for lunch and breaks; you'll come back refreshed. Don't ever eat lunch at your desk unless you have to.
- Allow yourself longer than you think you need for a project so you don't have to stay up all night.
- Avoid having to cram for school or work projects by starting early.
- Don't get too involved with outside organizations and commitments that steal your time and make you look slack at work.

- Start on the most difficult, boring jobs first. Reward yourself with something you enjoy after you have completed a good block of work.

- Weed out personal belongings; get rid of clutter that takes your time. Streamline your house, your workspace, your home desk, and your garage.

- File things as you go; don't pile them in stacks. Don't allow yourself to be one of those people who would rather "pile than file," because you will never be able to find important documents.

- If you have children, give each one a workspace with his or her own supplies. Give each child a file drawer or box to keep important papers that he or she will need again. You are teaching your children time management and organization skills.

- Handle paperwork immediately and only once.

- Organize your workspace and designate a specific place for your supplies. Keep supplies on hand so you don't run out at a crucial time.

- Prepare to be successful at work or school by getting ready the evening before. Decide what you are going to wear; press your clothes if they need it; polish your shoes.

- Keep a Rolodex file, iPod, or other system for important phone numbers and addresses you use frequently.

- Organize as effectively at home as you do at work.

- Plan a rotation schedule for housework. Clean one room each day.

- Organize your closets and dresser drawers, ridding yourself of clutter and things you don't use anymore.

- Fill up your gas tank the night before to avoid stress in the morning.

- If you are a perfectionist, get over it! Some things need to be perfect, but most don't.

- Take time to do things you love and create a healthy balance in your life. If you reward the completion of a big job by immediately beginning another big job, you have a good chance of becoming a workaholic.

- If you have children, schedule at least one hour a week with each one. Make this a happy, special time. Sunday nights are great for family night.

- Make family meals happy. Sit down together at least three times a week. Let the children help prepare the meal and set the table. Allow each person to tell about his or her day.

- Put fun days on your calendar and keep them sacred.

- Put family days on your calendar and have everyone help get things done so you can have a great family event.

STRESS? I DON'T HAVE ENOUGH TIME FOR STRESS!

Do You Feel Like You're Going to Explode?

The word *stress* is derived from the Latin word *strictus,* meaning "to draw tight." Stress is your body's response to people and events in your life; it is the mental and physical wear and tear on your body as a result of everyday life and all that you have to accomplish. Stress is inevitable, and it is not in itself bad. It is your response to stress that determines whether it is good stress (**eustress**) or bad stress (**distress**). Positive stress

iStockphoto

Do you find it difficult or easy to simplify and de-clutter your life? Why?

improves productivity, provided it doesn't persist too long. Negative stress, on the other hand, can affect you both physically and mentally.

Good stress can help you become more motivated and even more productive. It helps your energy level, too. It is only when stress gets out of hand that your body becomes distressed. Some physical signs of distress are:

Headaches	Muscular tension and pain	Fatigue
Coughs	Abdominal pain and diarrhea	Mental disorders
Dry mouth	Hypertension and chest pain	Insomnia
Impotence	Heartburn and indigestion	Suicidal tendencies
Twitching/Trembling	Abdominal pain	Apprehension
Jitters	Diminished performance	Decreased coping ability

If you begin to experience any of these reactions for an extended period of time, your body and mind are probably suffering from undue stress, anxiety, and pressure. This can lead to a very unhealthy situation. You may even require medical attention for hypertension. Take the stress assessment in Figure 17.13 to determine the level of distress you are currently experiencing in your life.

Figure 17.13 Test Your Stress

Check the items that reflect your behavior at home, work, or school, or in a social setting.

☐ 1. Your stomach tightens when you think about your work and all that you have to do.

☐ 2. You are not able to sleep at night.

☐ 3. You race from place to place trying to get everything done that is required of you.

☐ 4. Small things make you angry.

☐ 5. At the end of the day, you are frustrated that you did not accomplish all that you needed to do.

☐ 6. You get tired throughout the day.

☐ 7. You need some type of drug, alcohol, or tobacco to get through the day.

☐ 8. You often find it hard to be around people.

☐ 9. You don't take care of yourself physically or mentally.

☐ 10. You tend to keep everything inside.

☐ 11. You overreact.

☐ 12. You fail to find the humor in many situations others see as funny.

☐ 13. You do not eat properly.

☐ 14. Everything upsets you.

☐ 15. You are impatient and get angry when you have to wait for things.

☐ 16. You don't trust others.

☐ 17. You feel that most people move too slowly for you.

☐ 18. You feel guilty when you take time for yourself or your friends.

☐ 19. You interrupt people so that you can tell them your side of the story.

☐ 20. You experience memory loss.

Total Number of Check Marks

0–5   Low, manageable stress

6–10 Moderate stress

11+   High stress, could cause medical or emotional problems

I DON'T THINK I FEEL SO WELL

What Is the Relationship Between Poor Time Management, Monumental Stress, and Your Health?

There are probably as many stressors in this world as there are people alive. For some people, loud music causes stress. For others, a hectic day at the office with people demanding things and equipment breaking down causes stress. For others, that loud music and a busy day at the office are just what the doctor ordered—they love it and thrive off of the energy and demands. For some people, being idle and sitting around reading a book cause stress, whereas others long for a moment of peace walking on the beach or just sitting out in the backyard with a good book. One thing is for sure: poor planning and running out of time are on most people's list of major stressors. Medical research has shown that exposure to stress over a long period of time can be damaging to your health.

Consider the following tips for dealing with and reducing stress in your life:

- Become a dedicated goal setter and list maker and follow your plans carefully. One of the greatest causes of stress is floundering, not knowing where you are going.

- Reduce intake of alcohol, which can cause your moods to fluctuate and can make you edgy.

- Eat well. Certain foods give your body energy, while others drain your vitality. Reduce sweets and carbohydrates, and increase proteins such as lean baked turkey. Put more fruits and vegetables in your diet.

- Exercise! Physical exercise actually takes stress out of your body. If you feel yourself getting uptight, stop what you are doing and take a brisk 15-minute walk. Do the same thing for your children with homework. If they are getting frustrated, take the entire family on a walk.

- Get rid of all the clutter in your life. Sometimes we can become "possessed by our possessions."

- Use relaxation techniques such as visualization, listening to music, and practicing yoga.

- Get enough rest. You may not need eight hours, but your body needs a certain amount of sleep to regenerate itself.

- Let minor hassles and annoyances go. Ask yourself, "Is this situation worth a heart attack, stroke, or high blood pressure?"

- Don't be afraid to take a break.

- Learn to relax, and even take a little nap if it helps renew your energy.

- Laugh often! Laughter has been shown to increase learning and retention by 800 percent! Joy and laughter are great stress relievers.

Other physical symptoms include ***exhaustion,*** in which one part of the body weakens and shifts its responsibility to another part and causes complete failure of key organ functions. ***Chronic muscle pain*** and malfunction are also affected by unchecked stress. "Chronically tense muscles also result in numerous stress-related disorders including headaches, backaches, spasms of the esophagus and colon (causing diarrhea and constipation), posture problems, asthma, tightness in the throat and chest cavity, some eye problems, lockjaw, muscle tears and pulls, and perhaps rheumatoid arthritis" (Girdano, Dusek, & Everly, 2009).

As you can see from this medical research, stress is not something that you can just ignore and hope it will go away. Examine Figure 17.14.

Figure 17.14 Three Types of Major Stressors in Life

Cause	What You Can Do to Reduce Stress
Situational	
Change in physical environment	■ If at all possible, change your residence or physical environment to better suit your needs. ■ If you can't change it, talk to the people involved and explain your feelings.
Change in social environment	■ Work hard to meet new friends who support you and on whom you can rely in times of need. ■ Get involved in some type of activity outside of work. ■ Join a group activity or sports team.
Daily hassles	■ Try to keep things in perspective, and work to reduce the things that you allow to stress you out. ■ Allow time in your schedule for unexpected events. ■ Find a quiet place to relax and think.
Poor time management	■ Work out a time management plan that allows time to get your work complete while allowing time for rest and joy, too. ■ Create to do lists.
Conflicts at work and home	■ Read about conflict management and realize that conflict can result in stress. ■ Avoid "hot" topics such as religion or politics if you feel this causes you to engage in conflicts. ■ Be assertive, not aggressive or rude.
People	■ Try to avoid people who stress you out. ■ Put people into perspective and realize that we're all different, with different needs, wants, and desires. ■ Realize that not everyone is going to be like you, and not everyone is going to like you.
Relationships	■ Work hard to develop healthy, positive relationships. ■ Move away from toxic, unhealthy relationships and people who bring you down. ■ Understand that you can never change the way another person feels, acts, or thinks.
Death of a loved one	■ Try to focus on the good times you shared and what they meant to your life. ■ Remember that death is as much a part of life as living. ■ Talk about the person with your friends and family—share your memories. ■ Consider what the deceased person would have wanted you to do.
Financial problems	■ Cut back on your spending. ■ Seek the help of a financial planner. ■ Determine why your financial planning or spending patterns are causing you problems.
Psychological	
Unrealistic expectations	■ Surround yourself with positive people and work hard to set realistic goals with doable time-lines and results. ■ Expect and anticipate less.
Loneliness	■ Surround yourself with people who support you. ■ Call or visit home as often as you can until you get more comfortable. ■ Meet new friends at work or in your neighborhood.
Fear	■ Plan and execute carefully to help you feel more confident. ■ Visualize success and not failure. ■ Do one thing every day that scares you to expand your comfort zone.

Cause	What You Can Do to Reduce Stress
Psychological *(continued)*	
Anxiety over your future and what is going to happen	▪ Put things into perspective and work hard to plan and prepare, but accept that life is about constant change. ▪ Don't try to control the uncontrollable. ▪ Try to see the big picture and how "the puzzle" is going to come together.
Anxiety over your past	▪ Work hard to overcome past challenges and remember that your past does not have to dictate your future. ▪ Learn to forgive. ▪ Focus on your future and what you really want to accomplish.
Biological	
Insomnia	▪ Watch your caffeine intake. ▪ Avoid naps. ▪ Do not exercise two hours prior to your normal bedtime. ▪ Complete all of your activities before going to bed (working, watching TV, e-mailing, texting, etc.). Your bed is for sleeping.
Anxiety	▪ Laugh more. Share a joke. ▪ Enjoy your friends and family. ▪ Practice breathing exercises. ▪ Talk it out with friends. ▪ Learn to say "no" and mean it. ▪ Turn off the TV if the news makes you anxious or nervous.
Weight loss/gain	▪ Develop an exercise and healthy eating plan. ▪ Meet with a nutrition specialist. ▪ Join a health-related club or gym.
Reduced physical activities	▪ Increase your daily activity. ▪ If possible, walk to work or lunch instead of driving. ▪ Take the stairs instead of the elevator.
Sexual difficulties/ dysfunction	▪ Seek medical help in case something is physically wrong. ▪ Determine if your actions are in contradiction with your value system.

TIME, STRESS, DEPRESSION, AND ANXIETY

What Does One Have to Do with the Other?

Most people never make the connection, but not managing your time properly can cause more than stress—it can cause depression, anxiety, and a host of other mental, emotional, and physical problems. When you're rushing around trying to complete a project at the last moment, your stress level rises, and with higher levels of stress, depression and anxiety begin to creep in. Many of our mental and emotional issues can be addressed by allowing ourselves enough time to do a project well and not stress out over it. Yes, there are many causes of depression and anxiety, but managing your time well can help with reducing the levels of both.

SILENT PROBLEMS OF THE MIND

How Do You Control Depression and Anxiety Disorders?

Depression is a term used to describe feelings ranging from feeling blue to utter hopelessness. The use of "I'm depressed" to mean "I'm sad" or "I'm down" is a far cry from the illness of clinical depression. Depression is a sickness that can creep up on an individual and render that person helpless if it is not detected and properly treated.

There are several major types of depressions. They include the following:

- **Situational depression.** Situational depression is a feeling of sadness due to disappointments, bad news, daily frustrations, or "people problems."

- **Clinical depression.** Clinical depression is major depression and is characterized by the inability to enjoy life, loss of interest in things you once loved doing, self-hatred, feelings of utter worthlessness, and suicidal thoughts. Clinical depression is diagnosed when these feelings last at least two weeks.

- **Dysthymia.** Dysthymia is classified as mild to moderate depression and can last a long time—two years or more. There are times that you can't remember not being depressed and it is hard to enjoy life, family, or friends.

- **Seasonal depression.** Seasonal depression is caused by the weather or by the changing seasons of the year. Some people are depressed by rain; others are depressed by a lack of sunshine.

- **Postpartum depression.** Postpartum depression, sometimes called "the baby blues," occurs after the birth of a child. It can be a very serious condition where the mother avoids the child or even wants to cause harm to the child. It can occur up to a year or more after birth.

- **Anxiety.** According to the Anxiety Disorders Associations of America, anxiety disorders are the most common mental illness in the United States—with more than 13 percent of adults suffering from some form of anxiety disorder. Learning to cope with anxiety allows you to focus and maintain balance in your health and academic welfare. There are several ways to proactively approach dealing with anxiety: relaxation techniques such as yoga, music or dance therapy, and meditation; cognitive behavior therapy or other forms of therapy; and medication.

If you are feeling depressed or your anxiety has reached a level where you cannot control it, but your depression seems minor or situational, try some of these helpful hints for picking yourself up out of the blues:

- Get physical exercise—it releases endorphins, which help to stimulate you and give you a personal high.

- Spend time talking with a good friend; share your thoughts and feelings.

- Control your self-talk. If you're feeding yourself negative words, change to positive thoughts.

- Do something special for yourself: Take a long walk in the park, watch a favorite movie, listen to a special song, or visit a friend.

- Nurture yourself by doing things you love and enjoy and that bring you peace.

- *Never* be afraid or ashamed to seek professional assistance.

Reflections:
PUTTING IT ALL TOGETHER

Managing your time and reducing your levels of stress are two skills that you will need for the rest of your life. By learning to avoid procrastination and taking the time to enhance the quality of your life, you are actually increasing your value as an employee. Technological advances, fewer people doing more work, and pressure to perform at unprecedented levels can put your life in a tailspin, but with the ability to plan your time and reduce your own stress level, you are making a contribution to your own success.

DIGITAL BRIEFCASE

LEARNING TO USE A SOCIAL MEDIA MONITORING SYSTEM

Assume you have accepted a job with a startup company, headed by a young, ambitious technology guru. The company has been financially backed by angel investors (look up the definition for this term) and is under a great deal of pressure to produce quick results. The CEO and her management team are trying to maximize the use of social media for marketing, data collection, feedback, and other purposes.

Most people know how popular Facebook and Twitter are for personal use, but companies have caught on quickly that social media tools are also for business and creating lasting relationships with customers. Your boss is being pushed hard by his managers to increase the use of social media and to have employees actively engaged in constantly researching and finding new ideas and solutions to grow the business. As a member of this team, your job is to help find solutions and to generate new business using social media. You have found that tracking related websites is very time consuming, so you are seeking software that will help you track data while simultaneously helping you manage your time. Your job is very stressful and high pressure, so it helps to manage your time well.

Access the website www.omillion.com. Activate the free demo and learn the main points of this social media monitoring system. Write a two-paragraph report for your busy supervisor explaining how this software works and why it would be good for employees in your department. You can create fictitious information if you need to. In this report, explain the terminology "single dashboard" and "social media monitoring."

REFERENCES

Baca, M. (2009). *Get More Done*. Retrieved January 3, 2011, from www.getmoredone.com.

Girando, D., Dusek, D., & Everly, G. (2009). *Controlling stress and tension* (8th ed.). Boston: Benjamin Cummings.

U.S. Bureau of Labor Statistics. (2008). *Education and training pay.* Washington, DC: U.S. Government Printing Office.

Waitley, D. (1997). *Psychology of success: Developing your self-esteem.* Boston: Irwin Career Education Division.

Wetmore, D. (2008). Time management facts and figures. Accessed December 1, 2008, from www.balancetime.com.

Zen Habits. (2008). Simple living manifesto: 72 ways to simplify your life. Retrieved July 20, 2011, from http://zenhabits.net.

chapter eighteen

SOCIALIZE

AVOID WORKPLACE LAND MINES AND PERFECT YOUR PERSONAL IMAGE

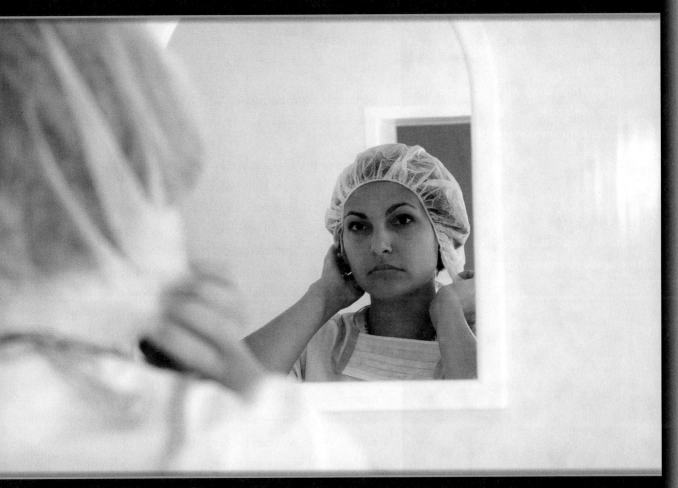

Never go to bed at night wondering if you were a conversational gun in the slandering of a person's character or the endangerment of his/her future.
—Letitia Baldridge

Why read this chapter?

Because you'll learn...

- To recognize and avoid "water cooler" gossip groups
- To be careful when dealing with office politics and workplace romances
- To select a classic business wardrobe, including business casual

Because you'll be able to...

- Work a room or a cocktail party like a pro
- Dine with dignity in any setting

PROFESSIONALS from the Field

Name: Lee Templeton

Business: Supervisor, Rush's

One of the biggest workplace land mines and conflicts can arise from hearsay, rumors, and gossip. Often, unfounded rumors are spread about how managers treat one employee one way and others a different way. Untrue rumors begin about relationships and workplace romances. Hearsay begins about favoritism. This almost always leads to conflict and causes unrest. When you assume a leadership role, it is extremely important to treat everyone equally, show respect to all, and avoid sharing private information. It will also be vitally important to never spread rumors or hearsay—not on the job, not in a social setting with coworkers or employees, not anywhere for that matter. While you can be empathetic and offer professional assistance, treat everyone equally and avoid the rumor mill at all costs.

NAVIGATING LAND MINES

How Do I Avoid Problems from Day One?

From the first day on, it is very important to perform your duties in an outstanding manner and convince your bosses that they made a good decision in hiring you. You should perform at your highest level every day and be willing to learn. Sometimes this means being willing to do the "dirty work" that no one else wants to do. It might mean arriving early and staying late at times. It will almost certainly mean that you will be sitting in classes or studying some phase of company regulations in front of a computer screen as you become oriented to the company.

In some cases, you will be on probation for a certain period of time, usually 90 days, so it is imperative that you perform at the top of your game during this time. The majority of companies conduct regular, formal performance appraisals. Ask for a copy of the evaluation instrument, study the items on which you will be evaluated, and be sure you are performing all of them at a high level. You don't want any surprises when the boss evaluates you. It is not unusual for employees to think they are doing what is expected of them only to learn at evaluation time that they have missed the mark. Although doing your job well is key, it is also important to be looking toward a promotion and your next career opportunity. Observe people in leadership roles who have done well and are respected by their colleagues: What is their educational background? How do they communicate? What do they do that sets them apart? Study the trends in your industry. Read good books, business journals, and trade journals in your field. What can you learn from books and journals that you can apply to your own work and perhaps do a better, more creative job?

"WATER COOLER" GOSSIP GROUPS

How Much Can a Little Gossip Hurt?

There are very few people who don't like to gossip. The workplace is no exception to this rule. Rumors fly around all the time, many of which have no real substance whatsoever; in fact, some people love to take a little tidbit of information and embellish it until there is no truth whatsoever. The problem with this little exercise is that it hurts the people who are the subjects of this unfounded gossip. The other problem is that everybody knows who the rumormongers are, and nobody trusts them. It's not hard to tell who goes up and down the halls spreading malicious gossip. A sure way to damage your personal reputation is to become one of these people. A good thing to remember is that stepping on one's feelings is as painful as stepping on one's toes, and it lasts a lot longer.

Never Speak Negatively about Your Boss or Former Employer

Think about this quote: "If you work for a man, work for him, or find another job." This is good advice whether your boss is a man or woman! While it is absolutely certain that some bosses won't earn your respect or

POSITIVE HABITS *at Work*

Do everything possible to make your boss look good. Find out what your boss is trying to accomplish and do everything you can to help him or her be successful. Bosses typically reward people who work hard, try to help in reaching the organization's goals, and are loyal. Avoid getting involved with the gossipers and naysayers.

BIGGEST INTERVIEW *Blunders*

Marie Hanson went on a job interview and was asked to describe her current boss. She proceeded to blast him with a stream of negative comments. Marie was highly qualified for this position based on her education and skill sets, but she didn't get the job. She made the classic mistake of bad-mouthing her former boss.

LESSON: Never say anything bad about your former boss or anyone else at your former company no matter how much you dislike him or her. People at the company where you are interviewing will assume that you will do the same about your new colleagues.

deserve your loyalty, he or she is the boss nevertheless. Not every boss is a good supervisor, but he or she is still the boss. You will be very fortunate if you get a boss who is visionary, fair, honest, ethical, and caring, and who tries to help all employees grow and to learn. Even if you have a lousy boss, if you are going to take the paycheck, you need to give a good day's work for a good day's pay.

Many bosses will tell you that the number one quality they value is loyalty. This doesn't mean that you can't disagree with the boss. It just means that you disagree with him or her in person and that you do it respectfully. Should you choose to disagree with your boss, you need to choose your words carefully and say something like this: "Mrs. Brown, I know you have so much more experience than I do, and I may be way off base, but it seems to me that the decision to close that branch might be a little premature. Are you aware that XYZ company is getting ready to build a big plant within half a mile of that branch?"

Never make the boss look bad in front of anyone to show how smart and clever you are. If you have a boss who truly encourages speaking up and disagreeing in meetings—and these are rare—be sure that even then you use a respectful tone of voice and that you don't say or do anything that causes the boss to lose face. No one—including a boss—ever forgets being embarrassed in front of his or her colleagues.

Figure out what is near and dear to the boss's heart and work hard to make it happen. This is not being underhanded; it's just using good sense. Don't let your boss hear bad news from someone else if you know about it. Bosses don't like surprises. They especially don't like to hear about it from their own bosses.

When you go for an interview, never say anything bad about the company or your present or former boss. Even if he or she deserves to be attacked, the person interviewing you will assume that you will be negative when you go to work with the new company, and most likely, you won't get the job offer.

Paying Attention to Workplace Politics

Politics is rampant in the workplace! You will see "kissing up," "brown-nosing," lying, bullying, exaggerating, people taking credit for others' work—the list goes on and on. The secret is to know what is going on without being a participant in the negative aspects of office politics. Most people know which colleagues are spreading the rumors, attacking others, playing up to the boss, and so on. You can't stop politics, so don't waste your time trying.

The only way you can avoid politics is to go to work in the middle of a forest and never see anyone else. The good news is that not all politics are bad. You don't have to change who you are to be successful at office politics. Nice guys do finish first most of the time. J. W. Marriott, CEO of Marriott Corporation, said, "The closer you get to the top, the nicer people are." You can be thoughtful, sincere, considerate, and interested in others, and your chances of succeeding are far better than those who choose to use dirty politics.

Some people believe that office politics are only played by people who can't get ahead by any other means, but according to Herminia Ibarra, associate professor at Harvard Business School, "You don't have to be a jerk to make things happen. Integrity can be a source of power." Lou DiNatale, senior fellow at the McCormick Institute of Public Affairs at the University of Massachusetts, says, "Real political power is about pulling other people to your ideas, and then pushing those ideas through to other people." Today it seems that people value knowledge and skills far more than they do negative politics. Politics will only take you so far, and if your power is attached to someone else's, when he or she falls from grace, so will you, especially if you have been a backstabber to other people.

There will always be a grapevine. It has been said that 80 percent of what comes down the grapevine is true. If you are the boss, you need to put the truth down the grapevine as often as you can. If you hear a rumor and you know it is not true, simply say, "That's not true. I was in that meeting, and Mr. Carter didn't say that. This is what he said."

Politics will always exist. Know what is going on around you at all times, but refuse to be a player in underhanded, dirty politics. Practice honesty, integrity, fairness, and decency, and if you are good at your job, you will succeed. Take time to get to know people on a personal level; don't judge them based on what anyone else says. Just because one person has a problem with a colleague doesn't mean you have to.

What does this statement mean?

Never judge another person through someone else's eyes.

_____

_____

_____

_____

_____

Avoid Backstabbing and Trampling on Others

There are many ways to trample on others' feelings, and you will probably encounter or observe most of them. The important thing is for you to avoid participating in such behavior. Some of the typical behaviors that people hate most are:

- Having someone take credit for their work
- Colleagues who don't perform their work well and on time so someone else falls behind and looks bad
- Unfounded rumors, such as untrue accusations about having an affair
- Schmoozing those at the top and scorning those below them
- Spreading rumors about people to cause animosity with the idea that the gossiper will come out on top
- Resisting requests for information that a person needs to do his or her job
- Bullying by loud, intimidating colleagues
- Laughter at some off-color or inappropriate joke that hurts another colleague
- Being left out of the loop intentionally on things that should be common knowledge

Just as these behaviors hurt you, they also hurt other employees. You will be respected if you refuse to participate in these games. If someone mistreats you, gather your courage, go to his or her office, and say something like, "I was told that you were spreading a rumor about me that isn't true, so I decided to ask you if you did this. Did you say I was having an affair with Mr. Kendall?" Since most people who trample on others and backstab their colleagues are chickens underneath their loud exteriors, the person will probably deny having said it and probably won't say it again. You can respond, "Well, I didn't think you were that kind of person, and I'm glad to know you aren't doing such a despicable thing. So we don't have a problem." The chances are good that this person will not target you again.

One in five employees reports being bullied at work.
—Valerie Cade, *Bullyfree Workplace*

WORKPLACE ROMANCES

What's Love Got to Do with It?

Is it something in the air? Or is it the music that plays constantly in many offices? Or is it the close proximity of office cubicles? No one seems to know what causes so many office romances, but "almost half of us have been romantically tied to someone from work, and many more would like to find amour in a neighboring cubicle" (Vault.com, 2010). Office romances seem to be rather common today. After all, employees spend up to one-third of their time at work in close quarters with other people. While office romances are not as taboo as they once were, for best results, cupid is best left out of the office.

What does your company's policy say about office relationships? Read this as soon as possible, before an office romance is even remotely possible. Before you jump into a romantic relationship with a coworker, you really need to think about it carefully. This may seem like the love of your life, the soulmate you have longed for. But what happens if this romance goes sour? What have you got to lose if it doesn't work out? Or even if it does work out?

In a worst-case scenario, you could lose your job. Some companies' corporate regulations forbid romantic relationships. You could damage your professional reputation, and in some cases, even be charged for sexual harassment if you get your life tangled up with the wrong person. Certainly, you know by now that everyone is not honest and ethical, much less responsible. If you have a relationship that doesn't work out, naturally, it would be much easier if this took place somewhere besides your office.

According to Joni Johnston, president and CEO of WorkRelationships.com, "Most dating relationships end. Think of the number of people we date and the number we end up marrying—the odds are not good." Is this relationship worth the gossip that will surely go on around you? (Remember, there are very few secrets at work.) Could you become involved in some kind of jealous triangle? Are the quarters too close for comfort to keep an office romance going? You have always heard the old expression, "Look before you leap." This is one of those times when you really need to weigh all the consequences before jumping in and getting in way over your head.

All that said, and even if it is not a good idea, it is virtually impossible to stop love from happening. Because you obviously have similar work interests, it stands to reason that you might share other mutually rewarding interests in hobbies, sports, movies, and the like. You might even have a group of friends to which you both belong, and perhaps you all go out together after work. One thing leads to another, and you find yourself in an office romance.

While we highly recommend not getting involved romantically at work, it would be wrong to say that everything is negative about a workplace romance. Because you work with the person, you can observe his or her behaviors frequently and determine if this person is a good match for you. You could have the opportunity to go to lunch or work out together in the company exercise facility. You can get an idea if this person is a good love interest or simply a wolf in sheep's clothing.

> There is no greater hatred than the hatred between two people who once loved.
> —Sophocles

You need to maintain a good balance between romance and work. Review the pointers in Figure 18.1 that might help you as you deal with office relationships.

While office romances may bring happiness, they have the potential to bring just as much sadness and anger, and at the same time, damage your career. Try very hard to avoid compromising situations. Proceed with caution, maturity, and wisdom.

DON'T PARTY AT THE COMPANY PARTY

Is It Really Worth Ruining Your Professional Reputation?

The company party is not the place to party! You should be seen, be sociable, and be gone. You should arrive a little late and leave a little early. If everyone else is staying very late and drinking too much, this is a good reason for you to excuse yourself and leave. You should never have more than one drink at a company function. Nurse that drink as long as you are there, and refrain from drinking simply because the liquor is free. This is not the place for you to have too much to drink and make a fool of yourself. You don't have to drink more than anyone else just because the drinks are free.

Figure 18.1 Tips for Managing Workplace Relationships

- Never have a relationship with your boss or a subordinate! You increase the risk of a sexual harassment lawsuit, you damage morale in the office, and you might get accused of preferential treatment. If you are a colleague competing for promotions, salaries, and other perks, naturally, people will say that you get better treatment. Managers tend to lose respect if they are caught dallying around with a subordinate. What about evaluations? How can a boss be unbiased in evaluating a love interest? "Just don't date anyone in your direct chain of command. Just don't do it," according to Taylor (2005).

- Never get involved with a married person—at work or anywhere else. You will quickly ruin your reputation. If this person will cheat on his or her spouse, he or she will cheat on you.

- If you sense that a work relationship is getting too serious, spend less time working and more time doing things that take your mind off this person. Go to places where you might meet someone with similar interests; spend more time working out; look up old friends.

- If you fall in love and you think you absolutely must have this person, one of you needs to move to another department or even to another company. Is this person worth giving up your job?

- If you become involved with a colleague, move very slowly into a serious relationship. It takes very mature people to handle a romantic relationship in the office.

- Kersten (2002) offers good advice: "Once you enter into a relationship, there are two people contributing to the way you are perceived in the company. It doesn't matter if you're being professional, if that other person is not, it's still going to impact you." What if your love interest shares intimate information with a colleague and it gets out around the watercooler?

- Do your homework. Does your company forbid interoffice dating? Are there unwritten rules that everyone seems to follow? What is the policy on harassment? Does your relationship with this person pose situations that may be harmful to the company? Are there any older, long-term employees in relationships with colleagues? Do you have very conservative bosses? Are other peers dating, and how has this affected their standing with their colleagues and bosses? If you were discussed in the same way as they are, could you live with it? How would you feel toward your romantic interest if the relationship cost you a promotion or your job?

- If you do get involved, make some hard-and-fast rules that you both will follow. No contact at work, no discussion of dating, no physical contact, and no talk of love. Perhaps the most important rule to agree on is this one: How will you treat each other if the relationship doesn't work out? Of course, there is no guarantee that either of you will live up to these promises. Can you be sure of what will happen if things don't turn out well? In extreme cases, one person or the other can't turn loose of their love interest, and it creates a bad scene at work, even resulting in violence and loss of job.

- Don't fall in love, get all starry-eyed, and stop paying attention to your job. You need to go to work, be prompt, meet deadlines, and handle your assignments in an excellent manner so your work doesn't suffer. Avoid e-mailing on company computers, and don't spend lots of time text-messaging when you should be working. Your computer at work belongs to the company, and anything you write can be examined by someone above your head if he or she chooses to do so. If this prince or princess doesn't work out, you still need your job and your reputation.

- If you break up—and you most likely will, according to statistics—handle it with maturity. Don't say bad things about your love interest; don't jump into another relationship at work or anywhere else right away; cool off. No one gets over a broken heart easily, but this is one of those times when you must deal with it in a very mature manner.

Wear something that is in good taste. This is a work function—not a laid-back social gathering with your best buddies. Women certainly want to look attractive, but not overly sexy. Women in upper management are not likely to dress in skimpy, tight clothes. You want to fit in with them. Men should also dress like the company executives do. They won't have on jeans and t-shirts.

If you are attending a pool party, don't swim. You will look like a drowned rat while everyone else is still fresh and attractive. Don't parade around in a swimsuit even if you look like a movie star. Neither men nor women will win friends by insisting on showing off a great body. This is not the place!

At every party there are two kinds of people—those who want to go home and those who don't. Trouble usually follows those who don't.

—Unknown

Figure 18.2 How to Work a Room Like a Pro

- Survey the room before you enter to get "the lay of the land."

- If you have a drink, hold it in your left hand so your right hand is free to shake hands. Don't have more than one drink!

- Avoid eating. It is difficult to talk, eat, balance a plate, and shake hands. Eat before you go! You are there to do business, not eat. The worst thing you can do is to load up your plate and act like this is your last meal.

- Don't cluster in the corner with the only person you know! Move around the room, shaking hands and introducing yourself. Take the initiative. Most people will be glad you did.

- Focus on the other person. Smile and be friendly. Talk for a few minutes and move on.

- Sell yourself with a sound bite—something interesting about yourself. For example: "I'm John Martin, the new admissions coordinator at Marion Hospital."

- Don't look around the room or over the other person's shoulder while you're talking to someone. Look at the person as though he or she is the most interesting person in the room. Use the person's name.

- Don't talk about politics, make fun of a state, or tell religious or ethnic jokes. You never know whom you might offend.

- Don't talk about your health. People find this very boring. No one wants to hear about your operation or extensive details about your vacation.

- Converse a few minutes, excuse yourself, and move on. The idea is to meet people and network.

How to Work a Room

As a businessperson, you probably will attend cocktail parties. You should consider them an extension of work. You are there to make contacts, make a good impression, network, expand your client base, and generally represent your company in a positive manner. In other words, you should work the room. Consider the basic tips in Figure 18.2 for working a room.

Business parties, receptions, and cocktail parties should be treated as an extension of work. You should look your best, present yourself well, and consider these events as a great opportunity to network.

ALCOHOL AND SUBSTANCE ABUSE

What Is the Cost to Companies and Individuals?

Alcohol and substance abuse by employees creates expensive problems for business and industry, including injuries on the job, increased premiums for health insurance, and missed work that affects others' jobs. "The loss to companies in the United States due to alcohol and drug-related abuse by employees totals $100 billion a year, according to the the National Clearinghouse for Alcohol and Drug Information (NCADI). These staggering numbers do not include the cost of diverting company resources that could be used for other purposes, toward addressing substance abuse issues. Nor does it include the 'pain and suffering' aspects, which cannot be measured in economic terms" (Buddy, 2011). Costs add up quickly in terms of expense of absenteeism, injuries, health insurance claims, loss of productivity, employee morale, theft, and fatalities.

According to NCADI statistics alcohol and drug users:

- Are far less productive.
- Use three times as many sick days.

- Are more likely to injure themselves or someone else.
- Are five times more likely to file worker's compensation claims.

One survey found that nine percent of heavy drinkers and 10 percent of drug users had missed work because of a hangover, six percent had gone to work high or drunk in the past year, and 11 percent of heavy drinkers and 18 percent of drug users had skipped work in the past month. (Buddy, 2011)

There is no doubt that alcohol and substance abuse create serious problems at work and can cause you to lose your job. You are urged to use good judgment related to any type of substance abuse for your health, as well as your career.

People abuse substances such as drugs, tobacco, and alcohol for many complex reasons, but our society pays a terrible price because of these abuses. People harm themselves and others, work suffers, families are adversely affected, relationships are ruined, and many people end up in prison due to substance abuse. There is a strong correlation between drug dependence and crime. While the use of cocaine has declined, use of other drugs such as heroin and "club drugs" has increased (Daly & Richards, 2007).

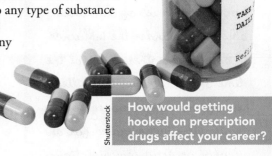

How would getting hooked on prescription drugs affect your career?

Friends, family, and coworkers may see some of the signs of substance abuse in people they know and care about listed in Figure 18.3.

While we cannot go into great depth on the issue of substance abuse here, suffice it to say that it is an increasingly serious problem among U.S. workers, and many people are not well-educated on the potential harmful effects of substance abuse. Many people, for example, have the mistaken idea that marijuana is harmless and non-habit-forming. According to Hoffman and Froemke (2007), "The odds of marijuana dependence in adulthood are six times higher for those who start using pot before the age of 15 than for those who begin after 18." Residual damage from substance abuse includes unwanted pregnancies, sexually transmitted diseases, and driving fatalities and accidents.

> *The estimated number of users of illicit drugs in the United States is about 13 million. About 10% of the population is dependent on alcohol and 25% of Americans smoke cigarettes.*
> —*National Household Survey*

Figure 18.3 Signs of Substance Abuse

- Showing a decline in grades or work performance
- Using room deodorizers and incense to hide odors
- Using drug paraphernalia such as baggies, pipes, or rolling paper
- Giving up hobbies and sports that he or she used to enjoy
- Getting drunk or high on a regular basis
- Lying about how much he or she is consuming
- Appearing rundown, hopeless, depressed, or suicidal
- Driving while under the influence of alcohol
- Avoiding friends and family to get drunk
- Hiding alcohol or drinking alone
- Becoming aggressive or hostile
- Getting suspended from school or work because of substance abuse–related incidents
- Getting in trouble with the police

Source: Adapted from Daly and Richards, 2007.

Eighty-five percent of the U.S. prison population either meets the medical criteria for substance abuse or addiction, or had histories of substance abuse; were under the influence of alcohol or other drugs at the time of their crime; committed their offense to get money to buy drugs; were incarcerated for an alcohol or drug law violation; or shared some combination of these characteristics.

—"Behind Bars II: Substance Abuse and America's Prison Population"

Binge drinking is drinking for the primary purpose of getting drunk. Cooper (2002) reported that 61 percent of men who binge drink practice unprotected sex, as compared to only 23 percent who do not binge drink. Forty-eight percent of women who participate in binge drinking practice unprotected sex, compared to 8 percent of women who do not practice binge drinking.

A substance abuse dependency started in college is very likely to carry over into the workplace. Many companies today will require a drug test before they will hire you. We offer the concerned advice of being very careful not to develop a substance abuse problem that can affect you for the rest of your life. If you have a problem or know of someone who does, get help at your earliest convenience.

PERFECT YOUR PROFESSIONAL IMAGE

How Do You Dress and Dine to Be Remembered for All the Right Reasons?

Should I use the shortest fork for my appetizer or the salad? Should I wear French cuffs on an interview? Should I extend my hand to be shaken or wait until a hand is offered?

Many people have the mistaken idea that everyone knows how to dress, how to dine properly, and how to demonstrate good manners. Some even believe that these qualities are not important. The truth is that these things are not taught at home as much as they once were, and many people grow up not knowing these basic points. However, do not be mistaken—first impressions, manners, etiquette, and basic grooming remain very important.

Several years ago, John Malloy, an "image guru," said, "As much as one-third of your success depends on what you wear." In Malloy's opinion, your appearance, image, and presence contribute greatly to your overall success in your career. When you combine a powerful first impression, professional dress, good basic manners, excellent dining etiquette, proper language skills, and add a winning smile, you have all the makings of an outstanding professional package. More and more colleges and schools are providing educational experiences in all these areas for their students. The professional package is the "icing on the cake" that helps students secure the job they want and then move up rapidly in the ranks.

What Is Image, Exactly?

What do we mean by image? And why do you have to have one? Image is the mental picture that people have of you when you pass through their minds. Image is what people see when they think of you. Whether you like it or not, you have an image. Take a minute right now if you can, and go stand in front of a full-length mirror. Pretend this person who is looking back at you is someone other than you. Try to look at your image with an unbiased eye. What do you see? Are you dressed well? Are you clean and pressed? Does your hair look well groomed? Are you smiling? Are your clothes altered correctly and professionally? Do you think you present an upper-middle-class image? If not, you have work to do, because image has a great deal to do with how people treat you and respect you.

Your image and attire combine to make up one component of your overall ability to practice good judgment. You want to dress like you have good judgment and demonstrate an image that makes people look at you as a professional. Knowing how to dress for work can be challenging and confusing. Because dressing can be daunting, many people, especially women, fail at making the right selections.

First, you should determine if your company has a dress code. If so, get a copy from your HR department and abide by the policies. Second, consider your long-term career goals and dress for the position you aspire to rather than the one you are in today. Third, pay attention to how the company leaders dress and take your cue from this group of successful people. Fourth, determine if your position dictates what you wear. If you are in accounting, for example, you might need to wear dark suits, blazers, and other professional outfits. Finally, consider your business wardrobe an investment. It should last for years if you buy classic clothing and avoid putting too much money into fads.

Dress to Impress

Many people like to demonstrate their own style and pay little attention to what constitutes appropriate dress at work. Frequently, companies today don't spell out exactly what they are looking for in employee dress, so you need to pay attention to what the successful people are wearing. Even if you are required to wear a uniform, notice how others present themselves. Is the uniform clean and pressed? Does it fit well?

You have to be able to determine for yourself what looks good on you, what is over-the-top dressing for your particular environment, and what is considered dress that will impress your superiors, colleagues, and customers. Look carefully at the people who have already made it and those who appear to be on a fast track. What do they wear to work? Are they overly casual? Do they wear jeans to work on casual day? Do you see any of them with earrings, tongue studs, or bright red streaks in their hair? Do you find any who have tattoos on their necks, heads, and other conspicuous places? Companies are hiring you to represent them, and they want a positive appearance from all their employees. The appearance that was appropriate at school and in a casual environment may not be acceptable in the work environment.

Women's Dress

Women have so many more choices than men—and so many more ways to get it right or wrong. Getting it right can be a great asset to someone thinking about promotions or making positive impressions. You have many choices that can complement your individual style and body type and still present you in a positive light. You should use dress to reinforce how serious you are about your work and your career.

Whatever your profession, you want to look the part. You don't necessarily want to wear clothes that make you stand out; rather, you want to look good so that people will respond to you appropriately. The mark of a well-dressed woman is that she always looks professional and well-dressed, but you don't necessarily remember exactly what she had on. If you stand out, you have to be sure it is for the right reasons—perhaps a flair for color, style, jewelry, or the ability to mix styles.

If you need to (or are required to) wear business suits, they should be dark colors and preferably should be natural fabrics like wool or linen. Shoes should be stylish, but comfortable, preferably leather, and jewelry should be well-made, preferably gold or silver. Women's professional shoes should not have open heels or toes, straps, platforms, or high spike heels.

Clothes should always be cleaned, pressed and immaculate—no spots, safety pins, or hems or cuffs that are in bad repair. Purses and belts should be leather and in good repair. Your blouses should be tailored; you should avoid busy prints, frilly lace, and sexy garments. Likewise, you should avoid pastel colors for major pieces of your wardrobe, especially light pink (which screams "baby girl") and bright, garish colors. Appearance is a cultivated practice, and you can learn to look and act successful, which will go a long way toward making you successful. To get an idea of how people dress in your profession, purchase magazines or journals that have pictures of people who work in your profession. You might also consider visiting an office where you would like to work and observing the dress of the women who work there. You want to have an image that says "understated elegance."

Shutterstock

If you saw this person at lunch, would she impress you as a professional?

> *Fashions fade, style is eternal.*
> *— Yves Saint Laurent*

Although pants are acceptable in most business offices, women should typically stick to pantsuits that have matching blazer and pants. The pants should be hemmed at the proper length according to what is in style. Sleeves should be hemmed so they do not extend below the wrist. Most clothes require some alterations. Avoid buying clothes off the rack that do not fit well or wearing them without having them altered properly to fit you. No matter what salespeople tell you, clothes off the rack almost always need alterations.

The information presented previously primarily relates to business dress for women who are working in business offices. Naturally, if you are working in aviation mechanics, you can't wear pumps and a business suit. Likewise, if you are working in a cubicle as a computer programmer, you will find that most of your colleagues aren't wearing dark business suits. Some positions, such as nursing, will require you to wear a uniform. When it comes to dress in non-traditional fields and fields other than business, you should observe what others in your position or department are wearing and follow suit. No matter what your position or dress code, you should always wear clean, pressed clothes in good repair. Some universal dress tips are presented in Figure 18.4.

Figure 18.4 Universal Dress Tips for Women in a Business Office Environment

Remember that you cannot be sexy and professional in the same outfit—so make up your mind what you want to be known for. No one will take you seriously if you dress provocatively at work.

- The best colors for business suits are navy, black, gray, burgundy, olive, tan, and khaki.

- Pantsuits should preferably have a matching blazer and pants, should be hemmed to the right length, and should never be too short.

- Sleeves should be hemmed so they do not extend below the wrist.

- If you wear a skirt, it should come at least to the top of your knees, even if very short skirts are in style—fashions may dictate changes in skirt lengths, but they should never be too short at work. When you sit, your thighs should be covered.

- Business dresses and pantsuits are fine for most days, but if you have an important meeting, wear a business suit with a skirt. If you wear a dress, wear a blazer or jacket over it.

- Your clothing should not be louder than your voice or personality.

- Avoid overpowering perfume that may be offensive to others. Some people are allergic to strong perfumes.

- Your hair should be clean, well-groomed, and fashionable and should not distract from your overall appearance.

- Avoid clothes that are too tight, see-through, or have long slits in the front that expose too much leg.

- Have your clothes altered to fit well.

- Avoid all extremes such as trendy clothes; bleached hair; or unnatural hair colors such as green, blue, or bright red streaks.

- Have no visible tattoos.

- Avoid any kind of body piercings that are obvious, especially facial piercings or multiple earrings.

- Jewelry should be simple—gold or silver is best.

- Wear no more than one ring on each hand, except for wedding and engagement rings.

- A nice gold watch and one bracelet are nice touches at work.

- Hose should coordinate with your outfit, but usually a barely black or suntan color works for most business occasions. You should always wear hose in the winter.

- Avoid colored, fishnet, and patterned hose at work.

- Carry a cordovan briefcase and no purse so you don't look like a pack horse when you go to an important meeting.

- Carry a briefcase or leather portfolio even if you have nothing in it. It is the image you are going for—a professional with her accessories.

- If you carry a purse, organize it, and don't be seen digging around in it searching for an item.

- Walk briskly and act like you know where you are going. Never drag around at work. This behavior becomes part of your image.

Your image should match your ambitions. If you were going to work today, would your wardrobe reflect your ambitions? Would you look chic and stylish, or would you appear frumpy and nondescript? Would you look like a student or like a professional? What would people say about your grooming? What does your body language say about you? Image is a complete package, and anyone can improve personal image. Some people are naturally more attractive than others, and some are more graceful and charming, but anyone can learn to develop presence and build a better image.

Women: Considering all the tips for dress and image improvement that we have shared with you, list several things about your typical dress that you think you could (and should) improve so that your appearance more closely matches that of your potential coworkers and your career goals.

_____

_____

_____

_____

_____

_____

Men's Dress

One of the best ways for men to stand out is by dressing in an outstanding manner. The typical male does not give a great deal of attention to his appearance, so when a man does it right, he gets a lot of positive attention. As stated earlier, women have many more choices than men—and many more ways of making bad decisions. Any man can become a very good dresser if he is willing to work at it.

While you may not work in a job that requires a suit, you need at least one nice suit and preferably two, especially for the interview. You want interviewers to think they are getting a bargain in you. The best times for men to buy suits are after Christmas and after the Fourth of July, when most nice men's stores put their suits on sale. You might also look for warehouse sales, which often provide excellent bargains if you know how to shop for them.

Many suits can be worn year-round, except perhaps on the coldest or hottest days. If you live in the South or Southwest, you don't need heavy wool clothes—you will get very little wear from them. Regardless of where you live, however, the fabric in your suits should contain wool because it helps suits keep their shape better after cleaning. If you are taking a traveling position, you need clothes that won't wrinkle badly.

Certainly, the rules of dress for a business office do not apply to many professional careers such as plumbing, electrical engineering, auto mechanics, computer programming, and medical assistant positions. In such positions, men should observe what others at their level are wearing and dress accordingly. If you are a computer programmer, for example, you may be allowed to wear jeans and a golf shirt. If this is the case, be sure your jeans are clean, pressed, and do not have holes or frayed cuffs, even if this is a fashion statement.

Review the tips for men's dress presented in Figure 18.5.

Shutterstock

Do you think a company would be interested in hiring this man?

Figure 18.5 Universal Dress Tips for Men in a Business Office Environment

- If you are going to work in a company where you need to wear suits, start building a good wardrobe now. Suits and blazers are expensive and should be accumulated over a period of time.

- Most men need to own at least two suits—navy and charcoal gray work well for most men and fit in well in most companies.

- As a new graduate, you can interview in a blue blazer and charcoal gray slacks if you don't have a suit. A nice sport coat is a good wardrobe addition.

- If you are required to wear dress shirts to work, you should own at least 6–10 of them, including several white shirts and at least two light blue shirts. French blue is also a versatile color that can be worn with most of the colors mentioned above. Of course, you can gradually accumulate this collection.

- The only color shirt to wear to an interview is white, and it should be starched and immaculate.

- Dress shirts should be starched—always! Do not rely on permanent pressed because they always look unkempt if not pressed.

- Dress shirts should always be long-sleeved, even in the summer. Never wear short-sleeved dress shirts—especially to an interview!

- A small monogram on your left cuff is a nice touch.

- You might want to consider at least one shirt with French cuffs and cufflinks.

- Suits should either be two- or three-button. Stay away from trendy suits that will go out of style soon.

- Purchase black and brown belts and shoes; they will look good with almost everything.

- The dressiest shoe a man can wear is a lace-up wing-tip, but young men can wear tasseled loafers or cap-toe lace-up shoes just as well. If you don't understand these terms, ask a shoe salesperson to explain them to you.

- Heels of shoes should not look worn, and shoes should always be polished and shined.

- Socks should be black if worn with gray, navy, or black. Bare leg should not show if you cross your legs, so buy long socks.

- Never wear white socks with a business suit or sport coat. Patterned socks are the mark of a well-dressed man if they are coordinated well.

- Ties should be stylish and bought with careful consideration. If you don't know how to choose a tie, get help from a salesperson at a nice men's store. Unless she has excellent taste, don't let your girlfriend or your wife choose your ties.

- Ties should be made of silk in a stylish width and should have no spots on them.

- Men should learn to tie a knot that is in style. The bottom part of the tie should reach right below your belt. Do not wear a tie that sits on your stomach and indicates that you do not know how to dress professionally.

- Men should wear a mild, non-offensive cologne.

- Remove fat wallets, large key rings, and excessive change from your pockets. You want to look streamlined and put together.

- Buy a nice leather briefcase, and use it even if you have nothing in it but your lunch!

GRADUATE Quote

Jonathan T. Ellis
Graduate!
The University of South Carolina, Columbia, SC
Career: Network Administrator, The University of South Carolina

The most important lesson I learned was this: Perfect your capacity to articulate your abilities and skills because you never know what employers are really looking for. Never be discouraged. Your dream position is out there.

Dress for interviews should be based on the kind of job you for which are interviewing. If you are dressing to be machine technician, you would dress differently from someone interviewing for a position in allied health. "The first judgment an interviewer makes is going to be based on how you look and what you are wearing" (Doyle, 2011).

Men: Considering all the tips we have discussed with you, list several things about your dress that you think you could (and should) improve so your dress more closely matches that of your potential coworkers and your career goals.

_____

_____

_____

_____

_____

Business Casual—The Type of Professional Dress That Stumps Many Men and Women

The important thing to remember about business casual is this: "While casual may be optional, looking professional is not. Exercising poor work attire choices can convey an unfavorable message to your superiors and colleagues and ultimately stunt your growth within an organization" (Zuri, 2011). Business casual should be crisp, clean, neat, and pressed. You should feel well-dressed even if you bump into the president.

Many businesses allow employees to "dress down," especially on Friday. Dressing down does not mean "anything goes." Some people really mess up with casual dress, and they stand out for all the wrong reasons because they don't take it seriously enough.

Although you don't want to overdress when others are casual, you don't want to go to great extremes with your casual dress either. Actually, it is just as expensive to dress well for casual occasions as it is to dress for business—and more difficult for many people because they fail to take it seriously. A general rule of thumb for dressing for success is this: Observe what others, including your supervisors, are wearing.

Some basic tips for business casual dress are listed below:

- On casual days, men should wear a good pair of dress slacks and a golf shirt or a knit shirt with a blazer.

- Men can also wear a button-down shirt with slacks and a blazer. Women can wear simple slacks that are pressed, the right length, and not too tight.

- Under no circumstances should you wear t-shirts and wrinkled khakis or unpressed jeans. Tennis shoes, sandals, or hiking boots are never appropriate.

Shutterstock

Does this man pass the test as a well-dressed professional?

- Showing cleavage for women is never appropriate, no matter what you see on television or in magazines.

- Facial hair should be worn only if higher-ranking company executives do so, and should be well-groomed.

- Makeup should be conservative and natural looking. Nails should be groomed and cleaned. Women should avoid very bright polish for business. Likewise, they should avoid all the fashion design nails done by salons for work.

DINE WITH CLASS

Who Cares If I Don't Use the Right Fork?

The mark of a very polished person is the ability to use outstanding dining etiquette, to order food and beverage with confidence. The finer points of dining etiquette need to be studied and used as you enter your career and consider moving up. No one is exempt from needing to know how to sit and eat a meal with dignity and grace. No one! Read a good etiquette book and take it seriously. Research shows that only about 12 percent of new hires are skilled in the social graces. In fact, many companies hire consultants to teach their employees how to practice good etiquette. Etiquette or the lack of it may mean the difference between success or failure. Excellent manners will set you apart early in your career. Manners will also make a positive impression on almost everyone, especially your customers and clients!

We assume you know the basics, such as chew with your mouth closed, keep your elbows off the table, pass food to the right, cut your meat only one piece at a time, and butter only one small piece of bread at a time—but many people don't know these rules! You also need to know the following basic rules of good etiquette and dining:

Do these employees look dressed professionally for work on business casual day?

Shutterstock

- A utensil that has been used should never be placed on a tablecloth. Place it on the edge of your plate.

- If you use a sweetener or other item that has been wrapped in paper, slip the paper under your bread plate. Don't leave it on the table in a conspicuous manner.

- Remember LR, LR, LR—liquids to the right. This means that you should only drink from or use the glasses on your right. Solids, such as bread plates, are always on your left.

- As part of your interview, you may be taken to a nice restaurant. People will be observing to determine if you can represent them well.

- Order something that is easy to eat and not the most expensive thing on the menu. A good rule is to follow the price range of the host who is taking you to dinner.

- Avoid messy foods. Spaghetti is difficult to manage, soup might drip on your clothes, and ribs can't be eaten easily.

- If you eat soup, dip your spoon away from you, rather than towards you.

- Do not push food onto your fork with your knife or a piece of bread.

- If the host orders dessert, you can do so, but you should not if he or she does not.

- Under no circumstances should you drink or smoke, even if others at the table do. If your host orders wine, you may have one glass of wine if you would like to, but you should not have any more.

- If you share foods—and this is not advised on an interview—do not pass your plate back and forth. Using a clean, unused utensil, place a portion on your bread plate and pass it to the person for whom it is intended or ask your server for a small plate.

Figure 18.6 is a diagram of a formal table setting. Study it carefully so you will know what to do if you are dining at a formal restaurant. Starting at the outer edge, use the appropriate fork with each course. Again, the rule to remember is: Solids on the left, liquids on the right; in other words, your personal bread plate is on the upper left hand side of your plate, and your drink will be on the right. If you can't remember this, wait and watch others at the table, then do what they do.

If you leave the table, place your napkin on your chair; do not put it on the table until the meal has been completed and you are leaving the restaurant. When you finish your meal and are leaving the table, fold your napkin loosely and place it back on the table.

When women approach or leave the table, men should stand. If it is a business occasion, women should stand at the beginning of the meal and shake hands as the men are doing. Women do not need to stand when someone leaves the table or returns. A man should help the woman to his right with her chair and then help the woman on his left if no one else is doing so. Take your seat from the right side of the chair.

You may be saying to yourself, "Who cares?" or "What difference does it make which fork I use?" The answer is simple and complex—no one and everyone. However, consider this: It is always better to have knowledge and skills and not need them than to need them and not have them. You will use this often!

There is much to learn en route to developing a professional presence, and you might make some mistakes. Learn from them and keep working until you are comfortable in any setting.

Figure 18.6   Formal Place Setting

Reflections:
PUTTING IT ALL TOGETHER

Avoiding workplace land mines can be quite tricky, but it's just a part of going to work every day. If you go to work with the right attitude, give your best, support your boss, and build a network of people who have goals and dreams like yours, you will be able to navigate the mine field.

In the beginning, you may have difficulty learning to dress well, to dine correctly, or simply to avoid office politics, but you will learn if you put your mind to it, and you will be surprised how much all these little things contribute to your big picture.

DIGITAL BRIEFCASE

CONDUCTING A POLL AND REPORTING DATA

Use Poll Everywhere (www.polleverywhere.com) and set up a poll that queries your social media friends on the "mistakes" they have seen people make, such as posting negative remarks about their boss or company, sending e-mails that contain obscenities on a company computer, sexting, posting pictures of drunken parties on Facebook, and others.

Also, ask them to describe in detail what the offense was, what the consequences were, and if this mistake can be rectified. Then make a three-column table with the headings "Offense," "Consequence," and "How to Resolve the Problem." Report what you learned using a chart similar to the one below. Research and write two brief paragraphs on "Avoiding Poor Choices Using Social Media."

Offense	Consequence	Resolution (if possible)
Sent offensive e-mail based on race to friend, who forwarded it to others.	Person was reprimanded by his boss and placed on probation because of violation of company policy.	Apologize to his boss and the person who was offended, and refrain from ever sending e-mails that are not work-related at work.

Offense	Consequence	Resolution (if possible)

REFERENCES

Behind bars II: Substance abuse and America's prison population. (2011). Retrieved May 14, 2011, from www.casacolumbia.org/templates/PressReleases.aspx?articleid=592&zoneid=79.

Buddy, T. (2011). Substance abuse in the workplace: A dangerous and expensive problem. Retrieved June 2, 2011, from http://alcoholism.about.com/cs/work/a/aa990120.htm.

Cooper, M. (2002). Alcohol use and risky sexual behavior among college students and youth. *Journal of Studies on Alcohol, 63*(2), 101.

Daly, K., & Richards, J. (2007). Substance abuse. Retrieved July 18, 2011, from www .emedicinehealth.com/substanceabuse/articleem.htm.

Doyle, A. (2010). How to dress for an interview. Retrieved July 18, 2011, from http:// jobsearch.about.com/od/interviewattire/a/interviewdress.htm.

Hoffman, J., & Froemke, S. (2007). *Addiction: Why can't they just stop?* Emmaus, PA: Rodale.

Kersten, D. (2002). Office romances can be risky. USA TODAY. Retrieved July 21, 2011, from www.usatoday.com/money.jobcenter/workplace/relationships/2002-11-12-office-romance.

Taylor, D. (2005). The intuitive life blog. "Why are office romances such a bad idea?" Retrieved May 18, 2011, from http://www.intuitive.com/blog/why_are_office_romances_such_a_bad_idea.html

Vault.com. (2010). Office Romance Survey 2010. Retrieved May 19, 2011, from www.vault .com/wps/portal/usa/vcm/detail/Career-Advice/Office-Romance/Office-Romance-Survey-2010?id=5519&filter_type=0&filter_id=0

Zuri, I. (2011). How to dress for work for women. Retrieved May 15, 2011, from www.ehow .com/how6223951dress-work-women.html#ixzz1MQBf9L4M.

chapter nineteen

MANAGE

NAVIGATING THE HUMAN RESOURCE MAZE

The only place where success comes before work is in the dictionary. —Vince Lombardi

Why
read this chapter?

Because you'll learn...

- The functions of human resources departments
- The differences in corporate benefits and which ones best serve you
- How companies are organized and where you fit in the structure

Because you'll be able to...

- Select benefits that protect you, your family, and your future
- Discuss various benefit packages and understand their importance to your future.

PROFESSIONALS
from the
Field

Name: Tina Petrie

Business: Director of Salary Administration and Benefits, The College of Southern Nevada

Your human resources (HR) office will be your center of information from application to retirement. Often, people think of HR as a place that hires and fires, but my advice would be to lean on your HR department for things like tax and estate planning, health spending accounts, medical plans, career path advice, professional development, and group discounts to large chains and entertainment venues. The HR department can also help you gather data to complete projects for your own department. Basically, use your HR department to leverage your benefits, information, and life planning.

OVERVIEW OF THE HUMAN RESOURCES DEPARTMENT

How Do They Manage All These Requirements?

Human resource management (HRM) is engaging people (employees) in a variety of ways and at different levels to accomplish an organization's goals and objectives. Human resource managers and employees work on a diverse array of responsibilities, ranging from recruiting to staffing to training to compensating to evaluating employees. This department is in charge of annual leave and vacations, sick leave, discrimination policies, social security deductions, taxes, retirement funds, and employee privacy. In addition, they must comply with government laws and rules such as safety regulations, and they must oversee internal corporate policies and procedures. At times, HR professionals must deal with unions and labor relations and negotiations. The illustration in Figure 19.1 shows the major functions in the HR process.

"In a large corporation, the *director of human resources* may supervise several departments, each headed by an experienced manager who most likely specializes in one human resources

Figure 19.1 Human Resource Functions

activity, such as employment and placement, compensation and benefits, training and development, or labor relations. The director may report to a top human resources executive" (U.S. Department of Labor, 2010–2011). In small companies, the HR department may consist of a manager and a few employees with multiple responsibilities.

Changes in HR Functions

Although the divisions of HR departments remain rather static, the functions are changing dramatically with shifts in technology and the global economy. "The world economy is going through a seismic shift from capital investment to intellectual capital. This shift, along with the change in the pace of business dynamics, is leading to compelling changes in the way people are managed. The boardroom has moved into the HR function, and most CEOs now don the hat of the Chief Talent Officers. As the workforce gets younger and the businesses increasingly become global and virtual, the challenge that HR faces is to engage the diverse workforce and align them to the business's objectives" (Murali, 2011). Today the HR department is heavily involved in using technology to recruit, receive and review resumés, conduct interviews, educate employees, and keep people informed about new rules and regulations.

GETTING ORIENTED AT YOUR NEW JOB

Research indicates that workers have three prime needs: Interesting work, recognition for doing a good job, and being let in on things that are going on in the company.

—Zig Ziglar, motivational speaker

Will Someone Help Me Understand All These Rules and Regulations?

From the very beginning of your contact with a company, you will be dealing with some aspect of HR. Someone from HR might interview you in addition to managers from the area where you are trying to find employment. If you are offered a position, HR will handle your employment paperwork. HR professionals will inform you about benefits the company offers. They will most likely provide training, and they are in charge of developing forms for evaluation purposes.

GRADUATE Quote

William Paddock
Graduate!
Louisville Technical Institute, Louisville, KY
Career: IT Security Specialist, First Technology

Completing your degree does not complete your learning—especially in fields that change rapidly, such as information technology and health science. Learning never stops. If you stop learning, you stop growing and then no one will hire you. You have to continually upgrade your knowledge base. You will also need to learn how to deal with the massive amounts of change in today's workplace. If I had not done this, I would not have survived.

One of the first ways you might be engaged with the HR department staff is through the company's orientation program for new employees. During this time, you will be provided a great deal of information about the company, including the company's history, the products and services it provides, policies and procedures, and financial data. You will most likely be provided information relative to the company's organizational structure, vision statement, mission statement, and goals and objectives. You will learn the names of people on the executive team. You may hear from a higher-level executive at some point in the process, and you might be given information about the company's primary competitors, clients, and market region.

In addition, you will complete a number of forms related to the hiring process. These forms will include a W-4, which informs HR how to withhold your taxes. At this time, you will also be informed about the company's benefits program. If your company requires that you wear an identification badge, this will be given to you. You might also be given keys to certain areas to which you will need access. At some point during the orientation process, you may be given a copy of the employee handbook. An HR person will go over some of the most important points, but you should read the entire handbook and keep it in your work area as a reference. You will probably need to refer to it often as you become familiar with your new position.

You may feel a little overwhelmed when hearing all of this data in a short period of time. Take good notes and take home any information provided to study it carefully. Do not hesitate to ask questions if there is anything that you do not understand. One of the most important areas for you to comprehend is the benefits section. It is much better to ask questions than to make a major mistake in selecting benefits.

UNDERSTANDING AND SELECTING BENEFITS

How Can I Get the 411 on My 401(k)?

Even in economic downturns, employers are always looking for ways to attract high-quality employees. Offering an outstanding benefits program is one way of attracting good people. Employers are always looking for unique ways to reward employees in order to retain their services. When you are interviewing for a new position, one of the areas you need to examine most closely is the benefits program, and after you accept a position, you really need to pay close attention. Benefits are **indirect compensation** (financial rewards that are not included in your paycheck such as paid holidays, medical insurance, or child care). Another name for benefits is "perks," and you might hear it mentioned in the workplace.

According to the U.S. Bureau of Labor Statistics, the cost to companies in supplying benefits to their employees has risen sharply. Many companies provide thousands of dollars in benefits to each employee annually. "U.S. businesses pay an average of $7.40 per hour that each employee works. The average cost of health care benefits is approximately $8424 annually per person" (Mondy, 2010). Because of the extraordinary costs of providing employee benefits, some companies are taking a less paternalistic approach and shifting more of the responsibility to employees themselves. Rather than provide retirement programs, more and more companies are moving to 401(k) programs to which employees contribute and manage themselves.

Usually only full-time employees receive benefits, although some companies provide limited benefits for part-time employees. You should consider benefits as part of your compensation package, and you should weigh their value very carefully when making an employment decision. Benefits are very expensive if you have to pay for them yourself. For example, if you have small children and your company provides child care as a benefit, this can save you thousands of dollars every year, plus give you the satisfaction of knowing your children are taken care of while you work.

> People are definitely a company's greatest asset. It doesn't make any difference whether the product is cars or cosmetics. A company is only as good as the people it keeps.
>
> —Mary Kay Ash, founder of Mary Kay Cosmetics

Full-time employees usually receive **direct benefits** (monetary value) and **indirect benefits** (such as sick leave and vacation). Due to rapidly rising costs, many companies are reducing the amounts of some of their benefits and eliminating others altogether. The list of potential employee benefits offered by companies usually includes a retirement plan, 401(k) plan, vacation, sick leave, personal leave, health insurance, life insurance, dental insurance, disability insurance, employee stock ownership plans, maternity leave, paternity leave, vision plans, and parking.

Some benefits such as paid vacation and holidays are considered company paid. Benefits to which the employee contributes are considered employee paid—employees are usually required to make a contribution to the cost of their health insurance, for example, because it is so expensive. Study Figure 19.2 for information on 10 of the most frequently provided benefits.

Benefits such as unemployment insurance, worker's compensation, social security, and family and medical leave are mandated by the federal government. "Approximately 95 percent of the workers in this country pay into and may draw Social Security benefits" (Mondy, 2010). The looming retirement of the "baby boomers" has endangered the solvency of social security if it continues on its current path. Congress has to find solutions and make changes in the next two decades or the program will not be able to pay full benefits.

> *The flatter the corporate hierarchy, the more likely it is that employees will communicate bad news and act upon it.*
> —Bill Gates

Figure 19.2 Understanding Benefits Programs

Type of Benefit	Explanation
Health Care	The most expensive benefit provided. Includes **HMOs** (exercises control over which doctors and facilities you can use); **PPOs** (encourages employees to use services specified by the system, with out-of-system services costing more); **defined contribution health care plans** (provides employees a specified amount of money, which they can use to purchase health insurance of their choice); and **major medical** (designed to cover large medical expenses brought about by long-term illness or serious diseases or accidents).
Dental and Vision Care	The costs provided for these benefits vary by company, but they usually require a small deductible before paying approximately 50 to 100 percent of the costs for dental preventive services. Some plans cover partial costs of orthodontics. Vision plans may cover the costs of eye examinations and all or part of the cost of glasses.
Retirement Plans	**Defined benefit plans** provide a fixed amount of money each month to retired employees and are usually based on years of service and an average of the employee's salary during the last years of work. Employees know exactly how much money they will receive each month under this program. Because of extraordinary costs, this type of program is declining, and the burden of planning for retirement is now on the employee. In **defined contribution plans,** employers make specific contributions to employees' retirement programs. The amount of money available to the employee at retirement under this plan will depend on how well investments made by the employee performed. **401(k) plans** fall under this category.
Paid Vacations	A very popular program with employees that allows them to rejuvenate and rest. Usually, the number of days increases with seniority.
Sick Leave	Employees who are too sick to come to work are still paid for a certain number of days each year.
Employee Stock Options (ESOP)/Profit Sharing	Companies who offer this benefit contribute shares of stock to employees based on their salaries. Some people believe that ESOP participation causes employees to work harder and to be more concerned about productivity. The downside to ESOPs is that employees cannot sell their stock until they retire, meaning that they cannot capitalize on an upswing in the stock market.

Type of Benefit	Explanation
Life Insurance	Many companies provide life insurance for employees in the amount of 1½ times their salaries, with options to purchase more for their themselves and their families.
Child Care	For employees who have small children, this is a very important benefit. Usually, the child care program is not paid 100 percent, but is subsidized, thus reducing the very expensive cost of child care. Some companies provide emergency care for children when babysitting services are not available on a temporary basis.
Education Reimbursement	Many employers will pay for employees to go back to school. Benefits vary but usually reimburse expenses based on achieving a certain grade. Some will pay only for courses or programs related to an employee's work.
Flextime or Flexible Scheduling	For many employees, this is a great benefit because it gives them the opportunity to choose some of the hours they work, and they can fit their work around family needs. Usually, employees are required to be at work during a core time (for example, 10:00–2:00) but are allowed to choose to come in early or stay late.

Choosing the Right Benefits

In some companies, all employees are provided the same basic benefits. In other companies, a **cafeteria benefits plan** is used. This type of plan allows employees to select certain benefits. Some companies provide the basic benefits such as health insurance for everyone in addition to the ones selected by the employee; others allow employees to choose from the cafeteria plan for all their benefits. An employee who has small children might select child care, whereas an employee who is taking care of older parents might select elder care. Employees select benefits based on their current stage of life and on what their individual needs are.

The following is a list of benefits your employer may offer:

Retirement plan	Child care	Parking
401(k) plan	Educational assistance	Company car (provided for certain positions)
Prescription drug program	Scholarships for dependents	Free meals in the cafeteria
Dental insurance	Vision care	Chiropractic visits
Family medical program	Legal assistance	Relocation benefits
Major medical insurance	Elder care	Flextime schedule
Flexible spending medical account	Paid vacation	Telecommuting
Medical insurance	Paid holidays	Compressed work week
Dental insurance	Paid personal days	Employee stock options
Life insurance	Company discounts	Health center

As you review the extensive list of benefits above, think about how your choice of benefits might change according to your age and family status. If you were going to work today and were offered a cafeteria plan for all your benefits and could choose only five to seven from the list, which ones would benefit you most? List them below:

1. _____

2. _____

3. _____

4. _____

5. _____

MAKING AN IMPORTANT CHOICE

How Do I Decide Which Job to Accept?

One of the most effective ways to make a decision is to use a numerical scale to actually assign a "grade" to each choice before you. This exercise is designed to help you make a choice between two job offers in relation to benefits. Of course, benefits are not the only major factor you have to consider when choosing between two jobs, but it is one of the most important components. This decision chart works in the following way:

- **Create an Element (benefit) column.** This column lists the aspects of the decision that are important to you, such as pay, potential for growth, joy of work, and so on.
- **Create a Rating of Importance column.** This column gives each element a rating that *you* assign. Using a scale of 1 to 10, you will decide if a particular benefit is very important (an 8, 9, or 10) or if it is not very important (a 1, 2, or 3).
- **Create a Choice 1 column.** This column will list the numerical calculations for your first job offer. You will decide how good this company's benefits program is in terms of a specific benefit and then multiply that number by your importance rating.
- **Create a Choice 2 column.** This column will list the numerical calculations for your second job offer. You will decide how good this company's benefits program is in terms of a specific benefit and then multiply that number by your importance rating.

Once you have created your columns (see Figure 19.3), you will work through your decisions using your head and your heart. Assume Samantha has been offered two jobs. Review how she

---

Figure 19.3 Samantha's Decision-Making Chart

The following example shows a decision-making chart between two job offers for Samantha. The Element (benefit) column lists the items that are most important to Samantha in selecting a new job.

Element (benefit)	My Rating of Importance 1–10	Choice 1 Job at Mercy Hospital	Choice 2 Job at Grace Hospital
Health insurance	10	Rating = 5 $10 \times 5 = 50$	Rating = 8 $10 \times 8 = 80$
Child care	10	Rating = 9 $10 \times 9 = 90$	Rating = 7 $10 \times 7 = 70$
Flexible schedule	7	Rating = 2 $7 \times 2 = 14$	Rating = 5 $7 \times 5 = 35$
Retirement plan	9	Rating = 9 $9 \times 9 = 81$	Rating = 5 $9 \times 5 = 45$
Paid vacation	8	Rating = 8 $8 \times 8 = 64$	Rating = 6 $8 \times 6 = 48$
		TOTAL SCORE = 299	TOTAL SCORE = 278

Figure 19.4 Decision-Making Chart

Element (benefit)	My Rating of Importance 1–10	Choice 1	Choice 2
		TOTAL SCORE =	**TOTAL SCORE =**

rated each benefit for the two different companies to help her make a decision about which job to accept.

As you can see, Samantha's best option in terms of benefits is Mercy Hospital. A numerical score may not be the ultimate way to make a decision, but at least you have taken the time to think about what is important to you, what is offered within the choices, and how it ranks in importance to you. By using this system, you are calling on your head and your heart to make decisions that could affect your life for a very long time.

Now, using the top five benefits that you selected above, insert them into the Decision-Making Chart in Figure 19.4. For purposes of this exercise, you can make up information about the two jobs.

PERFORMANCE APPRAISALS

How Do I Earn a Good Score?

Performance evaluations make everyone a little nervous, but there are ways to prepare for them that should relieve you of worry. When you are in an orientation program, find out when you will be evaluated and by whom. You will probably be evaluated at the end of your probationary period and thereafter on an annual basis. Ask for a copy of the appraisal instrument and go over it carefully to be sure you are doing everything that falls under your job description. You may be doing a great job in almost everything but get a low rating in one category because you simply ignored it.

Some companies will have you complete a **self-appraisal** prior to the one conducted by your supervisor. Self-appraisals are documents that are completed by the employee in advance of the formal evaluation and are designed to inform the boss. Most people tend to evaluate

BIGGEST INTERVIEW *Blunders*

Quan landed an interview with a company that was seeking a person for her dream job. She prepared carefully, dressed well, and arrived on time. But only a few minutes into the interview, Quan interrupted the interviewer to ask about benefits, telling the interviewer, "Benefits are my main consideration in accepting a position." Quan should have waited until the second interview to bring up benefits, or she should have given the interviewer time to introduce the subject during the interview. Because Quan appeared to be much more interested in her own compensation than she was in doing a good job for the company, she did not get the job.

LESSON: Wait until the second interview to mention salary and benefits. The interviewer knows you are interested and will most likely discuss it with you before you have to ask.

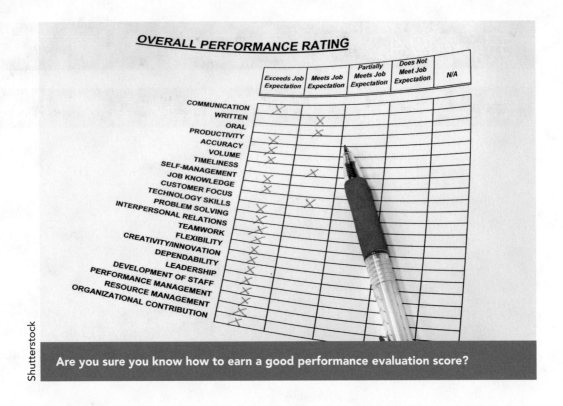

Are you sure you know how to earn a good performance evaluation score?

Shutterstock

themselves fairly accurately and are often tougher on themselves than their bosses are. A self-appraisal is a good opportunity to make sure your boss knows everything you have been doing. Remember, your boss is very busy and does not always know exactly what you are doing or how hard you are working. Tell the truth and do not be overly critical of yourself. This is a time to "toot your own horn" in an appropriate manner. Attach a list of major accomplishments that you have achieved since the last evaluation period. If you are not asked to complete a self-appraisal form, provide the list of accomplishments to your boss in a memo prior to the formal evaluation.

There are numerous appraisal methods and systems, including the rating scale method, the critical incident method, the work standards method, the forced distribution method, and the popular 360-degree feedback evaluation method, to name a few. The important thing is to find out exactly how you will be evaluated, get a copy of the instrument, evaluate yourself periodically, and be sure you are performing all aspects of your job in an outstanding manner.

MAXIMIZING PRODUCTIVITY

What Makes a Company Run?

Many people go to work and just try to learn only their own job. Most entry-level jobs are rather narrow in scope, and if that is all you learn, you are not likely to progress very fast. You should go to work with the idea that you "own the company" and that you want to learn everything you can possibly uncover. Ideally, you have already learned a great deal about the company when you were preparing to interview, but now you are on the inside and there is so much more to grasp. Pay attention to what the top executives do. What do they wear? How do they conduct themselves? What are their goals? Ask questions, read company documents, and observe carefully. Your eyes should be like little cameras—clicking, clicking, clicking, and storing up knowledge and information to help you be more productive and efficient.

Some of the things you need to familiarize yourself with are the company's **mission statement** (the purpose of the company, which answers the question, "Why does this company exist?"), **vision statement** (where the company is trying to go, which might be described as a picture of the company in the future), and **core values statement (a** guide for the company's internal conduct, which determines its relationship with the external world).

A mission statement should be clear and brief so that everyone in the company can quote it from memory. An example of a mission statement follows. This one belongs to Aflac:

Mission Statement

To combine aggressive strategic marketing with quality products and services at competitive prices to provide the best insurance value for consumers.

There is no doubt as to the purpose of this company. The employees know what they are trying to accomplish, the customers can understand what the company stands for, and the marketing and advertising are geared to match the mission.

Examples of vision statements follow:

Disney: To make people happy.

Walmart: Worldwide leader in retail.

Ritz Carlton: We are ladies and gentlemen serving ladies and gentlemen.

There is no doubt in anyone's mind what these companies are trying to accomplish.

An example of a core value statement follows.

1. **Accountability.** To accept responsibility for all our actions and all subsequent effects upon the community.

2. **Community.** To be an organization that gives back to the community, both with the services we provide and the charitable work we do.

3. **Diversity.** To appreciate the richness of a diverse staff and strive to build a team that reflects the diversity of the community we serve.

4. **Ethics.** To foster a workplace environment in which honesty and integrity are valued.

5. **Excellence.** To perform our services better than any of our competitors.

6. **Profit.** To give our valued shareholders the return they deserve by being financially successful.

7. **Leadership.** To provide visionary leadership that includes employee development.

A company's administrators and leaders typically develop the **strategic plan,** which might be described as a roadmap that flows from the mission and vision statements. This plan encompasses the strategy, the action plan, and the deadlines of how the company will accomplish its vision. Each department within the company will have certain **goals and objectives** to carry out that are part of the master plan. Goals are broad statements that are connected to the mission statement, and objectives are more clearly defined statements that detail exactly what the company plans to do. Figure 19.5 provides a visual illustration of what a strategic plan is all about.

When you go to work, ask for copies of the mission, vision, and core values statements. If possible, secure these documents and read them before you interview with a company. Take time to study them and strive to work in such a way as to help your company's leaders accomplish their goals for the business, employees, and customers. Some companies do not distribute the entire strategic plan, but if yours does, read it carefully. You'll be ahead of most of your colleagues in understanding what your leaders are trying to accomplish and how you can help.

Figure 19.5 Strategic Planning Diagram

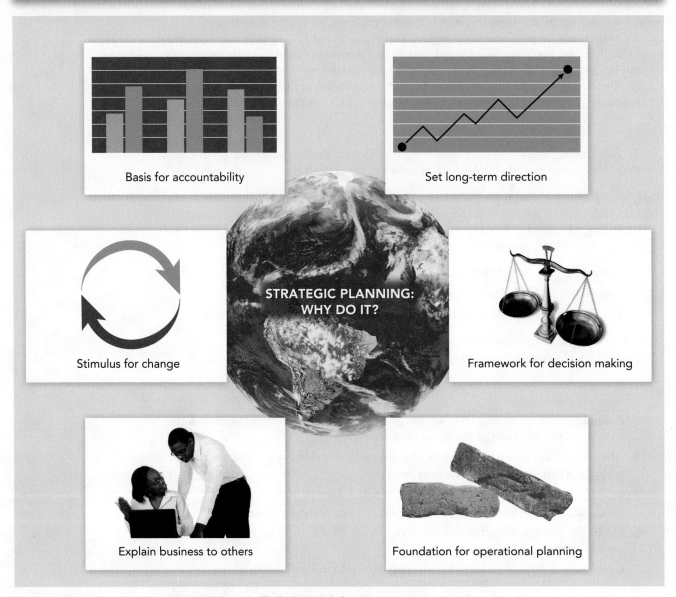

Basis for accountability

Set long-term direction

STRATEGIC PLANNING: WHY DO IT?

Stimulus for change

Framework for decision making

Explain business to others

Foundation for operational planning

Source: Adapted from NovaMind Strategic Planning Mind Mapping Software.

COMPANY ORGANIZATIONAL STRUCTURE

What Is the Big Picture?

The **organizational structure** of a company is a critical part of corporate effectiveness and internal customer satisfaction. The organizational structure determines how the company uses its resources and how it arranges itself. The structure may be one that divides employees into departments, each of which has a specific function. The organizational structure determines how the **five critical functions of management**—planning, organizing, staffing, leading, and controlling—will be carried out. Figure 19.6 illustrates the five functions of management.

Figure 19.6 The Five Functions of Management

Planning	Organizing	Staffing	Leading	Controlling
Plan strategy, set goals, establish deadlines, and develop action plan.	Decide what has to be done, how it will be accomplished, and who will do it.	Decide how employees will be organized, recruited, trained, and developed.	Determine how to motivate employees to carry out strategic plan, direct employee tasks and projects, and resolve conflicts.	Oversee corporate activities, projects, and plans to ensure satisfactory completion in a timely manner.

Every company has an **organizational chart**. Most people go to work every day and try to do their jobs well, but they don't have a clue as to how their company is organized, where they fit in the big picture, and who reports to whom. You should get a copy of your company's organizational structure and study it carefully. This chart will detail for you exactly what your career path might be as you move up the ladder, as well as other possible options. An example of one type of organizational chart is shown in Figure 19.7. The chart details key functions in this company and shows the lines of authority. Companies are typically organized around the functions that employees carry out. In the case of this company, the business is organized around the functions of marketing, finance, operations, human resources, and information systems.

Companies have a board of directors to which the CEO (chief executive officer and the company leader) reports directly. The board's job is to work with the CEO in developing

Figure 19.7 Organizational Chart

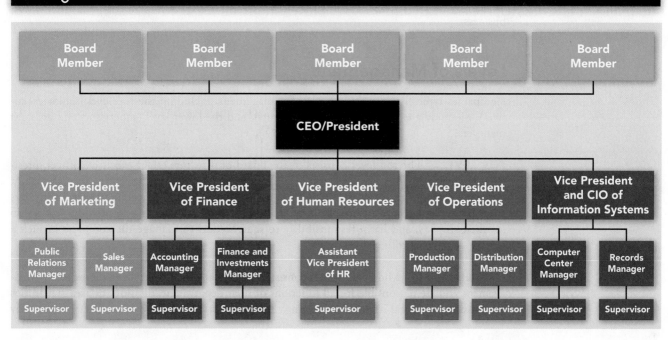

Three Rules of Work:
Out of clutter find simplicity;
From discord find harmony;
In the middle of difficulty
lies opportunity.
—Albert Einstein

the corporate strategy. The board members are elected to their positions by the shareholders (people who own stock in the company). Some companies have a CEO and a president; in some cases, one person serves as both the president and the CEO. The vice president of information systems is also frequently referred to as the CIO (chief information officer).

Responsibilities of Each Department

The **marketing department** handles the functions of creating the company's image and promoting and distributing the products or services. The **finance department** is responsible for controlling, managing, and growing the company's financial assets. The finance department is also responsible for developing and managing budgets. The **accounting department** handles payroll, incoming and outgoing cash and checks, and invoices and purchase orders. The **human resources department** takes care of all personnel issues, including recruiting, hiring, compensation packages, training programs, promotions, and terminations. The **operations department** is in charge of producing and distributing the products or services offered by the company. The **information systems department** deals with everything related to electronic management of information and all operations having to do with computers, including evaluating, purchasing, installing, and managing new software and computers.

There are many different types of organization charts and ways of organizing a company or institution. You should find your immediate supervisor on the chart and see to whom he or she reports. You should also be able to identify the top corporate officers if you see them in the building or meet them on some occasion, assuming you go to work for a big company and may not know the top officers. An important thing to remember: Do not go over your boss's head to his or her boss. Follow the lines of authority.

Although many corporate structures are organized differently depending on the business of the company, most will have a similar structure to the one that follows in Figure 19.8. Each level of employees has a specific function to perform, again depending on the nature of the company's business.

Levels of Management

Companies typically have three levels of management, including the top level (senior executives), the middle level (managers and directors), and the lower level (supervisors and assistant managers).

TOP LEVEL. The top level consists of the board of directors, chief executive officer, president, or managing director. The top level of management has the authority to make major decisions, to manage goals, and to develop policies for the company. The top level considers strategic decisions, controls activities of all departments and employees, provides leadership for the company, and has a responsibility to shareholders to manage the company in such a way as to make a profit.

MIDDLE LEVEL. Middle managers consist of managers and directors who report to top management and are responsible for all functions of their department, division, or area. Their jobs are considered tactical in nature, meaning they tie the strategy to the department's day-to-day

Figure 19.8 Corporate Structure

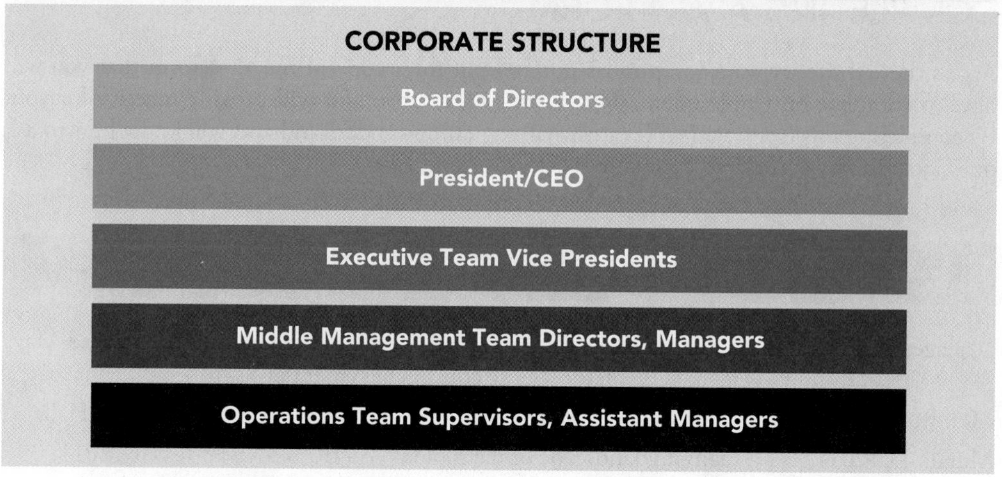

CORPORATE STRUCTURE

Board of Directors

President/CEO

Executive Team Vice Presidents

Middle Management Team Directors, Managers

Operations Team Supervisors, Assistant Managers

functions. They are primarily involved in organizing and directing functions for the area for which they are responsible. This group of managers must follow company policies, provide training for their subordinates, carry out directives from top management, write reports and send critical data to top management, evaluate employees' performance, and provide leadership for their division.

LOWER LEVEL.   The lower level of management is the operations level, or the level where the actual day-to-day work is performed. Managers at this level may be called supervisors, assistant managers, foremen, or superintendents. They are concerned with getting the job done and use the direction and controlling functions of management. Their job consists of assigning jobs and tasks to employees, providing guidance as to how to perform a task, ensure quality control, make recommendations to higher level managers, provide training to new employees, procure the products needed to do the job, prepare and deliver reports to higher levels of management, and discipline and motivate employees (Management Study Guide, Columbia College).

> *I'm a great believer in luck, and I find the harder I work the more I have of it.*
>
> —Thomas Jefferson

Reflections: PUTTING IT ALL TOGETHER

Learning everything you can about your company makes you a better and more engaged employee. When you go to work, try not to focus only on the narrow aspects of your particular position. Instead, try to understand how what you are doing fits into the big picture. What is happening around you? Who is doing what? Who is performing extraordinarily well and would be someone to emulate?

Who might be a good mentor for you? How does the expansion into international markets affect you, and what opportunities does it offer? What new degrees or courses could you take to enhance your career opportunities? Turn yourself into an inquisitive, involved, and concerned employee who is career oriented and at the same time, willing to give 100 percent back to the company that writes your paycheck.

DIGITAL BRIEFCASE

COMPLETING A W-4 FORM

Access the website www.irs.gov/pub/irs-pdf/fw4.pdf for a copy of the W-4 form that you will have to complete on employment. This form is interactive and will provide practice for you. By completing this form, you will learn what you do not understand and will know how to ask questions before you have to complete this form at a real job.

REFERENCES

Management Study Guide, Columbia College. (2010). Levels of management. Retrieved May 9, 2010, from www.managementstudyguide.com/managementlevels.htm.

Mondy, R. W. (2010). *Human resource management.* Upper Saddle River, NJ: Prentice Hall.

Murali, D. (2011). The changing landscape of technology in HR. Retrieved June 6, 2011, from www.thehindu.com/business/Industry/article2076741.ece.

U. S. Department of Labor. (2010–2011). *Occupational outlook handbook.* Human resources, training and labor relations managers and specialists. Retrieved June 4, 2011, from www .bls.gov/oco/ocos021.htm.

Part VI: Connections

Chapters taken from:
Cornerstones for Professionalism, Second Edition
by Robert M. Sherfield and Patricia G. Moody

chapter twenty

CONNECT

WORKING WITH TECHNOLOGY IN A KNOWLEDGE ECONOMY

Never before in history has innovation offered so much promise to so many in such a short time.
—Bill Gates, Microsoft founder

Why read this chapter?

Because you'll learn...

- To define digital workplace, social media, and the knowledge economy
- Qualifications for working in the knowledge economy
- How technology can assist you in all phases of your career

Because you'll be able to...

- Access tutorials to assist you in learning certain programs
- Identify specific programs that you need to know in any workplace

PROFESSIONALS from the Field

Name: Cathy Lanier

Business: CEO/President Technology Solutions

Few things are more important to a successful career today than a comprehensive knowledge of technology. Not only must you be adept at using word processing, spreadsheet and presentation software, and e-mail, but effective use of social media is becoming increasingly important for an employee's business profile. In addition to being technology efficient, you must be good at writing effective messages, using appropriate netiquette rules, and making good decisions about what to spend your time on when at work. You also need to learn the technologies that allow you to collaborate and share documents because so much work is now done collectively from a variety of offices all over the world. The basic point you need to know and embrace about technology is this: Technology is always changing, and you have to change with it or you will be left behind in this "brave new world."

THE KNOWLEDGE ECONOMY

What's It Got to Do with You?

Over the past decade the world has gone through traumatic times—financial crisis, mortgage meltdown, several simultaneous wars, and political stalemates, just to name a few. At the same time, a somewhat silent "event" was taking place in the U.S. workplace. Slowly but surely, the economy has become a knowledge economy as opposed to a manufacturing economy. This new workplace requires a complex set of skills that includes decision making, problem solving, communication, analysis, relationship building, collaboration, and technology abilities. "Today 48 million of the more than 137 million U.S. workers are knowledge workers, making this group the fastest growing talent pool in most organizations . . . 70 percent of all U.S. jobs created since 1998—4.5 million jobs, or roughly the combined workforce of the fifty-six largest public companies by market capitalization—require a set of conceptual tacit skills" (Meister & Willyerd, 2010).

> The global economy is giving more of our own people, and billions around the world, the chance to work and live and raise their families with dignity.
>
> —Bill Clinton

"Knowledge workers fuel innovation and growth . . . The heart of what knowledge workers do on the job is collaborate, which in the broadest terms means they interact to solve problems, serve customers, engage with partners, and nurture new ideas . . . Those able to use new technologies to reshape how they work are finding significant productivity gains" (Manyika, Sprague, & Yee, 2009). The knowledge economy is all about working smarter and using technology to build an innovative, collaborative, and frequently, global workforce.

This path to working smarter is characterized by:

I. Using technology to enhance the connections between people and establish a collaborative environment to improve productivity and quality,

II. Optimizing workflows to reduce costs and ensure that work gets done by the right person and the right team in the right sequence at the right time,

III. Ensuring that accurate and consistent information about business can be accessed by all who need it, when they need it,

IV. Integrating applications with business processes so they serve the needs of the business, and

V. Creating a continuous improvement in business processes with the help of analytics and metrics. (IBM, 2009)

What does the knowledge economy have to do with you? Everything! Everything about how work is done in this country—from nursing to welding to accounting—is changing rapidly and will continue to evolve. U.S. companies are shifting much of their manufacturing and lower-level tasks to less expensive workers in developing countries while simultaneously creating a wave of knowledge jobs here.

Why would you want to be one of the new breed of knowledge workers? Because these employees "earn a wage premium that ranges from 55 percent to 75 percent over the pay of workers who perform more basic production and transaction tasks" (Manyika, Sprague, & Yee, 2009). Regardless of what career you pursue, you will most likely use a computer and perform at least some tasks of a knowledge worker.

Thomas Friedman, author of *The World Is Flat,* has called today's global economy "a world without walls." The term *flat world* means that the playing field has been leveled because of technological advances. It doesn't matter if you live in a highly developed country or a developing country, because if you can "plug and play," you can compete. Changes are happening so fast and worldwide competition is increasing so rapidly that companies can ill afford to focus on one change at a time; rather, they must address many fronts at once. Headquarters of the world's largest companies have made major shifts in recent years, with the United States losing 38 companies. Many corporations are moving to the so-called BRIC countries (Brazil, Russia, India, and China). "By 2020, the BRIC countries will be the dominant centers of economic influence" (Meister & Willyerd, 2010).

U.S. corporations have reached out all over the world to find employees who have the knowledge and skills to help them become more productive at lower costs. The world's largest corporations and the newest high-tech start-up companies are tapping into a global talent pool as they develop a virtual workforce. Today's employees may become part of a global team with members who telecommute from home. These workers from the "flat world" communicate using innovative technology such as instant messaging, collaborative software, global conference calls, and document-sharing sites. Professional athletic teams have long recruited stars from all over the world. Now businesses are following suit, making the competition for technology jobs even tougher.

As the changing global workplace closes some doors for U.S. workers, it will open new ones for those who are properly prepared. If you can speak a second language such as Spanish or Mandarin, you may have an opportunity to work in an international arena or interface between foreign employees and U.S. workers. A solid language skill could provide an opportunity to be an interpreter, marketer, or salesperson in an international market. As you develop your "personal brand," use every skill you have worked hard to learn. A second language is a major asset.

The good news? You can do this. You can become the marketer of your own brand if you can use technology skillfully, make good decisions, work collaboratively, communicate across language barriers, and think innovatively. Many tutorial programs exist online that are free and easy to use and enable you to teach yourself many of the new programs. Here we will discuss many of the technologies you need to learn and how to access tutorial programs.

You can prepare yourself to become a knowledge worker in a global economy if you are willing to work hard and smart. You can also prepare yourself to be a knowledge worker in a small business in Anytown, USA. Regardless of what field you pursue, you will no doubt, in some ways, become a knowledge worker.

Will the communication habits of today's Millenial Generation carry over into the workplace?

Shutterstock

THE NEW CONNECTIVITY CULTURE

What Role Will You Play?

Today we live in a constantly connected world, and people all over the world are players. You might say, "They are always on, always available." The lines have blurred

Figure 20.1   Who Are the Hyperconnected Players?

- They are located all over the world, but more heavily concentrated in Latin America and Asia Pacific.
- They tend to be clustered in the banking and tech industries.
- They come in all ages, but over 60 percent are under age 35.
- Sixty-three percent of them have WiFi at home.
- They play more networked games than others.
- Their culture includes men and women, but most are men.
- They tend to work in companies that have a high concentration of high-tech equipment and the latest technologies.
- The hyperconnected can be found throughout a company, but most are in management.
- They might be located in any job but tend to work in a high-tech industry.
- They are most likely to live in a city.
- If they leave their homes for 24 hours, they are more likely to take their laptops than their wallets.
- They look at connectedness as normal and tend to blur lines between work and leisure. They are always checking their messages.

Source: Adapted partially from Aducci et al., 2008.

between work and social use of technology, becoming somewhat addictive for many who use multiple devices.

Today's youth are growing up as part of the so-called hyperconnected community. Those who fit this mold are always connected—at the movies, at home, in a restaurant, at work, on a trip—everywhere. If you observe a teenager, you will most likely see him texting on his cell phone, IMing, reading a message on Facebook or Twitter, doing homework with an iPod stuck in his ear, and perhaps interacting with others' avatars in an online video game. Today's youth are always in touch with their family, friends, and coworkers. Exactly who are these hyperconnected people and what are their characteristics? Study Figure 20.1 for a more detailed explanation.

> 96% of Millennials, also known as Generation Y, have joined a social network and 80% of companies use social media for recruitment.
>
> —Eric Qualman, *Socialnomics*

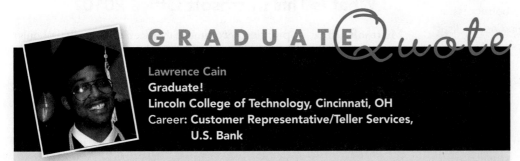

GRADUATE Quote

Lawrence Cain
Graduate!
Lincoln College of Technology, Cincinnati, OH
Career: **Customer Representative/Teller Services,**
            U.S. Bank

You control your own destiny. As long as you know and live by this, you have no excuses. You have to create your own future through goal setting, knowledge, and hard work. There will be people who help you along the way, but basically your future is what you make of it. No one is coming to rescue you. No one is going to save you. You have to save yourself and make your own way.

BIGGEST INTERVIEW *Blunders*

Ramon was excited when he was granted an interview with the largest plumbing company in his city. His goal was to become an entrepreneur and he planned to start his own company after he gained experience. In the interview, Ramon was asked if he knew how to use accounting software such as Quicken or QuickBooks. Without hesitating, Ramon answered, "Oh, I took a course that had a unit on that, but I didn't pay much attention to it because I was primarily interested in just the plumbing courses." The interviewer explained to him that this was a very progressive company. "Our plumbing associates all carry handheld electronic devices that require them to know QuickBooks. Our system requires our associates to submit invoices and other information directly to our central system." Ramon realized he had made a bad statement and quickly added, "Now that I realize how important it is, I'll go back and learn this software, and I'll start immediately." Ramon was fortunate. He got the job, but he learned a valuable lesson: technology is used in almost every job today, and you can never know too much.

LESSON: When you interview and begin work in a new company, be willing to do what needs to be done to be successful. You must always be learning new skills if you are going to be successful in the workforce today.

We are likely to see as much as 40 percent of the labor force in the hyperconnected culture within the next few years.

DEFINING THE DIGITAL WORKPLACE

Are You Ready for the Future?

The digital workplace has become a reality and is expected to grow exponentially in years to come. The digital universe is defined as "information that is created, captured, or replicated in digital form" (Meister & Willyerd, 2010). This revolution is redefining what constitutes work, how we perform work, how we measure work, and how we lead and manage employees who may be working on site or from distant workspaces. Study Figure 20.2 to understand some of these major changes. Regardless of where you work and what job you are doing, your work will be affected in some ways by the digital universe.

In the next few sections, we will introduce you to a number of technology programs that you need to be able to use in today's workplace. You can't possibly learn everything that is available or keep up with all the new programs that are constantly emerging, but you need to always be familiar with the most popular and widely used.

One of the best ways to learn new technology is to use the tutorials that you can find on websites such as YouTube and www.butterscotch.com. You can teach yourself how to use many new programs if you are persistent and patient.

THE SOFTWARE PACKAGE THAT YOU ABSOLUTELY MUST KNOW!

So What Is This Microsoft Office 2010?

Microsoft Office is a proprietary commercial office suite of several popular interrelated desktop applications, servers, and services for the Microsoft Windows and Mac OS X operating systems. This package was introduced by Microsoft in 1989 and has been refined several times since then. The current version for PC is Microsoft Office Suite 2010. Few offices operate today without Microsoft Office, and because it is so dominant, it is a "must know" for anyone entering the workforce.

The major desktop applications are Word (word processing), Excel (spreadsheets), Outlook (e-mail), PowerPoint (presentations), OneNote (digital notebook), and Publisher (desktop publishing). We highly advise you to spend as much time as necessary to become proficient in Microsoft Office. Screen captures of Microsoft Word, Excel, PowerPoint, Outlook, OneNote, and Publisher are shown on the following pages.

Figure 20.2 Impact of the Digital Universe

- More video was uploaded to YouTube in the past two months than if ABC, CBS, and NBC had been airing new content continuously since 1948.
- Launched in 2001, Wikipedia now features over 13 million articles in over 200 languages.
- Newspapers and traditional advertising are in steep decline, but digital advertising is growing rapidly.
- The average American teen sends 2,272 text messages per month.
- The mobile device will be the world's primary connection to the Internet in 2020.
- Ninety-three percent of adults in the United States own a cell phone.
- In February of 2008, John McCain raised $11 million for his U.S. presidential bid. Barack Obama attended no campaign fundraisers but utilized online social networks to raise $55 million in 29 days.

Source: Based on XPLANE, The Economist, Karl Fisch, Scott McLeod, and Laura Bestler, "Did You Know? 4.0" [video]. Retrieved May 28, 2011, from http://www.youtube.com/watch?v=rhe2XUKZ-fU&noredirect=1

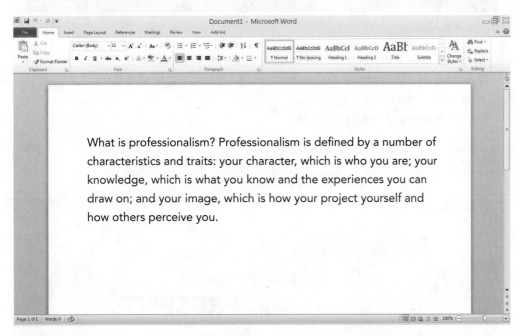

Used with permission from Microsoft.

The three main things you need to be able to do with **Word** are:

- Set up and produce documents, letters, and memos
- Import pictures, graphs, and other items from the Internet
- Back up and transport your work by downloading documents to a flash drive

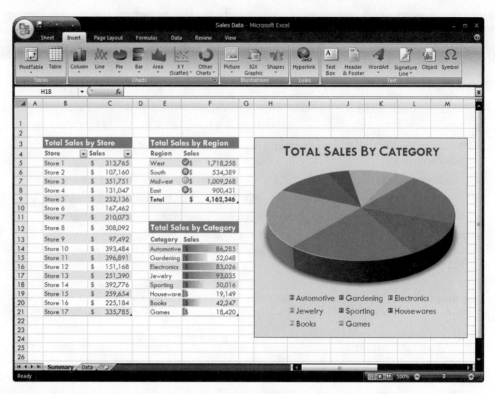

Used with permission from Microsoft.

The three main things you need to be able to do with **Excel** are:

- Understand the parts of a spreadsheet and what you can do with them
- Set up a spreadsheet
- Store values and make calculations

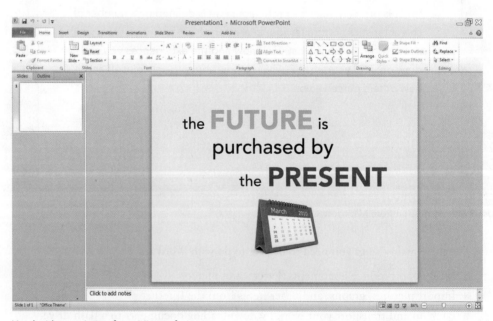

Used with permission from Microsoft.

The three main things you should be able to do with **PowerPoint** are:

- Understand the basics in making slideshows appealing and interesting
- Use the program to design and build a presentation
- Design slides that include animation and imported art and pictures

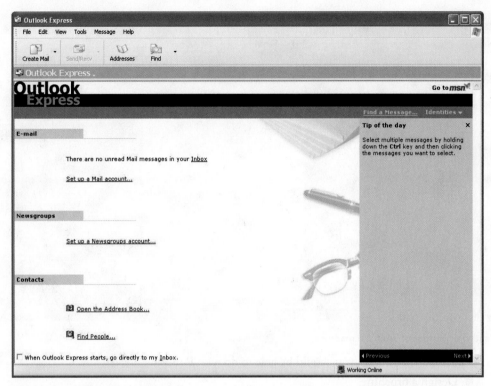

Used with permission from Microsoft.

The three main things you should be able to do with **Outlook** are:

- Send and receive e-mail
- Manage your calendar and share it with colleagues
- Manage your to do list

Used with permission from Microsoft.

The three main things you should be able to do with **OneNote** are:

- Organize your work into various levels of folders, sections, and pages
- Use note flags to denote importance and action to be taken
- Organize your current responsibilities and be able to find everything in one place

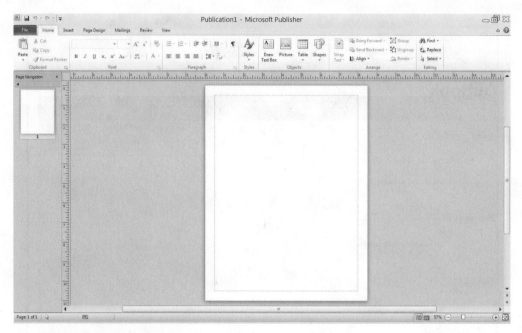

Used with permission from Microsoft.

The three main things you should be able to do with **Publisher** are:

- Design a brochure
- Design a newsletter
- Access and use Microsoft clip art

THE SOCIAL NETWORK GENERATION

What Is the S-Decade?

You might think of the past decade as the e-decade, where the focal points were e-learning, e-books, e-commerce, and the like. The current decade might be labeled the s-decade because of the way cultures and businesses worldwide have embraced social media, social learning, and social networking. Today's students are being challenged to use social media in ways other than communicating with their friends; businesses are scrambling to implement social media strategies for marketing, tracking their customers, and communicating with their customers; and rapidly increasing numbers of people are using social media such as Facebook, Twitter, YouTube, and Second Life. Businesses and universities are using social media to recruit employees and students. Contributors are uploading 13 hours of video every minute of the day, and the number of lurkers (people who follow blogs, discussions, and message boards but do not contribute) is growing at a rapid pace. Many companies are now searching resumés for evidence that candidates are Facebook and Twitter savvy. There is little doubt that social media is becoming the primary method of recruiting and retaining employees from the digital generation.

In the report "Global Faces and Networked Places," Nielsen Online reported that social networks and blogs have now surpassed e-mail as the most popular form of communication. According to the Nielsen report (2009), "Facebook started out as a service for university students, but now almost one third of its global audience is aged 35–49 years of age and almost one quarter is over 50 years."

> *Fifty seven percent of active online users (those people who are online regularly) have joined a social network.*
>
> —*Marta Z. Kagan,*
> *social media evangelist*

SO YOU NEED TO LEARN SOCIAL MEDIA

Where Do You Start?

Many businesses and institutions are using social networking sites in numerous ways to interact with customers, send messages, deliver positive advertising, and even connect with internal customers. We highly recommend that you familiarize yourself with all of them, become an expert on at least one of them by practicing and reading everything you can find, and list your expertise on your resumé. Regardless of what field you enter today, most employers will be looking for social media experts to help them develop, expand, and connect with their customer base. Information regarding a few of the most popular and widely used social media are discussed below.

> Social media is only going to become more pervasive, and as such, become a critical factor in the success or failure of any business.
>
> —Brian Solis, social media expert

Facebook is one of the most widely used and rapidly growing social media in existence. It is used to connect and communicate across social and business lines. Companies are using Facebook to promote their products, announce new products, interact with customers, track their customers' buying habits, and recruit and retain employees. "The fastest growing demographic of Facebook users is those twenty-five years and older" (Kabani, 2010). According to Kabani, Facebook is like a coffee shop; it is a great place to strike up a conversation. Research shows that many people use Facebook to share their personal information and identity. Google has introduced a new social media site called Google+. Google Circles are groups of friends you organize by topic: Friends, Family, College Buddies, Roommates, and so on. Both Facebook and Google+ have changed the way we live and work in the world. You can access Facebook and start your own page at www.facebook.com, and Google+ at https://plus.google.com.

LinkedIn is considered the professionals' site and is described by Kabani (2010) as a "buttoned-down office-networking event. If Facebook is happy hour, LinkedIn is all business,

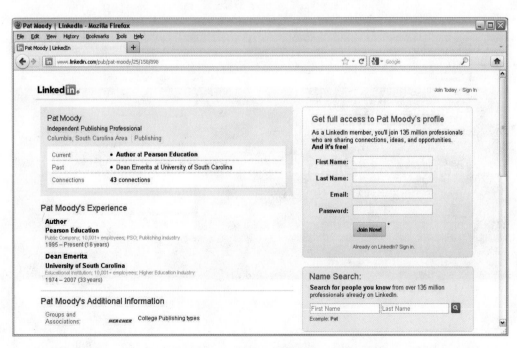

Used with permission. LinkedIn Corporation is in no way affiliated with the author or publisher, and does not endorse the content contained within this publication.

suit and tie." This is a site that should be treated as strictly business, and is certainly not the place to post unflattering pictures or information that might be damaging to you if a potential or current employer happened to see it. This site usually attracts well-educated people who tend to be more affluent. LinkedIn is a great place to post your resumé because other members might be searching for good employees. You can post recommendations from references (with their permission, of course) or glowing letters of appreciation from customers. If someone posts a recommendation for you, you will get a message giving you an opportunity to accept or reject the recommendation's posting.

You will be provided a space to post a summary of your background and accomplishments. You should give careful thought to this and you should update and improve it often. Consider using keywords that are related to the industry in which you are interested; human resource personnel often search LinkedIn for outstanding employees by using keywords from job descriptions. Discuss your specialties, education, and accomplishments, being sure to use spell check. Since this is a business site, the participants are likely to be much more picky than those who frequent Twitter or Facebook. You can access LinkedIn at www.linkedin.com.

Twitter falls in the category of microblog. A microblog is a brief message (no more than 140 characters long) that typically uses abbreviations or Internet acronyms such as OMG (oh my God or gosh) or LOL (laugh out loud) in order to pack more information in a message. Some people are constantly sending "tweets," telling their friends every move they make. As a professional, you need to leave this behavior to teenage girls and learn how to use Twitter to deliver time-sensitive information to clients or to inform your group about a special event or a big sale. Twitter is an excellent way to grab online visibility and to attract traffic for your company because it allows you to establish a dialogue with your customers and your community of friends.

Your Twitter home page will randomly display a number of messages sent to you by people you are following. If someone sends you an @ reply, the message will show up on your home page and it will also be filed under your replies tab. You need to know that replies are public. Everyone can see them! If you choose to do so, you can send direct messages to people that are not visible to everyone, but these messages are still out there if someone decides to share them.

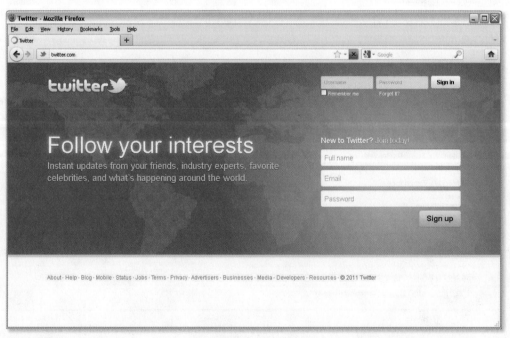

Used with permission.

Collaborative Communication Programs

Today many employees work in virtual teams (teams that work together but are not physically located in the same place) and they find collaborative communication programs to be very helpful and effective. While there are several available, we are going to discuss three of the most popular.

WIKIS. A wiki is a webpage that can be viewed and modified by anybody with a web browser and access to the Internet—it might be called a webpage with an edit button. This means that any visitor to the wiki can change its content if he or she desires, enabling people to collaborate with others online easily. While the potential for mischief exists because access to is open to anyone, wikis can be surprisingly robust and open-ended. They can be password protected if desired. One good way to use wikis is to post an agenda prior to a meeting, add notes during the meeting, and then save them to a public archive where everyone involved can access the notes and minutes. Teams can also use wikis to work collaboratively on documents.

GOOGLE DOCS. Google Docs is a great tool for virtual teams because it is absolutely free and it enables you to create documents, spreadsheets, presentations, forms, and drawings from anywhere around the world simply by accessing the Internet. Some people refer to it as an online alternative to Microsoft Office, which, of course, is not free. You can share documents with anyone you want from within Google Docs itself without manually finding a file and attaching it as an e-mail. It is also easy to download documents to your hard drive if you want to save them on your computer.

Used with permission.

SKYPE. Skype is another collaborative program for working, communicating, and celebrating together, although users may be miles apart. This program can be used between two or more people and is a great way to hold a conference when numerous people need to participate. You can hold meetings, have a work session with fellow employees, or just visit with friends. The great thing about Skype is that the basic program is free and can be downloaded to your computer from the Internet. For a small fee, you can communicate internationally with friends and virtual team members. Skype allows you to connect with customers, colleagues, friends, and family, and is a great way to complete business tasks when people need to meet but work miles apart.

> There has been a fundamental shift in the way we communicate—world famous singers are discovered through a video post on YouTube (the second largest search engine in the world), brands build their names through Tweeting, and debates and conversations form over Facebook groups.
> —MWEB, South Africa's leading Internet service provider

Presentation Software

PowerPoint continues to be the most popular presentation software, but **Prezi** has introduced an exciting package as well. You absolutely need to know PowerPoint, but you are also highly encouraged to review the up-and-coming Prezi presentation package at http://prezi.com.

Almost everyone has had to develop a slide presentation while in school, and all of us have tried to stay awake during a long, boring, tedious computerized presentation. This is an area of technology and communications that you need to be able to do well. While entire books have been written on making effective slideshows, we are going to share a few major points with you here:

- You might want to begin your presentation by building a storyboard or using index cards to lay out your program and your slides. Your first slide sets the stage, so be sure it gets attention in a positive way and includes your name, your company, and the title of your presentation.

- Use real pictures instead of clip art—they are more interesting. If you can use photos that fill the complete slide, the visual is more appealing.

- Avoid wordiness! Never put every word you are going to say on a slide and then proceed to read to your audience. This is deadly! Nothing is worse than one slide after another filled with text in a 12-point font that no one can see. Words in the body should be at least 14 points or larger. Titles and headings should be at least four points larger than the body.

- Light text on a dark background is harder to read than dark text on a light background.

- Present no more than one concept per slide.

- Try not to use more than three or four bullet points per slide.

- Number your points to show order and use bullets to emphasize certain points.

- Use no more than one or two fonts and avoid the fancy, hard-to-read styles.

- Use simple, clear graphs and charts that complement your remarks. Photos, graphs, and diagrams can often be used to explain a concept better than words.

- Your slideshow should use one screen design throughout.

- End with a summary slide that reviews your main points.

- Never read your slides word for word. They should be used to complement what you are saying.

- If you've made a handout for the audience, distribute it at the end of the presentation; otherwise people will be focused on reading the handout instead of your slideshow.

Figure 20.3 illustrates a slide that is boring and has too much information. Contrast this with Figure 20.4, which shows an interesting, appealing slide.

Online Videos

> There have been 100,000,000 videos posted on YouTube.
> —Marta Z. Kagan, social media expert

YouTube is the most popular video-sharing website. Participants have posted over 100,000,000 videos on YouTube since its inception. Using YouTube, participants can upload, share, and view videos produced by people all over the world. You can find videos on almost any subject. Some are professionally produced and others are rather amateurish. In order to play YouTube videos, you must install the Adobe Flash Player plug-in in your browser. You can access YouTube at www.youtube.com and input keywords to search for videos.

Figure 20.3 Slide with Too Much Information

MAKE STUDENTS FEEL IMPORTANT

Remember that every student wants to be somebody. Ask them what they want to be. Help them research what it takes to become this person they dream about.

Remember the power of the gold star.

Pay attention to students' strengths and weaknesses.

Create activities that cause interaction.

Be expressive—smile.

Bring high fives to your classroom!

Figure 20.4 Visually Appealing Slide

the **FUTURE** is
purchased by
the **PRESENT**

EVALUATING YOUR TECHNOLOGY SKILLS

How Will I Ever Learn All These New Programs?

One of the most wonderful things about the world of technology is that if you have never heard of a program or don't know how to use a certain application, there is immediate, useful help online at sites such as www.butterscotch.com and www.youtube.com. If you don't know how to create a movie using Camtasia, all you have to do is go to YouTube and you'll find a tutorial to assist you. This is the beauty of technology. The curse? It seems to change every day. Learning to keep up with the latest technologies and how to apply them at work is imperative. Learning the programs, applications, and terminology is also important.

Figure 20.5 details some of the major programs and applications used in today's workplace. You may not be required to use them all, but it will be helpful to familiarize yourself with some

Figure 20.5 Types of Technology

Description	Program	Website
Software Programs		
Used for word processing and creating presentations, charts, and graphs on PCs and Macs	Microsoft Office (Word, Excel, PowerPoint) PreziPages for Mac	www.office.microsoft.com www.prezi.com www.apple.com/iwork/pages
Group Communication Tools		
Used to communicate in groups and share information on your computer screen with others around the world	Twitter VoiceThread GoToMeeting WebEx	www.twitter.com www.voicethread.com www.gotomeeting.com www.webex.com
Social Networking/Sharing Sites		
Used to network with businesspeople who might help you get a job, chat, make friends, keep in touch, and post the latest news and photos	Facebook Twitter LinkedIn	www.facebook.com www.twitter.com www.linkedin.com
Photo/Video Building and Viewing		
Used to create and/or view videos and share them with friends or colleagues	Jing YouTube Hulu Flickr Camtasia	www.jingproject.com www.youtube.com www.hulu.com www.flickr.com www.techsmith.com
Search/Research Engines		
Used to research topics for work projects; it is wise to use a variety of these sites instead of relying on just one	Google Dogpile Yahoo Ask Lycos Wikipedia Bing Alta Vista	www.google.com www.dogpile.com www.yahoo.com www.ask.com www.lycos.com www.wikipedia.com www.bing.com www.altavista.com
Tools to Help You Learn to Use New Technology		
Offer easy-to-use video tutorials to help you use some of the technologies that may be required in your workplace	YouTube eHow Butterscotch	www.youtube.com www.ehow.com www.butterscotch.com
Document-Sharing Tools		
Used to share your word processing documents with colleagues onsite or at sites around the world	PBWorks Google Docs WorkZone WorkShare	www.pbworks.com www.docs.google.com www.workzone.com www.workshare.com
Digital Note-Taking Systems		
Used to take notes online	MyNoteIt Yahoo! Notes Notefish Ubernote Springnote	www.mynoteit.com www.widgets.yahoo.com/widgets/notes www.notefish.com www.ubernote.com www.springnote.com

different applications and their websites so you can at least speak with some knowledge of each application.

LEARNING THE LANGUAGE OF TECHNOLOGY

What Is a Worm and Why Is It in My Computer?

As you begin to familiarize yourself with the many aspects of computer literacy, there may be terms that pop up that you have not heard before. You will hear many of these terms in the workplace, so it is best to familiarize yourself with them now. The list of terms defined in Figure 20.6 will help you as you discover more about the world of technology and computer literacy.

Technology makes it possible for people to gain control over everything, except over technology.
—John Tutor

PRIVACY AND SECURITY ISSUES

Did You Know You're a Published Author?

Congratulations! You're an author—that is, if you have ever sent a tweet. As of 2010, the Library of Congress has archived *every tweet ever sent* since Twitter's inception in 2006. If you have ever sent a tweet—good or bad, nice or naughty, serious or silly—you are a part of the Library of Congress collection. This is just one of the many examples of lack of privacy on the web. Privacy issues can be monumental obstacles to you now and later in your life. Therefore, it is important that you guard your privacy and watch your online activities. What you post online now in a silly or romantic moment can come back later to cost you that dream job. Complaints about your boss, colleagues, or company are also short-sighted comments when posted in any public venue. Be careful what you post online—nothing on the Internet is private. In a world of WikiLeaks, hackers, and savvy researchers, your words and photos are public words and photos.

To protect yourself and your online information as much as possible, consider the following tips and suggestions:

- Create a strong, uncommon password for your accounts. Try to use a combination of at least eight letters, numbers, and symbols, such as RO#99@SH.
- Do not share your passwords with anyone, not even your best friends. Friendships change, and you may later regret sharing this information.
- Do not use common events such as your birthday, anniversary, or child's birthday as your password.
- Be careful where you post your photo. Even if you post your photo on your personal Facebook page, it can be found by a simple web search.
- Use only secure websites for any type of financial transaction. Look for security seals such as Verisign, Comodo, and GeoTrust. Do *not* use your debit card online. If you must purchase from an online site, use a credit card or consider getting a PayPal account to protect your credit information.
- Learn how to use online security features and privacy settings. These are offered for your safety and for the protection of your information.
- Don't tell your Facebook or online friends that you will not be home. This invites break-ins and burglary at your home.
- Install and run your security and spyware protections at least twice per week.
- Turn off or delete cookies from other sites and retailers.

Figure 20.6 The Techno-Pedia

Bookmarks	These allow you to tag popular sites so you can easily access them again—usually with one click.
Cookie	This term refers to data that is sent to your computer by a company's computer to monitor your actions while on their site. Cookies remember your log-in and password information and track what you viewed or purchased the last time you visited that site.
Dot com	.com is the most common ending for Internet addresses. However, there are many others. The following will help you direct your Internet searches: .com: Used to search commercial, for-profit businesses .edu: Used to search educational institutions, colleges, and universities .net: Used by Internet service providers .gov: Used to search documents within the U.S. government .org: Used to search non-profit organizations .mil: Used to search information from the U.S. military .us: Used to search any organization in specific countries such as United States (.us), United Kingdom (.uk), France (.fr), Sweden (.se), or Germany (.de)
Hacker	A modern-day bank robber. This is a person who electronically breaks into your computer and steals your private and sensitive information—often to use for illegal purposes.
HDTV/HDV	High-definition television or high-definition video. They are high-quality, crisp, visually appealing TV or video recordings.
Phishing	A scheme by hackers to acquire your private information such as passwords, log-in codes, and credit card information by using real companies' logos in their correspondence. They trick you into updating your information for a company or site you trust, when in actuality, you are directly providing the hacker your information.
PDF	The portable document format was created by Adobe as a document-sharing format that is independent of software programs and applications such as Word and PowerPoint.
Podcast	Combines the terms *iPod* and *broadcast* into a single word. It is a video or audio file you can access on your iPhone.
Malware	Meaning "malicious software," malware are programs that are placed on your computer without your knowledge to cause technological harm. Common types of malware (viruses) are trojan horses, worms, and spyware, which delete files or directory information and cause your computer to function improperly. To avoid them, do not open files from unknown sites or people and keep your spyware and virus programs up to date.
Right click	Refers to clicking the right button of your mouse to reveal additional menus and pop-ups. A mouse is automatically set to the left click for common tasks.
RTF	Rich text format (RTF) was developed by Microsoft as a document file format to make files easier to open in most formats and programs on most computers.
URL	Standing for universal retrieval language, the URL is the Internet address that you type into your search bar, such as www.yahoo.com, www.youtube.com, or www.pearsonhighered.com.
Web 2.0	Web 2.0 is the new age of the Internet. Web 1.0 was created as a one-sided, "you search it; we define it" tool, whereas Web 2.0 is more interactive and includes social media (Facebook, Twitter, etc.), blogs, document sharing, videos, and interactive searches.

- Be very wary of anyone asking for personal information to "update company records." It is probably a phishing scheme. This tactic may be initiated by phone or computer. Reputable companies will not ask for your personal information.

- Teach your children not to provide private information or to go onto unknown sites and rooms.

THE ART OF USING NETIQUETTE TO MAKE A POSITIVE IMPRESSION

Who Cares If I Use Proper Manners in E-Mail?

Netiquette, or Internet etiquette, refers to courteous practices that have evolved over the years since almost everyone started using the Internet. Netiquette, as etiquette, is always related to courtesy or good manners. This term simply means to use your manners when communicating with someone on the Internet. Your messages on the Internet are just as much a part of your image as your other written communications. Study the rules of netiquette in Figure 20.7 carefully to avoid offending internal and external customers.

Figure 20.7 Understanding the Rules of Netiquette

- Never, ever send an e-mail, IM, tweet or any other type of e-communication that you would not want anyone else to read. E-communication is not private, especially when done from a company/work computer. Information is available on the web for a long, long time.

- Not everyone is ethical and some will share your information with others. There is no such thing as privacy online!

- Remember that e-mail messages may be seen by anyone. Never write anything that you might find embarrassing if it were shared with others.

- Remember that e-mail is not anonymous and can be traced back to you.

- Be brief and use lots of white space so the message does not appear foreboding. People are too busy for long e-mails.

- Be sure you complete the subject line and that you are descriptive in the words you use.

- Copy only the people who need to receive the message.

- Be careful not to omit someone from the message list who might be offended if he or she does not receive the e-mail.

- Avoid flaming or using all capital letters, which is an indication that you are angry.

- If you receive a message in which the other person is obviously angry, try to talk to the person face-to-face so you can read his or her body language. Do not respond in a similar manner!

- When responding to a piece of correspondence, use the 24-hour rule if you are angry or if you have to make a very important decision. Do not respond in anger or fear. Once the "send" button has been pressed, you can't take it back. Use restraint, reread the correspondence, and once you have cooled off and thought it through, make your decision.

- If you receive a message in which the other person has gone out of his or her way to be rude, ignore it and do not respond.

- Remember that you do not have your nonverbal communication abilities when sending e-mails. Well-intentioned humor and satire can easily be misunderstood and can cause hard feelings.

- If you are going to disagree with someone, be very gentle and careful in phrasing your words. You might want to point out the good points that the person made and then offer the points with which you disagree.

(continued)

Figure 20.7 Understanding the Rules of Netiquette (*continued*)

- Never forward e-mails that were meant to be confidential to you. If you want to share an e-mail, ask for permission from the writer.

- Be careful not to forward attachments without carefully reading them—you may be highly embarrassed once you know the content.

- Text language (LOL, OMG, BFF, :-(, BTW, FYI) is fine when texting or IMing with your friends, but not for e-mails at work.

- Don't forward e-mail hoaxes, urban legends, or chain letters. Many people find it annoying and viruses are often passed along this way. Anything promising 10 million dollars from an overseas account is a scam, and Bill Gates is not going to give you any money for e-mailing your friends—even if your friend's lawyer checked it out!

- Don't forward chain letters, junk mail, spam, or jokes at work. In fact, don't do this anywhere, because most people find it very annoying.

- If you are constantly sending out blanket e-mails of spam, jokes, stories, and chain letters, people all over the company know you are not working. You are documenting this fact for them. People have been fired for spending their time on this kind of activity when they are supposed to be working.

- If you use someone else's work, document your source or sources correctly.

- Never send inappropriate e-mails to anyone at work— for example, sexually explicit jokes or stories. Actually, you should never send this kind of message to anyone because you have no idea where it will end up.

- Refrain from passing along ethnic or religious or obscene jokes and/or stories. Many people will find them offensive, and you may hurt someone's feelings.

- Assume that Internet mail is not secure. If you wouldn't write something on a postcard, don't write it in e-mail.

- Since we have a diverse workforce today, remember that recipients are human beings who may have a culture, sense of humor, religion, language, and customs that are very different from yours.

- Online e-communications, especially e-mails, should contain proper opening and closing salutations if a person does not know you well or if the e-mail is to an external person.

By adhering to these suggestions, you will soon find that your online correspondence is more effective.

Reflections: PUTTING IT ALL TOGETHER

The world of technology changes rapidly. Because of constant innovations and new inventions, it is sometimes difficult to keep up. However, if you can master the right technologies that are in demand by employers and use them to solve problems, generate creative ideas, and work collaboratively with virtual colleagues, you can leapfrog over many others who may not be as informed. There is no doubt that you will use technology in any job you accept today, and the more you learn, the more valuable you will become. Do yourself a big favor—make up your mind to keep learning and growing and mastering all the appropriate technology you can in your field.

DIGITAL BRIEFCASE

USING TECHNOLOGY EFFECTIVELY

Learn to use Facebook, LinkedIn, or Twitter by going online and setting up an account. After you have spent some time familiarizing yourself with the program you selected, design a PowerPoint or Prezi slideshow with no more than five slides that explains how to access this program and how to use some features. Follow the guidelines in this chapter for designing interesting and appealing slides.

REFERENCES

Aducci, R., Bilderbeek, P., Brown, H., Dowling, S., Freedman, N., Gantz, J., Germanow, A., Manabe, T., Manfridez, D., & Verma, R. (2008). The hyperconnected: Here they come. IDC White Paper.

IBM. (2009). Using technology to work smarter. Retrieved May 24, 2011, from www-01 .ibm.com/software/success/cssdb.nsf/CS/CHUY7YKMJA?OpenDocument&Site= default&cty=enus.

Kabani, S. H. (2010). *The zen of social media*. Dallas, TX: BenBella Books.

Manyika, J., Sprague, K., and Yee, L. (2009). Using technology to improve workforce collaboration. Retrieved May 24, 2011, from http://whatmatters.mckinseydigital.com/internet /using-technology-to-improve-workforce-collaboration.

Meister, J. C., & Willyerd, K. (2010). *The 2020 workplace: How innovative companies attract, develop, and keep tomorrow's employees today.* New York: HarperCollins Publishers.

Nielsen Report. (2009). Global faces and networked places. A Nielsen Report on Social Networking's New Global Footprint.

chapter twenty one

PLAN

CREATING A DYNAMIC EMPLOYMENT PACKAGE AND JOB SEARCH PLAN

*No one can tell you what your life's work is,
but it is important that you find it. There is a part
of you that already knows; affirm that part.*
—Willis W. Harman

Why read this chapter?

Because you'll learn...

- How to write a career objective
- About cover letters and resumés
- How to use action verbs to sell your skills and talents

Because you'll be able to...

- Use the D.O.C.T.O.R. system to write a powerful cover letter and resumé
- Effectively complete an online application
- Design attractive personal business cards

PROFESSIONALS from the Field

Name: Mark Jones

Business: Senior Customer Service Trainer SCANA Corporation

My advice would be to tailor your cover letter and resumé to the position for which you are applying. Never send a generic cover letter or resumé. Make sure your resumé is typed and can be scanned or sent electronically. Carefully read the company's job advertisement and then use keywords from their advertisement in your cover letter and resumé. Be specific about your skills. Do not state that you are fluent in Microsoft Office Suite; rather state that you know how to use PowerPoint, Word, Excel, and Outlook. This makes your resumé and cover letter stand out from the others, and keywords can be picked up by scanning software.

PLANNING FOR THE FUTURE

What Am I Going to Do for the Rest of My Life?

"What am I going to do for the rest of my life?" is an overwhelming question for anyone, especially in a dramatically changing, global, technologically driven environment. What was true last year—and sometimes even last week—is no longer true. While many things that worked for your parents and grandparents are still important and relevant today—like ethics, integrity, hard work, education, honesty, teamwork—many practices that were true in their time are no longer valid. Your grandfather may have gone to work for a company and stayed there all his life. Employers were loyal to employees, and employees were loyal to the company. Work stayed pretty much the same one year to the next. All that has changed. You will have many different jobs during your lifetime—you will most likely have at least three or four different careers, and what constitutes your work will be constantly changing.

iStockPhoto

What changes do you foresee coming in your chosen career field in the next five years?

Getting a job, the *right job*, is hard work. Many people in the career development field would say that finding the right job is a full-time job. We agree. One thing that you should have in mind as you begin your job search is that this process is not easy and it is totally yours. No one can complete your job search plan, application packet, and interview but you. Sure, people from your institution's career planning office will help you, but ultimately, you are on your own.

You will need to use every tool in your toolbox to find the job for which you've prepared. You will need to call on the career services office at your institution, scour the Internet for job postings—including corporate websites—use all of your personal and social networking contacts, quiz your instructors about possible leads, read the want-ads, post your resumé with an online job bank or a site such as Monster or LinkedIn, attend job fairs, and possibly even contact an employment or "headhunter" agency. In today's crazy, upside-down job market, you'll need to do everything you can to get your foot in the door. This chapter will help you create an outstanding impression through your cover letter, resumé, reference choices, and business cards so that you can do just that.

> *The four great questions: Why are you here? Where have you been? Where are you going? What difference will you make?*
>
> —Hal Simon

Your Positive Attitude and the Job Search

Today is the day that I am going to find my dream job. Today is the day that I am going to put my talents, knowledge, and experience to use. Today is the day that I will get to show people just what I can do. Today is the day that I am going to start my professional career.

Do you see the difference between these two people? Granted, a positive attitude is not the only thing that you need as you begin your job search, but it is certainly important. Will you hit walls during your search? Yes. Will you meet with rejection? Yes. Will you be frustrated? Yes. These things happen in the best of times. They most certainly are happening now. However, when you have a positive attitude about your search and what you have to offer, this comes across to the people who will be hiring you. Conversely, your negative attitude will also show. You may not notice it, but your attitude affects your actions, speech, interview responses, and nonverbal communication. Choose to be positive.

Career Objective

As you begin your job search both mentally and in writing, the place to begin is with a career objective. A career objective is an introductory statement written for your resumé. It is the only place on your resumé where you can use the words *I, me,* or *my.* This is a personal statement that briefly (usually one sentence) describes your desires, talents, skills, and interest in a specific position. Your career objective will not only make your resumé stronger, it also forces you to prepare mentally for what you really have to offer and what you want in a career.

Think of your career objective as *"an elevator speech."* Pretend you are on an elevator with your dream employer. You have the time span of two floors to tell Mr. Jamison about yourself, your skills, and what you want. Period. Wham! Two floors. What would you say? You need to be able to answer this question before you begin searching for a position, writing a cover letter, or preparing your resumé.

Two career objectives are shown below:

Weak Objective
I want to work as a marketing manager with a major corporation.

Strong Objective
Seeking a marketing position that will utilize my organization talents, oral communication skills, and expertise with Word, Excel, PowerPoint, Prezi, and Facebook in a competitive, engaging, and high-energy environment.

WORKIN' 9 TO 5—OR TRYING TO

Is It Really Possible to Sell Yourself Through a Cover Letter and Resumé?

You've got it all together—education, experience, and a strong sense of self. A positive attitude. What do you do now? How do you pull all of this together? How do you find the job of your dreams? The job for which you have prepared?

Know this! Getting a job—the *right job*—is hard work! Regardless of your status in school, now is the time to begin your job search. If you are in the last months of your program, your job search should be a top priority. If you are just beginning your educational plan, it is never too early to begin assembling a dynamic employment package.

Selling Yourself

Remember the old saying, "You are what you eat"? When searching for a professional position, you could change that to read, "You are what you write." Most likely, the people conducting the job search have never met you and know nothing about you except what you provide to them. A carefully crafted resumé communicates your past history (skills and experience) that makes you the ideal candidate for their position. Your resumé is the first marketing piece and in many cases must stand alone when a recruiter is determining whether to interview you. Just as a well-designed and well-written resumé can be a wonderful first step, a poorly designed and written resumé can doom you before you ever leave your house. A good thing to remember is this: A resumé gets you the interview; the interview gets you the job. Although there is no single way to develop your career resumé and formats may vary from discipline to discipline, this chapter will outline the key components of resumés and discuss how to develop a resumé that will represent your best efforts.

Your second "advertising tool" is your cover letter. A cover letter is basically an expansion of your resumé. A cover letter gives you the chance to link your resumé, skills, and experience together with your interest in a specific company's position. You will need to write many cover letters to make this link work properly; in other words, you most likely need to write a cover letter designed for each job for which you apply. Your cover letter will often be the stepping stone to get an employer to even look at your resumé. Consider it "a teaser," if you will, to all of your talents and experience. Just as you would never send someone a greeting card and not sign it, you would never send a resumé and not tell the person or committee why you sent it. Your cover letter tells why.

Shutterstock
What is your elevator speech?

WRITE A POWERFUL AND CONCISE COVER LETTER

How Do You Get Your Foot in the Door?

Careful preparation must be done ***prior to starting*** the interview process. Two key elements of this preparation are your cover letter and resumé. Both are key components in your career search.

Whenever you send your resumé to a company, whether it is in response to a posted advertisement or was requested by someone, you must send a cover letter with it. Cover letters are extremely important; in fact, most recruiters say that they read four times as many cover letters as they do resumés because if the cover letter does not "strike a chord," then they never look past it to the resumé.

Career development expert, author, and speaker Carol Robins (2006) states, "During my 25 plus years that I've been involved in career development, I have found that of all the paperwork associated with job searching, cover letters give job searchers the most difficulty." The information presented here will help you overcome any anxiety associated with writing your cover letter or resumé.

As you the process of building your cover letter and resumé, consider the general tips in Figure 21.1.

Simply put, the cover letter's purpose is to get the interviewer to read your resumé. It sets the tone for who you are, what you have to offer, and what you want. "It screams—ever so politely—that you have the intelligence, experience, and soft skills to be the answer to an employer's staffing problem" (Britton-Whitcomb, 2003). The cover letter should say to the reader, "You have an opening and a detailed description of what you need, and I can fill your opening and be the person who gets the job done—and done well."

Figure 21.1 Tips You Can't Skip to Build an Effective Resumé

- Both your resumé and cover letter *must be typed.* There are no exceptions to this rule. Ever!

- Your cover letter and resumé must be printed on the same type and color of fine-quality paper. Cheap paper sends the message that you don't care. This is not the place or time to pinch pennies; buy excellent quality, 100 percent cotton stock, resumé-quality paper.

- Check your printer and be sure that the print quality is impeccable. Never send a cover letter or resumé with smudges, ink smears, or poor print quality.

- When you print your cover letter and resumé, be certain that the watermark on the paper is turned in the correct direction. Hold it up to the light and you will see the watermark embedded in the paper. This may sound silly and picky, but people notice attention to detail.

- Do not fold your cover letter or resumé. Purchase a packet of 9" × 13" envelopes in which to send your materials.

- Do not handwrite the address on the envelope. Use a label or type the address directly on the envelope. Remember, first impressions are important.

- Never send a generic photocopy of a cover letter or resumé, even on the finest paper.

- Layout, design, font, spacing, and color must be considered in the building of your cover letter and resumé.

- Unless you are specifically asked to do so, never discuss money or salary history in either your cover letter or resumé. This could work against you. When asked for a salary history, use ranges.

- Your resumé and cover letter must be free of errors. That's right, not one single error is acceptable, including grammar, spelling, punctuation, layout/spacing, dates, or content.

- Each cover letter must be signed, preferably in black ink.

Consider the following **four steps to success** when writing your cover letter:

1. An effective cover letter will be *personally addressed and job specific.* If at all possible (and yes, it is possible with just a little research), address your letter to a specific person. Avoid at all costs the dreaded "Dear Sir or Madam" or "To Whom It May Concern." In most cases, a phone call to the company will provide the name of the person along with his or her title and address. Always verify spelling, even with common names. This single step can set you apart from lazy job-seekers. Also, make sure you spell the company's name correctly.

2. Once your letter is correctly addressed, your first paragraph should be an "attention grabber" and it should answer the question "Why am I writing?" Susan Britton-Whitcomb, author of *Resumé Magic* (2003), calls this "the carrot." This simply means that your first paragraph should have an interesting fact, an appeal, or maybe even a quote—something that makes the reader (hopefully, your future employer) read further. Your first paragraph should also have a transition statement that makes the reader want to read on. For example, your last statement might read, "With a degree in medical assisting and four years of experience at Desert Medical Center, I know that I can make a valued contribution to Grace Care Center."

3. Your second (and maybe third) paragraph(s) should clearly state why you are qualified for the position you are seeking. Use your cover letter to highlight those areas of your experience that specifically qualify you for the job. Your cover letter is not the time to list all of your qualifications, but to indicate the two or three components that most qualify you for the position and closely match the position announcement. You may also include specific attributes that may not be on your resumé. The emphasis here is your value. Relate your education, experience, and talents to the company's need. Mention facts and statistics of how you've been successful in the past. Remember, "Employers are not interested in you for your sake, but rather because of what you can bring to the organization. This might sound harsh, but businesspeople have an obligation to improve the success of their organization. If you consistently show how you can help them do this . . . they will be much more motivated to talk to you" (Farr and Kursmark, 2005).

4. Your final paragraph should address the question of "Where do we go from here?" Do not be ambiguous by saying something trite like "I hope to hear from you in the near future," or "If you have any questions please do not hesitate to call me." Remember, your job search is none of the company's business, nor is it their responsibility. Be proactive by stating that you will be following up with a phone call to discuss your resumé and experience(s) in more detail. Make sure that once you have said that you are going to call that you actually do call. Your final paragraph should also continue to express what you can do for the company. You should end your letter with a statement about your qualities and the company's needs, such as "Mr. Thompson, I will call you on Monday, January 24th at 11:30 a.m. to discuss how my past experiences can help streamline operations and continue superior patient care at Grace Care Center."

Don't forget to **sign your letter.** Figure 21.2 provides a sample cover letter and indicates the correct format and spacing to the left of the letter's content.

POSITIVE HABITS *at Work*

After you have found the position for which you have prepared, you need to think into the future and begin planning for your next job search. "What?" you might be saying. "My next job?" Yes! After you begin your new position, you need to create an e-file where you will save information about your successes, acquired skills, and accomplishments so that you can add them to your next resumé. Your resumé is a living document and must be updated extensively each time you apply for a new position. The best way to keep this information organized is to keep an e-file that lists what you have learned from this job. If you learned how to create an Excel spreadsheet, add that to your file. If you sat on a hiring committee, add that to your file. If you were asked to lead a team, add that to your file. Then, when it comes time to update your resumé, you have all of your successes and updated skills in one place.

UNDERSTAND THE DO'S AND DON'TS OF MEMORABLE RESUMÉS

How Do You Sell Yourself?

Eight seconds. That is all you have to gain the attention of your potential employer, according to author and consultant Susan Ireland (2003). "In eight seconds, an employer scans your resumé and decides whether she will invest more time to consider you as a job *candidate*. The secret to passing the eight-second test is to make your resumé look inviting and quick to read" (p. 14).

A resumé is the blueprint that details what you have accomplished with regards to education, experience, skills acquisition, workplace successes, and progressive responsibility and/or leadership. It is a painting (that you are able to "paint") of how your professional life looks. It is the ultimate advertisement of you! Your resumé must create interest and hopefully a *desire* to find out more about you!

As you begin to develop your resumé, make sure to allow plenty of time to develop it. Plan to enlist several qualified proofreaders to check your work. We cannot stress strongly enough the need for your resumé to be perfect. A simple typo or misuse of grammar can disqualify you from the job of your dreams. Don't allow a lack of attention to detail to stand between you and your future career.

Figure 21.2 Sample Cover Letter with Formatting

Your name and address. Your name should be larger and/or in a different font to call attention. →

The date (then double space) →

The specific person, title, and address to whom you are writing (then double space) →

The formal salutation followed by a colon (then double space) →

Paragraph 1 (then double space) →

Paragraph 2 (then double space) →

Paragraph 3 (then double space) →

Final paragraph or closing (then double space) →

The complimentary close (then four spaces) →

Your handwritten signature in black or blue ink within the four spaces →

Your typed name →

Enclosure contents →

BENJAMIN SHAW

1234 Lake Shadow Drive   (123) 555-1234
Maple City, PA 12345   ben.shaw@online.com

January 3, 2011

Mr. James Pixler, RN, CAN
Director of Placement and Advancement
Grace Care Center
123 Sizemore Street, Suite 444
Philadelphia, PA 12345

Dear Mr. Pixler:

Seven years ago, my mother was under the treatment of two incredible nurses at Grace Care Center in Philadelphia. My family and I agree that the care she was given was extraordinary. When I saw your ad in today's *Philadelphia Carrier*, I was extremely pleased to know that I now have the qualifications to be a part of the Grace Care Team as a Medical Assistant.

Next month, I will graduate with an Occupational Associate's Degree from Victory College of Health and Technology as a certified Medical Assistant. As my resumé indicates, I was fortunate to do my internship at Mercy Family Care Practice in Harrisburg. During this time, I was directly involved in patient care, records documentation, and family outreach.

As a part of my degree from Victory, I received a 4.0 in the following classes:

- Management Communications
- Microsoft Office (Word, Excel, Outlook, PowerPoint)
- Business Communications I, II, III
- Anatomy and Physiology I, II, III
- Medical Coding I, II
- Principles of Pharmacology
- Immunology I, II, III, IV
- Urinalysis and Body Fluids
- Clinical Practicum I, II, III

This, along with my past certificate in Medical Transcription and my immense respect for Grace Care Center, makes me the perfect candidate for your position.

I have detailed all of my experience on the enclosed resumé. I will call you on Monday, January 24, at 11:30 a.m. to discuss how my education and experiences can help streamline operations and continue superior patient care at Grace. In the meantime, please feel free to contact me at the number above.

Sincerely,

Benjamin Shaw
BENJAMIN SHAW

Enclosure: Resumé

Derwin Wallace
**Graduate: Devry University and Keller Graduate
School of Management
Career: Director of Corporate Investor Relations
National Association of Investor Corps**

In my position, my main responsibility is to put companies that trade in the stock market in front of investors in hopes they may purchase that company's stock. Just as my education gave me limitless opportunities, yours will too. Corporate America is a battlefield and you must get your armor ready. Your education is your preparation for battle—it is your boot camp for the real world.

When you land your new position, live below your means. Doing this gives you freedom. If you buy that BMW, the designer clothes, and the mansion on a hill and all of your money goes to pay the bills, you have lost your freedom and flexibility—you're a slave to a paycheck. The major stressor in life is to be tied to a job that you hate and can't leave because without it you will lose all your material possessions.

Further, your resumé must be 100 percent accurate and truthful. Do not fabricate information or fudge dates to make yourself look better. It will only come back to haunt you in the long run. Dennis Reina, organizational psychologist and author of *Trust and Betrayal in the Workplace,* states, "I think that what you put in a resume absolutely has to be rock-solid, concrete, and verifiable. If there are any questions, it will immediately throw both your application and your credibility into question" (Dresang, 2007). People have been fired from positions after they were hired because they misrepresented themselves on their resumés, cover letters, or applications.

As you begin to build your resumé, remember to "call in the **D.O.C.T.O.R.**"

D: Design

Visual **design** and format are imperative to a successful resumé. You need to think about the font that you plan to use; whether color is appropriate (usually, it is not); the use of bullets, lines, or shading; and where you are going to put information. You also need to pay attention to the text balance on the page (centered left/right, top/bottom). The visual aspect of your resumé will be the first impression. "Make it pretty" (Britton-Whitcomb, 2003).

O: Objective

Writing a clear and specific **objective** can help get your foot in the door. The reader, usually your potential employer, needs to be able to scan your resumé and gather as much detail as possible as quickly as possible. A job-specific objective can help. Consider the following two objectives:

- **Vague objective:** To get a job as an elementary school teacher in the Dallas Area School District.
- **Specific objective:** To secure an elementary teaching position that will enable me to use my 14 years of creative teaching experience, curriculum development abilities, supervisory skills, and commitment to superior instruction in a team environment.

C: Clarity

Clarity is of paramount importance, especially when including your past responsibilities, education, and job responsibilities. Be certain that you let the reader know exactly what you have done, what specific education you have gained, and what progress you have made. Being vague and unclear can cost you an interview.

T: Truth

When writing your resumé, you may be tempted to fudge a little bit here and there to make yourself look better. Perhaps you were out of work for a few months and you think it looks bad to have this gap in your chronological history. Avoid the urge to fudge. Telling the absolute **truth** on a resumé is essential. A lie, even a small one, can (and usually will) come back to haunt you.

O: Organization

Before you begin your resumé, think about the **organization** of your data. We will provide a model resumé; however, there are several other formats you might select. It is most important that you present your information in an attractive, easy-to-read, comprehensive format.

R: Review

Reviewing your resumé and cover letter is important, but having someone else review them for clarity, accuracy, spelling, grammar, formatting, and overall content can be one of the best things you can do for your job search.

The basic tips in Figure 21.3 will help you as you begin building a dynamic resumé. Some other basic tips include the following:

- Do not date stamp or record the preparation date of your resumé in any place.
- Limit your resumé (and cover letter) to one page each (a two-page resumé is appropriate if you have more than 10 years of experience).
- Use standard resumé paper colors, such as white, cream, gray, or beige.
- Use bullets (such as these) to help profile lists.
- Avoid fancy or hard-to-read fonts.
- Use a standard font size between 10 and 14 points.
- Do not staple anything to your resumé (or cover letter).
- Try to avoid the use of *I, me,* or *my* in your resumé (if you must use them, do so sparingly).
- Avoid contractions such as *don't,* and do not use abbreviations.

Figure 21.3   General Inclusion Tips

Contact information (name, complete mailing address, phone and cell numbers, fax number, e-mail address, webpage URL)	MUST include
Education, degrees, certificates, advanced training (to include dates and names of degrees)	MUST include
Current and past work history, experience and responsibilities	MUST include
Past accomplishments (this is *not* the same as work history or responsibilities)	MUST include
Specific licensures	MUST include
Specific career objective (different for each position for which you apply)	SHOULD include
Summary or list of qualifications, strengths, specializations	SHOULD include
Special skills (including special technical skills or multiple language skills)	SHOULD include
Volunteer work, public service, and/or community involvement	SHOULD include
Internships, externships, and/or extracurricular activities	SHOULD include
Awards, honors, certificates of achievement, special recognitions (at work or in the community)	SHOULD include
Military experience	CONSIDER including
Professional/preprofessional memberships, affiliations, and/or associations	CONSIDER including
Publications and presentations	CONSIDER including
Current business phone number and/or address (where you are working at the moment)	DO NOT include
Availability (date/time to begin work)	DO NOT include
Geographic limitations	DO NOT include
Personal hobbies or interests	DO NOT include
Personal information such as age, sex, health status, marital status, parental status, ethnicity, or religious affiliation	DO NOT include
Photos	DO NOT include
Salary requirements or money issues	DO NOT include (unless specifically asked to provide a salary history)
References	DO NOT include unless specifically asked but have the information ready on a separate sheet of paper that matches your resumé

Figure 21.4 Chronological Resumé

BENJAMIN SHAW

1234 Lake Shadow Drive, Maple City, PA 12345   (123) 555-1234   ben@online.com

OBJECTIVE: To work as a medical assistant in a professional atmosphere that uses my organizational skills, compassion for people, desire to make a difference, and impeccable work ethic.

PROFESSIONAL EXPERIENCE:

January 2007–Present	**Medical Assistant Intern** Mercy Family Care Practice, Harrisburg, PA ■ Responsible for completing patient charts ■ Took patients' vitals ■ Assisted with medical coding
February 2003–December 2006	**Medical Transcriptionist** The Office of Brenda Wilson, MD, Lancaster, PA ■ Interpreted and typed medical reports ■ Worked with insurance documentation ■ Assisted with medical coding ■ Served as Office Manager (1/05–12/06)
March 1998–February 2003	**Ward Orderly** Wallace Hospital, Lancaster, PA ■ Assisted nurses with patient care ■ Cleaned patient rooms ■ Served patient meals
August 1995–March 1998	**Administrative Assistant** Ellen Abbot Nursing Care Facility ■ Typed office reports ■ Organized patient files

EDUCATION:

Occupational Associate's Degree—Medical Assistant
Victory Health Institute, Harrisburg, PA
May 2008 (with honors)

Certificate of Completion—Medical Transcription
Philadelphia Technical Institute
December 2002

Vocational High School Diploma—Health Sciences
Philadelphia Vocational High School
August 1995

- Use action verbs such as *designed, managed, created, recruited, simplified,* and *built.*
- Avoid the use of full sentences; fragments are fine on a resumé, but not in a cover letter.
- Use the correct verb tense. You will use past tense (such as *recruited*), except when referring to your current job.
- Do not include irrelevant information that does not pertain to this particular job search.
- Choose a format that puts your "best foot" or greatest assets forward.

Remember that the job market is highly competitive. Your job is to write a resumé that is solid, appealing, comprehensive, and brief. The idea is to get someone to read it and make him or her want to know more about you.

BUILDING YOUR RESUMÉ

What Are the Major Differences?

There are different types of resumés, but primarily they can be classified as chronological resumés, functional resumés, accomplishment resumés, or a combination of the three. Your job package may also contain a portfolio. You might consider submitting a video resumé or a resumé that can be easily scanned and sent electronically. Each is described below.

- A **chronological resumé** (Figure 21.4) organizes education and work experience in reverse chronological order (your last or present job is listed first).
- A **functional resumé** (Figure 21.5) organizes your work and experience around specific skills and duties.
- An **accomplishment resumé** (Figure 21.6) allows you to place your past accomplishments into categories that are not necessarily associated with an employer, but shows your track record of "getting the job done." This type of resumé is usually reserved for those with previous work experience.
- A **video resumé** is a resumé that showcases your experiences and talent through a brief (three- to five-minute) video recording. A video resumé is often used to supplement a traditional resumé and shows your creative and technological skills. Some employers will not accept video resumés because they can lead to claims of bias.
- A **scannable resumé** (Figure 21.7) is a resumé with very little formatting and a clear font such as Courier, Arial, or Times New Roman. These resumés may appear to be less visually appealing, but they are easier to read once scanned. You may be asked to send your resumé as a PDF. A PDF file basically takes a snapshot of your document exactly as it was prepared and ensures that your electronic resumé remains just as you designed it.
- An **electronic (or plain text) resumé** (Figure 21.8) is one that can be easily sent online and scanned electronically for *keywords and skills* based on the company's needs and job advertisement. It is saved in American Standard Code for Information Interchange (ASCII) format. When designing your electronic resumé, consider the spacing, formatting, and fonts. Avoid italics, bullets (use asterisks instead), and columns. Align the text on the left. Do not indent with tabs or use parentheses or brackets. To save your current or future resumé as an electronic or plain text resumé, simply click "Save as" and in the "Save as type" box, select "Plain Text." Then re-open your file and make adjustments, corrections, and additions.
- A *portfolio* is a binder, website, CD-ROM, flash drive, or cloud file that showcases your very best work. It details your projects, awards, certificates, certifications, degrees, transcripts, military experience, and major accomplishments. Your portfolio should always be specific to the position for which you are applying.

Figure 21.5 Functional Resumé

BENJAMIN SHAW

1234 Lake Shadow Drive, Maple City, PA 12345   (123) 555-1234   ben@online.com

OBJECTIVE: To work as a medical assistant in an atmosphere that uses my organization abilities, people skills, compassion for patients, desire to make a difference, and impeccable work ethic.

SKILLS:

Bilingual (English/Spanish)	Data Protection
Claims Reimbursement	Client Relations
Highly Organized	Problem-Solving Skills
Motivated, Self-starter	Team Player
Priority Management Skills	Delegating Ability
Strategic Planning	Budget Management

PROFESSIONAL PREPARATION:

Occupational Associate's Degree—Medical Assistant
Victory Health Institute, Harrisburg, PA
May 2008 (with honors)

Certificate of Completion—Medical Transcription
Philadelphia Technical Institute
December 2002

Vocational High School Diploma—Health Sciences
Philadelphia Vocational High School
August 1995

PROFESSIONAL EXPERIENCE:

January 2007–Present	Medical Assistant Intern Mercy Family Care Practice, Harrisburg, PA
February 2003–December 2006	Medical Transcriptionist The Office of Brenda Wilson, MD, Lancaster, PA
March 1998–February 2003	Ward Orderly Wallace Hospital, Lancaster, PA
August 1995–March 1998	Administrative Assistant Ellen Abbot Nursing Care Facility

REFERENCES: Provided upon request

Figure 21.6 Accomplishment Resumé

BENJAMIN SHAW

1234 Lake Shadow Drive
Maple City, PA 12345
(123) 555-1234

ben@online.com
www.bjs@netconnect.com

Career Target:

MEDICAL ASSISTANT

A highly qualified medical professional with eight years' experience in patient care, client relations, and medical coding seeking a challenging career that uses my strong problem-solving skills, deep compassion for the people, and medical training.

PROFESSIONAL ACCOMPLISHMENTS

Mercy Family Care Practice

✓ Revised and updated medical coding procedures
✓ Increased insurance payments by 11%
✓ Revised and streamlined new patient intake process
✓ Assisted Lead MA with ethics plan revision
✓ Revamped treatment procedure guidelines

Office of Brenda Wilson, MD

✓ Developed new medication administration checklist
✓ Implemented new guidelines for lab specimen collection
✓ Assisted with compliance of OSHA regulations

SKILLS / STRENGTHS

✓ Highly organized
✓ Team player
✓ Impeccable work ethic
✓ Bilingual (English and Spanish)
✓ Budget minded
✓ Motivated, self-starter
✓ Excellent client relations
✓ Superior time management skills

PROFESSIONAL PREPARATION

Occupational Associate's Degree—Medical Assistant
Victory Health Institute, Harrisburg, PA
May 2008 (with high honors)

Certificate of Completion—Medical Transcription
Philadelphia Technical Institute
December 2002 (with honors)

Vocational High School Diploma—Health Sciences
Philadelphia Vocational High School
August 1995

PROFESSIONAL EXPERIENCE

January 2007–Present	Medical Assistant Intern
	Mercy Family Care Practice
February 2003–December 2006	Medical Transcriptionist
	The Office of Brenda Wilson, MD
March 1998–February 2003	Ward Orderly
	Wallace Hospital
August 1995–March 1998	Administrative Assistant
	Ellen Abbot Nursing Care Facility

Figure 21.7 Scannable Resumé

BENJAMIN SHAW

1234 Lake Shadow Drive, Maple City, PA 12345   (H) 123-456-7890 (C) 123-456-1232

OBJECTIVE
Seeking a position as a medical assistant in an atmosphere that uses my organizational abilities, communication skills, computer expertise, compassion for patients, desire to make a difference, and impeccable work ethic.

PROFESSIONAL EXPERIENCE

January 2006–Present

Medical Assistant Intern
Mercy Family Care Practice, Harrisburg, PA

- Responsible for completing patient charts
- Took patients' vitals
- Assisted with medical coding

February 2003–December 2006

Medical Transcriptionist
The Office of Brenda Wilson, MD, Lancaster, PA

- Interpreted and typed medical reports
- Worked with insurance documentation
- Served as Office Manager (1/05–12/06)

March 1998–February 2003

Ward Orderly
Wallace Hospital, Lancaster, PA

- Assisted nurses with patient care
- Cleaned patient rooms
- Served patient meals

EDUCATION:

Occupational Associate's Degree—Medical Assistant
Victory Health Institute, Harrisburg, PA
May 2008 (with Honors)

Certificate of Completion—Medical Transcription
Philadelphia Technical Institute
December 2002

Vocational High School Diploma—Health Sciences
Philadelphia Vocational High School
August 1995

Figure 21.8 Electronic (or Plain Text) Resumé

BENJAMIN SHAW

Box F-123   Pittsburgh, PA 12345   Phone: 555-123-4567   E-mail: ben@online.com

----

OBJECTIVE
Seeking a position as a medical assistant in an atmosphere that uses my organizational abilities, communication skills, computer expertise, compassion for patients, desire to make a difference, and impeccable work ethic.

QUALIFICATIONS SUMMARY
Health management, client relations, order processing, data protection, interpersonal skills, accounting, marketing, health policy, claims reimbursement, problem solving, leadership, responsible, management skills

----

COMPUTER SKILLS
Word, PowerPoint, Excel, Outlook, Publisher, Prezi, HTML/Web publishing, Facebook, and Twitter

----

PROFESSIONAL EXPERIENCE
January 2006-Present
Medical Assistant Intern
Mercy Family Care Practice, Harrisburg, PA
*Responsible for completing patient charts
*Took patients' vitals
*Assisted with medical coding and billing

February 2003-December 2006
Medical Transcriptionist
The Office of Brenda Wilson, MD, Lancaster, PA
*Interpreted and typed medical reports
*Worked with insurance documentation
*Assisted with medical coding
*Served as Office Manager (1/05-12/06)

EDUCATION
Occupational Associate's Degree, Medical Assistant
Victory Health Institute, Harrisburg, PA
May 2008 (with Honors)

Certificate of Completion, Medical Transcription
Philadelphia Technical Institute
December, 2002

RELEVANT COURSES and SKILLS
Human Anatomy & Physiology I, II, III
Public Health Policy
Organizational Health Care
Human Resource Management
Bilingual (English and Spanish)
Excellent Client Relations
Treatment Procedure Guidelines

CHOOSE YOUR WORDS CAREFULLY

Why Are "Power Words" Important to Use?

When constructing your resumé, you will be writing powerful, succinct statements that demonstrate your talents and accomplishments. The best way to do this is to use *action verbs*. When writing your accomplishments, consider the following two examples. As you can see, the active statement is stronger and more concise.

Passive Statements

I was responsible for controlling costs at the front desk

I learned how to train employees on the RoomKey System

Active Statements

Controlled costs at the front desk

Trained front desk employees to use the RoomKey Reservation System

Some action verbs for your resumé include the following. To find more, type "action verbs for resumés" into your search engine.

accomplished	achieved	adopted	applied
assisted	attained	built	charted
conducted	constructed	controlled	contributed
delegated	devised	earned	employed
enforced	exceeded	formed	fulfilled
helped	invested	managed	mastered
organized	oversaw	participated	planned
programmed	regulated	restored	secured
sponsored	undertook	used	verified

CHOOSE APPROPRIATE REFERENCES

Who Can Speak Positively about My Talents and Skills?

If an employer is interested in you, he or she will most likely ask that you provide three to five references: people who can attest to your professional skills, work ethic, and workplace knowledge. There are five steps for successfully soliciting letters of reference.

1. Select three to five people with whom you have had professional contact. As you determine the best ones to select, choose people who are very familiar with your work ability. Current and former employers with whom you have experienced a good working relationship are excellent sources of references. Your instructors are also excellent sources. If you do not have anyone who falls into these two categories, consider asking friends of your family who are respected members of the community. As you consider possible reference sources, be sure to choose individuals who are responsible and timely in their reply to your request. Typically, you should not use your minister, rabbi, or other religious figures as references. References are a reflection of you, and if the reference sources do not respond in the appropriate manner, they will cast a shadow on your credibility. Your references should have excellent written communication skills. A poorly written recommendation letter reflects badly on you.

2. Request permission from your reference sources. Always ask someone before you list them as a reference on an application or resumé. During your conversation with the individual, discuss your career goals and aspirations. Give him or her a copy of your resumé and cover letter. Ask for a critique and make any necessary changes. You should also ask the person to put your letter on his or her company letterhead and send your potential employer an original copy, not a photocopy.

3. Obtain all necessary contact information from them. You should know each reference's professional name, job title, business address, e-mail address, phone number, and fax number so that your potential employer can contact him or her with ease.

4. Send thank you letters to those who agree to serve as references for you. Stay in contact with them throughout your job search. Give them updates and a periodic thank you in the form of a card, an e-mail, or a phone call. At the end of your job search, a small token of your appreciation may be appropriate, but a thank you note is essential.

5. Develop a typed list of all references—including contact information—and take it with you to all interviews. It is now customary that you do not include the names of references on your resumé. You simply state: "References available upon request" or do not mention references at all. Employers will ask if they need them.

In the space provided in Figure 21.9, list three people you could ask to serve as references (or write you a reference letter). Once you have identified these three people, list the skills that each person could speak to on your behalf. Think about this carefully, as it is important to choose references who can speak to your many qualifications, not just one or two. Choose people who know you in different areas of success.

Figure 21.9 Selecting References

Person	Qualifications He or She Can Write About
JoAnna Thompson	My oral communication skills My attention to detail My ability to get along with others
Beau DeTiberious	My ability to form a team My ability to motivate team members My ability to meet deadlines
Person 1	Qualifications he or she can write about
Person 2	Qualifications he or she can write about
Person 3	Qualifications he or she can write about

ONLINE APPLICATIONS

How Can I Make a Strong Impression Electronically?

Often, employers will ask you to complete an *online application* instead of sending a resumé and cover letter. Some will require all three. Employers have found that online applications are easier to disseminate to the right people at the right time. The following tips will help you complete a successful online application and made a strong, lasting impression.

- Verify the existence and authenticity of the company before you complete an online application.
- Complete an online job application package with online sites such as Monster.com, Careerbuilder.com, or LinkedIn.com before you begin filling out company-specific online applications, as the company may ask for a link to your material.
- Read the instructions. Mistakes on an online application are as bad as mistakes on a hard-copy resumé or cover letter.
- Download the application as a hard copy and fill it out in writing before you complete the application online. This gives you the opportunity to polish your wording and check the accuracy of your dates, names, and numbers.
- Use keywords found in the company's job announcement so the computer will select your application.
- If possible, examine sample online applications from the company before completing your application.
- Complete all fields (boxes) of the online application.
- Do not provide any personal information such as mother's maiden name, bank account, or credit card numbers. No reputable company will ask for these in an online application.
- As with your resumé, strive for truth and accuracy in dates, names, locations, skills, and accomplishments. Your online application should match your resumé.
- As with a resumé, tailor your online application to the specific job for which you are applying.
- Send references only if requested.
- Keep a file (hard copy or electronic) of all online applications, materials sent, dates on which they were sent, attachments, and the actual job announcements.
- Reread your application for spelling and grammar. If possible, have someone read the application with you before you send it.
- If at all possible, follow up your online application with a personal e-mail or phone call to the employer.

BIGGEST INTERVIEW *Blunders*

Terrell received the call from Omni Environmental Controls. He had applied for a position as an HVAC industrial specialist. He was certain that the training he received in industrial heating, air conditioning, and ventilation at Century Technical College would give him the upper hand over applicants who had no degree and over those who had not had an internship with one of the major HVAC companies in town. The morning of the interview, Terrell dressed in a t-shirt, jeans, and a baseball cap. Everything was cleaned and pressed. He knew that technicians in his field did not wear suits, ties, and fancy clothes. During the interview, he was able to answer all of the questions that were asked of him with confidence and knowledge. He touted his internship experience. He was pleased. However, toward the end of the interview, Mr. Jamison, the owner of the company, looked at Terrell and said, "Son, if I hire you and send you out to bid on a job, do you have anything else to wear?" Terrell was shocked but answered, "Yes, sir, I do." "Good," stated Mr. Jamison, "You'll need them. We like to present ourselves as professionals to our clients."

LESSON: Always present your best self to any potential employer—in dress, attitude, knowledge, and poise. Even if you think you are being too formal, being overdressed and overpolished is always better than being underdressed and underpolished.

DESIGN AND DISTRIBUTE ATTRACTIVE PERSONAL BUSINESS CARDS

Does a Small Card Really Help?

Setting yourself apart from other job seekers is important, and designing and distributing attractive personal business cards can help with this endeavor. Business cards give you a professional edge, provide your potential employer another contact source, and help contacts stay in touch with you.

Business cards should be the standard size of 2" × 3.5" and should, if possible, be professionally designed and printed. If this is not possible, there are many computer programs and graphic packages to assist you in making your own. You can also purchase sheets of blank business cards for your home printer. You simply design, print, and separate them.

While including a simple graphic is fine (and can be very helpful), avoid flashy, unprofessional colors or "cutesy" graphics. Be certain to include your vital information such as:

Full name
Full address with zip code
Phone numbers (residence, business, cellular, and fax)
E-mail address
Website

Study the examples of appropriate and inappropriate personal business cards in Figure 21.10.

Figure 21.10   Sample Business Cards

Benjamin Shaw

BIKER • SKIER • ALL AROUND COOL DUDE

Babes, call me at
(702) 555-1212

or email me at
realDude@shaw.net

Inappropriate personal card for business use.

Benjamin Shaw

1234 Lake Shadow Drive, Maple City, PA 12345
702-555-1212 • ben.shaw@online.com

Student
Victory Health Institute
Medical Assistant Program

More appropriate personal card for business use.

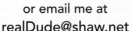

NETWORKING

How Do I Form a Circle of Peers in the World of Work?

It will be important for you to develop a network among the people you know who may work for a company in which you have an interest. People on the inside have an advantage in helping you get your foot in the door. What about your dad's coworker? Your wife's friend? What about a friend who knows your work style and works for a company in which you have an interest? Use every legal, moral, and ethical method you have to get the interview. Some important networking opportunities include:

- Attending events and conferences on and off campus
- Joining professional organizations in your field of study
- Shadowing professionals in your field
- Volunteering within your community
- Working in externships or internships in your field
- Contacting family and friends about opportunities
- Logging onto websites and job search sites such as:
    - www.monster.com
    - www.career.com
    - www.careerbuilder.com
    - www.indeed.com
    - www.craigslist.com
- Talking to your instructors
- Working with headhunters or recruiters
- Contacting a temp agency in the city in which you hope to work
- Working with your school's counselors and career officers
- Interviewing and connecting with guest speakers who came to your class

Reflections:
PUTTING IT ALL TOGETHER

This is your one lifetime! You need to prepare to do something you love. No matter how much money you make, you won't be happy unless you are doing something that matters to you, something that allows you to keep learning and becoming, something that provides you opportunities to give back—perhaps the best gift of all.

As you reflect on this chapter, keep the following pointers in mind:

- Learn how to make yourself a desirable employee.
- Set yourself apart with a dynamic cover letter and resumé.
- Select references who can speak to your many talents and skills.
- Learn to promote and sell yourself in an interview.
- Send thank you notes after your interview.
- Present yourself in a professional, educated manner.

DIGITAL BRIEFCASE

YOUR RESUMÉ WORKSHEET

Now, it is your turn. After reviewing the information for resumé writing and the examples of several resumés, begin compiling information to build your own resumé using the template below.

After you have completed this template, go online and find a free resumé building tool such as www.resumebuildertemplate.com.

You can go to any search engine and type in "free resumé template builder."

RESUMÉ INFORMATION

Personal Information

Name _____

Address _____

Phone number(s) _____

E-mail address _____ Website _____

Work Experience (Employment History)

1. (most recent)

   Company name _____

   Your position _____

   Your duties _____

2. (next most recent)

   Company name _____

   Your position _____

   Your duties _____

3. (next most recent)

   Company name _____

   Your position _____

   Your duties _____

Education and Training

1. (latest degree)

   Name of institution _____

   Name and date of degree _____

   Honors/Recognition _____

2. (degree)

   Name of institution _____

   Name and date of degree _____

   Honors/Recognition _____

Additional Training

Name of institution _____

Name and date of certificate or training program _____

Name of institution _____

Name and date of certificate or training program _____

Special Skills and Qualifications

List any skills and qualifications that you possess that may be of interest to an employer.

_____

_____

_____

College or Community Service (optional)

List any relevant service that you have performed that the potential employer might need to know.

_____

_____

_____

Personal References

List the names, addresses, and phone numbers of at least three people you could call on to serve as references for you if needed.

1. _____

2. _____

3. _____

Locate a position for which you would like to apply. Practice writing a job-specific objective.

_____

_____

_____

REFERENCES

Britton-Whitcomb, S. (2003). *Resume magic: Trade secrets of a professional resume writer.* Indianapolis, IN: JIST Works Publishing, Inc.

Dresang, J. (2007, April 23). "Liar! Liar! Won't Get Hired. In age of easy information, resume fibs can sabotage hunts for work." *The Las Vegas Review Journal,* reprinted from *The Milwaukee Journal Sentinel.*

Farr, M., & Kursmark, L. (2005). *15 minute cover letter: Write an effective cover letter right now.* Indianapolis, IN: JIST Works Publishing, Inc.

Ireland, S. (2003). *The complete idiot's guide to the perfect resume.* Indianapolis, IN: Alpha Publishing Company.

Robbins, C. (2006). *The job searcher's handbook* (3rd ed.). Upper Saddle River, NJ: Prentice Hall.

Part VII:
Growth and Change

Chapters taken from:
Cornerstones for Professionalism, Second Edition
by Robert M. Sherfield and Patricia G. Moody

Professionalism: Skills for Workplace Success, Third Edition
by Lydia E. Anderson and Sandra B. Bolt

chapter twenty two

GROW

BUILDING A LIFE PLAN
THROUGH GOAL SETTING

Success and happiness are not accidents.
They are created by conscious effort and actions.
—Cecile Peterkin

Why
read **this chapter?**

Because you'll learn...

- How to write a personal mission statement
- To list your key values and the role they play in your life
- To write goals with deadlines and measurements

Because you'll be able to...

- Eliminate roadblocks to your success and understand the importance of risk taking
- Understand the role your comfort zone plays in your life

PROFESSIONALS
from the
Field

Name: C. Steven Spearman

Business: Vice President, J. P. Morgan/Chase

Years ago when interviewing for a new position, the interviewer asked me, "*Where do you want to be in five years and what is your ultimate career goal.*" My response was, "*I'd like to move to the next level.*" He looked at me with a surprised face and said, "*Don't you want to be President of this bank one day?*" I was shocked. I had never thought that far into the future. At that time, I did not have any goals beyond Friday. My advice to you as you enter your career is to think in the long term—plan for five, ten, fifteen years down the road and do things today that will get you there. Learn all you can, act responsibly, lead with ethics, and your future goals will come true.

WHY I AM HERE

What Is My Main Mission and Purpose in Life?

First, an important statement: This chapter can change your life! But you have to remember this key fact: Nothing works unless you work. Vince Lombardi, the famous coach of the Green Bay Packers, made this statement: "The only place success comes before work is in the dictionary." We can almost guarantee you that you will have a more rewarding life, a more successful life, and a more eventful life if you will follow the instructions given here. We can also guarantee you that you will have to work hard and stay focused. For everything worth having, you will pay a price. You have to decide what is worth the price in your one lifetime. If you truly want to and are willing to work very hard, you can create the life of your dreams. In this chapter, we will teach you to write a personal vision statement, a personal mission statement, and an action plan made up of long-term and short-term goals.

Trying to decide exactly why you exist and what you want to do with your life is hard work, but it is an important first step in determining what goals you want to accomplish. We should tell you that most people never take this important step, and they never come close to realizing their potential. If you ask a group of 1000 people, "Are you as good as you can be?" chances are very good that not a single hand will be raised. And if you continued to talk to the group, you would find that most think they are using very little of their abilities. So why does this happen? The truth is that most people simply don't stop and think about who they want to become, what they want to have, where they want to go, what they want to do, and what kind of life they want to build. We encourage you to take the following advice very seriously and get ready to see significant changes in your life.

Pushing Yourself Out of Your Comfort Zone

If your personal mission statement and goals are worthwhile and worthy of your efforts, you are going to get pushed out of your *comfort zone*. What is a comfort zone, you may ask? This is that place where you are very relaxed, not challenged or stretched, just moseying along with no direction and not making much effort. You can easily do what you have to do when you are stuck in your comfort zone. Well, we are going to make a radical statement: *If you are comfortable, you are not doing anything but wasting your time and your life.* We want you to start *today* pushing yourself out of your comfort zone every day. Imagine a set of concentric circles like the ones in Figure 22.1. Consider each circle to be a step out of the comfort zone.

To accomplish anything worthwhile, you absolutely have to push yourself out of your comfort zone, and you must enlarge your comfort zone every day.

Bananastock

How can your friends, classmates, and peers help you achieve your goals?

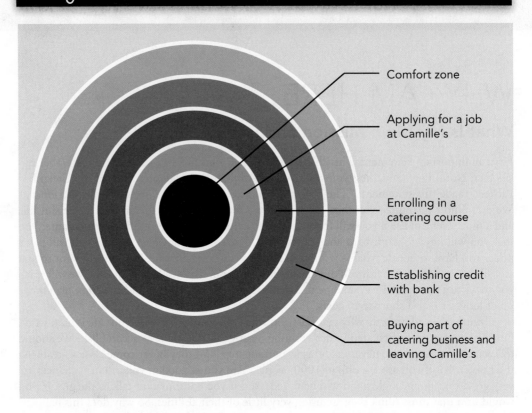

Figure 22.1 Comfort Zone

Comfort zone

Applying for a job at Camille's

Enrolling in a catering course

Establishing credit with bank

Buying part of catering business and leaving Camille's

WORKING HARD AND WORKING SMART

How Can You Change Your Life Through Goal Setting?

Have you ever known people who worked hard all their lives and never accomplished very much? The reason for this is that they did the same thing every day, and all along, they kept thinking something magical was going to happen. Their ship was going to come in. They were going to win the lottery. Someone was going to leave them a fortune. You need to know right now that those things rarely ever happen. If they do happen to you, great! But just in case they don't, you need to make something happen in your life. Your future success is up to you. You need to work hard and you need to work smart. And most likely, you need to change.

Someone once said, "Insanity is doing the same thing day after day and expecting a different result." Change means doing something different! Reaching goals means you have to change what you are doing now to something that is more focused and rewarding. Change means focusing on who you are now and who you want to become and then doing something about it. Most people spend more time deciding what they are going to wear to dinner on Friday night than they do deciding where they want to go with their life. As a result, they feel like a rudderless ship adrift on a sea of frustrations.

People who have no goals live lives of grinding monotony and low fulfillment. They have no direction in their lives, and they become very frustrated at the lack of progress they are making. They wonder, "Why am I making so little progress when I am working so hard?" Goal setting encompasses both working hard and working smart—you can't do one without the other. Goal setters have a vision for their lives, and they have formulated an action plan to accomplish that vision. Because of this vision, they know where to concentrate their time and efforts, and they learn to recognize distractions that deter them from becoming who they want to become or having what they want to have.

What Do You Really Value?

Take a little time and think about what and who are truly important to you. What and who make a difference in your life? Your next assignment is to list the things that you value. This list could include family, education, prestige, fame, money, home, beauty, belonging, contentment, daring, faith, harmony, opportunity, risk taking, romance, optimism, love, honor, religion, peace, joy, fun, sports, recreation—the list can go on and on indefinitely—but only some of these are at the top of your personal list. Before you can decide what you want out of life and what you want to become, you have to decide what you value, what really matters to you. After you think about this assignment very carefully, in the space below, write a list of the top 10 things you value in your life.

My Top 10 Personal Values

1. _____
2. _____
3. _____
4. _____
5. _____
6. _____
7. _____
8. _____
9. _____
10. _____

Before you begin writing your personal vision and mission statements, we want you to think about the end of your life, hopefully many, many years from now. Pretend you are an old man or woman and someone is writing your obituary. What would you want said about you?

As you begin to write, just say whatever passes through your mind. Just start writing. Don't worry about spelling, grammar, or sentence structure. For now, you are to think only about the end of your life and what you wish you could have accomplished.

- What did you achieve?
- Who did you influence or help? Why did you do this?
- What kind of character did you develop over all these years?
- Were you highly respected for your integrity?
- What kind of family did you have? Did they love and adore you?
- What did you accomplish at 40, 50, 60, 70?
- What were your passions?
- Did you travel?
- What legacy did you leave for your family and friends to remember you?

Think big! Stretch your imagination! Dream of what you could become by the end of your life, and think of all the good you could do!

Now, in the space below, write your obituary. The sky is the limit!

_____

_____

_____

_____

_____

_____

_____

_____

_____

_____

_____

_____

_____

_____

_____

_____

VISION—THE BIG PICTURE

Where Do I See Myself Going?

We want to provide the tools for you to build and lead a powerful, fulfilled life. One of the tools you need is a **personal vision statement.** This is the "big picture" of your life and what you want it to become. To write a vision statement, you have to think of yourself in the future and imagine how you are going to look, feel, and act. "See the person you are; what you are doing, who you are with, what you have accomplished, what is important to you, and how people relate to you. How does it feel to be you? Feel the person you are, your true self. Now, open your eyes and see your life and yourself in the present, through those eyes. You will begin to notice the changes you need to make to honor this vision and lead a powerful life" (Peterkin, 2003).

We want you to become your true self—who you were meant to be, the person you are comfortable with—and to be able to be this person all the time. That takes work! Your personal vision statement should encompass all the important things you want to build for your future life. "Although your personal vision helps you to see into the future, it must be grounded in the present. It is a statement of who you are, and who you are becoming. It is the framework for the process of creating your life. Your vision is where you are headed; how you get there is your mission statement" (Peterkin, 2003). Your vision statement should flow from things you enjoy doing, people you enjoy

How can a vision statement help you stay focused and working hard?

IndexOpen

being with, things you are good at, what you want to become, and how you want to feel about yourself.

Throughout these exercises on writing vision statements, mission statements, and goals, we are going to have you follow Samantha Hawthorne and to be involved with her as she works through her future plans and goals. Samantha's personal vision statement follows:

> I have graduated from college and have the job of my dreams. I am working as the manager of Camille's and am well on my way to owning my own restaurant. I have created a successful part-time catering business. My life is connected to many wonderful people with whom I have positive relationships. My spiritual life is rewarding and calming and provides a compass for my decisions. I am in a great personal relationship with the one I plan to marry. I have become involved in community service through an organization called Sister Care, on which I hope to model my own shelter in the future. I am earning $65,000 a year and am well on my way to achieving my personal mission and goals. I feel happy, joyful, optimistic, and blessed. I can see myself becoming exactly the person I have dreamed of becoming. In most of my interactions with people, I am truly myself. I try to be respectful of other's feelings, but I first try to be true to myself.

Now it's your turn to dream. In the space below, write your personal vision statement.

My Personal Vision Statement

_____

_____

_____

_____

_____

_____

_____

_____

_____

_____

_____

_____

_____

_____

_____

_____

Shutterstock

Can you see yourself accomplishing your dreams?

Once you have the "big picture" solidified, you are ready to make it come true by writing your personal mission statement.

POSITIVE HABITS
at Work

Colleen began her new job this past week. As soon as she was acclimated to her surroundings and responsibilities, she reviewed the corporate strategic plan and the organization chart. She then started her personal career plan, including her vision statement, mission statement, and long- and short-term goals. Colleen believes she has a much better chance of being successful and of moving up rapidly if she is focused and goal oriented.

PERSONAL MISSION STATEMENT

What Do I Want to Do with My One Lifetime?

Your personal mission statement is your plan for making your personal vision statement come true. Many expert life coaches believe that creating a powerful personal mission statement is one of the best ways to change your life. It is important to get it right because your goals and plans for the future will emanate from this mission statement.

Your personal mission statement should be focused on these things:

1. What is the purpose of my life?
2. What do I value, believe in, and stand for?
3. What action plan do I need to put in place to complement my purpose in life?

Important components of mission statements can be answered with the following three questions: **What do I want to be, what do I want to do, and what do I want to have?**

Samantha might answer the be, do, and have questions like this:

I would like to be a fine-dining restaurant owner, an owner of my own catering business, a wife and mother, a good daughter to my parents, a good sibling to my brother and sister, and a good community servant to people who need help.

I would like to do exciting things with my life, like travel to all the continents and visit all the major cities in this country. I would like to take my family and parents to Broadway plays and scenic vacations. I would like to sponsor homeless children for camps.

I would like to have my own restaurant and later three more of different types. I would like to have my own catering business that will support my charitable efforts. I would like to have a nice home for my family on 10 acres of land with horses and a pond. I would like to have Samantha's Women's and Children's Happy Place, where battered women and children could find a new start. I would like to have financial security when I am old and retired.

Now, you should answer these questions carefully and truthfully. You should please you—not someone else.

What do I want to *be?*

_____

_____

What do I want to *do?*

_____

_____

What do I want to *have?*

_____

_____

When writing personal mission statements, you should begin with the end in mind. Look way down the road and imagine you have come to the end of your life. What will you want to have accomplished? In whose life will you hope you made a difference? What character and values do you want to be known for? Who do you want to be as a person, employee, spouse, parent, colleague, friend? What do you dream of having and doing? If you have ever thought about what makes you happy, who brings you joy, what you value, what you enjoy doing, or what you dream about, you were actually taking some of the first steps in tying down your personal mission statement.

Now that you have determined what is really important to you, you are ready to begin writing your personal mission statement. This might take some time and you may want to continue to edit and adjust it for several days; you might even change this statement months from now. But get started *now!* You need to start with a statement and fill in the blanks with the things you value. Think about what is most important to you. Imagine yourself living a much more enlarged life than you are leading now. Remember, no one can put boundaries on you but you. Don't worry about what anyone else will think about your ambitions and purpose. People around you have no idea how hard you are willing to work or how big your dreams are.

Shutterstock

Do you have a guiding statement for your life?

Having a personal mission statement is like having a compass with you at all times to guide your decisions. You are always pointed in the right direction, and you don't wander around lost. Samantha's mission statement follows. As you can see, it is more specific about what she is actually going to do than her vision statement, which focused a great deal on her feelings.

I want to start my own business and own several restaurants and a catering business. My plan is to employ homeless people and people who have lost their jobs and give them a chance to own part of the business. When I have established four successful restaurants, I want to build a women's and children's shelter called Samantha's Happy Place. I will use this shelter to teach women how to work in the restaurant and catering business and help them get jobs so they can take care of their children. I want to change lives, make a difference, and be an example to my own children. I want to marry my soulmate and live in the country in a nice home with our children. I want to travel to all the continents with my husband and children, and I want to retire financially secure.

Some other examples of personal mission statements using values follow:

- I want to use my love of physical fitness to start a family-oriented gym with programs for people of all ages. I want to live a clean, healthy life and raise a family with children who are proud of me and who I am as a person. My goal is to help other people learn to eat healthy foods and exercise frequently. I would like to take my programs into schools, and I hope to make videotapes to sell that will help me help others.

- I want to start a plumbing company and own the largest company in Oklahoma City. I want to be able to take my family on international trips and provide them with a good living. I want to buy my mother a nice home and make her life comfortable. I would like to provide scholarships for deserving children who have grown up on Native American reservations.

- I want to use my talents of singing and playing the guitar to become a famous country and western artist. When I am wealthy, I want to use my fame and money to help educate children from the inner-city area of New York. I want to be remembered as one who gave more than I took.

None of these may relate to you—and they don't have to. This is *your* mission statement, so make it belong to you; make it appealing and exciting enough that you want to spend your life working toward accomplishing it. Now write your personal mission statement using the values you listed previously and your be, do, and have statements. Remember, you can erase and change and edit as much as you want to—just make it yours! You can start on this today and finish it next month. The important thing, however, is to think about it every day until you get it right for you.

My Personal Mission Statement

_____

_____

_____

_____

_____

_____

_____

_____

_____

_____

_____

_____

When you have defined your mission, you are ready to set long- and short-term goals, the building blocks and the foundation to a well-lived life.

TAKING THE ALL-IMPORTANT STEP OF WRITING GOALS

Why Do I Need to Write Goals?

Few people take the time to sit down and think about where they are going with their lives when it is a proven fact that having a clear, well-defined, personal mission statement and written goals makes a major difference in how much one accomplishes in life. Most people tend to drift around aimlessly with little purpose in what they do. They simply get up every day and do the same thing over and over again and wonder why their lives seem empty and meaningless and why they never seem to get ahead. They may go backward as often as they move forward. Life is a series of choices, but most people just make decisions without thinking about the ramifications to their lives and the lives of their families. Choose! Choose intentionally! We want you to make conscious choices about what you are doing and where you are going.

Some people have loosely configured goals in their minds and a general direction of where they are headed with their lives, but the roadmap has not been clearly defined, so they detour frequently and rarely ever get to their hoped-for destination. You might compare life with no direction to taking a trip with no destination. You don't have any idea what route you should take. You have no idea what stops you should make along the way. You don't know how much money you will need. You don't know how long it will take. You don't know what to pack in your luggage or what tools you might need on your journey. You don't even know when you get there because you have no idea where you are going.

> _A goal properly set is halfway reached._
> —Abraham Lincoln

> _Experts estimate that only 5 to 10% of people bother to think about their goals on a regular basis, and only 1% to 3% have clearly written goals._
> —Rodger Constandse

GRADUATE *Quote*

Mary Harris
Graduate!
Pima Medical Institute,
Las Vegas, NV
Career: Respiratory Therapist

Have confidence in yourself. Believe that you can do the job, meet new people, and be successful with the training that you have received. Self-doubt can only lead to trouble. Age does not matter. Determination, preparation, and confidence do. Use them all to your advantage.

Some reasons for writing goals follow:

- Writing goals makes you clarify what you really want in life. You have to be specific and you have to set deadlines. You have to do *something!*

- To be successful, you have to write your goals and take action on them. You need to post them where you can see them several times a day. Goals should not be written as an academic exercise and put on the shelf. You need to see them and live with them and think about them all the time.

- Putting direction in your life using a list of goals will often bring other associated opportunities. You may even have to rewrite your goals and specify bigger ambitions, and this is fine. Just get started now!

- Putting definition in your life will help you overcome inertia and the urge to just lie on the couch and watch another mindless television show. You have to do the work associated with goals if you are going to be successful. Merely writing them down is not enough.

- When you write goals with deadlines and you actually accomplish something, you begin to feel good about yourself and where you are going. You are no longer just doing the same thing day after day, but you are actually moving forward and making conscious choices. Accomplishing goals gives you reason to celebrate! You are enlarging your life!

Writing Long-Term and Short-Term Goals

In the beginning, you should write a rather short list of goals. A shorter list will enable you to experience success that will be motivating to you. As you grow and learn, you will alter your goals and increase your list to fit your current circumstances. **Long-term goals** are exactly what they appear to be—they take time to accomplish. Long-term goals may take a year, five years, or even 20 years. Because they do take a long time, we tend to get discouraged, so we need to set **short-term goals** that are like intermediate steps en route to the bigger goals. Some people refer to short-term goals as *enabling goals*—they enable you to take the steps that help you reach your long-term plans. Short-term goals are based on your long-term goals and should be the steps that lead you to accomplishing the long-term goal. Review Samantha Hawthorne's personal mission statement and then study a portion of her long-term and short-term goals:

- **Long-Term Goal 1:** I will own a fine dining restaurant in Portland, Oregon, within five years. (Notice that Samantha said "I

The tragedy of life doesn't lie in not reaching your goal. The tragedy lies in having no goals to reach.

—*Benjamin Mays*

will." She knows what she wants to do and where she wants to do it. She described the type of restaurant specifically.)

- **Short-Term Goal 1 (related to long-term goal):** I will secure a job in a fine-dining restaurant, preferably Camille's, and begin learning how to operate this type of restaurant by August 15.
- **Long-Term Goal 2:** I will own my own catering business, Samantha's Catering, within three years.
  - **Short-Term Goal 1:** I will enroll in the online catering program through the local community college and begin learning this business by August 15.
  - **Short-Term Goal 2:** I will work part-time in my neighbor's catering business to learn how to operate and manage this type of business and will begin within one month of finishing my catering certificate.
- **Long-Term Goal 3:** I will purchase a facility and equipment for my first restaurant within 4½ years.
  - **Short-Term Goal 1:** I will save 15 percent of my salary to use as a down payment in purchasing a facility and equipment and will begin as soon as I go to work. I will save all the money I make from catering to use in purchasing my first restaurant.
  - **Short-Term Goal 2:** By September 30, I will begin establishing an excellent credit record with First State Bank by borrowing a small amount of money, paying it back, and borrowing again to be in a position to get a loan.
- **Long-Term Goal 4:** Within 10 years, I will build a women's and children's shelter and involve the women and older children in the catering and restaurant business.
  - **Short-Term Goal 1:** By January 1, 20XX, I will begin volunteering at the Portland Homeless Shelter to learn how to best assist women and children in need of shelter and employment.

As you can see, Samantha has a plan. She knows where she is going and how she is going to get there. There will be no wandering around lost for Samantha! This is just a portion of Samantha's list of goals. Of course, Samantha will add additional long- and short-term goals from other areas that are discussed later as she begins to accomplish some of these goals.

Long-Term Goals

You are probably saying, "Long-term goals? Are you crazy? I don't know what I need to do tomorrow." The reason you don't know is that you have not yet put direction in your life. This is what broad long-term goals do for you. They serve as a compass to guide your rudderless ship. They are like a full moon on a dark night. Figure 22.2 defines areas where you need long-term goals and provides questions you need to answer en route to making these important decisions.

After you have identified and solidified your long-term goals, you are ready to think about short-term goals, which are really action plans that you do every day en route to your lifetime achievements. Before you do that, let's focus on writing SMART goals. The acronym SMART is a mnemonic that has been around for quite some time and has been used by many organizations and individuals. Each letter in SMART indicates one criterion of a well-written goal. You can probably locate several versions of this plan, but for our purposes, we are going to define SMART as follows:

> *Decide you want it more than you're afraid of it.*
> —Bill Cosby

- **S—SPECIFIC AND SIGNIFICANT:** SMART goals are detail oriented and will make a significant difference in your life if you achieve them. Unless something is going to make a major difference in your life, why are you wasting time on it?
- **M—MEASURABLE:** You might have heard the phrase, "What gets measured, gets done." This is true of goals. You have to have a plan of how well you are going to do something or how much you are going to accomplish.

Figure 22.2   Long-Term Goal Categories—Seeing the "Big Picture"

Categories of Goals	Questions to Answer
Career	Exactly who do I want to be when I grow up? What do I want to achieve in my career? What level of position do I plan to reach? Have I established a career path that allows me to grow? What new skills and knowledge do I need to develop in order to progress?
Personal	What do I need to do to become a better person? What values do I need to change? How can I improve my attitude and optimism? What work do I need to do on my character?
Romantic Relationships	Who am I looking for as a romantic partner? If I have one, how can I improve my relationship? What are the characteristics I would like to have in a spouse or partner? Who would be an ideal soul mate for me?
Friends/Relationships	What do I need to do to be a better friend and colleague? How can I enlarge my circle of friends? Who needs my help and attention?
Education	Is there another degree or certification I need to earn? What journals and books do I need to read? What seminars do I need to identify to help me gain appropriate knowledge? How can I learn to adapt and function in a changing world economy?
Family	What do I need to learn to be a better parent? How can I find ways to be a better spouse or partner? Who do I need to spend more quality time with? What future needs do I need to help my family plan for? What kind of relationship do I want to build with my children? What kind of parenting style do I want to develop?
Spiritual/Emotional	Do I need to find balance in my life? Do I need to take more time for "joy breaks" with my family and friends? Do I need to meditate and have quiet time to think and rejuvenate? Do I need to attend a religious service? Could I establish a better atmosphere in my home for my family?
Financial	How much money do I need to live comfortably when I retire? How can I discover additional revenue streams? How much do I need to save for college for my children? How can I get rid of credit card debt and student loans? What financial lessons do I need to teach my family? Do I need to take my lunch and put that money into a savings plan for emergencies?
Physical	What steps do I need to take to ensure that I will have long-term good health? Do I need to establish a program of physical exercise? What health problems do I have that I need to work on? Do I need to lose weight in order to be healthy? Do my family and I need to prepare more meals at home and eat healthier snacks? What do I need to teach my children to be healthier?
Service/Community/ Legacy	Do I want to make a difference for a particular group—Girl Scouts, Big Brothers, Boys Club, homeless children, battered women? Could I coach a team for young children? Could I chair a fundraiser for a group? Could I collect bicycles and other toys for children? What do I want to be known for? How can I involve my children in service to the community?

- **A—ACTION-ORIENTED AND ACHIEVABLE:** You have to do something to make goals happen, so action is required. These actions have to be under your control.
- **R—REALISTIC AND RELEVANT:** Goals need to be realistically achievable so you don't get frustrated and quit. They need to be just out of reach so you have to stretch and grow to attain them. Do you believe you can do this?
- **T—TIME STRUCTURED OR TRACKABLE:** Goals need to be guided by a sense of urgency—you don't have forever to make something happen. So give yourself a realistic deadline for reaching your goals.

Characteristics of Attainable Goals

The following characteristics will help you in your quest to bring about change through effective short-term goal setting. Goals should be:

- **Reasonable:** Your goal should be a challenge for you, but also within reason based on your abilities.
- **Believable:** To achieve a goal, you must really believe it is within your capacity to reach it.
- **Measurable:** Your goal needs to be concrete and measurable in some way. Avoid such terms as "earn a lot" or "lose some."
- **Adaptable:** Your goals may need to be adapted to changing circumstances that may be happening in your life.
- **Controllable:** Your goals should be within your own control; they should not depend on the whims and opinions of anyone else.
- **Desirable:** To attain a difficult goal, you must want it very badly. You should never work toward something just because someone else wants it.

> *Whoever wants to reach a distant goal must take small steps.*
>
> —Helmut Schmidt

BIGGEST INTERVIEW *Blunders*

Latisha had worked in hospitals since she was a freshman in college. Finding a position in Mercy Hospital had always been her goal after she completed her nursing degree. The big day had arrived, and Latisha was being interviewed by the supervisor of nursing at Mercy Hospital. She was excited but calm because she knew she was highly qualified and had good experience. After a few questions, the supervisor asked Latisha this question: "What are your long-term goals in the nursing profession?" Latisha had never thought about this question before, and her answer was not impressive. Fortunately, her other qualifications overshadowed this mistake and she got the job, but she learned an important lesson about being prepared.

LESSON: Before going on an interview, be sure you have anticipated potential questions and that you have thought about career goals, because most interviewers will ask you something about your goals.

How to Write Your Goals to Bring about Positive Change

"I will prepare in every way possible to get my dream job when I interview in three weeks" is an example of a short-term goal. "I will purchase my first home in seven to ten years" is an example of a long-term goal. Goals can be lofty and soaring, but excellent and meaningful goals can also be as simple as "I will spend two hours at the park with my children tomorrow afternoon."

Well-written, exciting, and effective goals include:

- A goal statement with a target date
- Action steps
- A narrative statement
- An "I Deserve It" statement
- A personal signature

The **goal statement** should be specific and measurable—that is, it should entail some tangible evidence of its achievement—and it should have a **target date,** or a timeline for accomplishing your goal. Your goal statement must also use an action verb. An example of a goal statement with an action verb and target date is: "I will lose 10 pounds in six weeks" or "I am going to join a professional organization and get involved by the end of this month." This is a much more powerful statement than: "I am thinking about joining an organization" or "I wanna have a new car."

After you write the goal statement, you'll need to create **specific action steps** that explain exactly what you are going to do to reach your goal. There is no certain number of steps; it all depends on your goal and your personal commitment. An example of action steps for weight loss might be: (1) I will join a gym within two weeks; (2) I will meet with a personal trainer this week; (3) I will join my neighbors who walk a mile at 6:00 every morning; (4) I will . . .

The next step is to write a **narrative statement** about what your goal accomplishment will mean to you and how your life will change because of reaching this goal. For example, if your goal is to lose 30 pounds, paint a "verbal picture" of how your life is going to look once this goal has been reached. Your verbal picture may include statements such as: "I'll be able to wear nicer clothes," "I'll feel better," "I'll be able to ride my bicycle again," "My self-esteem will be stronger," or "I'll be able to do more activities with my children." If your goals don't offer you significant rewards, you are not likely to stick to your plan.

Next, write two reasons why you deserve this goal. This is called your **"I Deserve It" statement.** It may seem simple, but this is a complex question. Many people do not follow through on their goals because deep down, they don't feel they deserve them. The narrative statement helps you understand how your life will look once the goal is met, but your "I Deserve It" statement asks you to consider *why* you deserve this goal.

Finally, **sign your goal statement.** This is an imperative step, because your signature shows that you are making a personal commitment to see this goal to fruition. This is your name. Use it with pride. Before you write a goal statement of your own, review Samantha's first short-term goal statement, which is related to her long-term plans and mission and vision statements (Figure 22.3).

Once you have reviewed Samantha's Goal Sheet, use the goal sheet in Figure 22.4 to build your goals. To help you get started, use this goal-setting sheet as a template for this and future goals.

Figure 22.3 Samantha's Goal Sheet

Name Samantha Hawthorne

Goal Statement (with action verb and target date)
I will secure a job in a fine-dining restaurant, preferably Camille's, and begin learning how to operate this type of restaurant by August 15.

Action Steps (concrete things you plan to do to reach your goal)

1. I will get an application to Camille's by Friday, July 10.

2. I will send my application, cover letter, and resumé to Camille's owner by July 15.

3. I will call Mr. Robinson, who knows Camille's owner, and ask him to talk to her about me and my work ethic by July 15.

Narrative Statement (how your life will look when you reach your goal)
My life is going to be happy and I will feel fulfilled because I will have taken the first step toward reaching my long-term goal of owning my own fine-dining restaurant.

I deserve this goal because:

1. I am hard working and focused, and I know what I want in life.

2. I have earned very good grades in my college courses and have planned for this day all during my college career.

3. When I am successful, I will do good things to help other people. I will always be a "giving back" person.

I hereby make this commitment to myself.

Samantha Hawthorne

My Signature

June 15, 20XX

Date

Shutterstock

What exactly is it going to take to achieve your biggest, most important goals?

Figure 22.4 My Personal Goal

To help you get started, use this goal-setting sheet as a template for this and future goals.

Name_____

Goal Statement (with action verb and target date) _____

_____

_____

Action Steps (concrete things you plan to do to reach your goal)

1._____

2._____

3._____

Narrative Statement (how your life will look when you reach your goal) _____

_____

_____

_____

_____

I deserve this goal because:

1._____

_____

2._____

_____

I hereby make this commitment to myself.

_____   _____

My Signature   Date

Reflections: PUTTING IT ALL TOGETHER

The transition from one place to another is seldom easy, even when the change is what you want. Going to work will give you the opportunity to assume new roles, develop new friendships, meet new people, work under different circumstances, and perhaps adjust your lifestyle. It is an opportunity to improve on who you are at this moment or to build an entirely new person. Work helps you do this. Going to work gives you the opportunity to reflect on your strengths and consider areas where you might need to change. If you begin your career as a goal setter, you will accomplish so much more than you will if you just drift along and accept what happens to you. As you reflect on this chapter, keep the following pointers in mind:

- Evaluate your reason(s) for choosing your career and what it can mean for you.
- Use goal setting to help you direct changes in your life.
- Don't just let change happen; get involved in your own life and learning.
- Focus on the positive by eliminating your negative self-talk.
- Keep your sense of humor.
- Be courageous by facing your fears before they derail you.

DIGITAL BRIEFCASE

WRITING A SOLID MISSION STATEMENT

Although you have already practiced writing a mission statement, you can find more excellent assistance by accessing www.franklincovey.com/msb. Follow the steps on this site and build a mission statement that you can use as you begin your career.

REFERENCES

Covey, F. Building a mission statement. Retrieved June 12, 2011, from www.franklincovey .com/msb.

Peterkin, C. Writing your personal mission statement. Retrieved June 14, 2011, from www .selfgrowth.com/articles/Peterkin3.html.

Career Changes

chapter 23

Real success is finding your lifework in the work that you love.

David McCullough (b. 1933)

Objectives

- Explain the importance of *training* and *development*
- Define the importance of continual *formal learning* and *informal learning*
- Know the various ways employment status can change
- Define the various types of workplace terminations
- Demonstrate how to write a *letter of resignation*
- Know the appropriate behavior to exhibit when leaving a position
- Understand the opportunities of becoming an *entrepreneur*

How-Do-You-Rate

	Do you understand job transition?	True	False
1.	It is normal to change jobs within the same company.	❑	❑
2.	Being fired is not the same as being laid off.	❑	❑
3.	It is appropriate to look for a new job while still employed.	❑	❑
4.	With the exception of being fired, when leaving a job, an employee should always write a thank-you note to his or her former boss.	❑	❑
5.	Many people start their own business if they are unable to find a job.	❑	❑

If you answered "true" to the majority of these questions, well done. You are aware of important concepts related to career and life changes.

Career Changes

Where do you want to be in five years? While this is a common interview question, it is also part of goal setting. Based upon the career and life plan, career changes should be welcome, because they mean you are accomplishing and updating your goals. Career changes are normal and common occurrences. While most of these changes can be controlled, some career changes are unexpected. Make a commitment to become a lifelong learner so you have current knowledge and skills to deal with unexpected change. This chapter explores the various career changes that may occur and teaches you how to welcome change as an opportunity for both personal and career growth.

Training and Development

Many companies offer current and new employees **training** to learn new skills. The teaching of new skills may be used to promote employees and/or increase their responsibilities. With the increase of technology usage, employee training is important for many companies. Training is usually provided and/or paid for by the company.

In addition to learning new skills through training, make every effort to attend **development** sessions designed to enhance existing skills or increase your skills. Development sessions make employees more diverse in knowledge, skills, and abilities, which provides an advantage when promotional or other opportunities arise in the workplace. Even if you do not think a development session is in your area of expertise, continue expanding your knowledge and skills in as many areas as possible. This is especially helpful if you are considering a promotion into a management position.

As an employee who is considering a management position, learn not only the skills needed for your job, but also other skills. Be aware of the key duties within other departments. The development of these skills will increase your knowledge and understanding of the company's mission and goals. When you can see beyond your job, you become more aware of what you are contributing to the company and how you are helping make it more successful.

The marketing department for Cory's company invited all employees to meet in the conference room during lunch hour to learn more about how to conduct a media interview. Cory did not know a lot about marketing and did not think media interviews were a part of Cory's job. However, Cory attended because it would be not only a good skill to learn, but also a good way to meet people in other departments.

Continual Learning

In addition to training and development programs offered by a company, there are other ways to improve and increase your skills and knowledge. **Continual learning** is the ongoing process of increasing knowledge in the area of your career. This can be accomplished by formal and/or informal learning.

Formal learning involves returning to college to increase knowledge, improve skills, or receive an additional or advanced degree. This can be done while you continue working. Consider taking one or two night classes a semester while you work. Be cautious about taking too many classes while working full-time, because that might stress you to a point that you will perform poorly at both work and school. Many colleges offer online classes, which have become increasingly popular for working adults. These classes allow more freedom and flexibility by allowing students to complete coursework on the Internet.

In addition to college, seminars and conferences are available. Some of these seminars and conferences offer college credit. Many seminars and conferences are offered by vendors or industry experts. Although you may have to pay for a conference, your company may be willing to reimburse you or share the cost with you. Conferences may last one day or may take place over a period of several days. Seminars and conferences are also excellent methods of expanding your professional network.

Informal learning is increasing knowledge by reading career-related magazines, newsletters, and electronic articles associated with your job. Another means of informal learning is using the Internet to research career-related information. Informal learning is an ongoing process and can occur during informational interviews, in conversations with professionals in your career area, and by attending association meetings. Make every opportunity a learning opportunity.

Talk It Out

Based on your target career, name two professional conferences or associations you would like to join/attend.

Exercise 23-1   Additional Career Interests

What additional classes might be helpful to you when you start working in your new job? Name at least three classes.

1. _____

2. _____

3. _____

Changes in Employment Status

Throughout this text, we have stressed the importance of goal setting. As you begin meeting your stated career goals, establish new ones. If you are following your life plan, you will have the desire to change jobs as you advance in your area of expertise. If and when this job change occurs depends upon many factors. Some reasons for changing jobs include a(n):

- Acquired experience for an advanced position
- Opportunity for higher salary
- Desire for improved work hours
- Need for increased responsibility, status, and/or power
- Perceived decrease in stress
- Desire for different work environment and/or colleagues

It is normal for employees to move within and outside of their company. A poor economy forces some employees to change positions and, in some cases, careers. Changes in employment status include promotions, voluntary terminations, involuntary terminations, lateral transfers, and retirement. The following section presents and discusses these changes in employment status and provides tips on how to handle each situation in a proactive and professional manner.

New Job Searches

Depending on their work situation, some employees determine that they must find a new job immediately, while other employees are constantly exploring opportunities. No matter your situation, identify when to share your desire for a new job and when to keep your job search private. If you have recently received a college certification or degree that qualifies you for a higher position, approach your supervisor or human resource department to inform the appropriate individuals of your increased qualifications and desire for additional responsibilities and/or promotion. It is also appropriate to share your need to change jobs if a situation is requiring you to move out of the area. In this instance, your employer may have contacts to assist you in securing a new job in another city. If you have had good performance evaluations and are leaving voluntarily, ask your immediate supervisor, another superior, or coworkers if they are willing to serve as references for future employers. If they agree to serve as references, secure letters of recommendation written on company letterhead. It is helpful to write and provide a draft letter for your reference that highlights your accomplishments and favorable work attitude. Finally, if you have mastered your job duties, have had good performance evaluations, and are beginning to feel bored, respectfully share your desire for increased responsibilities with your boss.

Apart from the previously mentioned circumstances, do not share your desire to change jobs with anyone at work. This includes close coworkers. Oftentimes, sharing secrets at work can be used against you. Therefore, keep your job search private. Conduct your job search outside of work hours and schedule job interviews before or after work.

Exercise 23-2 Employer Recommendations

List at least four key points to include in a draft letter of recommendation from your employer. Provide an example for each key point.

Key Point (Quality)	Example
1.	
2.	
3.	
4.	

Grace and style are two key words to remember if coworkers learn you are looking for a new position. When confronted about your job search, be brief and positive. State that you desire a move, be it the need for additional responsibility or the need for more money, but keep your explanation simple. You do not have to share details as to why you want to move on. It is also not necessary to share details about potential employers or the status of your job search.

Promotions

A **promotion** is when someone moves to a position higher in the organization with increased pay and responsibility. The first step in securing a future promotion within your company is to begin behaving and dressing for advancement. Secure a copy of the job description and/or research key skills necessary for your desired position. Begin acquiring work experience in the target area by volunteering for assignments that provide the needed experience. Develop new skills through appropriate classes, job training, and other educational experiences to increase your qualifications. Watch and learn from those who are already in the position you desire. Implement this plan and you will gain the necessary qualifications and have the experience when an advanced position becomes available.

If you receive a promotion, congratulate yourself. Your hard work has been noticed by others within your company, and they want to reward your excellent behavior. A promotion also means that you are advancing toward your career goals. When you are promoted, thank your former boss either verbally or with a simple handwritten thank-you note. Communicate to your former boss how he or she has helped you acquire new skills. Be sincere. Even if your former boss was less than perfect, his or her behavior taught you how to lead and manage. Keep your note positive and professional. With your promotion, you most likely will see an increase in pay, a new title, and new responsibilities. If your promotion occurred within the same company, do not gloat; there were probably others within the company who also applied for the job. Behave in a positive, pleasant, and professional manner that reinforces that your company made the right choice in selecting you for the position.

In your new job, do not try to reinvent the wheel. Become familiar with the history of your department or area. Be sensitive to the needs and adjustments of your new employees. Review files and begin networking with people who can assist you in achieving department goals. When you are new to a position, you do not know everything. Ask for and accept help from others.

With a history of favorable performance evaluations, Cory wants a promotion. Cory decided to take responsibility and began evaluating potential positions for which Cory might qualify. While conducting research, Cory created a list of additional knowledge, skills, and abilities needed for the promotion. Cory began taking classes, attending training seminars, and watching leaders within the company to prepare for a future promotion.

Voluntary Terminations

Leaving a job on your own is called a **voluntary termination.** Voluntary terminations frequently occur when an employee has taken a job with a new employer or when retiring. While at times the workplace can be so unbearable that you want to quit without having another job, it is best to not quit your job unless you have another job waiting. No matter what the situation, when voluntarily leaving a job, be professional and do not burn bridges.

When taking a voluntary termination, resign with a formal letter of resignation. A **letter of resignation** is a written notice of your voluntary termination. Unless you are working with a contract that specifies an end date of your employment, you are technically not required to provide advance notice of your voluntary termination. It is, however, considered unprofessional to resign from work and make your last day the same day you resign. Typically, two weeks' notice is acceptable. State your last date of employment in your letter of resignation. Include a positive statement about the employer and remember to sign and date your letter. Figure 23-1 is a sample letter of resignation.

In your final days of employment, do not speak or behave negatively. Leave in a manner that would make the company want to rehire you tomorrow. Coworkers may want to share gossip or speak poorly of others, but you must remain professional. It is also inappropriate to damage or take property that belongs to the company. Do not behave unethically. Take only personal belongings, and leave your workspace clean and organized for whoever assumes your position. Preserve the confidentiality of your coworkers, department, and customers.

February 1, 2015

Susie Supervisor
ABC Company
123 Avenue 456
Anycity, USA 98765

Re: Notice of Resignation

Dear Ms. Supervisor:

While I have enjoyed working for ABC Company, I have been offered and have accepted a new position with another firm. Therefore, my last day of employment will be February 23, 2012.

In the past two years, I have had the pleasure of learning new skills and of working with extremely talented individuals. I thank you for the opportunities you have provided me and wish everyone at ABC Company continued success.

Sincerely,

Jennie New-Job

Jennie New-Job
123 North Avenue
Anycity, USA 98765

Figure 23-1

Cory had a coworker who had been looking for a job over the past few months. Cory knew this because the coworker not only told everyone, but used the company equipment to update and mail her résumé. Cory often heard the coworker talking to potential employers on the telephone. On the day Cory's coworker finally landed a new job, the coworker proudly announced to everyone in the office that she was "leaving the prison" and that afternoon would be her last day at work. The coworker went on to bad-mouth the company, her boss, and several colleagues. As she was cleaning out her desk, Cory noticed that the coworker started packing items that did not belong to her. When Cory shared this observation, the coworker said she deserved the items and that the company would never miss them. A few weeks later, Cory's former coworker came by the office to say hello. Cory asked her how her new job was going. "Well..." said the coworker, "the job fell through." The coworker explained that she was stopping by the office to see if she could have her old position back. Unfortunately, the former coworker left in such a negative manner that the company would not rehire her.

On the last day of employment with your company, you may meet with a representative from the human resource department or with your immediate supervisor to receive your final paycheck. This paycheck should include all unpaid wages and accrued vacation. This is also when you will formally return all company property, including your keys and name badge. You may receive an

exit interview. An exit interview is when an employer meets with an employee who is voluntarily leaving a company to identify opportunities for improving the work environment. During this interview, a company representative will ask questions regarding the job you are leaving, the boss, and the work environment. The company's goal is to secure any information that provides constructive input on how to improve the company. Share opportunities for improvement, but do not turn your comments into personal attacks. While it is sometimes tempting to provide negative information in the interview, remain positive and professional.

Involuntary Terminations

Involuntary terminations are when you lose your job against your will. Types of involuntary terminations include **firing,** which happens when you are terminated because of a performance issue; a **layoff,** which is a result of the company's financial inability to keep your position; or a restructuring, which is when the company has eliminated your position due to a change in strategy.

If you are fired, you have lost your job as a result of a performance issue. Unless you have done something outrageous (such as blatant theft or harassment), you should have received a poor performance warning prior to being fired. Typically, this progressive discipline includes a verbal and/or written warning prior to termination. If you are totally unaware of why you are being fired, ask for documentation to support the company's decision. Firing based on outrageous behavior will be supported by a policy, while any performance issue should be supported with prior written documentation. When you are informed of your firing, you should immediately receive your final paycheck. You will also be asked to return all company property on the spot (including keys and name badge). Do not damage company property. Doing so is not only immature, but punishable by law. While you may be angry or caught off guard, do not make threats against the company or its employees. Remain calm and professional. If you think you are being wrongfully terminated, your legal recourse is to seek assistance from your state's labor commission or a private attorney.

Many people consider a layoff a form of firing. This is not true. Firing is a result of poor performance. A layoff is a result of a company's change of strategy or its inability to financially support a position. While some companies lay off employees based upon performance, most do it on seniority. Frequently, when the company's financial situation improves, employees may be recalled. A **work recall** is when employees are called back to work after being laid off. If you have been laid off, remain positive and ask your employer for a letter of reference and job-search assistance. This job-search assistance may include support with updating a résumé, counseling, job training, and job leads. Some companies require employees to take unpaid work days, called **furloughs.** Employees are required to take these unpaid work days. Work furloughs are not a result of poor performance. They are a result of employers trying to save financial resources. If your company implements a work furlough program, make the best of the situation. Be happy you still have a job, and find ways to assist the company in improving

Talk It Out

If you were to be laid off, what are the first three things you would do, and why?

Talk It Out

What is the best way to use your time during a furlough day?

its financial situation. Knowing your current employer is experiencing economic challenges provides you an opportunity to update your résumé and create a plan should your employer need to take additional steps toward saving resources.

In today's competitive environment, it is common for companies to restructure. **Restructuring** involves a company changing its strategy and reorganizing resources. This commonly results in eliminating unnecessary positions. If your position is eliminated, remain positive and inquire about new positions. In a restructuring situation, it is often common for new positions to be created. Once again, do not bad-mouth anyone or openly express your anger or dissatisfaction over the situation. If you have recently acquired new skills, now is the time to communicate and demonstrate them. Keep a record of your workplace accomplishments, and keep your ears open for new positions for which to apply.

Other Moves Within the Organization

In addition to promotions and terminations, there are several other methods of moving within and outside the company. These include lateral moves, demotions, and retirement. A **lateral move** is when you are transferred to another area of the organization with the same level of responsibility. Lateral moves involve only a change in department or work area. A change in pay is not involved in a lateral move. If you are moved to a different position and experience a pay increase, it is considered a promotion. If you are moved to a different position and experience a pay decrease, you have been demoted. While **demotions** are rare, they can occur if one's performance is not acceptable but the employee chooses to not leave the company. Of all the changes an employee can make, a demotion is by far the most difficult. You experience not only a decrease in pay, but also a decrease in job title and status. If you are demoted, remain professional and be respectful of your new boss.

The final change in employment status is called **retirement.** Retirement is when you are voluntarily leaving your employment and will no longer be working. Although this text addresses those entering the workforce, it is never too early to start planning for your retirement, both mentally and financially. This can be done by establishing career goals and deadlines, in addition to contributing to a retirement fund.

Entrepreneurship

Some individuals do not want to work for others and have a desire to be their own boss. A final and common form of career transition is that of becoming an entrepreneur. An **entrepreneur** is someone who assumes the risk of succeeding or failing in business through owning and operating a business. While owning and operating your own business may sound glamorous, doing so involves work. Individuals become entrepreneurs for several reasons. The most common reason is when someone has identified a business

Web Quiz

Take this web quiz or find another online quiz to identify if entrepreneurship is for you

http://www.sba.gov/
smallbusinessplanner/plan/
getready/SERV_SBPLANNER_
ISENTFORU.html

opportunity he or she wants to exploit. People also become entrepreneurs because they would rather work for themselves, want more control of their work environment, want more income, or have lost their jobs and have been unable to find another.

Talk It Out

What kind of business would you like to own? What steps would you need to take to make this occur?

Individuals with full-time jobs sometimes supplement their income by running a business on the side. It is unethical to run a side business that competes with or utilizes your employer's resources or confidential information. If your current employer allows employees to run side businesses, do not allow your side business to interfere with your full-time employment. Keep the two ventures separate.

Entrepreneurship is a rewarding career option for many and plays a valuable role in the U.S. economy. There are various methods of becoming an entrepreneur. You can start your own business, purchase an existing business, or operate a franchise. From a home-based business to running a chain of retail sites, every entrepreneur started with a dream. To be a successful entrepreneur, you need to have a passion for your business. You also need to know how to plan, manage finances, and make yourself creatively and professionally stand out from a crowd. These are all skills you have started to develop by reading this text.

If you are interested in becoming an entrepreneur, there are many resources available to you. Start by exploring the Small Business Administration website at www.sba.gov. Here you will find online, local, and national resources to get you started on the road to entrepreneurial success.

Career Success

As you have learned, there are several methods of advancing your career both within and outside of an organization. Although it is not good to change jobs too frequently, those with healthy careers move and rarely stay in one position their entire career. Personal issues frequently influence the choices we make in our careers. Health matters, changes in marital status, children, and elder care are just a few of these issues. There is a French proverb that states that some work to live, while others live to work. While there are trade-offs, your personal life must be a priority. Any change in your career will not only affect you, but those to whom you are close. Therefore, make them a consideration in your career decisions.

Career success is all about personal choice and maintaining an attitude of success. Regardless of when you plan to advance your career, keep your résumé updated, make a commitment to continuous learning, and display leadership. Doing so keeps you motivated to take on additional responsibilities and increases your knowledge, skills, and abilities. This will prepare you if some unforeseen opportunity comes your way. Keep focused on your life plan and consistently display professionalism. By consistently displaying professionalism, you will possess skills that position you for a lifetime of workplace success.

Workplace Dos and Don'ts

Do continually update your skills and knowledge through training and development	*Don't* assume additional skills and knowledge are not necessary for advancement
Do keep an open mind for job advancement opportunities	*Don't* openly share your dissatisfaction for your current job
Do write a formal resignation letter when leaving a company and a thank-you note to a boss or mentor when receiving a promotion	*Don't* leave your job abruptly without providing adequate notice to your current employer
Do behave professionally when leaving a position	*Don't* take or ruin company property when leaving a position
Do provide valuable feedback and opportunities for improvement during an exit interview	*Don't* turn an exit interview into a personal attack on your former boss or coworkers

Concept Review and Application

Summary of Key Concepts

- Continue learning new skills to help reach your career potential
- Formal learning is another way to increase skills and knowledge
- Changes in employment status include promotions, voluntary terminations, involuntary terminations, lateral moves, and retirement
- Be cautious about sharing your desire for a new job
- There are two types of terminations: voluntary and involuntary
- When leaving voluntarily, submit a letter of resignation
- When leaving in an involuntary manner, do not burn bridges or behave in an unprofessional or unethical manner
- There is a difference between being fired and being laid off
- It is never too early to begin planning for your retirement
- Becoming an entrepreneur is an additional form of career transition

Key Terms

continual learning

entrepreneur

formal learning

involuntary
   termination

restructuring

voluntary termination

demotion

exit interview

furlough

lateral move

letter of resignation

retirement

work recall

development

firing

informal learning

layoff

promotion

training

If You Were the Boss

1. Why would it be important to encourage training and development sessions within your department?
2. You hear through the grapevine that one of your best employees is looking for another job. What should you do?
3. Management has told you that you must lay off four of your employees. How do you determine whom to lay off and how best to tell them? How do you defend your decision?

Web Links

http://marciaconner.com/intros/informal.html

http://careerplanning.about.com/od/quittingyourjob

http://www.insiderreports.com/bizltrs/resign1.htm

Activities

Activity 23-1

Based on your career plan identify additional training, development, and continual learning you will need for professional success.

Training	Development	Continual Learning

Activity 23-2

Identify your ideal job. What continual learning will you need to secure this job?

Job Move	Continual Learning

Activity 23-3

Name at least five ways you can begin to develop additional skills for a future promotion.

1. _____

2. _____

3. _____

4. _____

5. _____

Activity 23-4

Throughout this text, you have learned good human relations for the workplace. Name at least three things you can do to decrease your chances of being laid off if that becomes necessary within your company.

1. _____

2. _____

3. _____

Activity 23-5

Write a draft letter of reference for yourself.

_____

_____

_____

_____

_____

_____

_____

1. To make you more diverse in your skills, attend _____ and _____.

2. The process of increasing knowledge in your career area is referred to as _____ and _____.

3. Changes in employment status include promotions, _____ terminations, involuntary _____, lateral moves, and _____.

4. If you have had positive performance evaluations and are leaving voluntarily, secure a _____.

5. A/An _____ is a written notice of your voluntary termination.

6. Your _____ should include all unpaid wages and _____.

7. Employees who are _____ are terminated due to a/an _____ issue.

8. Employees who are _____ are terminated due to the company's _____.

9. A/An _____ is when you are transferred to another area of the organization. A change in pay is not involved.

10. A/An _____ is someone who assumes the risk of _____ or _____ through owning and operating a _____.

chapter twenty four

CHANGE

DIRECTING YOUR LIFE THROUGH CONTINUOUS POSITIVE CHANGE

*We cannot become what we are capable
of being by remaining who we are.*
—Unknown

Why read this chapter?

Because you'll learn...

- To accept change as a natural part of life
- To distinguish between drivers, skaters, and defeatists
- To practice "carpe mañana"

Because you'll be able to...

- Understand the skills employers are looking for in employees
- Develop your own career plan

PROFESSIONALS from the Field

Name: Sheriff James Metts

Business: Sheriff of Lexington County, Lexington, SC

As a professional in the criminal justice system, I am continuously learning new life skills, adjusting to change, and reinventing myself. One of the biggest life skill changes I ever made was to earn my Ph.D. from the University of South Carolina, and today I am the only sheriff in the country who has a doctorate. I believe in education and encourage you to always continue learning. One of my jobs as the sheriff of a large county in South Carolina is to lead people in my department in developing themselves by providing training and educational programs. Our team is always learning about illegal drug trafficking, handling domestic violence, dealing with traffic violators, and many other areas of law enforcement—we can never learn too much and neither can you. To be successful in any position,

(continued)

you have to become an entrepreneur of your own life, so I encourage people to have a plan for their lives with goals and directions and action plans. I encourage my team to go back to school, to become involved in the community where they can gain positive recognition, and to accept change because it is constant.

YOU ARE ON YOUR WAY

How Do You Plan to G4I (Go for It)?

Once you get a position and begin to prove yourself in this new job, you need to think about long-range plans, thriving in your career, and making a name for yourself as a hard-working, creative team player. There are many ways to do this. Of course, the most important thing you need to do is to excel at the entry-level job you accept in the beginning. You may not like some of the menial tasks assigned to you, and in your heart, you may know that you can do bigger and better things. The fact remains, however, that if you don't do this first job well, there won't be any promotions. So you need to start strong and never let up. Start strong and finish stronger! You should do everything possible to be a good colleague who gets along well with everyone. But this doesn't mean you can't simultaneously plan and strategize to move up the ladder, get a position with more authority and higher pay, and gain recognition for your accomplishments. The best way to make this happen is to plan for it. As you have already learned, you need short-term and long-term goals, you need to brand yourself, and you also need a career plan.

As you mature and gain confidence, your priorities and interests will change. When you begin working in your first job, you may be willing to go anywhere and explore the world. At certain times in your career, you may welcome change, and at others, you may just want things to hold steady. "At some stages, there are likely to be significant pressures on your career due to family commitments" (Eby, Casper, Lockwood, Bordeaux, and Brinley, 2005). For now, you need to focus first on the job at hand while looking down the road at where you want your career to go. So what do you need to do besides doing a good job right out of the gate? In this chapter, we will provide many ways you can make a name for yourself, find rewards inside and outside of work, build your personal brand, continue learning and growing—and most importantly, continue changing.

You will learn soon enough that you are responsible for you. Even if you have an excellent mentor and supportive network, you are still in charge of your life, and it's basically up to you to make things happen. You may encounter many people who are willing to help you, but no one is going to make things happen in your career but you. While doing a good job is imperative, working hard by itself may not get you ahead. Haven't you known people who worked hard all their lives and never really got ahead? We will show you how to work hard and smart and to embrace change as a natural part of your life.

Previously, we asked you to set goals and to know what you want. This chapter is about doing the extras, taking the next step, going out of your way, giving back to others, and finding many ways to grow and expand your potential so you can accomplish your goals and dreams. It is designed to help you focus more attention on your own personal brand and to learn to gain positive visibility that can help you earn promotions and respect. And most

A NATURAL PART OF LIFE

How Can I Learn to Embrace Change When It Scares Me to Death?

Change is the one constant that you can expect when you go to work. It is a myth that change will go away! Most people are afraid of change, even good change, because they are leaving their comfort zone. It is much less frightening to us if we just keep going on the way we are. The good news is that you can learn strategies for accepting change and making positive things happen. Choose to be a navigator of change rather than a victim.

You will probably hear the term *paradigm* used in the workplace. A paradigm is simply a way of doing things—it's a pattern and a system of how things are working right now. A *paradigm shift* is a rapid change from doing things one way to a totally new way—it's a transformation or a revolution. Paradigm shifts don't just happen; they are usually driven by a leader or a management team that shakes things up. When people are heavily invested in an old paradigm and have worked hard to get to this position, they are very likely to resist the new paradigm. You can't afford to be one of these people. When a company makes a paradigm shift, there is usually a good reason: The competition is getting keener; the global economy is putting pressure on production; or the old ways are simply not working anymore. If the leader of the company or your division wants to change, you need to help make his or her ideas work. If you embrace change, you will become a navigator of change; if you reject it, you will become a victim. Change is coming! How you deal with it is up to you.

Choose to be happy!
—Michael J. Fox

DRIVERS, DODGERS, AND DEFEATISTS

Which Will You Become?

When we are faced with rapid change or a dramatic loss of some kind, people become **drivers, dodgers,** or **defeatists.** Drivers make up their minds to embrace the change that has come their way and take control by driving their own lives and decisions. Others, dodgers, dodge the change and just let life happen to them; still others, the defeatists, let hard times and rapid change defeat them.

How you deal with change is in your hands. You can choose to be a driver or you can choose to be a defeatist. A great deal of how you become a driver rather than a dodger or defeatist will depend on your attitude. Study Figure 24.1 for traits that explain each category.

STRATEGIES FOR DEALING WITH CHANGE

How Can I Practice Carpe Mañana?

You might ask, "What in the world is **carpe mañana?**" You have probably heard of carpe diem, which means "seize the day." Carpe mañana means "seize tomorrow." That term probably describes better than anything what we want you to be prepared to do after reading and studying

Figure 24.1   Drivers, Dodgers, or Defeatists

Drivers	Dodgers	Defeatists
Realize that change is coming and they can't stop it. They know that to reduce their personal anxiety, they have to go to work and embrace the changes.	Try to pretend that they are accepting change but secretly work against it; they may feel entitled to having things stay the same because they have been there a long time.	Are frequently scared and uneasy and afraid of what is coming; will say things like "We are doing fine. Why do we need to change?" or "We've never done this before." Uncertainty breeds fear.
Are genuinely excited about the changes that are happening and the new opportunities it presents for their career.	Are only focused on themselves and no one else or the company; worry about their job changing; wonder if they will have to do more work or a job they don't like.	Think the world is against them and their boss is out to get them; fear losing control over their work or personal situation; worry about losing status that they have gained in the past.
Try to learn everything they can about where the organization is headed so they can participate in leading change; anticipate change.	Complain a lot and try to undercut the boss without being open about it while secretly hoping things will stay the same.	Usually openly resist change and try to stop it by sabotaging ideas; pull back; undercut the boss with negative remarks and actions.
Think about ways change can enhance their personal career; attack the future instead of protecting the past.	Are passive-aggressive in many ways; make no efforts to embrace change or to lead.	Many times leave their job voluntarily or are among the first to be downsized because they have shown they cannot or will not change.

this chapter. We want you to learn to work hard and smart today as you prepare for more success tomorrow. In the world we live in, you cannot afford to be focused only on today.

Life seems to just serve up change, ready or not. It is simply a part of life. Change happens, and with it comes some level of discomfort, but what change does to you is really up to you. We tend to pay more attention to bad or disastrous change than we do to things that actually bring

GRADUATE Quote

Zack Karper
Honor Graduate!
The Art Institute of Philadelphia
Career: Head of Video Production
buggleproductions.com, Dream Camp Foundation

The biggest lesson that I learned in college was to treat every project, whether a paper, a speech, or a film, as if it was your baby. Nurture it. Care for it. Feed it. Make it great and never raise it halfway. Give your baby your all. Today, as head of video production at Buggle Productions, I live my dream of working in film and I get to help troubled kids who were in the same shoes I was in. I get to make a difference. If you work hard and put 100 percent into your projects, you will get to help people, too.

Figure 24.2 How to Practice Carpe Mañana When Dealing with Change

- Focus on carpe mañana, which means "seize tomorrow." Don't allow yourself to get comfortable with what is happening today. Be prepared for what is coming by making yourself better. *Prepare* is a keyword for being able to deal with change of any kind. Anticipate!

- Practice *kaizen*, a Japanese term that means "continuous improvement," by doing little things better and by setting and achieving increasingly higher standards.

- Face change by embracing it—good or bad—and look for the new opportunities that change brings. View change as growth. You cannot get better unless you change.

- Deal with change by understanding its phases:
  - Denial (includes focusing on the past, apathy, withdrawal)
  - Resistance (includes blame, anxiety, depression)
  - Adaptation (includes loss of energy, confusion, frustration, and beginning to adjust)
  - Commitment (includes clearer focus, new ideas, working better with others)

- When dealing with change, we encourage you to move up to the next level—create. In other words, make things happen; don't just accept things as they are. Turn the challenge of change into a positive. What new opportunities does change bring for you?

- If change puts everyone back at zero, seize the opportunity! You now have a level playing field with other employees who have been there a long time. Make the most of it!

- Associate with people who are embracing change, not resisting it. You want to be seen as a navigator, not a victim. Avoid those who are negative and pulling back. They will be among the first to go.

- Look for the signs of change so you are not shocked when they happen. Try to spot trends. Don't bury your head in the sand and keep doing the same things you have always done. Is the company changing leadership? Is the stock doing well? Are factories moving overseas? In the old days of chariot warfare, a dust storm was an indication of an approaching enemy. Do you see the dust storms before they engulf you?

- Think differently—obviously, things are changing in your company, or they should be. In what ways is your company changing and how do you fit in better? Help create value by making yourself useful and available to try new things.

- Revise your personal budget and save more money so you can survive a loss of job or any other bad event; increase your cash reserves; and reduce your debt.

- Reach out to friends and your support system for help during difficult changes, such as loss of job, death of a family member, or a painful divorce, but do not overburden them by focusing on your problems all the time. Seek professional counseling if you are severely depressed.

- Avoid negative coping mechanisms such as alcohol, denial, overeating, blaming, passiveness, and revenge. All of these just make a bad situation worse.

- Begin today to look down the road and try to figure out what is happening next. How can you learn strategies that help you "leapfrog" over people who are sitting still and pulling back and refusing to change?

- Ask yourself these questions on a regular basis: "How do I span the distance between what I am today and what I want to become? How do I continue to make the right changes that promote growth and success?"

- Keep moving! Exercise to remove stress from your body. Do not lie on the couch and watch endless television. Convert fear into energy! Get out of the ditch of depression and up on the road, where you are in the driver's seat. If you want milk, go find a cow instead of waiting for the cow to find you.

- Balance yourself. Find ways to bring joy into your life. Simplify your life. Take care of yourself and those whom you love.

us joy and happiness. In addition to being prepared for difficult change, we need to prepare for joyful change, and we need to set ourselves up to have joy and happiness in our lives. Abraham Lincoln said, "We are just about as happy as we make up our minds to be." We need to make up our minds to be happy and joyful and to deal with what comes our way.

No matter how optimistic and prepared we are, however, some bad things are going to happen to us. This kind of change may take more time to work through, but there are special ways of coping with difficult changes. Since you know change will always be coming, you can always be prepared, to some extent, to deal with it. To prepare for change, you have to have a good attitude, you must be flexible, and you have to be optimistic that you can handle it. Having a positive self-worth is very important to being able to deal with change. Figure 24.2 provides some ways for handling change effectively.

SKILLS AND ABILITIES VALUED BY EMPLOYERS

Do You Have the Right Stuff?

As you begin to map out your career plan, you need to give careful attention to certain skills that employers value highly. Although some positions require very specific job skills and knowledge, almost all jobs today require a set of universally sought-after skills. These skills can be developed if you are missing some, but it is important to be able to showcase all of them on your resumé. Figure 24.3 is a list of the top 10 skills most valued by employers (ASVAB, 2009).

As you can see, all these skills can be developed. You have to be honest with yourself and identify the ones you need to work on most. So exactly what do employers want in each of these categories?

What Employers Are Saying

According to the report *College Learning for the New Global Century* (Association of American Colleges and Universities, 2007), "Employers want college graduates to acquire versatile knowledge and skills. Fully sixty-three percent of employers believe that too many recent college graduates do not have the skills they need to succeed in the global economy and a majority of

Shutterstock

Have you ever used negative coping mechanisms? If so, what did you learn?

Figure 24.3 Skills Highly Valued by Employers

Review the list. Then rank the skills from 1–10 by each skill according to which ones you think are most highly valued.

Analytical skills	_____	Interpersonal skills	_____
Communication skills	_____	Problem-solving skills	_____
Computer skills	_____	Strong work ethic	_____
Flexibility/Adaptability	_____	Teamwork skills	_____
Initiative	_____	Technical skills	_____

Once you have ranked the skills, check them against the answers that were most selected by participants in the survey, which are provided below.

Skills Rank

1. Communication skills
2. Strong work ethic
3. Teamwork skills
4. Initiative
5. Analytical skills
6. Computer skills
7. Flexibility/Adaptability
8. Interpersonal skills
9. Problem-solving skills
10. Technical skills

> *Life is about change, and about movement and about being something other than what you are at this very moment.*
>
> —Oprah Winfrey

employers believe that only half or fewer recent graduates have the skills or knowledge needed to advance or to be promoted in their companies."

Whether we like it or not, a massive transformation is going on all around us in this country, as well as all over the world. Thriving in the coming years is going to be more difficult than in the past and will require certain new and different abilities and attitudes to be successful. You will need to learn the skills that will make you competitive, give you an edge, and help you master a life filled with changes and challenges.

Many of these skills are outlined in the following section. These skills will be needed for your success, personal independence, and growth in the new economy. Study them carefully, as each one will help you create a positive transition to the world of work.

CORNERSTONES FOR SUCCESS IN A CHANGING WORLD

What Major Skills Do I Need to Be Successful on the Job?

SEEK EXCELLENCE AS A COMMUNICATOR. Writing, speaking, and listening skills are constantly listed by employers as mandatory for success in any profession. Few people actually possess these qualities—especially all three. If you want to put yourself ahead of the competition, enroll in classes, attend seminars, join Toastmasters—anything that will help you learn more effective writing, speaking, and listening skills.

BECOME A SOUGHT-AFTER EMPLOYEE. A strong work ethic is another valuable quality that sets you apart from the other job seekers. A work ethic can include a variety of characteristics, including your pride, passion, professionalism, ability to work on a team, and ability to adapt, grow, and change. Your work ethic is how you perform at work without a job description, constant supervision, or someone threatening you. Your work ethic is not tied to what you do to get a raise or a promotion, but rather what you do because it is the right thing to do. In today's work environment, employers want to make sure that you are dedicated to your job, your company, and your colleagues.

Shutterstock

Are your communication skills an asset or a liability?

PRACTICE LOYALTY AND TRUSTWORTHINESS.   Loyalty to your employer is a highly valued trait. However, one's loyalty cannot be measured by a resumé or determined by a simple interview. Proving that you have the characteristics of loyalty and trustworthiness comes over time. It may take years to establish loyalty and trustworthiness with your company and within your industry, but with hard work, dedication, and honesty, it can and will be achieved. Be forewarned, however. While it takes years to build trust, it only takes seconds to destroy it.

ACT WITH CONFIDENCE AND MAKE BOLD DECISIONS.   Appropriate confidence and boldness are important to employers. There is a difference between having confidence in yourself, your work, and your decision-making ability and being "cocky." Confidence comes from experience, calculated risk taking, and previous successes. Employers are looking for confident people who are not afraid to make hard decisions. They are also seeking individuals who have confidence through experience. There is a difference between bragging about doing something and actually doing it. There is a difference between being hard and making hard decisions.

> The future belongs to those who see possibilities before they become obvious. When you see the bandwagon coming down the road, it is too late.
>
> —Unknown

USE CRITICAL-THINKING SKILLS.   The ability to think your way through problems and challenges is highly valued by employers. Employers are looking for people who can distinguish fact from opinion; identify fallacies; analyze, synthesize, and determine the value of a piece of information; think beyond the obvious; see things from varying angles; and arrive at sound solutions. They also want people who possess the emotional intelligence to critically and creatively work to resolve challenges.

MANAGE YOUR PRIORITIES WELL.   Setting priorities and managing time are essential to success in today's stressful workplace. Today, maybe more than any other time in mankind's history, we are faced with more and more to do and what seems like less and less time in which to do it. Your success depends on how well you manage your priorities, both personally and professionally. Priority management not only involves getting today's work accomplished, it also involves the ability to plan for your personal and professional future. Use your time wisely at work, at home, and in leisure.

MULTIPLY BY MULTITASKING.   The ability to multitask, or accomplish several things at once, will serve you well in the workplace and at home. A recent newspaper cartoon suggested that you are too busy if you are multitasking in the shower. This may be true, but in keeping pace with today's workforce, this is another essential task—the ability to do more than one thing at a time, and the ability to do them all very well. If you have not had much experience in multitasking, we suggest that you begin slowly. Don't take on too many things at one time. As you understand more about working on and completing several tasks at a time, you can expand your abilities in this arena. An example of multitasking at home is to have a casserole baking while clothes are washing at the same time you are researching a project on the Internet. To be successful in today's fast-paced world, you must be able to manage several tasks at once—without burning dinner.
Shutterstock

STAY CURRENT AND BUILD TRANSFERABLE SKILLS.   Keeping your skills and knowledge current is essential to your success. Building skills that can be transferred from one position to another is essential in today's workplace. Fine-tuning your computer skills

Shutterstock

Can you multitask without getting too distracted and accomplishing nothing?

Are you sure you are not posting photos that can come back to haunt you?

can set you apart from many of today's applicants. Your skills should include the ability to work with word-processing programs, spreadsheets, databases, and Power-Point. Some careers will require knowledge and expertise of industry software, and you will need to be an expert if this is true in your field. Learn to develop webpages, and create your own website that reflects a professional, career-oriented person. Learn to use social media for more than socializing.

CONTINUE TO GET EXPERIENCE AND EDUCATION.   Never stop learning! You may not want to hear it, but your education will never end. Your formal schooling will eventually come to an end, but as long as you are working in today's global economy, you will need to keep abreast of the changes in your field. Seek out opportunities to expand your knowledge base. Get certified in areas that will make you more marketable. Take a continuing education course to brush up on changing workplace skills. Earn an advanced degree. Make yourself the best, most knowledgeable, well-rounded applicant in the field.

AVOID INTERNET AND SOCIAL MEDIA BLUNDERS.   Don't let social media mistakes come back to haunt you and cause you to miss out on your dream job! You may think that posting that photo of yourself half-naked with a bottle of bourbon in one hand and a stuffed poodle in the other is cute and that your friends will love it. They may. Your current or future employer may not. Whether you like it or not, employers don't want people who do not represent them well. What you post online today may very well come back to haunt you in the future—even if you remove it, it can still be accessed. You may not lose your current position over a crazy, spur-of-the-moment posting, but it could cost you a future position. You may tell yourself that your Facebook, LinkedIn, or webpage is private and no one's business, but remember, nothing is private online, and everything is someone's business in the world of business.

Would your credit rating help or hurt your career? What can you do to improve it?

WATCH YOUR CREDIT RATING.   Building a good credit rating is one of the most important jobs you have. "Really?" you may think. "My credit rating? What in the world does my credit score have to do with my employment?" The answer: A great deal. More and more, employers are accessing your credit history and score as a part of the hiring procedure. Why? Because some employers believe that your credit history paints a clear picture of your working future. Bad credit history means a bad employee. Missed payments mean missed work. Low score means low morale. Careless errors mean a careless job performance. This is just one of the many ways that your credit history and score can follow you for years.

You want to be the most educated, the most brilliant, the most exciting, the most versatile, the most creative individual in the world because then, you can give it away. The only reason you have anything is to give it away.
—Leo Buscaglia, Ph.D.

REMAIN OPEN-MINDED.   The ability to accept, appreciate, and interact with a highly diverse workplace and the inherent differences and cultures that will be commonplace is important. You will need to develop the ability to listen to others with whom you disagree or with whom you may have little in common and learn from them and their experiences. The ability to learn a new language (even if your mastery is only at a primitive, broken, conversational level) and the ability to conduct yourself in a respectable and professional style will set you apart from other employees.

PRACTICE ACCOUNTABILITY.   The ability to accept responsibility and be accountable for all aspects of your future—including your psychological and spiritual well being, your relationships, your health, your finances, and your overall survival skills—is vitally important. Basically, you must develop a plan for the future that states, "If this fails, I'll do this," or "If this job is phased out, I'll do this," or "If this resource is gone, I'll use this," or "If this person won't help me, this one will."

POLISH YOUR HUMAN RELATIONS SKILLS. Polish your people skills and learn to get along with people from all walks of life. We saved this one for last, certainly not because it is least important, but because this quality is an overriding characteristic of everything listed previously. Employers are looking for individuals who have "people skills." This concept goes so much further than being a team player; it goes to the heart of many workplaces. It touches on your most basic nature, and it draws from your most inner self. The ability to get along with grouchy, cranky, mean, disagreeable, burned-out coworkers is, indeed, a rare quality. But don't be mistaken: There are those who do this, and do it well. Peak performers, or those at the "top of their game," have learned that this world is made up of many types of people, and there is never going to be a time when one of those cranky, grumpy people is not in our midst. Smile. Be nice. Remain positive.

Take some time now and work through the exercise in Figure 24.4. You will find several skills and traits for which employers are looking in the left-hand column. In the right-hand column, create two tips that outline ways *you* can impress an employer.

MOVING UP THE LADDER

How Do I Get Promoted?

When you start to work, you should make every effort to do an outstanding job in your current position, but you should also start thinking about how you are going to get promoted to your next position. You might even need to make a lateral move that better positions you to move up, so don't rule out such an offer before thinking about it carefully. Does a lateral move better position you in a track that will allow you to move up faster? In addition to the items previously listed, you need to pay attention to these hints:

- Give your employer an honest day's work for an honest day's pay. Don't slack off even if everyone else does. Get to work on time; don't take an extra long lunch; don't take sick leave unless you are sick; don't waste time chatting and gossiping when you should be working; and don't play games and send unprofessional e-mail at work.

- Plan every day in detail. Don't go to work and wander around in the desert. Hit the ground running. Do the big, important jobs that will get you noticed first.

- Be nice to your coworkers. Write thoughtful notes; send birthday cards; bring snacks; and use your manners.

- Try to get a mentor who can provide guidance for you. Mentors can spread good news about you and help you get noticed for your accomplishments. People above you on the career ladder often know information that will be helpful to you. If someone mentors you, you need to be prepared to return the favor by helping him or her.

- Support your boss! Make the boss look good, and he or she will not forget! Make your boss look bad, and he or she won't forget this either. When you

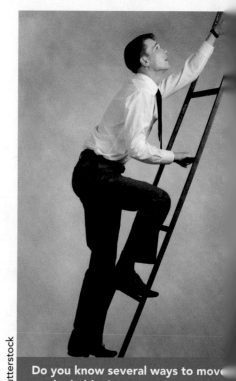

Shutterstock

Do you know several ways to move up the ladder?

Figure 24.4 Skills for Gainful Employment

Skill/Trait Employers Seek	Two Tips To Impress
Priority/Time management	1. 2.
Attitude	1. 2.
Written communication	1. 2.
Interpersonal communication/Relationships	1. 2.
Ethics	1. 2.
Dress/Personal grooming	1. 2.
Computer/Technology skills	1. 2.
Decision-making / Problem-solving skills	1. 2.
Confidence	1. 2.
Advanced training/Certifications	1. 2.

POSITIVE HABITS at Work

Plan to be successful by developing a career plan. Work on your plan every day by observing what successful people are doing. Adjust your plan when you find a better way of doing things. Pay the price to be successful by going back to school, taking in-house seminars, or learning a language. Build good relationships with internal and external customers. Include in your plan the ability to survive and thrive if you are outsourced.

have a formal evaluation, let your boss know that you want to move up and seek his or her advice as to what you need to do to be successful.

■ Sell yourself. Send reports to your boss detailing your accomplishments. Do this in a modest way, but be sure your boss knows what you are doing. There is an old saying that is very true: "He who tooteth not his own horn, the same shall not be tooted."

■ Build a network inside and outside the company. The more people you know, the better. Take advantage of any opportunity to make good connections. Join professional organizations, volunteer for jobs, and go to lunch with different people in a variety of positions and companies. The next promotion you get may be in an entirely different company.

■ Stand out from the pack. Come early; stay late. Go the extra mile. Dress sharp, regardless of what everyone else is doing. Help other people when they are swamped, as long as you have done your work. Never say, "That's not in my job description." Have something worthwhile to say in meetings—do your homework!

- Take solutions to your boss. Bosses get problems reported to them and dumped on their desks every day. It's fine to tell your boss there's a problem. It's great to be able to say, "Here's how to solve it."

- Be willing to move! Some people are willing to go anywhere. They'll jump at the chance to go work in India or China, whereas others don't want to leave their hometown. If you are willing to move—at least for the first few years—your chances of moving up faster are increased.

CREATING MULTIPLE REVENUE STREAMS

How Can I Earn and Save Money in Addition to My Salary?

Smart people learn early the value of multiple sources of income. There are many reasons to earn extra money: First, you can save it or invest it; second, you can develop new skills that might lead to your own business; and third, this income can tide you over if you lose your main source of income. Because of today's volatile job market, we highly encourage you to develop at least one alternate source of income. "How do I do this?" you might ask. Be creative. What are your talents and skills? Who can you partner with to start a part-time business? Some suggestions follow (though this is by no means a complete list):

- Are you musically talented? Can you play in a band? Can you perform children's music at parties? Can you be a disk jockey? Can you be a pianist for a small church that needs a part-time musician?

- Can you paint houses on the weekends?

- Can you have a booth at craft shows and sell materials?

- Can you make jewelry and sell it on the Internet?

- Can you buy and sell things on eBay?

- Can you design websites or perform other computing services for small companies?

- Are you good with accounting? Could you keep books and file reports for small companies?

- Are you good with children? Can you babysit on the weekends? Can you start a service using reliable friends?

- Are you good with landscaping? Could you and a friend start a part-time landscaping business?

- Are you especially talented in an academic subject? Can you provide tutoring for a high school or middle school student? Can you start a service business? Can you work for an established tutoring service?

The list of creative ideas is endless. The point is: Get started now! If and when you really need this money to survive, you will have saved enough to pay your bills, and you will still have income. If the worst-case scenario never happens, you can take a great vacation to China or Africa or buy a house or work on a master's degree. Use your talents to build security and confidence.

Shutterstock

What skills do you have that you could turn into additional revenue streams?

DOWNSIZING, RIGHTSIZING, RIFS, TERMINATIONS, OUTSOURCING, LAYOFFS

How Would I Survive Losing My Job?

Today it is quite common for employees to get the dreaded "pink slip" (letter telling an employee that they have been let go from their job) when they have done nothing to deserve it. If this happens to you, you should know that it is normal to be scared, disoriented, and depressed, but it is not the end of the world. You can overcome it and perhaps even do better.

> *Barn's burnt down . . .*
> *now I can see the moon.*
> *—Masahide, Japanese philosopher*
> *(1657-1723)*

In a tight economy, many companies find that they have too many employees to support relative to the income they are producing, so they have to reduce their workforce. If this happens to you, you need to be prepared. There are lots of qualified people looking for work, so you have to be focused and strategic when finding your next employment. Hopefully, you have initiated another source of income and can survive a few months while you search for the right job. You should always keep your resumé updated and ready to use at a minute's notice.

Try not to become adrift and depressed; instead, look at this event as an opportunity to do something totally new that might be a better fit for you. Sometimes it takes something like losing a job to force us out of our comfort zone and help us realize our potential. This may be the perfect time to reinvent yourself as the person you always wished you could be.

Being prepared for loss of job includes the following steps:

- Sign up for unemployment benefits the same day you lose your job. There is a period of about three weeks before you will start receiving benefits.
- Before you leave your job, copy all e-mail addresses, phone numbers, and contacts.
- If you have a company cell phone, copy the information to your own phone.
- Get your own personal e-mail address if you don't have one so employers can reach you and so you can file resumés online.
- Protect your credit rating. Try to make your minimum payments, but let your creditors know if you are having problems.
- Put your resumé on LinkedIn, Monster.com, Careerbuilder, and TheLadders.
- Look up the term "resumé blasting" and follow the directions for this process.
- Don't burn any bridges with the employer who laid you off. Your next job may be a recall from that company.
- Mobilize yourself. Quit moping about your bad luck, get off the couch, and mix and mingle with people who might have leads for jobs. Let your friends and colleagues know that you are looking for a job, and provide them with your resumé.
- If you have joined professional organizations, let the people you know in these groups that you are searching for a job.
- Attend career fairs and employment agencies that might be able to help you find work.
- Go to the gym. Exercise will produce chemicals that are a natural high, and it takes stress out of your body. If you feel better, you are likely to "sell" better to people looking for employees. Protect your health during this stressful time.
- Consider temporary employment that can help you pay the bills.

- If you have children, keep them at home temporarily instead of using expensive day care.
- Cut your grocery bills by eating less expensively.
- Rent movies instead of going to the theater.

As you can see, there are strategies to follow to avoid outsourcing or to survive it and thrive when it happens to you. You might want to consider this tip: "Go where the puck is going!" Sound crazy? The great hockey champ Wayne Gretzky made the comment that this one step had been his key to success. What does it mean? He said that when he was playing hockey, he did not skate to where the puck was at the moment—he skated to where the puck was going. He anticipated the direction of where the puck was going to be hit, and when it came his way, he was already there—ready to play.

Think of your career in this light. Go to companies that will be bright in the future, not necessarily where it is bright at this moment. Look ahead and try to determine what is going to be "hot" in the coming years, not what is hot right now. Plan ahead. Look at trends. Read. Ask questions. Stay prepared. Try to work in *sunrise industries* (those businesses that are new and emerging, such as solar energy), not *sunset industries* (textile factories). Think in the future tense, not the present.

Can you learn to anticipate "where the puck is going" when it relates to your future?

DESIGNING A CAREER PLAN

What Steps Do I Need to Take to Chart My Course?

This is not an easy, one-hour assignment. It takes time to think through your entire career and to design a plan that will take you where you aspire to go. You should know that this plan will change as you move up the ladder and as your confidence, skills, and knowledge grow. There is no doubt, however, that you will be far better off with a plan than you are just drifting along hoping someone will notice you and give you a promotion. A career plan will focus your efforts on doing all the right things to be successful. Simply looking at the next job down the road is not designing a career plan!

Before you chart your career path, you need to take an introspective look by considering the questions in Figure 24.5. You need to know what brings you happiness before you move toward the wrong career. After you have studied Figure 24.5, begin developing your own career plan. Don't be concerned if you can't complete the plan right now; the important thing is to start and continue.

Now you are ready to begin charting your path. Remember, this may take months, even years, because it will change as you move forward. The important thing is to always have a career plan. The great majority of people will not have a career plan; this plan puts you way ahead of the competition because you know what you want and have determined what you must do to get it. Study the sample career plan in Figure 24.6.

> *Rings and gems are not gifts. They are only imitations of gifts. The only true gift one can give is himself.*
>
> —Unknown

Figure 24.5   A Career Plan

1. What kind of work do you want to do? _____
   _____

2. What are you passionate about? _____
   _____

3. Are you a people person? Why or why not? _____
   _____

4. Do you want to live in a large city? _____
   _____

5. Are you willing to move around? Would you like a job that leads to an international position? _____
   _____

6. What are your strongest values? Does the company you are interested in match your values? _____
   _____

7. What kind of organization best fits your needs? Do you need to work for a large company or a small company, or do you need to start your own business? _____
   _____

8. Can you deal with the stress of a high-powered career, or would you be happier in a more laid-back type of work?
   _____
   _____

9. Are your career aspirations really yours, or are you trying to please someone else? _____
   _____

10. Are you driven by money or a feeling of satisfaction in doing a good job and in doing what you always wanted to do?
    _____
    _____

Now, answer two more questions before you begin designing your career plan.

What does "happiness" mean to you? (What would it look like? How would it feel? What would you be doing? What would you have? Who would you be with? How do you spend your leisure time? Do you have a family?)

What is "success" for you? (What does it look like? What are you doing? Who are you working for or with? How much money are you making? How does it feel? What are the rewards of success?)

Figure 24.6 Model Career Plan

What I Want to Achieve:

Having majored in business, I want to find an entry-level position that offers upward mobility according to how hard I work and how I use my education and abilities. I would like to begin my career as a consultant with a major consulting firm that will expose me to a variety of aspects of business and provide an entry into a company that matches my goals and aspirations. From that position, I would like to move into management, begin my MBA in international business, learn to speak Mandarin, and move to my dream company, XYZ, where I hope to attain a management position that will lead me to an executive management position.

Job 1: Business consultant

Skills required: Degree in business administration; in-house training with company, working with a team to learn the consulting area; excellent soft skills; specific technology and software skills; report-writing skills.

Skills assessment: I have degree, excellent soft skills, need more training on software, need to improve report-writing skills.

Duties and responsibilities: I will be working with a team to recommend IT practices, accounting systems, and interviewing skills.

Plan to get this job: Take a course in report writing, teach myself accounting software, send resumés to top 10 companies for business consulting, network with people I know who are doing this kind of work.

[After getting his first consulting position, Josh should then begin preparing to become a manager. He needs to pay attention to other managers, as well as his own. He needs to let HR and his supervisor know that he would like to move toward a supervisor position and would like to take advantage of any special training.]

Job 2: Supervisor of business consultants

Skills required: Ability to lead and manage other people, ability to delegate, ability to shape a vision for a group; skills in evaluation, excellent soft skills, sales ability.

Skills assessment: I need to take seminars in leading and managing and salesmanship; need to study visionary planning, how to evaluate people.

Duties and responsibilities: I will be leading a team of consultants and evaluating their performance; I will have

to sell our team to businesses as consultants; I will have to be able to delegate and make decisions.

Plan to get this job: Do an excellent job as a consultant; let management know I want to be a supervisor, take advantage of any in-house training available; take courses at the community college; build excellent relationships with people internally and externally; begin working on MBA in international business at night and on weekends; taking a course in Mandarin at community college; spend vacation in China.

[Assume Josh has done well in the first two jobs and he is now ready to seek employment in management with another company. You cannot plan to stay with the same company for your entire career; that rarely happens today. Remember, "go where the puck is going." XYZ is an international company that can ultimately offer Josh the opportunity to work in China, which is one of his top career goals. Do you see how Josh's plan is building on each previous position and how he will ultimately reach his top goal?]

Job #3: Sales position in XYZ Company

Skills required: Degree in business administration; Mandarin is an asset; international travel is considered a plus; sales and management experience required; ability to build relationships with clients; ability to learn XYZ software and technology.

Skills assessment: Have degree and working on MBA; learning Mandarin; have been to China; have sales and management experience; have built excellent relationships with external clients and could get recommendations from them; have ability to learn the software and technology based on past experience.

Duties and responsibilities: I will be a member of a team that sells XYZ software to international companies; some international travel required; ability to interact with international customers; must demonstrate software and technology and be able to make excellent presentations.

Plan to get this job: Send resumé with recommendations from several external clients; ask Mr. Robinson, who works at XYZ, to put in a good word for me; have my Mandarin professor write a letter about how well I am doing in this class; emphasize my international travel experience and desire to travel internationally; emphasize that I have almost completed MBA in international business.

[Notice how Josh is anticipating what is required for his next career move. He is not "letting things happen"; he

(continued)

Figure 24.6 Model Career Plan (continued)

is making things happen. He has prepared to be success-ful by anticipating what skills and knowledge are required and gradually accumulating all of them. Success does not just happen. Success is planned!]

Job 4: Manager of international sales team in XYZ Company

Skills required: Master's degree in business administration; experience in a variety of business areas including account-ing and IT; knowledge of software and technology; ability to shape a vision for a department; ability to lead a team and to build external relationships with customers; fluent Mandarin or Spanish skills; excellent salesmanship abilities.

Skills assessment: Lack one course in MBA program; pro-gram included Advanced Salesmanship and Advanced Communications and Presentation Skills; have experi-ence in leading others and shaping a vision for a team; have excellent relationships with external businesses; need to learn company-specific software for XYZ; learning Mandarin.

Duties and responsibilities: I lead a team that will sell XYZ's exclusive software to international companies; must be able to set priorities for team; shape a vision; interact with international clients; be able to travel internationally; must speak Mandarin; must have excellent communication and presentation skills.

Plan to get this job: Let the management team making the selection know I want this job and tell them what I have been doing to prepare for it; share my portfolio that includes travel to China, Mandarin course, com-munications and presentation skills, and examples of presentations I have made; try to get my manager to recommend me.

[If Josh gets this job and continues to prepare as he has been doing, he will most likely reach his goal of being a member of the Executive Team at XYZ. His career opportunities and desires may change along the way, but regardless, he has set himself up to be successful because he had a plan, he worked hard and smart, and he went where the puck was going.]

Reflections: PUTTING IT ALL TOGETHER

After reading this chapter, you have realized that change will be an important part of your life and career, and how you deal with it will no doubt have a big impact on your success. We encourage you to embrace change, antici-pate changes that are coming down the road, and plan for change. It is very important for you to develop a career plan that will guide you and help you realize your ambi-tions much faster. We hope you will also prepare for a potential loss of employment at some time during your career by using multiple sources of revenue to cushion the blow, as well as provide more income for investments, savings, and entertainment.

DIGITAL BRIEFCASE

CONNECTING WITH BUSINESS COLLEAGUES THROUGH LINKEDIN

LinkedIn is a professional network designed to help businesspeople interact. Think of it as Facebook for business. It is a great tool for increasing visibility and can assist you in showcasing your expertise. When beginning your job search, a great place to start is by creating a profile on

LinkedIn and then making connections with people you know. You can use LinkedIn to connect with current and former colleagues, supervisors, and clients.

Use the following tips to get started in creating and using your LinkedIn profile.

- Before you begin, think about what your want to accomplish with your LinkedIn profile. Do you want to expand your network, are you looking for a job, or are you looking to reconnect with colleagues from former jobs who may be able to recommend you?

- First, follow the steps to register on the LinkedIn.com site.

- Click on the "Profile" link.

- Click on "Edit Contact Settings" and choose the types of people with whom you want to connect.

- Click "Save Changes."

- Next, select an attractive, professional headshot.

- Post a profile summary that is honest and discusses results of things you have accomplished that might interest an employer. Keep it simple and straightforward and not too long. You can list your education, honors, and awards in other sections of your profile, but your summary should be brief and to the point.

- For ***each company you have worked for***, fill in the job title and describe your duties. You can click on the link right below the position field, which can provide you assistance in describing your duties.

- When you have finished listing your positions, you can enter information about your education into your profile. You will see that LinkedIn provides a pull-down menu that allows you to search for your institution. You can add information about your degree, your major, the date your attended the school, and other information about your educational experience.

- Work experience and education are the two main parts of your profile, but if you scroll down, you will see places where you can add information such as your website, interests, awards, and other items.

- Once you have completed your profile, read it one more time to check for errors and to be sure that it represents you in an exemplary manner. You can always go back and change or add things later.

- Click the tab "View My Profile" at the top of the profile screen to see how others will see your profile.

- Finally, look over to the right and locate a link that says "Edit Public Profile Settings" and select "Full View." Then you can choose the features that you want to be visible to anyone who accesses your profile.

- Finally, if you are happy with your profile, click "Save Changes" down at the bottom of the screen.

REFERENCES

Association of American Colleges and Universities. (2007). *College learning for the new global century.* Retrieved June 28, 2011, from www.aacu.org/leap/documents/GlobalCentury_final.pdf.

ASVAB. (2009). Career exploration program. Retrieved June 23, 2011, from www.asvab program.com/downloads/ASVABIdeaSkillsMostValued.pdf.

Eby, L. T., Casper, W. J., Lockwood, A., Bordeaux, C., & Brinley, A. (2005). *Work interference with life domains.* Retrieved July 29, 2011, from www.shrm.org/about/foundation /research/Documents/Ryan%20Final%20Report%20610.pdf

INDEX